Pure Mathematics 1 & 2

Hugh Neill and
Douglas Quadling

Series editor Hugh Neill

CAMBRIDGE
UNIVERSITY PRESS

PUBLISHED BY THE PRESS SYNDICATE OF THE UNIVERSITY OF CAMBRIDGE
The Pitt Building, Trumpington Street, Cambridge, United Kingdom

CAMBRIDGE UNIVERSITY PRESS
The Edinburgh Building, Cambridge CB2 2RU, UK
40 West 20th Street, New York, NY 10011–4211, USA
10 Stamford Road, Oakleigh, VIC 3166, Australia
Ruiz de Alarcón 13, 28014 Madrid, Spain
Dock House, The Waterfront, Cape Town 8001, South Africa

http://www.cambridge.org

First published 2000
Fifth printing 2001

Printed in the United Kingdom at the University Press, Cambridge

Typefaces Times, Helvetica   *Systems* Microsoft Word, MathType™

A catalogue record for this book is available from the British Library

ISBN 0 521 78369 0 paperback

Cover image: Images Colour Library

Contents

Introduction

Cambridge Advanced Level Mathematics has been written especially for the OCR modular examinations. It consists of one book or half-book corresponding to each module. This book combines the first two Pure Mathematics modules, P1 and P2.

The books are divided into chapters roughly corresponding to syllabus headings. Occasionally a section includes an important result that is difficult to prove or outside the syllabus. These sections are marked with an asterisk (*) in the section heading, and there is usually a sentence early on explaining precisely what it is that the student needs to know.

Occasionally within the text paragraphs appear in *this type style*. These paragraphs are usually outside the main stream of the mathematical argument, but may help to give insight, or suggest extra work or different approaches.

The authors have assumed that the students have access to graphic calculators. Although these are not permitted in parts of the examination, it is assumed that students will use them throughout the course to assist their learning of mathematics.

Numerical work is presented in a form intended to discourage premature approximation. In ongoing calculations inexact numbers appear in decimal form like 3.456..., signifying that the number is held in a calculator to more places than are given. Numbers are not rounded at this stage; the full display could be 3.456 123 or 3.456 789. Final answers are then stated with some indication that they are approximate, for example '1.23 correct to 3 significant figures'.

There are plenty of exercises, and each chapter contains a Miscellaneous exercise which includes some questions of examination standard. Questions which go beyond examination requirements are marked by an asterisk. The authors thank Charles Parker, Lawrence Jarrett and Tim Cross, the OCR examiners who contributed to these exercises, and also Peter Thomas, who read the book very carefully and made many extremely useful comments. Throughout the book there are Revision exercises.

The authors thank OCR and Cambridge University Press for their help in producing this book. However, the responsibility for the text, and for any errors, remains with the authors.

Module P1

Pure Mathematics 1

1 Coordinates, points and lines

This chapter uses coordinates to describe points and lines in two dimensions. When you have completed it, you should be able to

- find the distance between two points
- find the mid-point of a line segment, given the coordinates of its end points
- find the gradient of a line segment, given the coordinates of its end points
- find the equation of a line though a given point with a given gradient
- find the equation of the line joining two points
- recognise lines from different forms of their equations
- find the point of intersection of two lines
- tell from their gradients whether two lines are parallel or perpendicular.

1.1 The distance between two points

When you choose an origin, draw an x-axis to the right on the page and a y-axis up the page and choose scales along the axes, you are setting up a coordinate system. The coordinates of this system are called **cartesian coordinates** after the French mathematician René Descartes, who lived in the 17th century.

In Fig. 1.1, two points A and B have cartesian coordinates $(4,3)$ and $(10,7)$. The part of the line AB which lies between A and B is called a **line segment**. The length of the line segment is the distance between the points.

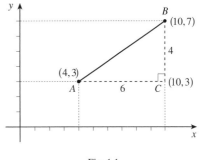

Fig. 1.1

A third point C has been added to Fig. 1.1 to form a right-angled triangle. You can see that C has the same x-coordinate as B and the same y-coordinate as A; that is, C has coordinates $(10,3)$.

It is easy to see that AC has length $10-4=6$, and CB has length $7-3=4$. Using Pythagoras' theorem in triangle ABC shows that the length of the line segment AB is

$$\sqrt{(10-4)^2+(7-3)^2} = \sqrt{6^2+4^2} = \sqrt{36+16} = \sqrt{52}.$$

You can use your calculator to give this as $7.21\ldots$, if you need to, but often it is better to leave the answer as $\sqrt{52}$.

The idea of coordinate geometry is to use algebra so that you can do calculations like this for any points A and B, and not just for the particular points of Fig. 1.1. It often helps to use a notation which shows at a glance which point a coordinate refers to. One way of doing this is with suffixes, calling the coordinates of the first point (x_1, y_1), and the coordinates of the second point (x_2, y_2). Thus, for example, x_1 stands for 'the x-coordinate of the first point'.

Fig. 1.2 shows this general triangle. You can see that C now has coordinates (x_2, y_1), and that $AC = x_2 - x_1$ and $CB = y_2 - y_1$. Pythagoras' theorem now gives

$$AB = \sqrt{(x_2 - x_1)^2 + (y_2 - y_1)^2}.$$

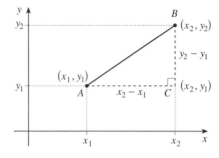

Fig. 1.2

An advantage of using algebra is that this formula works whatever the shape and position of the triangle. In Fig. 1.3, the coordinates of A are negative, and in Fig. 1.4 the line slopes downhill rather than uphill as you move from left to right. Use Figs. 1.3 and 1.4 to work out for yourself the length of AB in each case. You can then use the formula to check your answers.

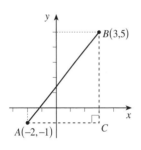

Fig. 1.3

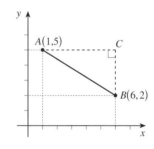

Fig. 1.4

In Fig. 1.3,

$$x_2 - x_1 = 3 - (-2) = 3 + 2 = 5 \quad \text{and} \quad y_2 - y_1 = 5 - (-1) = 5 + 1 = 6,$$

so $\quad AB = \sqrt{(3 - (-2))^2 + (5 - (-1))^2} = \sqrt{5^2 + 6^2} = \sqrt{25 + 36} = \sqrt{61}.$

And in Fig. 1.4,

$$x_2 - x_1 = 6 - 1 = 5 \quad \text{and} \quad y_2 - y_1 = 2 - 5 = -3,$$

so $\quad AB = \sqrt{(6 - 1)^2 + (2 - 5)^2} = \sqrt{5^2 + (-3)^2} = \sqrt{25 + 9} = \sqrt{34}.$

Also, it doesn't matter which way round you label the points A and B. If you think of B as 'the first point' (x_1, y_1), and A as 'the second point' (x_2, y_2), then the formula doesn't change. In Fig. 1.1, it would give

$$BA = \sqrt{(4 - 10)^2 + (3 - 7)^2} = \sqrt{(-6)^2 + (-4)^2} = \sqrt{36 + 16} = \sqrt{52}, \text{ as before.}$$

The distance between the points (x_1, y_1) and (x_2, y_2) (or the length of the line segment joining them) is

$$\sqrt{(x_2 - x_1)^2 + (y_2 - y_1)^2}.$$

1.2 The mid-point of a line segment

You can also use coordinates to find the mid-point of a line segment.

Fig. 1.5 shows the same line segment as Fig. 1.1, but with the mid-point M added. The line through M parallel to the y-axis meets AC at D. Then the lengths of the sides of the triangle ADM are half of those of triangle ACB, so that

$$AD = \tfrac{1}{2} AC = \tfrac{1}{2}(10 - 4) = \tfrac{1}{2}(6) = 3,$$

$$DM = \tfrac{1}{2} CB = \tfrac{1}{2}(7 - 3) = \tfrac{1}{2}(4) = 2.$$

The x-coordinate of M is the same as the x-coordinate of D, which is

$$4 + AD = 4 + \tfrac{1}{2}(10 - 4) = 4 + 3 = 7.$$

The y-coordinate of M is

$$3 + DM = 3 + \tfrac{1}{2}(7 - 3) = 3 + 2 = 5.$$

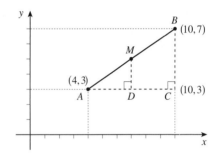

Fig. 1.5

So the mid-point M has coordinates $(7, 5)$.

In Fig. 1.6 points M and D have been added in the same way to Fig. 1.2. Exactly as before,

$$AD = \tfrac{1}{2} AC = \tfrac{1}{2}(x_2 - x_1), \text{ and}$$

$$DM = \tfrac{1}{2} CB = \tfrac{1}{2}(y_2 - y_1).$$

So the x-coordinate of M is

$$x_1 + AD = x_1 + \tfrac{1}{2}(x_2 - x_1) = x_1 + \tfrac{1}{2}x_2 - \tfrac{1}{2}x_1$$

$$= \tfrac{1}{2}x_1 + \tfrac{1}{2}x_2 = \tfrac{1}{2}(x_1 + x_2).$$

The y-coordinate is

$$y_1 + DM = y_1 + \tfrac{1}{2}(y_2 - y_1) = y_1 + \tfrac{1}{2}y_2 - \tfrac{1}{2}y_1$$

$$= \tfrac{1}{2}y_1 + \tfrac{1}{2}y_2 = \tfrac{1}{2}(y_1 + y_2).$$

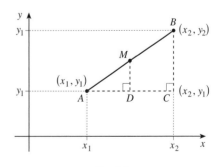

Fig. 1.6

The mid-point of the line segment joining (x_1, y_1) and (x_2, y_2) has coordinates

$$\left(\tfrac{1}{2}(x_1 + x_2), \tfrac{1}{2}(y_1 + y_2)\right).$$

Now that you have an algebraic form for the coordinates of M you can use it for any two points. For example, for Fig. 1.3 the mid-point of AB is

$$\left(\tfrac{1}{2}((-2)+3), \tfrac{1}{2}((-1)+5)\right) = \left(\tfrac{1}{2}(1), \tfrac{1}{2}(4)\right) = \left(\tfrac{1}{2}, 2\right).$$

And for Fig. 1.4 it is $\left(\tfrac{1}{2}(1+6), \tfrac{1}{2}(5+2)\right) = \left(\tfrac{1}{2}(7), \tfrac{1}{2}(7)\right) = \left(3\tfrac{1}{2}, 3\tfrac{1}{2}\right).$

Again, it doesn't matter which you call the first point and which the second. In Fig. 1.5, if you take (x_1, y_1) as $(10, 7)$ and (x_2, y_2) as $(4, 3)$, you find that the mid-point is $\left(\tfrac{1}{2}(10+4), \tfrac{1}{2}(7+3)\right) = (7, 5)$, as before.

1.3 The gradient of a line segment

The gradient of a line is a measure of its steepness. The steeper the line, the larger the gradient.

Unlike the distance and the mid-point, the gradient is a property of the whole line, not just a particular line segment. If you take any two points on the line and find the increases in the x- and y-coordinates as you go from one to the other, as in Fig. 1.7, then the value of the fraction

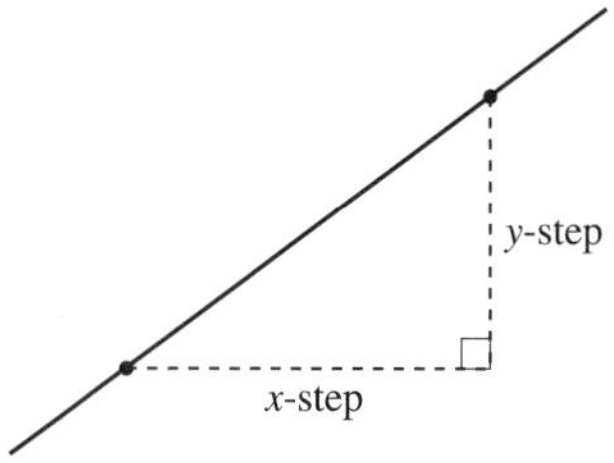

Fig. 1.7

$$\frac{y\text{-step}}{x\text{-step}}$$

is the same whichever points you choose. This is the **gradient** of the line.

In Fig. 1.2 on page 4 the x-step and y-step are $x_2 - x_1$ and $y_2 - y_1$, so that:

> The gradient of the line joining (x_1, y_1) to (x_2, y_2) is $\dfrac{y_2 - y_1}{x_2 - x_1}$.

This formula applies whether the coordinates are positive or negative. In Fig. 1.3, for example, the gradient of AB is $\dfrac{5-(-1)}{3-(-2)} = \dfrac{5+1}{3+2} = \dfrac{6}{5}$.

But notice that in Fig. 1.4 the gradient is $\dfrac{2-5}{6-1} = \dfrac{-3}{5} = -\dfrac{3}{5}$; the negative gradient tells you that the line slopes downhill as you move from left to right.

As with the other formulae, it doesn't matter which point has the suffix 1 and which has the suffix 2. In Fig. 1.1, you can calculate the gradient as either $\dfrac{7-3}{10-4} = \dfrac{4}{6} = \dfrac{2}{3}$, or $\dfrac{3-7}{4-10} = \dfrac{-4}{-6} = \dfrac{2}{3}$.

Two lines are **parallel** if they have the same gradient.

Example 1.3.1

The ends of a line segment are $(p-q, p+q)$ and $(p+q, p-q)$. Find the length of the line segment, its gradient and the coordinates of its mid-point.

For the length and gradient you have to calculate

$$x_2 - x_1 = (p+q) - (p-q) = p+q-p+q = 2q$$

and $\quad y_2 - y_1 = (p-q) - (p+q) = p-q-p-q = -2q.$

The length is $\sqrt{(x_2 - x_1)^2 + (y_2 - y_1)^2} = \sqrt{(2q)^2 + (-2q)^2} = \sqrt{4q^2 + 4q^2} = \sqrt{8q^2}.$

The gradient is $\dfrac{y_2 - y_1}{x_2 - x_1} = \dfrac{-2q}{2q} = -1.$

For the mid-point you have to calculate

$$x_1 + x_2 = (p-q) + (p+q) = p-q+p+q = 2p$$

and $\quad y_1 + y_2 = (p+q) + (p-q) = p+q+p-q = 2p.$

The mid-point is $\left(\frac{1}{2}(x_1 + x_2), \frac{1}{2}(y_1 + y_2)\right) = \left(\frac{1}{2}(2p), \frac{1}{2}(2p)\right) = (p, p).$

Try drawing your own figure to illustrate the results in this example.

Example 1.3.2

Prove that the points $A(1,1)$, $B(5,3)$, $C(3,0)$ and $D(-1,-2)$ form a parallelogram.

There are a number of ways in which you can approach this problem, but whichever method you use, it is worth drawing a sketch. This is shown in Fig. 1.8.

Method 1 (using distances)   In this method find the lengths of the opposite sides. If both pairs of opposite sides are equal, then $ABCD$ is a parallelogram.

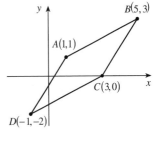

Fig. 1.8

$$AB = \sqrt{(5-1)^2 + (3-1)^2} = \sqrt{20}.$$
$$DC = \sqrt{(3-(-1))^2 + (0-(-2))^2} = \sqrt{20}.$$
$$CB = \sqrt{(5-3)^2 + (3-0)^2} = \sqrt{13}.$$
$$DA = \sqrt{(1-(-1))^2 + (1-(-2))^2} = \sqrt{13}.$$

Therefore $AB = DC$ and $CB = DA$, so $ABCD$ is a parallelogram.

Method 2 (using mid-points)   In this method, begin by finding the mid-points of the diagonals AC and BD. If these points are the same, then the diagonals bisect each other, so the quadrilateral is a parallelogram.

The mid-point of AC is $\left(\frac{1}{2}(1+3), \frac{1}{2}(1+0)\right)$, which is $\left(2, \frac{1}{2}\right)$. The mid-point of BD is $\left(\frac{1}{2}(5+(-1)), \frac{1}{2}(3+(-2))\right)$, which is also $\left(2, \frac{1}{2}\right)$. So $ABCD$ is a parallelogram.

Method 3 (using gradients)   In this method find the gradients of the opposite sides. If both pairs of opposite sides are parallel, then $ABCD$ is a parallelogram.

The gradients of AB and DC are $\frac{3-1}{5-1} = \frac{2}{4} = \frac{1}{2}$ and $\frac{0-(-2)}{3-(-1)} = \frac{2}{4} = \frac{1}{2}$ respectively, so AB is parallel to DC. The gradients of DA and CB are both $\frac{3}{2}$, so DA is parallel to CB. As the opposite sides are parallel, $ABCD$ is a parallelogram.

Exercise 1A

Do not use a calculator. Where appropriate, leave square roots in your answers.

1 Find the lengths of the line segments joining these pairs of points. In parts (e) and (h) assume that $a > 0$; in parts (i) and (j) assume that $p > q > 0$.

(a) $(2,5)$ and $(7,17)$ (b) $(-3,2)$ and $(1,-1)$

(c) $(4,-5)$ and $(-1,0)$ (d) $(-3,-3)$ and $(-7,3)$

(e) $(2a,a)$ and $(10a,-14a)$ (f) $(a+1,2a+3)$ and $(a-1,2a-1)$

(g) $(2,9)$ and $(2,-14)$ (h) $(12a,5b)$ and $(3a,5b)$

(i) (p,q) and (q,p) (j) $(p+4q,p-q)$ and $(p-3q,p)$

2 Show that the points $(1,-2)$, $(6,-1)$, $(9,3)$ and $(4,2)$ are vertices of a parallelogram.

3 Show that the triangle formed by the points $(-3,-2)$, $(2,-7)$ and $(-2,5)$ is isosceles.

4 Show that the points $(7,12)$, $(-3,-12)$ and $(14,-5)$ lie on a circle with centre $(2,0)$.

5 Find the coordinates of the mid-points of the line segments joining these pairs of points.

(a) $(2,11),(6,15)$ (b) $(5,7),(-3,9)$

(c) $(-2,-3),(1,-6)$ (d) $(-3,4),(-8,5)$

(e) $(p+2,3p-1),(3p+4,p-5)$ (f) $(p+3,q-7),(p+5,3-q)$

(g) $(p+2q,2p+13q),(5p-2q,-2p-7q)$ (h) $(a+3,b-5),(a+3,b+7)$

6 $A(-2,1)$ and $B(6,5)$ are the opposite ends of the diameter of a circle.
   Find the coordinates of its centre.

7 $M(5,7)$ is the mid-point of the line segment joining $A(3,4)$ to B. Find the coordinates of B.

8 $A(1,-2)$, $B(6,-1)$, $C(9,3)$ and $D(4,2)$ are the vertices of a parallelogram.
   Verify that the mid-points of the diagonals AC and BD coincide.

9 Which one of the points $A(5,2)$, $B(6,-3)$ and $C(4,7)$ is the mid-point of the other two?
   Check your answer by calculating two distances.

10 Find the gradients of the lines joining the following pairs of points.

(a) $(3,8),(5,12)$ (b) $(1,-3),(-2,6)$

(c) $(-4,-3),(0,-1)$ (d) $(-5,-3),(3,-9)$

(e) $(p+3,p-3),(2p+4,-p-5)$ (f) $(p+3,q-5),(q-5,p+3)$

(g) $(p+q-1,q+p-3),(p-q+1,q-p+3)$ (h) $(7,p),(11,p)$

11 Find the gradients of the lines AB and BC where A is $(3,4)$, B is $(7,6)$ and C is $(-3,1)$. What can you deduce about the points A, B and C?

12 The point $P(x,y)$ lies on the straight line joining $A(3,0)$ and $B(5,6)$. Find expressions for the gradients of AP and PB. Hence show that $y = 3x - 9$.

13 A median of a triangle is a line joining one vertex to the mid-point of the opposite side. Find the length of the median AM in the triangle $A(-1,1)$, $B(0,3)$, $C(4,7)$.

14 A triangle has vertices $A(-2,1)$, $B(3,-4)$ and $C(5,7)$.

    (a) Find the coordinates of M, the mid-point of AB, and N, the mid-point of AC.

    (b) Show that MN is parallel to BC.

15 The points $A(2,1)$, $B(2,7)$ and $C(-4,-1)$ form a triangle. M is the mid-point of AB and N is the mid-point of AC.

    (a) Find the lengths of MN and BC.   (b) Show that $BC = 2MN$.

16 The vertices of a quadrilateral $ABCD$ are $A(1,1)$, $B(7,3)$, $C(9,-7)$ and $D(-3,-3)$. The points P, Q, R and S are the mid-points of AB, BC, CD and DA respectively.

    (a) Find the gradient of each side of $PQRS$.   (b) What type of quadrilateral is $PQRS$?

17 The origin O and the points $P(4,1)$, $Q(5,5)$ and $R(1,4)$ form a quadrilateral.

    (a) Show that OR is parallel to PQ.   (b) Show that OP is parallel to RQ.

    (c) Show that $OP = OR$.   (d) What shape is $OPQR$?

18 The origin O and the points $L(-2,3)$, $M(4,7)$ and $N(6,4)$ form a quadrilateral.

    (a) Show that $ON = LM$.   (b) Show that ON is parallel to LM.

    (c) Show that $OM = LN$.   (d) What shape is $OLMN$?

19 The vertices of a quadrilateral $PQRS$ are $P(1,2)$, $Q(7,0)$, $R(6,-4)$ and $S(-3,-1)$.

    (a) Find the gradient of each side of the quadrilateral.

    (b) What type of quadrilateral is $PQRS$?

20 The vertices of a quadrilateral are $T(3,2)$, $U(2,5)$, $V(8,7)$ and $W(6,1)$. The mid-points of UV and VW are M and N respectively. Show that the triangle TMN is isosceles.

21 The vertices of a quadrilateral $DEFG$ are $D(3,-2)$, $E(0,-3)$, $F(-2,3)$ and $G(4,1)$.

    (a) Find the length of each side of the quadrilateral.

    (b) What type of quadrilateral is $DEFG$?

22 The points $A(2,1)$, $B(6,10)$ and $C(10,1)$ form an isosceles triangle with AB and BC of equal length. The point G is $(6,4)$.

    (a) Write down the coordinates of M, the mid-point of AC.

    (b) Show that $BG = 2GM$ and that BGM is a straight line.

    (c) Write down the coordinates of N, the mid-point of BC.

    (d) Show that AGN is a straight line and that $AG = 2GN$.

1.4   What is meant by the equation of a straight line or of a curve?

How can you tell whether or not the points $(3,7)$ and $(1,5)$ lie on the curve $y = 3x^2 + 2$? The answer is to substitute the coordinates of the points in the equation and see whether they fit; that is, whether the equation is **satisfied** by the coordinates of the point.

For $(3,7)$: the right side is $3 \times 3^2 + 2 = 29$ and the left side is 7, so the equation is not satisfied. The point $(3,7)$ does not lie on the curve $y = 3x^2 + 2$.

For $(1,5)$: the right side is $3 \times 1^2 + 2 = 5$ and the left side is 5, so the equation is satisfied. The point $(1,5)$ lies on the curve $y = 3x^2 + 2$.

> The equation of a curve is a rule for determining whether or not the point with coordinates (x, y) lies on the curve.

This is an important way of thinking about the equation of a curve.

1.5   The equation of a line

Example 1.5.1

Find the equation of the line with gradient 2 which passes through the point $(2,1)$.

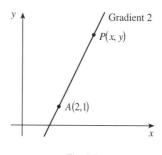

Fig. 1.9 shows the line of gradient 2 through $A(2,1)$, with another point $P(x, y)$ lying on it. P lies on the line if (and only if) the gradient of AP is 2.

Fig. 1.9

The gradient of AP is $\dfrac{y-1}{x-2}$. Equating this to 2 gives $\dfrac{y-1}{x-2} = 2$, which is $y - 1 = 2x - 4$, or $y = 2x - 3$.

In the general case, you need to find the equation of the line with gradient m through the point A with coordinates (x_1, y_1). Fig. 1.10 shows this line and another point P with coordinates (x, y) on it. The gradient of AP is $\dfrac{y - y_1}{x - x_1}$.

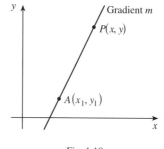

Equating to m gives $\dfrac{y - y_1}{x - x_1} = m$, or $y - y_1 = m(x - x_1)$.

> The equation of the line through (x_1, y_1) with gradient m is $y - y_1 = m(x - x_1)$.

Fig. 1.10

Notice that the coordinates of A satisfy this equation.

Example 1.5.2

Find the equation of the line through the point $(-2,3)$ with gradient -1.

Using the equation $y - y_1 = m(x - x_1)$, the equation is $y - 3 = -1(x - (-2))$, which is $y - 3 = -x - 2$ or $y = -x + 1$. As a check, substitute the coordinates $(-2,3)$ into both sides of the equation, to make sure that the given point does actually lie on the line.

Example 1.5.3

Find the equation of the line joining the points $(3,4)$ and $(-1,2)$.

To find this equation, first find the gradient of the line joining $(3,4)$ to $(-1,2)$. Then you can use the equation $y - y_1 = m(x - x_1)$.

The gradient of the line joining $(3,4)$ to $(-1,2)$ is $\dfrac{2-4}{(-1)-3} = \dfrac{-2}{-4} = \dfrac{1}{2}$.

The equation of the line through $(3,4)$ with gradient $\frac{1}{2}$ is $y - 4 = \frac{1}{2}(x - 3)$. After multiplying out and simplifying you get $2y - 8 = x - 3$, or $2y = x + 5$.

Check this equation mentally by substituting the coordinates of the other point.

1.6 Recognising the equation of a line

The answers to Examples 1.5.1–3 can all be written in the form $y = mx + c$, where m and c are numbers.

It is easy to show that any equation of this form is the equation of a straight line. If $y = mx + c$, then $y - c = m(x - 0)$, or

$$\frac{y-c}{x-0} = m \qquad \text{(except when } x = 0\text{).}$$

This equation tells you that, for all points whose coordinates satisfy the equation, the line joining $(0,c)$ to (x,y) has gradient m. That is, (x,y) lies on the line through $(0,c)$ with gradient m.

The point $(0,c)$ lies on the y-axis. The number c is called the **y-intercept** of the line.

To find the x-intercept, put $y = 0$ in the equation, which gives $x = -\dfrac{c}{m}$. But notice that you can't do this division if $m = 0$. In that case the line is parallel to the x-axis, so there is no x-intercept.

When $m = 0$, all the points on the line have the coordinates $(\text{something}, c)$. Thus the points $(1,2)$, $(-1,2)$, $(5,2)$, ... all lie on the straight line $y = 2$, shown in Fig. 1.11.

Similarly, a straight line parallel to the y-axis has an equation of the form $x = k$. All points on it have coordinates of the form $(k, \text{something})$. Thus the points $(3,0)$, $(3,2)$, $(3,4)$, ... all lie on the line $x = 3$, shown in Fig. 1.12.

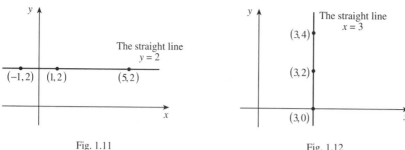

Fig. 1.11   Fig. 1.12

This line does not have a gradient; its gradient is undefined. Its equation cannot be written in the form $y = mx + c$.

1.7   The equation $ax + by + c = 0$

Suppose you have the equation $y = \frac{2}{3}x + \frac{4}{3}$. It is natural to multiply by 3 to get $3y = 2x + 4$, which can be rearranged to get $2x - 3y + 4 = 0$. This equation is in the form $ax + by + c = 0$ where a, b and c are constants.

A simple way to find the gradient of $ax + by + c = 0$ is to rearrange it into the form $y = \dots$. Here are some examples.

Notice that the straight lines $y = mx + c$ and $ax + by + c = 0$ both contain the letter c, but it doesn't have the same meanings. For $y = mx + c$, c is the y-intercept, but there is no similar meaning for the c in $ax + by + c = 0$.

Example 1.7.1
Find the gradient of the line $2x + 3y - 4 = 0$.
Write this equation in the form $y = \dots$, and then use the fact that the straight line $y = mx + c$ has gradient m.

From $2x + 3y - 4 = 0$ you find that $3y = -2x + 4$ and $y = -\frac{2}{3}x + \frac{4}{3}$. Therefore, comparing this equation with $y = mx + c$, the gradient is $-\frac{2}{3}$.

Example 1.7.2
One side of a parallelogram lies along the straight line with equation $3x - 4y - 7 = 0$. The point $(2, 3)$ is a vertex of the parallelogram. Find the equation of one other side.

The line $3x - 4y - 7 = 0$ is the same as $y = \frac{3}{4}x - \frac{7}{4}$, so its gradient is $\frac{3}{4}$. The line through $(2, 3)$ with gradient $\frac{3}{4}$ is $y - 3 = \frac{3}{4}(x - 2)$, or $3x - 4y + 6 = 0$.

1.8   The point of intersection of two lines

Suppose that you have two lines with equations $2x - y = 4$ and $3x + 2y = -1$. How do you find the coordinates of the point of intersection of these lines?

You want the point (x, y) which lies on both lines, so the coordinates (x, y) satisfy both equations. Therefore you need to solve the equations simultaneously.

From these two equations, you find $x = 1$, $y = -2$, so the point of intersection is $(1, -2)$.

This argument applies to straight lines with any equations provided they are not parallel. To find points of intersection, solve the equations simultaneously. The method can also be used to find the points of intersection of two curves.

Exercise 1B

1 In each part test whether the given point lies on the curve (or straight line) with the given equation.

(a) $(1, 2)$ on $y = 5x - 3$

(b) $(3, -2)$ on $y = 3x - 7$

(c) $(3, -4)$ on $x^2 + y^2 = 25$

(d) $(2, 2)$ on $3x^2 + y^2 = 40$

(e) $\left(1, 1\frac{1}{2}\right)$ on $y = \dfrac{x + 2}{3x - 1}$

(f) $\left(5p, \dfrac{5}{p}\right)$ on $y = \dfrac{5}{x}$

(g) $\left(p, (p-1)^2 + 1\right)$ on $y = x^2 - 2x + 2$

(h) $\left(t^2, 2t\right)$ on $y^2 = 4x$

2 Find the equations of the straight lines through the given points with the gradient shown. Your final answers should not contain any fractions.

(a) $(2, 3)$, gradient 5

(b) $(1, -2)$, gradient -3

(c) $(0, 4)$, gradient $\frac{1}{2}$

(d) $(-2, 1)$, gradient $-\frac{3}{8}$

(e) $(0, 0)$, gradient -3

(f) $(3, 8)$, gradient 0

(g) $(-5, -1)$, gradient $-\frac{3}{4}$

(h) $(-3, 0)$, gradient $\frac{1}{2}$

(i) $(-3, -1)$, gradient $\frac{3}{8}$

(j) $(3, 4)$, gradient $-\frac{1}{2}$

(k) $(2, -1)$, gradient -2

(l) $(-2, -5)$, gradient 3

(m) $(0, -4)$, gradient 7

(n) $(0, 2)$, gradient -1

(o) $(3, -2)$, gradient $-\frac{5}{8}$

(p) $(3, 0)$, gradient $-\frac{3}{5}$

(q) $(d, 0)$, gradient 7

(r) $(0, 4)$, gradient m

(s) $(0, c)$, gradient 3

(t) $(c, 0)$, gradient m

3 Find the equations of the lines joining the following pairs of points. Leave your final answer without fractions and in one of the forms $y = mx + c$ or $ax + by + c = 0$.

(a) $(1, 4)$ and $(3, 10)$

(b) $(4, 5)$ and $(-2, -7)$

(c) $(3, 2)$ and $(0, 4)$

(d) $(3, 7)$ and $(3, 12)$

(e) $(10, -3)$ and $(-5, -12)$

(f) $(3, -1)$ and $(-4, 20)$

(g) $(2, -3)$ and $(11, -3)$

(h) $(2, 0)$ and $(5, -1)$

(i) $(-4, 2)$ and $(-1, -3)$

(j) $(-2, -1)$ and $(5, -3)$

(k) $(-3, 4)$ and $(-3, 9)$

(l) $(-1, 0)$ and $(0, -1)$

(m) $(2, 7)$ and $(3, 10)$

(n) $(-5, 4)$ and $(-2, -1)$

(o) $(0, 0)$ and $(5, -3)$

(p) $(0, 0)$ and (p, q)

(q) (p, q) and $(p + 3, q - 1)$

(r) $(p, -q)$ and (p, q)

(s) (p, q) and $(p + 2, q + 2)$

(t) $(p, 0)$ and $(0, q)$

4 Find the gradients of the following lines.

(a) $2x + y = 7$ (b) $3x - 4y = 8$ (c) $5x + 2y = -3$

(d) $y = 5$ (e) $3x - 2y = -4$ (f) $5x = 7$

(g) $x + y = -3$ (h) $y = 3(x + 4)$ (i) $7 - x = 2y$

(j) $3(y - 4) = 7x$ (k) $y = m(x - d)$ (l) $px + qy = pq$

5 Find the equation of the line through $(-2, 1)$ parallel to $y = \frac{1}{2}x - 3$.

6 Find the equation of the line through $(4, -3)$ parallel to $y + 2x = 7$.

7 Find the equation of the line through $(1, 2)$ parallel to the line joining $(3, -1)$ and $(-5, 2)$.

8 Find the equation of the line through $(3, 9)$ parallel to the line joining $(-3, 2)$ and $(2, -3)$.

9 Find the equation of the line through $(1, 7)$ parallel to the x-axis.

10 Find the equation of the line through $(d, 0)$ parallel to $y = mx + c$.

11 Find the points of intersection of the following pairs of straight lines.

(a) $3x + 4y = 33,\ 2y = x - 1$ (b) $y = 3x + 1,\ y = 4x - 1$

(c) $2y = 7x,\ 3x - 2y = 1$ (d) $y = 3x + 8,\ y = -2x - 7$

(e) $x + 5y = 22,\ 3x + 2y = 14$ (f) $2x + 7y = 47,\ 5x + 4y = 50$

(g) $2x + 3y = 7,\ 6x + 9y = 11$ (h) $3x + y = 5,\ x + 3y = -1$

(i) $y = 2x + 3,\ 4x - 2y = -6$ (j) $ax + by = c,\ y = 2ax$

(k) $y = mx + c,\ y = -mx + d$ (l) $ax - by = 1,\ y = x$

12 Let P, with coordinates (p, q), be a fixed point on the 'curve' with equation $y = mx + c$ and Q, with coordinates (r, s), be any other point on $y = mx + c$. Use the fact that the coordinates of P and Q satisfy the equation $y = mx + c$ to show that the gradient of PQ is m for all positions of Q.

13* There are some values of a, b and c for which the equation $ax + by + c = 0$ does not represent a straight line. Give an example of such values.

1.9 The gradients of perpendicular lines

In Section 1.3 you saw that if two lines are parallel they have the same gradient. But what can you say about the gradients of two lines which are perpendicular? Firstly, if a line has a positive gradient, then the perpendicular line has a negative gradient, and vice versa. But you can be more exact than this. In Fig. 1.13, if the gradient of PB is m, you can draw a 'gradient triangle' PAB in which PA is one unit and AB is m units.

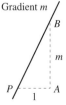

Fig. 1.13

In Fig 1.14, the gradient triangle PAB has been
rotated through a right-angle to $PA'B'$, so that
PB' is perpendicular to PB. The y-step for
$PA'B'$ is 1 and the x-step is $-m$, so

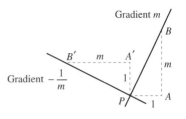

$$\text{gradient of } PB' = \frac{y\text{-step}}{x\text{-step}} = \frac{1}{-m} = -\frac{1}{m}.$$

Fig. 1.14

Therefore the gradient of the line perpendicular to PB is $-\dfrac{1}{m}$.

Thus if the gradients of the two perpendicular lines are m_1 and m_2, then $m_1 m_2 = -1$. It
is also true that if two lines have gradients m_1 and m_2, and if $m_1 m_2 = -1$, then the lines
are perpendicular. To prove this, see Miscellaneous exercise 1 Question 21.

Two lines with gradients m_1 and m_2 are perpendicular if

$$m_1 m_2 = -1, \quad \text{or} \quad m_1 = -\frac{1}{m_2}, \quad \text{or} \quad m_2 = -\frac{1}{m_1}.$$

Notice that the condition does not work if the lines are parallel to the axes. However,
you can see that a line $x = \text{constant}$ is perpendicular to one of the form $y = \text{constant}$.

Example 1.9.1
Show that the points $(0, -5)$, $(-1, 2)$, $(4, 7)$ and $(5, 0)$ form a rhombus.

*There are a number of ways that you could tackle this question. This solution shows that
the points form a parallelogram, and then that its diagonals are perpendicular.*

The mid-points of the diagonals are $\left(\frac{1}{2}(0 + 4), \frac{1}{2}(-5 + 7)\right)$, or $(2, 1)$, and

$\left(\frac{1}{2}((-1) + 5), \frac{1}{2}(2 + 0)\right)$, or $(2, 1)$. As these are the same point, the quadrilateral is a
parallelogram.

The gradients of the diagonals are $\dfrac{7 - (-5)}{4 - 0} = \frac{12}{4} = 3$ and $\dfrac{0 - 2}{5 - (-1)} = \frac{-2}{6} = -\frac{1}{3}$. As
the product of the gradients is -1, the diagonals are perpendicular. Therefore the
parallelogram is a rhombus.

Example 1.9.2
Find the coordinates of the foot of the perpendicular from $A(-2, -4)$ to the line joining
$B(0, 2)$ and $C(-1, 4)$.

*Always draw a diagram, like Fig. 1.15, which need not be to scale. The foot of the
perpendicular is the point of intersection, P, of BC and the line through A
perpendicular to BC. First find the gradient of BC and its equation.*

The gradient of BC is $\dfrac{4-2}{-1-0} = \dfrac{2}{-1} = -2$.

The equation of BC is $y - 2 = -2(x - 0)$,
which simplifies to $2x + y = 2$.

The gradient of the line through A

perpendicular to BC is $-\dfrac{1}{-2} = \frac{1}{2}$.

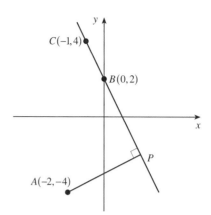

The equation of this line is

$$y - (-4) = \tfrac{1}{2}(x - (-2)),$$

or $x - 2y = 6$.

Fig. 1.15

These lines meet at the point P, whose
coordinates satisfy the simultaneous
equations $2x + y = 2$ and $x - 2y = 6$.
This is the point $(2, -2)$.

Exercise 1C

1   In each part write down the gradient of a line which is perpendicular to the one with the
given gradient.

(a) 2

(b) -3

(c) $\frac{3}{4}$

(d) $-\frac{5}{6}$

(e) -1

(f) $1\frac{3}{4}$

(g) $-\dfrac{1}{m}$

(h) m

(i) $\dfrac{p}{q}$

(j) 0

(k) $-m$

(l) $\dfrac{a}{b-c}$

2   In each part find the equation of the line through the given point which is perpendicular to
the given line. Your final answer should not contain any fractions.

(a) $(2,3)$ $y = 4x + 3$

(b) $(-3,1)$ $y = -\frac{1}{2}x + 3$

(c) $(2,-5)$ $y = -5x - 2$

(d) $(7,-4)$ $y = 2\frac{1}{2}$

(e) $(-1,4)$ $2x + 3y = 8$

(f) $(4,3)$ $3x - 5y = 8$

(g) $(5,-3)$ $2x = 3$

(h) $(0,3)$ $y = 2x - 1$

(i) $(0,0)$ $y = mx + c$

(j) (a,b) $y = mx + c$

(k) (c,d) $ny - x = p$

(l) $(-1,-2)$ $ax + by = c$

3   Find the equation of the line through the point $(-2,5)$ which is perpendicular to the line
$y = 3x + 1$. Find also the point of intersection of the two lines.

4   Find the equation of the line through the point $(1,1)$ which is perpendicular to the line
$2x - 3y = 12$. Find also the point of intersection of the two lines.

5   An altitude of a triangle is a line through a vertex which is perpendicular to the opposite
side. Find the equation of the altitude through the vertex A of the triangle ABC where A is
the point $(2,3)$, B is $(1,-7)$ and C is $(4,-1)$.

6 $P(2,5)$, $Q(12,5)$ and $R(8,-7)$ form a triangle.

   (a) Find the equations of the altitudes through (i) R and (ii) Q.

   (b) Find the point of intersection of these altitudes.

   (c) Show that the altitude through P also passes through this point.

Miscellaneous exercise 1

1 Show that the triangle formed by the points $(-2,5)$, $(1,3)$ and $(5,9)$ is right-angled.

2 Find the coordinates of the point where the lines $2x+y=3$ and $3x+5y-1=0$ meet.

3 A triangle is formed by the points $A(-1,3)$, $B(5,7)$ and $C(0,8)$.

   (a) Show that the angle ACB is a right angle.

   (b) Find the coordinates of the point where the line through B parallel to AC cuts the x-axis.

4 $A(7,2)$ and $C(1,4)$ are two vertices of a square $ABCD$.

   (a) Find the equation of the diagonal BD.

   (b) Find the coordinates of B and of D.

5 A quadrilateral $ABCD$ is formed by the points $A(-3,2)$, $B(4,3)$, $C(9,-2)$ and $D(2,-3)$.

   (a) Show that all four sides are equal in length.

   (b) Show that $ABCD$ is not a square.

6 P is the point $(7,5)$ and l_1 is the line with equation $3x+4y=16$.

   (a) Find the equation of the line l_2 which passes through P and is perpendicular to l_1.

   (b) Find the point of intersection of the lines l_1 and l_2.

   (c) Find the perpendicular distance of P from the line l_1.

7 Prove that the triangle with vertices $(-2,8)$, $(3,20)$ and $(11,8)$ is isosceles. Find its area.

8 The three straight lines $y=x$, $7y=2x$ and $4x+y=60$ form a triangle. Find the coordinates of its vertices.

9 Find the equation of the line through $(1,3)$ which is parallel to $2x+7y=5$. Give your answer in the form $ax+by=c$.

10 Find the equation of the perpendicular bisector of the line joining $(2,-5)$ and $(-4,3)$.

11 The points $A(1,2)$, $B(3,5)$, $C(6,6)$ and D form a parallelogram. Find the coordinates of the mid-point of AC. Use your answer to find the coordinates of D.

12 The point P is the foot of the perpendicular from the point $A(0,3)$ to the line $y=3x$.

   (a) Find the equation of the line AP.

   (b) Find the coordinates of the point P.

   (c) Find the perpendicular distance of A from the line $y=3x$.

13 Show that the points $(-1, 3)$, $(4, 7)$ and $(-11, -5)$ are collinear (lie on the same straight line).

14 Find the equation of the straight line that passes through the points $(3, -1)$ and $(-2, 2)$, giving your answer in the form $ax + by + c = 0$. Hence find the coordinates of the point of intersection of the line and the x-axis.   (OCR)

15 The coordinates of the points A and B are $(3, 2)$ and $(4, -5)$ respectively. Find the coordinates of the mid-point of AB, and the gradient of AB.

   Hence find the equation of the perpendicular bisector of AB, giving your answer in the form $ax + by + c = 0$, where a, b and c are integers.   (OCR)

16 The curve $y = 1 + \dfrac{1}{2 + x}$ crosses the x-axis at the point A and the y-axis at the point B.

   (a) Calculate the coordinates of A and of B.

   (b) Find the equation of the line AB.

   (c) Calculate the coordinates of the point of intersection of the line AB and the line with equation $3y = 4x$.   (OCR)

17 The straight line p passes through the point $(10, 1)$ and is perpendicular to the line r with equation $2x + y = 1$. Find the equation of p.

   Find also the coordinates of the point of intersection of p and r, and deduce the perpendicular distance from the point $(10, 1)$ to the line r.   (OCR)

18 Show by calculation that the points $P(0, 7)$, $Q(6, 5)$, $R(5, 2)$ and $S(-1, 4)$ are the vertices of a rectangle.

19 The line $3x - 4y = 8$ meets the y-axis at A. The point C has coordinates $(-2, 9)$. The line through C perpendicular to $3x - 4y = 8$ meets it at B. Calculate the area of the triangle ABC.

20 The points $A(-3, -4)$ and $C(5, 4)$ are the ends of the diagonal of a rhombus $ABCD$.

   (a) Find the equation of the diagonal BD.

   (b) Given that the side BC has gradient $\frac{5}{3}$, find the coordinates of B and hence of D.

21 A median of a triangle is a line joining one vertex to the mid-point of the opposite side. Find the equations of the medians of the triangle with vertices $(0, 2)$, $(6, 0)$ and $(4, 4)$. Show that the medians are concurrent (all pass through the same point).

22* Two lines have equations $y = m_1 x + c_1$ and $y = m_2 x + c_2$, and $m_1 m_2 = -1$. Prove that the lines are perpendicular.

2 Surds

This chapter is about expressions involving square and cube roots. When you have completed it, you should

- be able to simplify expressions involving square, cube and other roots.

2.1 Different kinds of number

At first numbers were used only for counting, and 1, 2, 3, ... were all that was needed. These are **natural numbers**, or **positive integers**.

Then it was found that numbers could also be useful for measurement and in commerce. For these purposes fractions were also needed. Integers and fractions together make up the **rational numbers**. These are numbers which can be expressed in the form $\frac{p}{q}$ where p and q are integers, and q is not 0.

One of the most remarkable discoveries of the ancient Greek mathematicians was that there are numbers which cannot be expressed in this way. These are called **irrational numbers**. The first such number to be found was $\sqrt{2}$, which is the length of the diagonal of a square with side 1 unit, by Pythagoras' theorem. The argument that the Greeks used to prove this can be adapted to show that the square root, cube root, ... of any positive integer is either an integer or an irrational number. You will find a proof that $\sqrt{2}$ is irrational later in the course. Many other numbers are now known to be irrational, of which the most famous is π.

Rational and irrational numbers together make up the **real numbers**. Integers, rational and irrational numbers and real numbers can all be either positive or negative.

When rational numbers are written as decimals, they either come to a stop after a number of places, or the sequence of decimal digits eventually starts repeating in a regular pattern. For example,

$$\tfrac{7}{10} = 0.7, \quad \tfrac{7}{11} = 0.6363..., \quad \tfrac{7}{12} = 0.5833..., \quad \tfrac{7}{13} = 0.538\,461\,538\,461\,53...,$$
$$\tfrac{7}{14} = 0.5, \quad \tfrac{7}{15} = 0.466..., \quad \tfrac{7}{16} = 0.4375, \quad \tfrac{7}{17} = 0.411\,764\,705\,882\,352\,941\,176...$$

The reverse is also true, that if a decimal number stops or repeats indefinitely then it is a rational number. So if an irrational number is written as a decimal, the pattern of the decimal digits never repeats however long you continue the calculation.

2.2 Surds and their properties

When you have met expressions such as $\sqrt{2}$, $\sqrt{8}$ and $\sqrt{12}$ before, it is likely that you have used a calculator to express them in decimal form. You might have written

$$\sqrt{2} = 1.414... \quad \text{or} \quad \sqrt{2} = 1.414 \text{ correct to three decimal places} \quad \text{or} \quad \sqrt{2} \approx 1.414.$$

Why is the statement '$\sqrt{2} = 1.414$' incorrect?

Expressions like $\sqrt{2}$ or $\sqrt[3]{9}$ are called **surds**. This section is about calculating with surds. You need to remember that $\sqrt{x}$ always means the **positive** square root of x, or zero.

The main properties that you will use are:

$$\sqrt{xy} = \sqrt{x} \times \sqrt{y} \quad \text{and} \quad \sqrt{\frac{x}{y}} = \frac{\sqrt{x}}{\sqrt{y}}.$$

As $\left(\sqrt{x} \times \sqrt{y}\right) \times \left(\sqrt{x} \times \sqrt{y}\right) = \left(\sqrt{x} \times \sqrt{x}\right) \times \left(\sqrt{y} \times \sqrt{y}\right) = x \times y = xy$, and as $\sqrt{x} \times \sqrt{y}$ is positive, it is the square root of xy. Therefore $\sqrt{xy} = \sqrt{x} \times \sqrt{y}$. Similar reasoning will convince you that $\sqrt{\frac{x}{y}} = \frac{\sqrt{x}}{\sqrt{y}}$.

The following examples illustrate these properties:

$$\sqrt{8} = \sqrt{4 \times 2} = \sqrt{4} \times \sqrt{2} = 2\sqrt{2}; \quad \sqrt{12} = \sqrt{4 \times 3} = \sqrt{4} \times \sqrt{3} = 2\sqrt{3};$$
$$\sqrt{18} \times \sqrt{2} = \sqrt{18 \times 2} = \sqrt{36} = 6; \quad \frac{\sqrt{27}}{\sqrt{3}} = \sqrt{\frac{27}{3}} = \sqrt{9} = 3.$$

It is well worth checking some or all of the calculations above on your calculator.

Example 2.2.1
Simplify   (a) $\sqrt{28} + \sqrt{63}$,   (b) $\sqrt{5} \times \sqrt{10}$.
Notice that alternative methods of solution may be possible, as in part (b).

(a) $\sqrt{28} + \sqrt{63} = \left(\sqrt{4} \times \sqrt{7}\right) + \left(\sqrt{9} \times \sqrt{7}\right) = 2\sqrt{7} + 3\sqrt{7} = 5\sqrt{7}$.

(b) **Method 1** $\sqrt{5} \times \sqrt{10} = \sqrt{5 \times 10} = \sqrt{50} = \sqrt{25 \times 2} = 5\sqrt{2}$

   Method 2 $\sqrt{5} \times \sqrt{10} = \sqrt{5} \times \left(\sqrt{5} \times \sqrt{2}\right) = \left(\sqrt{5} \times \sqrt{5}\right) \times \sqrt{2} = 5\sqrt{2}$.

It is sometimes useful to be able to remove a surd from the denominator of a fraction such as $\frac{1}{\sqrt{2}}$. You can do this by multiplying top and bottom by $\sqrt{2}$: $\frac{1 \times \sqrt{2}}{\sqrt{2} \times \sqrt{2}} = \frac{\sqrt{2}}{2}$.

Helpful results which you should try to use whenever possible are:

$$\frac{x}{\sqrt{x}} = \sqrt{x}, \text{ and its reciprocal } \frac{1}{\sqrt{x}} = \frac{\sqrt{x}}{x}.$$

Removing the surd from the denominator is called **rationalising the denominator**.

Example 2.2.2
Rationalise the denominator in the expressions   (a) $\dfrac{6}{\sqrt{2}}$,   (b) $\dfrac{3\sqrt{2}}{\sqrt{10}}$.

(a) $\dfrac{6}{\sqrt{2}} = \dfrac{3 \times 2}{\sqrt{2}} = 3 \times \dfrac{2}{\sqrt{2}} = 3\sqrt{2}$.

(b) $\dfrac{3\sqrt{2}}{\sqrt{10}} = \dfrac{3}{\sqrt{5}} = \dfrac{3\sqrt{5}}{5}$.

Similar rules to those for square roots also apply to cube roots and higher roots.

Example 2.2.3
Simplify   (a) $\sqrt[3]{16}$,   (b) $\sqrt[3]{12} \times \sqrt[3]{18}$.

(a) $\sqrt[3]{16} = \sqrt[3]{8 \times 2} = \sqrt[3]{8} \times \sqrt[3]{2} = 2 \times \sqrt[3]{2}$.

(b) $\sqrt[3]{12} \times \sqrt[3]{18} = \sqrt[3]{12 \times 18} = \sqrt[3]{216} = 6$.

Example 2.2.4
Fig. 2.1 shows the vertical cross-section of a roof of a building as a right-angled triangle ABC, with $AB = 15$ m. The height of the roof, BD, is 10 m. Calculate x and y.

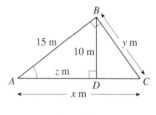

Fig. 2.1

Starting with triangle ADB, by Pythagoras' theorem $z^2 + 10^2 = 15^2$, so $z^2 = 225 - 100 = 125$ and

$$z = \sqrt{125} = \sqrt{25 \times 5} = 5\sqrt{5}.$$

Now notice that the triangles ADB and ABC are similar. You can see the similarity more clearly by flipping triangle ADB over to make the side AB horizontal, as in Fig. 2.2. The sides of triangles ADB and ABC must therefore be in the same proportion, so that

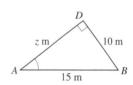

Fig. 2.2

$\dfrac{x}{15} = \dfrac{y}{10} = \dfrac{15}{z}$. Since $\dfrac{15}{z} = \dfrac{15}{5\sqrt{5}} = \dfrac{3}{\sqrt{5}} = \dfrac{3\sqrt{5}}{5}$,

$x = 15 \times \dfrac{3\sqrt{5}}{5} = 9\sqrt{5}$ and $y = 10 \times \dfrac{3\sqrt{5}}{5} = 6\sqrt{5}$.

As a check, using Pythagoras' theorem in triangle ABC shows that $x^2 = 15^2 + y^2$.

Exercise 2

1 Simplify the following without using a calculator.

(a) $\sqrt{3} \times \sqrt{3}$

(b) $\sqrt{10} \times \sqrt{10}$

(c) $\sqrt{16} \times \sqrt{16}$

(d) $\sqrt{8} \times \sqrt{2}$

(e) $\sqrt{32} \times \sqrt{2}$

(f) $\sqrt{3} \times \sqrt{12}$

(g) $5\sqrt{3} \times \sqrt{3}$

(h) $2\sqrt{5} \times 3\sqrt{5}$

(i) $3\sqrt{6} \times 4\sqrt{6}$

(j) $2\sqrt{20} \times 3\sqrt{5}$

(k) $\left(2\sqrt{7}\right)^2$

(l) $\left(3\sqrt{3}\right)^2$

(m) $\sqrt[3]{5} \times \sqrt[3]{5} \times \sqrt[3]{5}$

(n) $\left(2\sqrt[4]{3}\right)^4$

(o) $\left(2\sqrt[3]{2}\right)^6$

(p) $\sqrt[4]{125} \times \sqrt[4]{5}$

2 Simplify the following without using a calculator.

(a) $\sqrt{18}$ (b) $\sqrt{20}$ (c) $\sqrt{24}$ (d) $\sqrt{32}$

(e) $\sqrt{40}$ (f) $\sqrt{45}$ (g) $\sqrt{48}$ (h) $\sqrt{50}$

(i) $\sqrt{54}$ (j) $\sqrt{72}$ (k) $\sqrt{135}$ (l) $\sqrt{675}$

3 Simplify the following without using a calculator.

(a) $\sqrt{8}+\sqrt{18}$ (b) $\sqrt{3}+\sqrt{12}$ (c) $\sqrt{20}-\sqrt{5}$

(d) $\sqrt{32}-\sqrt{8}$ (e) $\sqrt{50}-\sqrt{18}-\sqrt{8}$ (f) $\sqrt{27}+\sqrt{27}$

(g) $\sqrt{99}+\sqrt{44}+\sqrt{11}$ (h) $8\sqrt{2}+2\sqrt{8}$ (i) $2\sqrt{20}+3\sqrt{45}$

(j) $\sqrt{52}-\sqrt{13}$ (k) $20\sqrt{5}+5\sqrt{20}$ (l) $\sqrt{48}+\sqrt{24}-\sqrt{75}+\sqrt{96}$

4 Simplify the following without using a calculator.

(a) $\dfrac{\sqrt{8}}{\sqrt{2}}$ (b) $\dfrac{\sqrt{27}}{\sqrt{3}}$ (c) $\dfrac{\sqrt{40}}{\sqrt{10}}$ (d) $\dfrac{\sqrt{50}}{\sqrt{2}}$

(e) $\dfrac{\sqrt{125}}{\sqrt{5}}$ (f) $\dfrac{\sqrt{54}}{\sqrt{6}}$ (g) $\dfrac{\sqrt{3}}{\sqrt{48}}$ (h) $\dfrac{\sqrt{50}}{\sqrt{200}}$

5 Rationalise the denominator in each of the following expressions, and simplify them.

(a) $\dfrac{1}{\sqrt{3}}$ (b) $\dfrac{1}{\sqrt{5}}$ (c) $\dfrac{4}{\sqrt{2}}$ (d) $\dfrac{6}{\sqrt{6}}$

(e) $\dfrac{11}{\sqrt{11}}$ (f) $\dfrac{2}{\sqrt{8}}$ (g) $\dfrac{12}{\sqrt{3}}$ (h) $\dfrac{14}{\sqrt{7}}$

(i) $\dfrac{\sqrt{6}}{\sqrt{2}}$ (j) $\dfrac{\sqrt{2}}{\sqrt{6}}$ (k) $\dfrac{3\sqrt{5}}{\sqrt{3}}$ (l) $\dfrac{4\sqrt{6}}{\sqrt{5}}$

(m) $\dfrac{7\sqrt{2}}{2\sqrt{3}}$ (n) $\dfrac{4\sqrt{2}}{\sqrt{12}}$ (o) $\dfrac{9\sqrt{12}}{2\sqrt{18}}$ (p) $\dfrac{2\sqrt{18}}{9\sqrt{12}}$

6 Simplify the following, giving each answer in the form $k\sqrt{3}$.

(a) $\sqrt{75}+\sqrt{12}$ (b) $6+\sqrt{3}\left(4-2\sqrt{3}\right)$

(c) $\dfrac{12}{\sqrt{3}}-\sqrt{27}$ (d) $\dfrac{2}{\sqrt{3}}+\dfrac{\sqrt{2}}{\sqrt{6}}$

(e) $\sqrt{2}\times\sqrt{8}\times\sqrt{27}$ (f) $\left(3-\sqrt{3}\right)\left(2-\sqrt{3}\right)-\sqrt{3}\times\sqrt{27}$

7 $ABCD$ is a rectangle in which $AB=4\sqrt{5}$ cm and $BC=\sqrt{10}$ cm. Giving each answer in simplified surd form, find

(a) the area of the rectangle,   (b) the length of the diagonal AC.

8 Solve the following equations, giving each answer in the form $k\sqrt{2}$.

(a) $x\sqrt{2}=10$ (b) $2y\sqrt{2}-3=\dfrac{5y}{\sqrt{2}}+1$ (c) $z\sqrt{32}-16=z\sqrt{8}-4$

9 Express in the form $k\sqrt[3]{3}$

(a) $\sqrt[3]{24}$ (b) $\sqrt[3]{81}+\sqrt[3]{3}$ (c) $\left(\sqrt[3]{3}\right)^{4}$ (d) $\sqrt[3]{3000}-\sqrt[3]{375}$.

10 Find the length of the third side in each of the following right-angled triangles, giving each answer in simplified surd form.

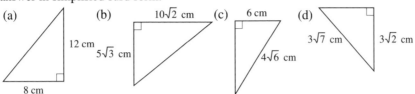

(a)   12 cm   8 cm

(b) $10\sqrt{2}$ cm $5\sqrt{3}$ cm

(c)   6 cm $4\sqrt{6}$ cm

(d) $3\sqrt{7}$ cm $3\sqrt{2}$ cm

11 You are given that, correct to twelve decimal places, $\sqrt{26} = 5.099\,019\,513\,593$.

  (a) Find the value of $\sqrt{104}$ correct to ten decimal places.

  (b) Find the value of $\sqrt{650}$ correct to ten decimal places.

  (c) Find the value of $\dfrac{13}{\sqrt{26}}$ correct to ten decimal places.

12 Solve the simultaneous equations $7x - \left(3\sqrt{5}\right)y = 9\sqrt{5}$ and $\left(2\sqrt{5}\right)x + y = 34$.

13 Simplify

  (a) $\left(\sqrt{2}-1\right)\left(\sqrt{2}+1\right)$ (b) $\left(2-\sqrt{3}\right)\left(2+\sqrt{3}\right)$

  (c) $\left(\sqrt{7}+\sqrt{3}\right)\left(\sqrt{7}-\sqrt{3}\right)$ (d) $\left(2\sqrt{2}+1\right)\left(2\sqrt{2}-1\right)$

  (e) $\left(4\sqrt{3}-\sqrt{2}\right)\left(4\sqrt{3}+\sqrt{2}\right)$ (f) $\left(\sqrt{10}+\sqrt{5}\right)\left(\sqrt{10}-\sqrt{5}\right)$

  (g) $\left(4\sqrt{7}-\sqrt{5}\right)\left(4\sqrt{7}+\sqrt{5}\right)$ (h) $\left(2\sqrt{6}-3\sqrt{3}\right)\left(2\sqrt{6}+3\sqrt{3}\right)$.

14 In Question 13, every answer is an integer. Copy and complete each of the following.

  (a) $\left(\sqrt{3}-1\right)\left(\quad\right) = 2$ (b) $\left(\sqrt{5}+1\right)\left(\quad\right) = 4$

  (c) $\left(\sqrt{6}-\sqrt{2}\right)\left(\quad\right) = 4$ (d) $\left(2\sqrt{7}+\sqrt{3}\right)\left(\quad\right) = 25$

  (e) $\left(\sqrt{11}+\sqrt{10}\right)\left(\quad\right) = 1$ (f) $\left(3\sqrt{5}-2\sqrt{6}\right)\left(\quad\right) = 21$

The examples in Questions 15 and 16 indicate a method for rationalising the denominator in cases which are more complicated than those in Question 5.

15* (a) Explain why $\dfrac{1}{\sqrt{3}-1} = \dfrac{1}{\sqrt{3}-1} \times \dfrac{\sqrt{3}+1}{\sqrt{3}+1}$ and hence show that $\dfrac{1}{\sqrt{3}-1} = \dfrac{\sqrt{3}+1}{2}$.

  (b) Show that $\dfrac{1}{2\sqrt{2}+\sqrt{3}} = \dfrac{2\sqrt{2}-\sqrt{3}}{5}$.

16* Rationalise the denominators of these fractions.

  (a) $\dfrac{1}{2-\sqrt{3}}$ (b) $\dfrac{1}{3\sqrt{5}-5}$ (c) $\dfrac{4\sqrt{3}}{2\sqrt{6}+3\sqrt{2}}$

Miscellaneous exercise 2

1 Simplify

  (a) $5\left(\sqrt{2}+1\right)-\sqrt{2}\left(4-3\sqrt{2}\right)$,   (b) $\left(\sqrt{2}\right)^4 + \left(\sqrt{3}\right)^4 + \left(\sqrt{4}\right)^4$,

  (c) $\left(\sqrt{5}-2\right)^2 + \left(\sqrt{5}-2\right)\left(\sqrt{5}+2\right)$,   (d) $\left(2\sqrt{2}\right)^5$.

2 Simplify

   (a) $\sqrt{27} + \sqrt{12} - \sqrt{3}$,   (b) $\sqrt{63} - \sqrt{28}$,

   (c) $\sqrt{100\,000} + \sqrt{1000} + \sqrt{10}$,   (d) $\sqrt[3]{2} + \sqrt[3]{16}$.

3 Rationalise the denominators of the following.

   (a) $\dfrac{9}{2\sqrt{3}}$ (b) $\dfrac{1}{5\sqrt{5}}$ (c) $\dfrac{2\sqrt{5}}{3\sqrt{10}}$ (d) $\dfrac{\sqrt{8}}{\sqrt{15}}$

4 Simplify

   (a) $\dfrac{4}{\sqrt{2}} - \dfrac{4}{\sqrt{8}}$,   (b) $\dfrac{10}{\sqrt{5}} + \sqrt{20}$,

   (c) $\dfrac{1}{\sqrt{2}}\left(2\sqrt{2} - 1\right) + \sqrt{2}\left(1 - \sqrt{8}\right)$,   (d) $\dfrac{\sqrt{6}}{\sqrt{2}} + \dfrac{3}{\sqrt{3}} + \dfrac{\sqrt{15}}{\sqrt{5}} + \dfrac{\sqrt{18}}{\sqrt{6}}$.

5 Express $\dfrac{5}{\sqrt{7}}$ in the form $k\sqrt{7}$ where k is a rational number.   (OCR)

6 In the diagram, angles ABC and ACD are right angles. Given that $AB = CD = 2\sqrt{6}$ cm and $BC = 7$ cm, show that the length of AD is between $4\sqrt{6}$ cm and $7\sqrt{2}$ cm.

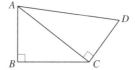

7 In the triangle PQR, Q is a right angle, $PQ = \left(6 - 2\sqrt{2}\right)$ cm and $QR = \left(6 + 2\sqrt{2}\right)$ cm.

   (a) Find the area of the triangle.   (b) Show that the length of PR is $2\sqrt{22}$ cm.

8 In the triangle ABC, $AB = 4\sqrt{3}$ cm, $BC = 5\sqrt{3}$ cm and angle B is $60°$. Use the cosine rule to find, in simplified surd form, the length of AC.

9 Solve the simultaneous equations $5x - 3y = 41$ and $\left(7\sqrt{2}\right)x + \left(4\sqrt{2}\right)y = 82$.

10 The coordinates of the points A and B are $(2,3)$ and $(4,-3)$ respectively. Find the length of AB and the coordinates of the midpoint of AB.   (OCR)

11 (a) Find the equation of the line l through the point $A(2,3)$ with gradient $-\frac{1}{2}$.

   (b) Show that the point P with coordinates $(2 + 2t, 3 - t)$ will always lie on l whatever the value of t.

   (c) Find the value of t such that the length AP is 5 units.

   (d) Find the value of t such that OP is perpendicular to l (where O is the origin). Hence find the length of the perpendicular from O to l.

12 P and Q are the points of intersection of the line $\dfrac{x}{a} + \dfrac{y}{b} = 1$ $(a > 0,\ b > 0)$

   with the x- and y-axes respectively. The distance PQ is 20 and the gradient of PQ is -3. Find the values of a and b.

13 The sides of a parallelogram lie along the lines $y = 2x - 4$, $y = 2x - 13$, $x + y = 5$ and $x + y = -4$. Find the length of one side, and the perpendicular distance between this and the parallel side. Hence find the area of the parallelogram.

3 Some important graphs

This chapter introduces the idea of a function and investigates the graphs representing functions of various kinds. When you have completed it, you should

- understand function notation
- know the shapes of the graphs of positive integer powers of x
- know the shapes of graphs of functions of the form $f(x) = ax^2 + bx + c$
- be able to suggest possible equations of such functions from their graphs
- know how to use factors to sketch graphs
- be able to find the point(s) of intersection of two graphs.

To get full value from this chapter you will need either a graphic calculator or a computer with graph-plotting software, so that you can check for yourself the graphs which accompany the text, and carry out further research along similar lines.

3.1 The idea of a function

You are already familiar with formulae which summarise calculations which need to be performed frequently, such as:

the area of a circle with radius x metres is πx^2 square metres;

the volume of a cube of side x metres is x^3 cubic metres;

the time that it takes to travel k kilometres at x kilometres per hour is $\dfrac{k}{x}$ hours.

You will often have used different letters from x in these formulae, such as r for radius or s for speed, but in this chapter x will always be used for the letter in the formula, and y for the quantity you want to calculate. Notice that some formulae also involve other letters, called **constants**; these might be either a number like π, which is irrational and cannot be written out in full, or a quantity like the distance k, which you choose for yourself depending on the distance you intend to travel.

Expressions such as πx^2, x^3 and $\dfrac{k}{x}$ are examples of **functions** of x. The essential feature of a function is that, having chosen x, you can get a unique value of y from it.

It is often useful to have a way of writing functions in general, rather than always having to refer to particular functions. The notation which is used for this is $f(x)$ (read 'f of x', or sometimes just 'f x'). The letter f stands for the function itself, and x for the number you choose for its evaluation.

If you want to refer to the value of the function when x has a particular value, say $x = 2$, then you write the value as $f(2)$. For example, if $f(x)$ stands for the function x^3, then $f(2) = 2^3 = 8$.

If a problem involves more than one function, you can use different letters for each function. Two functions can, for example, be written as $f(x)$ and $g(x)$.

Functions are not always defined by algebraic formulae. Sometimes it is easier to describe them in words, or to define them using a flow chart or a computer program. All that matters is that each value of x chosen leads to a unique value of $y = f(x)$.

3.2 Graphs

You are familiar with drawing graphs. You set up a coordinate system for cartesian coordinates using x- and y-axes, and choose the scales on each axis.

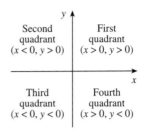

The axes divide the plane of the paper or screen into four quadrants, numbered as shown in Fig. 3.1. The first quadrant is in the top right corner, where x and y are both positive. The other quadrants then follow in order going anticlockwise round the origin.

Fig. 3.1

Example 3.2.1
In which quadrants is $xy > 0$?

If the product of two numbers is positive, either both are positive or both are negative. So either $x > 0$ and $y > 0$, or $x < 0$ and $y < 0$. The point (x, y) therefore lies in either the first or the third quadrant.

The graph of a function $f(x)$ is made up of all the points whose coordinates (x, y) satisfy the equation $y = f(x)$. When you draw such a graph on graph paper, you choose a few values of x and work out $y = f(x)$ for these. You then plot the points with coordinates (x, y), and join up these points by eye, usually with a smooth curve. If you have done this accurately, the coordinates of other points of the curve will also satisfy the equation $y = f(x)$. Calculators and computers make graphs in much the same way, but they can plot many more points much more quickly.

For some functions there is a restriction on the values of x you can choose.

Example 3.2.2
Draw the complete graph of $f(x) = \sqrt{4 - x^2}$.

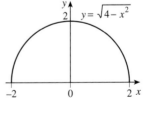

You can only calculate the values of the function $f(x) = \sqrt{4 - x^2}$ if x is between –2 and 2 inclusive, since if $x > 2$ or $x < -2$ the value of $4 - x^2$ is negative, and a negative number does not have a square root.

Also $y = f(x)$ cannot be negative (recall that square roots are positive or zero by definition) and it can't be greater than $\sqrt{4} = 2$. So the graph of $f(x) = \sqrt{4 - x^2}$, shown in Fig. 3.2, lies between –2 and 2 inclusive in the x-direction, and between 0 and 2 inclusive in the y-direction.

Fig. 3.2

However, many functions have a value when x is any real number, and then it is impossible to show the whole graph. The skill is to choose the values of x between which to draw the graph, so that you include all the important features.

3.3 Positive integer powers of x

This section looks at graphs of functions of the form $f(x) = x^n$, where n is a positive integer. Notice that $(0,0)$ and $(1,1)$ satisfy the equation $y = x^n$ for all these values of n, so that all the graphs include the points $(0,0)$ and $(1,1)$.

First look at the graphs when x is positive. Then x^n is also positive, so that the graphs lie entirely in the first quadrant. Fig. 3.3 shows the graphs for $n = 1$, 2, 3 and 4 for values of x from 0 to somewhere beyond 1.

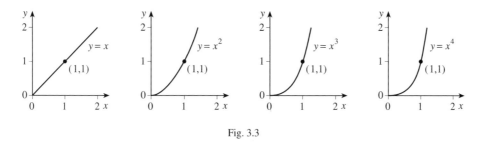

Fig. 3.3

Points to notice are:

- $n = 1$ is a special case: it gives the straight line $y = x$ through the origin, which makes an angle of $45°$ with each axis.
- For $n > 1$ the x-axis is a tangent to the graphs at the origin. This is because, when x is small, x^n is very small. For example, $0.1^2 = 0.01$, $0.1^3 = 0.001$, $0.1^4 = 0.0001$.
- For each increase in the index n, the graph stays closer to the x-axis between $x = 0$ and $x = 1$, but then climbs more steeply beyond $x = 1$. This is because $x^{n+1} = x \times x^n$, so that $x^{n+1} < x^n$ when $0 < x < 1$ and $x^{n+1} > x^n$ when $x > 1$.

What happens when x is negative depends on whether n is odd or even. To see this, suppose $x = -a$, where a is a positive number.

If n is even, $f(-a) = (-a)^n = a^n = f(a)$. So the value of y on the graph is the same for $x = -a$ and $x = a$. This means that the graph is symmetrical about the y-axis. This is illustrated in Fig. 3.4 for the graphs of $y = x^2$ and $y = x^4$. Functions with the property that $f(-a) = f(a)$ for all values of a are called **even functions**.

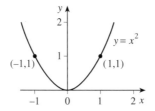
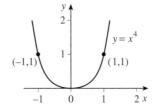

Fig. 3.4

If n is odd, $f(-a) = (-a)^n = -a^n = -f(a)$. The value of y for $x = -a$ is minus the value for $x = a$. Note that the points with coordinates (a, a^n) and $(-a, -a^n)$ are symmetrically placed on either side of the origin. This means that the whole graph is symmetrical about the origin. This is illustrated in Fig. 3.5 for the graphs of $y = x$ and $y = x^3$. Functions with the property that $f(-a) = -f(a)$ for all values of a are called **odd functions**.

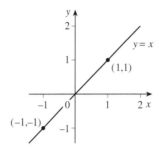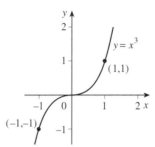

Fig. 3.5

Exercise 3A

1 Given $f(x) = 2x + 5$, find the values of
    (a) $f(3)$,   (b) $f(0)$,   (c) $f(-4)$,   (d) $f\left(-2\frac{1}{2}\right)$.

2 Given $f(x) = 3x^2 + 2$, find the values of
    (a) $f(4)$,   (b) $f(-1)$,   (c) $f(-3)$,   (d) $f(3)$.

3 Given $f(x) = x^2 + 4x + 3$, find the values of
    (a) $f(2)$,   (b) $f\left(\frac{1}{2}\right)$,   (c) $f(-1)$,   (d) $f(-3)$.

4 Given $g(x) = x^3$ and $h(x) = 4x + 1$,
    (a) find the value of $g(2) + h(2)$;   (b) find the value of $3g(-1) - 4h(-1)$;
    (c) show that $g(5) = h(31)$;   (d) find the value of $h(g(2))$.

5 Sketch the graphs of
    (a) $y = x^5$,   (b) $y = x^6$,   (c) $y = x^{10}$,   (d) $y = x^{15}$.

6 Given $f(x) = x^n$ and $f(3) = 81$, determine the value of n.

7 Of the following functions, one is even and two are odd. Determine which is which.
    (a) $y = x^7$ (b) $y = x^4 + 3x^2$ (c) $y = x\left(x^2 - 1\right)$

8 Given that $f(x) = ax + b$ and that $f(2) = 7$ and $f(3) = 12$, find a and b.

3.4 Graphs of the form $y = ax^2 + bx + c$

In Chapter 1, you found out how to sketch graphs of straight lines, and what the constants m and c mean in the equation $y = mx + c$.

Exercise 3B gives you experience of plotting the graphs of functions with equations of the form $y = ax^2 + bx + c$, and examining their properties using a graphic calculator or a computer. A summary of the main points appears after the exercise.

Exercise 3B

1 Display, on the same set of axes, the graphs of
  (a) $y = x^2 - 2x + 5$,   (b) $y = x^2 - 2x + 1$,
  (c) $y = x^2 - 2x$,   (d) $y = x^2 - 2x - 6$.

2 Display, on the same set of axes, the graphs of
  (a) $y = x^2 + x - 4$,   (b) $y = x^2 + x - 1$,
  (c) $y = x^2 + x + 2$,   (d) $y = x^2 + x + 5$.

3 The diagram shows the graph of $y = ax^2 - bx$. On a copy of the diagram, sketch the graphs of
  (a) $y = ax^2 - bx + 4$,
  (b) $y = ax^2 - bx - 6$.

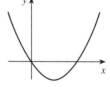

4 What is the effect on the graph of $y = ax^2 + bx + c$ of changing the value of c?

5 Display the graphs of
  (a) $y = x^2 - 4x + 1$,   (b) $y = x^2 - 2x + 1$,
  (c) $y = x^2 + 1$,   (d) $y = x^2 + 2x + 1$.

6 Display the graph of $y = 2x^2 + bx + 4$ for different values of b. How does changing b affect the curve $y = ax^2 + bx + c$?

7 Display the graphs of
  (a) $y = x^2 + 1$,   (b) $y = 3x^2 + 1$,
  (c) $y = -3x^2 + 1$,   (d) $y = -x^2 + 1$.

8 Display the graphs of
  (a) $y = -4x^2 + 3x + 1$,   (b) $y = -x^2 + 3x + 1$,
  (c) $y = x^2 + 3x + 1$,   (d) $y = 4x^2 + 3x + 1$.

9 Display the graph of $y = ax^2 - 2x$ for different values of a.

10 How does changing a affect the shape of the graph of $y = ax^2 + bx + c$?

11 Which of the following could be the equation of the curve shown in the diagram?

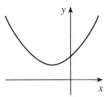

(a) $y = x^2 - 2x + 5$

(b) $y = -x^2 - 2x + 5$

(c) $y = x^2 + 2x + 5$

(d) $y = -x^2 + 2x + 5$

12 Which of the following could be the equation of the curve shown in the diagram?

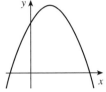

(a) $y = -x^2 + 3x + 4$

(b) $y = x^2 - 3x + 4$

(c) $y = x^2 + 3x + 4$

(d) $y = -x^2 - 3x + 4$

3.5 The shapes of graphs of the form $y = ax^2 + bx + c$

In Exercise 3B, you should have found a number of results, which are summarised below.

> All the graphs have the same general shape, which is called a **parabola**. These parabolas have a vertical **axis of symmetry**. The point where a parabola meets its axis of symmetry is called the **vertex**.
>
> Changing c moves the graph up and down in the y-direction.
>
> Changing b moves the axis of symmetry of the graph in the x-direction. If a and b have the same sign the axis of symmetry is to the left of the y-axis; if a and b have opposite signs the axis of symmetry is to the right of the y-axis.
>
> If a is positive the vertex is at the lowest point of the graph; if a is negative the vertex is at the highest point. The larger the size of a the more the graph is elongated.

3.6 The point of intersection of two graphs

The principle for finding the point of intersection of two curves is the same as that for finding the point of intersection of two graphs which are straight lines.

Suppose that you have two graphs, with equations $y = f(x)$ and $y = g(x)$. You want the point (x, y) which lies on both graphs, so the coordinates (x, y) satisfy both equations. Therefore x must satisfy the equation $f(x) = g(x)$.

Example 3.6.1

Find the point of intersection of the line $y = 2$ with the graph $y = x^2 - 3x + 4$ (see Fig. 3.6).

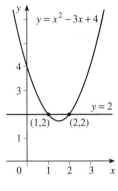

Solving these equations simultaneously gives $x^2 - 3x + 4 = 2$, which reduces to $x^2 - 3x + 2 = 0$. After factorising, you get $(x-1)(x-2) = 0$, giving $x = 1$ and $x = 2$.

Substituting these values in either equation ($y = 2$ is obviously easier!) to find y, the points of intersection are $(1,2)$ and $(2,2)$.

Fig. 3.6

Example 3.6.2

Find the point of intersection of the line $y = 2x - 1$ with the graph $y = x^2$ (see Fig. 3.7).

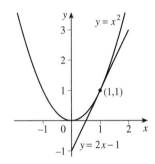

Solving these equations gives $2x - 1 = x^2$, which is $x^2 - 2x + 1 = 0$. Factorising, $(x-1)^2 = 0$, giving $x = 1$.

Substituting these values in either equation to find y gives the point of intersection as $(1,1)$.

The fact that there is only one point of intersection shows that this line is a tangent to the graph. You can check this by showing both graphs on your graphic calculator.

Fig. 3.7

Example 3.6.3

Find the point of intersection of the graphs $y = x^2 - 2x - 6$ and $y = 12 + x - 2x^2$.

Solving these equations simultaneously gives $x^2 - 2x - 6 = 12 + x - 2x^2$, which is $3x^2 - 3x - 18 = 0$. Dividing by 3 gives $x^2 - x - 6 = 0$, which factorises as $(x+2)(x-3) = 0$, giving $x = -2$ or $x = 3$.

Substituting these values in either equation to find y gives the points of intersection as $(-2,2)$ and $(3,-3)$.

Check the solution with your graphic calculator.

Exercise 3C

1 Find the point or points of intersection for the following lines and curves.

(a) $x = 3$ and $y = x^2 + 4x - 7$

(b) $y = 3$ and $y = x^2 - 5x + 7$

(c) $y = 8$ and $y = x^2 + 2x$

(d) $y + 3 = 0$ and $y = 2x^2 + 5x - 6$

2 Find the points of intersection for the following lines and curves. Check your answers in each case by displaying the graphs on a graphic calculator.

   (a) $y = x + 1$ and $y = x^2 - 3x + 4$ (b) $y = 2x + 3$ and $y = x^2 + 3x - 9$

   (c) $y = 3x + 11$ and $y = 2x^2 + 2x + 5$ (d) $y = 4x + 1$ and $y = 9 + 4x - 2x^2$

   (e) $3x + y - 1 = 0$ and $y = 6 + 10x - 6x^2$

3 In both the following, show that the line and curve meet only once, find the point of intersection and use a graphic calculator to check that the line touches the curve.

   (a) $y = 2x + 2$ and $y = x^2 - 2x + 6$ (b) $y = -2x - 7$ and $y = x^2 + 4x + 2$

4 Find the points of intersection between the curve $y = x^2 - x$ and the line

   (a) $y = x$,   (b) $y = x - 1$.

   Use a graphic calculator to see how the curves are related.

5 Find the points of intersection between the curve $y = x^2 + 5x + 18$ and the lines

   (a) $y = -3x + 2$,   (b) $y = -3x + 6$.

   Use a graphic calculator to see how the curve and the lines are related.

6 Find the points of intersection between the line $y = x + 5$ and the curves

   (a) $y = 2x^2 - 3x - 1$,   (b) $y = 2x^2 - 3x + 7$.

   Use a graphic calculator to see how the line and the curves are related.

7 Find the points of intersection of the following curves.

   (a) $y = x^2 + 5x + 1$ and $y = x^2 + 3x + 11$

   (b) $y = x^2 - 3x - 7$ and $y = x^2 + x + 1$

   (c) $y = 7x^2 + 4x + 1$ and $y = 7x^2 - 4x + 1$

8 Find the points of intersection of the following curves. Check your answers by using a graphic calculator.

   (a) $y = \frac{1}{2}x^2$ and $y = 1 - \frac{1}{2}x^2$ (b) $y = 2x^2 + 3x + 4$ and $y = x^2 + 6x + 2$

   (c) $y = x^2 + 7x + 13$ and $y = 1 - 3x - x^2$ (d) $y = 6x^2 + 2x - 9$ and $y = x^2 + 7x + 1$

   (e) $y = (x - 2)(6x + 5)$ and $y = (x - 5)^2 + 1$ (f) $y = 2x(x - 3)$ and $y = x(x + 2)$

3.7 Using factors to sketch graphs

The graphs of some functions of the form $f(x) = ax^2 + bx + c$ which factorise can also be drawn in another way. For example, take the functions

$$f(x) = x^2 - 6x + 5 = (x - 1)(x - 5)   \quad \text{and} \quad   g(x) = 12x - 4x^2 = 4x(3 - x).$$

In the first case, $f(1) = 0$ and $f(5) = 0$, so that the points $(1, 0)$ and $(5, 0)$ lie on the graph of $f(x)$. This is shown in Fig. 3.8.

Similarly $g(0) = g(3) = 0$, so that $(0, 0)$ and $(3, 0)$ lie on the graph of $g(x)$. This is shown in Fig. 3.9.

You can draw the graph of any function of this type which can be factorised as

$$a(x-r)(x-s),$$

by first noting that it cuts the x-axis at the points $(r,0)$ and $(s,0)$. The sign of the constant a tells you whether it 'bends upwards' (like $y=x^2$) or 'bends downwards'.

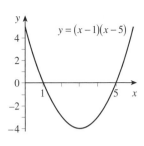

Fig. 3.8

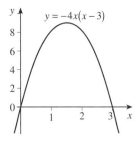

Fig. 3.9

Note that in Figs. 3.8 and 3.9 different scales have been used on the two axes. If equal scales had been used the elongation in both figures would have been more obvious.

Example 3.7.1

Draw a sketch of the graph of $f(x) = 3x^2 - 2x - 1$.

You can factorise the expression as $f(x) = (3x+1)(x-1)$, but to apply the method you need to write it as

$$f(x) = 3\left(x+\tfrac{1}{3}\right)(x-1).$$

So the graph passes through $\left(-\tfrac{1}{3},0\right)$ and $(1,0)$. The constant 3 tells you that the graph faces upwards and is elongated.

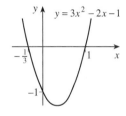

Fig. 3.10

This is enough information to give a good idea of the shape of the graph, from which you can draw a sketch like Fig. 3.10. It is also worth noting that $f(0) = -1$, so that the graph cuts the y-axis at the point $(0,-1)$.

Note that the sketch does not have marks against the axes, except to say where the graph cuts them.

3.8 Predicting functions from their graphs

You can also use the factor form to predict the equation of a function of the type $f(x) = ax^2 + bx + c$, if you know the points where its graph crosses the x-axis and the coordinates of one other point on the graph.

Example 3.8.1

Find the equation of the graph of the type $y = ax^2 + bx + c$ which crosses the x-axis at the points $(1,0)$ and $(4,0)$ and also passes through the point $(3,-4)$.

Since the curve cuts the axes at $(1,0)$ and $(4,0)$, the equation has the form

$$y = a(x-1)(x-4).$$

Since the point $(3,-4)$ lies on this curve, $-4 = a(3-1)(3-4)$, giving $-4 = -2a$, so $a = 2$. The equation of the curve is therefore

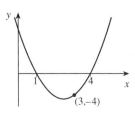

Fig. 3.11

$$y = 2(x-1)(x-4), \quad \text{or} \quad y = 2x^2 - 10x + 8.$$

You can extend this method to drawing graphs of functions with more than two factors. For example,

$$f(x) = a(x-r)(x-s)(x-t)$$

defines a function whose equation, when multiplied out, starts with $f(x) = ax^3 - \dots$.

The graph passes through the points $(r,0)$, $(s,0)$ and $(t,0)$. The constant a tells you whether, for large values of x, the graph lies in the first or the fourth quadrant.

This is shown in Figs. 3.12 and 3.13, which show the graphs of $y = 2x(x-1)(x-4)$ and $y = -(x+2)(x-1)^2$.

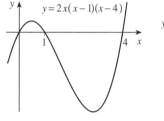
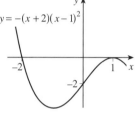

Notice that, in Fig. 3.13, the factor $(x-1)$ is squared, so that there are only two points of the graph on the x-axis. At $(1,0)$ the x-axis is a tangent to the graph.

Fig. 3.12   Fig. 3.13

Exercise 3D

1 Sketch each of the following graphs.

(a) $y = (x-2)(x-4)$ (b) $y = (x+3)(x-1)$ (c) $y = x(x-2)$

(d) $y = (x+5)(x+1)$ (e) $y = x(x+3)$ (f) $y = 2(x+1)(x-1)$

2 Sketch each of the following graphs.

(a) $y = 3(x+1)(x-5)$ (b) $y = -2(x-1)(x-3)$ (c) $y = -(x+3)(x+5)$

(d) $y = 2\left(x+\frac{1}{2}\right)(x-3)$ (e) $y = -3(x-4)^2$ (f) $y = -5(x-1)\left(x+\frac{4}{5}\right)$

3 By first factorising the function, sketch each of the following graphs.

(a) $y = x^2 - 2x - 8$ (b) $y = x^2 - 2x$ (c) $y = x^2 + 6x + 9$

(d) $y = 2x^2 - 7x + 3$ (e) $y = 4x^2 - 1$ (f) $y = -(x^2 - x - 12)$

(g) $y = -x^2 - 4x - 4$ (h) $y = -(2x^2 - 7x + 12)$ (i) $y = 11x - 4x^2 - 6$

4 Find the equation, in the form $y = x^2 + bx + c$, of the parabola which

(a) crosses the x-axis at the points $(2,0)$ and $(5,0)$,

(b) crosses the x-axis at the points $(-7,0)$ and $(-10,0)$,

(c) passes through the points $(-5,0)$ and $(3,0)$,

(d) passes through the points $(-3,0)$ and $(1,-16)$.

5 Sketch each of the following graphs.

(a) $y = (x+3)(x-2)(x-3)$ (b) $y = x(x-4)(x-6)$

(c) $y = x^2(x-4)$ (d) $y = x(x-4)^2$

(e) $y = -(x+6)(x+4)(x+2)$ (f) $y = -3(x+1)(x-3)^2$

6 Find the equation, in the form $y = ax^2 + bx + c$, of the parabola which

(a) crosses the x-axis at $(1,0)$ and $(5,0)$ and crosses the y-axis at $(0,15)$,

(b) crosses the x-axis at $(-2,0)$ and $(7,0)$ and crosses the y-axis at $(0,-56)$,

(c) passes through the points $(-6,0)$, $(-2,0)$ and $(0,-6)$,

(d) crosses the x-axis at $(-3,0)$ and $(2,0)$ and also passes through $(1,16)$,

(e) passes through the points $(-10,0)$, $(7,0)$ and $(8,90)$.

7 Sketch each of the following graphs.

(a) $y = x^2 - 4x - 5$ (b) $y = 4x^2 - 4x + 1$ (c) $y = -x^2 - 3x + 18$

(d) $y = 2x^2 - 9x + 10$ (e) $y = -(x^2 - 4x + 9)$ (f) $y = 3x^2 + 9x$

8 Here are the equations of nine parabolas.

A $y = (x-3)(x-8)$ B $y = 14 + 5x - x^2$ C $y = 6x^2 - x - 70$

D $y = x(3-x)$ E $y = (x+2)(x-7)$ F $y = -3(x+3)(x+7)$

G $y = x^2 + 2x + 1$ H $y = x^2 + 8x + 12$ I $y = x^2 - 25$

Answer the following questions without drawing the graphs of these parabolas.

(a) Which of the parabolas cross the y-axis at a positive value of y?

(b) For which of the parabolas is the vertex at the highest point of the graph?

(c) For which of the parabolas is the vertex to the left of the y-axis?

(d) Which of the parabolas pass through the origin?

(e) Which of the parabolas does not cross the x-axis at two separate points?

(f) Which of the parabolas has the y-axis as its axis of symmetry?

(g) Which two of the parabolas have the same axis of symmetry?

(h) Which of the parabolas have the vertex in the fourth quadrant?

9 Suggest a possible equation for each of the graphs shown below.

(a)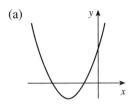

(b)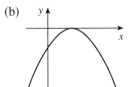

(c)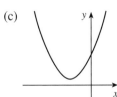

(d)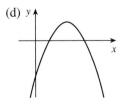

(e)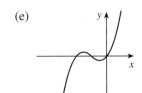

(f)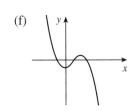

Miscellaneous exercise 3

1   The function f is defined by $f(x) = 7x - 4$.

    (a)   Find the values of $f(7)$, $f(\frac{1}{2})$ and $f(-5)$.

    (b)   Find the value of x such that $f(x) = 10$.

    (c)   Find the value of x such that $f(x) = x$.

    (d)   Find the value of x such that $f(x) = f(37)$.

2   The function f is defined by $f(x) = x^2 - 3x + 5$. Find the two values of x for which $f(x) = f(4)$.

3   The diagram shows the graph of $y = x^n$, where n is an integer. Given that the curve passes between the points $(2, 200)$ and $(2, 2000)$, determine the value of n.

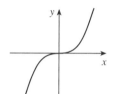

4   Find the points of intersection of the curves $y = x^2 - 7x + 5$ and $y = 1 + 2x - x^2$.

5   Find the points of intersection of the line $y = 2x + 3$ and the curve $y = 2x^2 + 3x - 7$.

6   Show that the line $3x + y - 2 = 0$ is a tangent to the curve $y = (4x - 3)(x - 2)$ and find the point of contact.

7   Find the coordinates of any points of intersection of the curves $y = (x - 2)(x - 4)$ and $y = x(2 - x)$. Sketch the two curves to show the relationship between them.

8   Given that k is a positive constant, sketch the graphs of

    (a) $y = (x + k)(x - 2k)$,   (b) $y = (x + 4k)(x + 2k)$,

    (c) $y = x(x - k)(x - 5k)$,   (d) $y = (x + k)(x - 2k)^2$.

9   The function f is defined by $f(x) = ax^2 + bx + c$. Given that $f(0) = 6$, $f(-1) = 15$ and $f(1) = 1$, find the values of a, b and c.

10   Find the point where the line $y = 3 - 4x$ meets the curve $y = 4(4x^2 + 5x + 3)$.

11   Sketch the graphs of

    (a) $y = (x + 4)(x + 2) + (x + 4)(x - 5)$,   (b) $y = (x + 4)(x + 2) + (x + 4)(5 - x)$.

12   A function f is defined by $f(x) = ax + b$. Given that $f(-2) = 27$ and $f(1) = 15$, find the value of x such that $f(x) = -5$.

13   A curve with equation $y = ax^2 + bx + c$ crosses the x-axis at $(-4, 0)$ and $(9, 0)$ and also passes through the point $(1, 120)$. Where does the curve cross the y-axis?

14*   The curve $y = ax^2 + bx + c$ passes through the points $(-1, 22)$, $(1, 8)$, $(3, 10)$, $(-2, p)$ and $(q, 17)$. Find the value of p and the possible values of q.

15 Show that the curves $y = 2x^2 + 5x$, $y = x^2 + 4x + 12$ and $y = 3x^2 + 4x - 6$ have one point in common and find its coordinates.

16 Suggest a possible equation for each of the graphs shown below.

(a)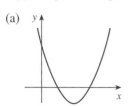

(b)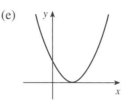

(c)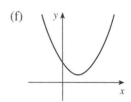

(d)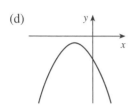

(e)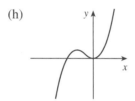

(f)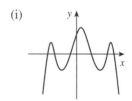

(g)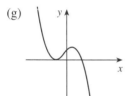

(h)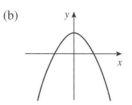

(i)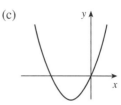

17 Given that the curves $y = x^2 - 3x + c$ and $y = k - x - x^2$ meet at the point $(-2, 12)$, find the values of c and k. Hence find the other point where the two curves meet.

18 Find the value of the constant p if the three curves $y = x^2 + 3x + 14$, $y = x^2 + 2x + 11$ and $y = px^2 + px + p$ have one point in common.

19 The straight line $y = x - 1$ meets the curve $y = x^2 - 5x - 8$ at the points A and B. The curve $y = p + qx - 2x^2$ also passes through the points A and B. Find the values of p and q.

20 The line $y = 10x + c$ is a tangent to the curve $y = x^2$. Determine the value of c.

21 Find, in surd form, the points of intersection of the curves $y = x^2 - 5x - 3$ and $y = 3 - 5x - x^2$.

22 The line $y = 6x + 1$ meets the curve $y = x^2 + 2x + 3$ at two points. Show that the coordinates of one of the points are $\left(2 - \sqrt{2}, 13 - 6\sqrt{2}\right)$, and find the coordinates of the other point.

23 Show that the curves $y = 2x^2 - 7x + 14$ and $y = 2 + 5x - x^2$ meet at only one point and use a graphic calculator to confirm the relationship between the curves. Without further calculation or sketching, deduce the number of points of intersection of

(a) $y = 2x^2 - 7x + 12$ and $y = 2 + 5x - x^2$, (b) $y = 2x^2 - 7x + 14$ and $y = 1 + 5x - x^2$,

(c) $y = 2x^2 - 7x + 34$ and $y = 22 + 5x - x^2$.

4 Quadratics

This chapter is about quadratic expressions of the form $ax^2 + bx + c$ and their graphs. When you have completed it, you should

- know how to complete the square in a quadratic expression
- know how to locate the vertex and the axis of symmetry of the quadratic graph $y = ax^2 + bx + c$
- be able to solve quadratic equations
- know that the discriminant of the quadratic expression $ax^2 + bx + c$ is the value of $b^2 - 4ac$, and know how to use it
- be able to solve a pair of simultaneous equations involving a quadratic equation and a linear equation
- be able to recognise and solve equations which can be reduced to quadratic equations by a substitution.

4.1 Quadratic expressions

You know that the equation $y = bx + c$ is a straight line. What happens if you add on a term ax^2, giving $y = ax^2 + bx + c$? The expression $ax^2 + bx + c$, where a, b and c are constants, is called a **quadratic**. Thus x^2, $x^2 - 6x + 8$, $2x^2 - 3x + 4$ and $-3x^2 - 5$ are all examples of quadratics.

You can write any quadratic as $ax^2 + bx + c$, where a, b and c are constants. The values of b and c can be any numbers you please, including 0, but a cannot be 0 (the expression would not then be a quadratic). The numbers a, b and c are called **coefficients**: a is the coefficient of x^2, b is the coefficient of x and c is often called the constant term.

The coefficients of x^2, x and the constant term in $2x^2 - x + 4$ are 2, –1 and 4.

4.2 Completed square form

You can write a quadratic expression such as $x^2 - 6x + 8$ in a number of ways. These include the factor form $(x - 4)(x - 2)$, useful for solving the quadratic equation $x^2 - 6x + 8 = 0$; and the form $(x - 3)^2 - 1$, useful for locating the vertex of the parabola which is the graph of $y = x^2 - 6x + 8$, shown in Fig. 4.1.

Note that you cannot always write a quadratic expression in factor form. For instance, try $x^2 + 1$ or $x^2 + 2x + 3$.

If you write the equation of the graph $y = x^2 - 6x + 8$ in the form $y = (x - 3)^2 - 1$, you can locate the axis of symmetry and the vertex quite easily. Since $(x - 3)^2$ is a

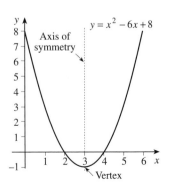

Fig. 4.1

perfect square its value is always greater than or equal to 0, and only 0 when $x = 3$. That is, $(x-3)^2 \geqslant 0$, and since $y = (x-3)^2 - 1$, it follows that $y \geqslant -1$. Since $(x-3)^2 = 0$ when $x = 3$, the vertex is at the point $(3, -1)$. The axis of symmetry is the line $x = 3$.

The form $(x-3)^2 - 1$ is called the **completed square form**. Here are some more examples of using it.

Example 4.2.1
Locate the vertex and the axis of symmetry of the quadratic graph $y = 3 - 2(x+2)^2$.

> Since $2(x+2)^2 \geqslant 0$, and $2(x+2)^2 = 3 - y$, it follows that $3 - y \geqslant 0$, so $y \leqslant 3$. As $(x+2)^2 = 0$ when $x = -2$, the vertex of the graph is the point with coordinates $(-2, 3)$, the greatest value of y is 3 and the axis of symmetry is $x = -2$.

Example 4.2.2
Solve the equation $3(x-2)^2 - 2 = 0$.

> As $3(x-2)^2 - 2 = 0$, $3(x-2)^2 = 2$ and $(x-2)^2 = \frac{2}{3}$.
>
> Therefore $(x-2) = \pm\sqrt{\frac{2}{3}}$, so $x = 2 \pm \sqrt{\frac{2}{3}}$.

4.3   Completing the square

When you try to write the quadratic expression $x^2 + bx + c$ in completed square form, the key point is to note that when you square $\left(x + \frac{1}{2}b\right)$ you get

$$\left(x + \tfrac{1}{2}b\right)^2 = x^2 + bx + \tfrac{1}{4}b^2, \text{ so } x^2 + bx = \left(x + \tfrac{1}{2}b\right)^2 - \tfrac{1}{4}b^2.$$

Now add c to both sides:

$$x^2 + bx + c = \left(x^2 + bx\right) + c = \left(x + \tfrac{1}{2}b\right)^2 - \tfrac{1}{4}b^2 + c.$$

Example 4.3.1
Write $x^2 + 10x + 32$ in completed square form.

> $$x^2 + 10x + 32 = \left(x^2 + 10x\right) + 32 = \left\{(x+5)^2 - 25\right\} + 32 = (x+5)^2 + 7.$$

Don't try to learn the form $x^2 + bx + c = \left(x + \frac{1}{2}b\right)^2 + c - \frac{1}{4}b^2$. Learn that you halve the coefficient of x, and write $x^2 + bx = \left(x + \frac{1}{2}b\right)^2 - \frac{1}{4}b^2$. Then add c to both sides.

If you need to write $ax^2 + bx + c$ in completed square form, but the coefficient a of x^2 is not 1, you can rewrite $ax^2 + bx + c$ by taking out the factor a from the first two terms:

$$ax^2 + bx + c = a\left(x^2 + \frac{b}{a}x\right) + c.$$

Then complete the square of the quadratic expression $x^2 + \dfrac{b}{a}x$ inside the bracket.

Example 4.3.2

Express $2x^2 + 10x + 7$ in completed square form.

Start by taking out the factor 2 in the terms which involve x:

$$2x^2 + 10x + 7 = 2(x^2 + 5x) + 7.$$

Dealing with the term inside the bracket,

$$x^2 + 5x = \left(x + \tfrac{5}{2}\right)^2 - \tfrac{25}{4},$$

so $2x^2 + 10x + 7 = 2(x^2 + 5x) + 7 = 2\left\{\left(x + \tfrac{5}{2}\right)^2 - \tfrac{25}{4}\right\} + 7$

$$= 2\left(x + \tfrac{5}{2}\right)^2 - \tfrac{25}{2} + 7 = 2\left(x + \tfrac{5}{2}\right)^2 - \tfrac{11}{2}.$$

It's worth checking your result mentally at this stage.

If the coefficient of x^2 is negative, the technique is similar to Example 4.3.2.

Example 4.3.3

Express $3 - 4x - 2x^2$ in completed square form.

Start by taking out the factor -2 in the terms which involve x:

$$3 - 4x - 2x^2 = 3 - 2(x^2 + 2x).$$

Dealing with the term inside the bracket, $x^2 + 2x = (x + 1)^2 - 1$,

so $3 - 4x - 2x^2 = 3 - 2(x^2 + 2x) = 3 - 2\left\{(x + 1)^2 - 1\right\}$

$$= 3 - 2(x + 1)^2 + 2 = 5 - 2(x + 1)^2.$$

Example 4.3.4

Express $12x^2 - 7x - 12$ in completed square form, and use your result to find the factors of $12x^2 - 7x - 12$.

$$12x^2 - 7x - 12 = 12\left(x^2 - \tfrac{7}{12}x\right) - 12 = 12\left\{\left(x - \tfrac{7}{24}\right)^2 - \tfrac{49}{576}\right\} - 12$$

$$= 12\left\{\left(x - \tfrac{7}{24}\right)^2 - \tfrac{625}{576}\right\} = 12\left\{\left(x - \tfrac{7}{24}\right)^2 - \left(\tfrac{25}{24}\right)^2\right\}.$$

You can now use the formula $a^2 - b^2 = (a - b)(a + b)$ with a as $x - \tfrac{7}{24}$ and b as $\tfrac{25}{24}$ to factorise the expression inside the brackets as the difference of two squares:

$$12\left\{\left(x - \tfrac{7}{24}\right)^2 - \left(\tfrac{25}{24}\right)^2\right\} = 12\left\{x - \tfrac{7}{24} - \tfrac{25}{24}\right\}\left\{x - \tfrac{7}{24} + \tfrac{25}{24}\right\}$$

$$= 12\left(x - \tfrac{4}{3}\right)\left(x + \tfrac{3}{4}\right) = 3\left(x - \tfrac{4}{3}\right) \times 4\left(x + \tfrac{3}{4}\right)$$

$$= (3x - 4)(4x - 3).$$

Exercise 4A

1 Find (i) the vertex and (ii) the equation of the line of symmetry of each of the following quadratic graphs.

(a) $y = (x-2)^2 + 3$

(b) $y = (x-5)^2 - 4$

(c) $y = (x+3)^2 - 7$

(d) $y = (2x-3)^2 + 1$

(e) $y = (5x+3)^2 + 2$

(f) $y = (3x+7)^2 - 4$

(g) $y = (x-3)^2 + c$

(h) $y = (x-p)^2 + q$

(i) $y = (ax+b)^2 + c$

2 Find (i) the least (or, if appropriate, the greatest) value of each of the following quadratic expressions and (ii) the value of x for which this occurs.

(a) $(x+2)^2 - 1$

(b) $(x-1)^2 + 2$

(c) $5 - (x+3)^2$

(d) $(2x+1)^2 - 7$

(e) $3 - 2(x-4)^2$

(f) $(x+p)^2 + q$

(g) $(x-p)^2 - q$

(h) $r - (x-t)^2$

(i) $c - (ax+b)^2$

3 Solve the following quadratic equations. Leave surds in your answer.

(a) $(x-3)^2 - 3 = 0$

(b) $(x+2)^2 - 4 = 0$

(c) $2(x+3)^2 = 5$

(d) $(3x-7)^2 = 8$

(e) $(x+p)^2 - q = 0$

(f) $a(x+b)^2 - c = 0$

4 Express the following in completed square form.

(a) $x^2 + 2x + 2$

(b) $x^2 - 8x - 3$

(c) $x^2 + 3x - 7$

(d) $5 - 6x + x^2$

(e) $x^2 + 14x + 49$

(f) $2x^2 + 12x - 5$

(g) $3x^2 - 12x + 3$

(h) $7 - 8x - 4x^2$

(i) $2x^2 + 5x - 3$

5 Use the completed square form to factorise the following expressions.

(a) $x^2 - 2x - 35$

(b) $x^2 - 14x - 176$

(c) $x^2 + 6x - 432$

(d) $6x^2 - 5x - 6$

(e) $14 + 45x - 14x^2$

(f) $12x^2 + x - 6$

6 Use the completed square form to find as appropriate the least or greatest value of each of the following expressions, and the value of x for which this occurs.

(a) $x^2 - 4x + 7$

(b) $x^2 - 3x + 5$

(c) $4 + 6x - x^2$

(d) $2x^2 - 5x + 2$

(e) $3x^2 + 2x - 4$

(f) $3 - 7x - 3x^2$

7 By completing the square find (i) the vertex, and (ii) the equation of the line of symmetry, of each of the following parabolas.

(a) $y = x^2 - 4x + 6$

(b) $y = x^2 + 6x - 2$

(c) $y = 7 - 10x - x^2$

(d) $y = x^2 + 3x + 1$

(e) $y = 2x^2 - 7x + 2$

(f) $y = 3x^2 - 12x + 5$

4.4 Solving quadratic equations

You will be familiar with solving quadratic equations of the form $x^2 - 6x + 8 = 0$ by factorising $x^2 - 6x + 8$ into the form $(x-2)(x-4)$, and then using the argument:

if $(x-2)(x-4) = 0$

then either $x - 2 = 0$ or $x - 4 = 0$

so $x = 2$ or $x = 4$.

The **solution** of the equation $x^2 - 6x + 8 = 0$ is $x = 2$ or $x = 4$. The numbers 2 and 4 are the **roots** of the equation.

If the quadratic expression has factors which you can find easily, then this is certainly the quickest way to solve it. However, the expression may not have factors, or they may be hard to find: try finding the factors of $30x^2 - 11x - 30$.

If you cannot factorise a quadratic expression easily to solve an equation, then you will be used to using the quadratic formula:

The solution of $ax^2 + bx + c = 0$, where $a \neq 0$, is

$$x = \frac{-b \pm \sqrt{b^2 - 4ac}}{2a}.$$

It is useful to know how this formula is derived by expressing $ax^2 + bx + c$ in completed square form. Start by dividing both sides of the equation by a (which cannot be zero, otherwise the equation would not be a quadratic equation):

$$x^2 + \frac{b}{a}x + \frac{c}{a} = 0.$$

Completing the square of the expression on the left side, you find that

$$x^2 + \frac{b}{a}x + \frac{c}{a} = \left(x + \frac{b}{2a}\right)^2 - \frac{b^2}{4a^2} + \frac{c}{a} = \left(x + \frac{b}{2a}\right)^2 - \frac{b^2 - 4ac}{4a^2}.$$

So you can continue with the equation:

$$\left(x + \frac{b}{2a}\right)^2 - \frac{b^2 - 4ac}{4a^2} = 0, \quad \text{which is} \quad \left(x + \frac{b}{2a}\right)^2 = \frac{b^2 - 4ac}{4a^2}.$$

There are two possibilities, $x + \dfrac{b}{2a} = +\sqrt{\dfrac{b^2 - 4ac}{4a^2}}$ or $-\sqrt{\dfrac{b^2 - 4ac}{4a^2}}$, giving

$$x = -\frac{b}{2a} \pm \frac{\sqrt{b^2 - 4ac}}{2a} = \frac{-b \pm \sqrt{b^2 - 4ac}}{2a}.$$

This shows that if $ax^2 + bx + c = 0$ and $a \neq 0$, then $x = \dfrac{-b \pm \sqrt{b^2 - 4ac}}{2a}$.

Example 4.4.1
Use the quadratic equation formula to solve the equations
(a) $2x^2 - 3x - 4 = 0$, (b) $2x^2 - 3x + 4 = 0$, (c) $30x^2 - 11x - 30 = 0$.

(a) Comparing this with $ax^2 + bx + c = 0$, put $a = 2$, $b = -3$ and $c = -4$. Then

$$x = \frac{-(-3) \pm \sqrt{(-3)^2 - 4 \times 2 \times (-4)}}{2 \times 2} = \frac{3 \pm \sqrt{9 + 32}}{4} = \frac{3 \pm \sqrt{41}}{4}.$$

Sometimes you will be expected to leave the roots in surd form. At other times you may be required to give the roots in the form $\dfrac{3 + \sqrt{41}}{4} \approx 2.35$ *and* $\dfrac{3 - \sqrt{41}}{4} \approx -0.85$. *Try substituting these numbers in the equation and see what happens.*

(b) Putting $a = 2$, $b = -3$ and $c = 4$,

$$x = \frac{-(-3) \pm \sqrt{(-3)^2 - 4 \times 2 \times 4}}{2 \times 2} = \frac{3 \pm \sqrt{9 - 32}}{4} = \frac{3 \pm \sqrt{-23}}{4}.$$

But -23 does not have a square root. This means that the equation $2x^2 - 3x + 4 = 0$ has no roots.

Try putting $2x^2 - 3x + 4$ *in completed square form; what can you deduce about the graph of* $y = 2x^2 - 3x + 4$?

(c) Putting $a = 30$, $b = -11$ and $c = -30$,

$$x = \frac{-(-11) \pm \sqrt{(-11)^2 - 4 \times 30 \times (-30)}}{2 \times 30} = \frac{11 \pm \sqrt{121 + 3600}}{60}$$

$$= \frac{11 \pm \sqrt{3721}}{60} = \frac{11 \pm 61}{60}.$$

So $\quad x = \frac{72}{60} = \frac{6}{5}$ or $x = -\frac{50}{60} = -\frac{5}{6}$.

This third example factorises, but the factors are difficult to find. But once you know the roots of the equation you can deduce that $30x^2 - 11x - 30 = (6x + 5)(5x - 6)$.

4.5   The discriminant $b^2 - 4ac$

If you look back at Example 4.4.1 you will see that in part (a) the roots of the equation involved surds, in part (b) there were no roots, and in part (c) the roots were fractions.

You can predict which case will arise by calculating the value of the expression under the square root sign, $b^2 - 4ac$, and thinking about the effect that this value has in the quadratic equation formula $x = \dfrac{-b \pm \sqrt{b^2 - 4ac}}{2a}$.

- If $b^2 - 4ac$ is a perfect square, the equation will have solutions which are integers or fractions.
- If $b^2 - 4ac > 0$, the equation $ax^2 + bx + c = 0$ will have two roots.
- If $b^2 - 4ac < 0$, there will be no roots.
- If $b^2 - 4ac = 0$, the root has the form $x = -\dfrac{b \pm 0}{2a} = -\dfrac{b}{2a}$, and there is one root only. Sometimes it is said that there are two coincident roots, or a **repeated root**, because the root values $-\dfrac{b + 0}{2a}$ and $-\dfrac{b - 0}{2a}$ are equal.

The expression $b^2 - 4ac$ is called the **discriminant** of the quadratic expression $ax^2 + bx + c$ because, by its value, it discriminates between the types of solution of the equation $ax^2 + bx + c = 0$.

Example 4.5.1

What can you deduce from the values of the discriminants of these quadratic equations?

(a) $2x^2 - 3x - 4 = 0$ (b) $2x^2 - 3x - 5 = 0$

(c) $2x^2 - 4x + 5 = 0$ (d) $2x^2 - 4x + 2 = 0$

(a) As $a = 2$, $b = -3$ and $c = -4$, $b^2 - 4ac = (-3)^2 - 4 \times 2 \times (-4) = 9 + 32 = 41$. The discriminant is positive, so the equation $2x^2 - 3x - 4 = 0$ has two roots. Also, as 41 is not a perfect square, the roots are irrational.

(b) As $a = 2$, $b = -3$, and $c = -5$, $b^2 - 4ac = (-3)^2 - 4 \times 2 \times (-5) = 9 + 40 = 49$. The discriminant is positive, so the equation $2x^2 - 3x - 5 = 0$ has two roots. Also, as 49 is a perfect square, the roots are rational.

(c) $b^2 - 4ac = (-4)^2 - 4 \times 2 \times 5 = 16 - 40 = -24$. As the discriminant is negative, the equation $2x^2 - 4x + 5 = 0$ has no roots.

(d) $b^2 - 4ac = (-4)^2 - 4 \times 2 \times 2 = 16 - 16 = 0$. As the discriminant is zero, the equation $2x^2 - 4x + 2 = 0$ has only one (repeated) root.

Example 4.5.2

The equation $kx^2 - 2x - 7 = 0$ has two real roots. What can you deduce about the value of the constant k?

The discriminant is $(-2)^2 - 4 \times k \times (-7) = 4 + 28k$. As the equation has two real roots, the value of the discriminant is positive, so $4 + 28k > 0$, and $k > -\frac{1}{7}$.

Example 4.5.3

The equation $3x^2 + 2x + k = 0$ has a repeated root. Find the value of k.

The equation has repeated roots if $b^2 - 4ac = 0$; that is, if $2^2 - 4 \times 3 \times k = 0$. This gives $k = \frac{1}{3}$.

Notice how, in these examples, there is no need to solve the quadratic equation. You can find all you need to know from the discriminant.

Exercise 4B

1 Use the quadratic formula to solve the following equations. Leave irrational answers in surd form. If there is no solution, say so. Keep your answers for use in Question 8.

(a) $x^2 + 3x - 5 = 0$ (b) $x^2 - 4x - 7 = 0$ (c) $x^2 + 6x + 9 = 0$

(d) $x^2 + 5x + 2 = 0$ (e) $x^2 + x + 1 = 0$ (f) $3x^2 - 5x - 6 = 0$

(g) $2x^2 + 7x + 3 = 0$ (h) $8 - 3x - x^2 = 0$ (i) $5 + 4x - 6x^2 = 0$

2 Use the value of the discriminant $b^2 - 4ac$ to determine whether the following equations have two roots, one root or no roots.

(a) $x^2 - 3x - 5 = 0$ (b) $x^2 + 2x + 1 = 0$ (c) $x^2 - 3x + 4 = 0$

(d) $3x^2 - 6x + 5 = 0$ (e) $2x^2 - 7x + 3 = 0$ (f) $5x^2 + 9x + 4 = 0$

(g) $3x^2 + 42x + 147 = 0$ (h) $3 - 7x - 4x^2 = 0$

In parts (i) and (j), the values of p and q are positive.

(i) $x^2 + px - q = 0$ (j) $x^2 - px - q = 0$

3 The following equations have repeated roots. Find the value of k in each case. Leave your answers as integers, exact fractions or surds.

(a) $x^2 + 3x - k = 0$ (b) $kx^2 + 5x - 8 = 0$ (c) $x^2 - 18x + k = 0$

(d) $-3 + kx - 2x^2 = 0$ (e) $4x^2 - kx + 6 = 0$ (f) $kx^2 - px + q = 0$

4 The following equations have the number of roots shown in brackets. Deduce as much as you can about the value of k.

(a) $x^2 + 3x + k = 0$ (2)   (b) $x^2 - 7x + k = 0$ (1)

(c) $kx^2 - 3x + 5 = 0$ (0)   (d) $3x^2 + 5x - k = 0$ (2)

(e) $x^2 - 4x + 3k = 0$ (1)   (f) $kx^2 - 5x + 7 = 0$ (0)

(g) $x^2 - kx + 4 = 0$ (2)   (h) $x^2 + kx + 9 = 0$ (0)

5 Use the value of the discriminant to determine the number of points of intersection of the following graphs with the x-axis.

(a) $y = x^2 - 5x - 5$ (b) $y = x^2 + x + 1$ (c) $y = x^2 - 6x + 9$

(d) $y = x^2 + 4$ (e) $y = x^2 - 10$ (f) $y = 3 - 4x - 2x^2$

(g) $y = 3x^2 - 5x + 7$ (h) $y = x^2 + bx + b^2$ (i) $y = x^2 - 2qx + q^2$

6 If a and c are both positive, what can be said about the graph of $y = ax^2 + bx - c$?

7 If a is negative and c is positive, what can be said about the graph of $y = ax^2 + bx + c$?

8* You will need your answers to Question 1, in rational or surd form, not decimals.

(A) For Question 1 parts (a), (b) and (d), find (i) the sum and (ii) the product of the roots. What do you notice? What happens if there is only one (repeated) root?

(B) If α and β are the roots of the quadratic equation $x^2 + bx + c = 0$ then these arise from factors $(x - \alpha)$ and $(x - \beta)$ of $x^2 + bx + c$. Show that the equation $x^2 + bx + c = 0$ has roots which have sum $-b$ and product c.

(C) Extend (B) to find expressions in terms of a, b and c for (i) the sum and (ii) the product of the roots of the equation $ax^2 + bx + c = 0$.

4.6 Simultaneous equations

In this section, you will learn how to solve a pair of simultaneous equations such as $y = x^2$ and $5x + 4y = 21$. This takes forward the ideas in Section 3.6.

Example 4.6.1
Solve the simultaneous equations $y = x^2$, $x + y = 6$.

These equations are usually best solved by finding an expression for x or y from one equation and substituting it into the other. In this case, it is easier to substitute for y from the first equation into the second, giving $x + x^2 = 6$. This rearranges to $x^2 + x - 6 = 0$, so $(x + 3)(x - 2) = 0$, giving $x = 2$ or $x = -3$. You can find the corresponding y values from the original equations. They are $y = 4$ and $y = 9$ respectively. The solution is therefore $x = 2$, $y = 4$ or $x = -3$, $y = 9$.

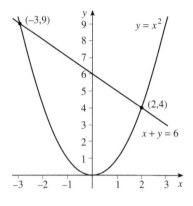

Fig. 4.2

Notice that the answers go together in pairs. It would be wrong to give the answer in the form $x = 2$ or $x = -3$ and $y = 4$ or $y = 9$, because $x = 2$ and $y = 9$ do not satisfy the original equations. You can see this if you interpret the equations as finding the points of intersection of the graphs $y = x^2$ and $x + y = 6$, as in Fig. 4.2.

Here is an example with a harder substitution.

Example 4.6.2
Solve the simultaneous equations $x^2 - 2xy + 3y^2 = 6$ and $2x - 3y = 3$.

It is not easy to find either x or y from the first equation, but you can find them from the second equation. You are less likely to make mistakes if you avoid fractions. From the second equation, $2x = 3 + 3y$, so, squaring this equation,

$$4x^2 = (3 + 3y)^2 = 9 + 18y + 9y^2.$$

When you substitute for $4x^2$ and $2x$ in the first equation, it is helpful to multiply the first equation by 4. Then

$$4x^2 - 8xy + 12y^2 = 24,$$
so $$\left(9 + 18y + 9y^2\right) - 4y(3 + 3y) + 12y^2 = 24.$$

This reduces to $9y^2 + 6y - 15 = 0$, and, dividing by 3, to $3y^2 + 2y - 5 = 0$. Solving this equation gives $(y - 1)(3y + 5) = 0$, so $y = 1$ or $y = -\frac{5}{3}$.

Substituting in the second equation to find x, you obtain $x = 3$ and $x = -1$. Therefore the solution is $x = 3$, $y = 1$ or $x = -1$, $y = -\frac{5}{3}$.

It is worth checking your answers in the original equations.

Example 4.6.3

At how many points does the line $x + 2y = 3$ meet the curve $2x^2 + y^2 = 4$?

From $x + 2y = 3$, $x = 3 - 2y$. Substituting in $2x^2 + y^2 = 4$, $2(3 - 2y)^2 + y^2 = 4$, so $2(9 - 12y + 4y^2) + y^2 = 4$, which reduces to $9y^2 - 24y + 14 = 0$.

The discriminant d of this equation is $d = 24^2 - 4 \times 9 \times 14 = 576 - 504 = 72$. As $d > 0$, this equation has two solutions, so the line meets the curve in two points.

4.7 Equations which reduce to quadratic equations

Sometimes you will come across equations which are not quadratic, but which can be changed into quadratic equations, usually by making the right substitution.

Example 4.7.1

Solve the equation $t^4 - 13t^2 + 36 = 0$.

This equation in t has degree 4 and is a quartic equation, but if you write t^2 as x you can see that it becomes $x^2 - 13x + 36 = 0$, which is a quadratic equation in x.

Then $(x - 4)(x - 9) = 0$, so $x = 4$ or $x = 9$.

Now recall that $x = t^2$, so $t^2 = 4$ or $t^2 = 9$, giving $t = \pm 2$ or $t = \pm 3$.

Example 4.7.2

Solve the equation $\sqrt{x} = 6 - x$
(a) by writing $\sqrt{x}$ as y,   (b) by squaring both sides of the equation.

(a) Writing $\sqrt{x} = y$, the equation becomes $y = 6 - y^2$ or $y^2 + y - 6 = 0$. Therefore $(y + 3)(y - 2) = 0$, so $y = 2$ or $y = -3$. But, as $y = \sqrt{x}$, and $\sqrt{x}$ is never negative, the only solution is $y = 2$, giving $x = 4$.

(b) Squaring both sides gives $x = (6 - x)^2 = 36 - 12x + x^2$ or $x^2 - 13x + 36 = 0$. Therefore $(x - 4)(x - 9) = 0$, so $x = 4$ or $x = 9$. Checking the answers shows that when $x = 4$, the equation $\sqrt{x} = 6 - x$ is satisfied, but when $x = 9$, $\sqrt{x} = 3$ and $6 - x = -3$, so $x = 9$ is not a root. Therefore $x = 4$ is the only root.

This is important. Squaring is not a reversible step, because it introduces the root or roots of the equation $\sqrt{x} = -(6 - x)$ as well. Notice that $x = 9$ does satisfy this last equation, but $x = 4$ doesn't! The moral is that, when you square an equation in the process of solving it, it is essential to check your answers.

Exercise 4C

1 Solve the following pairs of simultaneous equations.

(a) $y = x + 1$ $x^2 + y^2 = 25$ (b) $x + y = 7$ $x^2 + y^2 = 25$

(c) $y = x - 3$ $y = x^2 - 3x - 8$ (d) $y = 2 - x$ $x^2 - y^2 = 8$

(e) $2x + y = 5$ $x^2 + y^2 = 25$ (f) $y = 1 - x$ $y^2 - xy = 0$

(g) $7y - x = 49$ $x^2 + y^2 - 2x - 49 = 0$ (h) $y = 3x - 11$ $x^2 + 2xy + 3 = 0$

2 Find the coordinates of the points of intersection of the given straight lines with the given curves.

(a) $y = 2x + 1$ $y = x^2 - x + 3$ (b) $y = 3x + 2$ $x^2 + y^2 = 26$

(c) $y = 2x - 2$ $y = x^2 - 5$ (d) $x + 2y = 3$ $x^2 + xy = 2$

(e) $3y + 4x = 25$ $x^2 + y^2 = 25$ (f) $y + 2x = 3$ $2x^2 - 3xy = 14$

(g) $y = 2x - 12$ $x^2 + 4xy - 3y^2 = -27$ (h) $2x - 5y = 6$ $2xy - 4x^2 - 3y = 1$

3 In each case find the number of points of intersection of the straight line with the curve.

(a) $y = 1 - 2x$ $x^2 + y^2 = 1$ (b) $y = \frac{1}{2}x - 1$ $y = 4x^2$

(c) $y = 3x - 1$ $xy = 12$ (d) $4y - x = 16$ $y^2 = 4x$

(e) $3y - x = 15$ $4x^2 + 9y^2 = 36$ (f) $4y = 12 - x$ $xy = 9$

4 Solve the following equations; give irrational answers in terms of surds.

(a) $x^4 - 5x^2 + 4 = 0$ (b) $x^4 - 10x^2 + 9 = 0$ (c) $x^4 - 3x^2 - 4 = 0$

(d) $x^4 - 5x^2 - 6 = 0$ (e) $x^6 - 7x^3 - 8 = 0$ (f) $x^6 + x^3 - 12 = 0$

5 Solve the following equations.

(a) $x - 8 = 2\sqrt{x}$ (b) $x + 15 = 8\sqrt{x}$ (c) $t - 5\sqrt{t} - 14 = 0$

(d) $t = 3\sqrt{t} + 10$ (e) $\sqrt[3]{x^2} - \sqrt[3]{x} - 6 = 0$ (f) $\sqrt[3]{t^2} - 3\sqrt[3]{t} = 4$

6* Solve the following equations. (In most cases, multiplication by an appropriate expression will turn the equation into a form you should recognise.)

(a) $x = 3 + \dfrac{10}{x}$ (b) $x + 5 = \dfrac{6}{x}$ (c) $2t + 5 = \dfrac{3}{t}$

(d) $x = \dfrac{12}{x + 1}$ (e) $\sqrt{t} = 4 + \dfrac{12}{\sqrt{t}}$ (f) $\sqrt{t}\left(\sqrt{t} - 6\right) = -9$

(g) $x - \dfrac{2}{x + 2} = \frac{1}{3}$ (h) $\dfrac{20}{x + 2} - 1 = \dfrac{20}{x + 3}$ (i) $\dfrac{12}{x + 1} - \dfrac{10}{x - 3} = -3$

(j) $\dfrac{15}{2x + 1} + \dfrac{10}{x} = \frac{55}{2}$ (k) $y^4 - 3y^2 = 4$ (l) $\dfrac{1}{y^2} - \dfrac{1}{y^2 + 1} = \frac{1}{2}$

<hr style="height:6px;background:gray">

Miscellaneous exercise 4

1 Solve the simultaneous equations $x + y = 2$ and $x^2 + 2y^2 = 11$.   (OCR)

2 The quadratic polynomial $x^2 - 10x + 17$ is denoted by $f(x)$. Express $f(x)$ in the form $(x - a)^2 + b$ stating the values of a and b.

Hence find the least possible value that $f(x)$ can take and the corresponding value of x.   (OCR)

3 Solve the simultaneous equations $2x + y = 3$ and $2x^2 - xy = 10$.   (OCR)

4 For what values of k does the equation $2x^2 - kx + 8 = 0$ have a repeated root?

5 (a) Solve the equation $x^2 - (6\sqrt{3})x + 24 = 0$, giving your answer in terms of surds, simplified as far as possible.

   (b) Find all four solutions of the equation $x^4 - (6\sqrt{3})x^2 + 24 = 0$ giving your answers correct to 2 decimal places. (OCR)

6 Show that the line $y = 3x - 3$ and the curve $y = (3x + 1)(x + 2)$ do not meet.

7 Express $9x^2 - 36x + 52$ in the form $(Ax - B)^2 + C$, where A, B and C are integers. Hence, or otherwise, find the set of values taken by $9x^2 - 36x + 52$ for real x. (OCR)

8 Find the points of intersection of the curves $y = 6x^2 + 4x - 3$ and $y = x^2 - 3x - 1$, giving the coordinates correct to 2 decimal places.

9 (a) Express $9x^2 + 12x + 7$ in the form $(ax + b)^2 + c$ where a, b, c are constants whose values are to be found.

   (b) Find the set of values taken by $\dfrac{1}{9x^2 + 12x + 7}$ for real values of x. (OCR)

10 Find, correct to 3 significant figures, all the roots of the equation $8x^4 - 8x^2 + 1 = \frac{1}{2}\sqrt{3}$. (OCR)

11 Find constants a, b and c such that, for all values of x,

$$3x^2 - 5x + 1 = a(x + b)^2 + c.$$

Hence find the coordinates of the minimum point on the graph of $y = 3x^2 - 5x + 1$. (Note: the minimum point or maximum point is the vertex.) (OCR, adapted)

12 Find the points of intersection of the curve $xy = 6$ and the line $y = 9 - 3x$. (OCR)

13* The equation of a curve is $y = ax^2 - 2bx + c$, where a, b and c are constants with $a > 0$.

   (a) Find, in terms of a, b and c, the coordinates of the vertex of the curve.

   (b) Given that the vertex of the curve lies on the line $y = x$, find an expression for c in terms of a and b. Show that in this case, whatever the value of b, $c \geq -\dfrac{1}{4a}$. (OCR, adapted)

14 (a) The diagram shows the graphs of $y = x - 1$ and $y = kx^2$, where k is a positive constant. The graphs intersect at two distinct points A and B. Write down the quadratic equation satisfied by the x-coordinates of A and B, and hence show that $k < \frac{1}{4}$.

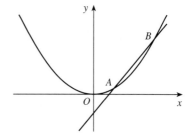

   (b) Describe briefly the relationship between the graphs of $y = x - 1$ and $y = kx^2$ in each of the cases   (i) $k = \frac{1}{4}$,   (ii) $k > \frac{1}{4}$.

   (c) Show, by means of a graphical argument or otherwise, that when k is a negative constant, the equation $x - 1 = kx^2$ has two real roots, one of which lies between 0 and 1.

15 Use the following procedure to find the least (perpendicular) distance of the point $(1,2)$ from the line $y = 3x + 5$, *without* having to find the equation of a line perpendicular to $y = 3x + 5$ (as you did in Chapter 1).

   (a) Let (x, y) be a general point on the line. Show that its distance, d, from $(1,2)$ is given by $d^2 = (x-1)^2 + (y-2)^2$.

   (b) Use the equation of the line to show that $d^2 = (x-1)^2 + (3x+3)^2$.

   (c) Show that $d^2 = 10x^2 + 16x + 10$.

   (d) By completing the square, show that the minimum distance required is $\frac{3}{5}\sqrt{10}$.

16 Using the technique of Question 15,

   (a) find the perpendicular distance of $(2,3)$ from $y = 2x + 1$,

   (b) find the perpendicular distance of $(-1,3)$ from $y = -2x + 5$,

   (c) find the perpendicular distance of $(2,-1)$ from $3x + 4y - 7 = 0$.

17 Point O is the intersection of two roads which cross at right angles; one road runs from north to south, the other from east to west. Car A is 100 metres due west of O and travelling east at a speed of 20 m s^{-1}, and Car B is 80 metres due north of O and travelling south at 20 m s^{-1}.

   (a) Show that after t seconds their distance apart, d metres, is given by
$$d^2 = (100 - 20t)^2 + (80 - 20t)^2.$$

   (b) Show that this simplifies to $d^2 = 400\big((5-t)^2 + (4-t)^2\big)$.

   (c) Show that the minimum distance apart of the two cars is $10\sqrt{2}$ metres.

18 Point O is the intersection of two roads which cross at right angles; one road runs from north to south, the other from east to west. Find the least distance apart of two cars A and B which are initially approaching O on different roads in the following cases.

   (a) Both cars are 10 metres from O. A is travelling at 20 m s^{-1}, B at 10 m s^{-1}.

   (b) A is 120 metres from O travelling at 20 m s^{-1}, B is 80 metres from O travelling at 10 m s^{-1}.

   (c) A is 120 metres from O travelling at 20 m s^{-1}, B is 60 metres from O travelling at 10 m s^{-1}.

5 Differentiation

This chapter is about finding the gradient of the tangent at a point on a graph. When you have completed it, you should be able to

- calculate an approximation to the gradient at a point on a curve given its equation
- calculate the exact gradient at a point on a quadratic curve and certain other curves
- find the equations of the tangent and normal to a curve at a point.

This chapter is divided into two parts. In the first part, Sections 5.1 to 5.5, you will develop results experimentally and use them to solve problems about tangents to graphs. In the second part, Sections 5.6 and 5.7, the experimental results are proved. You may, if you wish, omit the second part of the chapter on a first reading, but you should still tackle Miscellaneous exercise 5 at the end of the chapter.

5.1 Calculating gradients of chords

Think of a simple curve such as the graph of $y = x^2$. As your eye moves along the x-axis, can you describe, in mathematical terms, how the direction of the curve changes?

Just as a straight line has a numerical gradient, so any curve, provided it is reasonably smooth, has a steepness or **gradient** which can be measured at any given point. The difference is that for the curve the gradient will change as you move along it; mathematicians use this gradient to describe the curve's direction.

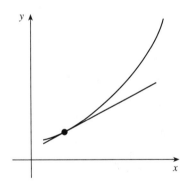

Fig. 5.1

In Chapter 1 you saw how to measure the gradient of a straight line through two points when you know their coordinates. You cannot use this method directly on a curve because it is not a straight line. Instead you find the gradient of the **tangent** to the curve at the point you have chosen, since (as you can see from Fig. 5.1) the tangent has the same steepness at that point. However, this creates another difficulty; you can only find the gradient of a line if you know the coordinates of two points on it.

Fig. 5.2 shows three chords (straight lines through two points of the curve) which get closer and closer to the tangent line; it turns out that a good way to begin is by finding the gradient of these chords, because for these you *can* use the techniques of Chapter 1.

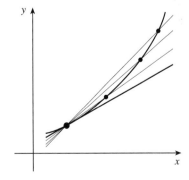

Fig. 5.2

Example 5.1.1

Find the gradient and the equation of the chord joining the points on the curve $y = x^2$ with coordinates $(0.4, 0.16)$ and $(0.7, 0.49)$.

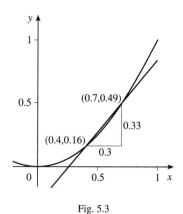

Fig. 5.3

From the formula in Section 1.3, the gradient of the chord is

$$\frac{0.49 - 0.16}{0.7 - 0.4} = \frac{0.33}{0.3} = 1.1.$$

The formula in Section 1.5 then gives the equation of the chord as

$$y - 0.16 = 1.1(x - 0.4), \quad \text{which is}$$
$$y = 1.1x - 0.28.$$

Fig. 5.3 shows that this is the equation of the whole line through the two points, not just the line segment between the two points which people often think of as the 'chord'.

At this point it is useful to introduce some new notation. The Greek letter δ (delta) is used as an abbreviation for 'the increase in'. Thus 'the increase in x' is written as δx, and 'the increase in y' as δy. These are the quantities called the 'x-step' and 'y-step' in Chapter 1. Thus in Example 5.1.1 from one end of the chord to the other the x-step is $0.7 - 0.4 = 0.3$ and the y-step is $0.49 - 0.16 = 0.33$, so you can write

$$\delta x = 0.3, \quad \delta y = 0.33.$$

With this notation, you can write the gradient of the chord as $\dfrac{\delta y}{\delta x}$.

Some people use the capital letter Δ rather than δ. Either is acceptable.

Notice that, in the fraction $\dfrac{\delta y}{\delta x}$, you cannot 'cancel out' the deltas. While you are getting used to the notation it is a good idea to read δ as 'the increase in', so that you are not tempted to treat it as an ordinary algebraic symbol. Remember also that δx or δy could be negative, making the x-step or y-step a decrease.

Using this notation for the gradient of the chord, the first line of Example 5.1.1 would read

$$\frac{\delta y}{\delta x} = \frac{0.49 - 0.16}{0.7 - 0.4} = \frac{0.33}{0.3} = 1.1.$$

Example 5.1.2

Find the gradient of the chord joining the points on the curve $y = x^2$ with x-coordinates 0.4 and 0.41.

First you need to calculate the y-coordinates of the two points. They are $0.4^2 = 0.16$ and $0.41^2 = 0.1681$.

Working in a similar way to Example 5.1.1,

$$\delta x = 0.41 - 0.4 = 0.01 \quad \text{and} \quad \delta y = 0.1681 - 0.16 = 0.0081,$$

so that the gradient of the chord is

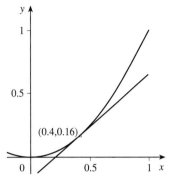

$$\frac{\delta y}{\delta x} = \frac{0.0081}{0.01} = 0.81.$$

Notice that Fig. 5.4 is not very useful as an illustration, because the two points are so close together. There is a small triangle there, like the triangle in Fig. 5.3, but you could be excused for missing it.

In Fig. 5.4 it has become difficult to distinguish between the chord joining two points close together and the tangent at the point with x-coordinate 0.4. This shows the way to find the gradient of the tangent at the point on the curve with $x = 0.4$.

Fig. 5.4

In Example 5.1.3, the two points have become even closer together.

Example 5.1.3
Find the gradient of the chord joining the points on the curve $y = x^2$ with x-coordinates 0.4 and 0.40001.

The coordinates of the two points are $\left(0.4, 0.4^2\right)$ and $\left(0.400\,01, 0.400\,01^2\right)$;

$$\delta x = 0.400\,01 - 0.4 = 0.000\,01 \quad \text{and} \quad \delta y = 0.400\,01^2 - 0.4^2 = 0.000\,008\,000\,1,$$

so that the gradient of the chord is

$$\frac{\delta y}{\delta x} = \frac{0.000\,008\,000\,1}{0.000\,01} = 0.800\,01.$$

This result, being so close to 0.8, seems to indicate that the gradient of the tangent to the curve $y = x^2$ at $x = 0.4$ is 0.8. But note that it doesn't prove it, because you are still finding the equation of the chord joining two points, no matter how close those points are.

Exercise 5A

In Questions 2 and 3 the parts of the questions could be divided, so that groups of students working together have answers to all the parts of each question, and can pool their results.

1 Find the equation of the line joining the points with x-values 1 and 2 on the graph $y = x^2$.

2 In each part of this question, find the gradient of the chord joining the two points with the given x-coordinates on the graph of $y = x^2$.

    (a) 1 and 1.001　　　　　　　　(b) 1 and 0.9999　　　　　　　　(c) 2 and 2.002

    (d) 2 and 1.999　　　　　　　　(e) 3 and 3.000 001　　　　　　　(f) 3 and 2.999 99

3 In each part of this question find the gradient of the chord from the given point on the graph $y = x^2$ to a nearby point. Vary the distance between the point given and the nearby point; make sure that some of the points that you choose are on the left of the given point.

    (a) $(-1, 1)$ (b) $(-2, 4)$ (c) $(10, 100)$

4 Use the results of Questions 2 and 3 to make a guess about the gradient of the tangent at any point on the graph of $y = x^2$.

5 (a)   Use a similar method to that of Questions 2 to 4 to make a guess about the gradients of the tangents at points on the graphs of $y = x^2 + 1$ and $y = x^2 - 2$.

    (b)   Use the results from part (a) to make a generalisation about the gradient at any point on the graph of $y = x^2 + c$, where c is any real number.

5.2   The gradient of a tangent to the curve $y = x^2 + c$

If you collected the results from Exercise 5A, you should have found that the gradient of the tangent to the curve $y = x^2$ at any point is twice the value of the x-coordinate of the point. Another way of saying this is that the gradient formula for the curve $y = x^2$ is $2x$.

For example, at the point $(-3, 9)$ on the curve $y = x^2$, the gradient is $2 \times (-3) = -6$. This means that the tangent to the curve at this point is the straight line which has gradient -6 and passes through the point $(-3, 9)$.

To find the equation of this tangent, you can use the method in Section 1.5. The equation of the line is

$$y - 9 = -6(x - (-3)), \quad \text{which is}$$
$$y - 9 = -6x - 18, \text{ or } y = -6x - 9.$$

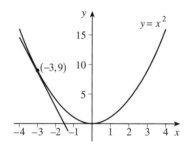

Fig. 5.5

You should also have seen that the gradient formula holds for the curve $y = x^2 + c$ where c is any constant: the gradient at x is also $2x$. After all, the curve $y = x^2 + c$ has the same shape as the curve $y = x^2$, but it is shifted in the y-direction.

Assume for the moment that these results can be proved. You will find proofs, if you need them, in Section 5.6.

5.3   The normal to a curve at a point

The line passing through the point of contact of the tangent with the curve which is perpendicular to the tangent is called the **normal** to the curve at that point.

Fig. 5.6 shows a curve with equation $y = f(x)$. The tangent and the normal at the point A have been drawn.

If you know the gradient of the tangent at A, you can

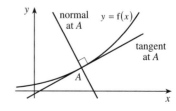

Fig. 5.6

calculate the gradient of the normal by using the result of Section 1.9. If the gradient of the tangent is m, then the gradient of the normal is $-\dfrac{1}{m}$, provided that $m \neq 0$.

Example 5.3.1
Find the equation of the normal to the curve $y = x^2$ at the point for which
(a) $x = -3$, (b) $x = 0$.

(a) You found in Section 5.2 that the gradient of the tangent at $(-3, 9)$ is -6.

The gradient of the normal is $-\dfrac{1}{-6} = \tfrac{1}{6}$ and it also passes through $(-3, 9)$.

Therefore the equation of the normal is $y - 9 = \tfrac{1}{6}(x - (-3))$, which simplifies to

$$6y = x + 57.$$

(b) At $(0, 0)$, the gradient of the tangent is 0, so the tangent is parallel to the x-axis. The normal is therefore parallel to the y-axis, and is therefore of the form $x = $ something. As the normal passes through $(0, 0)$, its equation is $x = 0$.

Try plotting the curve $y = x^2$, the tangent $y = -6x - 9$ and the normal $6y = x + 57$ on your graphic calculator. You may be surprised by the results.

You should realise that if you draw a curve together with its tangent and normal at a point, the normal will only appear perpendicular in your diagram if the scales are the same on both the x- and y-axes. However, no matter what the scales are, the tangent will always appear as a tangent.

At this stage you should recognise that you need to generalise the remark at the start of this section, that the gradient of the tangent at x to the curve $y = x^2 + c$ is $2x$, to curves with other equations.

Exercise 5B

In Questions 9 to 12 some of the work could be split up between different groups, so that collectively you have answers to all the parts of each question, and can pool your results.

1 Find the gradient of the tangent to the graph of $y = x^2$, at each of the points with the given x-coordinate.

(a) 1	(b) 4	(c) 0	(d) -2
(e) -0.2	(f) -3.5	(g) p	(h) $2p$

2 Find the gradient of the tangent to the graph of $y = x^2 - 2$, at each of the points with the given x-coordinate.

(a) 1	(b) 4	(c) 0	(d) -2
(e) -0.2	(f) -3.5	(g) p	(h) $2p$

3 The y-coordinate of a point P on the graph of $y = x^2 + 5$ is 9. Find the two possible values of the gradient of the tangent to $y = x^2 + 5$ at P.

4 Find the equation of the tangent(s) to each of the following graphs at the point(s) whose x- or y-coordinate is given.

(a) $y = x^2$ where $x = 2$

(b) $y = x^2 + 2$ where $x = -1$

(c) $y = x^2 - 2$ where $y = -1$

(d) $y = x^2 - 2$ where $y = -2$

5 Find the equations of the normals to each of the following graphs at the point whose x-coordinate is given.

(a) $y = x^2$ where $x = 1$

(b) $y = x^2 + 1$ where $x = -2$

(c) $y = x^2 + 1$ where $x = 0$

(d) $y = x^2 + c$ where $x = \sqrt{c}$

6 The tangent at P to the curve $y = x^2$ has gradient 3. Find the equation of the normal at P.

7 A normal to the curve $y = x^2 + 1$ has gradient -1. Find the equation of the tangent there.

8 Find the point where the normal at $(2,4)$ to $y = x^2$ cuts the curve again.

9 In each part of this question, find the gradient of the chord joining the two points with the given x-coordinates on the graphs of $y = 2x^2$, $y = 3x^2$ and $y = -x^2$.

(a) 1 and 1.001

(b) 1 and 0.9999

(c) 2 and 2.002

(d) 2 and 1.999

(e) 3 and 3.000 001

(f) 3 and 2.999 99

10 In each part of this question find the gradient of the chord from the point with the given x-coordinate to a nearby point for each of the curves $y = \frac{1}{2}x^2$ and $y = \frac{1}{2}x^2 + 2$. Vary the distance between the point given and the nearby point which you choose; make sure that some of the points that you choose are on the left of the given point.

(a) −1

(b) −2

(c) 10

11 Use the results of Questions 9 and 10 to make a guess about the gradient of the tangent at any point on the graph of $y = ax^2$, where a is any real number.

12 (a) Use a similar method to that of Questions 9 to 11 to make a guess about the gradients of the tangents at points on the graphs of $y = x^2 + 3x$ and $y = x^2 - 2x$.

(b) Use the results from part (a) to make a generalisation about the gradient at any point on the graph of $y = x^2 + bx$, where b is any real number.

5.4 The gradient formula for quadratic graphs

Chapter 3 introduced the idea of the general quadratic graph, whose equation can be written $y = ax^2 + bx + c$, where a, b and c are constants. What can you say about the gradient of the tangent to this curve?

From the results of the questions in Exercise 5B you should have found that the gradient formula for $y = ax^2$ is $2ax$. This means, for example, that the graph of $y = 3x^2$ is three times as steep at any given value of x as the graph of $y = x^2$. You should also have found that the gradient formula for $y = x^2 + bx$ is $2x + b$. This means that the gradient formula for $y = x^2 + 4x$ is $2x + 4$, which is the sum of the gradient formulae for x^2 and $4x$.

You already know that $y = x^2$ and $y = x^2 + c$ have the same gradient formula whatever the value of c.

So it seems reasonable to expect that:

> The gradient formula for the curve with equation
> $y = ax^2 + bx + c$ is $2ax + b$.

The importance of this result is that you can find the gradient of a function which is the sum of several parts by finding the gradient of each part in turn, and adding the results. You can also find the gradient of a constant multiple of a function by taking the same multiple of the gradient.

Section 5.6 will show how these results can be proved. Meanwhile here are some examples of their use. But first it would help to have some new notation.

Let the equation of a curve be $y = f(x)$. Then the gradient formula is denoted by $f'(x)$. This is pronounced 'f dashed x'.

The process of finding the gradient of the tangent to a curve is called **differentiation**. When you find the gradient formula, you are **differentiating**.

Just as $f(2)$ stands for the value of the function where $x = 2$, so $f'(2)$ stands for the gradient of $y = f(x)$ at $x = 2$. Thus the dash in $f'(x)$ tells you to differentiate: you then substitute the value of x at which you wish to find the gradient.

The quantity $f'(2)$ is called the **derivative** of $f(x)$ at $x = 2$.

Thus to find the gradient at $x = 2$ on the curve with equation $y = f(x)$, find $f'(x)$, and then substitute $x = 2$ to get $f'(2)$.

Example 5.4.1
(a) Differentiate $y = 3x^2 - 2x + 5$.
(b) Find the equation of the tangent and the normal to the graph of $y = 3x^2 - 2x + 5$ at the point for which $x = 1$.

(a) Let $f(x) = 3x^2 - 2x + 5$. For this function $a = 3$, $b = -2$ and $c = 5$. So, differentiating, $f'(x) = 2 \times 3 \times x - 2 = 6x - 2$.

(b) The y-coordinate of the point on the curve for which $x = 1$ is $3 - 2 + 5 = 6$.

When $x = 1$ the gradient of the tangent is $f'(1) = 6 \times 1 - 2 = 4$.

The equation of the tangent is therefore $y - 6 = 4(x - 1)$, or $y = 4x + 2$. The normal is perpendicular to the tangent, so its gradient is $-\frac{1}{4}$. The equation of the normal is therefore $y - 6 = -\frac{1}{4}(x - 1)$, which simplifies to $x + 4y = 25$.

Example 5.4.2

Differentiate   (a) $f(x) = 2(x^2 - 3x - 2)$,   (b) $(x+2)(2x-3)$

(a) **Method 1**   Multiplying out the bracket,

$$f(x) = 2(x^2 - 3x - 2) = 2x^2 - 6x - 4, \quad \text{so} \quad f'(x) = 4x - 6.$$

Method 2   The gradient of a constant multiple of a function is the same multiple of the gradient. In this case, the multiple is 2, so $f'(x) = 2(2x - 3)$.

(b) For $f(x) = (x+2)(2x-3)$, you cannot use Method 2 of part (a) because the multiple is not constant. But you can multiply out the brackets to get a quadratic which you can then differentiate.

$$f(x) = (x+2)(2x-3) = 2x^2 + x - 6, \quad \text{so} \quad f'(x) = 4x + 1.$$

If you cannot immediately differentiate a given function using the rules you know, see if you can write the function in a different form which enables you to apply one of the rules.

Example 5.4.3

Find the equation of the tangent to the graph of $y = x^2 - 4x + 2$ which is parallel to the x-axis.

From Section 1.6, a line parallel to the x-axis has gradient 0.

Let $f(x) = x^2 - 4x + 2$. Then $f'(x) = 2x - 4$.

To find when the gradient is 0 you need to solve $2x - 4 = 0$, giving $x = 2$.

When $x = 2$, $y = 2^2 - 4 \times 2 + 2 = -2$.

From Section 1.6, the equation of a line parallel to the x-axis has the form $y = c$. So the equation of the tangent is $y = -2$.

Exercise 5C

In Questions 13 to 16 some of the work could be split up between different groups, so that collectively you have answers to all the parts of each question, and can pool your results.

1 Find the gradient formula for each of the following functions.

(a) x^2 (b) $x^2 - x$ (c) $4x^2$ (d) $3x^2 - 2x$

(e) $2 - 3x$ (f) $x - 2 - 2x^2$ (g) $2 + 4x - 3x^2$ (h) $\sqrt{2}x - \sqrt{3}x^2$

2 For each of the following functions $f(x)$, find $f'(x)$. You may need to rearrange some of the functions before differentiating them.

(a) $3x - 1$ (b) $2 - 3x^2$ (c) 4 (d) $1 + 2x + 3x^2$

(e) $x^2 - 2x^2$ (f) $3(1 + 2x - x^2)$ (g) $2x(1 - x)$ (h) $x(2x + 1) - 1$

3 Find the derivative of each of the following functions $f(x)$ at $x = -3$.

(a) $-x^2$ (b) $3x$ (c) $x^2 + 3x$ (d) $2x - x^2$

(e) $2x^2 + 4x - 1$ (f) $-(3 - x^2)$ (g) $-x(2 + x)$ (h) $(x - 2)(2x - 1)$

4 For each of the following functions $f(x)$, find x such that $f'(x)$ has the given value.

(a) $2x^2$ 3 (b) $x - 2x^2$ -1 (c) $2 + 3x + x^2$ 0

(d) $x^2 + 4x - 1$ 2 (e) $(x - 2)(x - 1)$ 0 (f) $2x(3x + 2)$ 10

5 Find the equation of the tangent to the curve at the point with the given x-coordinate.

(a) $y = x^2$ where $x = -1$ (b) $y = 2x^2 - x$ where $x = 0$

(c) $y = x^2 - 2x + 3$ where $x = 2$ (d) $y = 1 - x^2$ where $x = -3$

(e) $y = x(2 - x)$ where $x = 1$ (f) $y = (x - 1)^2$ where $x = 1$

6 Find the equation of the normal to the curve at the point with the given x-coordinate.

(a) $y = -x^2$ where $x = 1$ (b) $y = 3x^2 - 2x - 1$ where $x = 1$

(c) $y = 1 - 2x^2$ where $x = -2$ (d) $y = 1 - x^2$ where $x = 0$

(e) $y = 2(2 + x + x^2)$ where $x = -1$ (f) $y = (2x - 1)^2$ where $x = \frac{1}{2}$

7 Find the equation of the tangent to the curve $y = x^2$ which is parallel to the line $y = x$.

8 Find the equation of the tangent to the curve $y = x^2$ which is parallel to the x-axis.

9 Find the equation of the tangent to the curve $y = x^2 - 2x$ which is perpendicular to the line $2y = x - 1$.

10 Find the equation of the normal to the curve $y = 3x^2 - 2x - 1$ which is parallel to the line $y = x - 3$.

11 Find the equation of the normal to the curve $y = (x - 1)^2$ which is parallel to the y-axis.

12 Find the equation of the normal to the curve $y = 2x^2 + 3x + 4$ which is perpendicular to the line $y = 7x - 5$.

13 Use an exploration method similar to that of Questions 9 and 10 in Exercise 5B to make a guess about the gradient formulas for the graphs of $y = x^3$ and $y = x^4$.

14 In each part of this question, find the gradient of the chord joining the two points with the given x-coordinates on the graphs of $y = \sqrt{x}$.

(a) 1 and 1.001 (b) 1 and 0.9999 (c) 4 and 4.002

(d) 4 and 3.999 (e) 0.25 and 0.250 001 (f) 0.25 and 0.249 999

15 In each part of this question find the gradient of the chord from the given point to a nearby point for the curve $y = \dfrac{1}{x}$.

Vary the distance between the given point and the nearby point which you choose; make sure that some of the points that you choose are on the left of the given point.

(a) $(-1, -1)$ (b) $(-2, -0.5)$ (c) $(10, 0.1)$

16 Use the results of Questions 14 and 15 to make a guess about the gradient of the tangent at any point on the graphs of $y = \sqrt{x}$ and $y = \dfrac{1}{x}$.

5.5 Some rules for differentiation

You already know the following rules:

If $f(x) = ax^2 + bx + c$, then $f'(x) = 2ax + b$.

If you add two functions, then the derivative of the sum is the sum of the derivatives: if $f(x) = g(x) + h(x)$, then $f'(x) = g'(x) + h'(x)$.

If you multiply a function by a constant, you multiply its derivative by the same constant: if $f(x) = ag(x)$, then $f'(x) = ag'(x)$.

You will have found from Exercise 5C that the derivative for $f(x) = x^3$ is $f'(x) = 3x^2$, and the derivative for $f(x) = x^4$ is $f'(x) = 4x^3$. You already know that if $f(x) = x^2$, then $f'(x) = 2x$, or $2x^1$. This suggests the rule:

If $f(x) = x^n$, where n is a positive integer, then $f'(x) = nx^{n-1}$.

Example 5.5.1
Find the coordinates of the points on the graph of $y = x^3 - 3x^2 - 4x + 2$ at which the gradient is 5.

Let $f(x) = x^3 - 3x^2 - 4x + 2$. Then $f'(x) = 3x^2 - 6x - 4$. The gradient is 5 when $f'(x) = 5$, that is when $3x^2 - 6x - 4 = 5$, leading to the quadratic equation $3x^2 - 6x - 9 = 0$, which simplifies to $x^2 - 2x - 3 = 0$.

Solving this equation, $(x + 1)(x - 3) = 0$, so $x = -1$ or $x = 3$.

Substituting these values into $y = x^3 - 3x^2 - 4x + 2$ to find the y-coordinates of the points, you find $y = (-1)^3 - 3 \times (-1)^2 - 4 \times (-1) + 2 = -1 - 3 + 4 + 2 = 2$ and $y = 3^3 - 3 \times 3^2 - 4 \times 3 + 2 = 27 - 27 - 12 + 2 = -10$. The coordinates of the required points are therefore $(-1, 2)$ and $(3, 10)$.

The results of Exercise 5C Questions 14 to 16 suggest two more rules:

If $f(x) = \sqrt{x}$, then $f'(x) = \dfrac{1}{2\sqrt{x}}$.

If $f(x) = \dfrac{1}{x}$, then $f'(x) = -\dfrac{1}{x^2}$.

Example 5.5.2

Find the equation of the tangent to the graph of $y = 2\sqrt{x}$ at the point $x = 9$.

Let $f(x) = 2\sqrt{x}$. Then, using results in the shaded boxes, $f'(x) = 2 \times \dfrac{1}{2\sqrt{x}} = \dfrac{1}{\sqrt{x}}$.

When $x = 9$, $f'(9) = \dfrac{1}{\sqrt{9}} = \frac{1}{3}$.

The tangent passes through the point $(9, 2\sqrt{9}) = (9, 6)$, so its equation is

$$y - 6 = \tfrac{1}{3}(x - 9), \quad \text{or} \quad 3y - x = 9.$$

Example 5.5.3

Differentiate each of the functions   (a) $x(1 + x^2)$,   (b) $(1 + \sqrt{x})^2$,   (c) $\dfrac{x^2 + x + 1}{x}$.

(a) Let $f(x) = x(1 + x^2)$ Then $f(x) = x + x^3$, so $f'(x) = 1 + 3x^2$.

(b) Let $f(x) = (1 + \sqrt{x})^2$. Then $f(x) = 1 + 2\sqrt{x} + x$, so $f'(x) = 2 \times \dfrac{1}{2\sqrt{x}} + 1 = \dfrac{1}{\sqrt{x}} + 1$.

(c) Let $f(x) = \dfrac{x^2 + x + 1}{x}$. Then, by division, $f(x) = x + 1 + \dfrac{1}{x}$, so $f'(x) = 1 - \dfrac{1}{x^2}$.

The results stated in this section can be assumed for the remainder of this book. Some of them are proved in Sections 5.6 and 5.7, but if you wish you may omit these final sections and, after working Exercise 5D, go straight to Miscellaneous exercise 5.

Exercise 5D

1 Differentiate the following functions.

  (a) $x^3 + 2x^2$ (b) $1 - 2x^3 + 3x^2$ (c) $x^3 - 6x^2 + 11x - 6$

  (d) $2x^3 - 3x^2 + x$ (e) $x(1 + x^2)$ (f) $(1 - x)(1 + x + x^2)$

2 Find $f'(-2)$ for each of the following functions $f(x)$.

  (a) $2x - x^3$ (b) $2x - x^2$ (c) $1 - 2x - 3x^2 + 4x^3$

  (d) $2 - x$ (e) $x^2(1 + x)$ (f) $(1 + x)(1 - x + x^2)$

3 For each of the following functions $f(x)$ find the value(s) of x such that $f'(x)$ is equal to the given number.

  (a) x^3 12   (b) $x^3 - x^2$ 8   (c) $3x - 3x^2 + x^3$ 108

  (d) $x^3 - 3x^2 + 2x$ −1   (e) $x(1 + x)^2$ 0   (f) $x(1 - x)(1 + x)$ 2

4 Differentiate the following functions.

  (a) $2\sqrt{x}$ (b) $(1 + \sqrt{x})^2$ (c) $y = x - \tfrac{1}{2}\sqrt{x}$ (d) $x\left(1 - \dfrac{1}{\sqrt{x}}\right)^2$

  (e) $x - \dfrac{1}{x}$ (f) $\dfrac{x^3 + x^2 + 1}{x}$ (g) $\dfrac{(x + 1)(x + 2)}{x}$ (h) $\left(\dfrac{\sqrt{x} + x}{\sqrt{x}}\right)^2$

5   Find the equation of the tangent to the curve $y = x^3 + x$ at the point for which $x = -1$.

6   One of the tangents to the curve with equation $y = 4x - x^3$ is the line with equation $y = x - 2$. Find the equation of the other tangent parallel to $y = x - 2$.

7   Find the equation of the tangent at the point $(4, 2)$ to the curve with equation $y = \sqrt{x}$.

8   Find the equation of the tangent at the point $\left(2, \frac{1}{2}\right)$ to the curve with equation $y = \frac{1}{x}$.

9   Find the equation of the normal at the point $(1, 2)$ to the graph $y = x + \frac{1}{x}$.

10 The graphs of $y = x^2 - 2x$ and $y = x^3 - 3x^2 - 2x$ both pass through the origin. Show that they share the same tangent at the origin.

11 Find the equation of the tangent to the curve with equation $y = x^3 - 3x^2 - 2x - 6$ at the point where it crosses the y-axis.

12 A curve has equation $y = x(x - a)(x + a)$, where a is a constant. Find the equations of the tangents to the graph at the points where it crosses the x-axis.

13 Find the coordinates of the point of intersection of the tangents to the graph of $y = x^2$ at the points at which it meets the line with equation $y = x + 2$.

5.6* The gradient formula for any quadratic graph

If you wish, you can omit these final sections and go straight on to Miscellaneous exercise 5.

The purpose of this section is to show you how to calculate the gradient of a quadratic graph without making any approximations.

Example 5.6.1
Find the gradient of the chord of $y = x^2$ joining the points with x-coordinates p and $p + h$.

The y-coordinates of the points are p^2 and $(p + h)^2$, so for this chord

$$\delta x = h, \quad \delta y = (p + h)^2 - p^2 = p^2 + 2ph + h^2 - p^2 = 2ph + h^2 = h(2p + h),$$

and the gradient is

$$\frac{\delta y}{\delta x} = \frac{2ph + h^2}{h} = 2p + h.$$

Notice that the gradients found in Examples 5.1.1 to 5.1.3 are special cases of this result, as shown in Table 5.7.

	p	$p+h$	h	$\dfrac{\delta y}{\delta x} = 2p+h$
Example 5.1.1	0.4	0.7	0.3	1.1
Example 5.1.2	0.4	0.41	0.01	0.81
Example 5.1.3	0.4	0.400 01	0.000 01	0.800 01

Table 5.7

The advantage of using algebra is that you don't have to work out the gradients each time from scratch. Table 5.8 shows some more results for $p = 0.4$ with different values of h, some positive and some negative.

Value of h	0.1	0.001	0.000 001	−0.1	−0.001	−0.000 001
Value of $\dfrac{\delta y}{\delta x}$	0.9	0.801	0.800 001	0.7	0.799	0.799 999

Table 5.8

If you have a graphic calculator, or some computer software for drawing graphs, it is interesting to produce a display showing the graph of $y = x^2$ and the chord through $(0.4, 0.16)$ with each of these gradients in turn. You will find that, when h is very close to 0, so that the two ends of the chord are very close together, it is almost impossible to distinguish the chord from the tangent to the curve. And you can see from Tables 5.7 and 5.8 that, for these chords, the gradient is very close to 0.8.

In fact, by taking h close enough to 0, you can make the gradient of the chord as close to 0.8 as you choose. From Example 5.6.1, the gradient of the chord is $0.8 + h$. So if you want to find a chord through $(0.4, 0.16)$ with a gradient between, say, $0.799\,999$ and $0.800\,001$, you can do it by taking h somewhere between $-0.000\,001$ and $+0.000\,001$.

The only value that you cannot take for h is 0 itself. But you can say that

'in the limit, as h tends to 0, the gradient of the chord tends to 0.8'.

The conventional way of writing this is

$$\lim_{h\to 0}(\text{gradient of chord}) = \lim_{h\to 0}(0.8 + h) = 0.8.$$

There is nothing special about taking p to be 0.4. You can use the same argument for any other value of p. Example 5.5.1 shows that the gradient of the chord joining (p, p^2) to $(p+h, (p+h)^2)$ is $2p+h$. If you keep p fixed, and let h take different values, then, by the same argument as before,

$$\lim_{h\to 0}(\text{gradient of chord}) = \lim_{h\to 0}(2p + h) = 2p.$$

Therefore the gradient at the point (p, p^2) on the curve $y = x^2$ is $2p$.

What this shows is that:

> The gradient formula for the curve $y = x^2$ is $2x$.

A similar approach can be used for any curve if you know its equation.

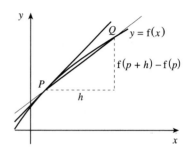

Fig. 5.9 shows a curve which has an equation of the form $y = f(x)$. Suppose that you want the gradient of the tangent at the point P, with coordinates $(p, f(p))$. The chord joining this point to any other point Q on the curve with coordinates $(p + h, f(p + h))$ has

$$\delta x = h, \quad \delta y = f(p + h) - f(p)$$

so that its gradient is

Fig. 5.9

$$\frac{\delta y}{\delta x} = \frac{f(p + h) - f(p)}{h}.$$

Now let the value of h change so that the point Q takes different positions on the curve. Then, if Q is close to P, so that h is close to 0, the gradient of the chord is close to the gradient of the tangent at p. In the limit, as h tends to 0, this expression tends to $f'(p)$.

> If the curve $y = f(x)$ has a tangent at $(p, f(p))$, then its gradient is
>
> $$\lim_{h \to 0} \frac{f(p + h) - f(p)}{h}.$$
>
> This quantity is called the derivative of $f(x)$ at $x = p$; it is denoted by $f'(p)$.
>
> In general the derivative is $f'(x)$, where $f'(x) = \lim_{h \to 0} \frac{f(x + h) - f(x)}{h}$.

Example 5.6.2

Find the derivative for the function $f(x) = 4x - 5$.

From the definition, $f'(x) = \lim_{h \to 0} \frac{f(x + h) - f(x)}{h}$ with $f(x) = 4x - 5$.

The top line is

$$f(x + h) - f(x) = (4(x + h) - 5) - (4x - 5) = 4x + 4h - 5 - 4x + 5 = 4h.$$

Therefore

$$\frac{f(x + h) - f(x)}{h} = \frac{4h}{h} = 4.$$

Then in the limit, as h tends to 0,

$$f'(x) = \lim_{h \to 0} \frac{f(x+h) - f(x)}{h} = \lim_{h \to 0} 4 = 4.$$

Notice that you could have predicted this result. From the work of Chapter 1, the graph of $f(x) = 4x - 5$ is a straight line with gradient 4. So it should not be a surprise that the derivative at x of $f(x) = 4x - 5$ is 4.

Similarly, you would expect the gradient at x of the function $f(x) = mx + c$, whose graph is the straight line $y = mx + c$, to be given by $f'(x) = m$.

Example 5.6.3
Find the derivative at x of the function $f(x) = 3x^2$.

For this function, $f(x+h) = 3(x+h)^2 = 3x^2 + 6xh + 3h^2$, so

$$f(x+h) - f(x) = \left(3x^2 + 6xh + 3h^2\right) - 3x^2 = 6xh + 3h^2 = h(6x + 3h)$$

and $\quad \dfrac{f(x+h) - f(x)}{h} = \dfrac{h(6x + 3h)}{h} = 6x + 3h.$

Then in the limit, as h tends to 0,

$$f'(x) = \lim_{h \to 0} \frac{f(x+h) - f(x)}{h} = \lim_{h \to 0} (6x + 3h) = 6x.$$

Notice that the derivative of $f(x) = x^2$ is $2x$ and the derivative of $f(x) = 3x^2$ is $6x$, which is $3 \times 2x$. This is an example of a general rule:

> If you multiply a function by a constant, then you multiply its derivative by the same constant.

Example 5.6.4
Find the derivative for the function $f(x) = 3x^2 + 4x - 5$.

For the function $f(x) = 3x^2 + 4x - 5$,

$$f(x+h) = 3(x+h)^2 + 4(x+h) - 5 = 3x^2 + 6xh + 3h^2 + 4x + 4h - 5,$$

so $\quad f(x+h) - f(x) = \left(3x^2 + 6xh + 3h^2 + 4x + 4h - 5\right) - \left(3x^2 + 4x - 5\right)$

$$= 3x^2 + 6xh + 3h^2 + 4x + 4h - 5 - 3x^2 - 4x + 5$$

$$= 6xh + 3h^2 + 4h = h(6x + 3h + 4),$$

and $\quad \dfrac{f(x+h) - f(x)}{h} = \dfrac{h(6x + 3h + 4)}{h} = 6x + 3h + 4.$

Then in the limit, as h tends to 0,

$$f'(x) = \lim_{h \to 0} \frac{f(x+h) - f(x)}{h} = \lim_{h \to 0} (6x + 3h + 4) = 6x + 4.$$

Examples 5.6.2 to 5.6.4 illustrate another general rule. The function in Example 5.6.4 is the sum of the functions in Examples 5.6.2 and 5.6.3, and the gradient in Example 5.6.4 is the sum of the gradients in Examples 5.6.2 and 5.6.3.

The general rule is:

> If you add two functions, then you find the derivative of the resulting function by adding the derivatives of the individual functions.

5.7* The gradient formula for some other functions

For some functions the method used in Section 5.6 lands you in some tricky algebra, and it is sometimes easier to use a different notation. Instead of finding the gradient of the chord joining the points with x-coordinates p and $p+h$ (or x and $x+h$), you can take the points to have coordinates $(p, f(p))$ and $(q, f(q))$, so that

$$\delta x = q - p \quad \text{and} \quad \delta y = f(q) - f(p).$$

Then the gradient is $\dfrac{\delta y}{\delta x} = \dfrac{f(q) - f(p)}{q - p}$.

To see how this works, here is Example 5.6.3 worked in this notation.

Example 5.7.1
Find the derivative at $x = p$ for the function $f(x) = 3x^2$.

For this function, $f(q) - f(p) = 3q^2 - 3p^2 = 3(q^2 - p^2) = 3(q - p)(q + p)$.

So $\dfrac{\delta y}{\delta x} = \dfrac{f(q) - f(p)}{q - p} = \dfrac{3(q - p)(q + p)}{q - p} = 3(q + p)$.

Now, in this method, q has taken the place of $p + h$, so that instead of taking the limit 'as h tends to 0' you take it 'as q tends to p'. It is easy to see that, as q tends to p, $3(q + p)$ tends to $3(p + p) = 3(2p) = 6p$.

Therefore, if $f(x) = 3x^2$, $f'(p) = 6p$. Since this holds for any value of p, you can write $f'(x) = 6x$.

With this notation, the definition of the derivative takes the form:

> The derivative of $f(x)$ at $x = p$ is $\quad f'(p) = \lim_{q \to p} \dfrac{f(q) - f(p)}{q - p}.$

Example 5.7.2

Use an algebraic method to find the derivative of the function $f(x) = x^4$ at $x = p$.

At $x = p$, $f(p) = p^4$ and at $x = q$, $f(q) = q^4$. The chord joining (p, p^4) and (q, q^4) has $\delta x = q - p$, $\delta y = q^4 - p^4$.

Notice that you can write δy as $(q^2)^2 - (p^2)^2$, so you can use the difference of two squares twice to obtain

$$\delta y = (q^2 - p^2)(q^2 + p^2) = (q - p)(q + p)(q^2 + p^2).$$

Therefore

$$\frac{\delta y}{\delta x} = \frac{(q - p)(q + p)(q^2 + p^2)}{q - p} = (q + p)(q^2 + p^2).$$

Then in the limit, as q tends to p,

$$f'(p) = \lim_{q \to p} \frac{f(q) - f(p)}{q - p} = \lim_{q \to p}\left((q + p)(q^2 + p^2)\right) = 2p(2p^2) = 4p^3.$$

Example 5.7.3

Use an algebraic method to find the derivative of the function $f(x) = \sqrt{x}$ at $x = p$.

At $x = p$, $f(p) = \sqrt{p}$ and at $x = q$, $f(q) = \sqrt{q}$. The chord joining $(p, \sqrt{p})$ and $(q, \sqrt{q})$ has $\delta x = q - p$, $\delta y = \sqrt{q} - \sqrt{p}$.

Notice that you can write δx as the difference of two squares in the form

$$\delta x = q - p = (\sqrt{q})^2 - (\sqrt{p})^2 = (\sqrt{q} - \sqrt{p})(\sqrt{q} + \sqrt{p}),$$

so $$\frac{\delta y}{\delta x} = \frac{\sqrt{q} - \sqrt{p}}{(\sqrt{q} - \sqrt{p})(\sqrt{q} + \sqrt{p})} = \frac{1}{\sqrt{q} + \sqrt{p}}.$$

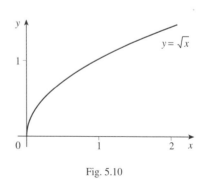

Then in the limit, as q tends to p,

$$f'(p) = \lim_{q \to p} \frac{f(q) - f(p)}{q - p}$$

$$= \lim_{q \to p} \frac{1}{\sqrt{q} + \sqrt{p}}$$

$$= \frac{1}{\sqrt{p} + \sqrt{p}} = \frac{1}{2\sqrt{p}}.$$

Fig. 5.10

Notice that this does not work when $p = 0$. In this case $\dfrac{\delta y}{\delta x} = \dfrac{1}{\sqrt{q}}$, which does

not have any limit as $q \to 0$. You can see from the graph of $y = \sqrt{x}$ in Fig. 5.10 that the tangent at $x = 0$ is the y-axis, which does not have a gradient.

Example 5.7.4

Find the derivative of the function $f(x) = \dfrac{1}{x}$ at $x = p$.

At $x = p$, $f(p) = \dfrac{1}{p}$, and at $x = q$, $f(q) = \dfrac{1}{q}$. The chord joining $\left(p, \dfrac{1}{p}\right)$ and $\left(q, \dfrac{1}{q}\right)$

has $\delta x = q - p$, $\quad \delta y = \dfrac{1}{q} - \dfrac{1}{p} = \dfrac{p-q}{pq} = -\dfrac{q-p}{pq}$, and

$$\frac{\delta y}{\delta x} = \frac{-\left(\dfrac{q-p}{qp}\right)}{q-p} = -\frac{1}{qp}.$$

Then, in the limit as q tends to p,

$$f'(p) = \lim_{q \to p} \frac{f(q) - f(p)}{q - p} = \lim_{q \to p}\left(-\frac{1}{qp}\right) = -\frac{1}{p^2}.$$

Display this curve on a graphic calculator and see why the gradient is always negative.

Exercise 5E*

1 Use an algebraic method to find the derivative of the function $f(x) = x^3$ at $x = p$.
   (You will need to use either the expansion $(p+h)^3 = p^3 + 3p^2h + 3ph^2 + h^3$ or the
   product of factors $(q - p)(q^2 + qp + p^2) = q^3 - p^3$.)

2 Use an algebraic method to find the derivative of the function $f(x) = x^8$ at $x = p$. (Let
   $p + h = q$ and use the difference of two squares formula on $q^8 - p^8$ as often as you can.)

3 Use an algebraic method to find the derivative of the function $f(x) = \dfrac{1}{x^2}$ at $x = p$.

Miscellaneous exercise 5

1 Find the equation of the tangent to $y = 5x^2 - 7x + 4$ at the point $(2,10)$.

2 Given the function $f(x) = x^3 + 5x^2 - x - 4$, find
   (a) $f'(-2)$ (b) the values of a such that $f'(a) = 56$.

3 Find the equation of the normal to $y = x^4 - 4x^3$ at the point for which $x = \frac{1}{2}$.

4 Show that the equation of the tangent to $y = \dfrac{1}{x}$ at the point for which $x = p$ is

   $p^2 y + x = 2p$. At what point on the curve is the equation of the tangent $9y + x + 6 = 0$?

5 The tangent to the curve $y = 6\sqrt{x}$ at the point $(4,12)$ meets the axes at A and B. Show
   that the distance AB may be written in the form $k\sqrt{13}$, and state the value of k.

6 Find the coordinates of the two points on the curve $y = 2x^3 - 5x^2 + 9x - 1$ at which the gradient of the tangent is 13.

7 Find the equation of the normal to $y = (2x - 1)(3x + 5)$ at the point $(1,8)$. Give your answer in the form $ax + by + c = 0$, where a, b and c are integers.

8 The curve $y = x^2 - 3x - 4$ crosses the x-axis at P and Q. The tangents to the curve at P and Q meet at R. The normals to the curve at P and Q meet at S. Find the distance RS.

9 The equation of a curve is $y = 2x^2 - 5x + 14$. The normal to the curve at the point $(1,11)$ meets the curve again at the point P. Find the coordinates of P.

10 At a particular point of the curve $y = x^2 + k$, the equation of the tangent is $y = 6x - 7$. Find the value of the constant k.

11 Show that the curves $y = x^3$ and $y = (x + 1)(x^2 + 4)$ have exactly one point in common, and use differentiation to find the gradient of each curve at this point. (OCR)

12 At a particular point of the curve $y = 5x^2 - 12x + 1$ the equation of the normal is $x + 18y + c = 0$. Find the value of the constant c.

6 Inequalities

This chapter is about inequality relationships, and how to solve inequalities. When you have completed it, you should

- know the rules for working with inequality symbols
- be able to solve linear inequalities
- be able to solve quadratic inequalities.

6.1 Notation for inequalities

You often want to compare one number with another and say which is the bigger. This comparison is expressed by using the inequality symbols $>$, $<$, $\leqslant$ and $\geqslant$. You have already met inequalities in Chapters 3 to 5.

The symbol $a > b$ means that a is greater than b. You can visualise this geometrically as in Fig. 6.1 which shows three number lines, with a to the right of b.

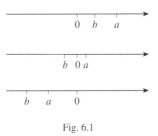

Notice that it does not matter whether a and b are positive or negative. The position of a and b in relation to zero on the number line is irrelevant. In all three lines, $a > b$. As an example, in the bottom line, $-4 > -7$.

Fig. 6.1

Similarly, the symbol $a < b$ means that a is less than b. You can visualise this geometrically on a number line, with a to the left of b.

> These expressions are equivalent.
>
> $a > b$ a is greater than b $b < a$ b is less than a

The symbol $a \geqslant b$ means that 'either $a > b$ or $a = b$'; that is, a is greater than or equal to, but not less than, b. You can also use the symbol $a \not< b$ for 'a is not less than b'. Thus $a \geqslant b$ and $a \not< b$ are equivalent. Similarly, the symbols $a \leqslant b$ and $a \not> b$ are also equivalent.

> These expressions are equivalent.
>
> $a \geqslant b$ a is greater than or equal to b $a \not< b$
> $b \not> a$ b is not greater than a $b \leqslant a$

The symbols $<$ and $>$ are called **strict** inequalities, and the symbols $\leqslant$ and $\geqslant$ are called **weak** inequalities.

6.2   Solving linear inequalities

When you solve an inequality such as $3x + 10 > 10x - 11$, you have to write a simpler statement with precisely the same meaning. In this case the simpler statement turns out to be $x < 3$. But how do you get from the complicated statement to the simple one?

Adding or subtracting the same number on both sides

You can add or subtract the same number on both sides of an inequality. For instance you can add the number 11 to both sides. In the example you would get

$$(3x + 10) + 11 > (10x - 11) + 11,$$
$$3x + 21 > 10x.$$

Justifying such a step involves showing that, for any number c, 'if $a > b$ then $a + c > b + c$'.

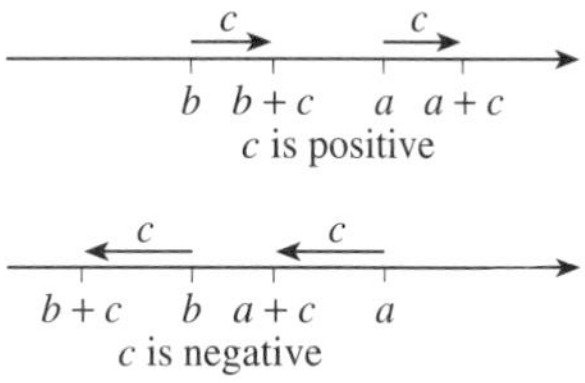

This is saying that if a is to the right of b on the number line, then $a + c$ is to the right of $b + c$. Fig. 6.2 shows that this is true whether c is positive or negative.

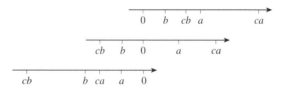

Fig. 6.2

Since subtracting c is the same as adding $-c$, you can also subtract the same number from both sides.

In the example, if you subtract $3x$ from both sides you get

$$(3x + 21) - 3x > 10x - 3x,$$
$$21 > 7x.$$

Multiplying both sides by a positive number

You can multiply (or divide) both sides of an inequality by a positive number. In the example above, you can divide both sides by the positive number 7 (or multiply both sides by $\frac{1}{7}$), and get:

$$21 \times \tfrac{1}{7} > 7x \times \tfrac{1}{7},$$
$$3 > x.$$

Here is a justification of the step , 'if $c > 0$ and $a > b$, then $ca > cb$'.

As $a > b$, a is to the right of b on the number line.

As $c > 0$, ca and cb are enlargements of the positions of a and b relative to the number 0.

Fig. 6.3

Fig. 6.3 shows that, whether a and b are positive or negative, ca is to the right of cb, so $ca > cb$.

Multiplying both sides by a negative number

If $a > b$, and you subtract $a + b$ from both sides, then you get $-b > -a$, which is the same as $-a < -b$. This shows that if you multiply both sides of an inequality by -1, then you change the direction of the inequality. Suppose that you wish to multiply the inequality $a > b$ by -2. This is the same as multiplying $-a < -b$ by 2, so $-2a < -2b$.

You can also think of multiplying by -2 as reflecting the points corresponding to a and b in the origin, and then multiplying by 2 as an enlargement.

You can summarise this by saying that if you multiply (or divide) both sides of an inequality by a negative number, you must change the direction of the inequality. Thus if $c < 0$ and $a > b$, then $ca < cb$ (see Fig. 6.4).

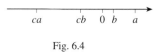

Fig. 6.4

Summary of operations on inequalities

- You can add or subtract a number on both sides of an inequality.
- You can multiply or divide an inequality by a positive number.
- You can multiply or divide an inequality by a negative number, but you must change the direction of the inequality.

The technique of solving inequalities is to use these three rules in a helpful way.

Example 6.2.1

Solve the inequality $-3x < 21$.

In this example you need to divide both sides by -3. Remembering to change the direction of the inequality, $-3x < 21$ becomes $x > -7$.

Example 6.2.2

Solve the inequality $\frac{1}{3}(4x + 3) - 3(2x - 4) \geqslant 20$.

Use the rule about multiplying by a positive number to multiply both sides by 3, in order to clear the fractions. In the solution, a reason is given only when an operation is carried out which affects the inequality.

$$\frac{1}{3}(4x + 3) - 3(2x - 4) \geqslant 20,$$
$$(4x + 3) - 9(2x - 4) \geqslant 60, \qquad \text{multiply both sides by 3}$$
$$4x + 3 - 18x + 36 \geqslant 60,$$
$$-14x + 39 \geqslant 60,$$
$$-14x \geqslant 21, \qquad \text{subtract 39 from both sides}$$
$$x \leqslant -\tfrac{3}{2}. \qquad \text{divide both sides by } -14, \text{ change } \geqslant \text{ to } \leqslant$$

Solving inequalities of this type is similar to solving equations. However, when you multiply or divide by a number, remember to reverse the inequality if that number is negative.

░░░░░░░░░░░░░░░ **Exercise 6A** ░░░░░░░░░░░░░░░

Solve the following inequalities.

1 (a) $x - 3 > 11$ (b) $x + 7 < 11$ (c) $2x + 3 \leqslant 8$ (d) $3x - 5 \geqslant 16$

   (e) $3x + 7 > -5$ (f) $5x + 6 \leqslant -10$ (g) $2x + 3 < -4$ (h) $3x - 1 \leqslant -13$

2 (a) $\dfrac{x+3}{2} > 5$ (b) $\dfrac{x-4}{6} \leqslant 3$ (c) $\dfrac{2x+3}{4} < -5$ (d) $\dfrac{3x+2}{5} \leqslant 4$

   (e) $\dfrac{4x-3}{2} \geqslant -7$ (f) $\dfrac{5x+1}{3} > -3$ (g) $\dfrac{3x-2}{8} < 1$ (h) $\dfrac{4x-2}{3} \geqslant -6$

3 (a) $-5x \leqslant 20$ (b) $-3x \geqslant -12$ (c) $5 - x < -4$ (d) $4 - 3x \leqslant 10$

   (e) $2 - 6x \leqslant 0$ (f) $6 - 5x > 1$ (g) $6 - 5x > -1$ (h) $3 - 7x < -11$

4 (a) $\dfrac{3-x}{5} < 2$ (b) $\dfrac{5-x}{3} \geqslant 1$ (c) $\dfrac{3-2x}{5} > 3$ (d) $\dfrac{7-3x}{2} < -1$

   (e) $\dfrac{5-4x}{2} \leqslant -3$ (f) $\dfrac{3-2x}{5} > -7$ (g) $\dfrac{3+2x}{4} < 5$ (h) $\dfrac{7-3x}{4} \leqslant -5$

5 (a) $x - 4 \leqslant 5 + 2x$ (b) $x - 3 \geqslant 5 - x$ (c) $2x + 5 < 4x - 7$

   (d) $3x - 4 > 5 - x$ (e) $4x \leqslant 3(2 - x)$ (f) $3x \geqslant 5 - 2(3 - x)$

   (g) $6x < 8 - 2(7 + x)$ (h) $5x - 3 > x - 3(2 - x)$ (i) $6 - 2(x + 1) \leqslant 3(1 - 2x)$

6 (a) $\frac{1}{3}(8x + 1) - 2(x - 3) > 10$ (b) $\frac{5}{2}(x + 1) - 2(x - 3) < 7$

   (c) $\dfrac{2x+1}{3} - \dfrac{4x+5}{2} \leqslant 0$ (d) $\dfrac{3x-2}{2} - \dfrac{x-4}{3} < x$

   (e) $\dfrac{x+1}{4} + \dfrac{1}{6} \geqslant \dfrac{2x-5}{3}$ (f) $\dfrac{x}{2} - \dfrac{3-2x}{5} \leqslant 1$

   (g) $\dfrac{x-1}{3} - \dfrac{x+1}{4} > \dfrac{x}{2}$ (h) $\dfrac{x}{3} \geqslant 5 - \dfrac{3x}{4}$

6.3 Quadratic inequalities

In Chapter 4, you saw that a quadratic function might take one of three forms:

$$f(x) = ax^2 + bx + c \qquad \text{the usual form}$$
$$f(x) = a(x - p)(x - q) \qquad \text{the factor form}$$
$$f(x) = a(x - r)^2 + s \qquad \text{the completed square form.}$$

If you need to solve a quadratic inequality of the form $f(x) < 0$, $f(x) > 0$, $f(x) \leqslant 0$ or $f(x) \geqslant 0$, by far the most convenient form is the factor form, so use that if you can.

Here are some examples which show ways of solving quadratic inequalities.

Example 6.3.1

Solve the inequality $(x-2)(x-4) < 0$.

Method 1   Sketch the graph of $y = (x-2)(x-4)$. The graph cuts the x-axis at $x = 2$ and $x = 4$. As the coefficient of x^2 is positive, the parabola bends upwards, as shown in Fig. 6.5.

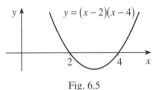

Fig. 6.5

You need to find the values of x such that $y < 0$.

From the graph you can see that this happens when x lies between 2 and 4, that is $x > 2$ and $x < 4$.

Remembering that $x > 2$ is the same as $2 < x$, you can write this as $2 < x < 4$, meaning that x is greater than 2 and less than 4.

Notice that when you write an inequality of the kind $r < x$ and $x < s$ in the form $r < x < s$, it is essential that $r < s$. It makes no sense to write $7 < x < 3$; how can x be both greater than 7 and less than 3?

Method 2   Find the values of x for which $(x-2)(x-4) = 0$. Call these values, $x = 2$ and $x = 4$, the **critical values** for the inequality.

Make a table showing the signs of the factors in the product $(x-2)(x-4)$.

	$x < 2$	$x = 2$	$2 < x < 4$	$x = 4$	$x > 4$
$x-2$	$-$	0	$+$	$+$	$+$
$x-4$	$-$	$-$	$-$	0	$+$
$(x-2)(x-4)$	$+$	0	$-$	0	$+$

Table 6.6

From Table 6.6 you can see that $(x-2)(x-4) < 0$ when $2 < x < 4$.

Example 6.3.2

Solve the inequality $(x+1)(5-x) \le 0$.

Fig. 6.7 shows the graph of $y = (x+1)(5-x)$. As the coefficient of x^2 is negative, the parabola has its vertex at the top. So $y \le 0$ when either $x \le -1$ or $x \ge 5$.

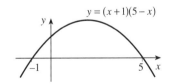

Fig. 6.7

Note that in this case the inequality is also satisfied by the critical values -1 and 5.

Here is an important general example.

Example 6.3.3

Solve the inequality $x^2 \leqslant a^2$, where $a > 0$.

This is the same as $x^2 - a^2 \leqslant 0$ or $(x+a)(x-a) \leqslant 0$. The critical values are $x = -a$ and $x = a$.

	$x < -a$	$x = -a$	$-a < x < a$	$x = a$	$x > a$
$x + a$	$-$	0	$+$	$+$	$+$
$x - a$	$-$	$-$	$-$	0	$+$
$(x+a)(x-a)$	$+$	0	$-$	0	$+$

Table 6.8

Table 6.8 shows that, if $x^2 \leqslant a^2$, then $-a \leqslant x \leqslant a$. It also shows that, if $-a \leqslant x \leqslant a$, then $x^2 \leqslant a^2$.

You can write the result of Example 6.3.3 more shortly as:

> If $a > 0$, then these statements are equivalent.
>
> $$x^2 \leqslant a^2 \qquad -a \leqslant x \leqslant a$$

It is usually easiest to solve inequalities by using graphical or tabular methods. If you have access to a graphic calculator, you can use it to obtain the sketch, which makes the whole process even easier.

Example 6.3.4 shows how inequality arguments can be expressed in a more algebraic form.

Example 6.3.4

Solve the inequalities (a) $(2x+1)(x-3) < 0$, (b) $(2x+1)(x-3) > 0$.

(a) If the product of two factors is negative, one of them must be negative, and the other positive. So there are two possibilities to consider.

If $2x+1$ is negative and $x-3$ is positive, then $x < -\frac{1}{2}$ and $x > 3$. This is obviously impossible.

But if $2x+1$ is positive and $x-3$ is negative, then $x > -\frac{1}{2}$ and $x < 3$, which happens if $-\frac{1}{2} < x < 3$.

(b) If the product of two factors is positive, either both are positive or both are negative.

If both $2x+1$ and $x-3$ are positive, then $x > -\frac{1}{2}$ and $x > 3$, which happens if $x > 3$.

If both $2x+1$ and $x-3$ are negative, then $x < -\frac{1}{2}$ and $x < 3$, which happens if $x < -\frac{1}{2}$.

So $(2x+1)(x-3) > 0$ if $x > 3$ or $x < -\frac{1}{2}$.

You could solve both parts at once by constructing a table as in Example 6.3.3, and reading off the sign from the last line.

There may be occasions where you don't have access to a graphic calculator, or when factorising the given expression is difficult or impossible. In those circumstances, you should complete the square, as described in Section 4.3.

Example 6.3.5
Solve algebraically the inequalities   (a) $2x^2 - 8x + 11 \leqslant 0$,   (b) $2x^2 - 8x + 5 \leqslant 0$.

(a) By completing the square, $2x^2 - 8x + 11 = 2(x-2)^2 + 3$.
The smallest value of $2(x-2)^2 + 3$ is 3, and it occurs when $x = 2$. So there are no values of x for which $2x^2 - 8x + 11 \leqslant 0$.

(b) $2x^2 - 8x + 5 = 2(x-2)^2 - 3$,
so $2(x-2)^2 - 3 \leqslant 0$,
$$(x-2)^2 - \tfrac{3}{2} \leqslant 0,$$
$$(x-2)^2 \leqslant \tfrac{3}{2}.$$

Using the result in the shaded box on page 75,
$$-\sqrt{\tfrac{3}{2}} \leqslant x - 2 \leqslant \sqrt{\tfrac{3}{2}}, \quad \text{or} \quad 2 - \sqrt{\tfrac{3}{2}} \leqslant x \leqslant 2 + \sqrt{\tfrac{3}{2}}.$$

Exercise 6B

1 Use sketch graphs to solve the following inequalities.
(a) $(x-2)(x-3) < 0$ (b) $(x-4)(x-7) > 0$ (c) $(x-1)(x-3) < 0$
(d) $(x-4)(x+1) \geqslant 0$ (e) $(2x-1)(x+3) > 0$ (f) $(3x-2)(2x+5) \leqslant 0$
(g) $(x+2)(4x+5) \geqslant 0$ (h) $(1-x)(3+x) < 0$ (i) $(3-2x)(5-x) > 0$
(j) $(x-5)(x+5) < 0$ (k) $(3-4x)(3x+4) > 0$ (l) $(2+3x)(2-3x) \leqslant 0$

2 Use a table based on critical values to solve the following inequalities.
(a) $(x-3)(x-6) < 0$ (b) $(x-2)(x-8) > 0$ (c) $(x-2)(x+5) \leqslant 0$
(d) $(x-3)(x+1) \geqslant 0$ (e) $(2x+3)(x-2) > 0$ (f) $(3x-2)(x+5) \leqslant 0$
(g) $(x+3)(5x+4) \geqslant 0$ (h) $(2-x)(5+x) < 0$ (i) $(5-2x)(3-x) > 0$
(j) $(3x+1)(3x-1) \geqslant 0$ (k) $(2-7x)(3x+4) < 0$ (l) $(5+3x)(1-3x) \leqslant 0$

3 Use an algebraic method to solve the following inequalities. Leave irrational numbers in terms of surds. Some inequalities may be true for all values of x, others for no values of x.
(a) $x^2 + 3x - 5 > 0$ (b) $x^2 + 6x + 9 < 0$ (c) $x^2 - 5x + 2 < 0$
(d) $x^2 - x + 1 \geqslant 0$ (e) $x^2 - 9 < 0$ (f) $x^2 + 2x + 1 \leqslant 0$
(g) $2x^2 - 3x - 1 < 0$ (h) $8 - 3x - x^2 > 0$ (i) $2x^2 + 7x + 1 \geqslant 0$

4 Use any method you like to solve the following inequalities.

(a) $x^2 + 5x + 6 > 0$ (b) $x^2 - 7x + 12 < 0$ (c) $x^2 - 2x - 15 \leqslant 0$

(d) $2x^2 - 18 \geqslant 0$ (e) $2x^2 - 5x + 3 \geqslant 0$ (f) $6x^2 - 5x - 6 < 0$

(g) $x^2 + 5x + 2 > 0$ (h) $7 - 3x^2 < 0$ (i) $x^2 + x + 1 < 0$

(j) $2x^2 - 5x + 5 > 0$ (k) $12x^2 + 5x - 3 > 0$ (l) $3x^2 - 7x + 1 \leqslant 0$

Miscellaneous exercise 6

1 Solve the inequality $x^2 - x - 42 \leqslant 0$.

2 Solve the inequality $(x + 1)^2 < 9$.

3 Solve the inequality $x(x + 1) < 12$.   (OCR)

4 Solve the inequality $x - x^3 < 0$.

5 Solve the inequality $x^3 \geqslant 6x - x^2$.

Use the discriminant '$b^2 - 4ac$' in answering Questions 6 to 8. You may need to check the value $k = 0$ separately.

6 Find the values of k for which the following equations have two real, separate roots.

(a) $kx^2 + kx + 2 = 0$ (b) $kx^2 + 3x + k = 0$ (c) $x^2 - 2kx + 4 = 0$

7 Find the values of k for which the following equations have no real roots.

(a) $kx^2 - 2kx + 5 = 0$ (b) $k^2 x^2 + 2kx + 1 = 0$ (c) $x^2 - 5kx - 2k = 0$

8 Find the range of values of k for which the equation $x^2 + 3kx + k = 0$ has any real roots.

9 Find the set of values of x for which $9x^2 + 12x + 7 > 19$.   (OCR)

10 Sketch, on the same diagram, the graphs of $y = \dfrac{1}{x}$ and $y = x - \dfrac{3}{2}$. Find the solution set of the inequality $x - \dfrac{3}{2} > \dfrac{1}{x}$.   (OCR)

11 Solve each of the following inequalities.

(a) $\dfrac{x}{x - 2} < 5$

(b) $x(x - 2) < 5$ (OCR, adapted)

Revision exercise 1

1 The line l_1 passes through the points $A(4,8)$ and $B(10,26)$. Show that an equation for l_1 is $y = 3x - 4$.

   The line l_1 intersects the line l_2, which has equation $y = 5x + 4$, at C. Find the coordinates of C.

2 Simplify (a) $3\sqrt{3} + 3\sqrt{27}$,   (b) $3\sqrt{2} \times 4\sqrt{8}$.

3 Show that any root of the equation $5 + x - \sqrt{3 + 4x} = 0$ is also a root of the equation $x^2 + 6x + 22 = 0$. Hence show that the equation $5 + x - \sqrt{3 + 4x} = 0$ has no solutions.

4 Write $x^2 + 10x + 38$ in the form $(x + b)^2 + c$ where the values of b and c are to be found.

   (a) State the minimum value of $x^2 + 10x + 38$ and the value of x for which this occurs.

   (b) Determine the values of x for which $x^2 + 10x + 38 \geqslant 22$.

5 A tangent to the curve $y = 3 - 5x - 2x^2$ has gradient -1. Find the coordinates of the point of contact, and the equation of the tangent.

6 Solve the inequalities   (a) $2x^2 - 5x + 2 \leqslant 0$,   (b) $(2x - 3)^2 < 16$,   (c) $\frac{1}{3}x - \frac{1}{4}(2x - 5) < \frac{1}{5}$.

7 Find the equation of the tangent at $x = 3$ to the curve with equation $y = 2x^2 - 3x + 2$.

8 Find the values of k such that the straight line $y = 2x + k$ meets the curve with equation $x^2 + 2xy + 2y^2 = 5$ exactly once.

9 Display on the same axes the curves with equations $y = x^3$ and $y = \sqrt[3]{x}$, and give the coordinates of their points of intersection.

10 Find the coordinates of the vertex of the parabola with equation $y = 3x^2 + 6x + 10$

   (a) by using the completed square form,

   (b) by using differentiation.

11 Find the coordinates of the point on the curve $y = 2x^2 - 3x + 1$ where the tangent has gradient 1.

12 A mail-order photographic developing company offers a picture-framing service to its customers. It will enlarge and mount any photograph, under glass and in a rectangular frame. Its charge is based on the size of the enlargement. It charges £6 per metre of perimeter for the frame and £15 per square metre for the glass. Write down an expression for the cost of enlarging and mounting a photograph in a frame which is x metres wide and y metres high.

   A photograph was enlarged and mounted in a square frame of side z metres at a cost of £12. Formulate and solve a quadratic equation for z.

13 Find the equation of the straight line through $A(1,4)$ which is perpendicular to the line passing through the points $B(2,-2)$ and $C(4,0)$. Hence find the area of the triangle ABC, giving your answer in the simplest possible form.

14 Solve the inequalities (a) $2(3-x) < 4-(2-x)$, (b) $(x-3)^2 < x^2$, (c) $(x-2)(x-3) \geqslant 6$.

15 Find the coordinates of the point where the normal to the curve with equation $y = x^2$ at the point for which $x = 2$ meets the curve again.

16 A normal to the curve $y = x^2$ has gradient 2. Find where it meets the curve.

17 The quadratic equation $(p-1)x^2 + 4x + (p-4) = 0$ has a repeated root. Find the possible values of p.

18 Prove that the triangle with vertices at the points $(1,2)$, $(9,8)$ and $(12,4)$ is right-angled, and calculate its area.

19 Find where the line $y = 5-2x$ meets the curve $y = (3-x)^2$. What can you deduce from your answer?

20 A rhombus has opposite vertices at $(-1,3)$ and $(5,-1)$. Find the equations of its diagonals. One of the other vertices is $(0,-2)$. Find the fourth vertex.

21 Simplify (a) $\sqrt{75} - \sqrt{27}$, (b) $\dfrac{\sqrt{18}}{2\sqrt{2}}$, (c) $\left(\dfrac{4}{2\sqrt{2}}\right)^3$.

22 Find the equation of the tangent to the curve with equation $y = 2x^2 - x - 2$ which is perpendicular to the straight line with equation $2x - 3y + 4 = 0$.

23 Points A and B have coordinates $(-1,2)$ and $(7,-4)$ respectively.
(a) Write down the coordinates of M, the mid-point of AB.
(b) Calculate the distance MB.
(c) The point P lies on the circle with AB as diameter and has coordinates $(2,y)$ where y is positive. Calculate the value of y, giving your answer in surd form.

24 Solve the inequalities (a) $x^2 - x - 2 > 0$, (b) $(x+1)(x-2)(x-3) > 0$.

25 Solve the simultaneous equations
$$2x + 3y = 5,$$
$$x^2 + 3xy = 4.$$

26 Find the equation of the normal to the curve with equation $y = \sqrt{x}$ at the point $(1,1)$. Calculate the coordinates of the point at which this normal meets the graph of $y = -\sqrt{x}$.

27 Two of the sides of a triangle have lengths $4\,\text{cm}$ and $6\,\text{cm}$, and the angle between them is $120°$. Calculate the length of the third side, giving your answer in the form $m\sqrt{p}$, where m and p are integers, and p is prime.

7 Index notation

You have already used index notation in the form of squares, cubes and other integer powers. In this chapter the notation is extended to powers which are zero, negative numbers and fractions. When you have completed it you should

- know the rules of indices
- know the meaning of negative, zero and fractional indices
- be able to simplify expressions involving indices
- know how to draw the graph of $y = x^n$ when n is negative or a fraction
- know that the derivative of $f(x) = x^n$ is given by $f'(x) = nx^{n-1}$ for all rational values of n.

7.1 Working with indices

In the 16th century, when mathematics books began to be printed, mathematicians were finding how to solve cubic and quartic equations. They found it was more economical to write and to print the products xxx and $xxxx$ as x^3 and x^4.

This is how index notation started. But it turned out to be much more than a convenient shorthand. The new notation led to important mathematical discoveries, and mathematics as it is today would be inconceivable without index notation.

You will already have used simple examples of this notation. In general, the symbol a^m stands for the result of multiplying m as together:

$$a^m = \overbrace{a \times a \times a \times \ \ldots \ \times a}^{m \text{ of these}}.$$

The number a is called the **base**, and the number m is the **index** (plural 'indices'). Notice that, although a can be any kind of number, m must be a positive integer. Another way of describing this is 'a raised to the mth power', or more shortly 'a to the power m'. When this notation is used, expressions can often be simplified by using a few simple rules.

One of these is the **multiplication rule**,

$$a^m \times a^n = \overbrace{a \times a \times \ \ldots \ \times a}^{m \text{ of these}} \times \overbrace{a \times a \times \ \ldots \ \times a}^{n \text{ of these}} = \overbrace{a \times a \times \ \ldots \ \times a}^{m+n \text{ of these}} = a^{m+n}.$$

This is used, for example, in finding the volume of a cube of side a:

$$\text{volume} = \text{base area} \times \text{height} = a^2 \times a = a^2 \times a^1 = a^{2+1} = a^3.$$

Closely linked with this is the **division rule**,

$$a^m \div a^n = \overbrace{(a \times a \times \ \ldots \ \times a)}^{m \text{ of these}} \div \overbrace{(a \times a \times \ \ldots \ \times a)}^{n \text{ of these}}$$

$$= \overbrace{a \times a \times \ \ldots \ \times a}^{m-n \text{ of these}} \quad (\text{since } n \text{ of the '}a\text{'s cancel out})$$

$$= a^{m-n}, \quad \text{provided that } m > n.$$

Another rule is the **power-on-power rule**,

$$(a^m)^n = \overbrace{\overbrace{a \times a \times \ \ldots \ \times a}^{m \text{ of these}} \times \overbrace{a \times a \times \ \ldots \ \times a}^{m \text{ of these}} \times \ldots \times \overbrace{a \times a \times \ \ldots \ \times a}^{m \text{ of these}}}^{n \text{ of these brackets}}$$

$$= \overbrace{a \times a \times \ \ldots \ \times a}^{m \times n \text{ of these}} = a^{m \times n}.$$

One further rule, the **factor rule**, has two bases but just one index:

$$(a \times b)^m = \overbrace{(a \times b) \times (a \times b) \times \ldots \times (a \times b)}^{m \text{ of these brackets}} = \overbrace{a \times a \times \ \ldots \ \times a}^{m \text{ of these}} \times \overbrace{b \times b \times \ \ldots \ \times b}^{m \text{ of these}} = a^m \times b^m.$$

In explaining these rules multiplication signs have been used. But, as in other parts of algebra, they are usually omitted if there is no ambiguity. For completeness, here are the rules again.

The multiplication rule:	$a^m \times a^n = a^{m+n}$
The division rule:	$a^m \div a^n = a^{m-n}$, provided that $m > n$
The power-on-power rule:	$(a^m)^n = a^{m \times n}$
The factor rule:	$(a \times b)^m = a^m \times b^m$

Example 7.1.1
Simplify $(2a^2 b)^3 \div (4a^4 b)$.

$$(2a^2 b)^3 \div (4a^4 b) = \left(2^3 (a^2)^3 b^3\right) \div (4a^4 b) \qquad \text{factor rule}$$

$$= (8a^{2 \times 3} b^3) \div (4a^4 b) \qquad \text{power-on-power}$$

$$= (8 \div 4) \times (a^6 \div a^4) \times (b^3 \div b^1) \qquad \text{rearranging}$$

$$= 2a^{6-4} b^{3-1} \qquad \text{division rule}$$

$$= 2a^2 b^2.$$

7.2 Zero and negative indices

The definition of a^m in Section 7.1, as the result of multiplying m as together, makes no sense if m is zero or a negative integer. You can't multiply -3 as or 0 as together. But extending the meaning of a^m when the index is zero or negative is possible, and useful, since it turns out that the rules still work with such index values.

Look at this sequence: $2^5 = 32$, $2^4 = 16$, $2^3 = 8$, $2^2 = 4$, ...

On the left sides, the base is always 2, and the indices go down by 1 at each step. On the right, the numbers are halved at each step. So you might continue the process

$$... , \; 2^2 = 4, \; 2^1 = 2, \; 2^0 = 1, \; 2^{-1} = \tfrac{1}{2}, \; 2^{-2} = \tfrac{1}{4}, \; 2^{-3} = \tfrac{1}{8}, \; ...$$

and you can go on like this indefinitely. Now compare

$$2^1 = 2 \text{ with } 2^{-1} = \tfrac{1}{2}, \qquad 2^2 = 4 \text{ with } 2^{-2} = \tfrac{1}{4}, \qquad 2^3 = 8 \text{ with } 2^{-3} = \tfrac{1}{8}.$$

It looks as if 2^{-m} should be defined as $\dfrac{1}{2^m}$, with the special value in the middle $2^0 = 1$.

This can be standardised, for any base a (except 0), and any positive integer m, as the **negative power rule**.

$$a^{-m} = \frac{1}{a^m} \text{ and } a^0 = 1.$$

Here are some examples to show that, with these definitions, the rules established in Section 7.1 for positive indices still work with negative indices. Try making up other examples for yourself.

The multiplication rule: $a^3 \times a^{-7} = a^3 \times \dfrac{1}{a^7} = \dfrac{1}{a^7 \div a^3}$

$$= \frac{1}{a^{7-3}} \qquad \text{using the division rule} \atop \text{for positive indices}$$

$$= \frac{1}{a^4} = a^{-4} = a^{3+(-7)}.$$

The power-on-power rule: $(a^{-2})^{-3} = \left(\dfrac{1}{a^2}\right)^{-3} = \dfrac{1}{(1/a^2)^3} = \dfrac{1}{1/(a^2)^3}$

$$= \frac{1}{1/a^6} \qquad \text{using the power-on-power} \atop \text{rule for positive indices}$$

$$= a^6 = a^{(-2)\times(-3)}.$$

The factor rule: $(ab)^{-3} = \dfrac{1}{(ab)^3} = \dfrac{1}{a^3 b^3}$ $\text{using the factor rule} \atop \text{for positive indices}$

$$= \frac{1}{a^3} \times \frac{1}{b^3} = a^{-3} b^{-3}.$$

Example 7.2.1

If $a = 5$, find the value of $4a^{-2}$.

The important thing to notice is that the index -2 goes only with the a and not with the 4. So $4a^{-2}$ means $4 \times \dfrac{1}{a^2}$. When $a = 5$, $4a^{-2} = 4 \times \dfrac{1}{25} = 0.16$.

Example 7.2.2

Simplify   (a) $4a^2 b \times (3ab^{-1})^{-2}$,   (b) $\left(\dfrac{\text{MLT}^{-2}}{\text{L}^2}\right) \div \left(\dfrac{\text{LT}^{-1}}{\text{L}}\right)$.

(a) **Method 1**   Turn everything into positive indices.

$$4a^2b \times (3ab^{-1})^{-2} = 4a^2b \times \frac{1}{(3a \times 1/b)^2} = 4a^2b \times \frac{1}{9a^2 \times 1/b^2} = 4a^2b \times \frac{b^2}{9a^2}$$

$$= \tfrac{4}{9}b^{1+2} = \tfrac{4}{9}b^3.$$

Method 2   Use the rules directly with positive and negative indices.

$$4a^2b \times (3ab^{-1})^{-2} = 4a^2b \times \left(3^{-2}a^{-2}(b^{-1})^{-2}\right) \qquad\qquad \text{factor rule}$$

$$= 4a^2b \times (3^{-2}a^{-2}b^2) \qquad\qquad \text{power-on-power rule}$$

$$= \left(4 \times \tfrac{1}{3^2}\right) \times (a^2a^{-2}) \times (bb^2) = \tfrac{4}{9}a^0b^3 = \tfrac{4}{9}b^3.$$

(b) This is an application in mechanics: M, L, T stand for dimensions of mass, length and time in the measurement of viscosity. Taking the brackets separately,

$$\left(\frac{\text{MLT}^{-2}}{\text{L}^2}\right) = \text{ML}^{1-2}\text{T}^{-2} = \text{ML}^{-1}\text{T}^{-2} \text{ and } \left(\frac{\text{LT}^{-1}}{\text{L}}\right) = \text{L}^{1-1}\text{T}^{-1} = \text{L}^0\text{T}^{-1} = \text{T}^{-1},$$

so $\quad \left(\dfrac{\text{MLT}^{-2}}{\text{L}^2}\right) \div \left(\dfrac{\text{LT}^{-1}}{\text{L}}\right) = \left(\text{ML}^{-1}\text{T}^{-2}\right) \div \text{T}^{-1} = \text{ML}^{-1}\text{T}^{-2-(-1)} = \text{ML}^{-1}\text{T}^{-1}.$

One application of negative indices is in writing down very small numbers. You probably know how to write very large numbers in standard form, or scientific notation. For example, it is easier to write the speed of light as $3.00 \times 10^8 \text{ m s}^{-1}$ than as $300\,000\,000 \text{ m s}^{-1}$. Similarly, the wavelength of red light, about $0.000\,000\,75$ metres, is more easily appreciated written as 7.5×10^{-7} metres.

Computers and calculators often give users the option to work in scientific notation, and if numbers become too large (or too small) to be displayed in ordinary numerical form they will switch into standard form, for example 3.00E8 or 7.5E–7. The symbol E stands for 'exponent', yet another word for 'index'. You can write this in scientific notation by simply replacing the symbol E m by $\times 10^m$, for any integer m.

Example 7.2.3
Calculate the universal constant of gravitation, G, from $G = \dfrac{gR^2}{M}$ where, in SI units,

$g \approx 9.81$, $R \approx 6.37 \times 10^6$ and $M \approx 5.97 \times 10^{24}$. ($R$ and M are the earth's radius and mass, and g is the acceleration due to gravity at the earth's surface.)

$$G \approx \frac{9.81 \times (6.37 \times 10^6)^2}{5.97 \times 10^{24}} = \frac{9.81 \times (6.37)^2}{5.97} \times \frac{(10^6)^2}{10^{24}}$$

$$\approx 66.7 \times \frac{10^{12}}{10^{24}} = 6.67 \times 10^1 \times 10^{-12} = 6.67 \times 10^{1-12} = 6.67 \times 10^{-11}.$$

7.3 Graphs of $y = x^n$ for negative n

In Section 3.3 you investigated the shapes of graphs with equations $y = x^n$ for positive integer values of n. You can now extend this to negative values of n.

You can write a negative integer n as $-m$, where m is a positive integer. Then x^n becomes x^{-m}, or $\dfrac{1}{x^m}$.

It is simplest to begin with the part of the graph for which x is positive. Then $\dfrac{1}{x^m}$ is also positive, so the graph lies in the first quadrant. Just as when n is positive, the point $(1,1)$ lies on the graph. But there is an important difference when $x = 0$, since then $x^m = 0$ and $\dfrac{1}{x^m}$ is not defined. So there is no point on the graph for which $x = 0$.

To look at this more closely, take a value of x close to 0, say 0.01. Then for $n = -1$ the corresponding value of y is $0.01^{-1} = \dfrac{1}{0.01^1} = \dfrac{1}{0.01} = 100$; and for $n = -2$ it is $0.01^{-2} = \dfrac{1}{0.01^2} = \dfrac{1}{0.0001} = 10\,000$. Even if you use a very small scale, the graph will disappear off the top of the page or screen as x is reduced towards zero.

What happens if x is large? For example, take $x = 100$. Then for $n = -1$ the corresponding value of y is $100^{-1} = \dfrac{1}{100^1} = \dfrac{1}{100} = 0.01$; and for $n = -2$ it is $100^{-2} = \dfrac{1}{100^2} = \dfrac{1}{10\,000} = 0.0001$. So x^n becomes very small, and the graph comes very close to the x-axis.

Use a graphic calculator to produce the graphs of $y = x^{-m}$ for various positive integer values of m. How do the graphs change as m increases?

Now consider the part of the graph for which x is negative. You found in Chapter 3 that, for positive n, this depends on whether n is odd or even. The same is true when n is negative, and for the same reason. If n is even, x^n is an even function and its graph is symmetrical about the y-axis. If n is odd, x^n is an odd function and its graph is symmetrical about the origin.

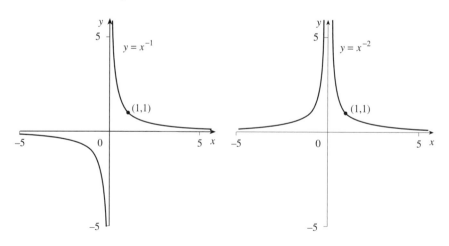

Fig. 7.1

All these properties are shown by the graphs of $y = x^n$ for $n = -1$ and $n = -2$ in Fig. 7.1.

Exercise 7A

1 Simplify the following expressions.

(a) $a^2 \times a^3 \times a^7$ (b) $(b^4)^2$ (c) $c^7 \div c^3$

(d) $d^5 \times d^4$ (e) $(e^5)^4$ (f) $(x^3y^2)^2$

(g) $5g^5 \times 3g^3$ (h) $12h^{12} \div 4h^4$ (i) $(2a^2)^3 \times (3a)^2$

(j) $(p^2q^3)^2 \times (pq^3)^3$ (k) $(4x^2y)^2 \times (2xy^3)^3$ (l) $(6ac^3)^2 \div (9a^2c^5)$

(m) $(3m^4n^2)^3 \times (2mn^2)^2$ (n) $(49r^3s^2)^2 \div (7rs)^3$ (o) $(2xy^2z^3)^2 \div (2xy^2z^3)$

2 Simplify the following, giving each answer in the form 2^n.

(a) $2^{11} \times (2^5)^3$ (b) $(2^3)^2 \times (2^2)^3$ (c) 4^3 (d) 8^2

(e) $\dfrac{2^7 \times 2^8}{2^{13}}$ (f) $\dfrac{2^2 \times 2^3}{(2^2)^2}$ (g) $4^2 \div 2^4$ (h) $2 \times 4^4 \div 8^3$

3 Express each of the following as an integer or a fraction.

(a) 2^{-3} (b) 4^{-2} (c) 5^{-1} (d) 3^{-2}

(e) 10^{-4} (f) 1^{-7} (g) $\left(\frac{1}{2}\right)^{-1}$ (h) $\left(\frac{1}{3}\right)^{-3}$

(i) $\left(2\frac{1}{2}\right)^{-1}$ (j) 2^{-7} (k) 6^{-3} (l) $\left(1\frac{1}{3}\right)^{-3}$

4 If $x = 2$, find the value of each of the following.

(a) $4x^{-3}$ (b) $(4x)^{-3}$ (c) $\frac{1}{4}x^{-3}$

(d) $\left(\frac{1}{4}x\right)^{-3}$ (e) $(4 \div x)^{-3}$ (f) $(x \div 4)^{-3}$

5 If $y = 5$, find the value of each of the following.

(a) $(2y)^{-1}$ (b) $2y^{-1}$ (c) $\left(\frac{1}{2}y\right)^{-1}$

(d) $\frac{1}{2}y^{-1}$ (e) $\dfrac{1}{(2y)^{-1}}$ (f) $\dfrac{2}{y^{-1}}$

6 Express each of the following in as simple a form as possible.

(a) $a^4 \times a^{-3}$ (b) $\dfrac{1}{b^{-1}}$ (c) $(c^{-2})^3$

(d) $d^{-1} \times 2d$ (e) $e^{-4} \times e^{-5}$ (f) $\dfrac{f^{-2}}{f^3}$

(g) $12g^3 \times (2g^2)^{-2}$ (h) $(3h^2)^{-2}$ (i) $(3i^{-2})^{-2}$

(j) $\left(\frac{1}{2}j^{-2}\right)^{-3}$ (k) $(2x^3y^{-1})^3$ (l) $(p^2q^4r^3)^{-4}$

(m) $(4m^2)^{-1} \times 8m^3$ (n) $(3n^{-2})^4 \times (9n)^{-1}$ (o) $(2xy^2)^{-1} \times (4xy)^2$

(p) $(5a^3c^{-1})^2 \div (2a^{-1}c^2)$ (q) $(2q^{-2})^{-2} \div (4/q)^2$ (r) $(3x^{-2}y)^2 \div (4xy)^{-2}$

7 Solve the following equations.

(a) $3^x = \frac{1}{9}$ (b) $5^y = 1$ (c) $2^z \times 2^{z-3} = 32$

(d) $7^{3x} \div 7^{x-2} = \frac{1}{49}$ (e) $4^y \times 2^y = 8^{120}$ (f) $3^t \times 9^{t+3} = 27^2$

8 The length of each edge of a cube is 3×10^{-2} metres.

(a) Find the volume of the cube.   (b) Find the total surface area of the cube.

9   An athlete runs 2×10^{-1} km in 7.5×10^{-3} hours. Find her average speed in km h^{-1}.

10 The volume, V m^3, of l metres of wire is given by $V = \pi r^2 l$, where r metres is the radius of the circular cross-section.

(a) Find the volume of 80 m of wire with radius of cross-section 2×10^{-3} m.

(b) Another type of wire has radius of cross-section 5×10^{-3} m. What length of this wire has a volume of 8×10^{-3} m^3?

(c) Another type of wire is such that a length of 61 m has a volume of 6×10^{-3} m^3. Find the radius of the cross-section.

11 An equation which occurs in the study of waves is $y = \dfrac{\lambda d}{a}$.

(a) Calculate y when $\lambda = 7 \times 10^{-7}$, $d = 5 \times 10^{-1}$ and $a = 8 \times 10^{-4}$.

(b) Calculate λ when $y = 10^{-3}$, $d = 0.6$ and $a = 2.7 \times 10^{-4}$.

12 Solve the equation $\dfrac{3^{5x+2}}{9^{1-x}} = \dfrac{27^{4+3x}}{729}$.

13 Find the point(s) of intersection of these pairs of graphs. Illustrate your answers with sketch graphs.

(a) $y = 8x^2$, $y = 8x^{-1}$ (b) $y = x^{-1}$, $y = 3x^{-2}$ (c) $y = x$, $y = 4x^{-3}$

(d) $y = 8x^{-2}$, $y = 2x^{-4}$ (e) $y = 9x^{-3}$, $y = x^{-5}$ (f) $y = \frac{1}{4}x^4$, $y = 16x^{-2}$

14 Three graphs have equations   (p) $y = x^{-2}$,   (q) $y = x^{-3}$,   (r) $y = x^{-4}$.
A line $x = k$ meets the three graphs at points P, Q and R, respectively. Give the order of the points P, Q and R on the line (from the bottom up) when k takes the following values.

(a) 2   (b) $\frac{1}{2}$ (c) $-\frac{1}{2}$ (d) -2

15 For what values of x are these inequalities satisfied? Sketch graphs illustrating your answers.

(a) $0 < x^{-3} < 0.001$ (b) $x^{-2} < 0.0004$ (c) $x^{-4} \geqslant 100$ (d) $8x^{-4} < 0.000\,05$

16* Draw sketch graphs with these equations. Check your answers with a graphic calculator.

(a) $y = x^2 + x^{-1}$ (b) $y = x + x^{-2}$ (c) $y = x^2 - x^{-1}$

(d) $y = x^{-2} - x^{-1}$ (e) $y = x^{-2} - x^{-3}$ (f) $y = x^{-2} - x^{-4}$

7.4 Fractional indices

In Section 7.2, you saw that the four index rules still work when m and n are integers, but not necessarily positive. What happens if m and n are not necessarily integers? If you put $m = \frac{1}{2}$ and $n = 2$ in the power-on-power rule, you find that

$$\left(x^{\frac{1}{2}}\right)^2 = x^{\frac{1}{2} \times 2} = x^1 = x.$$

Putting $x^{\frac{1}{2}} = y$, this equation becomes $y^2 = x$, so $y = \sqrt{x}$ or $y = -\sqrt{x}$, which is $x^{\frac{1}{2}} = \sqrt{x}$ or $-\sqrt{x}$. *Defining* $x^{\frac{1}{2}}$ as the positive square root of x, you get $x^{\frac{1}{2}} = \sqrt{x}$.

Similarly, if you put $m = \frac{1}{3}$ and $n = 3$, you can show that $x^{\frac{1}{3}} = \sqrt[3]{x}$. Then, by putting $m = \dfrac{1}{n}$, you find that $\left(x^{\frac{1}{n}}\right)^n = x^{\frac{1}{n} \times n} = x$, which leads to the result

$$x^{\frac{1}{n}} = \sqrt[n]{x}.$$

Notice that for the case $x^{\frac{1}{2}} = \sqrt{x}$, you must have $x \geqslant 0$, but for the case $x^{\frac{1}{3}} = \sqrt[3]{x}$ you do not need $x \geqslant 0$, because you can take the cube root of a negative number.

A slight extension of the $x^{\frac{1}{n}} = \sqrt[n]{x}$ rule can show you how to deal with expressions of the form $x^{\frac{2}{3}}$. There are two alternatives:

$$x^{\frac{2}{3}} = x^{\frac{1}{3} \times 2} = \left(x^{\frac{1}{3}}\right)^2 = \left(\sqrt[3]{x}\right)^2 \quad \text{and} \quad x^{\frac{2}{3}} = x^{2 \times \frac{1}{3}} = \left(x^2\right)^{\frac{1}{3}} = \sqrt[3]{x^2}.$$

(If x has an exact cube root it is usually best to use the first form, otherwise the second form is better.) In general, similar reasoning leads to the **fractional power rule**,

$$x^{\frac{m}{n}} = \left(\sqrt[n]{x}\right)^m = \sqrt[n]{x^m}.$$

Example 7.4.1
Simplify   (a) $9^{\frac{1}{2}}$ (b) $3^{\frac{1}{2}} \times 3^{\frac{3}{2}}$ (c) $16^{-\frac{3}{4}}$.

(a) $9^{\frac{1}{2}} = \sqrt{9} = 3$.   (b) $3^{\frac{1}{2}} \times 3^{\frac{3}{2}} = 3^{\frac{1}{2}+\frac{3}{2}} = 3^2 = 9$.

(c) **Method 1** $16^{-\frac{3}{4}} = \left(2^4\right)^{-\frac{3}{4}} = 2^{-3} = \frac{1}{8}$.

Method 2 $16^{-\frac{3}{4}} = \dfrac{1}{16^{\frac{3}{4}}} = \dfrac{1}{\left(\sqrt[4]{16}\right)^3} = \dfrac{1}{2^3} = \frac{1}{8}$.

There are often good alternative ways for solving problems involving indices, and you should try experimenting with them. Many people prefer to think with positive indices rather than negative ones; if you are one of them, writing $16^{-\frac{3}{4}} = \dfrac{1}{16^{\frac{3}{4}}}$, as in Method 2 of Example 7.4.1 (c), makes good sense as a first step.

Example 7.4.2
Simplify   (a) $\left(2\frac{1}{4}\right)^{-\frac{1}{2}}$ (b) $2x^{\frac{1}{2}} \times 3x^{-\frac{5}{2}}$ (c) $\dfrac{\left(2x^2y^2\right)^{-\frac{1}{2}}}{\left(2xy^{-2}\right)^{\frac{3}{2}}}$.

(a) $\left(2\frac{1}{4}\right)^{-\frac{1}{2}} = \left(\frac{9}{4}\right)^{-\frac{1}{2}} = \left(\frac{4}{9}\right)^{\frac{1}{2}} = \sqrt{\frac{4}{9}} = \frac{2}{3}$.

(b) $2x^{\frac{1}{2}} \times 3x^{-\frac{5}{2}} = 6x^{\frac{1}{2}-\frac{5}{2}} = 6x^{-2} = \dfrac{6}{x^2}$.

(c) **Method 1**   The numerator is $(2x^2y^2)^{-\frac{1}{2}} = \dfrac{1}{(2x^2y^2)^{\frac{1}{2}}} = \dfrac{1}{2^{\frac{1}{2}}xy}$, so

$$\frac{(2x^2y^2)^{-\frac{1}{2}}}{(2xy^{-2})^{\frac{3}{2}}} = \frac{1}{2^{\frac{1}{2}}xy} \times \frac{1}{2^{\frac{3}{2}}x^{\frac{3}{2}}y^{-3}} = \frac{1}{2^2x^{\frac{5}{2}}y^{-2}} = \frac{y^2}{4x^{\frac{5}{2}}}.$$

Method 2   The denominator is $(2xy^{-2})^{\frac{3}{2}} = (2xy^{-2})^{-\frac{3}{2}}$, so

$$\frac{(2x^2y^2)^{-\frac{1}{2}}}{(2xy^{-2})^{\frac{3}{2}}} = (2x^2y^2)^{-\frac{1}{2}}(2xy^{-2})^{-\frac{3}{2}} = (2^{-\frac{1}{2}}x^{-1}y^{-1})(2^{-\frac{3}{2}}x^{-\frac{3}{2}}y^3) = 2^{-2}x^{-\frac{5}{2}}y^2.$$

Notice that in part (c) the final answer has been given in different forms for the two methods. Which is 'simpler' is to some extent a matter of taste.

7.5 An application to differentiation

In Chapter 5 you found that, for positive integer powers of n, the derivative of $f(x) = x^n$ is given by the formula $f'(x) = nx^{n-1}$. The question now arises of whether this formula remains true for indices n which are not positive integers.

There are two particular values of n for which you can test this.

Exercise 5C showed numerically and Example 5.7.3 showed algebraically that, if $f(x) = \sqrt{x}$, then $f'(x) = \dfrac{1}{2\sqrt{x}}$. You can now write both these expressions in index notation: $f(x)$ is $x^{\frac{1}{2}}$ and $f'(x)$ is $\frac{1}{2}x^{-\frac{1}{2}}$, which you can write as $\frac{1}{2}x^{(\frac{1}{2}-1)}$.

Exercise 5C and Example 5.7.4 showed that, if $f(x) = \dfrac{1}{x}$, then $f'(x) = -\dfrac{1}{x^2}$. In index notation $f(x)$ is x^{-1} and $f'(x)$ is $-x^{-2}$, which you can write as $-x^{(-1-1)}$.

So the positive integer rule for differentiation also works for the indices $n = \frac{1}{2}$ and $n = -1$. In fact it works for all rational indices (and for all real indices, though you do not yet know the meaning of x^n when n is irrational). The proof of this will have to wait until later in the course, but for the time being you can use it with confidence.

Example 7.5.1
Find the equation of the tangent to $y = \sqrt[3]{x}$ at the point $(8,2)$.

In index notation $\sqrt[3]{x} = x^{\frac{1}{3}}$. So the rule gives the derivative as $\frac{1}{3}x^{(\frac{1}{3}-1)}$ or $\frac{1}{3}x^{-\frac{2}{3}}$, which in surd notation is $\dfrac{1}{3(\sqrt[3]{x})^2}$. At $(8,2)$, this is $\dfrac{1}{3(\sqrt[3]{8})^2} = \dfrac{1}{12}$.

Thus the equation of the tangent is $y - 2 = \frac{1}{12}(x-8)$, or $x - 12y + 16 = 0$.

7.6 Graphs of $y = x^n$ for fractional n

When n is a fraction, the function x^n may or may not be defined for negative values of x. For example, $x^{\frac{1}{3}}$ (the cube root of x) and $x^{-\frac{4}{5}}$ have values when $x < 0$, but $x^{\frac{1}{2}}$ (the square root of x) and $x^{-\frac{3}{4}}$ do not. Even when x^n is defined for negative x, some calculators and computers are not programmed to do the calculation. So it is simplest to restrict the discussion to values of $x \geqslant 0$.

It is easy to sketch the graphs of many of these functions by comparison with those of integral powers. Here are two examples.

The graph of $y = x^{\frac{5}{2}}$ must lie between the graphs of $y = x^2$ and $y = x^3$.

The graph of $y = x^{-\frac{1}{2}}$ is not defined when $x = 0$; its graph is broadly similar to the graph of $y = \dfrac{1}{x}$ (see Fig. 7.1), but lies below it when $x < 1$ and above it when $x > 1$.

It is worth experimenting for yourself with various other fractional powers, using a calculator or a computer. You will find that:

- it is still true that the graph of $y = x^n$ contains the point $(1,1)$;
- if n is positive it also contains the point $(0,0)$;
- if $n > 1$ the x-axis is a tangent to the graph; if $0 < n < 1$ the y-axis is a tangent. (To show this convincingly you may need to zoom in to display an enlarged version of the graph close to the origin.)

This last point follows if you substitute $x = 0$ in the expression nx^{n-1} to find the gradient at $(0,0)$. This has the value 0 if $n - 1 > 0$, but is undefined if $n - 1 < 0$.

Much the most important of these graphs is that of $y = x^{\frac{1}{2}}$, or $y = \sqrt{x}$. The clue to finding the shape of this graph is to note that if $y = x^{\frac{1}{2}}$, then $x = y^2$. The graph can therefore be obtained from that of $y = x^2$ by swapping the x- and y-axes. This has the effect of tipping the graph on its side, so that instead of facing upwards it faces to the right.

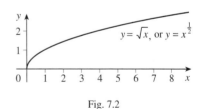

Fig. 7.2

But this is not quite the whole story. If $x = y^2$, then either $y = +\sqrt{x}$ or $y = -\sqrt{x}$. Since you want only the first of these possibilities, you must remove the part of the graph of $x = y^2$ below the x-axis, leaving only the part shown in Fig. 7.2 as the graph of $y = x^{\frac{1}{2}}$, or $y = \sqrt{x}$.

Exercise 7B

1 Evaluate the following without using a calculator.

   (a) $25^{\frac{1}{2}}$ (b) $8^{\frac{1}{3}}$ (c) $36^{\frac{1}{2}}$ (d) $32^{\frac{1}{5}}$

   (e) $81^{\frac{1}{4}}$ (f) $9^{-\frac{1}{2}}$ (g) $16^{-\frac{1}{4}}$ (h) $49^{-\frac{1}{2}}$

   (i) $1000^{-\frac{1}{3}}$ (j) $(-27)^{\frac{1}{3}}$ (k) $64^{\frac{2}{3}}$ (l) $(-125)^{-\frac{4}{3}}$

2 Evaluate the following without using a calculator.

(a) $4^{\frac{1}{2}}$　　(b) $\left(\frac{1}{4}\right)^{2}$　　(c) $\left(\frac{1}{4}\right)^{-2}$　　(d) $4^{-\frac{1}{2}}$

(e) $\left(\frac{1}{4}\right)^{-\frac{1}{2}}$　　(f) $\left(\frac{1}{4}\right)^{\frac{1}{2}}$　　(g) 4^{2}　　(h) $\left(\left(\frac{1}{4}\right)^{\frac{1}{4}}\right)^{2}$

3 Evaluate the following without using a calculator.

(a) $8^{\frac{2}{3}}$　　(b) $4^{\frac{3}{2}}$　　(c) $9^{-\frac{3}{2}}$　　(d) $27^{\frac{4}{3}}$

(e) $32^{\frac{2}{5}}$　　(f) $32^{\frac{3}{5}}$　　(g) $64^{-\frac{5}{6}}$　　(h) $4^{2\frac{1}{2}}$

(i) $10\,000^{-\frac{3}{4}}$　　(j) $\left(\frac{1}{125}\right)^{-\frac{4}{3}}$　　(k) $\left(3\frac{3}{8}\right)^{\frac{2}{3}}$　　(l) $\left(2\frac{1}{4}\right)^{-\frac{1}{2}}$

4 Simplify the following expressions.

(a) $a^{\frac{1}{3}}\times a^{\frac{5}{3}}$　　(b) $3b^{\frac{1}{2}}\times 4b^{-\frac{3}{2}}$　　(c) $\left(6c^{\frac{1}{4}}\right)\times\left(4c\right)^{\frac{1}{2}}$

(d) $\left(d^{2}\right)^{\frac{1}{3}}\div\left(d^{\frac{1}{3}}\right)^{2}$　　(e) $\left(2x^{\frac{1}{2}}y^{\frac{1}{3}}\right)^{6}\times\left(\frac{1}{2}x^{\frac{1}{4}}y^{\frac{3}{4}}\right)^{4}$　　(f) $\left(24e\right)^{\frac{1}{3}}\div\left(3e\right)^{\frac{1}{3}}$

(g) $\dfrac{\left(5p^{2}q^{4}\right)^{\frac{1}{3}}}{\left(25pq^{2}\right)^{-\frac{1}{3}}}$　　(h) $\left(4m^{3}n\right)^{\frac{1}{4}}\times\left(8mn^{3}\right)^{\frac{1}{2}}$　　(i) $\dfrac{\left(2x^{2}y^{-1}\right)^{-\frac{1}{4}}}{\left(8x^{-1}y^{2}\right)^{-\frac{1}{2}}}$

5 Solve the following equations.

(a) $x^{\frac{1}{2}}=8$　　(b) $x^{\frac{1}{3}}=3$　　(c) $x^{\frac{2}{3}}=4$　　(d) $x^{\frac{3}{2}}=27$

(e) $x^{-\frac{3}{2}}=8$　　(f) $x^{-\frac{2}{3}}=9$　　(g) $x^{\frac{3}{2}}=x\sqrt{2}$　　(h) $x^{\frac{3}{2}}=2\sqrt{x}$

6 The time, T seconds, taken by a pendulum of length l metres to complete one swing is given by $T=2\pi l^{\frac{1}{2}}g^{-\frac{1}{2}}$ where $g\approx 9.81\,\mathrm{m\,s}^{-2}$.

(a) Find the value of T for a pendulum of length 0.9 metres.

(b) Find the length of a pendulum which takes 3 seconds for a complete swing.

7 The radius, $r\,\mathrm{cm}$, of a sphere of volume $V\,\mathrm{cm}^{3}$ is given by $r=\left(\dfrac{3V}{4\pi}\right)^{\frac{1}{3}}$. Find the radius of a sphere of volume $1150\,\mathrm{cm}^{3}$.

8 Solve the following equations.

(a) $4^{x}=32$　　(b) $9^{y}=\frac{1}{27}$　　(c) $16^{z}=2$　　(d) $100^{x}=1000$

(e) $8^{y}=16$　　(f) $8^{z}=\frac{1}{128}$　　(g) $\left(2^{t}\right)^{3}\times4^{t-1}=16$　　(h) $\dfrac{9^{y}}{27^{2y+1}}=81$

9 On each of the graphs　(a) $y=x^{\frac{1}{3}}$,　(b) $y=x^{\frac{2}{3}}$,　(c) $y=x^{-\frac{2}{3}}$,　(d) $y=x^{-\frac{4}{3}}$,

P is the point where $x=8$ and Q is the point where $x=8.1$. Find
(i)　the y-coordinate of Q,　　(ii)　the gradient of the chord PQ,
(iii) the gradient of the tangent at P,　　(iv) the equation of the tangent at P.

10 For each of the graphs　(a) $y=x^{\frac{1}{2}}$,　(b) $y=x^{-\frac{1}{2}}$,　(c) $y=x^{-2}$,　(d) $y=x^{-3}$,

P is the point where $x=4$, Q is the point where $x=3.99$ and R is the point where $x=4.01$. Find
(i)　the gradient of the chord QR,
(ii)　the gradient of the tangent at P,
(iii) the equation of the tangent at P.

11 Sketch the graphs of these equations for $x > 0$. Use a graphic calculator to check your answers.

(a) $y = x^{\frac{3}{2}}$

(b) $y = x^{\frac{1}{3}}$

(c) $y = -2x^{\frac{1}{2}}$

(d) $y = 4x^{-\frac{1}{4}}$

(e) $y = x^{-\frac{4}{3}}$

(f) $y = x^{\frac{2}{3}} - x^{-\frac{2}{3}}$

12 Differentiate each of these functions $f(x)$. Give your answers $f'(x)$ in a similar form, without negative or fractional indices.

(a) $\dfrac{1}{4x}$

(b) $\dfrac{3}{x^2}$

(c) x^0

(d) $\sqrt[4]{x^3}$

(e) $6\sqrt[3]{x}$

(f) $\dfrac{4}{\sqrt{x}}$

(g) $\dfrac{3}{x} + \dfrac{1}{3x^3}$

(h) $\sqrt{16x^5}$

(i) $x\sqrt{x}$

(j) $\dfrac{1}{\sqrt[3]{8x}}$

(k) $\dfrac{x-2}{x^2}$

(l) $\dfrac{1+x}{\sqrt[4]{x}}$

13 (a) Without using a calculator, state which of these expressions has a value when $x = -64$. Find this value when it exists.

(i) $x^{\frac{2}{3}}$

(ii) $x^{\frac{3}{2}}$

(iii) $x^{-\frac{1}{3}}$

(iv) $\left(\frac{1}{2}x\right)^{\frac{4}{5}}$

(v) $x^{\frac{1}{6}}$

(vi) $(4x)^{\frac{3}{4}}$

(b) Investigate whether your calculator gives the answers you obtained in part (a).

(c) What can you say about p or q if $x^{\frac{p}{q}}$ has a value when x is negative?

14 Sketch these graphs, including negative values of x where appropriate. Compare your graphs with those given by a graphic calculator.

(a) $y = x^{\frac{2}{3}}$

(b) $y = x^{\frac{3}{4}}$

(c) $y = x^{\frac{4}{5}}$

(d) $y = x^{-\frac{1}{3}}$

(e) $y = x^{\frac{4}{3}}$

(f) $y = x^{-\frac{3}{2}}$

Miscellaneous exercise 7

1 Evaluate the following without using a calculator.

(a) $\left(\frac{1}{2}\right)^{-1} + \left(\frac{1}{2}\right)^{-2}$

(b) $32^{-\frac{4}{5}}$

(c) $\left(4^{\frac{3}{2}}\right)^{-\frac{1}{3}}$

(d) $\left(1\frac{7}{9}\right)^{1\frac{1}{2}}$

2 Simplify

(a) $\left(4p^{\frac{1}{4}} q^{-3}\right)^{\frac{1}{2}}$,

(b) $\dfrac{(5b)^{-1}}{(8b^6)^{\frac{1}{3}}}$,

(c) $(2x^6 y^8)^{\frac{1}{4}} \times (8x^{-2})^{\frac{1}{4}}$,

(d) $\left(m^{\frac{1}{3}} n^{\frac{1}{2}}\right)^2 \times \left(m^{\frac{1}{6}} n^{\frac{1}{3}}\right)^4 \times (mn)^{-2}$.

3 Express $\left(9a^4\right)^{-\frac{1}{2}}$ as an algebraic fraction in simplified form. (OCR)

4 Express $\dfrac{1}{\left(\sqrt{a}\right)^{\frac{4}{3}}}$ in the form a^n, stating the value of n. (OCR)

5 By letting $y = x^{\frac{1}{3}}$, or otherwise, find the values of x for which $x^{\frac{1}{3}} - 2x^{-\frac{1}{3}} = 1$. (OCR)

6 Solve the equation $4^{2x} \times 8^{x-1} = 32$.

7 Given that, in standard form, $3^{236} \approx 4 \times 10^{112}$, and $3^{-376} \approx 4 \times 10^{-180}$, find approximations, also in standard form, for

(a) 3^{376} (b) 3^{612} (c) $\left(\sqrt{3}\right)^{236}$ (d) $\left(3^{-376}\right)^{\frac{5}{2}}$

8 The table below shows, for three of the planets in the solar system, details of their mean distance from the sun and the time taken for one orbit round the sun.

Planet	Mean radius of orbit r metres	Period of revolution T seconds
Mercury	5.8×10^{10}	7.6×10^{6}
Jupiter	7.8×10^{11}	3.7×10^{8}
Pluto	5.9×10^{12}	7.8×10^{9}

(a) Show that $r^3 T^{-2}$ has approximately the same value for each planet in the table.

(b) The earth takes one year for one orbit of the sun. Find the mean radius of the earth's orbit around the sun.

9 Simplify

(a) $2^{-\frac{3}{2}} + 2^{-\frac{1}{2}} + 2^{\frac{1}{2}} + 2^{\frac{3}{2}}$, giving your answer in the form $k\sqrt{2}$,

(b) $\left(\sqrt{3}\right)^{-3} + \left(\sqrt{3}\right)^{-2} + \left(\sqrt{3}\right)^{-1} + \left(\sqrt{3}\right)^{0} + \left(\sqrt{3}\right)^{1} + \left(\sqrt{3}\right)^{2} + \left(\sqrt{3}\right)^{3}$, giving your answer in the form $a + b\sqrt{3}$.

10 Express each of the following in the form 2^n.

(a) $2^{70} + 2^{70}$ (b) $2^{-400} + 2^{-400}$ (c) $2^{\frac{1}{3}} + 2^{\frac{1}{3}} + 2^{\frac{1}{3}} + 2^{\frac{1}{3}}$

(d) $2^{100} - 2^{99}$ (e) $8^{0.1} + 8^{0.1} + 8^{0.1} + 8^{0.1} + 8^{0.1} + 8^{0.1} + 8^{0.1} + 8^{0.1}$

11 Solve the equation $\dfrac{125^{3x}}{5^{x+4}} = \dfrac{25^{x-2}}{3125}$.

12 The graphs of $y = x^m$ and $y = x^n$ intersect at the point $P(1,1)$. Find the connection between m and n if the tangent at P to each curve is the normal to the other curve.

13 The formulae for the volume and the surface area of a sphere are $V = \frac{4}{3}\pi r^3$ and $S = 4\pi r^2$ respectively, where r is the sphere's radius. Find expressions for

(a) S in terms of V,   (b) V in terms of S,

giving your answer in the form $(S \text{ or } V) = 2^m 3^n \pi^p (V \text{ or } S)^q$.

14 The tangents at $x = \frac{1}{4}$ to $y = \sqrt{x}$ and $y = \dfrac{1}{\sqrt{x}}$ meet at P. Find the coordinates of P.

15 The normals at $x = 2$ to $y = \dfrac{1}{x^2}$ and $y = \dfrac{1}{x^3}$ meet at Q. Find the coordinates of Q.

16 The kinetic energy, K joules, possessed by an object of mass m kg moving with speed $v \, \text{m s}^{-1}$ is given by the formula $K = \frac{1}{2}mv^2$. Find the kinetic energy possessed by a bullet of mass 2.5×10^{-2} kg moving with speed $8 \times 10^2 \, \text{m s}^{-1}$.

8 Functions and graphs

You now know about a lot of particular functions and their graphs. This chapter is about functions in general. When you have completed it, you should

- understand the terms 'domain' and 'range', and appreciate the importance of defining the domain of a function
- recognise that the derivative of a function is itself a function
- be able to modify equations of the form $y = f(x)$ so as to translate, stretch or reflect their graphs.

8.1 The domain of a function

When you produce a graph of $y = mx + c$ or $y = x^2$ you are aware that you cannot show the whole graph. However small the scale, and however large the screen or the paper, the graph will eventually spill over the edge. This is because x can be any real number, as large as you like in both positive and negative directions.

You have met functions which cannot be defined for all real numbers. Examples are $\frac{1}{x}$, which has no meaning when x is 0; and $\sqrt{x}$, which has no meaning when x is negative. Another example is $\sqrt{x(6-x)}$, which only has a meaning when $x(6-x) \geq 0$, or $0 \leq x \leq 6$. You will see later that this last function only takes values in the range $0 \leq y \leq 3$, so that with suitable scales you can show the whole graph on the screen or paper.

There are also times when you use a function which has a meaning for all real numbers x, but you are interested in it only when x is restricted in some way. For example, the formula for the volume of a cube is $V = x^3$. Although you can calculate x^3 for any real number x, you would only use this formula for $x > 0$.

Here is an example when x is restricted to a finite interval.

Example 8.1.1
A wire of length 4 metres is cut into two pieces, and each piece is bent into a square. How should this be done so that the two squares together have
(a) the smallest area,   (b) the largest area?

Let the two pieces have lengths x metres and $(4-x)$ metres. The areas of the squares are then $\left(\frac{1}{4}x\right)^2$ and $\left(\frac{1}{4}(4-x)\right)^2$ square metres. So the total area, y square metres, is given by

$$y = \frac{1}{16}\left(x^2 + \left(16 - 8x + x^2\right)\right)$$

$$= \frac{1}{8}\left(x^2 - 4x + 8\right).$$

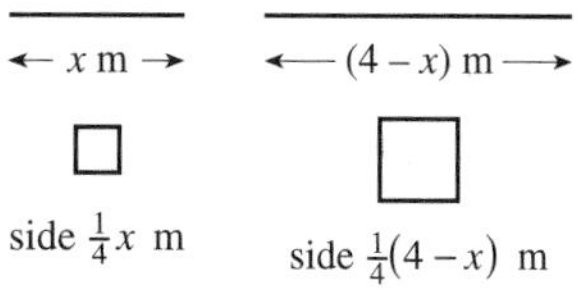

$\leftarrow x\text{ m} \rightarrow$ $\leftarrow (4-x)\text{ m} \rightarrow$

$\square$ $\square$

side $\frac{1}{4}x$ m   side $\frac{1}{4}(4-x)$ m

Fig. 8.1

Writing this in completed square form,

$$y = \tfrac{1}{8}\big((x-2)^2 + 4\big).$$

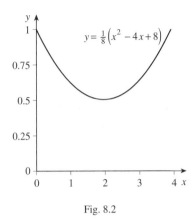

You can evaluate this expression for any real number x, but the problem only has meaning if $0 < x < 4$. Fig. 8.2 shows the graph of the area function for this interval. As $(x-2)^2 \geq 0$, the area is least when $x = 2$, when it is 0.5 m^2.

From the graph it looks as if the largest area is 1 m^2, when $x = 0$ and $x = 4$; but these values of x are excluded, since they do not produce two pieces of wire. You can get areas as near to 1 m^2 as you like, but you cannot achieve this target. There is therefore no largest area.

Fig. 8.2

So two possible reasons why a function $f(x)$ might not be defined for all real numbers x are

- the algebraic expression for $f(x)$ may only have meaning for some x
- only some x are relevant in the context in which the function is being used.

The set of numbers x for which a function $f(x)$ is defined is called the **domain** of the function. For example, the domain of the function in Example 8.1.1 is the interval $0 < x < 4$. The largest possible domain of the function $\dfrac{1}{x}$ is all the real numbers except 0, but if the function is used in a practical problem you may choose a smaller domain, such as all positive real numbers.

8.2 The range of a function

Once you have decided the domain of a function $f(x)$, you can ask what values $f(x)$ can take. This is called the **range** of the function.

In Example 8.1.1 the graph shows that the range is $\tfrac{1}{2} \leq y < 1$. Note that the value $y = \tfrac{1}{2}$ is attained when $x = 2$, but the value $y = 1$ is not attained if $0 < x < 4$.

The function $f(x) = \dfrac{1}{x}$, with domain all real numbers except 0, takes all values except 0.

Example 8.2.1
Find the range of the function $\sqrt{x(6-x)}$ over its largest possible domain $0 \leq x \leq 6$.

Writing $y = \sqrt{x(6-x)}$, note first that $y \geq 0$ by the definition of a square root.

Also $y^2 = x(6-x)$, so $x^2 - 6x + y^2 = 0$.

Now if you give y any value this is a quadratic equation for x. This equation has real roots provided that the discriminant is greater than or equal to 0. That is,

$(-6)^2 - 4 \times 1 \times y^2 \geq 0$, so $y^2 \leq 9$.

Recalling that y cannot be negative, it follows that $0 \leq y \leq 3$. This is the range of the function. Its graph is shown in Fig. 8.3.

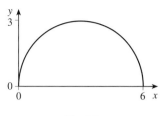

Fig. 8.3

8.3 Some useful language

Suppose that you want to find the difference between the heights of two people. With numerical information, the answer is quite straightforward: if their heights are 90 cm and 100 cm, you would answer 10 cm; and if their heights were 100 cm and 90 cm, you would still answer 10 cm. But how would you answer the question if their heights were H cm and h cm? The answer is, it depends which is bigger: if $H > h$, you would answer $(H - h)$ cm; if $h > H$ you would answer $(h - H)$ cm; and if $h = H$ you would answer 0 cm, which is either $(H - h)$ cm or $(h - H)$ cm.

Questions like this, in which you want an answer which is always positive or zero, lead to the idea of the modulus.

> The **modulus** of x, written $|x|$ and pronounced 'mod x', is defined by
>
> $|x| = x$ if $x \geq 0$,
>
> $|x| = -x$ if $x < 0$.

Using the modulus notation, you can now write the difference in heights as $|H - h|$ whether $H > h$, $h > H$ or $h = H$.

Another situation when the modulus is useful is when you talk about numbers which are large numerically, but which are negative, such as -1000 or -1000000. These are 'negative numbers with large modulus'.

For example, for large positive values of x, the value of $\frac{1}{x}$ approaches 0. The same is true for negative values of x with large modulus. So you can say that, when $|x|$ is large, $\left|\frac{1}{x}\right|$ is close to zero; or in a numerical example, when $|x| > 1000$, $\left|\frac{1}{x}\right| < 0.001$. (See Fig. 8.4.)

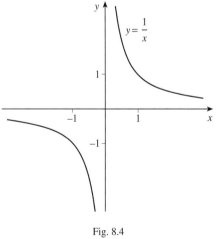

Fig. 8.4

Some calculators have a key which converts any number in the display to its modulus. This key is often labelled [ABS], which stands for 'absolute value'.

Exercise 8A

1 Find the largest possible domain of each of the following functions.

(a) $\sqrt{x}$ (b) $\sqrt{-x}$ (c) $\sqrt{x-4}$ (d) $\sqrt{4-x}$

(e) $\sqrt{x(x-4)}$ (f) $\sqrt{2x(x-4)}$ (g) $\sqrt{x^2-7x+12}$ (h) $\sqrt{x^3-8}$

(i) $\dfrac{1}{x-2}$ (j) $\dfrac{1}{\sqrt{x-2}}$ (k) $\dfrac{1}{1+\sqrt{x}}$ (l) $\dfrac{1}{(x-1)(x-2)}$

2 Find the range of each of the following functions. All the functions are defined for the largest possible domain of values of x.

(a) $f(x)=x^2+4$ (b) $f(x)=2(x^2+5)$ (c) $f(x)=(x-1)^2+6$

(d) $f(x)=-(1-x)^2+7$ (e) $f(x)=3(x+5)^2+2$ (f) $f(x)=2(x+2)^4-1$

3 Each of the following functions is defined for all real values of x. By writing them in completed-square form, find their ranges.

(a) $f(x)=x^2-6x+10$ (b) $f(x)=x^2+7x+1$ (c) $f(x)=x^2-3x+4$

(d) $f(x)=2x^2+8x+1$ (e) $f(x)=3x^2+5x-12$ (f) $f(x)=-x^2-6x+12$

4 These functions are each defined for the given domain. Find their ranges.

(a) $f(x)=2x$ for $0\leqslant x\leqslant 8$ (b) $f(x)=3-2x$ for $-2\leqslant x\leqslant 2$

(c) $f(x)=x^2$ for $-1\leqslant x\leqslant 4$ (d) $f(x)=x^2$ for $-5\leqslant x\leqslant -2$

5 The domain of each of the following functions is the set of all positive real numbers. Find the range of each function.

(a) $f(x)=2x+7$ (b) $f(x)=-5x$ (c) $f(x)=3x-1$

(d) $f(x)=x^2-1$ (e) $f(x)=(x+2)(x+1)$ (f) $f(x)=(x-1)(x-2)$

6 Find the range of each of the following functions. All the functions are defined for the largest possible domain of values of x.

(a) $f(x)=x^8$ (b) $f(x)=x^{11}$ (c) $f(x)=\dfrac{1}{x^3}$ (d) $f(x)=\dfrac{1}{x^4}$

(e) $f(x)=x^4+5$ (f) $f(x)=\frac{1}{4}x+\frac{1}{8}$ (g) $f(x)=\sqrt{4-x^2}$ (h) $f(x)=\sqrt{4-x}$

7 A piece of wire 24 cm long has the shape of a rectangle. Given that the width is w cm, show that the area, A cm^2, of the rectangle is given by the function $A=w(12-w)$. Find the greatest possible domain and the corresponding range of this function in this context.

8 Sketch the graph of $y=x(8-2x)(22-2x)$.
Given that y cm^3 is the volume of a cuboid with height x cm, length $(22-2x)$ cm and width $(8-2x)$ cm, state an appropriate domain for the function given above.

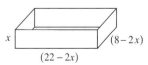

9 State the values of the following.

(a) $|-7|$ (b) $\left|-\frac{1}{200}\right|$ (c) $|9-4|$

(d) $|4-9|$ (e) $|\pi-3|$ (f) $|\pi-4|$

10 Find the values of $\left|x-x^2\right|$ when x takes the values

(a) 2,   (b) $\frac{1}{2}$,   (c) 1,

(d) -1,   (e) 0.

11 You are given that $y = \dfrac{1}{x^2}$. What can you say about y if

(a) $|x| > 100$,   (b) $|x| < 0.01$?

12 You are given that $y = \dfrac{1}{x^3}$.

(a) What can you say about y if $|x| < 1000$?

(b) What can you say about x if $|y| > 1000$?

13 The number, N, of people at a football match was reported as '37 000 to the nearest thousand'. Write this statement as an inequality using the modulus sign.

14 The mathematics marks, m and n, of two twins never differ by more than 5. Write this statement as an inequality using the modulus sign.

15 A line has length x cm. You are given that $|x-5.23| < 0.005$. How would you explain this in words?

8.4 Derivatives as functions

In Chapter 5 you were introduced to differentiation by carrying out a number of 'explorations'. For example, in Exercise 5A Question 5(a) you were asked to make guesses about the gradient of the tangent at various points on the graph of $y = f(x)$, where $f(x) = x^2 - 2$. Table 8.5 shows the results you were expected to get.

p	-2	-1	1	2	3	10
$f(p)$	2	-1	-1	2	7	98
$f'(p)$	-4	-2	2	4	6	20

Table 8.5

What this suggests is that the gradient is also a function of x, given by the formula $2x$. In Chapter 5 this formula was called the derivative. But when you are thinking of it as a function rather than using its value for a particular x, it is sometimes called the **derived function**. It is denoted by $f'(x)$, and in this example $f'(x) = 2x$.

Also, just as you can draw the graph of the
function $f(x)$, so it is possible to draw the
graph of the derived function $f'(x)$. It is
interesting to show these two graphs aligned
one above the other on the page, as in
Fig. 8.6.

Notice that on the left half of the graph for
$x < 0$, the graph of $f'(x)$ is below the x-axis,
indicating that the gradient of $f(x)$ is
negative. On the right, where the gradient of
$f(x)$ is positive, the graph of $f'(x)$ is above
the x-axis.

You can now write down what you know
about differentiation in terms of the derived
function:

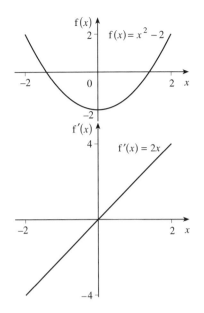

Fig. 8.6

> If $f(x) = x^n$, where n is a constant, then $f'(x) = nx^{n-1}$.
>
> The derived function of $f(x) + g(x)$ is $f'(x) + g'(x)$.
>
> The derived function of $cf(x)$, where c is a constant, is $cf'(x)$.

Example 8.4.1
Find the derived function of $f(x) = x^2 - \frac{1}{3}x^3$.

Using the results from the shaded box, the derived function is $f'(x) = 2x - x^2$.

The graphs of $f(x)$ and $f'(x)$ in this Example are drawn
in Fig. 8.7. Notice that when $x < 0$ the gradient of the
graph of $f(x) = x^2 - \frac{1}{3}x^3$ is negative, and the values of
the derived function are also negative.

When $x = 0$, the gradient of $f(x)$ is 0, so the value of
$f'(0)$ is 0.

Between $x = 0$ and $x = 2$ the gradient of $f(x)$ is positive,
so $f'(x)$ is positive.

When $x = 2$, the gradient of $f(x)$ is 0, so $f'(0) = 0$.

When $x > 2$, the gradient of $f(x)$ is negative, and the
values of the derived function are also negative.

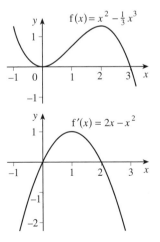

Fig. 8.7

═══════════════ **Exercise 8B** ═══════════════

1 Draw and compare the graphs of $y = f(x)$ and $y = f'(x)$ in each of the following cases.

    (a) $f(x) = 4x$ (b) $f(x) = 3 - 2x$ (c) $f(x) = x^2$

    (d) $f(x) = 5 - x^2$ (e) $f(x) = x^2 + 4x$ (f) $f(x) = 3x^2 - 6x$

2 Draw and compare the graphs of $y = f(x)$ and $y = f'(x)$ in each of the following cases.

    (a) $f(x) = (2 + x)(4 - x)$ (b) $f(x) = (x + 3)^2$ (c) $f(x) = x^4$

    (d) $f(x) = x^2(x - 2)$ (e) $f(x) = \sqrt{x}$ for $x \geqslant 0$ (f) $f(x) = \dfrac{1}{x}$ for $x \neq 0$

3 In each part of the question, the diagram shows the graph of $y = f(x)$. Draw a graph of the derived function $y = f'(x)$.

    (a) 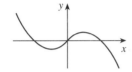   (b)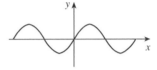

    (c) 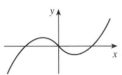   (d)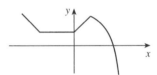

4 In each part of the question, the diagram shows the graph of the derived function $y = f'(x)$. Draw a possible graph of $y = f(x)$.

    (a)    (b)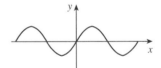

8.5 Translating graphs

Fig. 8.8 shows a graph whose equation is $y = f(x)$. What is the graph whose equation is $y = f(x) + k$?

For each particular value of x, the y-coordinate on the second graph is k more than the y-coordinate on the first. So the whole of the second graph must lie k units higher than the first graph.

Of course, if k is negative, the second graph will lie $|k|$ units lower than the first.

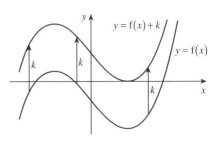

Fig. 8.8

The transformation which converts the first graph into the second is called a **translation**. A translation is defined by its magnitude and direction; this one is a translation of k units in the y-direction.

Notice that you can write the equation $y = f(x) + k$ as $y - k = f(x)$. This shows that:

> Replacing y by $y - k$ in the equation of a graph produces a translation of k units in the y-direction.

Similarly:

> Replacing x by $x - k$ in the equation of a graph produces a translation of k units in the x-direction.

This second result is illustrated in Fig. 8.9. The graph of $y = f(x - k)$ is obtained from that of $y = f(x)$ by a shift to the right of k units.

You may be surprised by the minus sign in the equation $y = f(x - k)$, but it can easily be justified by expressing the result in different words:

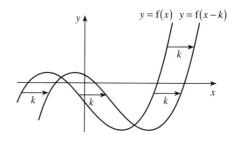

> If the point with coordinates (r, s) lies on the graph $y = f(x)$, then the point $(r + k, s)$ lies on the graph $y = f(x - k)$.

Fig. 8.9

So you have to show that, if $s = f(r)$, then $s = f((r + k) - k)$. The two equations are clearly the same, since $(r + k) - k = r$.

Example 8.5.1
Describe the graph of $y = x^2 - 6x + 4$.

In completed square form,
$x^2 - 6x + 4 = (x - 3)^2 - 5$. You can get from $y = x^2$ to $y = (x - 3)^2 - 5$ via the graph of $y = (x - 3)^2$.

Replacing x by $x - 3$ in the equation $y = x^2$ produces a translation of 3 units parallel to the x-axis. Then you obtain $y = (x - 3)^2 - 5$ from $y = (x - 3)^2$ by a translation of -5 parallel to the y-axis. The combination of the two translations is shown in Fig. 8.10.

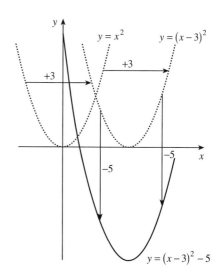

Fig. 8.10

This example takes you a stage further than Chapter 4, where the completed square form was used to find the vertex of a quadratic. Now you can see that as the graph is obtained from $y = x^2$ by a pair of translations, the two graphs have the same shape and size.

8.6 Stretching graphs

If you multiply a function by a constant c, then for each particular value of x the y-coordinate is c times as large as before. What this means geometrically depends on whether c is positive or negative. First suppose that $c > 0$.

Imagine that the graph $y = f(x)$ is drawn on an elastic sheet, and that this is pinned along the x-axis. If then the sheet is held along the top and bottom edges and pulled, the y-coordinate of each point on the sheet will be increased in the same ratio. This is called a **stretch**.

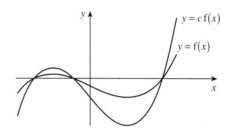

A stretch in the y-direction with $c = 2.5$

Fig. 8.11

So the graph of $y = f(x)$ is converted into $y = cf(x)$ by a stretch of factor c (the ratio is $c : 1$). This is illustrated in Fig. 8.11.

The word 'stretch' is rather misleading, since if c is less than 1 the y-coordinates are reduced, so that the transformation would more aptly be described as a 'squash'. But there is no mathematical advantage in separating the cases $c < 1$ and $c > 1$.

Notice that you can write the equation $y = cf(x)$ as $\dfrac{y}{c} = f(x)$. This shows that:

> Replacing y by $\dfrac{y}{c}$ in the equation of a graph produces a stretch of factor c in the y-direction.

Similarly:

> Replacing x by $\dfrac{x}{c}$ in the equation of a graph produces a stretch of factor c in the x-direction.

For example, to get from the graph of $y = f(x)$ to that of $y = f(2x)$, you need to write $2x$ as $\dfrac{x}{1/2}$. So this is a stretch of factor $\frac{1}{2}$, which is a squash in which the x-coordinate of each point of the graph is halved. This is illustrated in Fig. 8.12.

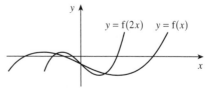

A stretch in the x-direction with a factor $\frac{1}{2}$

Fig. 8.12

Example 8.6.1

The graph $y = x^2$ is stretched by a factor of 4 in the y-direction, then by a factor of 4 in the x-direction. How else could you achieve the final result?

The double stretch is equivalent to an all-round enlargement of factor 4, like a photographic enlargement, which doesn't distort the shape of the graph. It is achieved by replacing y by $\frac{1}{4}y$ and x by $\frac{1}{4}x$. So the equation of the final graph is

$$\tfrac{1}{4}y = \left(\tfrac{1}{4}x\right)^2.$$

You can write this equation as $y = \frac{1}{4}x^2$, which is a squash in the y-direction alone in which the y-coordinate of each point of the graph is multiplied by $\frac{1}{4}$. Or it can be written as $y = \left(\frac{1}{2}x\right)^2$, a stretch of factor 2 in the x-direction alone.

Try drawing with the same axes the graphs of $y = x^2$ and $y = \frac{1}{4}x^2$, and think how the first can be transformed into the second by each of the three transformations described in Example 8.6.1.

Finally, what happens if $c < 0$? The simplest way of dealing with this is to regard multiplication by c as a combination of multiplication by $|c|$ and a change of sign. Since $|c| > 0$, you already know how to deal with the first transformation. Now it is necessary to interpret the effect of changing the sign of the x- or y-coordinate.

8.7 Reflecting graphs

If you draw with the same axes the graphs of $y = f(x)$ and $y = -f(x)$, then for each value of x the values of y on the two graphs have the same modulus but opposite signs, so that the corresponding points are mirror images in the x-axis. The complete graphs are therefore mirror images of each other.

You have to imagine a 'mathematical' mirror, capable of reflection in both directions. If $f(x)$ takes both positive and negative values, then the reflection converts positive to negative and negative to positive.

Since you can write $y = -f(x)$ as $-y = f(x)$, another way of expressing this is:

Replacing y by $-y$ in the equation of a graph produces a reflection in the x-axis.

Similarly:

Replacing x by $-x$ in the equation of a graph produces a reflection in the y-axis.

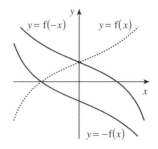

Fig. 8.13

With these results it is possible to make precise the ideas of even functions (such as x^2 or x^4) and odd functions (such as x^3) introduced in Section 3.4.

The graph of an even function is symmetrical about the y-axis, so reflection in the y-axis leaves it unchanged. This means that $y = f(x)$ and $y = f(-x)$ are the same equation, so that $f(-x) = f(x)$.

The graph of an odd function is symmetrical about the origin, so a combination of reflections in the x- and y-axes leaves it unchanged. This means that $y = f(x)$ and $-y = f(-x)$ are the same equation, so that $f(-x) = -f(x)$.

However, in using the terms 'odd' and 'even', there is an important difference between integers and functions. Every integer is either odd or even, but there are many functions, such as $x^2 + x$, which are neither odd nor even.

8.8 Combining transformations

From the graph of $y = f(x)$ a great variety of graphs can be obtained by a combination of translations, stretches and reflections, and the results of the last three sections can be used to find their equations.

Example 8.8.1

Suggest a possible equation for the graph shown in Fig. 8.14.

It is best to work through this example with a graphic calculator or computer. Whenever the instruction [PLOT] appears, you should add the graph of the stated equation to your screen display.

The graph has some resemblance to that of $y = x^3$ [PLOT], but it is the wrong way up. You can correct this by reflecting $y = x^3$ in the x-axis to obtain $y = -x^3$ [PLOT]. (Notice that reflecting $y = x^3$ in the y-axis, giving $y = (-x)^3$, will do just as well.)

You now want to shift this graph to the left, by a translation of -1 in the x-direction. The equation then becomes $y = -(x - (-1))^3$, or

$$y = -(x+1)^3 \text{ [PLOT]}.$$

This is close to the desired shape, but you will notice that, when $x = 0$, your equation gives $y = -1$, but the graph in Fig. 8.13 cuts the y-axis where $y = -2$. You can now give the graph $y = -(x+1)^3$ a stretch of factor 2, giving the equation

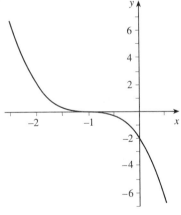

Fig. 8.14

$$y = -2(x+1)^3 \text{ [PLOT]}.$$

In this example, you cannot be sure that the final equation was the one which produced Fig. 8.13. For example, the graph of $y = -2(x+1)^5$ looks very similar, but is somewhat flatter round $x = -1$. Try plotting both on the screen.

Example 8.8.2

A water engineer, who is studying the motion of a wave travelling at 2 metres per second along a narrow channel without change of shape, starts measurements when the wave has equation $y = f(x)$, as shown in Fig. 8.15.

(a) Find the equation of the wave 4 seconds later.

(b) Find the equation of the wave t seconds later.

(c) The engineer has placed a sensor on the y-axis to plot the height of the wave at this position against the time. Find the shape of the graph.

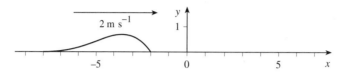

Fig. 8.15

(a) The wave travels 8 metres in 4 seconds, so the graph is translated 8 metres in the x-direction (see Fig. 8.16). Its equation is then $y = f(x-8)$.

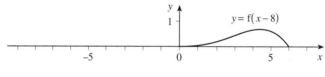

Fig. 8.16

(b) The wave travels $2t$ metres in t seconds, so its equation is then $y = f(x-2t)$.

(c) Substituting $x = 0$ in the equation in (b) gives the equation of the height on the y-axis as $y = f(-2t)$.

Now Fig. 8.15 is shown as a graph of y against x with equation $y = f(x)$, but changing the letter x to t, and the x-axis to a t-axis, would not change the shape of the graph. To convert $y = f(t)$ into $y = f(-2t)$ you need a reflection in the y-axis combined with a stretch of factor $\frac{1}{2}$ (see Fig. 8.12). This produces the graph shown in Fig. 8.17.

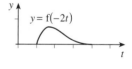

Fig. 8.17

Exercise 8C

1 The following translations are each applied to the graph of $y = x^2 + 3x$. Find the equation of each of the transformed graphs, giving your answer in as simple a form as possible.

(a) A translation of 3 units in the positive x-direction.

(b) A translation of 4 units in the positive y-direction.

(c) A translation of 3 units in the positive x-direction followed by a translation of 4 units in the positive y-direction.

2 The following translations are each applied to the graph of $y = x^2 - 5x + 7$. Find the equation of each of the transformed graphs, giving your answer in as simple a form as possible.

(a) A translation of -2 units in the positive x-direction.

(b) A translation of -5 units in the positive y-direction.

(c) A translation of -5 units in the positive y-direction followed by a translation of -2 units in the positive x-direction.

3 Give details of

(a) the translation which will convert the graph with equation $y = (x+3)^2$ into the graph with equation $y = x^2$,

(b) the translations which will convert the graph of $y = (x-5)^2$ into the graph with equation $y = (x-8)^2 - 3$.

4 Describe the relationship of the graph of $y = x^2 + 8x + 14$ with that of the graph of $y = x^2$. Illustrate by means of a sketch graph.

5 The graph $y = 2x^2$ is stretched by a factor of 2 in the y-direction and then by a factor of 3 in the x-direction. Find the new equation of the graph and state clearly how you could achieve the same final result with

(a) just one stretch in the x-direction,   (b) just one stretch in the y-direction.

6 In which axis is the graph of $y = x^2 - 7x + 6$ reflected if its new equation is

(a) $y = x^2 + 7x + 6$,   (b) $y = -x^2 + 7x - 6$?

7 The graph of $y = (x-2)^2$ is transformed into the graph of $y = (x+2)^2$ when it is reflected in one of the coordinate axes. Which axis is it?

8 Find the transformed equation when the graph of $y = x^2$ is transformed by the given three transformations. Give your final equation in the form $y = f(x)$. In each case, a translation is denoted by T, a stretch by S and a reflection by R.

1st transformation	2nd transformation	3rd transformation
(a) T, 2, x-direction	S, factor 3, x-direction	R, x-axis
(b) S, factor $\frac{1}{2}$, x-direction	R, y-axis	T, -3, x-direction
(c) R, y-axis	T, 4, y-direction	S, factor 2, y-direction

9 The graph of $y = -3(x+1)^4$ has been produced from the graph of $y = x^4$ by three successive transformations: a translation, a stretch and then a reflection. Define each of the transformations clearly.

10 Describe clearly the transformations which convert the graph of $y = f(x)$ into

(a) $y = af(x)$ (b) $y = f(x) + a$

(c) $y = f(x+a)$ (d) $y = f(ax)$

where a is a positive constant.

11* Determine if the following functions are 'even', 'odd' or 'neither even nor odd'.

(a) $f(x) = x^3 + 3x$ (b) $f(x) = 7x^2 - 8$

(c) $f(x) = (x-1)(x-3)$ (d) $f(x) = x^5 + 3x^3 + 1$

Find $f'(x)$ for each of the four functions and determine if it is even, odd or neither even nor odd. What does this suggest about derivatives of even and odd functions?

12 Prove that if (r, s) lies on $y = f(x)$, then (cr, s) lies on $y = f\left(\dfrac{x}{c}\right)$.

Miscellaneous exercise 8

1 The following functions are defined for all real values of x. Find their ranges.

(a) $f(x) = 9 - 2x^2$ (b) $f(x) = 5x - 7$

(c) $f(x) = x^2 + 16x - 5$ (d) $f(x) = (2x+5)(2x-7)$

2 The graph of the straight line $y = x$ is transformed as follows:

translation by 4 units in the positive x-direction,

followed by stretch in the y-direction with scale factor 2,

followed by reflection in the x-axis.

Find the equation of the final transformed graph.

3 Sketch the graph of the curve with equation $y = x(1-x)$. Determine the greatest and least values of y when $-1 \leqslant x \leqslant 1$.   (OCR)

4 The diagram shows the graph of $y = f(x)$. The curve passes through the origin O and the point A with coordinates $(a, 0)$, where a is a positive constant. Sketch, on separate diagrams, the graphs of

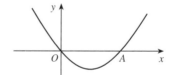

(a) $y = f(x+a)$ (b) $y = f(-x)$ (OCR)

5 The graph of $y = \dfrac{1}{x}$ is first stretched by a factor of 3 in the x-direction and then stretched by a factor of $\frac{1}{3}$ in the y-direction. What is the effect on the original curve?

6 The function $f(x)$ is defined by $f(x) = 5(x+2)^2 - 7$ for all real values of x.

(a) Sketch the graph of $y = f(x)$ and state the range of the function.

(b) Describe clearly the sequence of transformations which will transform the graph of $y = x^2$ to the graph of $y = f(x)$.

(c) Describe the sequence of transformations which will transform the graph of $y = f(x)$ to the graph of $y = x^2$.

(d) Find $f'(x)$ and sketch the graph of $y = f'(x)$.

(e) Describe the sequence of transformations which will transform the graph of $y = 2x$ to the graph of $y = f'(x)$.

7   The function $f(x) = 16 - 6x - x^2$ has domain all real values of x. Find the maximum value of $f(x)$ and state the range of $f(x)$.

8   The graph of $y = x^2$ can be transformed to that of $y = 2(x+1)^2$ by means of a translation and a stretch, in that order. State the magnitude and direction of the translation, and the scale factor and direction of the stretch.   (OCR)

9   The function $y = x^2 - 4ax$, where a is a positive constant, is defined for all real values of x. Given that the range is $y \geqslant -7$, find the exact value of a.

10 The diagram shows the curve $y = f(x + a)$, where a is a positive constant. The maximum and minimum points on the curve are $(-a, 3a)$ and $(a, 0)$ respectively. Sketch the following curves, on separate diagrams, in each case stating the coordinates of the maximum and minimum points:

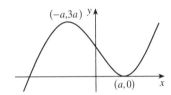

(a) $y = f(x)$ (b) $y = -2f(x + a)$ (OCR)

11 The straight line $y = ax + b$ is transformed by two translations. One translation is by 4 units in the positive x-direction and the other is by 7 units in the positive y-direction. Given that the equation of the transformed line is $y = 6x - 27$, find the values of a and b.

12 The curve $y = cx^2 + d$ is transformed by a translation, a stretch and a reflection in that order. The translation is by 2 units in the negative x-direction, the stretch is in the y-direction with scale factor 4 and the reflection is in the y-axis. Given that the equation of the final curve is $y = 12x^2 - 48x + 20$ find the values of c and d.

13 If the graph of $y = f(x)$ is reflected in the x-axis and then in the y-axis, what is its new equation? If the graph is the same as the original, what type of function is $f(x)$?

14* What can you say about $\dfrac{|x|}{x}$ if   (a) $x > 0$,   (b) $x < 0$?

15* Draw a sketch of the graph of an even function $f(x)$ which has a derivative at every point. Let P be the point on the graph for which $x = p$ (where $p > 0$) and draw the tangent at P on your sketch. Also draw the tangent at the point P' for which $x = -p$.

(a)   What is the relationship between the gradient at P' and the gradient at P? What can you deduce about the relationship between $f'(p)$ and $f'(-p)$? What does this tell you about the derivative of an even function?

(b)   Show that the derivative of an odd function is even.

16* The function $\text{int}(x)$, sometimes called the integer part of x, is defined to be the greatest integer less than or equal to x.

Sketch the graphs of $y = \text{int}(x)$ and $y = x - \text{int}(x)$ for the domain $-2 \leqslant x \leqslant 3$. What are the ranges of $\text{int}(x)$ and $y = x - \text{int}(x)$ for this domain?

17 The curve with equation $y = 2x^2 - 3x + 7$ is translated by p units in the negative y-direction, then stretched in the x-direction by the positive scale factor q and finally translated in the positive x-direction by r units. If the final curve has equation $y = \frac{1}{2}x^2 - \frac{19}{2}x + 46$ find the values of p, q and r.

9 Applications of differentiation

In the last few chapters you have learnt what differentiation means and how to differentiate a lot of functions. This chapter shows how you can use this to sketch graphs and apply it to real-world problems. When you have completed it, you should

- appreciate the significance of positive, negative and zero derivatives
- be able to locate maximum and minimum points on graphs
- know that you can interpret a derivative as a rate of change of one variable with respect to another
- be familiar with the notation $\dfrac{dy}{dx}$ for a derivative
- be able to apply these techniques to solve real-world problems.

9.1 Increasing and decreasing functions

For simplicity, the word 'function' in this chapter will mean functions which are **continuous** within their domains. This includes all the functions you have met so far, but cuts out functions such as 'the fractional part of x', which is defined for all positive real numbers but whose graph (shown in Fig. 9.1) has jumps in it.

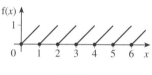

Fig. 9.1

In the last chapter, in Example 8.5.1, you saw that the graph of $y = x^2 - 6x + 4$ has the same shape as $y = x^2$, but translated so that its vertex is at $(3, -5)$. Another way of investigating the shape of the graph is to use differentiation.

Example 9.1.1
Find the interval in which $f(x) = x^2 - 6x + 4$ is increasing, and the interval in which it is decreasing.

The derivative is $f'(x) = 2x - 6 = 2(x - 3)$. This means that the graph has a positive gradient for $x > 3$. Look back to Fig. 8.10, and you will see that over this interval the values of y are getting larger as x gets larger. That is, $f(x)$ is increasing for $x > 3$.

For $x < 3$ the gradient is negative, and the values of y are getting smaller as x gets larger. That is, $f(x)$ is decreasing for $x < 3$.

What about $x = 3$ itself? At first sight you might think that this has to be left out of both the increasing and the decreasing intervals, but this would be wrong! If you imagine moving along the curve from left to right, then as soon as you have passed through $x = 3$ the gradient becomes positive and the curve starts to climb. However close you are to $x = 3$, the value of y is greater than $f(3) = -5$. So you can say that $f(x)$ is increasing for $x \geq 3$, and decreasing for $x \leq 3$.

You can use the reasoning in Example 9.1.1 for any function. Fig. 9.2 shows the graph of a function $y = f(x)$ whose derivative $f'(x)$ is positive in an interval $p < x < q$. You can see that larger values of y are associated with larger values of x. More precisely, if x_1 and x_2 are two values of x in the interval $p \leqslant x \leqslant q$, and if $x_2 > x_1$, then $f(x_2) > f(x_1)$. A function with this property is said to be **increasing** over the interval $p \leqslant x \leqslant q$.

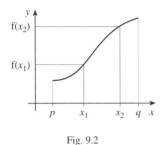

Fig. 9.2

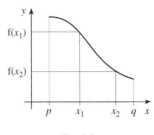

Fig. 9.3

If $f'(x)$ is negative in the interval $p < x < q$, as in Fig. 9.3, the function has the opposite property; if $x_2 > x_1$, then $f(x_2) < f(x_1)$. A function with this property is **decreasing** over the interval $p \leqslant x \leqslant q$.

If $f'(x) > 0$ in an interval $p < x < q$, then $f(x)$ is increasing over the interval $p \leqslant x \leqslant q$.

If $f'(x) < 0$ in $p < x < q$, then $f(x)$ is decreasing over $p \leqslant x \leqslant q$.

Notice that, for $f(x)$ to be increasing for $p \leqslant x \leqslant q$, the gradient $f'(x)$ does not have to be positive at the ends of the interval, where $x = p$ or $x = q$. At these points it may be 0, or even undefined. This may seem a minor distinction, but it has important consequences. It is a pay-off from the decision to work only with continuous functions.

The word 'interval' is used not only for a finite part of the domain, but also for values of x satisfying inequalities $x > p$ or $x < q$, which extend indefinitely in either the positive or negative direction.

Example 9.1.2
For the function $f(x) = x^4 - 4x^3$, find the intervals in which $f(x)$ is increasing and those in which it is decreasing.

Begin by expressing $f'(x)$ in factors as

$$f'(x) = 4x^3 - 12x^2 = 4x^2(x - 3).$$

Notice that x^2 is always positive (except at $x = 0$), so to find where $f'(x) > 0$ you need only solve the inequality $x - 3 > 0$, giving $x > 3$. Therefore $f(x)$ is increasing over the interval $x \geqslant 3$, including the end-point.

The solution of $x - 3 < 0$ is $x < 3$; but to find

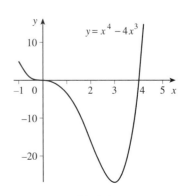

Fig. 9.4

where $f'(x) < 0$ you have to exclude $x = 0$, so that $f'(x) < 0$ if $x < 0$ or $0 < x < 3$. Therefore $f(x)$ is decreasing over the intervals $x \leq 0$ and $0 \leq x \leq 3$.

However, these last two intervals have the value $x = 0$ in common, so you can combine them as a single interval $x \leq 3$. It follows that $f(x)$ is decreasing over the interval $x \leq 3$.

Note also that $f'(x) = 0$ when $x = 0$ and $x = 3$. You can check all these properties from the graph of $y = f(x)$ shown in Fig. 9.4.

Example 9.1.2 shows that the rule given above, connecting the sign of $f'(x)$ with the property that $f(x)$ is increasing or decreasing, can be slightly relaxed.

> If $f'(x) > 0$ in an interval $p < x < q$ except at isolated points where $f'(x) = 0$, then $f(x)$ is increasing in the interval $p \leq x \leq q$.
>
> If $f'(x) < 0$ in an interval $p < x < q$ except at isolated points where $f'(x) = 0$, then $f(x)$ is decreasing over $p \leq x \leq q$.

The next example is about a function which involves fractional powers of x for $x < 0$. These were avoided in Chapter 7, because often such functions are not defined when x is negative. But the indices in this example involve only cube roots. There is no difficulty in taking the cube root of a negative number.

Example 9.1.3
Find the intervals in which the function $f(x) = x^{\frac{2}{3}}(1 - x)$ is increasing and those in which it is decreasing.

To differentiate, write the expression as $f(x) = x^{\frac{2}{3}} - x^{\frac{5}{3}}$, so that

$$f'(x) = \tfrac{2}{3}x^{-\frac{1}{3}} - \tfrac{5}{3}x^{\frac{2}{3}},$$

which you can write as

$$f'(x) = \tfrac{1}{3}x^{-\frac{1}{3}}(2 - 5x).$$

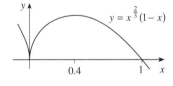
Fig. 9.5

In this last expression, $x^{-\frac{1}{3}}$ is positive when $x > 0$ and negative when $x < 0$. The factor $2 - 5x$ is positive when $x < 0.4$ and negative when $x > 0.4$. Fig. 9.5 shows that

$f(x)$ is increasing in the interval $0 \leq x \leq 0.4$,

$f(x)$ is decreasing in the intervals $x \leq 0$ and $x \geq 0.4$.

9.2 Maximum and minimum points

Example 9.1.1 showed that, for $f(x) = x^2 - 6x + 4$, $f(x)$ is decreasing for $x \leq 3$ and increasing for $x \geq 3$. It follows from the definition of decreasing and increasing functions that, if $x_1 < 3$, then $f(x_1) > f(3)$; and that, if $x_2 > 3$, then $f(x_2) > f(3)$. That is, for every value of x other than 3, $f(x)$ is greater than $f(3) = -5$. You can say that $f(3)$ is the minimum value of $f(x)$, and that $(3, -5)$ is the minimum point on the graph of $y = f(x)$.

A minimum point does not have to be the lowest point on the whole graph, but is the lowest point in its immediate neighbourhood. In Example 9.1.3, $(0, 0)$ is a minimum point; this is shown by the fact that $f(x) > 0$ for every number $x < 1$ except $x = 0$, although $f(x) < 0$ when $x > 1$.

This leads to a definition, which is illustrated by Fig. 9.6.

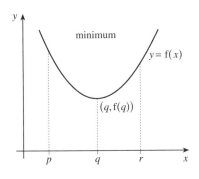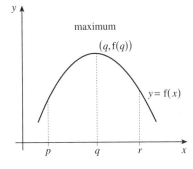

Fig. 9.6

A function $f(x)$ has a **minimum** at $x = q$ if there is an interval $p < x < r$ containing q in which $f(x) > f(q)$ for every value of x except q.

It has a **maximum** if $f(x) < f(q)$ for every value of x in the interval except q.

The point $(q, f(q))$ is called a **minimum point**, or a **maximum point**.

Thus, in Example 9.1.3, $f(x)$ has a minimum at $x = 0$, and a maximum at $x = 0.4$.

Minimum and maximum points are sometimes also called **turning points**.

You will see that at the minimum point in Fig. 9.4 and the maximum point in Fig. 9.5 the graph has gradient 0. But at the minimum point $(0, 0)$ in Fig. 9.5 the tangent to the graph is the y-axis, so that the gradient is undefined. These examples illustrate a general rule:

If $(q, f(q))$ is a minimum or maximum point of the graph of $y = f(x)$, then either $f'(q) = 0$ or $f'(q)$ is undefined.

Notice, though, that Fig. 9.4 has another point at which the gradient is 0, which is neither a minimum nor a maximum, namely the point $(0, 0)$. A point of a graph where the gradient is 0 is called a **stationary point**. So Figs. 9.4 and 9.5 illustrate the fact that a stationary point may be a minimum or maximum point, but may be neither.

A way to decide between a minimum and a maximum point is to find the sign of the gradient $f'(x)$ on either side of $x = q$. To follow the details you may again find it helpful to refer to Fig. 9.6.

If $f'(x) < 0$ in an interval $p < x < q$, and $f'(x) > 0$ in an interval $q < x < r$, then $(q, f(q))$ is a minimum point.

If $f'(x) > 0$ in $p < x < q$, and $f'(x) < 0$ in $q < x < r$, then $(q, f(q))$ is a maximum point.

You may be happy to accept this on the evidence of the graph, but it can also be argued from statements which you have already met. Consider the minimum case.

Suppose that x_1 is a number in $p < x < q$. Then, since $f'(x) < 0$ in that interval, it follows from Section 9.1 that $f(x_1) > f(q)$.

Now suppose that x_2 is a number in $q < x < r$. Since $f'(x) > 0$ in that interval, $f(q) < f(x_2)$.

This shows that, if x is any number in the interval $p < x < r$ other than q, then $f(x) > f(q)$. From the definition, this means that $f(x)$ has a minimum at $x = q$.

All these results can be summed up in a set of procedures.

To find the minimum and maximum points on the graph of $y = f(x)$:

Step 1   Decide the domain in which you are interested.

Step 2   Find an expression for $f'(x)$.

Step 3   List the values of x in the domain for which $f'(x)$ is either 0 or undefined.

Step 4   Taking each of these values of x in turn, find the sign of $f'(x)$ in intervals immediately to the left and to the right of that value.

Step 5   If these signs are – and + respectively, the graph has a minimum point. If they are + and – it has a maximum point. If the signs are the same, it has neither.

Step 6   For each value of x which gives a minimum or maximum, calculate $f(x)$.

Example 9.2.1

Find the minimum point on the graph with equation $y = \sqrt{x} + \dfrac{4}{x}$.

Let $f(x) = \sqrt{x} + \dfrac{4}{x}$.

Step 1   As $\sqrt{x}$ is defined for $x \geqslant 0$ but $\dfrac{1}{x}$ is not defined for $x = 0$, the largest possible domain for $f(x)$ is the positive real numbers.

Step 2   The derivative $f'(x) = \frac{1}{2}x^{-\frac{1}{2}} - 4x^{-2}$ can be written as $f'(x) = \dfrac{x^{\frac{3}{2}} - 8}{2x^2}$.

Step 3   The derivative is defined for all positive real numbers, and is 0 when $x^{\frac{3}{2}} = 8$. Raising both sides to the power $\frac{2}{3}$ and using the power-on-power rule,

$$x = \left(x^{\frac{3}{2}}\right)^{\frac{2}{3}} = 8^{\frac{2}{3}} = 4.$$

Step 4   If $0 < x < 4$, the bottom line, $2x^2$, is positive, and

$$x^{\frac{3}{2}} - 8 < 4^{\frac{3}{2}} - 8 = 8 - 8 = 0, \text{ so that } f'(x) < 0.$$

If $x > 4$, $2x^2$ is still positive, but $x^{\frac{3}{2}} - 8 > 4^{\frac{3}{2}} - 8 = 0$, so that $f'(x) > 0$.

Step 5   The sign of $f'(x)$ is $-$ on the left of 4 and $+$ on the right, so the function has a minimum at $x = 4$.

Step 6   Calculate $f(4) = \sqrt{4} + \dfrac{4}{4} = 2 + 1 = 3$. The minimum point is $(4, 3)$.

It is interesting to use a graphic calculator to display $y = f(x)$ together with $y = \sqrt{x}$ and $y = \dfrac{4}{x}$, from which it is made up. You will find that $y = f(x)$ is very flat around the minimum; it would be difficult to tell by eye exactly where the minimum occurs.

Notice that this theory gives you another way of finding the range of some functions. For the function in Example 9.2.1 with domain $x > 0$, the range is $y \geqslant 3$.

Exercise 9A

1 For each of the following functions $f(x)$, find $f'(x)$ and the interval in which $f(x)$ is increasing.

(a) $x^2 - 5x + 6$ (b) $x^2 + 6x - 4$ (c) $7 - 3x - x^2$

(d) $3x^2 - 5x + 7$ (e) $5x^2 + 3x - 2$ (f) $7 - 4x - 3x^2$

2 For each of the following functions $f(x)$, find $f'(x)$ and the interval in which $f(x)$ is decreasing.

(a) $x^2 + 4x - 9$ (b) $x^2 - 3x - 5$ (c) $5 - 3x + x^2$

(d) $2x^2 - 8x + 7$ (e) $4 + 7x - 2x^2$ (f) $3 - 5x - 7x^2$

3 For each of the following functions $f(x)$, find $f'(x)$ and any intervals in which $f(x)$ is increasing.

(a) $x^3 - 12x$ (b) $2x^3 - 18x + 5$ (c) $2x^3 - 9x^2 - 24x + 7$

(d) $x^3 - 3x^2 + 3x + 4$ (e) $x^4 - 2x^2$ (f) $x^4 + 4x^3$

(g) $3x - x^3$ (h) $2x^5 - 5x^4 + 10$ (i) $3x + x^3$

4 For each of the following functions $f(x)$, find $f'(x)$ and any intervals in which $f(x)$ is decreasing. In part (i), n is an integer.

(a) $x^3 - 27x$ for $x \geqslant 0$ (b) $x^4 + 4x^2 - 5$ for $x \geqslant 0$ (c) $x^3 - 3x^2 + 3x - 1$

(d) $12x - 2x^3$ (e) $2x^3 + 3x^2 - 36x - 7$ (f) $3x^4 - 20x^3 + 12$

(g) $36x^2 - 2x^4$ (h) $x^5 - 5x$ (i) $x^n - nx$ $(n > 1)$

5 For each of the following functions $f(x)$, find $f'(x)$, the intervals in which $f(x)$ is decreasing, and the intervals in which $f(x)$ is increasing.

(a) $x^{\frac{3}{2}}(x - 1)$, for $x > 0$ (b) $x^{\frac{3}{4}} - 2x^{\frac{7}{4}}$, for $x > 0$ (c) $x^{\frac{2}{3}}(x + 2)$

(d) $x^{\frac{1}{3}}\left(x^2 - 13\right)$ (e) $x + \dfrac{3}{x}$, for $x \neq 0$ (f) $\sqrt{x} + \dfrac{1}{\sqrt{x}}$, for $x > 0$

6 For the graphs of each of the following functions:
(i)   find the coordinates of the stationary point;
(ii)   say, with reasoning, whether this is a maximum or a minimum point;
(iii)   check your answer by using the method of 'completing the square' to find the vertex;
(iv)   state the range of values which the function can take.

(a) $x^2 - 8x + 4$ (b) $3x^2 + 12x + 5$ (c) $5x^2 + 6x + 2$

(d) $4 - 6x - x^2$ (e) $x^2 + 6x + 9$ (f) $1 - 4x - 4x^2$

7 Find the coordinates of the stationary points on the graphs of the following functions, and find whether these points are maxima or minima.

(a) $2x^3 + 3x^2 - 72x + 5$ (b) $x^3 - 3x^2 - 45x + 7$ (c) $3x^4 - 8x^3 + 6x^2$

(d) $3x^5 - 20x^3 + 1$ (e) $2x + x^2 - 4x^3$ (f) $x^3 + 3x^2 + 3x + 1$

(g) $x + \dfrac{1}{x}$ (h) $x^2 + \dfrac{54}{x}$ (i) $x - \dfrac{1}{x}$

(j) $x - \sqrt{x}$, for $x > 0$ (k) $\dfrac{1}{x} - \dfrac{3}{x^2}$ (l) $x^2 - \dfrac{16}{x} + 5$

(m) $x^{\frac{1}{3}}(4 - x)$ (n) $x^{\frac{1}{5}}(x + 6)$ (o) $x^4(1 - x)$

8 Find the ranges of each of these functions $f(x)$, defined over the largest possible domains.

(a) $x^2 + x + 1$ (b) $x^4 - 8x^2$ (c) $x + \dfrac{1}{x}$

9.3 Derivatives as rates of change

The quantities x and y in a relationship $y = f(x)$ are often called **variables**, because x can stand for any number in the domain and y for any number in the range. When you draw the graph you have a free choice of the values of x, and then work out y. So x is called the **independent variable** and y the **dependent variable**.

These variables often stand for physical or economic quantities, and then it is convenient to use other letters which suggest what these quantities are: for example t for time, V for volume, C for cost, P for population, and so on.

To illustrate this consider a situation familiar to deep sea divers, that pressure increases with depth below sea level. The independent variable is the depth, z metres, below the surface.

It will soon be clear why the letter d was avoided for the depth. The letter z is often used for distances in the vertical direction.

The dependent variable is the pressure, p, measured in bars. At the surface the diver experiences only atmospheric pressure, about 1 bar, but the pressure increases as the diver descends. At off-shore (coastal) depths the variables are connected approximately by the equation

$$p = 1 + 0.1z.$$

The (z, p) graph is a straight line, shown in Fig. 9.7.

The constant 0.1 in the equation is the amount that the pressure goes up for each extra metre of depth. This is the 'rate of change of pressure with respect to depth'.

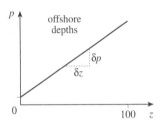

Fig. 9.7

If the diver descends a further distance of δz metres, the pressure goes up by δp bars; this rate of change is $\dfrac{\delta p}{\delta z}$.

It is represented by the gradient of the graph.
But at ocean depths the (z, p) graph is no longer a straight line: it has the form of Fig. 9.8. The quantity $\dfrac{\delta p}{\delta z}$ now

represents the average rate of change over the extra depth δz. It is represented by the gradient of the chord in Fig. 9.8.

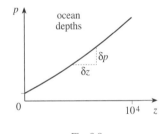

Fig. 9.8

The rate of change of pressure with respect to depth is the limit of $\dfrac{\delta p}{\delta z}$ as δz tends to 0. The f'( ) notation, which has so far been used for this limit, is not very convenient, and it is useful to have a notation which includes the letters used for the variables. An alternative symbol $\dfrac{dp}{dz}$ was devised, obtained by replacing the letter δ in the average rate by d in the limit. Formally,

$$\frac{dp}{dz} = \lim_{\delta z \to 0} \frac{\delta p}{\delta z}.$$

There is no new idea here. It is simply a different way of writing the definition of the derivative given in Chapter 5. The advantage is that it can be adapted, using different letters, to express the rate of change whenever there is a function relationship between two variables.

If x and y are the independent and dependent variables respectively in a functional relationship, then the derivative,

$$\frac{dy}{dx} = \lim_{\delta x \to 0} \frac{\delta y}{\delta x},$$

measures the **rate of change of y with respect to x**.

If $y = f(x)$, then $\dfrac{dy}{dx} = f'(x)$.

Although $\dfrac{dy}{dx}$ looks like a fraction, for the time being you should treat it as one inseparable symbol made up of four letters and a horizontal line. By themselves, the symbols dx and dy have no meaning. (Later on, though, you will find that in some ways the symbol $\dfrac{dy}{dx}$ *behaves* like a fraction. This is another advantage of using it in preference to the $f'(\ )$ notation.)

The notation can be used in a wide variety of contexts. For example, if the area of burnt grass, t minutes after a fire has started, is A square metres, then $\dfrac{dA}{dt}$ measures the rate at which the fire is spreading in square metres per minute. If, at a certain point on the Earth's surface, distances of x metres on the ground are represented by distances of y metres on a map, then $\dfrac{dy}{dx}$ represents the scale of the map at that point.

Example 9.3.1

A sprinter in a women's 100-metre race reaches her top speed of 12 metres per second after she has run 36 metres. Up to that distance her speed is proportional to the square root of the distance she has run. Show that until she reaches full speed the rate of change of her speed with respect to distance is inversely proportional to her speed.

Suppose that after she has run x metres her speed is S metres per second. You are told that, up to $x = 36$, $S = k\sqrt{x}$, and also that $S = 12$ when $x = 36$. So

$$12 = k\sqrt{36}, \quad \text{giving} \quad k = \tfrac{12}{6} = 2.$$

The (x, S) relationship is therefore

$$S = 2\sqrt{x} \text{ for } 0 < x < 36.$$

The rate of change of speed with respect to distance is the derivative $\dfrac{dS}{dx}$, and the derivative of $\sqrt{x}$ (from Section 5.7) is $\dfrac{1}{2\sqrt{x}}$. Therefore

$$\frac{dS}{dx} = 2 \times \frac{1}{2\sqrt{x}} = \frac{1}{\sqrt{x}}.$$

Since $\sqrt{x} = \dfrac{S}{2}$, $\dfrac{dS}{dx}$ can be written as $\dfrac{2}{S}$.

The rate of change is therefore inversely proportional to her speed.

If she maintains her top speed for the rest of the race, the rate of change of speed with respect to distance drops to 0 for $x > 36$. Fig. 9.9 shows that the gradient, which represents the rate of change, gets smaller as her speed increases, and then becomes zero once she reaches her top speed.

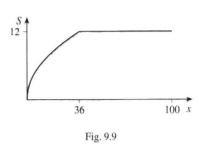

Fig. 9.9

Example 9.3.2

A line of cars, each 5 metres long, is travelling along an open road at a steady speed of S km per hour. There is a recommended separation between each pair of cars given by the formula $\left(0.18S + 0.006S^2\right)$ metres. At what speed should the cars travel to maximise the number of cars that the road can accommodate?

It is a good idea to write the separation formula as $\left(aS + bS^2\right)$, where $a = 0.18$ and $b = 0.006$. This gives a neater formula, and will also enable you to investigate the effect of changing the coefficients in the formula. But remember when you differentiate that a and b are simply constants, and you can treat them just like numbers.

A 'block', consisting of a car's length and the separation distance in front of it, occupies $5 + aS + bS^2$ metres of road, or $\dfrac{5 + aS + bS^2}{1000}$ km. For the largest number of blocks passing a checkpoint in an hour, the time T (in hours) for a single block to pass the checkpoint should be as small as possible. Since the block is moving at speed S km per hour,

$$T = \frac{5 + aS + bS^2}{1000S} = 0.001\left(5S^{-1} + a + bS\right).$$

Now follow the procedure for finding the minimum value of T.

Step 1 Since the speed must be positive, the domain is $S > 0$.

Step 2 The derivative is $\dfrac{dT}{dS} = 0.001\left(-5S^{-2} + b\right)$.

Step 3 This derivative is defined everywhere in the domain, and is zero when $-\dfrac{5}{S^2} + b = 0$, which is at $S = \sqrt{\dfrac{5}{b}}$.

Step 4 As S increases, $\dfrac{5}{S^2}$ decreases, so $-\dfrac{5}{S^2} + b$ increases. Since $\dfrac{dT}{dS}$ is 0 when $S = \sqrt{\dfrac{5}{b}}$, the sign of $\dfrac{dT}{dS}$ is $-$ when $S < \sqrt{\dfrac{5}{b}}$, and $+$ when $S > \sqrt{\dfrac{5}{b}}$.

Step 5   Since $\dfrac{\mathrm{d}T}{\mathrm{d}S}$ changes from $-$ to $+$, T is a minimum when $S = \sqrt{\dfrac{5}{b}}$.

Step 6   Substituting $a = 0.18$ and $b = 0.006$ gives $S = \sqrt{\dfrac{5}{0.006}} \approx 28.87$ and
$T \approx 0.000\,526\,4$ at the minimum point.

This shows that the cars flow best at a speed of just under 29 km/h. Each block
then takes approximately $0.000\,526$ hours (or 1.89 seconds) to pass the
checkpoint, so that the number of cars which pass in an hour is approximately
$\dfrac{1}{0.000\,526} \approx 1900$.

Example 9.3.3

A hollow cone with base radius a cm and height b cm is placed on a table. What is the
volume of the largest cylinder that can be hidden underneath it?

The volume of a cylinder of radius r cm and height h cm is V cm^3, where

$$V = \pi r^2 h.$$

You can obviously make this as large as you like by choosing r and h large
enough. But in this problem the variables are restricted by the requirement that the
cylinder has to fit under the cone. Before you can follow the procedure for finding
a maximum, you need to find how this restriction affects the values of r and h.

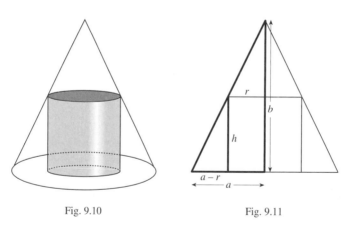

Fig. 9.10   Fig. 9.11

Fig. 9.10 shows the three-dimensional set-up, and Fig. 9.11 is a vertical section
through the top of the cone. The similar triangles picked out with heavy lines in
Fig. 9.11 show that r and h are connected by the equation

$$\frac{h}{a-r} = \frac{b}{a}, \text{ so that } h = \frac{b(a-r)}{a}.$$

Substituting this expression for h in the formula for V then gives

$$V = \frac{\pi r^2 b(a-r)}{a} = \left(\frac{\pi b}{a}\right)\left(ar^2 - r^3\right).$$

Notice that the original expression for V contains two independent variables r and h. The effect of the substitution is to reduce the number of independent variables to one; h has disappeared, and only r remains. This makes it possible to apply the procedure for finding a maximum.

The physical problem only has meaning if $0 < r < a$, so take this interval as the domain of the function. Differentiating by the usual rule (remembering that π, a and b are constants) gives

$$\frac{dV}{dr} = \left(\frac{\pi b}{a}\right)\left(2ar - 3r^2\right) = \left(\frac{\pi b}{a}\right)r(2a - 3r).$$

The only value of r in the domain for which $\dfrac{dV}{dr} = 0$ is $\frac{2}{3}a$. It is easy to check that the sign of $\dfrac{dV}{dr}$ is $+$ for $0 < r < \frac{2}{3}a$ and $-$ for $\frac{2}{3}a < r < a$.

So the cylinder of maximum volume has radius $\frac{2}{3}a$, height $\frac{1}{3}b$, and volume $\frac{4}{27}\pi a^2 b$. Since the volume of the cone is $\frac{1}{3}\pi a^2 b$, the cylinder of maximum volume occupies $\frac{4}{9}$ of the space under the cone.

Exercise 9B

1   In each part of this question express each derivative as 'the rate of change of … with respect to …', and state its physical significance.

   (a) $\dfrac{dh}{dx}$, where h is the height above sea level, and x is the horizontal distance travelled, along a straight road

   (b) $\dfrac{dN}{dt}$, where N is the number of people in a football stadium at time t before kick-off

   (c) $\dfrac{dM}{dr}$, where M is the magnetic force at a distance r from a magnet

   (d) $\dfrac{dv}{dt}$, where v is the velocity of a particle moving in a straight line at time t

   (e) $\dfrac{dq}{dS}$, where q is the rate at which petrol is used in a car in litres per km, and S is the speed of the car in km per hour

2   Defining suitable notation and units, express each of the following as a derivative.

   (a) the rate of change of atmospheric pressure with respect to height above sea level

   (b) the rate of change of temperature with respect to the time of day

   (c) the rate at which the tide is rising

   (d) the rate at which a baby's weight increases in the first weeks of life

3 (a) Find $\dfrac{dz}{dt}$ where $z = 3t^2 + 7t - 5$. (b) Find $\dfrac{d\theta}{dx}$ where $\theta = x - \sqrt{x}$.

   (c) Find $\dfrac{dx}{dy}$ where $x = y + \dfrac{3}{y^2}$. (d) Find $\dfrac{dr}{dt}$ where $r = t^2 + \dfrac{1}{\sqrt{t}}$.

   (e) Find $\dfrac{dm}{dt}$ where $m = (t+3)^2$. (f) Find $\dfrac{df}{ds}$ where $f = 2s^6 - 3s^2$.

   (g) Find $\dfrac{dw}{dt}$ where $w = 5t$. (h) Find $\dfrac{dR}{dr}$ where $R = \dfrac{1 - r^3}{r^2}$.

4 A particle moves along the x-axis. Its displacement at time t is $x = 6t - t^2$.

   (a) What does $\dfrac{dx}{dt}$ represent?

   (b) Is x increasing or decreasing when   (i) $t = 1$,   (ii) $t = 4$?

   (c) Find the greatest (positive) displacement of the particle. How is this connected to your answer to part (a)?

5 Devise suitable notation to express each of the following in mathematical form.

   (a) The distance travelled along the motorway is increasing at a constant rate.

   (b) The rate at which a savings bank deposit grows is proportional to the amount of money deposited.

   (c) At the slimming club Mary is losing weight faster than John.

   (d) The rate at which the diameter of a tree increases is a function of the air temperature.

6 At a speed of S km per hour my car will travel y kilometres on each litre of petrol, where

$$y = 5 + \tfrac{1}{5}S - \tfrac{1}{800}S^2.$$

Calculate the speed at which the car should be driven for maximum economy.

7 A cricket ball is thrown vertically upwards. At time t seconds its height h metres is given by $h = 20t - 5t^2$. Calculate the ball's maximum height above the ground.

8 The sum of two real numbers x and y is 12. Find the maximum value of their product xy.

9 The product of two positive real numbers x and y is 20. Find the minimum possible value of their sum.

10 The volume of a cylinder is given by the formula $V = \pi r^2 h$. Find the greatest and least values of V if $r + h = 6$.

11 A loop of string of length 1 metre is formed into a rectangle with one pair of opposite sides each x cm. Calculate the value of x which will maximise the area enclosed by the string.

12 One side of a rectangular sheep pen is formed by a hedge. The other three sides are made using fencing. The length of the rectangle is x metres; 120 metres of fencing is available.

   (a) Show that the area of the rectangle is $\tfrac{1}{2}x(120 - x)\,\text{m}^2$.

   (b) Calculate the maximum possible area of the sheep pen.

13 A rectangular sheet of metal measures 50 cm by 40 cm. Equal squares of side x cm are cut from each corner and discarded. The sheet is then folded up to make a tray of depth x cm. What is the domain of possible values of x? Find the value of x which maximises the capacity of the tray.

14 An open rectangular box is to be made with a square base, and its capacity is to be 4000 cm^3. Find the length of the side of the base when the amount of material used to make the box is as small as possible. (Ignore 'flaps'.)

15 An open cylindrical wastepaper bin, of radius r cm and capacity V cm^3, is to have a surface area of 5000 cm^2.

   (a) Show that $V = \frac{1}{2}r\left(5000 - \pi r^2\right)$.

   (b) Calculate the maximum possible capacity of the bin.

16 A circular cylinder is cut out of a sphere of radius 10 cm. Calculate the maximum possible volume of the cylinder. (It is probably best to take as your independent variable the height, or half the height, of the cylinder.)

Miscellaneous exercise 9

1 Use differentiation to find the coordinates of the stationary points on the curve

$$y = x + \frac{4}{x}$$

and determine whether each stationary point is a maximum point or a minimum point.

Find the set of values of x for which y increases as x increases.   (OCR)

2 The rate at which a radioactive mass decays is known to be proportional to the mass remaining at that time. If, at time t, the mass remaining is m, this means that m and t satisfy the equation

$$\frac{dm}{dt} = -km$$

where k is a positive constant. (The negative sign ensures that $\frac{dm}{dt}$ is negative, which indicates that m is decreasing.)

Write down similar equations which represent the following statements.

   (a) The rate of growth of a population of bacteria is proportional to the number, n, of bacteria present.

   (b) When a bowl of hot soup is put in the freezer, the rate at which its temperature, $\theta\,°C$, decreases as it cools is proportional to its current temperature.

   (c) The rate at which the temperature, $\theta\,°$, of a cup of coffee decreases as it cools is proportional to the excess of its temperature over the room temperature, $\beta°$.

3 A car accelerates to overtake a truck. Its initial speed is u, and in a time t after it starts to accelerate it covers a distance x, where $x = ut + kt^2$.

   Use differentiation to show that its speed is then $u + 2kt$, and show that its acceleration is constant.

4 A car is travelling at 20 m s^{-1} when the driver applies the brakes. At a time t seconds later the car has travelled a further distance x metres, where $x = 20t - 2t^2$. Use differentiation to find expressions for the speed and the acceleration of the car at this time. For how long do these formulae apply?

5 A boy stands on the edge of a cliff of height 60 m. He throws a stone vertically upwards so that its distance, $h \text{ m}$, above the cliff top is given by $h = 20t - 5t^2$.

   (a) Calculate the maximum height of the stone above the cliff top.

   (b) Calculate the time which elapses before the stone hits the beach. (It just misses the boy and the cliff on the way down.)

   (c) Calculate the speed with which the stone hits the beach.

6 Find the least possible value of $x^2 + y^2$ given that $x + y = 10$.

7 The sum of the two shorter sides of a right angled triangle is 18 cm. Calculate

   (a) the least possible length of the hypotenuse,

   (b) the greatest possible area of the triangle.

8 (a) Find the stationary points on the graph of $y = 12x + 3x^2 - 2x^3$ and sketch the graph.

   (b) How does your sketch show that the equation $12x + 3x^2 - 2x^3 = 0$ has exactly three real roots?

   (c) Use your graph to show that the equation $12x + 3x^2 - 2x^3 = -5$ also has exactly three real roots.

   (d) For what range of values of k does the equation $12x + 3x^2 - 2x^3 = k$ have
        (i) exactly three real roots,   (ii) only one real root?

9 Find the coordinates of the stationary points on the graph of

   $$y = x^3 - 12x - 12$$

   and sketch the graph.

   Find the set of values of k for which the equation

   $$x^3 - 12x - 12 = k$$

   has more than one real solution.   (OCR)

10 Find the coordinates of the stationary points on the graph of $y = x^3 + x^2$. Sketch the graph and hence write down the set of values of the constant k for which the equation $x^3 + x^2 = k$ has three distinct real roots.

11 Find the coordinates of the stationary points on the graph of $y = 3x^4 - 4x^3 - 12x^2 + 10$, and sketch the graph. For what values of k does the equation $3x^4 - 4x^3 - 12x^2 + 10 = k$ have
    (a) exactly four roots,   (b) exactly two roots?

12 Find the coordinates of the stationary points on the curve with equation $y = x(x - 1)^2$. Sketch the curve.

   Find the set of real values of k such that the equation $x(x - 1)^2 = k^2$ has exactly one real root.   (OCR, adapted)

13   The cross-section of an object has the shape of a quarter-circle of radius r adjoining a rectangle of width x and height r, as shown in the diagram.

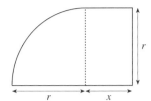

(a) The perimeter and area of the cross-section are P and A respectively. Express each of P and A in terms of r and x, and hence show that $A = \frac{1}{2}Pr - r^2$.

(b) Taking the perimeter P of the cross-section as fixed, find x in terms of r for the case when the area A of the cross-section is a maximum, and show that, for this value of x, A is a maximum and not a minimum.   (OCR)

14   A curve has equation $y = \dfrac{1}{x} - \dfrac{1}{x^2}$. Use differentiation to find the coordinates of the stationary point and determine whether the stationary point is a maximum point or a minimum point. Deduce, or obtain otherwise, the coordinates of the stationary point of each of the following curves.

(a) $y = \dfrac{1}{x} - \dfrac{1}{x^2} + 5$ (b) $y = \dfrac{2}{x-1} - \dfrac{2}{(x-1)^2}$

15   The costs of a firm which makes climbing boots are of two kinds:
Fixed costs (plant, rates, office expenses): £2000 per week;
Production costs (materials, labour): £20 for each pair of boots made.

Market research suggests that, if they price the boots at £30 a pair they will sell 500 pairs a week, but that at £55 a pair they will sell none at all; and between these values the graph of sales against price is a straight line.

If they price boots at £x a pair $(30 \leqslant x \leqslant 55)$ find expressions for

(a) the weekly sales,   (b) the weekly receipts,   (c) the weekly costs
(assuming that just enough boots are made).

Hence show that the weekly profit, £P, is given by
$$P = -20x^2 + 1500x - 24\,000.$$

Find the price at which the boots should be sold to maximise the profit.   (OCR)

16   The manager of a supermarket usually adds a mark-up of 20% to the wholesale prices of all the goods he sells. He reckons that he has a loyal core of F customers and that, if he lowers his mark-up to $x\%$ he will attract an extra $k(20 - x)$ customers from his rivals. Each week the average shopper buys goods whose wholesale value is £A. Show that with a mark-up of $x\%$ the supermarket will have an anticipated weekly profit of
$$£\tfrac{1}{100}Ax\big((F + 20k) - kx\big).$$

Show that the manager can increase his profit by reducing his mark-up below 20% provided that $20k > F$.   (OCR)

10 Integration

Integration is the reverse process of differentiation. When you have completed this chapter, you should

- understand the term 'indefinite integral' and the need to add an arbitrary constant
- be able to integrate functions which can be expressed as sums of powers of x, and be aware of any exceptions
- know how to find the equation of a graph given its derivative and a point on the graph
- know how to evaluate a definite integral
- be able to use definite integrals to find areas
- understand the possibility that infinite and improper integrals may exist, and be able to evaluate them.

10.1 Finding a function from its derivative

It was shown in Section 8.4 that some features of the graph of a function can be interpreted in terms of the graph of its derived function.

Suppose now that you know the graph of the derived function. What does this tell you about the graph of the original function?

It is useful to begin by trying to answer this question geometrically. Fig. 10.1 shows the graph of the derived function $f'(x)$ of some function. The problem is to sketch the graph of $f(x)$. Scanning the domain from left to right, you can see that:

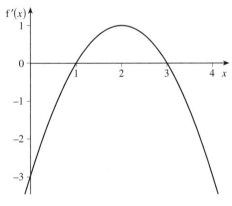

Fig. 10.1

For $x < 1$ the gradient is negative, so $f(x)$ is decreasing.

At $x = 1$ the gradient changes from – to +, so $f(x)$ has a minimum.

For $1 < x < 3$ the gradient is positive, so $f(x)$ is increasing. Notice that the gradient is greatest when $x = 2$, so that is where the graph climbs most steeply.

At $x = 3$ the gradient changes from + to –, so $f(x)$ has a maximum.

Fig. 10.2

For $x > 3$ the gradient is negative, so $f(x)$ is again decreasing.

Using this information you can make a sketch like Fig. 10.2 which gives an idea of the shape of the graph of $f(x)$. But there is no way of deciding precisely where the graph is located. You could translate it in the y-direction by any amount, and it would still have the same gradient $f'(x)$. So there is no unique answer to the problem; there are many functions $f(x)$ with the given derived function.

This can be shown algebraically. The graph in Fig. 10.1 comes from the equation

$$f'(x) = (x-1)(3-x) = 4x - x^2 - 3.$$

What function has this expression as its derivative? The key is to note that in differentiating x^n the index decreases by 1, from n to $n-1$. So to reverse the process the index must go up by 1. The three terms $4x$, $-x^2$ and -3 must therefore come from multiples of x^2, x^3 and x. These functions have derivatives $2x$, $3x^2$ and 1, so to get the correct coefficients in $f'(x)$ you have to multiply by 2, $-\frac{1}{3}$ and -3. One possible answer is therefore

$$f(x) = 2x^2 - \tfrac{1}{3}x^3 - 3x.$$

But, as argued above, this is only one of many possible answers. You can translate the graph of $f(x)$ in the y-direction by any amount k without changing its gradient. This is because the derivative of any constant k is zero. So the complete solution to the problem is

$$f(x) = 2x^2 - \tfrac{1}{3}x^3 - 3x + k \text{ for any constant } k.$$

The process of getting from $f'(x)$ to $f(x)$ is called **integration**, and the general expression for $f(x)$ is called the **indefinite integral** of $f'(x)$. Integration is the reverse process of differentiation.

The indefinite integral always includes an added constant k, which is called an **arbitrary constant**. The word 'arbitrary' means that, in any application, you can choose its value to fit some extra condition; for example, you can make the graph of $y = f(x)$ go through some given point.

It is easy to find a rule for integrating functions which are powers of x. Because differentiation reduces the index by 1, integration must increase it by 1. So the function x^n must be derived from some multiple of x^{n+1}. But the derivative of x^{n+1} is $(n+1)x^n$, so to reduce the coefficient to 1 you have to multiply by $\dfrac{1}{n+1}$. The rule is therefore that one integral of x^n is $\dfrac{1}{n+1}x^{n+1}$.

But notice an important exception to this rule. The formula has no meaning if $n+1$ is 0, so it does not give the integral of x^{-1}, or $\dfrac{1}{x}$. You will find later that the integral of $\dfrac{1}{x}$ is not a power of x, but a quite different kind of function. (See P2 Section 12.4.)

The extension to functions which are sums of powers of x then follows from the equivalent rules for differentiation:

> The indefinite integral of a function made up of the sum of multiples of x^n, where $n \neq -1$, is the corresponding sum of multiples of $\dfrac{1}{n+1}x^{n+1}$, together with an added arbitrary constant.

Example 10.1.1

The graph of $y = f(x)$ passes through $(2,3)$, and $f'(x) = 6x^2 - 5x$. Find its equation.

The indefinite integral is $6\left(\frac{1}{3}x^3\right) - 5\left(\frac{1}{2}x^2\right) + k$, so the graph has equation

$$y = 2x^3 - \tfrac{5}{2}x^2 + k$$

for some constant k. The coordinates $x = 2$, $y = 3$ have to satisfy this equation, so

$$3 = 2 \times 8 - \tfrac{5}{2} \times 4 + k, \text{ giving } k = 3 - 16 + 10 = -3.$$

The equation of the graph is therefore $y = 2x^3 - \tfrac{5}{2}x^2 - 3$.

Example 10.1.2

A gardener is digging a plot of land. As he gets tired he works more slowly; after t minutes he is digging at a rate of $\dfrac{2}{\sqrt{t}}$ square metres per minute. How long will it take him to dig an area of 40 square metres?

Let A square metres be the area he has dug after t minutes. Then his rate of digging is measured by the derivative $\dfrac{dA}{dt}$. So you know that $\dfrac{dA}{dt} = 2t^{-\frac{1}{2}}$; in this case $n = -\frac{1}{2}$, so $n + 1 = \frac{1}{2}$ and the indefinite integral is

$$A = 2\left(\tfrac{1}{1/2}\right)t^{\frac{1}{2}} + k = 4\sqrt{t} + k.$$

To find k, you need to know a pair of values of A and t. Since A is 0 when he starts to dig, which is when t is 0, $0 = 4\sqrt{0} + k$ and so $k = 0$.

The equation connecting A with t is therefore $A = 4\sqrt{t}$.

To find how long it takes to dig 40 square metres, substitute $A = 40$:

$$40 = 4\sqrt{t}, \text{ so that } \sqrt{t} = 10, \text{ and hence } t = 100.$$

It will take him 100 minutes to dig an area of 40 square metres.

Exercise 10A

1   Find a general expression for the function $f(x)$ in each of the following cases.

(a) $f'(x) = 4x^3$ (b) $f'(x) = 6x^5$ (c) $f'(x) = 2x$

(d) $f'(x) = 3x^2 + 5x^4$ (e) $f'(x) = 10x^9 - 8x^7 - 1$ (f) $f'(x) = -7x^6 + 3x^2 + 1$

2 Find a general expression for the function $f(x)$ in each of the following cases.

(a) $f'(x) = 9x^2 - 4x - 5$

(b) $f'(x) = 12x^2 + 6x + 4$

(c) $f'(x) = 7$

(d) $f'(x) = 16x^3 - 6x^2 + 10x - 3$

(e) $f'(x) = 2x^3 + 5x$

(f) $f'(x) = x + 2x^2$

(g) $f'(x) = 2x^2 - 3x - 4$

(h) $f'(x) = 1 - 2x - 3x^2$

3 Find y in terms of x in each of the following cases.

(a) $\dfrac{dy}{dx} = x^4 + x^2 + 1$

(b) $\dfrac{dy}{dx} = 7x - 3$

(c) $\dfrac{dy}{dx} = 2x^2 + x - 8$

(d) $\dfrac{dy}{dx} = 6x^3 - 5x^2 + 3x + 2$

(e) $\dfrac{dy}{dx} = \frac{2}{3}x^3 + \frac{1}{2}x^2 + \frac{1}{3}x + \frac{1}{6}$

(f) $\dfrac{dy}{dx} = \frac{1}{2}x^3 - \frac{1}{3}x^2 + x - \frac{1}{3}$

(g) $\dfrac{dy}{dx} = x - 3x^2 + 1$

(h) $\dfrac{dy}{dx} = x^3 + x^2 + x + 1$

4 The graph of $y = f(x)$ passes through the origin and $f'(x) = 8x - 5$. Find $f(x)$.

5 A curve passes through the point $(2, -5)$ and satisfies $\dfrac{dy}{dx} = 6x^2 - 1$. Find y in terms of x.

6 A curve passes through $(-4, 9)$ and is such that $\dfrac{dy}{dx} = \frac{1}{2}x^3 + \frac{1}{4}x + 1$. Find y in terms of x.

7 Given that $f'(x) = 15x^2 - 6x + 4$ and $f(1) = 0$, find $f(x)$.

8 Each of the following diagrams shows the graph of a derived function $f'(x)$. In each case, sketch the graph of a possible function $f(x)$.

(a)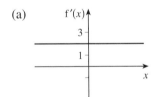

(b)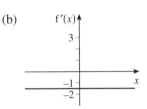

(c)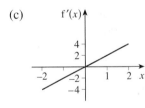

(d)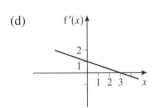

(e)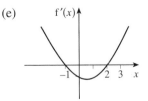

(f)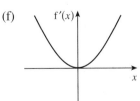

9 Find a general expression for the function $f(x)$ in each of the following cases.

(a) $f'(x) = x^{-2}$

(b) $f'(x) = 3x^{-4}$

(c) $f'(x) = \dfrac{6}{x^3}$

(d) $f'(x) = 4x - \dfrac{3}{x^2}$

(e) $f'(x) = \dfrac{1}{x^3} - \dfrac{1}{x^4}$

(f) $f'(x) = \dfrac{2}{x^2} - 2x^2$

10 Find y in terms of x in each of the following cases.

(a) $\dfrac{dy}{dx} = x^{\frac{1}{2}}$ 　　　　　　(b) $\dfrac{dy}{dx} = 4x^{-\frac{2}{3}}$ 　　　　　　(c) $\dfrac{dy}{dx} = \sqrt[3]{x}$

(d) $\dfrac{dy}{dx} = 2\sqrt{x} - \dfrac{2}{\sqrt{x}}$ 　　　(e) $\dfrac{dy}{dx} = \dfrac{5}{\sqrt[3]{x}}$ 　　　　　(f) $\dfrac{dy}{dx} = \dfrac{-2}{\sqrt[3]{x^2}}$

11 The graph of $y = f(x)$ passes through $(4, 25)$ and $f'(x) = 6\sqrt{x}$. Find its equation.

12 The graph of $y = f(x)$ passes through $\left(\frac{1}{2}, 5\right)$ and $f'(x) = \dfrac{4}{x^2}$. Find its equation.

13 A curve passes through the point $(25, 3)$ and is such that $\dfrac{dy}{dx} = \dfrac{1}{2\sqrt{x}}$ Find the equation of the curve.

14 A curve passes through the point $(1, 5)$ and is such that $\dfrac{dy}{dx} = \sqrt[3]{x} - \dfrac{6}{x^3}$. Find the equation of the curve.

15 In each of the following cases, find y in terms of x.

(a) $\dfrac{dy}{dx} = 3x(x + 2)$ 　　　(b) $\dfrac{dy}{dx} = (2x - 1)(6x + 5)$ 　　　(c) $\dfrac{dy}{dx} = \dfrac{4x^3 + 1}{x^2}$

(d) $\dfrac{dy}{dx} = \dfrac{x + 4}{\sqrt{x}}$ 　　　(e) $\dfrac{dy}{dx} = \left(\sqrt{x} + 5\right)^2$ 　　　(f) $\dfrac{dy}{dx} = \dfrac{\sqrt{x} + 5}{\sqrt{x}}$

16 A tree is growing so that, after t years, its height is increasing at a rate of $\dfrac{30}{\sqrt[3]{t}}$ cm per year. Assume that, when $t = 0$, the height is 5 cm.

(a) Find the height of the tree after 4 years.

(b) After how many years will the height be 4.1 metres?

17 A pond, with surface area 48 square metres, is being invaded by a weed. At a time t months after the weed first appeared, the area of the weed on the surface is increasing at a rate of $\frac{1}{3}t$ square metres per month. How long will it be before the weed covers the whole surface of the pond?

18 The function $f(x)$ is such that $f'(x) = 9x^2 + 4x + c$, where c is a particular constant. Given that $f(2) = 14$ and $f(3) = 74$, find the value of $f(4)$.

10.2 Calculating areas

An important application of integration is to calculate areas and volumes. Many of the formulae you have learnt, such as for the volume of a sphere or a cone, can be proved by using integration. This chapter deals only with areas.

The method can be illustrated by finding the area in Fig. 10.1 between the x-axis and the graph of $y = (x - 1)(3 - x)$ from $x = 1$ to $x = 3$. The key is to begin by asking a more general question: what is the area, A, between the x-axis and the graph from $x = 1$ as far as any value of x? This is illustrated by the region with dark shading in Fig. 10.3.

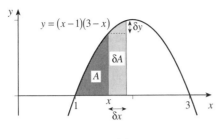

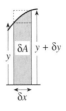

Fig. 10.3

Fig. 10.4

The point of doing this is that x can now be varied. Suppose that x is increased by δx. Since both y and A are functions of x, you can write the corresponding increases in y and A as δy and δA. This is represented in Fig. 10.3 by the region with light shading.

This region is drawn by itself in Fig. 10.4. Dotted lines have been added to this figure, which show that the area δA of the region is between the areas of two rectangles, each with width δx and having heights of y and $y + \delta y$. So

δA is between $y\delta x$ and $(y + \delta y)\delta x$,

from which it follows that

$\dfrac{\delta A}{\delta x}$ is between y and $y + \delta y$.

Now consider the effect of making δx tend to 0. From the definition, $\dfrac{\delta A}{\delta x}$ tends to the derivative $\dfrac{dA}{dx}$. Also δy tends to 0, so that $y + \delta y$ tends to y. It follows that

$\dfrac{dA}{dx} = y.$

So A is a function whose derivative is $y = (x - 1)(3 - x)$, that is A is an integral of $(x - 1)(3 - x)$, and you found in Section 10.1 that this has equation

$A = 2x^2 - \tfrac{1}{3}x^3 - 3x + k$, for some number k.

To find k, you need to know A for some value of x. In this case it is obvious that $A = 0$ when $x = 1$, so that $0 = 2 - \tfrac{1}{3} - 3 + k$, which gives $k = \tfrac{4}{3}$.

The original problem was to find the area when $x = 3$, which is

$2 \times 3^2 - \tfrac{1}{3} \times 3^3 - 3 \times 3 + \tfrac{4}{3} = 18 - 9 - 9 + \tfrac{4}{3} = \tfrac{4}{3}.$

Notice that the answer has been given without a unit, because it is not usual to attach a unit to the variables x and y when graphs are drawn. But if in a particular application x and y each denote numbers of units, then a corresponding unit (the x-unit $\times$ the y-unit) should be attached to the value of A.

Exercise 10B

1 Find the following indefinite integrals.

  (a) $\displaystyle\int 4x\,dx$ (b) $\displaystyle\int 15x^2\,dx$ (c) $\displaystyle\int 2x^5\,dx$

  (d) $\displaystyle\int 9\,dx$ (e) $\displaystyle\int \tfrac{1}{2}x^8\,dx$ (f) $\displaystyle\int \tfrac{2}{3}x^4\,dx$

2 Evaluate the following definite integrals.

  (a) $\displaystyle\int_1^2 3x^2\,dx$ (b) $\displaystyle\int_2^5 8x\,dx$ (c) $\displaystyle\int_0^2 x^3\,dx$

  (d) $\displaystyle\int_{-1}^1 10x^4\,dx$ (e) $\displaystyle\int_0^{\frac{1}{2}} \tfrac{1}{2}x\,dx$ (f) $\displaystyle\int_0^1 2\,dx$

3 Find the following indefinite integrals.

  (a) $\displaystyle\int (6x+7)\,dx$ (b) $\displaystyle\int \left(6x^2-2x-5\right)dx$

  (c) $\displaystyle\int \left(2x^3+7x\right)dx$ (d) $\displaystyle\int \left(3x^4-8x^3+9x^2-x+4\right)dx$

  (e) $\displaystyle\int (2x+5)(x-4)\,dx$ (f) $\displaystyle\int x(x+2)(x-2)\,dx$

4 Evaluate the following definite integrals.

  (a) $\displaystyle\int_0^2 (8x+3)\,dx$ (b) $\displaystyle\int_2^4 (5x-4)\,dx$

  (c) $\displaystyle\int_{-2}^2 \left(6x^2+1\right)dx$ (d) $\displaystyle\int_0^1 (2x+1)(x+3)\,dx$

  (e) $\displaystyle\int_{-3}^4 \left(6x^2+2x+3\right)dx$ (f) $\displaystyle\int_{-3}^3 \left(6x^3+2x\right)dx$

5 Find the area under the curve $y=x^2$ from $x=0$ to $x=6$.

6 Find the area under the curve $y=4x^3$ from $x=1$ to $x=2$.

7 Find the area under the curve $y=12x^3$ from $x=2$ to $x=3$.

8 Find the area under the curve $y=3x^2+2x$ from $x=0$ to $x=4$.

9 Find the area under the curve $y=3x^2-2x$ from $x=-4$ to $x=0$.

10 Find the area under the curve $y=x^4+5$ from $x=-1$ to $x=1$.

11 The diagram shows the region under $y=4x+1$ between $x=1$ and $x=3$. Find the area of the shaded region by

  (a) using the formula for the area of a trapezium,

  (b) using integration.

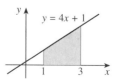

12 The diagram shows the region bounded by $y = \frac{1}{2}x - 3$, by $x = 14$ and the x-axis. Find the area of the shaded region by

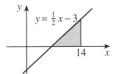

(a) using the formula for the area of a triangle,

(b) using integration.

13 Find the area of the region shaded in each of the following diagrams.

(a)

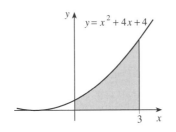

$y = x^2 + 4x + 4$

(b)

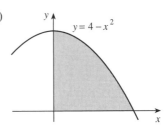

$y = 4 - x^2$

(c)

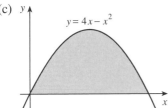

$y = 4x - x^2$

(d)

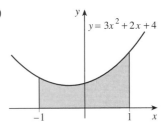

$y = 3x^2 + 2x + 4$

(e)

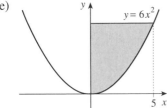

$y = 6x^2$

(f)

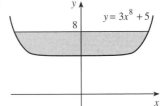

$y = 3x^8 + 5$

14 Find the following indefinite integrals.

(a) $\displaystyle\int \frac{1}{x^3}\,dx$

(b) $\displaystyle\int \left(x^2 - \frac{1}{x^2}\right)dx$

(c) $\displaystyle\int \sqrt{x}\,dx$

(d) $\displaystyle\int 6x^{\frac{2}{3}}\,dx$

(e) $\displaystyle\int \frac{6x^4 + 5}{x^2}\,dx$

(f) $\displaystyle\int \frac{1}{\sqrt{x}}\,dx$

15 Evaluate the following definite integrals.

(a) $\displaystyle\int_0^8 12\sqrt[3]{x}\,dx$

(b) $\displaystyle\int_1^2 \frac{3}{x^2}\,dx$

(c) $\displaystyle\int_1^4 \frac{10}{\sqrt{x}}\,dx$

(d) $\displaystyle\int_1^2 \left(\frac{8}{x^3} + x^3\right)dx$

(e) $\displaystyle\int_4^9 \frac{2\sqrt{x} + 3}{\sqrt{x}}\,dx$

(f) $\displaystyle\int_1^8 \frac{1}{\sqrt[3]{x^2}}\,dx$

16 Find the area under the curve $y = \dfrac{6}{x^4}$ between $x = 1$ and $x = 2$.

17 Find the area under the curve $y = \sqrt[3]{x}$ between $x = 1$ and $x = 27$.

18 Find the area under the curve $y = \dfrac{5}{x^2}$ between $x = -3$ and $x = -1$.

19 Given that $\displaystyle\int_0^a 12x^2\,\mathrm{d}x = 1372$, find the value of the constant a.

20 Given that $\displaystyle\int_0^9 p\sqrt{x}\,\mathrm{d}x = 90$, find the value of the constant p.

21 Find the area of the shaded region in each of the following diagrams.

(a)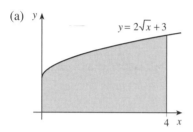

(b)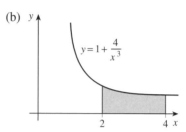

22 The diagram shows the graph of $y = 9x^2$. The point P has coordinates $(4, 144)$. Find the area of the shaded region.

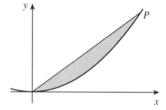

23 The diagram shows the graph of $y = \dfrac{1}{\sqrt{x}}$. Show that the area of the shaded region is $3 - \dfrac{5\sqrt{3}}{3}$.

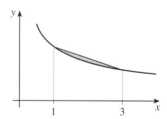

24 Find the area of the region between the curve $y = 9 + 15x - 6x^2$ and the x-axis.

10.4 Some properties of definite integrals

In definite integral notation the calculation in Section 10.2 of the area in Fig. 10.1 would be written

$$\int_1^3 (x-1)(3-x)\,\mathrm{d}x = \left[2x^2 - \tfrac{1}{3}x^3 - 3x\right]_1^3 = (0) - \left(-\tfrac{4}{3}\right) = \tfrac{4}{3}.$$

But what is the interpretation of the calculation

$$\int_0^3 (x-1)(3-x)\,\mathrm{d}x = \left[2x^2 - \tfrac{1}{3}x^3 - 3x\right]_0^3 = (0) - (0) = 0\,?$$

Clearly the area between the graph and the x-axis between $x = 0$ and $x = 3$ is not zero, as the value of the definite integral suggests.

You can find the clue by calculating the integral between $x = 0$ and $x = 1$:

$$\int_0^1 (x-1)(3-x)\,dx = \left[2x^2 - \tfrac{1}{3}x^3 - 3x\right]_0^1 = \left(-\tfrac{4}{3}\right) - (0) = -\tfrac{4}{3}.$$

This shows that you need to be careful in identifying the definite integral as an area. In Fig. 10.1 the area of the region contained between the curve and the two axes is $\tfrac{4}{3}$, and the negative sign attached to the definite integral indicates that between $x = 0$ and $x = 1$ the graph lies below the x-axis.

The zero answer obtained for the integral from $x = 0$ to $x = 3$ is then explained by the fact that definite integrals are added by the usual rules of algebra:

$$\int_0^3 (x-1)(3-x)\,dx = \int_0^1 (x-1)(3-x)\,dx + \int_1^3 (x-1)(3-x)\,dx = -\tfrac{4}{3} + \tfrac{4}{3} = 0.$$

This is a special case of a general rule:

$$\int_a^b f(x)\,dx + \int_b^c f(x)\,dx = \int_a^c f(x)\,dx.$$

To prove this, let $I(x)$ denote the simplest indefinite integral of $f(x)$.

Then the sum of the integrals on the left side is equal to

$$\left[I(x)\right]_a^b + \left[I(x)\right]_b^c = \{I(b) - I(a)\} - \{I(c) - I(b)\} = I(c) - I(a) = \int_a^c f(x)\,dx.$$

Another way in which negative definite integrals can arise is by interchanging the bounds of integration. Since

$$\left[I(x)\right]_b^a = I(a) - I(b) = -\{I(b) - I(a)\} = -\left[I(x)\right]_a^b,$$

it follows that

$$\int_b^a f(x)\,dx = -\int_a^b f(x)\,dx.$$

You are not likely to use this in numerical examples, but such integrals may turn up if a or b are algebraic expressions.

10.5 Infinite and improper integrals

Example 10.5.1
Find the areas under the graphs of (a) $y = \dfrac{1}{x^2}$, (b) $y = \dfrac{1}{\sqrt{x}}$ in the intervals

(i) $x = 1$ to $x = s$, where $s > 1$, (ii) $x = r$ to $x = 1$, where $0 < r < 1$.

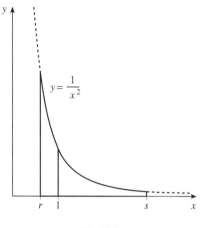

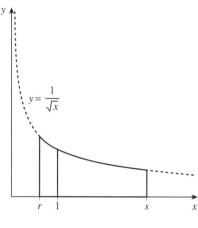

Fig. 10.7   Fig. 10.8

These areas are shown in Figs. 10.7 and 10.8.

The functions are (a) x^{-2} and (b) $x^{-\frac{1}{2}}$, so the simplest indefinite integrals are

(a) $-x^{-1} = -\dfrac{1}{x}$ and   (b) $2x^{\frac{1}{2}} = 2\sqrt{x}$.

(a) (i) $\displaystyle\int_1^s \frac{1}{x^2}\,dx = \left[-\frac{1}{x}\right]_1^s = 1 - \frac{1}{s}.$

(a) (ii) $\displaystyle\int_r^1 \frac{1}{x^2}\,dx = \left[-\frac{1}{x}\right]_r^1 = \frac{1}{r} - 1.$

(b) (i) $\displaystyle\int_1^s \frac{1}{\sqrt{x}}\,dx = \left[2\sqrt{x}\right]_1^s = 2\sqrt{s} - 2.$

(b) (ii) $\displaystyle\int_r^1 \frac{1}{\sqrt{x}}\,dx = \left[2\sqrt{x}\right]_r^1 = 2 - 2\sqrt{r}.$

The interesting feature of these results appears if you consider what happens in (i) if s becomes indefinitely large, and in (ii) if r comes indefinitely close to 0.

Consider s first. By taking a large enough value for s, you can make $1 - \dfrac{1}{s}$ as close to 1 as you like, but it always remains less than 1. You can say that the integral (a)(i) 'tends to 1 as s tends to infinity' (written '$\to 1$ as $s \to \infty$'). A shorthand for this is

$$\int_1^\infty \frac{1}{x^2}\,dx = 1.$$

This is called an **infinite integral**.

However, $2\sqrt{s} - 2$ can be made as large as you like by taking a large enough value for s, so the integral (b)(i) 'tends to infinity as s tends to infinity' (or '$\to \infty$ as $s \to \infty$').

Since 'infinity' is not a number, you cannot give a meaning to the symbol

$$\int_1^\infty \frac{1}{\sqrt{x}}\,dx\,.$$

In the case of r, the situation is reversed. The expression $2-2\sqrt{r}$ tends to 2 as r tends to 0. So you can write

$$\int_0^1 \frac{1}{\sqrt{x}}\,dx = 2$$

even though the integrand $\dfrac{1}{\sqrt{x}}$ is not defined when $x=0$. This is called an **improper integral**. But in the final example, $\dfrac{1}{r}-1$ tends to infinity as r tends to 0, so you cannot give a meaning to the symbol

$$\int_0^1 \frac{1}{x^2}\,dx\,.$$

You can see from the graphs that, as you would expect, the cases where the integrals are defined correspond to regions in which the graph is very close to the asymptote. You can then say that the region has a finite area, even though it is unbounded.

10.6 The area between two graphs

You sometimes want to find the area of a region bounded by the graphs of two functions $f(x)$ and $g(x)$, and two lines $x=a$ and $x=b$, as in Fig. 10.9.

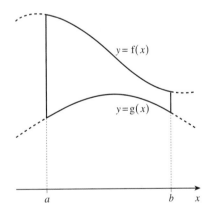

Although you could find this as the difference of the areas of two regions of the kind illustrated in Fig. 10.5, calculated as

$$\int_a^b f(x)\,dx - \int_a^b g(x)\,dx,$$

it is often simpler to find this as a single integral

$$\int_a^b \big(f(x)-g(x)\big)\,dx\,.$$

Fig. 10.9

Example 10.6.1

Show that the graphs of $f(x)=x^3-x^2-6x+8$ and $g(x)=x^3+2x^2-1$ intersect at two points, and find the area enclosed between them.

The graphs intersect where

$$x^3-x^2-6x+8 = x^3+2x^2-1,$$
$$0 = 3x^2+6x-9,$$
$$3(x+3)(x-1)=0.$$

The points of intersection are therefore $(-3, -10)$ and $(1, 2)$.

Before reading on, use a calculator to display the two graphs between $x = -3$ and $x = 1$. You will see that $f(x) > g(x)$ in this interval.

The area between the graphs is

$$\int_{-3}^{1} (f(x) - g(x)) \, dx = \int_{-3}^{1} \left(9 - 6x - 3x^2\right) dx = \left[9x - 3x^2 - x^3\right]_{-3}^{1}$$

$$= (9 - 3 - 1) - (-27 - 27 + 27) = 5 - (-27) = 32.$$

Notice that in this example, integrating $f(x) - g(x)$, rather than $f(x)$ and $g(x)$ separately, greatly reduces the amount of calculation.

Exercise 10C

1 Evaluate $\displaystyle\int_0^2 3x(x-2) \, dx$.

2 Find the total area of the region shaded in each of the following diagrams.

(a)
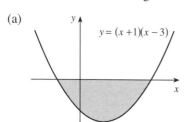

(b)
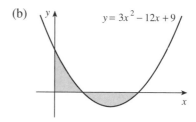

(c)
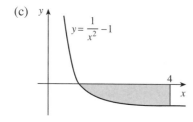

(d)
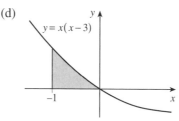

3 Find the values of the improper integrals (a) $\displaystyle\int_0^{16} \frac{1}{\sqrt[4]{x}} \, dx$, (b) $\displaystyle\int_0^{16} \frac{1}{\sqrt[4]{x^3}} \, dx$, (c) $\displaystyle\int_0^1 x^{-0.99} \, dx$.

4 Find the values of the infinite integrals (a) $\displaystyle\int_2^{\infty} \frac{6}{x^4} \, dx$, (b) $\displaystyle\int_4^{\infty} \frac{6}{x\sqrt{x}} \, dx$, (c) $\displaystyle\int_1^{\infty} x^{-1.01} \, dx$.

5 Find an expression for $\displaystyle\int_1^s \frac{1}{x^m} \, dx$ in terms of m and s, where m is a positive rational number, $m \neq -1$ and $s > 1$. Show that the infinite integral $\displaystyle\int_1^{\infty} \frac{1}{x^m} \, dx$ has a meaning if $m > 1$, and state its value in terms of m.

6 Find an expression for $\int_r^1 \dfrac{1}{x^m}\,dx$ in terms of m and r, where m is a positive rational number, $m \neq -1$ and $0 < r < 1$. For what values of m does the improper integral $\int_0^1 \dfrac{1}{x^m}\,dx$ have a meaning? State its value in terms of m.

7 The diagram shows the graphs of
$y = 2x + 7$ and $y = 10 - x$.
Find the area of the shaded region.

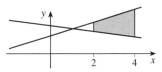

8 Find the area enclosed between the curves $y = x^2 + 7$ and $y = 2x^2 + 3$.

9 Find the area enclosed between the straight line $y = 12x + 14$ and the curve $y = 3x^2 + 6x + 5$.

10 The diagram shows the graphs of
$y = 16 + 4x - 2x^2$ and $y = x^2 - 2x - 8$.
Find the area of the region, shaded in the
diagram, between the curves.

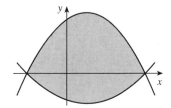

11 Find the area between the curves $y = (x - 4)(3x - 1)$ and $y = (4 - x)(1 + x)$.

12 Parts of the graphs of $f(x) = 2x^3 + x^2 - 8x$ and $g(x) = 2x^3 - 3x - 4$ enclose a finite region. Find its area.

13 The diagram shows the graph of $y = \sqrt{x}$.
Given that the area of the shaded region is
72, find the value of the constant a.

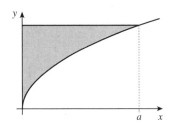

Miscellaneous exercise 10

1 A curve passes through $(2,3)$ and is such that $\dfrac{dy}{dx} = \dfrac{1}{2}x^2 - \dfrac{1}{3}x + 1$. Find y in terms of x.

2 The diagram shows the graph of $y = 12 - 3x^2$.

Determine the x-coordinate of each of the
points where the curve crosses the x-axis.

Find by integration the area of the region
(shaded in the diagram) between the curve
and the x-axis. (OCR)

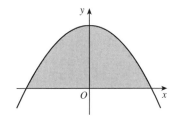

3 Find $\displaystyle\int 6\sqrt{x}\,dx$, and hence evaluate $\displaystyle\int_1^4 6\sqrt{x}\,dx$.   (OCR)

4 (a) Find $\displaystyle\int\left(\frac{1}{x^3}+x^3\right)dx$.   (b) Evaluate $\displaystyle\int_0^8 \frac{1}{\sqrt[3]{x}}\,dx$.   (OCR)

5 Find the area of the region enclosed between the curve $y=12x^2+30x$ and the x-axis.

6 Find the value of the improper integral $\displaystyle\int_0^4 \frac{(x+2)^2}{\sqrt{x}}\,dx$.

7 Given that $\displaystyle\int_{-a}^a 15x^2\,dx = 3430$, find the value of the constant a.

8 The diagram shows the curve $y=x^3$. The
point P has coordinates $(3,27)$ and PQ is
the tangent to the curve at P. Find the area
of the region enclosed between the curve,
PQ and the x-axis.

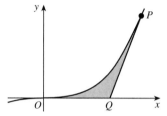

9 The diagram shows the curve
$y=(x-2)^2+1$ with minimum point P.
The point Q on the curve is such that the
gradient of PQ is 2. Find the area of the
region, shaded in the diagram, between
PQ and the curve.

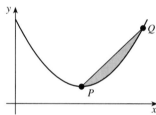

10 Evaluate $\displaystyle\int_0^2 x(x-1)(x-2)\,dx$ and explain your answer with reference to the graph of
$y=x(x-1)(x-2)$.

11 (a) Find $\displaystyle\int x\left(x^2-2\right)dx$.

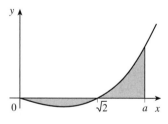

   (b) The diagram shows the graph of $y=x\left(x^2-2\right)$
       for $x\geqslant 0$. The value of a is such that the two
       shaded regions have equal areas. Find the value
       of a.   (OCR)

12 The diagram shows a sketch of the graph of $y=x^2$
and the normal to the curve at the point $A(1,1)$.

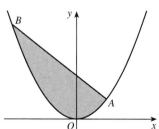

   (a) Use differentiation to find the equation of the
       normal at A. Verify that the point B where the
       normal cuts the curve again has coordinates
       $\left(-\frac{3}{2},\frac{9}{4}\right)$.

   (b) The region which is bounded by the   curve and
       the normal is shaded in the diagram. Calculate its
       area, giving your answer as an exact fraction.
                                                   (OCR)

13 Given that $\int_1^p \left(8x^3 + 6x\right)dx = 39,$ find two possible values of p. Use a graph to explain why there are two values.

14 Show that the area enclosed between the curves $y = 9 - x^2$ and $y = x^2 - 7$ is $\dfrac{128\sqrt{2}}{3}$.

15 Given that $f(x)$ and $g(x)$ are two functions such that $\int_0^4 f(x)\,dx = 17$ and $\int_0^4 g(x)\,dx = 11,$ find, where possible, the value of each of the following.

(a) $\displaystyle\int_0^4 \left(f(x) - g(x)\right)dx$ (b) $\displaystyle\int_0^4 \left(2f(x) + 3g(x)\right)dx$

(c) $\displaystyle\int_0^2 f(x)\,dx$ (d) $\displaystyle\int_0^4 \left(f(x) + 2x + 3\right)dx$

(e) $\displaystyle\int_0^1 f(x)\,dx + \int_1^4 f(x)\,dx$ (f) $\displaystyle\int_4^0 g(x)\,dx$

(g) $\displaystyle\int_1^5 f(x-1)\,dx$ (h) $\displaystyle\int_{-4}^0 g(-t)\,dt$

16 The diagram shows the graph of $y = \sqrt[3]{x} - x^2.$ Show by integration that the area of the region (shaded in the diagram) between the curve and the x-axis is $\frac{5}{12}.$ (OCR)

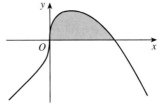

17 The diagram shows a sketch of the graph of the curve $y = x^3 - x$ together with the tangent to the curve at the point $A(1,0).$

(a) Use differentiation to find the equation of the tangent to the curve at A, and verify that the point B where the tangent cuts the curve again has coordinates $(-2,-6).$

(b) Use integration to find the area of the region bounded by the curve and the tangent (shaded in the diagram), giving your answer as a fraction in its lowest terms.   (OCR)

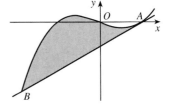

18 The diagram shows part of the curve $y = x^n,$ where $n > 1.$

The point P on the curve has x-coordinate $a.$ Show that the curve divides the rectangle $OAPB$ into two regions whose areas are in the ratio $n:1.$

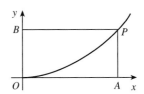

19 Find the stationary points on the graph of $y = x^4 - 8x^2$. Use your answers to make a sketch of the graph. Show that the graphs of $y = x^4 - 8x^2$ and $y = x^2$ enclose two finite regions. Find the area of one of them.

20 Using the same axes, make sketches of the graphs of $y = x^3$ and $y = (x+1)^3 - 1$. Then sketch on a larger scale the finite area enclosed between them.

Given that $(x+1)^3 = x^3 + 3x^2 + 3x + 1$, find the area of the region.

21 A function $f(x)$ with domain $x > 0$ is defined by $f(x) = \dfrac{6}{x^4} - \dfrac{2}{x^3}$.

(a) Find the values of $\displaystyle\int_2^3 f(x)\,dx$ and $\displaystyle\int_2^\infty f(x)\,dx$.

(b) Find the coordinates of (i) the point where the graph of $y = f(x)$ crosses the x-axis, (ii) the minimum point on the graph.

Use your answers to draw a sketch of the graph, and hence explain your answers to part (a).

11 Trigonometry

This chapter develops work on sines, cosines and tangents. When you have completed it, you should

- know the shapes of the graphs of sine, cosine and tangent for all angles
- know, or be able to find, exact values of the sine, cosine and tangent of certain special angles
- be able to solve simple trigonometric equations
- know and be able to use identities involving $\sin\theta°$, $\cos\theta°$ and $\tan\theta°$.

11.1 The graph of $\cos\theta°$

Letters of the Greek alphabet are often used to denote angles. In this chapter, θ (theta) and ϕ (phi) will usually be the letters that are used.

You probably first used $\cos\theta°$ in calculations with right-angled triangles, so that $0 < \theta < 90$. Then you may have used it in any triangle, with $0 < \theta < 180$. However, you will find that a graphic calculator produces a graph of $\cos\theta°$ like that in Fig. 11.3. This section extends the definition of $\cos\theta°$ to angles of any size, positive and negative.

Fig. 11.1 shows a circle of radius 1 unit with centre O; the circle meets the x-axis at A. Draw a line OP at an angle θ to the x-axis, to meet the circle at P. Draw a perpendicular from P to meet OA at N. Let $ON = x$ units and $NP = y$ units, so that the coordinates of P are (x, y).

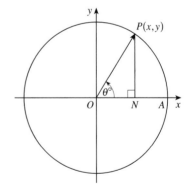

Look at triangle ONP. Using the definition
$$\cos\theta° = \frac{ON}{OP}, \text{ you find that } \cos\theta° = \frac{x}{1} = x.$$

This result, $\cos\theta° = x$, is used as the definition of $\cos\theta°$ for all values of θ.

Fig. 11.1

You can see the consequences of this definition whenever θ is a multiple of 90.

Example 11.1.1
Find the value of $\cos\theta°$ when   (a) $\theta = 180$,   (b) $\theta = 270$.

(a) When $\theta = 180$, P is the point $(-1, 0)$. As the x-coordinate of P is -1, $\cos 180° = -1$.

(b) When $\theta = 270$, P is the point $(0, -1)$, so $\cos 270° = 0$.

As θ increases, the point P moves round the circle. When $\theta = 360$, P is once again at A, and as θ becomes greater than 360, the point P moves round the circle again. It follows immediately that $\cos(\theta - 360)° = \cos\theta°$, and that the values of $\cos\theta°$ repeat themselves every time θ increases by 360.

If $\theta < 0$, the angle θ is drawn in the opposite direction, starting once again from A. Fig. 11.2 shows the angle $-150°$ drawn. Thus, if $\theta = -150$, P is in the third quadrant, and, since the x-coordinate of P is negative, $\cos(-150)°$ is negative.

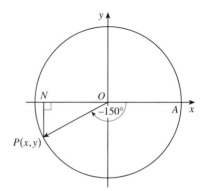

Your calculator will give you values of $\cos\theta°$ for all values of θ, and you should get it to display the graph of $\cos\theta°$, shown in Fig. 11.3.

You will have to input the equation of the graph of $\cos\theta°$ as $y = \cos x$ into your calculator, and make sure that your calculator is in degree mode.

Fig. 11.2

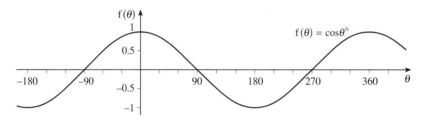

Fig. 11.3

Note that the range of the cosine function is $-1 \leqslant \cos\theta° \leqslant 1$. The maximum value of 1 is taken at $\theta = 0, \pm 360, \pm 720, \dots$, and the minimum of -1 at $\theta = \pm 180, \pm 540, \dots$.

The graph of the cosine function keeps repeating itself. Functions with this property are called **periodic**. The **period** of a periodic function is the smallest interval for which the function repeats itself, so the period of the cosine function is 360. The property that $\cos(\theta \pm 360)° = \cos\theta°$ is called the **periodic property**. Many natural phenomena have periodic properties, and the cosine is often used in applications involving them.

Example 11.1.2
The height in metres of the water in a harbour is given approximately by the formula $d = 6 + 3\cos 30t°$ where t is the time in hours from noon. Find (a) the height of the water at 9.45 p.m., and (b) the highest and lowest water levels, and when they occur.

At 9.45 p.m., $t = 9.75$, so $d = 6 + 3\cos(30 \times 9.75)° = 6 + 3\cos 292.5° = 7.148\dots$. Therefore the height of the water is 7.15 metres, correct to 3 significant figures.

The maximum value of the height occurs when the value of the cosine function is 1, and is therefore $6 + 3 \times 1 = 9$. Similarly, the minimum value is $6 + 3 \times (-1) = 3$. The maximum and minimum heights are 9 metres and 3 metres. The first times that they occur after noon are when $30t = 360$ and $30t = 180$; that is, at midnight and 6.00 p.m.

11.2 The graphs of $\sin\theta°$ and $\tan\theta°$

Using the same construction as for the cosine (see Fig. 11.1), the sine function is defined by

$$\sin\theta° = \frac{NP}{OP} = \frac{y}{1} = y.$$

Like the cosine graph, the sine graph (shown in Fig. 11.4) is periodic, with period 360. It also lies between -1 and 1 inclusive.

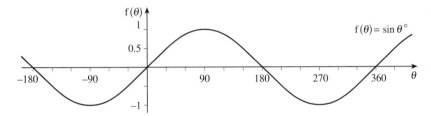

Fig. 11.4

If you return to Fig. 11.1, you will see that $\tan\theta° = \dfrac{NP}{ON} = \dfrac{y}{x}$; this is taken as the definition of $\tan\theta°$. The domain of $\tan\theta°$ does not include those angles for which x is zero, namely $\theta = \pm90, \pm270, \ldots$. Fig. 11.5 shows the graph of $\tan\theta°$.

If you draw the graph of $y = \tan x$ on your calculator for values of x from -180 to 180 you may find that the calculator puts in some incorrect near-vertical lines near -90 and 90 as it attempts to join positive and negative values of y with large moduli.

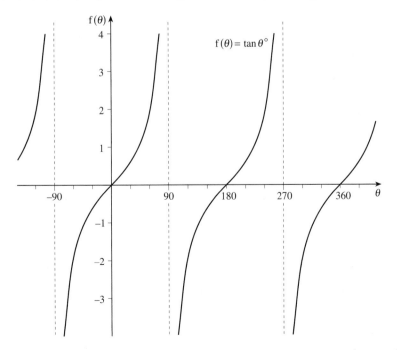

Fig. 11.5

Like the graphs of $\cos\theta°$ and $\sin\theta°$, the graph of $\tan\theta°$ is periodic, but its period is 180. Thus $\tan(\theta\pm180)° = \tan\theta°$.

As $\cos\theta° = x$, $\sin\theta° = y$ and $\tan\theta° = \dfrac{y}{x}$, it follows that $\tan\theta° = \dfrac{\sin\theta°}{\cos\theta°}$. You could use this as an alternative definition of $\tan\theta°$.

11.3 Exact values of some trigonometric ratios

There are a few angles which are a whole number of degrees and whose sines, cosines and tangents you can find exactly. The most important of these are $45°$, $60°$ and $30°$.

To find the sine, cosine and tangent of $45°$, draw a right-angled isosceles triangle of side 1 unit, as in Fig. 11.6. The length of the hypotenuse is then $\sqrt{2}$ units. Then

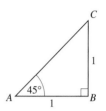

Fig. 11.6

$$\cos 45° = \frac{1}{\sqrt{2}}; \quad \sin 45° = \frac{1}{\sqrt{2}}; \quad \tan 45° = 1.$$

If you rationalise the denominators you get

$$\cos 45° = \frac{\sqrt{2}}{2}; \quad \sin 45° = \frac{\sqrt{2}}{2}; \quad \tan 45° = 1.$$

To find the sine, cosine and tangent of $60°$ and $30°$, draw an equilateral triangle of side 2 units, as in Fig. 11.7. Drop the perpendicular from one vertex, bisecting the opposite side. This perpendicular has length $\sqrt{3}$ units, and it makes an angle of $30°$ with AC. Then

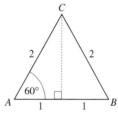

Fig. 11.7

$$\cos 60° = \frac{1}{2}; \quad \sin 60° = \frac{\sqrt{3}}{2}; \quad \tan 60° = \sqrt{3};$$

$$\cos 30° = \frac{\sqrt{3}}{2}; \quad \sin 30° = \frac{1}{2}; \quad \tan 30° = \frac{1}{\sqrt{3}} = \frac{\sqrt{3}}{3}.$$

You should learn these results, or be able to reproduce them quickly.

Exercise 11A

1 In each of the following cases find, correct to four decimal places, the values of
   (i) $\cos\theta°$,   (ii) $\sin\theta°$,   (iii) $\tan\theta°$,   for the given value of θ.

   (a) 25   (b) 125   (c) 225   (d) 325
   (e) −250   (f) 67.4   (g) 124.9   (h) 554

2 Find (i) the maximum value, and (ii) the minimum value, of each of the following functions. In each case, give the least positive value of x at which they occur.

   (a) $2+\sin x°$ (b) $7-4\cos x°$ (c) $5+8\cos 2x°$

   (d) $\dfrac{8}{3-\sin x°}$ (e) $9+\sin(4x-20)°$ (f) $\dfrac{30}{11-5\cos\left(\frac{1}{2}x-45\right)°}$

3 (Do not use a calculator for this question.) In each part of the question a trigonometric ratio of a number is given. Find all possible numbers x, $0 \leqslant x \leqslant 360$, such that the same function of x is equal to the given trigonometric ratio. For example, if the given ratio is $\sin 80°$, then $x = 100$, since $\sin 100° = \sin 80°$.

(a) $\sin 20°$ (b) $\cos 40°$ (c) $\tan 60°$ (d) $\sin 130°$

(e) $\cos 140°$ (f) $\tan 160°$ (g) $\sin 400°$ (h) $\cos(-30)°$

(i) $\tan 430°$ (j) $\sin(-260)°$ (k) $\cos(-200)°$ (l) $\tan 1000°$

4 (Do not use a calculator for this question.) In each part of the question a trigonometric ratio of a number is given. Find any numbers x, $-180 \leqslant x \leqslant 180$, such that the same function of x is equal to the given trigonometric ratio. For example, if the given ratio is $\sin 80°$, then $x = 100$, since $\sin 100° = \sin 80°$.

(a) $\sin 20°$ (b) $\cos 40°$ (c) $\tan 60°$ (d) $\sin 130°$

(e) $\cos 140°$ (f) $\tan 160°$ (g) $\sin 400°$ (h) $\cos(-30)°$

(i) $\tan 430°$ (j) $\sin(-260)°$ (k) $\cos(-200)°$ (l) $\tan 1000°$

5 Without using a calculator, write down the exact values of these trigonometric ratios.

(a) $\sin 135°$ (b) $\cos 120°$ (c) $\sin(-30)°$ (d) $\tan 240°$

(e) $\cos 225°$ (f) $\tan(-330)°$ (g) $\cos 900°$ (h) $\tan 510°$

(i) $\sin 225°$ (j) $\cos 630°$ (k) $\tan 405°$ (l) $\sin(-315)°$

(m) $\sin 210°$ (n) $\tan 675°$ (o) $\cos(-120)°$ (p) $\sin 1260°$

6 Without using a calculator, write down the smallest positive angle which satisfies the following equations.

(a) $\cos\theta° = \frac{1}{2}$ (b) $\sin\phi° = -\frac{1}{2}\sqrt{3}$ (c) $\tan\theta° = -\sqrt{3}$ (d) $\cos\theta° = \frac{1}{2}\sqrt{3}$

(e) $\tan\theta° = \frac{1}{3}\sqrt{3}$ (f) $\tan\phi° = -1$ (g) $\sin\theta° = -\frac{1}{2}$ (h) $\cos\theta° = 0$

7 Without using a calculator, write down the angle with the smallest modulus which satisfies the following equations. (If there are two such angles, choose the positive one.)

(a) $\cos\theta° = -\frac{1}{2}$ (b) $\tan\phi° = \sqrt{3}$ (c) $\sin\theta° = -1$ (d) $\cos\theta° = -1$

(e) $\sin\phi° = \frac{1}{2}\sqrt{3}$ (f) $\tan\theta° = -\frac{1}{3}\sqrt{3}$ (g) $\sin\phi° = -\frac{1}{2}\sqrt{2}$ (h) $\tan\phi° = 0$

8 The water levels in a dockyard on Humberside follow (approximately) a twelve-hour cycle, and are modelled by the equation $D = A + B\sin 30t°$, where D is the depth of water in the dock in metres, A and B are positive constants, and t is the time in hours after the start of the working day at 8 a.m.

Given that the greatest and least depths of water in the dock are 7.8 m and 2.2 m respectively, find

(a) the value of A and the value of B

(b) the depth of water in the dock at noon, giving your answer correct to the nearest cm.

11.4 Symmetry properties of the graphs of $\cos\theta°$, $\sin\theta°$ and $\tan\theta°$

If you examine the graphs of $\cos\theta°$, $\sin\theta°$, and $\tan\theta°$ you can see that they have many symmetry properties. The graph of $\cos\theta°$ is shown in Fig. 11.8.

Recall from Section 8.5 that if you translate a graph by k in the direction of the positive x-axis, the graph changes from $y = f(x)$ to $y = f(x-k)$.

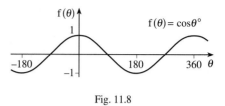

Fig. 11.8

In this case, θ is used instead of x; if you translate the graph of $\cos\theta°$ by 360 in the direction of either the positive or the negative θ-axis, you get the same graph. It follows that

$$\cos(\theta \pm 360)° = \cos\theta°.$$

If you reflect the graph of $\cos\theta°$ in the y-axis you get the same graph. Section 8.6 shows that this is produced by replacing θ by $-\theta$. Therefore

$$\cos(-\theta)° = \cos\theta°.$$

This shows that $\cos\theta°$ is an even function of θ (as defined in Section 3.3).

There are other symmetry properties. For example, if you translate the cosine graph by 180 in the direction of the positive θ-axis, you get the same result as reflecting it in the θ-axis. Therefore $y = \cos(\theta - 180)°$ is the same graph as $y = -\cos\theta°$, and

$$\cos(\theta - 180)° = -\cos\theta°,$$

which is called the translation property.

There is one more useful symmetry property. Using the even and translation properties,

$$\cos(180 - \theta)° = \cos(\theta - 180)° = -\cos\theta°.$$

You may have met this property in using the cosine formula for a triangle.

> The function $\cos\theta°$ has the following properties.
>
> Periodic property: $\cos(\theta \pm 360)° = \cos\theta°$
>
> Even property: $\cos(-\theta)° = \cos\theta°$
>
> Translation property: $\cos(\theta - 180)° = -\cos\theta°$
>
> $\cos(180 - \theta)° = -\cos\theta°$

There are similar properties for the graph of $\sin\theta°$, which is shown in Fig. 11.9. You are asked to prove them as part of Exercise 11B. Their proofs follow very similar lines to the cosine proofs.

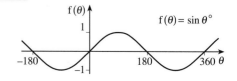

Fig. 11.9

The function $\sin\theta°$ has the following properties.

Periodic property: $\qquad \sin(\theta \pm 360)° = \sin\theta°$

Odd property: $\qquad \sin(-\theta)° = -\sin\theta°$

Translation property: $\quad \sin(\theta - 180)° = -\sin\theta°$

$\qquad\qquad\qquad\qquad \sin(180 - \theta)° = \sin\theta°$

If you refer back to the graph of $\tan\theta°$ in Fig. 11.7, and think in the same way as with the cosine and sine graphs, you can obtain similar results:

The function $\tan\theta°$ has the following properties.

Periodic property: $\qquad \tan(\theta \pm 180)° = \tan\theta°$

Odd property: $\qquad \tan(-\theta)° = -\tan\theta°$

$\qquad\qquad\qquad\qquad \tan(180 - \theta)° = -\tan\theta°$

Note that the period of the graph of $\tan\theta°$ is 180, and that the translation property of $\tan\theta°$ is the same as the periodic property.

There are also relations between $\cos\theta°$ and $\sin\theta°$. One is shown in Example 11.4.1.

Example 11.4.1

Establish the property that $\cos(90 - \theta)° = \sin\theta°$.

This is easy if $0 < \theta < 90$: consider a right-angled triangle. But it can be shown for any value of θ.

If you translate the graph of $\cos\theta°$ by 90 in the direction of the positive θ-axis, you obtain the graph of $\sin\theta°$, so $\cos(\theta - 90)° = \sin\theta°$. And since the cosine is an even function, $\cos(90 - \theta)° = \cos(\theta - 90)°$. Therefore $\cos(90 - \theta)° = \sin\theta°$.

Another example, which you are asked to prove in Exercise 11B, is $\sin(90 - \theta)° = \cos\theta°$.

Exercise 11B

1 Use the symmetric and periodic properties of the sine, cosine and tangent functions to establish the following results:

(a) $\sin(90 - \theta)° = \cos\theta°$

(b) $\sin(270 + \theta)° = -\cos\theta°$

(c) $\sin(90 + \theta)° = \cos\theta°$

(d) $\cos(90 + \theta)° = -\sin\theta°$

(e) $\tan(\theta - 180)° = \tan\theta°$

(f) $\cos(180 - \theta)° = \cos(180 + \theta)°$

(g) $\tan(360 - \theta)° = -\tan(180 + \theta)°$

(h) $\sin(-\theta - 90)° = -\cos\theta°$

2 Sketch the graphs of $y = \tan\theta°$ and $y = \dfrac{1}{\tan\theta°}$ on the same set of axes.

Deduce that $\tan(90 - \theta)° = \dfrac{1}{\tan\theta°}$.

3 In each of the following cases find the least positive value of the angle α for which

(a) $\cos(\alpha - \theta)° = \sin\theta°$,

(b) $\sin(\alpha - \theta)° = \cos(\alpha + \theta)°$,

(c) $\tan\theta° = \tan(\theta + \alpha)°$,

(d) $\sin(\theta + 2\alpha)° = \cos(\alpha - \theta)°$,

(e) $\cos(2\alpha - \theta)° = \cos(\theta - \alpha)°$,

(f) $\sin(5\alpha + \theta)° = \cos(\theta - 3\alpha)°$.

11.5 Solving equations involving the trigonometric functions

Solving the equation $\cos\theta° = k$

To solve the equation $\cos\theta° = k$, you need to assume that $-1 \leqslant k \leqslant 1$. If it does not, there is no solution. In Fig. 11.10, a negative value of k is shown. Note that, in general, there are two roots to the equation $\cos\theta° = k$ in every interval of $360°$, the exceptions being when $k = \pm 1$.

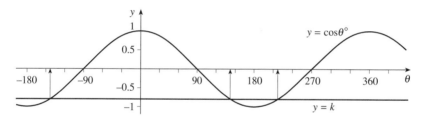

Fig. 11.10

Usually you would want to find all the roots of $\cos\theta° = k$ in a given interval (probably one of width 360). If you try using the $\cos^{-1}$ key on your calculator, you find that only one root is given. The problem then is how to find all the other roots in your required interval.

There are three steps in solving the equation of $\cos\theta° = k$.

Step 1   Find $\cos^{-1}k$.

Step 2   Use the symmetry property $\cos(-\theta)° = \cos\theta°$ to find another root.

Step 3   Use the periodic property $\cos(\theta \pm 360)° = \cos\theta°$ to find the roots in the required interval.

Example 11.5.1

Solve the equation $\cos\theta° = \frac{1}{3}$, giving all roots in the interval $0 \leqslant \theta \leqslant 360$ correct to one decimal place.

Step 1   Use your calculator to find $\cos^{-1}\frac{1}{3} = 70.52\ldots$. This is one root in the interval $0 \leqslant \theta \leqslant 360$.

Step 2   Use the symmetry property $\cos(-\theta)° = \cos\theta°$ to show that $-70.52\ldots$ is another root. Note that $-70.52\ldots$ is not in the required interval.

Step 3   Use the periodic property, $\cos(\theta \pm 360)° = \cos\theta°$, to say that $-70.52\ldots + 360 = 289.47\ldots$ is a root in the required interval.

Therefore the roots in the interval $0 \leqslant \theta \leqslant 360$ are 70.5 and 289.5, correct to one decimal place.

Example 11.5.2

Solve the equation $\cos 3\theta° = -\frac{1}{2}$, giving all the roots in the interval $-180 \leqslant \theta \leqslant 180$.

This example is similar to the previous example, except for an important extra step at the beginning, and another at the end.

Let $3\theta = \phi$. Then you have to solve the equation $\cos\phi° = -\frac{1}{2}$. But, as $3\theta = \phi$, if $-180 \leqslant \theta \leqslant 180$, then $3 \times (-180) \leqslant 3\theta \leqslant 3 \times 180$ so $-540 \leqslant \phi \leqslant 540$. So the original problem has become: solve the equation $\cos\phi° = -\frac{1}{2}$ with $-540 \leqslant \phi \leqslant 540$. (Note that you should expect six roots of the equation in this interval.)

Step 1 $\cos^{-1}\left(-\frac{1}{2}\right) = 120$.

Step 2   Another root is -120.

Step 3   Adding and subtracting multiples of 360 shows that $-120 - 360 = -480$, $-120 + 360 = 240$, $120 - 360 = -240$ and $120 + 360 = 480$ are also roots.

Therefore the roots of $\cos\phi° = -\frac{1}{2}$ in $-540 \leqslant \phi \leqslant 540$ are -480, -240, -120, 120, 240 and 480.

Returning to the original equation, and using the fact that $\theta = \frac{1}{3}\phi$, the roots are $-160, -80, -40, 40, 80$ and 160.

Solving the equation $\sin\theta° = k$

The same principles govern the solution of an equation of the form $\sin\theta° = k$, where $-1 \leqslant k \leqslant 1$. The only difference is that the symmetry property for $\sin\theta°$ is $\sin(180 - \theta)° = \sin\theta°$.

Step 1   Find $\sin^{-1}k$.

Step 2   Use the symmetry property $\sin(180 - \theta)° = \sin\theta°$ to find another root.

Step 3   Use the periodic property $\sin(\theta \pm 360)° = \sin\theta°$ to find the roots in the required interval.

Example 11.5.3

Solve the equation $\sin\theta° = -0.7$, giving all the roots in the interval $-180 \leqslant \theta \leqslant 180$ correct to one decimal place.

Step 1   Use your calculator to find $\sin^{-1}(-0.7) = -44.42\ldots$. This is one root in the interval $-180 \leqslant \theta \leqslant 180$.

Step 2   Use the symmetry property $\sin(180 - \theta)° = \sin\theta°$ to show that $180 - (-44.42\ldots) = 224.42\ldots$ is another root. Unfortunately it is not in the required interval.

Step 3   Use the periodic property, $\sin(\theta \pm 360)° = \sin\theta°$, to obtain $224.42\ldots - 360 = -135.57\ldots$, a root in the required interval.

Therefore the roots in the interval $-180 \leqslant \theta \leqslant 180$ are -44.4 and -135.6, correct to one decimal place.

Example 11.5.4

Solve the equation $\sin\frac{1}{3}(\theta - 30)° = \frac{1}{2}\sqrt{3}$, giving all the roots in the interval $0 \leqslant \theta \leqslant 360$.

Let $\frac{1}{3}(\theta - 30) = \phi$, so that the equation becomes $\sin\phi° = \frac{1}{2}\sqrt{3}$, with roots required in the interval $-10 \leqslant \phi \leqslant 110$.

Step 1 $\sin^{-1}\left(\frac{1}{2}\sqrt{3}\right) = 60$. This is one root in the interval $-10 \leqslant \phi \leqslant 110$.

Step 2   Another root is $180 - 60 = 120$, but this is not in the required interval.

Step 3   Adding and subtracting multiples of 360 will not give any more roots in the interval $-10 \leqslant \phi \leqslant 110$.

Therefore the only root of $\sin\phi° = \frac{1}{2}\sqrt{3}$ in $-10 \leqslant \phi \leqslant 110$ is 60.

Returning to the original equation, since $\theta = 3\phi + 30$, the root is $\theta = 210$.

Solving the equation $\tan\theta° = k$

The same principles govern the solution of equations of the form $\tan\theta° = k$. Note that there is generally one root for every interval of 180. Other roots can be found from the periodic property, $\tan(180 + \theta)° = \tan\theta°$. However the same principles govern the solution of $\tan\theta° = k$.

Step 1   Find $\tan^{-1}k$.

Step 2   Use the periodic property $\tan(180 + \theta)° = \tan\theta°$ to find the roots in the required interval.

Example 11.5.5

Solve the equation $\tan\theta° = -2$, giving all the roots correct to one decimal place in the interval $0 \leqslant \theta \leqslant 360$.

Step 1   Find $\tan^{-1}(-2) = -63.43\ldots$. Unfortunately, this root in not in the required interval.

Step 2   Add multiples of 180 to get roots in the required interval. This gives $116.56\ldots$ and $296.56\ldots$.

Therefore the roots of $\tan\theta° = -2$ in $0 \leqslant \theta \leqslant 360$ are 116.6 and 296.6, correct to one decimal place.

Revisiting Example 11.1.2, here is an application of solving equations of this type.

Example 11.5.6
The height in metres of the water in a harbour is given approximately by the formula $d = 6 + 3\cos 30t°$ where t is the time measured in hours from noon. Find the time after noon when the height of the water is 7.5 metres for the second time.

To find when the height is 7.5 metres, solve $6 + 3\cos 30t° = 7.5$. This gives $3\cos 30t° = 7.5 - 6 = 1.5$, or $\cos 30t° = 0.5$. After substituting $\phi = 30t$, the equation reduces to $\cos\phi° = 0.5$.

Now $\cos^{-1} 0.5 = 60$, but this gives only the first root, $t = 2$. So, using the symmetry property of the cos function, another root is -60. Adding 360 gives $\phi = 300$ as the second root of $\cos\phi° = 0.5$. Thus $30t = 300$, and $t = 10$.

The water is at height 7.5 metres for the second time at 10.00 p.m.

<hr>

Exercise 11C

1 Find, correct to 1 decimal place, the two smallest positive values of θ for which

(a) $\sin\theta° = 0.1$ (b) $\sin\theta° = -0.84$ (c) $\sin\theta° = 0.951$

(d) $\cos\theta° = 0.8$ (e) $\cos\theta° = -0.84$ (f) $\cos\theta° = \sqrt{\dfrac{2}{3}}$

(g) $\tan\theta° = 4$ (h) $\tan\theta° = -0.32$ (i) $\tan\theta° = 0.11$

(j) $\sin(180 + \theta)° = 0.4$ (k) $\cos(90 - \theta)° = -0.571$ (l) $\tan(90 - \theta)° = -3$

(m) $\sin(2\theta + 60)° = 0.3584$ (n) $\sin(30 - \theta)° = 0.5$ (o) $\cos(3\theta - 120)° = 0$

2 Find all values of θ in the interval $-180 \leqslant \theta \leqslant 180$ which satisfy each of the following equations, giving your answers correct to 1 decimal place where appropriate.

(a) $\sin\theta° = 0.8$ (b) $\cos\theta° = 0.25$ (c) $\tan\theta° = 2$

(d) $\sin\theta° = -0.67$ (e) $\cos\theta° = -0.12$ (f) $4\tan\theta° + 3 = 0$

(g) $4\sin\theta° = 5\cos\theta°$ (h) $2\sin\theta° = \dfrac{1}{\sin\theta°}$ (i) $2\sin\theta° = \tan\theta°$

3 Find all the solutions in the interval $0 < \phi \leqslant 360$ of each of the following equations.

(a) $\cos 2\phi = \dfrac{1}{3}$ (b) $\tan 3\phi = 2$ (c) $\sin 2\phi = -0.6$

(d) $\cos 4\phi = -\dfrac{1}{4}$ (e) $\tan 2\phi = 0.4$ (f) $\sin 3\phi = -0.42$

4 Find the roots in the interval $-180 \leqslant \phi \leqslant 180$ of each of the following equations.

(a) $\cos 3\phi° = \frac{2}{3}$ (b) $\tan 2\phi° = -3$ (c) $\sin 3\phi° = -0.2$

(d) $\cos 2\phi° = 0.246$ (e) $\tan 5\phi° = 0.8$ (f) $\sin 2\phi° = -0.39$

5 Find the roots (if there are any) in the interval $-180 \leqslant \theta \leqslant 180$ of the following equations.

(a) $\cos \frac{1}{2}\theta° = \frac{2}{3}$ (b) $\tan \frac{2}{3}\theta° = -3$ (c) $\sin \frac{1}{4}\theta° = -\frac{1}{4}$

(d) $\cos \frac{1}{3}\theta° = \frac{1}{3}$ (e) $\tan \frac{3}{4}\theta = 0.5$ (f) $\sin \frac{2}{5}\theta° = -0.3$

6 Without using a calculator, find the exact roots of the following equations, if there are any, giving your answers in the interval $0 < \phi \leqslant 360$.

(a) $\sin(2\phi - 30)° = \frac{1}{2}$ (b) $\tan(2\phi - 45)° = 0$ (c) $\cos(3\phi + 135)° = \frac{1}{2}\sqrt{3}$

(d) $\tan(\frac{3}{2}\phi - 45)° = -\sqrt{3}$ (e) $\cos(2\phi - 50)° = -\frac{1}{2}$ (f) $\sin(\frac{1}{2}\phi + 50)° = 1$

(g) $\cos(\frac{1}{5}\phi - 50)° = 0$ (h) $\tan(3\phi - 180)° = -1$ (i) $\sin(\frac{1}{4}\phi - 20)° = 0$

7 Find, to 1 decimal place, all values of x in the interval $-180 \leqslant \phi \leqslant 180$ satisfying

(a) $\sin \phi° = -0.16$ (b) $\cos \phi°(1 + \sin \phi°) = 0$ (c) $(1 - \tan \phi°)\sin \phi° = 0$

(d) $\sin 2\phi° = 0.23$ (e) $\cos(45 - \phi)° = 0.832$ (f) $\tan(3\phi - 17)° = 3$

8 Find all values of θ such that $0 \leqslant \theta \leqslant 360$ for which

(a) $\sin 2\theta° = \cos 36°$ (b) $\cos 5\theta° = \sin 70°$ (c) $\tan 3\theta° = \tan 60°$

9 Find all values of θ in the interval $0 \leqslant \theta \leqslant 180$, for which $2 \sin \theta° \cos \theta° = \frac{1}{2} \tan \theta°$.

10 For each of the following values of θ, give an example of a trigonometric function involving   (i) sine,   (ii) cosine,   (iii) tangent,   with period θ.

(a) $\theta = 90$ (b) $\theta = 20$ (c) $\theta = 48$

(d) $\theta = 120$ (e) $\theta = 720$ (f) $\theta = 600$

11 Sketch the graphs of each of the following in the interval $0 \leqslant \phi \leqslant 360$. In each case, state the period of the function.

(a) $y = \sin 3\phi°$ (b) $y = \cos 2\phi°$ (c) $y = \sin 4\phi°$ (d) $y = \tan \frac{1}{3}\phi°$

(e) $y = \cos \frac{1}{2}\phi°$ (f) $y = \sin(\frac{1}{2}\phi + 30)°$ (g) $y = \sin(3\phi - 20)°$ (h) $y = \tan 2\phi°$

12 At a certain latitude, the number d of hours of daylight in each day of the year is taken to be $d = A + B \sin kt°$, where A, B, k are positive constants and t is the time in days after the spring equinox.

(a) Assuming that the number of hours of daylight follows an annual cycle of 365 days, find the value of k, giving your answer correct to three decimal places.

(b) Given also that the shortest and longest days have 6 and 18 hours of daylight respectively, state the values of A and B. Find, in hours and minutes, the amount of daylight on New Year's Day, which is 80 days before the spring equinox.

(c) A town at this latitude holds a fair twice a year on those days having exactly 10 hours of daylight. Find, in relation to the spring equinox, which two days these are.

13 The road to an island close to the shore is sometimes covered by the tide. When the water rises to the level of the road, the road is closed. On a particular day, the water at high tide is a height 4.6 metres above mean sea level. The height, h metres, of the tide is modelled by using the equation $h = 4.6\cos kt°$, where t is the time in hours from high tide; it is also assumed that high tides occur every 12 hours.

(a) Determine the value of k.

(b) On the same day, a notice says that the road will be closed for 3 hours. Assuming that this notice is correct, find the height of the road above sea level, giving your answer correct to two decimal places.

(c) In fact, the road has been repaired, a process which has raised its level, and it will be impassable for only 2 hours 40 minutes. By how many centimetres has the road level been raised? (OCR)

11.6 Relations between the trigonometric functions

In algebra, you are used to solving equations, which involves finding a value of the unknown, often called x, in an equation such as $2x + 3 - x - 6 = 7$. You are also used to simplifying algebraic expressions like $2x + 3 - x - 6$, which becomes $x - 3$. You may not, however, have realised that these are quite different processes.

First, when you solve the equation $2x + 3 - x - 6 = 7$, you soon find that $x = 10$. Secondly, the expression $x - 3$ is identical to $2x + 3 - x - 6$ for all values of x. Sometimes it is important to distinguish between these two situations.

When two expressions take the same values for every value of x, they are said to be **identically** equal. This is written with the symbol $\equiv$, read as 'identically equal to'. The statement

$$2x + 3 - x - 6 \equiv x - 3$$

is called an **identity**. Thus an identity in x is an equation which is true for all values of x.

Similar ideas occur in trigonometry. At the end of Section 11.3, it was observed that $\tan\theta° = \dfrac{\sin\theta°}{\cos\theta°}$, provided, of course, that $\cos\theta° \neq 0$. Thus

$$\tan\theta° \equiv \frac{\sin\theta°}{\cos\theta°}.$$

There is another relationship which comes immediately from the definitions of $\cos\theta° = x$ and $\sin\theta° = y$ next to Fig. 11.1. As P lies on the circumference of a circle with radius 1 unit, Pythagoras' theorem gives $x^2 + y^2 = 1$, or $(\cos\theta°)^2 + (\sin\theta°)^2 \equiv 1$.

Conventionally, $(\cos\theta°)^2$ is written as $\cos^2\theta°$ and $(\sin\theta°)^2$ is written as $\sin^2\theta°$. Therefore $\cos^2\theta° + \sin^2\theta° \equiv 1$ for all values of θ. This is sometimes called Pythagoras' theorem in trigonometry.

For all values of θ:

$$\tan\theta° \equiv \frac{\sin\theta°}{\cos\theta°}, \quad \text{provided that } \cos\theta° \neq 0;$$

$$\cos^2\theta° + \sin^2\theta° \equiv 1.$$

There is the possibility of ambiguity in writing powers of $\cos\theta°$ and $\sin\theta°$ in this way, because $\cos^{-1}\theta$ might mean the angle whose cosine is θ. The way round this is never to write $\cos\theta°$ and $\sin\theta°$ to a negative power using this convention. If in doubt, you should write $(\cos\theta°)^2$ or $(\cos\theta°)^{-2}$ which is never ambiguous.

You can use the relation $\cos^2\theta° + \sin^2\theta° \equiv 1$ in the process of proving the cosine formula for a triangle.

Let ABC be a triangle, with sides $BC = a$, $CA = b$ and $AB = c$. Place the point A at the origin, and let AC lie along the x-axis in the positive x-direction, shown in Fig. 11.11.

The coordinates of C are $(b, 0)$, and those of B are $(c\cos A°, c\sin A°)$, where A stands for the angle BAC. Then the length BC equals a, so by using the distance formula

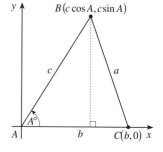

Fig. 11.11

$$a^2 = (b - c\cos A°)^2 + (c\sin A°)^2$$
$$= c^2\cos^2 A° - 2bc\cos A° + b^2 + c^2\sin^2 A°$$
$$= b^2 + c^2\left(\cos^2 A° + \sin^2 A°\right) - 2bc\cos A°$$
$$= b^2 + c^2 - 2bc\cos A°,$$

using $\cos^2 A° + \sin^2 A° \equiv 1$ at the end.

Example 11.6.1
Given that $\sin\theta° = \frac{3}{5}$, and that the angle $\theta°$ is obtuse, find, without using tables, the values of $\cos\theta°$ and $\tan\theta°$.

Since $\cos^2\theta° + \sin^2\theta° \equiv 1$, $\cos^2\theta° = 1 - \left(\frac{3}{5}\right)^2 = \frac{16}{25}$ giving $\cos\theta° = \pm\frac{4}{5}$. As the angle $\theta°$ is obtuse, $90 < \theta < 180$, so $\cos\theta°$ is negative. Therefore $\cos\theta° = -\frac{4}{5}$.

As $\sin\theta° = \frac{3}{5}$ and $\cos\theta° = -\frac{4}{5}$, $\tan\theta° = \frac{\sin\theta°}{\cos\theta°} = \frac{3/5}{-4/5} = -\frac{3}{4}$.

Example 11.6.2
Solve the equation $3\cos^2\theta° + 4\sin\theta° = 4$, giving all the roots in the interval $-180 < \theta \leqslant 180$ correct to one decimal place.

As it stands you cannot solve this equation, but if you write $\cos^2\theta° \equiv 1 - \sin^2\theta°$ you will obtain the equation $3(1 - \sin^2\theta°) + 4\sin\theta° = 4$, which reduces to

$$3\sin^2\theta° - 4\sin\theta° + 1 = 0.$$

This is a quadratic equation in $\sin\theta°$, which you can solve using factors:

$$(3\sin\theta° - 1)(\sin\theta° - 1) = 0, \text{ giving } \sin\theta° = \tfrac{1}{3} \text{ and } \sin\theta° = 1.$$

One root is $\sin^{-1}\tfrac{1}{3} = 19.47\ldots$, and the other root, obtained from the symmetry of $\sin\theta°$, is $(180 - 19.47\ldots) = 160.52\ldots$.

The only root for $\sin\theta° = 1$ is $\theta = 90$, so the roots are 19.5, 90 and 160.5, correct to one decimal place.

Exercise 11D

1 For each triangle sketched below,

   (i) use Pythagoras' theorem to find the length of the third side in an exact form;

   (ii) write down the exact values of $\sin\theta°$, $\cos\theta°$ and $\tan\theta°$.

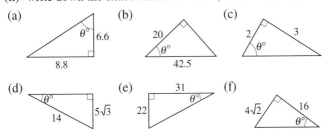

2 (a) Given that angle A is obtuse and that $\sin A° = \tfrac{5}{14}\sqrt{3}$, find the exact value of $\cos A°$.

   (b) Given that $180 < B < 360$ and that $\tan B° = -\tfrac{21}{20}$, find the exact value of $\cos B°$.

   (c) Find all possible values of $\sin C°$ for which $\cos C° = \tfrac{1}{2}$.

   (d) Find the values of D for which $-180 < D < 180$ and $\tan D° = 5\sin D°$.

3 Use $\tan\theta° \equiv \dfrac{\sin\theta°}{\cos\theta°}$, $\cos\theta° \neq 0$, and $\cos^2\theta° + \sin^2\theta° \equiv 1$ to establish the following:

   (a) $\dfrac{1}{\sin\theta°} - \dfrac{1}{\tan\theta°} \equiv \dfrac{1 - \cos\theta°}{\sin\theta°}$

   (b) $\dfrac{\sin^2\theta°}{1 - \cos\theta°} \equiv 1 + \cos\theta°$

   (c) $\dfrac{1}{\cos\theta°} + \tan\theta° \equiv \dfrac{\cos\theta°}{1 - \sin\theta°}$

   (d) $\dfrac{\tan\theta°\sin\theta°}{1 - \cos\theta°} \equiv 1 + \dfrac{1}{\cos\theta°}$

4 Solve the following equations for θ, giving all the roots in the interval $0 \leqslant \theta \leqslant 360$ correct to the nearest 0.1.

   (a) $4\sin^2\theta° - 1 = 0$

   (b) $\sin^2\theta° + 2\cos^2\theta° = 2$

   (c) $10\sin^2\theta° - 5\cos^2\theta° + 2 = 4\sin\theta°$

   (d) $4\sin^2\theta°\cos\theta° = \tan^2\theta°$

5 Find all values of θ, $-180 < \theta < 180$, for which $2\tan\theta° - 3 = \dfrac{2}{\tan\theta°}$.

Miscellaneous exercise 11

1 Write down the period of each of the following.

   (a) $\sin x°$ (b) $\tan 2x°$ (OCR)

2 By considering the graph of $y = \cos x°$, or otherwise, express the following in terms of $\cos x°$.

   (a) $\cos(360 - x)°$ (b) $\cos(x + 180)°$ (OCR)

3 Draw the graph of $y = \cos \frac{1}{2}\theta°$ for θ in the interval $-360 \le \theta \le 360$. Mark clearly the coordinates of the points where the graph crosses the θ- and y-axes.

4 Solve the following equations for θ, giving your answers in the interval $0 \le \theta \le 360$.

   (a) $\tan \theta° = 0.4$ (b) $\sin 2\theta° = 0.4$ (OCR)

5 Solve the equation $3\cos 2x° = 2$, giving all the solutions in the interval $0 \le x \le 180$ correct to the nearest 0.1.   (OCR)

6 (a) Give an example of a trigonometric function which has a period of 180.

   (b) Solve for x the equation $\sin 3x° = 0.5$, giving all solutions in the interval $0 < x < 180$.

                                                                     (OCR)

7 Find all values of $\theta°$, $0 \le \theta \le 360$, for which $2\cos(\theta + 30)° = 1$.   (OCR)

8 (a) Express $\sin 2x° + \cos(90 - 2x)°$ in terms of a single trigonometric function.

   (b) Hence, or otherwise, find all values of x in the interval $0 \le x \le 360$ for which

      $\sin 2x° + \cos(90 - 2x)° = -1$.   (OCR)

9 Find the least positive value of the angle A for which

   (a) $\sin A° = 0.2$ and $\cos A°$ is negative;   (b) $\tan A° = -0.5$ and $\sin A°$ is negative;

   (c) $\cos A° = \sin A°$ and both are negative;   (d) $\sin A° = -0.2275$ and $A > 360$.

10 Prove the following identities.

   (a) $\dfrac{1}{\sin \theta°} - \sin \theta° \equiv \dfrac{\cos \theta°}{\tan \theta°}$ (b) $\dfrac{1 - \sin \theta°}{\cos \theta°} \equiv \dfrac{\cos \theta°}{1 + \sin \theta°}$

   (c) $\dfrac{1}{\tan \theta°} + \tan \theta° \equiv \dfrac{1}{\sin \theta° \cos \theta°}$ (d) $\dfrac{1 - 2\sin^2 \theta°}{\cos \theta° + \sin \theta°} \equiv \cos \theta° - \sin \theta°$

11 For each of the following functions, determine the maximum and minimum values of y and the least positive values of x at which these occur.

   (a) $y = 1 + \cos 2x°$ (b) $y = 5 - 4\sin(x + 30)°$

   (c) $y = 29 - 20\sin(3x - 45)°$ (d) $y = 8 - 3\cos^2 x°$

   (e) $y = \dfrac{12}{3 + \cos x°}$ (f) $y = \dfrac{60}{1 + \sin^2(2x - 15)°}$

12 Solve the following equation for θ, giving solutions in the interval $0 \le \theta \le 360$.

   (a) $\sin \theta° = \tan \theta°$ (b) $2 - 2\cos^2 \theta° = \sin \theta°$

   (c) $\tan^2 \theta° - 2\tan \theta° = 1$ (d) $\sin 2\theta° - \sqrt{3}\cos 2\theta° = 0$

13 The function t is defined by $t(x) = \tan 3x°$.

   (a) State the period of $t(x)$.   (b) Solve the equation $t(x) = \frac{1}{2}$ for $0 \leqslant x \leqslant 180$.

   (c) Deduce the smallest positive solution of each of the following equations.

      (i) $t(x) = -\frac{1}{2}$ (ii) $t(x) = 2$ (OCR)

14 (a) Describe geometrically the transformations which map

      (i) the graph of $y = \cos x°$ onto the graph of $y = 4\cos x°$;

      (ii) the graph of $y = 4\cos x°$ onto the graph of $y = 4\cos x° - 3$.

   (b) (i) On a single diagram, sketch the graphs of $y = \tan x°$ and $y = 4\cos x° - 3$ for $0 \leqslant x \leqslant 180$.

      (ii) Deduce the number of solutions of the equation $f(x) = 0$ which exist for $0 \leqslant x \leqslant 180$, where $f(x) = 3 + \tan x° - 4\cos x°$.   (OCR)

15 In each of the following, construct a formula involving a trigonometric function which could be used to model the situations described.

   (a) water depths in a canal which vary between a minimum of 3.6 m and a maximum of 6 m over 24-hour periods

   (b) a 10-day cycle of petroleum refining at a chemical plant, with a minimum production of 15 000 barrels per day and a maximum of 28 000 barrels per day

   (c) the number of hours of daylight at a point on the Earth which has between 2 and 22 hours of daylight during a 360-day year

16 The population, P, of a certain type of bird on a remote Scottish island varies during the course of a year according to feeding, breeding, migratory seasons and predator-interactions. An ornithologist doing research into bird numbers for this species attempts to model the population on the island with the annually periodic equation

$$P = N - C\cos \omega t°,$$

where N, C and ω are constants, and t is the time in weeks, with $t = 0$ representing midnight on the first of January.

   (a) Taking the period of this function to be 50 weeks, find the value of ω.

   (b) Use this formula to describe, in terms of N and C,

      (i) the number of birds of this species on the island at the start of each year;

      (ii) the maximum number of these birds, and the time of year when this occurs.

17 A simple model of the tides in a harbour on the south coast of Cornwall assumes that they are caused by the attractions of the sun and the moon. The magnitude of the attraction of the moon is assumed to be nine times the magnitude of the attraction of the sun. The period of the sun's effect is taken to be 360 days and that of the moon is 30 days. A model for the height, h metres, of the tide (relative to a mark fixed on the harbour wall), at t days, is

$$h = A\cos \alpha t° + B\cos \beta t°,$$

where the term $A\cos \alpha t°$ is the effect due to the sun, and the term $B\cos \beta t°$ is the effect due to the moon. Given that $h = 5$ when $t = 0$, determine the values of A, B, α and β.

                                             (OCR, adapted)

12 Second derivatives

This chapter extends the idea of differentiation further. When you have completed it, you should

- understand the significance of the second derivative for the shape of graphs and in real-world applications
- be able to use second derivatives where appropriate to distinguish minimum and maximum points
- understand that at a point of inflexion the second derivative is zero.

12.1 Interpreting and sketching graphs

The results in Chapter 9, linking features of the graph of a function with values of the derivative, were restricted to functions which are continuous within their domains. These results used the idea that the derivative doesn't just measure the gradient at a particular point of a graph, but could itself be regarded as a function.

In this chapter a further restriction needs to be made, to functions which are 'smooth'; that is, those whose graphs do not have sudden changes of direction. This means that, with a function such as $x^{\frac{2}{3}}(1-x)$ (from Example 9.1.3), you must exclude the 'awkward' point (the origin in this example) from the domain.

The 'smooth' condition means that the derivative, considered as a function, is continuous and can itself be differentiated. The result is called the **second derivative** of the function, and it is denoted by $f''(x)$. It is sometimes called the 'second order derivative'. If you are using the $\dfrac{dy}{dx}$ notation, the second derivative is written as $\dfrac{d^2y}{dx^2}$. (The reason for this rather curious symbol is explained in Section 12.5.)

Example 12.1.1
In the graph of $y = f(x) = x^3 - 3x^2$, identify the intervals in which $f(x)$, $f'(x)$ and $f''(x)$ are positive, and interpret these graphically.

$$\frac{dy}{dx} = f'(x) = 3x^2 - 6x, \quad \text{and} \quad \frac{d^2y}{dx^2} = f''(x) = 6x - 6.$$

Fig. 12.1 shows the graphs of the function and its first and second derivatives.

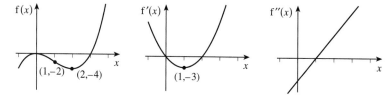

Fig. 12.1

Notice first that $f(x) = x^2(x-3)$, so that $f(x) > 0$ when $x > 3$. These are the values of x for which the graph of $f(x)$ (on the left) lies above the x-axis.

Since $f'(x) = 3x(x-2)$, $f'(x) > 0$ when $x < 0$ or $x > 2$. In the graph of $f(x)$, the gradient is positive in these intervals, so that $f(x)$ is increasing.

Lastly, $f''(x) = 6(x-1)$, so that $f''(x) > 0$ when $x > 1$. It appears that this is the interval in which the graph of $f(x)$ can be described as bending upwards.

To make this idea of 'bending upwards' more precise, it is helpful to use the letter g to denote the gradient of the graph on the left of Fig. 12.1, so that $g = f'(x)$. Then $f''(x) = \dfrac{dg}{dx}$, which is the rate of change of the gradient with respect to x. In an interval where $f''(x) > 0$, the gradient increases as x increases.

This can be seen in the middle graph of Fig. 12.1, which is a quadratic graph with its vertex at $(1, -3)$. So the gradient of the graph on the left increases from a value of -3 at the point $(1, -2)$, through zero at the minimum point $(2, -4)$ and then becomes positive and continues to increase when $x > 2$.

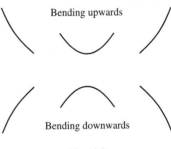

Fig. 12.2 shows three curves which would be described as bending upwards, for which $f''(x) > 0$, and three bending downwards for which $f''(x) < 0$. The important thing to notice is that this property does not depend on the sign of the gradient. A curve can bend upwards whether its gradient is positive, negative or zero.

Bending upwards

Bending downwards

Fig. 12.2

Example 12.1.2

Investigate the graph of $y = f(x)$, where $f(x) = \dfrac{1}{x} - \dfrac{1}{x^2}$ with domain $x > 0$.

You can write $f(x)$ either as $\dfrac{x-1}{x^2}$ or, with negative indices, as $x^{-1} - x^{-2}$. So

$$f'(x) = -x^{-2} + 2x^{-3} = -\frac{1}{x^2} + \frac{2}{x^3} = \frac{-x+2}{x^3},$$

and $\quad f''(x) = 2x^{-3} - 6x^{-4} = \dfrac{2}{x^3} - \dfrac{6}{x^4} = \dfrac{2(x-3)}{x^4}.$

It follows that, in the given domain,

$f(x) < 0$ for $x < 1$ $\quad$ and $\quad$ $f(x) > 0$ for $x > 1$;

$f'(x) > 0$ for $x < 2$ $\quad$ and $\quad$ $f'(x) < 0$ for $x > 2$;

$f''(x) < 0$ for $x < 3$ $\quad$ and $\quad$ $f''(x) > 0$ for $x > 3$.

So the graph lies below the x-axis when $0 < x < 1$ and above it when $x > 1$, crossing the axis at $(1, 0)$. It has positive gradient when $0 < x < 2$ and negative gradient for $x > 2$, with a maximum point at $\left(2, \frac{1}{4}\right)$. And the graph bends downwards for $0 < x < 3$ and upwards for $x > 3$.

This is enough information to give a good idea of the shape of the graph for values of x in an interval covering the critical values $x = 1$, 2 and 3, but to complete the investigation it would be helpful to know more about the graph for very small and very large values of x. This suggests calculating, say,

$$\text{f}(0.01) = 100 - 10000 = -9900 \quad \text{and} \quad \text{f}(100) = 0.01 - 0.0001 = 0.0099.$$

So when x is small, y is a negative number with large modulus; and when x is large, y is a small positive number.

Try to sketch the graph for yourself using the information found in the example, then check your sketch with a graphic calculator.

The skill in sketching a graph is to work out the coordinates of only those points where something significant occurs. Example 12.1.2 draws attention to the point $(1,0)$, where the graph crosses the x-axis, and to the maximum point $\left(2, \frac{1}{4}\right)$. Another interesting point is $\left(3, \frac{2}{9}\right)$, where the graph changes from bending downwards to bending upwards. Notice that $\text{f}''(x)$ changes from $-$ to $+$ at this point, and that $\text{f}''(3) = 0$.

> A point of a graph which separates a part of the curve which bends one way from a part which bends the other way is called a **point of inflexion** of the graph. If $(p, \text{f}(p))$ is a point of inflexion of the graph of a smooth function, $\text{f}''(p) = 0$.

12.2 Second derivatives in practice

There are many real-world situations in which second derivatives are important, because they give advance warning of future trends.

For example, the number of UK households possessing a computer has been increasing for a long time. Manufacturers will estimate the number of such households, H, in year t, and note that the graph of H against t has a positive gradient $\dfrac{\text{d}H}{\text{d}t}$. But to plan ahead they need to know whether this rate of increase is itself increasing (so that they should increase production of models for first-time users) or decreasing (in which case they might target existing customers to update to more sophisticated equipment). So it is the value of $\dfrac{\text{d}^2 H}{\text{d}t^2}$ which affects strategic planning decisions.

Similarly, a weather forecaster observing the pressure p at time t may not be too concerned if $\dfrac{\text{d}p}{\text{d}t}$ is negative; but if she also notices that $\dfrac{\text{d}^2 p}{\text{d}t^2}$ is negative, it may be time to issue a warning of severe weather.

Exercise 12A

In this exercise you should try to sketch the graphs using information about the first and second derivatives. When you have drawn your sketch, check it from a graphic calculator or computer display.

1 Consider the graph of $y = f(x)$ where $f(x) = x^3 - x$.

   (a) Use the fact that $f(x) = x(x^2 - 1) = x(x-1)(x+1)$ to find where the graph cuts the x-axis and hence sketch the graph.

   (b) Find $f'(x)$ and sketch the graph of $y = f'(x)$.

   (c) Find $f''(x)$ and sketch the graph of $y = f''(x)$.

   (d) Check the consistency of your sketches: for example, check that the graph of $y = f(x)$ is bending upwards where $f''(x) \geq 0$.

2 For the graph of $y = x^3 + x$

   (a) use factors to show that the graph crosses the x-axis once only;

   (b) find $\dfrac{dy}{dx}$ and $\dfrac{d^2y}{dx^2}$;

   (c) find the intervals in which the graph is bending upwards;

   (d) use the information gained to sketch the graph of $y = x^3 + x$;

   (e) check your work using a graphic calculator or a computer.

3 Use information about $f'(x)$ and $f''(x)$ to sketch the graph of $y = f(x)$, where $f(x) = x^3 - 3x^2 + 3x - 9$. (Note that $x^3 - 3x^2 + 3x - 9 = (x-3)(x^2 + 3)$.)

4 Sketch the graphs of the following, giving the coordinates of any points at which

   (i) $\dfrac{dy}{dx} = 0$ (ii) $\dfrac{d^2y}{dx^2} = 0$.

   Use a graphic calculator or computer to check your answers.

   (a) $y = x^4 - 4x^2$ (b) $y = x^3 + x^2$ (c) $y = x + \dfrac{1}{x}$

   (d) $y = x - \dfrac{1}{x}$ (e) $y = x + \dfrac{4}{x^2}$ (f) $y = x - \dfrac{4}{x^2}$

5 (a) This graph shows prices (P) plotted against time (t).

      The rate of inflation, measured by $\dfrac{dP}{dt}$, is increasing. What does $\dfrac{d^2P}{dt^2}$ represent and what can be said about its value?

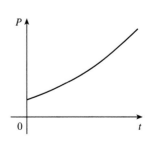

   (b) Sketch a graph showing that prices are increasing but that the rate of inflation is slowing down with an overall increase tending to 20%.

6 Write down the signs of $f'(x)$ and $f''(x)$ for the following graphs of $y = f(x)$. In parts (e) and (f) you will need to state the relevant intervals.

(a)

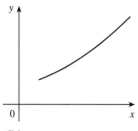

(b)

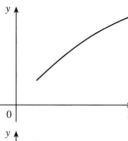

(c)

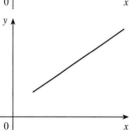

(d)

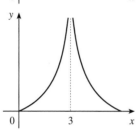

(e)

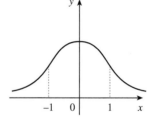

(f)

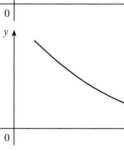

7 The graph shows the price S of shares in a certain company.

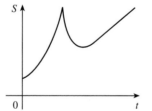

(a) For each stage of the graph comment on $\dfrac{dS}{dt}$ and $\dfrac{d^2S}{dt^2}$.

(b) Describe what happened in non-technical language.

8 Colin sets off for school, which is 800 m from home. His speed is proportional to the distance he still has to go. Let x metres be the distance he has gone, and y metres be the distance that he still has to go.

(a) Sketch graphs of x against t and y against t.

(b) What are the signs of $\dfrac{dx}{dt}$, $\dfrac{d^2x}{dt^2}$, $\dfrac{dy}{dt}$ and $\dfrac{d^2y}{dt^2}$?

9 The rate of decay of a radioactive substance is proportional to the number, N, of radioactive atoms present at time t.

(a) Write an equation representing this information.

(b) Sketch a graph of N against t.

(c) What is the sign of $\dfrac{d^2N}{dt^2}$?

10 Sketch segments of graphs of $y = f(x)$ in each of the following cases.

(For example, in part (a), you can only sketch the graph near the y-axis because you have no information for other values of x.)

(a) $f(0) = 3$, $\quad f'(0) = 2$, $\quad f''(0) = 1$ $\qquad$ (b) $f(5) = -2$, $\quad f'(5) = -2$, $\quad f''(5) = -2$

(c) $f(0) = -3$, $\quad f'(0) = 0$, $\quad f''(0) = 3$

12.3 Minima and maxima revisited

In the last exercise you will sometimes have found that different pieces of information reinforce each other. This is especially true at points where a graph has a minimum or maximum. If you have identified a minimum from changes in the sign of $f'(x)$, you will also have found from $f''(x)$ that the graph is bending upwards.

The curves on the right of Fig. 12.2 suggest a general result:

> If $f'(q) = 0$ and $f''(q) > 0$, then $f(x)$ has a minimum at $x = q$.
>
> If $f'(q) = 0$ and $f''(q) < 0$, then $f(x)$ has a maximum at $x = q$.

It is often simpler to use this instead of considering the change in sign of $f'(x)$ to decide whether a point on a graph is a minimum or a maximum. The procedures described in Section 9.2 can then be amended as follows.

> To find the minimum and maximum points on the graph of $y = f(x)$:
>
> **Step 1** Decide the domain in which you are interested.
>
> **Step 2** Find an expression for $f'(x)$.
>
> **Step 3** List the values of x in the domain for which $f'(x)$ is 0.
> (If there are values where $f'(x)$ is undefined, use the old procedure.)
>
> **Step 4** Find an expression for $f''(x)$.
>
> **Step 5** For each value of x in Step 3, find the sign of $f''(x)$. If the sign is +, the graph has a minimum point; if –, a maximum.
> (If the value of $f''(x)$ is 0, follow the old procedure.)
>
> **Step 6** For each value of x giving a minimum or maximum, calculate $f(x)$.

Notice that there are two ways in which this procedure can break down.

Firstly, the method only works for the graphs of smooth functions, so that it does not apply at points where $f'(x)$ is undefined.

Secondly, if $f'(q) = 0$ and $f''(q) = 0$, it is possible for $f(x)$ to have a minimum, or a maximum, or neither, at $x = q$. This can be shown by comparing $f(x) = x^3$ with

$g(x) = x^4$ at $x = 0$. You can easily check that $f'(0) = f''(0) = 0$ and that $g'(0) = g''(0) = 0$. But $g(x)$ has a minimum at $x = 0$, whereas $f(x)$ has neither a minimum nor a maximum. (In fact the graph of $y = f(x)$ has a point of inflexion at the origin, since $f''(x) = 6x$, which is negative when $x < 0$ and positive when $x > 0$.)

You will also find later on that for some functions it can be very laborious to find the second derivative. In that case, it is more efficient to use the old procedure. But this will not apply to any of the functions you have met so far.

Example 12.3.1

Find the minimum and maximum points on the graph of $f(x) = x^4 + x^5$.

Step 1   The function is defined for all real numbers.

Step 2 $f'(x) = 4x^3 + 5x^4 = x^3(4 + 5x)$.

Step 3 $f'(x) = 0$ when $x = 0$ or $x = -0.8$.

Step 4 $f''(x) = 12x^2 + 20x^3 = 4x^2(3 + 5x)$.

Step 5 $f''(-0.8) = 4 \times (-0.8)^2 \times (3 - 4) < 0$, so $x = -0.8$ gives a maximum.

$f''(0) = 0$, so revert to the old procedure. For $-0.8 < x < 0$, $x^3 < 0$ and $4 + 5x > 0$, so $f'(x) < 0$; for $x > 0$, $f'(x) > 0$. So $x = 0$ gives a minimum.

Step 6   The maximum point is $(-0.8, 0.08192)$; the minimum point is $(0, 0)$.

Example 12.3.2

Find the minimum and maximum points on the graph of $y = \dfrac{(x+1)^2}{x}$.

The function is defined for all real numbers except 0.

To differentiate, write $\dfrac{(x+1)^2}{x}$ as $\dfrac{x^2 + 2x + 1}{x} = x + 2 + x^{-1}$.

Then $\dfrac{dy}{dx} = 1 - x^{-2} = 1 - \dfrac{1}{x^2} = \dfrac{x^2 - 1}{x^2}$, so $\dfrac{dy}{dx} = 0$ gives $x^2 - 1 = 0$, or $x = \pm 1$.

The second derivative is $\dfrac{d^2 y}{dx^2} = 2x^{-3} = \dfrac{2}{x^3}$. This has values -2 when $x = -1$, and 2 when $x = 1$. So $(-1, 0)$ is a maximum point and $(1, 4)$ is a minimum point.

Note that the minimum value is greater than the maximum value. How can this happen?

Exercise 12B

Use first and second derivatives to locate and describe the stationary points on the graphs of the following functions and equations. If this method fails then you should use the change of sign of $\dfrac{dy}{dx}$ or $f'(x)$ to distinguish maxima, minima and points of inflexion.

1 (a) $f(x) = 3x - x^3$

(b) $f(x) = x^3 - 3x^2$

(c) $f(x) = 3x^4 + 1$

(d) $f(x) = 2x^3 - 3x^2 - 12x + 4$

(e) $f(x) = \dfrac{2}{x^4} - \dfrac{1}{x}$

(f) $f(x) = x^2 + \dfrac{1}{x^2}$

(g) $f(x) = \dfrac{1}{x} - \dfrac{1}{x^2}$

(h) $f(x) = 2x^3 - 12x^2 + 24x + 6$

2 (a) $y = 3x^4 - 4x^3 - 12x^2 - 3$

(b) $y = x^3 - 3x^2 + 3x + 5$

(c) $y = 16x - 3x^3$

(d) $y = \dfrac{4}{x^2} - x$

(e) $y = \dfrac{4 + x^2}{x}$

(f) $y = \dfrac{x - 3}{x^2}$

(g) $y = 2x^5 - 7$

(h) $y = 3x^4 - 8x^3 + 6x^2 + 1$

12.4 Logical distinctions

You have seen that, for the graphs of smooth functions, it is true that

> if $(q, f(q))$ is a minimum or maximum point, then $f'(q) = 0$;

but the **converse** statement, that

> if $f'(q) = 0$, then $(q, f(q))$ is a minimum or maximum point,

is false.

This can be shown by finding a **counterexample**; that is, an example of a function for which the 'if …' part of the statement holds, but the 'then …' part does not.

Such a function is $f(x) = x^3$ with $q = 0$. Since $f'(x) = 3x^2$, $f'(0) = 0$, but $(0,0)$ is not a minimum or maximum point of the graph of $y = x^3$.

A similar situation arises with points of inflexion. For the graphs of smooth functions it is true that

> if $(p, f(p))$ is a point of inflexion, then $f''(p) = 0$;

but the converse, that

> if $f''(p) = 0$, then $(p, f(p))$ is a point of inflexion,

is false.

A suitable counterexample in this case is $f(x) = x^4$ with $x = 0$. Since $f''(x) = 12x^2$, $f''(0) = 0$, but $(0,0)$ is a minimum point on the graph of $y = x^4$, not a point of inflexion.

Much of advanced mathematics involves applying general theorems to particular functions. There are many theorems (such as Pythagoras' theorem) whose converses are also true. But if, as in the examples above, the converse of a theorem is false, it is very important to be sure that you are applying the (true) theorem rather than its (false) converse.

12.5 Extending $\dfrac{dy}{dx}$ notation

Although $\dfrac{dy}{dx}$ is a symbol which should not be split into smaller bits, it can usefully be adapted by separating off the y, as

$$\frac{d}{dx}y$$

so that if $y = f(x)$, you can write

$$f'(x) = \frac{d}{dx}f(x).$$

This can be used as a convenient shorthand. For example, instead of having to write

$$\text{if } y = x^4 \text{ then } \frac{dy}{dx} = 4x^3$$

you can abbreviate this to

$$\frac{d}{dx}x^4 = 4x^3.$$

In this equation $\dfrac{d}{dx}$ can be thought of as an instruction to differentiate whatever comes after it.

You may have seen calculators which do algebra as well as arithmetic. With these, you can input a function such as x^4, key in 'differentiate', and the output $4x^3$ appears in the display. The symbol $\dfrac{d}{dx}$, sometimes called the **differential operator**, is the equivalent of pressing the 'differentiate' key.

This explains the notation used for the second derivative, which is what you get by differentiating $\dfrac{dy}{dx}$; that is,

$$\frac{d}{dx}\frac{dy}{dx}.$$

If you collect the elements of this expression into a single symbol, the top line becomes d^2y, and the bottom line $(dx)^2$. Dropping the brackets, this takes the form

$$\frac{d^2y}{dx^2}.$$

12.6* Higher derivatives

There is no reason to stop at the second derivative. Since $\dfrac{d^2y}{dx^2}$ is also a function, provided it is smooth, it can be differentiated to give a third derivative; and the process can continue indefinitely, giving a whole sequence of higher derivatives

$$\frac{d^3y}{dx^3}, \frac{d^4y}{dx^4}, \frac{d^5y}{dx^5}, \dots$$

In function notation these are written as

$$\mathrm{f}'''(x), \ \mathrm{f}^{(4)}(x), \ \mathrm{f}^{(5)}(x), \ ....$$

Notice that, from the fourth derivative onwards, the dashes are replaced by a small numeral in brackets.

These further derivatives do not often have useful interpretations in graph sketching or in real-world applications. But you will find later in the course that they are important in finding approximations and for expressing functions in series form.

Exercise 12C*

1 Find $\dfrac{dy}{dx}, \ \dfrac{d^2y}{dx^2}, \ \dfrac{d^3y}{dx^3}$ and $\dfrac{d^4y}{dx^4}$ for the following.

(a) $y = x^2 + 3x - 7$ (b) $y = 2x^3 + x + \dfrac{1}{x}$ (c) $y = x^4 - 2$

(d) $y = \sqrt{x}$ (e) $y = \dfrac{1}{\sqrt{x}}$ (f) $y = x^{\frac{1}{4}}$

2 Find $\mathrm{f}'(x)$, $\mathrm{f}''(x)$, $\mathrm{f}'''(x)$ and $\mathrm{f}^{(4)}(x)$ for the following.

(a) $\mathrm{f}(x) = x^2 - 5x + 2$ (b) $\mathrm{f}(x) = 2x^5 - 3x^2$ (c) $\mathrm{f}(x) = \dfrac{1}{x^4}$

(d) $\mathrm{f}(x) = x^2\left(3 - x^4\right)$ (e) $\mathrm{f}(x) = x^{\frac{3}{4}}$ (f) $\mathrm{f}(x) = x^{\frac{3}{8}}$

3 Find $\dfrac{d^n y}{dx^n}$ for $y = x^n$ in the case where n is a positive integer.

4 Find an expression for $\dfrac{d^n y}{dx^n}$ for $y = x^{n+2}$ where n is a positive integer.

5 Find $\dfrac{d^n y}{dx^n}$ where $y = x^m$ in the case where m is a positive integer and $n > m$.

Miscellaneous exercise 12

1 Give sketches of possible graphs for which the following data hold. Consider only the domain $0 \leqslant x \leqslant 5$, and assume that the graph of $y = \mathrm{f}''(x)$ is smooth.

(a) $\mathrm{f}(0) = 0$, $\mathrm{f}(2) = 5$, $\mathrm{f}'(2) = 0$, $\mathrm{f}''(2) < 0$, $\mathrm{f}(4) = 3$, $\mathrm{f}'(4) = 0$, $\mathrm{f}''(4) > 0$

(b) $\mathrm{f}(0) = 0$, $\mathrm{f}''(1) < 0$, $\mathrm{f}(2) = 5$, $\mathrm{f}'(2) = 0$, $\mathrm{f}''(3) > 0$, $\mathrm{f}(4) = 7$

(c) $\mathrm{f}(0) = 0$, $\mathrm{f}'(0) = -1$, $\mathrm{f}'(1) = 0$, $\mathrm{f}(3) = 0$, $\mathrm{f}'(3) = 2$, $\mathrm{f}''(3) = 0$, $\mathrm{f}''(4) < 0$

(d) $\mathrm{f}(0) = 1$, $\mathrm{f}'(0) = 1$, $\mathrm{f}''(0) = 1$ and $\mathrm{f}''(x)$ increases as x increases

(e) $\mathrm{f}(0) = 1$, $\mathrm{f}'(0) = 0$, $\mathrm{f}'(x) < 0$ for $0 < x < 5$, $\mathrm{f}(5) = \mathrm{f}'(5) = 0$

(f) $\mathrm{f}(0) = 3$, $\mathrm{f}'(0) = -2$, $\mathrm{f}''(x) > 0$ for $0 < x < 5$, $\mathrm{f}(5) = \mathrm{f}'(5) = 0$

2 The rate at which Nasreen's coffee cools is proportional to the difference between its temperature, $\theta°$, and room temperature, $\alpha°$. Sketch a graph of θ against t given that $\alpha = 20$ and that $\theta = 95$ when $t = 0$. State the signs of θ, $\dfrac{d\theta}{dt}$ and $\dfrac{d^2\theta}{dt^2}$ for $t > 0$.

9   Find the maximum and minimum values of $y = x^3 - 6x^2 + 9x - 8$.

10   Without using a calculator, draw a sketch of $y = x^4 - x^5$, indicating those points for which $\dfrac{d^2 y}{dx^2}$ is positive and those for which $\dfrac{d^2 y}{dx^2}$ is negative.

11   Let n be a positive integer. Sketch the graphs of $y = x^n$ and $y = x^{\frac{1}{n}}$ for $x \geqslant 0$ and find the area of the region between them.

12   Solve the following equations, giving values of θ in the interval $-180 \leqslant \theta \leqslant 180$ correct to one decimal place.

    (a) $3 \sin^2 \theta° - 2 \cos^2 \theta° = 1$ (b) $\cos \theta° \tan \theta° = -\frac{1}{2}$

    (b) $3 + 4 \tan 2\theta° = 5$ (d) $4 \cos^2 2\theta° = 3$

13   The graph of $y = f(x)$ is shown in the diagram; $f(x)$ is zero for $x \geqslant 3$ and $x \leqslant -2$.

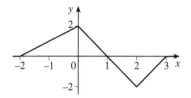

    On separate diagrams, sketch the graphs of

    (a) $y = f(x-1)$,

    (b) $y = f(2x)$.

14   A curve has equation $y = 2x^3 - 9x^2 + 12x - 5$. Show that one of the stationary points lies on the x-axis, and determine whether this point is a maximum or a minimum.

15   (a)   Solve the equation $\tan^2 2x° = \frac{1}{3}$ giving all solutions in the interval $0 \leqslant x \leqslant 360$.

    (b)   Prove that $\tan^2 \theta° \equiv \dfrac{1}{\cos^2 \theta°} - 1$.

    (c)   Write down the period of the graph of $y = \dfrac{3}{2 + \cos^2 2x°}$, and also the coordinates of a maximum value of y.

16   A curve has an equation which satisfies $\dfrac{d^2 y}{dx^2} = 5$. The curve passes through the point $(0, 4)$ and the gradient of the tangent at this point is 3. Find y in terms of x.

17   Differentiate $\sqrt{x} + \dfrac{1}{\sqrt{x}}$ and $\left(\sqrt{x} + \dfrac{1}{\sqrt{x}}\right)^2$ with respect to x.

18   Find the value of $\displaystyle\int_{1}^{3} \left(x^3 - 6x^2 + 11x - 6\right) dx$. Interpret your result geometrically.

19   By drawing suitable sketch graphs, determine the number of roots of the equation

    $$\cos x° = \dfrac{10}{x}$$

    which lie in the interval $-180 < x < 180$.   (OCR, adapted)

Mock examination 1 for P1

Time 1 hour 20 minutes

Answer all the questions.
Only scientific calculators are allowed.

1   Express $\left(3\sqrt{2} - 2\sqrt{3}\right)^2$ in the form $a - b\sqrt{c}$ where a, b and c are integers.   [3]

2   Express the quadratic polynomial $x^2 - 4x + 9$ in completed square form.   [2]

Hence solve the equation $x^2 - 4x + 9 = 11$, leaving your answers in surd form.   [2]

3   Draw a sketch of the graph of $y = \sqrt{x}$.   [1]

Hence sketch, on a single diagram, the graphs of
(i) $y = \sqrt{x + 1.5}$,
(ii) $y = \sqrt{2x + 3}$,
making clear which graph is which. Give the coordinates of any points of intersection of
the graphs with the axes.   [4]

4   Differentiate $2x^3 - \dfrac{1}{x} + 2\sqrt{x}$ with respect to x.   [5]

5   Sketch the graph of $y = \cos 2x°$ for $0 \leqslant x \leqslant 360$.   [2]

Solve the equation $\cos 2x° = -0.7$, for x in the interval $0 \leqslant x < 360$.   [4]

6

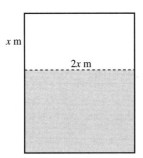

A window consists of two rectangles, one above the other. The width of each rectangle is $2x$ metres and the height of the upper rectangle is half its width (see diagram). The total perimeter of the window (not including the dotted line between the two parts of the window) is 6 metres. Show that height of the lower window is $(3 - 3x)$ metres.   [2]

The bottom part of the window is tinted, and the glass for this part costs £4 per m^2. The glass for the untinted part of the window costs £2 per m^2. Find an expression for the total cost of the glass, and show that this total cost is a maximum (and not a minimum) when $x = \frac{3}{5}$ metres.   [5]

7   Solve the simultaneous equations

$$2x^2 + xy = 10,$$
$$x + y = 3.$$ [5]

Show that the simultaneous equations

$$2x^2 + xy = 10,$$
$$x + y = a$$

always have two distinct solutions, for all possible values of the constant a.   [3]

8   Three points have coordinates $A(1,2)$, $B(4,6)$ and $C(2,4)$. The point D is such that the points A, B, C and D, in that order, form a parallelogram. Find the coordinates of D.   [2]

The line through B perpendicular to AC meets AC produced at E.
(i)   Calculate the coordinates of E.   [5]
(ii)   Calculate the area of $ABCD$.   [3]

9

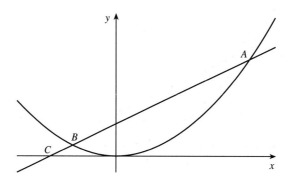

The diagram shows the curve $y = x^2$ and the line $y = 3 + 2x$. Prove algebraically that A is the point $(3,9)$ and calculate the coordinates of the other point of intersection, B, of the line with the curve.   [6]

(i)   Calculate the area of the region enclosed between the curve and the line segment AB.   [3]

(ii)   The line $y = 3 + 2x$ cuts the x-axis at C. Calculate the area of the region enclosed between the curve, the x-axis and the line segment BC.   [3]

Mock examination 2 for P1

Time 1 hour 20 minutes

Answer all the questions.
Only scientific calculators are allowed.

1 Points A and B have coordinates $(3,2)$ and $(-1,4)$ respectively. Find the equation of the straight line which is perpendicular to AB and which passes through its mid-point. [4]

2 Part of the graph of a function $y = f(x)$ defined for all values of x is shown in Fig. 1. For all the values of x not shown on Fig. 1, $f(x) = 1$.

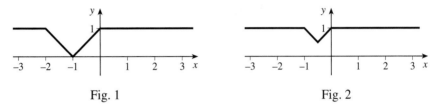

Fig. 1   Fig. 2

    (i) Sketch the graph of $y = f(x+2)$. [1]

    (ii) The equation of the graph in Fig. 2 can be written as $y = af(bx)+c$, where a, b and c are constants. Find a, b and c. [3]

3 Express the quadratic polynomial $x^2 + 6x + 16$ in completed square form. [2]

Hence find the coordinates of the vertex of the graph of $y = x^2 + 6x + 16$. [2]

4 Given that $\left(a\sqrt{5}+b\sqrt{3}\right)\left(2\sqrt{5}+4\sqrt{3}\right) = 4+10\sqrt{15}$, where a and b are constants, find the values of the integers a and b. [4]

5 Find $\displaystyle\int_{2}^{\infty} \frac{4}{x^2}\,dx.$ [2]

For what region does the definite integral $\displaystyle\int_{2}^{\infty} \frac{4}{x^2}\,dx$ give the area? Draw a sketch to illustrate your answer. [3]

6 Find the equation of the curve that passes through the point $(1,0)$ for which
$$\frac{dy}{dx} = 4x^2 - \frac{4}{x^3}.$$ [5]

7   The height h metres of the water in a harbour t hours after noon is given by the formula $h = 4 + 2\sin 30t°$.

(i)   Find the height at 5 p.m.   [1]

(ii)   Write down the maximum and minimum heights of the water.   [1]

(iii) A boat can enter the harbour provided that the height of the water is at least 3 metres. Find the times before midnight between which the boat cannot enter the harbour.   [5]

8   (i)   By writing $y = 3^x$, or otherwise, solve for x the equation $3^{2x+1} - 4 \times 3^x + 1 = 0$.   [5]

(ii)   Find the set of values of k for which the quadratic equation $3x^2 + kx + 4 = 0$ has no real roots.   [3]

9   Find the equation of the tangent at the point with x-coordinate 1 to the curve with equation $y = 4x^3 - 4x^2 - 10x + 12$.   [4]

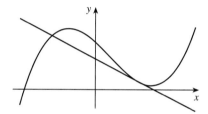

You are given that this tangent meets the curve again where $x = -1$ (see figure). Calculate the area of the region which lies between the tangent and the curve.   [5]

10   Differentiate $x + \dfrac{2}{x}$ with respect to x.   [2]

Use your answer to find the stationary value of $x + \dfrac{2}{x}$ for which x is positive, showing clearly whether it is a maximum or a minimum.   [5]

Show that the second derivative of $x + \dfrac{2}{x}$ is always positive for positive values of x. What information does this give you about the shape of the graph of $y = x + \dfrac{2}{x}$ for positive values of x?   [3]

Module P2

Pure Mathematics 2

1 Polynomials

This chapter is about polynomials, which include linear and quadratic expressions. When you have completed it, you should

- be able to add, subtract, multiply and divide polynomials
- understand the words 'quotient' and 'remainder' used in dividing polynomials
- be able to use the method of equating coefficients
- be able to use the remainder theorem and the factor theorem.

1.1 Polynomials

You already know a good deal about polynomials from your work on quadratics in Chapter 4 of Pure Mathematics 1 (module P1), because a quadratic is a special case of a polynomial. Here are some examples of polynomials.

$$3x^3 - 2x^2 + 1 \qquad 3 \qquad 4 - 2x \qquad x^2 \qquad 1$$
$$2x^4 \qquad 1 - 2x + 3x^5 \qquad \sqrt{2}x^2 \qquad \tfrac{1}{2}x^{17} \qquad x$$

A (non-zero) **polynomial**, $p(x)$, is an expression in x of the form

$$ax^n + bx^{n-1} + \ldots + jx + k$$

where $a, b, c, \ldots, k$ are real numbers, $a \neq 0$, and n is a non-negative integer.

The number n is called the **degree** of the polynomial. The expressions ax^n, bx^{n-1}, $\ldots$, jx and k which make up the polynomial are called **terms**. The numbers $a, b, c, \ldots, j$ and k are called **coefficients**; a is the **leading coefficient**. The coefficient k is the **constant term**.

Thus, in the quadratic polynomial $4x^2 - 3x + 1$, the degree is 2; the coefficients of x^2 and x, and the constant term, are 4, -3 and 1 respectively.

Polynomials with low degree have special names: if the polynomial has
- degree 0 it is called a **constant polynomial**, or a **constant**
- degree 1 it is called a **linear polynomial**
- degree 2 it is called a **quadratic polynomial**, or a **quadratic**
- degree 3 it is called a **cubic polynomial**, or a **cubic**
- degree 4 it is called a **quartic polynomial**, or a **quartic**.

When a polynomial is written as $ax^n + bx^{n-1} + \ldots + jx + k$, with the term of highest degree first and the other terms in descending degree order finishing with the constant term, the terms are said to be in **descending order**. If the terms are written in reverse order, they are said to be in **ascending order**. For example, $3x^4 + x^2 - 7x + 5$ is in descending order; in ascending order it is $5 - 7x + x^2 + 3x^4$. It is the same polynomial whatever order the terms are written in.

The functions $\dfrac{1}{x} = x^{-1}$ and $\sqrt{x} = x^{\frac{1}{2}}$ are not polynomials, because the powers of x are not non-negative integers.

Polynomials have much in common with integers. You can add them, subtract them and multiply them together and the result is another polynomial. You can even divide a polynomial by another polynomial, as you will see in Section 1.4.

1.2 Addition, subtraction and multiplication of polynomials

To add or subtract two polynomials, you simply add or subtract the coefficients of corresponding powers; in other words, you collect like terms. Suppose that you want to add $2x^3 + 3x^2 - 4$ to $x^2 - x - 2$. Then you can set out the working like this:

$$
\begin{array}{rrrrrrr}
2x^3 & + & 3x^2 & & & - & 4 \\
 & & x^2 & - & x & - & 2 \\
\hline
2x^3 & + & 4x^2 & - & x & - & 6 \\
\end{array}
$$

Notice that you must leave gaps in places where the coefficient is zero. You need to do addition so often that it is worth getting used to setting out the work in a line, thus:

$$\left(2x^3 + 3x^2 - 4\right) + \left(x^2 - x - 2\right) = (2+0)x^3 + (3+1)x^2 + (0+(-1))x + ((-4)+(-2))$$

$$= 2x^3 + 4x^2 - x - 6.$$

You will soon find that you can miss out the middle step and go straight to the answer.

Notice that the result of the polynomial calculation $\left(2x^3 + 3x^2 - 4\right) - \left(2x^3 + 3x^2 - 4\right)$ is 0. This is a special case, and it is called the **zero polynomial**. It has no degree.

Look back at the definition of a polynomial, and see why the zero polynomial was not included there.

Multiplying polynomials is harder. It relies on the rules for multiplying out brackets,

$$a(b + c + \ldots + k) = ab + ac + \ldots + ak \text{ and } (b + c + \ldots + k)a = ba + ca + \ldots + ka.$$

To apply these rules to multiplying the two polynomials $5x + 3$ and $2x^2 - 5x + 1$, replace $2x^2 - 5x + 1$ temporarily by z. Then

$$\left(5x + 3\right)\left(2x^2 - 5x + 1\right) = (5x + 3)z$$

$$= 5xz + 3z$$

$$= 5x\left(2x^2 - 5x + 1\right) + 3\left(2x^2 - 5x + 1\right)$$

$$= \left(10x^3 - 25x^2 + 5x\right) + \left(6x^2 - 15x + 3\right)$$

$$= 10x^3 - 19x^2 - 10x + 3.$$

In practice, it is easier to note that every term in the left bracket multiplies every term in the right bracket. You can show this by setting out the steps in the following way.

$$
\begin{array}{rrrr|l}
 & 2x^2 & - & 5x & + & 1 & \times \\
\hline
10x^3 & - & 25x^2 & + & 5x & & 5x \\
 & + & 6x^2 & - & 15x & + & 3 & +3 \\
\hline
10x^3 & + & (-25+6)x^2 & + & (5-15)x & + & 3 &
\end{array}
$$

giving the result $10x^3 - 19x^2 - 10x + 3$.

It is worth learning to work horizontally. The arrows in this method show the term $5x$ from the first bracket multiplied by $-5x$ from the second bracket to get $-25x^2$.

$$
(5x+3)(2x^2 - 5x + 1) = 5x(2x^2 - 5x + 1) + 3(2x^2 - 5x + 1)
$$
$$
= (10x^3 - 25x^2 + 5x) + (6x^2 - 15x + 3)
$$
$$
= 10x^3 - 19x^2 - 10x + 3.
$$

You could shorten the process and write

$$
(5x+3)(2x^2 - 5x + 1) = 10x^3 - 25x^2 + 5x + 6x^2 - 15x + 3
$$
$$
= 10x^3 - 19x^2 - 10x + 3.
$$

If you multiply a polynomial of degree m by a polynomial of degree n, you have a calculation of the type

$$
\left(ax^m + bx^{m-1} + \dots\right)\left(Ax^n + Bx^{n-1} + \dots\right) = aAx^{m+n} + \dots
$$

in which the largest power of the product is $m+n$. Also the coefficient aA is not zero because neither of a and A is zero. This shows that:

> When you multiply two polynomials, the degree of the product polynomial is the sum of the degrees of the two polynomials.

Exercise 1A

1 State the degree of each of the following polynomials.

(a) $x^3 - 3x^2 + 2x - 7$ (b) $5x + 1$

(c) $8 + 5x - 3x^2 + 7x + 6x^4$ (d) 3

(e) $3 - 5x$ (f) x^0

2 In each part find $p(x) + q(x)$, and give your answer in descending order.

(a) $p(x) = 3x^2 + 4x - 1,$ $q(x) = x^2 + 3x + 7$

(b) $p(x) = 4x^3 + 5x^2 - 7x + 3,$ $q(x) = x^3 - 2x^2 + x - 6$

(c) $p(x) = 3x^4 - 2x^3 + 7x^2 - 1,$ $q(x) = -3x - x^3 + 5x^4 + 2$

(d) $p(x) = 2 - 3x^3 + 2x^5,$ $q(x) = 2x^4 + 3x^3 - 5x^2 + 1$

(e) $p(x) = 3 + 2x - 4x^2 - x^3,$ $q(x) = 1 - 7x + 2x^2$

3 For each of the pairs of polynomials given in Question 2 find $p(x) - q(x)$.

4 Note that $p(x) + p(x)$ may be shortened to $2p(x)$. Let $p(x) = x^3 - 2x^2 + 5x - 3$ and $q(x) = x^2 - x + 4$. Express each of the following as a single polynomial.

   (a) $2p(x) + q(x)$ (b) $3p(x) - q(x)$ (c) $p(x) - 2q(x)$ (d) $3p(x) - 2q(x)$

5 Find the following polynomial products.

   (a) $(2x - 3)(3x + 1)$ (b) $(x^2 + 3x - 1)(x - 2)$

   (c) $(x^2 + x - 3)(2x + 3)$ (d) $(3x - 1)(4x^2 - 3x + 2)$

   (e) $(x^2 + 2x - 3)(x^2 + 1)$ (f) $(2x^2 - 3x + 1)(4x^2 + 3x - 5)$

   (g) $(x^3 + 2x^2 - x + 6)(x + 3)$ (h) $(x^3 - 3x^2 + 2x - 1)(x^2 - 2x - 5)$

   (i) $(1 + 3x - x^2 + 2x^3)(3 - x + 2x^2)$ (j) $(2 - 3x + x^2)(4 - 5x + x^3)$

   (k) $(2x + 1)(3x - 2)(x + 5)$ (l) $(x^2 + 1)(x - 3)(2x^2 - x + 1)$

6 In each of the following products find (i) the coefficient of x, and (ii) the coefficient of x^2.

   (a) $(x + 2)(x^2 - 3x + 6)$ (b) $(x - 3)(x^2 + 2x - 5)$

   (c) $(2x + 1)(x^2 - 5x + 1)$ (d) $(3x - 2)(x^2 - 2x + 7)$

   (e) $(2x - 3)(3x^2 - 6x + 1)$ (f) $(2x - 5)(3x^3 - x^2 + 4x + 2)$

   (g) $(x^2 + 2x - 3)(x^2 + 3x - 4)$ (h) $(3x^2 + 1)(2x^2 - 5x + 3)$

   (i) $(x^2 + 3x - 1)(x^3 + x^2 - 2x + 1)$ (j) $(3x^2 - x + 2)(4x^3 - 5x + 1)$

7 In each of the following the product of $Ax + B$ with another polynomial is given. Using the fact that A and B are constants, find A and B.

   (a) $(Ax + B)(x - 3) = 4x^2 - 11x - 3$ (b) $(Ax + B)(x + 5) = 2x^2 + 7x - 15$

   (c) $(Ax + B)(3x - 2) = 6x^2 - x - 2$ (d) $(Ax + B)(2x + 5) = 6x^2 + 11x - 10$

   (e) $(Ax + B)(x^2 - 1) = x^3 + 2x^2 - x - 2$ (f) $(Ax + B)(x^2 + 4) = 2x^3 - 3x^2 + 8x - 12$

   (g) $(Ax + B)(2x^2 - 3x + 4) = 4x^3 - x + 12$ (h) $(Ax + B)(3x^2 - 2x - 1) = 6x^3 - 7x^2 + 1$

1.3 Equations and identities

In this chapter so far you have learned how to add, subtract and multiply polynomials, and you can now carry out calculations such as

$$(2x + 3) + (x - 2) = 3x + 1,$$

$$(x^2 - 3x - 4) - (2x + 1) = x^2 - 5x - 5 \quad \text{and}$$

$$(1 - x)(1 + x + x^2) = 1 - x^3$$

fairly automatically.

However, you should realise that these are not equations in the normal sense, because they are true for all values of x.

In P1 Section 11.6, you saw that when two expressions take the same values for every value of the variable, they are said to be **identically** equal, and a statement such as

$$(1-x)(1+x+x^2) = 1 - x^3$$

is called an **identity**.

To emphasise that an equation is an identity, the symbol $\equiv$ is used. The statement $(1-x)(1+x+x^2) \equiv 1 - x^3$ means that $(1-x)(1+x+x^2)$ and $1-x^3$ are equal for all values of x.

But now suppose that $Ax + B \equiv 2x + 3$. What can you say about A and B? As $Ax + B \equiv 2x + 3$ is an identity, it is true for all values of x. In particular, it is true for $x = 0$. Therefore $A \times 0 + B = 2 \times 0 + 3$, giving $B = 3$. But the identity is also true when $x = 1$, so $A \times 1 + 3 = 2 \times 1 + 3$, giving $A = 2$. Therefore:

If $Ax + B \equiv 2x + 3$ then $A = 2$ and $B = 3$.

This is an example of the process called **equating coefficients**. The full result is:

If $ax^n + bx^{n-1} + \ldots + k \equiv Ax^n + Bx^{n-1} + \ldots + K$,

then $a = A, b = B, \ldots, k = K$.

The statement in the shaded box says that, if two polynomials are equal for all values of x, then all the coefficients of corresponding powers of x are equal.

This result may not surprise you, but you should realise that you are using it. Indeed, it is very likely that you have used it before now without realising it.

Example 1.3.1
One factor of $3x^2 - 5x - 2$ is $x - 2$. Find the other factor.

There is nothing wrong in writing down the answer by inspection as $3x + 1$. But the process behind this quick solution is as follows.

Suppose that the other factor is $Ax + B$. Then $(Ax + B)(x - 2) \equiv 3x^2 - 5x - 2$, and, multiplying out, you get

$$Ax^2 + (-2A + B)x - 2B \equiv 3x^2 - 5x - 2.$$

By equating coefficients of x^2, you get $A = 3$. Equating coefficients of x^0, the constant term, you get $-2B = -2$, giving $B = 1$. Therefore the other factor is $3x + 1$.

You can also check that the middle term, $-2A + B = -6 + 1 = -5$, is correct.

You should continue to write down the other factor by inspection if you can. However, in some cases, it is not easy to see what the answer will be without intermediate working.

Example 1.3.2

If $4x^3 + 2x^2 + 3 \equiv (x-2)(Ax^2 + Bx + C) + R$, find A, B, C and R.

Multiplying out the right side gives

$$4x^3 + 2x^2 + 3 \equiv Ax^3 + (-2A + B)x^2 + (-2B + C)x + (-2C + R).$$

Equating coefficients of x^3: $4 = A$

Equating coefficients of x^2: $2 = -2A + B = -2 \times 4 + B = -8 + B$, so $B = 10$.

Equating coefficients of x^3: $0 = -2B + C = -20 + C$, so $C = 20$.

Equating coefficients of x^0: $3 = -2C + R = -40 + R$, giving $R = 43$.

Therefore $A = 4$, $B = 10$, $C = 20$ and $R = 43$, so

$$4x^3 + 2x^2 + 3 \equiv (x-2)(4x^2 + 10x + 20) + 43.$$

In practice, people often use the symbol for equality, $=$, when they really mean the symbol for identity, $\equiv$. The context usually suggests which meaning of the $=$ sign is intended.

Exercise 1B

1 In each of the following quadratic polynomials one factor is given. Find the other factor.

(a) $x^2 + x - 12 \equiv (x+4)(\quad)$ (b) $x^2 + 14x - 51 \equiv (x-3)(\quad)$

(c) $3x^2 + 5x - 22 \equiv (x-2)(\quad)$ (d) $35x^2 + 48x - 27 \equiv (5x+9)(\quad)$

(e) $2x^2 - x - 15 \equiv (2x+5)(\quad)$ (f) $14x^2 + 31x - 10 \equiv (2x+5)(\quad)$

2 In each of the following identities find the values of A, B and R.

(a) $x^2 - 2x + 7 \equiv (x+3)(Ax + B) + R$ (b) $x^2 + 9x - 3 \equiv (x+1)(Ax + B) + R$

(c) $15x^2 - 14x - 8 \equiv (5x+2)(Ax + B) + R$ (d) $6x^2 + x - 5 \equiv (2x+1)(Ax + B) + R$

(e) $12x^2 - 5x + 2 \equiv (3x-2)(Ax + B) + R$ (f) $21x^2 - 11x + 6 \equiv (3x-2)(Ax + B) + R$

3 In each of the following identities find the values of A, B, C and R.

(a) $x^3 - x^2 - x + 12 \equiv (x+2)(Ax^2 + Bx + C) + R$

(b) $x^3 - 5x^2 + 10x + 10 \equiv (x-3)(Ax^2 + Bx + C) + R$

(c) $2x^3 + x^2 - 3x + 4 \equiv (2x-1)(Ax^2 + Bx + C) + R$

(d) $12x^3 + 11x^2 - 7x + 5 \equiv (3x+2)(Ax^2 + Bx + C) + R$

(e) $4x^3 + 4x^2 - 37x + 5 \equiv (2x-5)(Ax^2 + Bx + C) + R$

(f) $9x^3 + 12x^2 - 15x - 10 \equiv (3x+4)(Ax^2 + Bx + C) + R$

4 In each of the following identities find the values of A, B, C, D and R.

(a) $2x^4 + 3x^3 - 5x^2 + 11x - 5 \equiv (x+3)(Ax^3 + Bx^2 + Cx + D) + R$

(b) $4x^4 - 7x^3 - 2x^2 - 2x + 7 \equiv (x-2)(Ax^3 + Bx^2 + Cx + D) + R$

(c) $6x^4 + 5x^3 - x^2 + 3x + 2 \equiv (2x+1)(Ax^3 + Bx^2 + Cx + D) + R$

(d) $3x^4 - 7x^3 + 17x^2 - 14x + 5 \equiv (3x-1)(Ax^3 + Bx^2 + Cx + D) + R$

1.4   Division of polynomials

You can, if you wish, carry out division of polynomials using a layout like the one for long division of integers. You may already have seen and used such a process. However, you can also use the method of equating coefficients for division.

When you divide 112 by 9, you get an answer of 12 with 4 over. The number 9 is called the divisor, 12 is the quotient and 4 the remainder. You can express this as an equation in integers, $112 = 9 \times 12 + 4$. The remainder r has to satisfy the inequality $0 \leqslant r < 9$.

Now look back at Example 1.3.2. You will see that it is an identity of just the same shape, but with polynomials instead of integers. So you can say that, when $4x^3 + 2x^2 + 3$ is divided by the divisor $x - 2$, the quotient is $4x^2 + 10x + 20$ and the remainder is 43. The degree of the remainder (in this case 0) has to be less than the degree of the divisor.

> When a polynomial, $a(x)$, is divided by a non-constant **divisor**, $b(x)$, the **quotient** $q(x)$ and the **remainder** $r(x)$ are defined by the identity
>
> $$a(x) \equiv b(x)q(x) + r(x),$$
>
> where the degree of the remainder is less than the degree of the divisor.
>
> The degree of the quotient is equal to the degree of $a(x)$ – the degree of $b(x)$.

Example 1.4.1

Find the quotient and remainder when $x^4 + x + 2$ is divided by $x + 1$.

Using the result in the shaded box, as the degree of $x^4 + x + 2$ is 4 and the degree of $x + 1$ is 1, the degree of the quotient is $4 - 1 = 3$. And as the degree of the remainder is less than 1, it is a constant.

Let the quotient be $Ax^3 + Bx^2 + Cx + D$, and let the remainder be R. Then

$$x^4 + x + 2 \equiv (x + 1)\left(Ax^3 + Bx^2 + Cx + D\right) + R, \text{ so}$$

$$x^4 + x + 2 \equiv Ax^4 + (A + B)x^3 + (B + C)x^2 + (C + D)x + D + R.$$

Equating coefficients of x^4: $1 = A$.
Equating coefficients of x^3: $0 = A + B$, so $B = -A$, giving $B = -1$.
Equating coefficients of x^2: $0 = B + C$, so $C = -B$, giving $C = 1$.
Equating coefficients of x: $1 = C + D$, so $D = 1 - C$, giving $D = 0$.
Equating coefficients of x^0: $2 = D + R$, so $R = 2 - D$, giving $R = 2$.

The quotient is $x^3 - x^2 + x$ and the remainder is 2.

Example 1.4.2

Find the quotient and remainder when $x^4 + 3x^2 - 2$ is divided by $x^2 - 2x + 2$.

The shaded box result states that the degree of the remainder is less than 2, so assume that it is a linear polynomial. Let the quotient be $Ax^2 + Bx + C$, and the remainder be $Rx + S$.

$$x^4 + 3x^2 - 2 \equiv \left(x^2 - 2x + 2\right)\left(Ax^2 + Bx + C\right) + Rx + S,$$

so $x^4 + 3x^2 - 2 \equiv Ax^4 + (-2A + B)x^3 + (2A - 2B + C)x^2$
$$+ (2B - 2C + R)x + 2C + S.$$

Equating coefficients of x^4: $1 = A$.
Equating coefficients of x^3: $0 = -2A + B$, so $B = 2A$, giving $B = 2$.
Equating coefficients of x^2: $3 = 2A - 2B + C$, so $C = 3 - 2A + 2B$, giving $C = 5$.
Equating coefficients of x: $0 = 2B - 2C + R$, so $R = -2B + 2C$, giving $R = 6$.
Equating coefficients of x^0: $-2 = 2C + S$, so $S = -2 - 2C$, giving $S = -12$.

The quotient is $x^2 + 2x + 5$ and the remainder is $6x - 12$.

When you are dividing by a *linear* polynomial, there is a quick way of finding the remainder. For example, in Example 1.4.1, when $x^4 + x + 2$ was divided by $x + 1$, the first line of the solution was:

$$x^4 + x + 2 \equiv (x + 1)\left(Ax^3 + Bx^2 + Cx + D\right) + R.$$

Since this is an identity, it is true for all values of x and, in particular, it is true for $x = -1$. Putting $x = -1$ in the left side, you get $(-1)^4 + (-1) + 2 = 2$: putting $x = -1$ in the right side, you get $0 \times \left(A(-1)^3 + B(-1)^2 + C(-1) + D\right) + R = R$. Therefore $R = 2$.

Similar reasoning leads to the remainder theorem.

> **The remainder theorem**
> When a polynomial $p(x)$ is divided by $x - t$,
> the remainder is the constant $p(t)$.

Proof   When $p(x)$ is divided by $x - t$, let the quotient be $q(x)$ and the remainder be R. Then

$$p(x) \equiv (x - t)q(x) + R.$$

Putting $x = t$ in this identity gives $p(t) = 0 \times q(t) + R = R$, so $R = p(t)$. This proves that the remainder is the constant $p(t)$.

You will find more on theorems and proving them when you reach Chapter 8.

Example 1.4.3

Find the remainder when $x^3 - 3x + 4$ is divided by $x + 3$.

Let $p(x) \equiv x^3 - 3x + 4$. Then $p(-3) = (-3)^3 - 3 \times (-3) + 4 = -27 + 9 + 4 = -14$.
By the remainder theorem, the remainder is -14.

Example 1.4.4

When the polynomial $p(x) \equiv x^3 - 3x^2 + ax + b$ is divided by $x - 1$ the remainder is -4.
When $p(x)$ is divided by $x - 2$ the remainder is also -4. Find the remainder when
$p(x)$ is divided by $x - 3$.

By the remainder theorem, when $p(x)$ is divided by $x - 1$, the remainder is
$p(1) = 1^3 - 3 \times 1^2 + a + b = a + b - 2$. Therefore $a + b - 2 = -4$, so $a + b = -2$.

Similarly, $p(2) = 2^3 - 3 \times 2^2 + 2a + b = 2a + b - 4$, so $2a + b - 4 = -4$ and
$2a + b = 0$.

Solving the equations $a + b = -2$ and $2a + b = 0$ simultaneously gives $a = 2$ and
$b = -4$, making the polynomial $p(x) \equiv x^3 - 3x^2 + 2x - 4$.

The remainder on division by $x - 3$ is $p(3) = 3^3 - 3 \times 3^2 + 2 \times 3 - 4 = 2$.

The remainder theorem is useful when you want to find the remainder when you divide
a polynomial by a linear polynomial such as $x - 2$, but it doesn't tell you how to find
the remainder when you divide by a linear polynomial such as $3x - 2$. To do this, you
need the extended form of the remainder theorem.

> **The remainder theorem: extended form**
> When a polynomial $p(x)$ is divided by $sx - t$,
> the remainder is the constant $p\left(\dfrac{t}{s}\right)$.

Proof   When $p(x)$ is divided by $sx - t$, let the quotient be $q(x)$ and the
remainder be R. Then $p(x) \equiv (sx - t)q(x) + R$.

Putting $x = \dfrac{t}{s}$ in this identity,

$$p\left(\frac{t}{s}\right) = \left(s \times \frac{t}{s} - t\right) \times q\left(\frac{t}{s}\right) + R = 0 \times q\left(\frac{t}{s}\right) + R = R, \quad \text{so} \quad R = p\left(\frac{t}{s}\right).$$

This proves that the remainder is the constant $p\left(\dfrac{t}{s}\right)$.

Example 1.4.5

Find the remainder when $x^3 - 3x + 4$ is divided by $2x + 3$.

Let $p(x) \equiv x^3 - 3x + 4$. Then $p\left(-\frac{3}{2}\right) = \left(-\frac{3}{2}\right)^3 - 3 \times \left(-\frac{3}{2}\right) + 4 = -\frac{27}{8} + \frac{9}{2} + 4 = 5\frac{1}{8}$.
By the remainder theorem in its extended form, the remainder is $5\frac{1}{8}$.

Exercise 1C

1 Find the quotient and the remainder when

  (a) $x^2 - 5x + 2$ is divided by $x - 3$,   (b) $x^2 + 2x - 6$ is divided by $x + 1$,

  (c) $2x^2 + 3x - 1$ is divided by $x - 2$,   (d) $2x^2 + 3x + 1$ is divided by $2x - 1$,

  (e) $6x^2 - x - 2$ is divided by $3x + 1$,   (f) x^4 is divided by x^3.

2 Find the quotient and the remainder when the first polynomial is divided by the second.

  (a) $x^3 + 2x^2 - 3x + 1$, $x + 2$ (b) $x^3 - 3x^2 + 5x - 4$, $x - 5$

  (c) $2x^3 + 4x - 5$, $x + 3$ (d) $5x^3 - 3x + 7$, $x - 4$

  (e) $2x^3 - x^2 - 3x - 7$, $2x + 1$ (f) $6x^3 + 17x^2 - 17x + 5$, $3x - 2$

3 Find the quotient and the remainder when

  (a) $x^4 - 2x^3 - 7x^2 + 7x + 5$ is divided by $x^2 + 2x - 1$,

  (b) $x^4 - x^3 + 7x + 2$ is divided by $x^2 + x - 1$,

  (c) $2x^4 - 4x^3 + 3x^2 + 6x + 5$ is divided by $x^3 + x^2 + 1$,

  (d) $6x^4 + x^3 + 13x + 10$ is divided by $2x^2 - x + 4$.

4 Find the remainder when

  (a) $x^3 - 5x^2 + 2x - 3$ is divided by $x - 1$,   (b) $x^3 + x^2 - 6x + 5$ is divided by $x + 2$,

  (c) $2x^3 - 3x + 5$ is divided by $x - 3$,   (d) $4x^3 - 5x^2 + 3x - 7$ is divided by $x + 4$,

  (e) $x^3 + 3x^2 - 2x + 1$ is divided by $2x - 1$,   (f) $2x^3 + 5x^2 - 3x + 6$ is divided by $3x + 1$,

  (g) $x^4 - x^3 + 2x^2 - 7x - 2$ is divided by $x - 2$, (h) $3x^4 + x^2 - 7x + 6$ is divided by $x + 3$.

5 When $x^3 + 2x^2 - px + 1$ is divided by $x - 1$ the remainder is 5. Find the value of p.

6 When $2x^3 + x^2 - 3x + q$ is divided by $x - 2$ the remainder is 12. Find the value of q.

7 When $x^3 + 2x^2 + px - 3$ is divided by $x + 1$ the remainder is the same as when it is divided by $x - 2$. Find the value of p.

8 When $x^3 + px^2 - x - 4$ is divided by $x - 1$ the remainder is the same as when it is divided by $x + 3$. Find the value of p.

9 When $3x^3 - 2x^2 + ax + b$ is divided by $x - 1$ the remainder is 3. When divided by $x + 1$ the remainder is -13. Find the values of a and b.

10 When $x^3 + ax^2 + bx + 5$ is divided by $x - 2$ the remainder is 23. When divided by $x + 1$ the remainder is 11. Find the values of a and b.

11 When $x^3 + ax^2 + bx - 5$ is divided by $x - 1$ the remainder is -1. When divided by $x + 1$ the remainder is -5. Find the values of a and b.

12 When $2x^3 - x^2 + ax + b$ is divided by $x - 2$ the remainder is 25. When divided by $x + 1$ the remainder is -5. Find the values of a and b.

1.5   The factor theorem

When you solve an equation $p(x) = 0$ by factors, writing $p(x) \equiv (x - t)(x - u)(x - v)\ldots$, you deduce that $x = t$ or $x = u$ or $x = v$ or .... So when you substitute $x = t$ in $p(x)$, you find that $p(t) = 0$. It is not quite so obvious that, if $p(t) = 0$, then $x - t$ is a factor of $p(x)$. This result, a special case of the remainder theorem, is called the factor theorem.

> Let $p(x)$ be a polynomial. Then
>   (a)   if $x - t$ is a factor of $p(x)$ then $p(t) = 0$;
>   (b)   if $p(t) = 0$ then $x - t$ is a factor of $p(x)$.
>
> The second of these results is called the **factor theorem**.

Proof

(a) If $x - t$ is a factor of $p(x)$, then $p(x) \equiv (x - t)q(x)$, where $q(x)$ is a polynomial. Putting $x = t$ into this identity shows that $p(t) = (t - t)q(t) = 0$.

(b) When $p(x)$ is divided by $x - t$, let the quotient be $q(x)$ and the remainder be R. Then $p(x) \equiv (x - t)q(x) + R$.

Putting $x = t$ into this identity gives $p(t) = R$ (this is the remainder theorem again). Thus if $p(t) = 0$, $R = 0$, so $x - t$ is a factor of the polynomial $p(x)$.

You can use the factor theorem to search for factors of a polynomial when its coefficients are small.

When you search for factors of a polynomial such as $x^3 - x^2 - 5x - 3$, you need only try factors of the form $x - t$ where t divides the modulus of the constant coefficient, 3. Thus you need only try $x - 1$, $x + 1$, $x - 3$ and $x + 3$.

Example 1.5.1

Find the factors of $x^3 - x^2 - 5x - 3$, and hence solve the equation $x^3 - x^2 - 5x - 3 = 0$.

Denote $x^3 - x^2 - 5x - 3$ by $p(x)$.

Could $x - 1$ be a factor? $p(1) = 1^3 - 1^2 - 5 \times 1 - 3 = -8 \neq 0$, so $x - 1$ is not a factor.

Try $x + 1$ as a factor. $p(-1) = (-1)^3 - (-1)^2 - 5 \times (-1) - 3 = 0$, so $x + 1$ is a factor.

Dividing $x^3 - x^2 - 5x - 3$ by $x + 1$ in the usual way, you find

$$x^3 - x^2 - 5x - 3 \equiv (x + 1)(x^2 - 2x - 3).$$

Since $x^2 - 2x - 3 \equiv (x + 1)(x - 3)$, you can now factorise $x^3 - x^2 - 5x - 3$ completely to get

$$x^3 - x^2 - 5x - 3 \equiv (x + 1)(x + 1)(x - 3) \equiv (x + 1)^2(x - 3).$$

The solution of the equation $x^3 - x^2 - 5x - 3 = 0$ is $x = -1$ (repeated) and $x = 3$.

Example 1.5.2

Find the factors of $x^4 + x^3 - x - 1$ and solve the equation $x^4 + x^3 - x - 1 = 0$.

Let $p(x) \equiv x^4 + x^3 - x - 1$.

Since $p(1) = 1 + 1 - 1 - 1 = 0$, $x - 1$ is a factor of $p(x)$.

Writing $x^4 + x^3 - x - 1 \equiv (x - 1)(Ax^3 + Bx^2 + Cx + D)$ and multiplying out the right side shows that

$$x^4 + x^3 - x - 1 \equiv Ax^4 + (B - A)x^3 + (C - B)x^2 + (D - C)x - D.$$

Equating coefficients of x^4 and the constant terms gives $A = 1$ and $D = 1$, and you can see by inspection that the other coefficients are $B = 2$ and $C = 2$. So

$$p(x) \equiv (x - 1)(x^3 + 2x^2 + 2x + 1).$$

Let $q(x) \equiv x^3 + 2x^2 + 2x + 1$. Then $q(1) \neq 0$, so $x - 1$ is not a factor of $q(x)$, but $q(-1) = -1 + 2 - 2 + 1 = 0$, so $(x + 1)$ is a factor of $q(x)$.

Writing $x^3 + 2x^2 + 2x + 1 \equiv (x + 1)(Ex^2 + Fx + G)$ and equating coefficients shows that $E = 1$, $G = 1$ and $F = 1$.

Therefore $x^4 + x^3 - x - 1 \equiv (x - 1)(x + 1)(x^2 + x + 1)$.

As the discriminant of $x^2 + x + 1$ is $1^2 - 4 \times 1 \times 1 = -3 < 0$, $x^2 + x + 1$ does not split into linear factors, so, $x^4 + x^3 - x - 1$ cannot be factorised further.

Also the equation $x^2 + x + 1 = 0$ doesn't have real roots. So the solution of the equation $x^4 + x^3 - x - 1 = 0$ is $x = 1$ or $x = -1$.

Like the remainder theorem, the factor theorem has an extended form.

> Let $p(x)$ be a polynomial. Then
>
> (a) if $sx - t$ is a factor of $p(x)$ then $p\left(\dfrac{t}{s}\right) = 0$;
>
> (b) if $p\left(\dfrac{t}{s}\right) = 0$ then $sx - t$ is a factor of $p(x)$.
>
> The second result is the **extended form of the factor theorem**.

You can modify the proof of the factor theorem in the same way as the proof of the remainder theorem was modified in Section 1.4. Simply replace $p(x) \equiv (x - t)q(x)$ by $p(x) \equiv (sx - t)q(x)$, and put $x = \dfrac{t}{s}$ in the identity.

You can save a lot of effort when you apply this form of the factor theorem by using the fact that, if the coefficients of $p(x) \equiv ax^n + bx^{n-1} + \ldots + k$ are all integers, and if $sx - t$ is a factor of $p(x)$, then s divides a and t divides k. (This will be proved in Chapter 8.)

Example 1.5.3
Find the factors of $p(x) \equiv 3x^3 + 4x^2 + 5x - 6$.

Begin by noting that, if $sx - t$ is a factor, s divides 3 and t divides 6. So s can only be ± 1 or ± 3, and t can only be ± 1, ± 2, ± 3 or ± 6.

You can reduce the number of possibilities further in two ways.
- $sx - t$ is not really a different factor from $-sx + t$. So you need consider only positive values of s.
- The factors can't be $3x \pm 3$ or $3x \pm 6$ since then 3 would be a common factor of the coefficients of $p(x)$, which it isn't.

So there are only twelve possible factors: $x \mp 1$, $x \mp 2$, $x \mp 3$, $x \mp 6$, $3x \mp 1$ and $3x \mp 2$. You can test these by evaluating $p(x)$ for $x = \pm 1$, ± 2, ± 3, ± 6, $\pm \frac{1}{3}$ and $\pm \frac{2}{3}$ until you get a zero.

Working through these in turn, you will eventually find that

$$p\left(\tfrac{2}{3}\right) \equiv 3 \times \left(\tfrac{2}{3}\right)^3 + 4 \times \left(\tfrac{2}{3}\right)^2 + 5 \times \tfrac{2}{3} - 6 = \tfrac{8}{9} + \tfrac{16}{9} + \tfrac{10}{3} - 6 = 0.$$

So $3x - 2$ is a factor, and by division $p(x) \equiv (3x - 2)\left(x^2 + 2x + 3\right)$.

Since $x^2 + 2x + 3 \equiv (x + 1)^2 + 2$, which has no factors, $p(x)$ doesn't factorise further.

Exercise 1D

1 Use the factor theorem to factorise the following cubic polynomials $p(x)$. In each case write down the real roots of the equation $f(x) = 0$.

(a) $x^3 + 2x^2 - 5x - 6$ (b) $x^3 - 3x^2 - x + 3$ (c) $x^3 - 3x^2 - 13x + 15$

(d) $x^3 - 3x^2 - 9x - 5$ (e) $x^3 + 3x^2 - 4x - 12$ (f) $2x^3 + 7x^2 - 5x - 4$

(g) $3x^3 - x^2 - 12x + 4$ (h) $6x^3 + 7x^2 - x - 2$ (i) $x^3 + 2x^2 - 4x + 1$

2 Use the factor theorem to factorise the following quartic polynomials $p(x)$. In each case write down the real roots of the equation $p(x) = 0$.

(a) $x^4 - x^3 - 7x^2 + x + 6$ (b) $x^4 + 4x^3 - x^2 - 16x - 12$

(c) $2x^4 - 3x^3 - 12x^2 + 7x + 6$ (d) $6x^4 + x^3 - 17x^2 - 16x - 4$

(e) $x^4 - 2x^3 + 2x - 1$ (f) $4x^4 - 12x^3 + x^2 + 12x + 4$

3 Factorise the following.

(a) $x^3 - 8$ (b) $x^3 + 8$ (c) $x^3 - a^3$

(d) $x^3 + a^3$ (e) $x^4 - a^4$ (f) $x^5 + a^5$

4 (a) Show that $x - a$ is a factor of $x^n - a^n$.

(b) Under what conditions is $x + a$ a factor of $x^n + a^n$? Under these conditions, find the other factor.

Miscellaneous exercise 1

1 It is given that

$$(x+a)(x^2+bx+2) \equiv x^3 - 2x^2 - x - 6$$

where a and b are constants. Find the value of a and the value of b.   (OCR)

2 Find the remainder when $(1+x)^4$ is divided by $x+2$.

3 Show that $(x-1)$ is a factor of $6x^3 + 11x^2 - 5x - 12$, and find the other two linear factors of this expression.   (OCR)

4 The cubic polynomial $x^3 + ax^2 + bx - 8$, where a and b are constants, has factors $(x+1)$ and $(x+2)$. Find the values of a and b.   (OCR)

5 Find the value of a for which $(x-2)$ is a factor of $3x^3 + ax^2 + x - 2$.

Show that, for this value of a, the cubic equation $3x^3 + ax^2 + x - 2 = 0$ has only one real root.   (OCR)

6 Solve the equation $4x^3 + 8x^2 + x - 3 = 0$ given that one of the roots is an integer.   (OCR)

7 The cubic polynomial $x^3 - 2x^2 - 2x + 4$ has a factor $(x-a)$, where a is an integer.

(a) Use the factor theorem to find the value of a.

(b) Hence find exactly all three roots of the cubic equation $x^3 - 2x^2 - 2x + 4 = 0$.   (OCR)

8 The cubic polynomial $x^3 - 2x^2 - x - 6$ is denoted by $f(x)$. Show that $(x-3)$ is a factor of $f(x)$. Factorise $f(x)$. Hence find the number of real roots of the equation $f(x) = 0$, justifying your answer.

Hence write down the number of points of intersection of the graphs with equations

$$y = x^2 - 2x - 1 \quad \text{and} \quad y = \frac{6}{x},$$

justifying your answer.   (OCR)

9 Given that $(2x+1)$ is a factor of $2x^3 + ax^2 + 16x + 6$, show that $a = 9$.

Find the real quadratic factor of $2x^3 + 9x^2 + 16x + 6$. By completing the square, or otherwise, show that this quadratic factor is positive for all real values of x.   (OCR)

10 Show that both $(x - \sqrt{3})$ and $(x + \sqrt{3})$ are factors of $x^4 + x^3 - x^2 - 3x - 6$.

Hence write down one quadratic factor of $x^4 + x^3 - x^2 - 3x - 6$, and find a second quadratic factor of this polynomial.   (OCR)

11 The diagram shows the curve

$$y = -x^3 + 2x^2 + ax - 10.$$

The curve crosses the x-axis at $x = p$, $x = 2$ and $x = q$.

(a) Show that $a = 5$.

(b) Find the exact values of p and q.

(OCR)

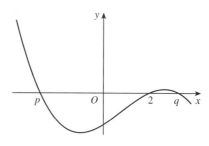

12 The polynomial $x^3 + 3x^2 + ax + b$ leaves a remainder of 3 when it is divided by $x + 1$ and a remainder of 15 when it is divided by $x - 2$. Find the remainder when it is divided by $(x - 2)(x + 1)$.

13 Find the quotient and the remainder when $x^4 + 4$ is divided by $x^2 - 2x + 2$.

14 Let $p(x) = 4x^3 + 12x^2 + 5x - 6$.

    (a) Calculate $p(2)$ and $p(-2)$, and state what you can deduce from your answers.

    (b) Solve the equation $4x^3 + 12x^2 + 5x - 6 = 0$.

15 It is given that $f(x) = x^4 - 3x^3 + ax^2 + 15x + 50$, where a is a constant, and that $x + 2$ is a factor of $f(x)$.

    (a) Find the value of a.

    (b) Show that $f(5) = 0$ and factorise $f(x)$ completely into exact linear factors.

    (c) Find the set of values of x for which $f(x) > 0$.   (OCR)

16 The diagram shows the graph of $y = x^2 - 3$ and the part of the graph of $y = \dfrac{2}{x}$ for $x > 0$.

The two graphs intersect at C, and A and B are the points of intersection of $y = x^2 - 3$ with the x-axis. Write down the exact coordinates of A and B.

Show that the x-coordinate of C is given by the equation $x^3 - 3x - 2 = 0$.

Factorise $x^3 - 3x - 2$ completely.

Hence

    (a) write down the x-coordinate of C,

    (b) describe briefly the geometrical relationship between the graph of $y = x^2 - 3$ and the part of the graph of $y = \dfrac{2}{x}$ for which $x < 0$.   (OCR)

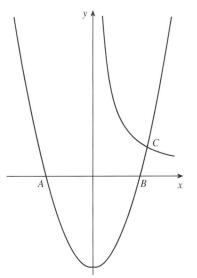

17 The polynomial $x^5 - 3x^4 + 2x^3 - 2x^2 + 3x + 1$ is denoted by $f(x)$.

    (a) Show that neither $(x - 1)$ nor $(x + 1)$ is a factor of $f(x)$.

    (b) By substituting $x = 1$ and $x = -1$ in the identity

$$f(x) \equiv (x^2 - 1)q(x) + ax + b,$$

        where $q(x)$ is a polynomial and a and b are constants, or otherwise, find the remainder when $f(x)$ is divided by $(x^2 - 1)$.

    (c) Show, by carrying out the division, or otherwise, that when $f(x)$ is divided by $(x^2 + 1)$, the remainder is $2x$.

    (d) Find all the real roots of the equation $f(x) = 2x$.   (OCR)

2 Combining and inverting functions

This chapter develops the idea of a function further, and more theoretically, than in P1 Chapters 3 and 8. It introduces a kind of algebra of functions, by showing how to find a composite function. When you have completed it, you should

- be able to use correct language and notation associated with functions
- know when functions can be combined by the operation of composition, and be able to form the composite function
- know the 'one–one' condition for a function to have an inverse, and be able to form the inverse function
- know the relationship between the graph of a one–one function and the graph of its inverse function.

The references to calculators in the chapter may not exactly fit your own machine. For example, on some calculators the [=] key is labelled [EXE] (which stands for 'execute').

2.1 Function notation

In using a calculator to find values of a function, you carry out three separate steps:

Step 1 Key in a number (the 'input').

Step 2 Key in the function instructions.

Step 3 Read the number in the display (the 'output').

Step 2 sometimes involves just a single key, such as 'square root', 'change sign' or 'sine'. For example:

$$
\begin{array}{lll}
\text{Input} & & \text{Output} \\
4 & \rightarrow \ [\ \sqrt{\ }\ ] \ \rightarrow & 2 \\
3 & \rightarrow \ [+/-] \ \rightarrow & -3 \\
30 & \rightarrow \ [\ \sin\ ] \ \rightarrow & 0.5
\end{array}
$$

In this chapter sin, cos *and* tan *stand for these functions as operated by your calculator in 'degree mode'. You enter a number* x, *and the output is* $\sin x°$, $\cos x°$ *or* $\tan x°$.

Other functions need several keys, such as 'subtract 3':

$$7 \ \rightarrow \ [\ -,\ 3,\ =\ ] \ \rightarrow \ 4.$$

But the principle is the same. The important point is that it is the key sequence inside the square brackets that represents the function. This sequence is the same whatever number you key in as the input in Step 1.

You can think of a function as a kind of machine. Just as you can have a machine which takes fabric and turns it into clothes, so a function takes numbers in the domain and turns them into numbers in the range. For a general input number x, you can write

$$x \;\rightarrow\; [\; +/-\;] \;\rightarrow\; -x,$$
$$x \;\rightarrow\; [\; -,\; 3,\; =\;] \;\rightarrow\; x-3,$$

and so on. And for a general function,

$$x \;\rightarrow\; [\; \mathrm{f}\;] \;\rightarrow\; \mathrm{f}(x),$$

where f stands for the key sequence of the function.

This book has often used phrases like 'the function x^2', 'the function $|x|$', or 'the function $\mathrm{f}(x)$', and you have understood what is meant. Working mathematicians do this all the time. But it is strictly wrong; x^2, $|x|$ and $\mathrm{f}(x)$ are symbols for the *output* when the input is x, not for the function itself. When you need to use precise language, you should refer to 'the function square', 'the function cos' or 'the function f'.

Unfortunately only a few functions have convenient names like 'square' or 'cos'. There is no simple name for a function whose output is given by an expression such as $x^2 - 6x + 4$. The way round this is to decide for the time being to call this function f (or any other letter you like). You can then write

$$\mathrm{f} : x \mapsto x^2 - 6x + 4.$$

You read this as ' f is the function which turns any input number x in the domain into the output number $x^2 - 6x + 4$'. Notice the bar at the blunt end of the arrow; this avoids confusion with the arrow which has been used to stand for 'tends to' in finding gradients of tangents.

Try to write a key sequence to represent this function. (You may need the memory keys.)

Example 2.1.1
If $\mathrm{f} : x \mapsto x(5-x)$, what is $\mathrm{f}(3)$?

The symbol $\mathrm{f}(3)$ stands for the output when the input is 3. The function called f turns the input 3 into the output $3(5-3) = 6$. So $\mathrm{f}(3) = 6$.

This idea of using an arrow to show the connection between the input and the output can also be linked to the graph of the function. Fig. 2.1 shows the graph of $y = x(5-x)$, with the input number 3 on the x-axis. An arrow which goes up the page from this point and bends through a right angle when it hits the graph takes you to the output number 6 on the y-axis.

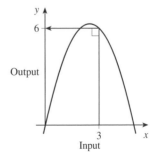

Fig. 2.1

2.2 Forming composite functions

If you want to work out values of $\sqrt{x-3}$, you would probably use the key sequence $-, 3, =, \sqrt{}$ with hardly a thought. But if you look carefully, you will see that three numbers appear in the display during the process. For example, if you use an input 7, the display will show in turn your input number 7, then (on keying $=$) 4, and finally the output 2. In fact, you are really working out two functions, 'subtract 3' then 'square root', in succession. You could represent the whole calculation:

$$7 \;\rightarrow\; [-,\, 3,\, =] \;\rightarrow\; 4 \;\rightarrow\; [\sqrt{}\,] \;\rightarrow\; 2.$$

The output of the first function becomes the input of the second.

Example 2.2.1
Find the output if the functions square, sin act in succession on inputs of
(a) 30,   (b) x.

    (a) $30 \;\rightarrow\; [\,\text{square}\,] \;\rightarrow\; 900 \;\rightarrow\; [\,\sin\,] \;\rightarrow\; 0.$

    (b) $x \;\rightarrow\; [\,\text{square}\,] \;\rightarrow\; x^2 \;\rightarrow\; [\,\sin\,] \;\rightarrow\; \sin(x^2)^{\circ}.$

Notice that since in (b) the input to the function sin is x^2, not x, the output is $\sin(x^2)^{\circ}$, not $\sin x^{\circ}$. For a general input, and two general functions f and g, this would become:

$$x \;\rightarrow\; [\,\text{f}\,] \;\rightarrow\; \text{f}(x) \;\rightarrow\; [\,\text{g}\,] \;\rightarrow\; \text{g}(\text{f}(x)).$$

Since the output of the composite function is $\text{g}(\text{f}(x))$, the composite function itself is denoted by gf. Notice that gf must be read as 'first f, then g'. You must get used to reading the symbol gf from right to left. Writing fg means 'first g, then f', which is almost always a different function from gf. For instance, if you change the order of the functions in Example 2.2.1 part (a), instead of the output 0 you get

$$30 \;\rightarrow\; [\,\sin\,] \;\rightarrow\; 0.5 \;\rightarrow\; [\,\text{square}\,] \;\rightarrow\; 0.25.$$

Example 2.2.2
Let $\text{f} : x \mapsto x + 3$ and $\text{g} : x \mapsto x^2$. Find gf and fg. Show that there is just one number x such that $\text{gf}(x) = \text{fg}(x)$.

    The composite function gf is represented by

$$x \;\rightarrow\; [\,\text{f}\,] \;\rightarrow\; x + 3 \;\rightarrow\; [\,\text{g}\,] \;\rightarrow\; (x + 3)^2$$

and fg is represented by

$$x \;\rightarrow\; [\,\text{g}\,] \;\rightarrow\; x^2 \;\rightarrow\; [\,\text{f}\,] \;\rightarrow\; x^2 + 3.$$

So $\text{gf} : x \mapsto (x + 3)^2$ and $\text{fg} : x \mapsto x^2 + 3$.

If $\text{gf}(x) = \text{fg}(x)$, $(x + 3)^2 = x^2 + 3$, so $x^2 + 6x + 9 = x^2 + 3$, or $x = -1$.

You can check this with your calculator. If you input -1 and then 'add 3' $[+, 3, =]$ followed by 'square', the display will show in turn $-1, 2, 4$. If you do 'square' followed by 'add 3', it will show $-1, 1, 4$. With this input, the outputs are the same although the intermediate displays are different.

Example 2.2.3
If $f : x \mapsto \cos x°$ and $g : x \mapsto \dfrac{1}{x}$, calculate   (a) $gf(60)$,   (b) $gf(90)$.

    (a)   With input 60, the calculator will show in turn $60, 0.5, 2$, so that $gf(60) = 2$.

    (b)   With input 90, the calculator will display 90 and 0 and then give an error message! This is because $\cos 90° = 0$ and $\frac{1}{0}$ is not defined.

What has happened in Example 2.2.3 part (b) is that the number 0 is in the range of the function f, but it is not in the domain of g. You always need to be aware that this may happen when you find the composite of two functions. It is time to look again at domains and ranges, so that you can avoid this problem.

2.3   Domain and range

When the letters x and y are used in mathematics, for example in an equation such as $y = 2x - 10$, it is generally understood that they stand for real numbers. But sometimes it is important to be absolutely precise about this. The symbol $\mathbb{R}$ is used to stand for 'the set of real numbers', and the symbol $\in$ for 'belongs to'. With these symbols, you can shorten the statement 'x is a real number', or 'x belongs to the set of real numbers', to $x \in \mathbb{R}$. So you can write

$$f : x \mapsto 2x - 10, \quad x \in \mathbb{R}$$

to indicate that f is the function whose domain is the set of real numbers which turns any input x into the output $2x - 10$.

Strictly, a function is not completely defined unless you state the domain as well as the rule for obtaining the output from the input. In this case the range is also $\mathbb{R}$, although you do not need to state this in describing the function.

You know from P1 Chapters 8 and 9 that for some functions the domain is only a part of $\mathbb{R}$, because the expression $f(x)$ only has meaning for some $x \in \mathbb{R}$. (Here $\in$ has to be read as 'belonging to' rather than 'belongs to'.) The set of real numbers for which $f(x)$ has a meaning will be called the 'natural domain' of f. With a calculator, if you input a number not in the natural domain, the output will be an 'error' display.

For the square root function, for example, the natural domain is the set of positive real numbers and zero, so you write

$$\text{square root} : x \mapsto \sqrt{x}, \quad \text{where } x \in \mathbb{R} \text{ and } x \geq 0.$$

If you are given a function described by a formula but no domain is stated, you should assume that the domain is the natural domain.

Example 2.3.1
Find the range of the functions
(a) sin, with natural domain $\mathbb{R}$,   (b) sin, with domain $x \in \mathbb{R}$ and $0 < x < 90$.

From the graph of $y = \sin x°$ shown in Fig. 2.2 you can read off the ranges:

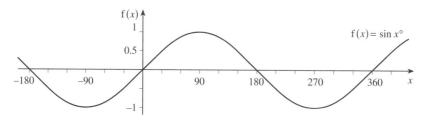

Fig. 2.2

(a)   For $x \in \mathbb{R}$, the range is $y \in \mathbb{R}, -1 \leqslant y \leqslant 1$.

(b)   For $x \in \mathbb{R}, 0 < x < 90$, the range is $y \in \mathbb{R}, 0 < y < 1$.

Although the letter x is usually used in describing the domain, and y for the range, this is not essential. The set of numbers $y \in \mathbb{R}, 0 < y < 1$ is the same set of numbers as $x \in \mathbb{R}, 0 < x < 1$ or $t \in \mathbb{R}, 0 < t < 1$.

It is especially important to understand this when you find composite functions. For example, in Example 2.2.3 part (a), the number 0.5 appears first as the output for the input 60 to the function $f : x \mapsto \cos x°$, so you might think of this as $y = \cos 60° = 0.5$. But for the input to the function $g : x \mapsto \dfrac{1}{x}$, it is natural to write $x = 0.5$. The number 0.5 belongs first to the range of f, then to the domain of g.

This is where Example 2.2.3 part (b) breaks down. The number 0, which appears as the output when the input to f is 90, is not in the natural domain of g. So although 90 is in the natural domain of f, it is not in the natural domain of gf.

The general rule is:

To form the composite function gf, the domain D of f must be chosen so that the whole of the range of f is included in the domain of g. The function gf is then defined as $gf : x \mapsto g(f(x))$, $x \in D$.

For the functions in Example 2.2.3, the domain of g is the set $\mathbb{R}$ excluding 0, so the domain of f must be chosen to exclude the numbers x for which $\cos x° = 0$. These are $\ldots, -450, -270, -90, +90, +270, +450, \ldots$, all of which can be summed up by the formula $90 + 180n$, where n is an integer.

There is a neat way of writing this, using the standard symbol $\mathbb{Z}$ for the set of integers $\ldots, -3, -2, -1, 0, 1, 2, 3, \ldots$. The domain of f can then be expressed as $x \in \mathbb{R}, x \neq 90 + 180n, n \in \mathbb{Z}$.

Example 2.3.2
Find the natural domain and the corresponding range of the function $x \mapsto \sqrt{x(x-3)}$.

You can express the function as gf, where $f: x \mapsto x(x-3)$ and $g: x \mapsto \sqrt{x}$.

The natural domain of g is $x \in \mathbb{R}, x \geqslant 0$, so you want the range of f to be included in $y \in \mathbb{R}, y \geqslant 0$. (Switching from x to y is not essential, but you may find it easier.) The solution of the inequality $y = x(x-3) \geqslant 0$ is $x \geqslant 3$ or $x \leqslant 0$.

The natural domain of gf is therefore $x \in \mathbb{R}, x \geqslant 3$ or $x \leqslant 0$.

With this domain the range of f is $y \in \mathbb{R}, y \geqslant 0$, so the numbers input to g are given by $x \in \mathbb{R}, x \geqslant 0$. With this domain, the range of g is $y \in \mathbb{R}, y \geqslant 0$. This is therefore the range of the combined function gf.

Try using a graphic calculator to plot the graph $y = \sqrt{x(x-3)}$, using a window of $-1 \leqslant x \leqslant 4$ and $0 \leqslant y \leqslant 2$. You should find that no points are plotted for the 'illegal' values of x in the interval $0 < x < 3$. If you were to input a number in this interval, such as 1, you will get as far as $1(1-3) = -2$, but the final $\sqrt{}$ key will give you an error message or some display which does not represent a real number.

Exercise 2A

1 Given $f: x \mapsto (3x+5)^2$, where $x \in \mathbb{R}$, find the values of
  (a) $f(2)$,
  (b) $f(-1)$,
  (c) $f(7)$.

2 Given $g: x \mapsto 3x^2 + 5$, where $x \in \mathbb{R}$, find the values of
  (a) $g(2)$,
  (b) $g(-1)$,
  (c) $g(7)$.

3 Given $f: x \mapsto \dfrac{4}{x+5}$, where $x \in \mathbb{R}$ and $x \neq -5$, find the values of
  (a) $f(-1)$,
  (b) $f(-4)$,
  (c) $f(3)$.

4 Given $g: x \mapsto \dfrac{4}{x} + 5$, where $x \in \mathbb{R}$ and $x \neq 0$, find the values of
  (a) $g(-1)$,
  (b) $g(-4)$,
  (c) $g(3)$.

5 Find the output if the functions 'square', 'subtract 4' act in succession on an input of
  (a) 2,
  (b) −5,
  (c) $\frac{1}{2}$,
  (d) x.

6 Find the output if the functions 'cos', 'add 2', 'cube' act in succession on an input of
  (a) 0,
  (b) 90,
  (c) 120,
  (d) x.

7 Find the output if the functions 'square root', 'multiply by 2', 'subtract 10', 'square', act in succession on an input of
  (a) 9,
  (b) 16,
  (c) $\frac{1}{4}$,
  (d) x.

8 Determine the key sequence needed to represent each of the following functions.
  (a) $f: x \mapsto 4x+9$
  (b) $f: x \mapsto 4(x+9)$
  (c) $f: x \mapsto 2x^2 - 5$
  (d) $f: x \mapsto 2(x-5)^2$
  (e) $f: x \mapsto (\sqrt{x}-3)^3, x \geqslant 0$
  (f) $f: x \mapsto \sqrt{(x-2)^2 + 10}$

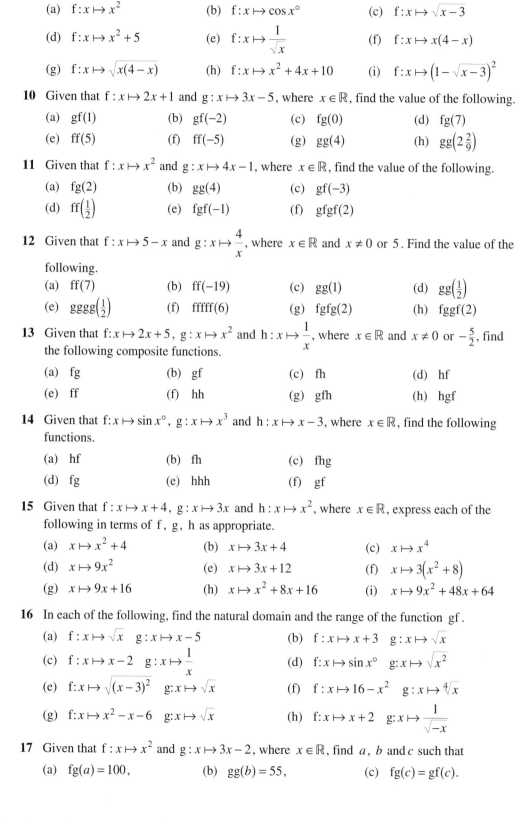

9 Find the natural domain and corresponding range of each of the following functions.

(a) $f : x \mapsto x^2$

(b) $f : x \mapsto \cos x°$

(c) $f : x \mapsto \sqrt{x-3}$

(d) $f : x \mapsto x^2 + 5$

(e) $f : x \mapsto \dfrac{1}{\sqrt{x}}$

(f) $f : x \mapsto x(4-x)$

(g) $f : x \mapsto \sqrt{x(4-x)}$

(h) $f : x \mapsto x^2 + 4x + 10$

(i) $f : x \mapsto \left(1 - \sqrt{x-3}\right)^2$

10 Given that $f : x \mapsto 2x + 1$ and $g : x \mapsto 3x - 5$, where $x \in \mathbb{R}$, find the value of the following.

(a) $gf(1)$

(b) $gf(-2)$

(c) $fg(0)$

(d) $fg(7)$

(e) $ff(5)$

(f) $ff(-5)$

(g) $gg(4)$

(h) $gg\left(2\tfrac{2}{9}\right)$

11 Given that $f : x \mapsto x^2$ and $g : x \mapsto 4x - 1$, where $x \in \mathbb{R}$, find the value of the following.

(a) $fg(2)$

(b) $gg(4)$

(c) $gf(-3)$

(d) $ff\left(\tfrac{1}{2}\right)$

(e) $fgf(-1)$

(f) $gfgf(2)$

12 Given that $f : x \mapsto 5 - x$ and $g : x \mapsto \dfrac{4}{x}$, where $x \in \mathbb{R}$ and $x \neq 0$ or 5. Find the value of the following.

(a) $ff(7)$

(b) $ff(-19)$

(c) $gg(1)$

(d) $gg\left(\tfrac{1}{2}\right)$

(e) $gggg\left(\tfrac{1}{2}\right)$

(f) $fffff(6)$

(g) $fgfg(2)$

(h) $fggf(2)$

13 Given that $f : x \mapsto 2x + 5$, $g : x \mapsto x^2$ and $h : x \mapsto \dfrac{1}{x}$, where $x \in \mathbb{R}$ and $x \neq 0$ or $-\tfrac{5}{2}$, find the following composite functions.

(a) fg

(b) gf

(c) fh

(d) hf

(e) ff

(f) hh

(g) gfh

(h) hgf

14 Given that $f : x \mapsto \sin x°$, $g : x \mapsto x^3$ and $h : x \mapsto x - 3$, where $x \in \mathbb{R}$, find the following functions.

(a) hf

(b) fh

(c) fhg

(d) fg

(e) hhh

(f) gf

15 Given that $f : x \mapsto x + 4$, $g : x \mapsto 3x$ and $h : x \mapsto x^2$, where $x \in \mathbb{R}$, express each of the following in terms of f, g, h as appropriate.

(a) $x \mapsto x^2 + 4$

(b) $x \mapsto 3x + 4$

(c) $x \mapsto x^4$

(d) $x \mapsto 9x^2$

(e) $x \mapsto 3x + 12$

(f) $x \mapsto 3\left(x^2 + 8\right)$

(g) $x \mapsto 9x + 16$

(h) $x \mapsto x^2 + 8x + 16$

(i) $x \mapsto 9x^2 + 48x + 64$

16 In each of the following, find the natural domain and the range of the function gf.

(a) $f : x \mapsto \sqrt{x} \quad g : x \mapsto x - 5$

(b) $f : x \mapsto x + 3 \quad g : x \mapsto \sqrt{x}$

(c) $f : x \mapsto x - 2 \quad g : x \mapsto \dfrac{1}{x}$

(d) $f : x \mapsto \sin x° \quad g : x \mapsto \sqrt{x^2}$

(e) $f : x \mapsto \sqrt{(x-3)^2} \quad g : x \mapsto \sqrt{x}$

(f) $f : x \mapsto 16 - x^2 \quad g : x \mapsto \sqrt[4]{x}$

(g) $f : x \mapsto x^2 - x - 6 \quad g : x \mapsto \sqrt{x}$

(h) $f : x \mapsto x + 2 \quad g : x \mapsto \dfrac{1}{\sqrt{-x}}$

17 Given that $f : x \mapsto x^2$ and $g : x \mapsto 3x - 2$, where $x \in \mathbb{R}$, find a, b and c such that

(a) $fg(a) = 100$,

(b) $gg(b) = 55$,

(c) $fg(c) = gf(c)$.

18 Given that $f : x \mapsto ax + b$ and that $ff : x \mapsto 9x - 28$, find the possible values of a and b.

19 For $f : x \mapsto ax + b$, $f(2) = 19$ and $ff(0) = 55$. Find the possible values of a and b.

20 The functions $f : x \mapsto 4x + 1$ and $g : x \mapsto ax + b$ are such that $fg = gf$ for all real values of x. Show that $a = 3b + 1$.

2.4 Reversing functions

If your sister is 2 years older than you, then you are 2 years younger than her. To get her age from yours you use the 'add 2' function; to get your age from hers you 'subtract 2'. The functions 'add 2' and 'subtract 2' are said to be **inverse functions** of each other. That is, 'subtract 2' is the inverse function of 'add 2' (and vice versa).

You know many pairs of inverse functions: 'double' and 'halve', 'cube' and 'cube root' are simple examples.

There are also some functions which are their own inverses, such as 'change sign'; to undo the effect of a change of sign, you just change sign again. Another example is 'reciprocal' $\left(x \mapsto \dfrac{1}{x} \right)$. These functions are said to be **self-inverse**.

The inverse of a function f is denoted by the symbol f^{-1}. If f turns an input number x into an output number y, then f^{-1} turns y into x. You can illustrate this graphically by reversing the arrow which symbolises the function, as in Fig. 2.3. The range of f becomes the domain of f^{-1}, and the domain of f becomes the range of f^{-1}.

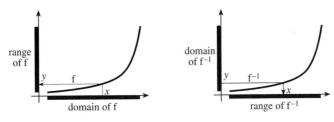

Fig. 2.3

You have used inverse functions in calculations about triangles. Often you know an angle, and calculate the length of a side by using one of the trigonometric functions such as $\tan$. But if you know the sides and want to calculate the angle you use the inverse function, which is denoted by $\tan^{-1}$.

On many calculators you find values of $\tan^{-1}$ by using a sequence of two keys: first an 'inverse' key (which on some calculators is labelled 'shift' or '2nd function') and then 'tan'. In what follows this is referred to as 'the $\tan^{-1}$ key', and similarly for the $\sin^{-1}$ and $\cos^{-1}$ functions.

Example 2.4.1
Find the values of $\cos^{-1} y$ when   (a) $y = 0.5$,   (b) $y = -1$,   (c) $y = 1.5$.

Using the $\cos^{-1}$ key with inputs 0.5, -1, 1.5 in turn gives output of 60, 180, and an error message!

So, in degree mode, (a) $\cos^{-1} 0.5 = 60$,
(b) $\cos^{-1}(-1) = 180$, but (c) $\cos^{-1} 1.5$ has no
meaning. Fig. 2.4 shows the graph of $y = \cos x°$
with domain $x \in \mathbb{R}, 0 \leqslant x \leqslant 180$. This shows that
the range of the function cos is $-1 \leqslant x \leqslant 1$. Since
this is the domain of the inverse function, the
answer to (c) is explained by the fact that 1.5 lies
outside this interval.

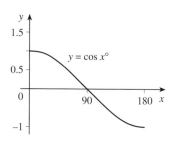

Fig. 2.4

If you try to check by finding the cosines of the answers to
this example, you get

(a) $0.5 \rightarrow [\cos^{-1}] \rightarrow 60 \rightarrow [\cos] \rightarrow 0.5$,

(b) $-1 \rightarrow [\cos^{-1}] \rightarrow 180 \rightarrow [\cos] \rightarrow -1$.

This is of course what you would expect; the function and its inverse cancel each other
out. In general, if $-1 \leqslant y \leqslant 1$, then

$$y \rightarrow [\cos^{-1}] \rightarrow [\cos] \rightarrow y.$$

You may therefore be surprised by the result of the next example.

Example 2.4.2
If $f : x \mapsto \sin x°$ and $g : x \mapsto \sin^{-1} x$, evaluate   (a) gf(50),   (b) gf(130).

Work this example for yourself using the calculator sequence

$$x \rightarrow [\sin] \rightarrow [\sin^{-1}] \rightarrow gf(x).$$

You should get the answers (a) 50 (as you would expect), (b) 50.

The answer to part (b) calls for a more careful look at the theory of inverse functions.

2.5   One–one functions

The answers to Example 2.4.2 can be explained by Fig. 2.5, which shows the graph of
$y = \sin x°$ over the interval $0 \leqslant x \leqslant 180$. The graph rises from $y = 0$ to $y = 1$ over the
values for x for which the angle is acute, and then falls symmetrically back to $y = 0$
over the values for which the angle is obtuse. This is because the sine of the obtuse
angle $x°$ is equal to the sine of the supplementary angle $(180 - x)°$. So
$\sin 130° = \sin 50°$, and the calculator gives the value $0.7660\ldots$ for both.

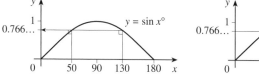

Fig. 2.5

When you use the $\sin^{-1}$ key to find $\sin^{-1}(0.7660\ldots)$, the calculator has to give the same answer in either case. It is programmed always to give the answer with the smallest modulus, which in this case is 50.

Exactly the same problem arises whenever you try to reverse a function which has the same output for more than one input. And in mathematics, such ambiguity is not acceptable. The solution adopted is a drastic one, to refuse to define an inverse for any function which has the same output for more than one input. That is, the only functions which have an inverse function are those for which each output in the range comes from only one input. These functions are said to be 'one–one'.

A function f defined for some domain D is **one–one** if, for each number y in the range R of f there is only one number $x \in D$ such that $y = f(x)$. The function with domain R defined by $f^{-1} : y \mapsto x$, where $y = f(x)$, is the **inverse function** of f.

This definition was illustrated above in Fig. 2.3, which was drawn to ensure that the function f was one–one.

The way in which this is achieved in practice is to restrict the domain of f. For example, the function $x \mapsto \sin x°$, $x \in \mathbb{R}$, whose graph is shown in Fig. 2.2 on page 198, is not one–one, so it does not have an inverse. But the function $x \mapsto \sin x°$, where $x \in \mathbb{R}$ and $-90 \leqslant x \leqslant 90$, shown in Fig. 2.6, is one–one; it is the inverse of this function which is denoted by $\sin^{-1}$, and activated by the familiar key sequence on the calculator.

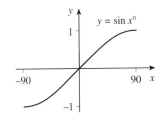

Fig. 2.6

Fig. 2.3 suggests that, if you combine a function with its inverse, you get back to the number you started with. That is,

$$f^{-1}f(x) = x, \quad \text{and} \quad ff^{-1}(y) = y.$$

The functions $f^{-1}f$ and ff^{-1} are called **identity functions** because their inputs and outputs are identical. But there is a subtle difference between these two composite functions, since their domains may not be the same; the first has domain D and the second has domain R.

2.6 Finding inverse functions

For very simple one-step functions it is easy to write down an expression for the inverse function. The inverse of 'add 2' is 'subtract 2', so

$$f : x \mapsto x + 2, x \in \mathbb{R} \quad \text{has inverse} \quad f^{-1} : x \mapsto x - 2, x \in \mathbb{R}.$$

Notice that the inverse could equally well be written as

$$f^{-1} : y \mapsto y - 2, y \in \mathbb{R}.$$

You can sometimes break down more complicated functions into a chain of simple steps. You can then find the inverse by going backwards through each step in reverse order. (This is sometimes called the 'shoes and socks' process: you put your socks on before your shoes, but you take off your shoes before your socks. In mathematical notation, $(gf)^{-1} = f^{-1}g^{-1}$, where f denotes putting on your socks and g your shoes.)

However, this method does not always work, particularly if x appears more than once in the expression for the function. You can then try writing $y = f(x)$, and turn the formula round into the form $x = g(y)$. Then g is the inverse of f.

Example 2.6.1
Find the inverse of $f : x \mapsto 2x + 5, x \in \mathbb{R}$.

Note first that f is one–one, and that the range is $\mathbb{R}$.

Method 1   You can break the function down as

$$x \;\rightarrow\; [\,\text{double}\,] \;\rightarrow\; [\,\text{add } 5\,] \;\rightarrow\; 2x + 5.$$

To find f^{-1}, go backwards through the chain (read from right to left):

$$\tfrac{1}{2}(x - 5) \;\leftarrow\; [\,\text{halve}\,] \;\leftarrow\; [\,\text{subtract } 5\,] \;\leftarrow\; x.$$

So $f^{-1} : x \mapsto \tfrac{1}{2}(x - 5), x \in \mathbb{R}$.

Method 2   If $y = 2x + 5$,

$$y - 5 = 2x$$
$$x = \tfrac{1}{2}(y - 5).$$

So the inverse function is $f^{-1} : y \mapsto \tfrac{1}{2}(y - 5), y \in \mathbb{R}$.

The two answers are the same, even though different letters are used.

Example 2.6.2
Restrict the domain of the function $f : x \mapsto x^2 - 2x$, so that an inverse function exists, and find an expression for f^{-1}.

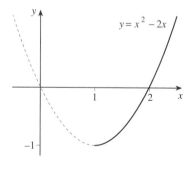

Fig. 2.7 shows the graph of $y = x^2 - 2x, x \in \mathbb{R}$, which is quadratic with its vertex at $(1, -1)$. For $y > -1$ there are two values of x for each y, so the graph does not represent a one–one function. One way of making it one–one is to chop off the part of the graph to the left of its axis of symmetry. The remainder has domain $x \in \mathbb{R}, x \geqslant 1$, and range $y \in \mathbb{R}, y \geqslant -1$.

Fig. 2.7

Method 1   Completing the square, $f(x) = (x - 1)^2 - 1$, so you can break the function down as

$$x \rightarrow [\,\text{subtract } 1\,] \rightarrow [\,\text{square}\,] \rightarrow [\,\text{subtract } 1\,] \rightarrow y.$$

In reverse,

$$1+\sqrt{y+1} \leftarrow [\text{add } 1] \leftarrow [\ \sqrt{\ }\ ] \leftarrow [\text{add } 1] \leftarrow y.$$

So the inverse function is $f^{-1} : y \mapsto 1 + \sqrt{y+1},\ y \in \mathbb{R},\ y \geq -1$.

Notice that the positive square root was chosen, to make $x > 1$.

Method 2 If $y = x^2 - 2x$, $x^2 - 2x - y = 0$.

This is a quadratic equation with roots

$$x = \frac{2 \pm \sqrt{4+4y}}{2} = 1 \pm \sqrt{1+y}.$$

Since $x \geq 1$, you must choose the positive sign, giving $x = 1 + \sqrt{1+y}$. So the inverse function is $f^{-1} : y \mapsto 1 + \sqrt{y+1},\ y \in \mathbb{R},\ y \geq -1$.

Example 2.6.3
Find the inverse of the function $y = \dfrac{x+2}{x-2}$, where $x \in \mathbb{R}$ and $x \neq 2$.

It is not obvious that this function is one–one, or what its range is. However, using the second method and writing $y = \dfrac{x+2}{x-2}$,

$$y(x-2) = x+2,$$
$$yx - 2y = x + 2,$$
$$yx - x = 2y + 2,$$
$$x(y-1) = 2(y+1),$$
$$x = \frac{2(y+1)}{y-1}.$$

This shows that, unless $y = 1$, there is just one value of x for each value of y. So f must be one–one, the inverse function therefore exists, and

$$f^{-1} : y \mapsto \frac{2(y+1)}{y-1} \text{ where } y \in \mathbb{R} \text{ and } y \neq -1.$$

2.7 Graphing inverse functions

Fig. 2.8 on the next page shows the graph of $y = f(x)$, where f is a one–one function with domain D and range R. Since f^{-1} exists, with domain R and range D, you can also write the equation as $x = f^{-1}(y)$. You can regard Fig. 2.8 as the graph of both f and f^{-1}.

But you sometimes want to draw the graph in the more conventional form, as $y = f^{-1}(x)$ with the domain along the x-axis. To do this you have to swap the x- and y-axes, which you do by reflecting the graph in Fig. 2.8 in the line $y = x$. (Make sure that you have the same scale on both axes!) Then the x-axis is reflected into the y-axis and vice versa, and the graph of $x = f^{-1}(y)$ is reflected into the graph of $y = f^{-1}(x)$. This is shown in Fig. 2.9.

If f is a one–one function, the graphs of $y = f(x)$ and $y = f^{-1}(x)$ are reflections of each other in the line $y = x$.

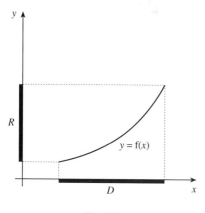

Fig. 2.8

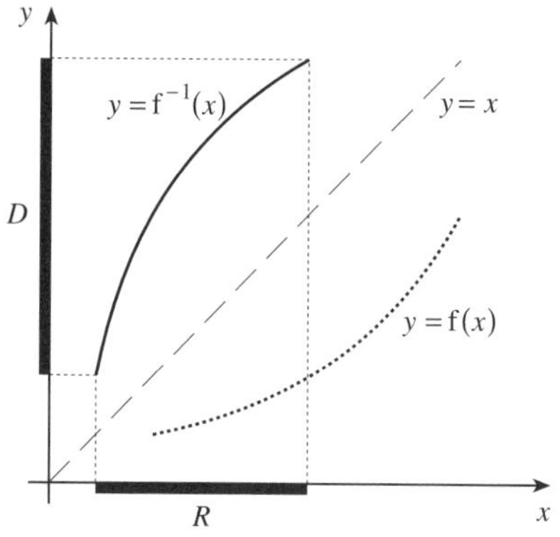

Fig. 2.9

Example 2.7.1

For the function in Example 2.6.2, draw the graphs of $y = f(x)$ and $y = f^{-1}(x)$.

Example 2.6.2 showed that
$f^{-1}(x) = 1 + \sqrt{x+1}$, $x \in \mathbb{R}$, $x \geqslant -1$.

Fig. 2.10 shows the graphs of
$y = f(x) = x^2 - 2x$ for $x \geqslant 1$ and
$y = f^{-1}(x) = 1 + \sqrt{x+1}$ for $x \geqslant -1$. You
can see that these graphs are reflections of
each other in the line $y = x$.

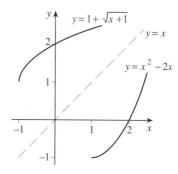

Fig. 2.10

Exercise 2B

1 Each of the following functions has domain $\mathbb{R}$. In each case use a graph to show that the function is one–one, and write down its inverse.

  (a) $f : x \mapsto x + 4$ (b) $f : x \mapsto x - 5$ (c) $f : x \mapsto 2x$

  (d) $f : x \mapsto \frac{1}{4}x$ (e) $f : x \mapsto x^3$ (f) $f : x \mapsto \sqrt[5]{x}$

2 Given the function $f : x \mapsto x - 6, x \in \mathbb{R}$, find the values of

  (a) $f^{-1}(4)$ (b) $f^{-1}(1)$ (c) $f^{-1}(-3)$ (d) $ff^{-1}(5)$ (e) $f^{-1}f(-4)$

3 Given the function $f : x \mapsto 5x, x \in \mathbb{R}$, find the values of

  (a) $f^{-1}(20)$ (b) $f^{-1}(100)$ (c) $f^{-1}(7)$ (d) $ff^{-1}(15)$ (e) $f^{-1}f(-6)$

4 Given the function $f : x \mapsto \sqrt[3]{x}, x \in \mathbb{R}$, find the values of

  (a) $f^{-1}(2)$ (b) $f^{-1}\left(\frac{1}{2}\right)$ (c) $f^{-1}(8)$ (d) $f^{-1}f(-27)$ (e) $ff^{-1}(5)$

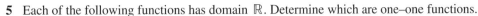

5 Each of the following functions has domain $\mathbb{R}$. Determine which are one–one functions.

(a) $f : x \mapsto 3x + 4$ (b) $f : x \mapsto x^2 + 1$ (c) $f : x \mapsto x^2 - 3x$

(d) $f : x \mapsto 5 - x$ (e) $f : x \mapsto \cos x°$ (f) $f : x \mapsto x^3 - 2$

(g) $f : x \mapsto \frac{1}{2}x - 7$ (h) $f : x \mapsto \sqrt{x^2}$ (i) $f : x \mapsto x(x - 4)$

(j) $f : x \mapsto x^3 - 3x$ (k) $f : x \mapsto x^9$ (l) $f : x \mapsto \sqrt{x^2 + 1}$

6 Determine which of the following functions, with the specified domains, are one–one.

(a) $f : x \mapsto x^2, x > 0$ (b) $f : x \mapsto \cos x°, -90 \leqslant x \leqslant 90$

(c) $f : x \mapsto 1 - 2x, x < 0$ (d) $f : x \mapsto x(x - 2), 0 < x < 2$

(e) $f : x \mapsto x(x - 2), x > 2$ (f) $f : x \mapsto x(x - 2), x < 1$

(g) $f : x \mapsto \sqrt{x}, x > 0$ (h) $f : x \mapsto x^2 + 6x - 5, x > 0$

(i) $f : x \mapsto x^2 + 6x - 5, x < 0$ (j) $f : x \mapsto x^2 + 6x - 5, x > -3$

7 Each of the following functions has domain $x \geqslant k$. In each case, find the smallest possible value of k such that the function is one–one.

(a) $f : x \mapsto x^2 - 4$ (b) $f : x \mapsto (x + 1)^2$ (c) $f : x \mapsto (3x - 2)^2$

(d) $f : x \mapsto x^2 - 8x + 15$ (e) $f : x \mapsto x^2 + 10x + 1$ (f) $f : x \mapsto (x + 4)(x - 2)$

(g) $f : x \mapsto x^2 - 3x$ (h) $f : x \mapsto 6 + 2x - x^2$ (i) $f : x \mapsto (x - 4)^4$

8 Use Method 1 of Example 2.6.1 to find the inverse of each of the following functions.

(a) $f : x \mapsto 3x - 1, x \in \mathbb{R}$ (b) $f : x \mapsto \frac{1}{2}x + 4, x \in \mathbb{R}$

(c) $f : x \mapsto x^3 + 5, x \in \mathbb{R}$ (d) $f : x \mapsto \sqrt{x} - 3, x > 0$

(e) $f : x \mapsto \dfrac{5x - 3}{2}, x \in \mathbb{R}$ (f) $f : x \mapsto (x - 1)^2 + 6, x \geqslant 1$

9 Use Method 2 of Example 2.6.2 to find the inverse of each of the following functions.

(a) $f : x \mapsto 6x + 5, x \in \mathbb{R}$ (b) $f : x \mapsto \dfrac{x + 4}{5}, x \in \mathbb{R}$

(c) $f : x \mapsto 4 - 2x, x \in \mathbb{R}$ (d) $f : x \mapsto \dfrac{2x + 7}{3}, x \in \mathbb{R}$

(e) $f : x \mapsto 2x^3 + 5, x \in \mathbb{R}$ (f) $f : x \mapsto \dfrac{1}{x} + 4, x \in \mathbb{R}$ and $x \neq 0$

(g) $f : x \mapsto \dfrac{5}{x - 1}, x \in \mathbb{R}$ and $x \neq 1$ (h) $f : x \mapsto (x + 2)^2 + 7, x \in \mathbb{R}$ and $x \geqslant -2$

(i) $f : x \mapsto (2x - 3)^2 - 5, x \in \mathbb{R}$ and $x \geqslant \frac{3}{2}$ (j) $f : x \mapsto x^2 - 6x, x \in \mathbb{R}$ and $x \geqslant 3$

10 For each of the following, find the inverse function and sketch the graphs of $y = f(x)$ and $y = f^{-1}(x)$.

(a) $f : x \mapsto 4x, x \in \mathbb{R}$ (b) $f : x \mapsto x + 3, x \in \mathbb{R}$

(c) $f : x \mapsto \sqrt{x}, x \in \mathbb{R}$ and $x \geqslant 0$ (d) $f : x \mapsto 2x + 1, x \in \mathbb{R}$

(e) $f : x \mapsto (x - 2)^2, x \in \mathbb{R}$ and $x \geqslant 2$ (f) $f : x \mapsto 1 - 3x, x \in \mathbb{R}$

(g) $f : x \mapsto \dfrac{3}{x}, x \in \mathbb{R}$ and $x \neq 0$ (h) $f : x \mapsto 7 - x, x \in \mathbb{R}$

11 Show that the following functions are self-inverse.

    (a) $f : x \mapsto 5 - x, \, x \in \mathbb{R}$

    (b) $f : x \mapsto -x, \, x \in \mathbb{R}$

    (c) $f : x \mapsto \dfrac{4}{x}, \, x \in \mathbb{R}$ and $x \neq 0$

    (d) $f : x \mapsto \dfrac{6}{5x}, \, x \in \mathbb{R}$ and $x \neq 0$

    (e) $f : x \mapsto \dfrac{x + 5}{x - 1}, \, x \in \mathbb{R}$ and $x \neq 1$

    (f) $f : x \mapsto \dfrac{3x - 1}{2x - 3}, \, x \in \mathbb{R}$ and $x \neq \frac{3}{2}$

12 Find the inverse of each of the following functions.

    (a) $f : x \mapsto \dfrac{x}{x - 2}, \, x \in \mathbb{R}$ and $x \neq 2$

    (b) $f : x \mapsto \dfrac{2x + 1}{x - 4}, \, x \in \mathbb{R}$ and $x \neq 4$

    (c) $f : x \mapsto \dfrac{x + 2}{x - 5}, \, x \in \mathbb{R}$ and $x \neq 5$

    (d) $f : x \mapsto \dfrac{3x - 11}{4x - 3}, \, x \in \mathbb{R}$ and $x \neq \frac{3}{4}$

13 The function $f : x \mapsto x^2 - 4x + 3$ has domain $x \in \mathbb{R}$ and $x > 2$.

    (a) Determine the range of f.

    (b) Find the inverse function f^{-1} and state its domain and range.

    (c) Sketch the graphs of $y = f(x)$ and $y = f^{-1}(x)$.

14 The function $f : x \mapsto \sqrt{x - 2} + 3$ has domain $x \in \mathbb{R}$ and $x > 2$.

    (a) Determine the range of f.

    (b) Find the inverse function f^{-1} and state its domain and range.

    (c) Sketch the graphs of $y = f(x)$ and $y = f^{-1}(x)$.

15 The function $f : x \mapsto x^2 + 2x + 6$ has domain $x \in \mathbb{R}$ and $x \leqslant k$. Given that f is one–one, determine the greatest possible value of k. When k has this value,

    (a) determine the range of f,

    (b) find the inverse function f^{-1} and state its domain and range,

    (c) sketch the graphs of $y = f(x)$ and $y = f^{-1}(x)$.

16 The inverse of the function $f : x \mapsto ax + b, \, x \in \mathbb{R}$ is $f^{-1} : x \mapsto 8x - 3$. Find a and b.

17 The function $f : x \mapsto px + q, \, x \in \mathbb{R}$, is such that $f^{-1}(6) = 3$ and $f^{-1}(-29) = -2$. Find $f^{-1}(27)$.

18 The function $f : x \mapsto x^2 + x + 6$ has domain $x \in \mathbb{R}$ and $x > 0$. Find the inverse function and state its domain and range.

19 The function $f : x \mapsto -2x^2 + 4x - 7$ has domain $x \in \mathbb{R}$ and $x < 1$. Find the inverse function and state its domain and range.

20 For each of the following functions, sketch the graph of $y = f^{-1}(x)$.

    (a) $f : x \mapsto \sin x^\circ, \, x \in \mathbb{R}$ and $-90 \leqslant x \leqslant 90$

    (b) $f : x \mapsto \cos x^\circ, \, x \in \mathbb{R}$ and $0 \leqslant x \leqslant 180$

    (c) $f : x \mapsto \tan x^\circ, \, x \in \mathbb{R}$ and $-90 \leqslant x \leqslant 90$

Miscellaneous exercise 2

1 The functions f and g are defined by

$$f: x \mapsto 4x + 9, \, x \in \mathbb{R}, \qquad g: x \mapsto x^2 + 1, \, x \in \mathbb{R}.$$

Find the value of each of the following.

(a) fg(2)　　　　　　(b) $fg(2\sqrt{3})$　　　　　　(c) gf(−2)

(d) ff(−3)　　　　　　(e) gg(−4)　　　　　　(f) $fgf(\frac{1}{2})$

2 Find the natural domain and corresponding range of each of the following functions.

(a) $f: x \mapsto 4 - x^2$　　　　(b) $f: x \mapsto (x+3)^2 - 7$　　　　(c) $f: x \mapsto \sqrt{x+2}$

(d) $f: x \mapsto 5x + 6$　　　　(e) $f: x \mapsto (2x+3)^2$　　　　(f) $f: x \mapsto 2 - \sqrt{x}$

3 The functions f and g are defined by

$$f: x \mapsto x^3, \, x \in \mathbb{R} \qquad g: x \mapsto 1 - 2x, \, x \in \mathbb{R}.$$

Find the functions

(a) fg,　　　(b) gf,　　　(c) gff,　　　(d) gg,　　　(e) g^{-1}.

4 The function f is defined by $f: x \mapsto 2x^3 - 6, \, x \in \mathbb{R}$. Find the values of the following.

(a) f(3)　　　(b) $f^{-1}(48)$　　　(c) $f^{-1}(-8)$　　　(d) $f^{-1}f(4)$　　　(e) $ff^{-1}(4)$

5 The function f is defined for all real values of x by $f(x) = x^{\frac{1}{3}} + 10$. Evaluate

(a) ff(−8),　　　　(b) $f^{-1}(13)$.　　　　　　　　　　　　　　　　　(OCR)

6 Show that the function $f: x \mapsto (x+3)^2 + 1$, with domain $x \in \mathbb{R}$ and $x > 0$, is one–one and find its inverse.

7 The function f is defined by $f: x \mapsto 4x^3 + 3, \, x \in \mathbb{R}$. Give the corresponding definition of f^{-1}. State a relationship between the graphs of f and f^{-1}.　　　(OCR)

8 Given that $f(x) = 3x^2 - 4, \, x > 0$, and $g(x) = x + 4, \, x \in \mathbb{R}$, find

(a) $f^{-1}(x), \, x > -4$,　　　　(b) $fg(x), \, x > -4$.　　　　　　　　　(OCR)

9 The functions f, g and h are defined by

$$f: x \mapsto 2x + 1, \, x \in \mathbb{R}, \qquad g: x \mapsto x^5, \, x \in \mathbb{R}, \qquad h: x \mapsto \frac{1}{x}, \, x \in \mathbb{R} \text{ and } x \neq 0.$$

Express each of the following in terms of f, g, h as appropriate.

(a) $x \mapsto (2x+1)^5$　　　(b) $x \mapsto 4x + 3$　　　(c) $x \mapsto x^{\frac{1}{5}}$　　　(d) $x \mapsto 2x^{-5} + 1$

(e) $x \mapsto \dfrac{1}{2x^5 + 1}$　　　(f) $x \mapsto \dfrac{x-1}{2}$　　　(g) $x \mapsto \sqrt[5]{\dfrac{2}{x^5} + 1}$　　　(h) $x \mapsto \dfrac{2}{x-1}$

10 The function f is defined by $f: x \mapsto x^2 + 1, \, x \geq 0$. Sketch the graph of the function f and, using your sketch or otherwise, show that f is a one–one function. Obtain an expression in terms of x for $f^{-1}(x)$ and state the domain of f^{-1}.

The function g is defined by $g: x \mapsto x - 3, \, x \geq 0$. Give an expression in terms of x for $gf(x)$ and state the range of gf.　　　　　　　　　　　　　　(OCR)

11 The functions f and g are defined by

   $$f:x \mapsto x^2 + 6x, \, x \in \mathbb{R}, \qquad g:x \mapsto 2x - 1, \, x \in \mathbb{R}.$$

   Find the two values of x such that $fg(x) = gf(x)$, giving each answer in the form $p + q\sqrt{3}$.

12 The function f is defined by $f : x \mapsto x^2 - 2x + 7$ with domain $x \leqslant k$. Given that f is a one–one function, find the greatest possible value of k and find the inverse function f^{-1}.

13 Functions f and g are defined by

   $$f:x \mapsto x^2 + 2x + 3, \, x \in \mathbb{R}, \qquad g:x \mapsto ax + b, \, x \in \mathbb{R}.$$

   Given that $fg(x) = 4x^2 - 48x + 146$ for all x, find the possible values of a and b.

14 The function f is defined by $f : x \mapsto 1 - x^2, \, x \leqslant 0$.

   (a) Sketch the graph of f.

   (b) Find an expression, in terms of x, for $f^{-1}(x)$ and state the domain of f^{-1}.

   (c) The function g is defined by $g : x \mapsto 2x, \, x \leqslant 0$. Find the value of x for which $fg(x) = 0$.

                                                                              (OCR)

15 Functions f and g are defined by $f:x \mapsto 4x + 5, \, x \in \mathbb{R}$ and $g:x \mapsto 3 - 2x, \, x \in \mathbb{R}$. Find

   (a) f^{-1},   (b) g^{-1},   (c) $f^{-1}g^{-1}$,   (d) gf,   (e) $(gf)^{-1}$.

16 Functions f and g are defined by $f:x \mapsto 2x + 7, \, x \in \mathbb{R}$ and $g:x \mapsto x^3 - 1, \, x \in \mathbb{R}$. Find

   (a) f^{-1},   (b) g^{-1},   (c) $g^{-1}f^{-1}$,   (d) $f^{-1}g^{-1}$,

   (e) fg,   (f) gf,   (g) $(fg)^{-1}$,   (h) $(gf)^{-1}$.

17 Given the function $f : x \mapsto 10 - x, \, x \in \mathbb{R}$, evaluate

   (a) $f(7)$,   (b) $f^2(7)$,   (c) $f^{15}(7)$,   (d) $f^{100}(7)$.

   (The notation f^2 represents the composite function ff, f^3 represents fff, and so on.)

18 Given the function $f:x \mapsto \dfrac{x+5}{2x-1}, \, x \in \mathbb{R}$ and $x \neq \frac{1}{2}$, find

   (a) $f^2(x)$,   (b) $f^3(x)$,   (c) $f^4(x)$,   (d) $f^{10}(x)$,   (e) $f^{351}(x)$.

19 Given the function $f(x) = \dfrac{2x-4}{x}, \, x \in \mathbb{R}$ and $x \neq 0$, find

   (a) $f^2(x)$,   (b) $f^{-1}(x)$,   (c) $f^3(x)$,

   (d) $f^4(x)$,   (e) $f^{12}(x)$,   (f) $f^{82}(x)$.

20 Show that a function of the form $x \mapsto \dfrac{x+a}{x-1}, \, x \in \mathbb{R}$ and $x \neq 1$, is self-inverse for all values of the constant a.

3 Sequences

This chapter is about sequences of numbers. When you have completed it, you should

- know that a sequence can be constructed from a formula or an inductive definition
- appreciate that a sequence can be regarded as a function whose domain is the natural numbers, or a consecutive subset of the natural numbers
- be familiar with triangle, factorial, Pascal and arithmetic sequences
- know how to find the sum of an arithmetic series.

3.1 Constructing sequences

Here are six rows of numbers, each forming a pattern of some kind. What are the next three numbers in each row?

(a) 1   4   9   16   25 ...

(b) $\frac{1}{2}$ $\frac{2}{3}$ $\frac{3}{4}$ $\frac{4}{5}$ $\frac{5}{6}$ ...

(c) 99   97   95   93   91 ...

(d) 1   1.1   1.21   1.331   1.4641 ...

(e) 2   4   8   14   22 ...

(f) 3   1   4   1   5 ...

Rows of this kind are called **sequences**, and the separate numbers are called **terms**.

The usual notation for the first, second, third, ... terms of a sequence is u_1, u_2, u_3, and so on. There is nothing special about the choice of the letter u, and other letters such as v, x, t and I are often used instead, especially if the sequence appears in some application. If r is a natural number, then the rth term will be u_r, v_r, x_r, t_r or I_r.

Sometimes it is convenient to begin numbering the terms $u_0, u_1, u_2, ...$ but you then have to be careful in referring to 'the first term': is this u_0 or u_1?

In (a) and (b) you would have no difficulty in writing a formula for the rth term of the sequence. The numbers in (a) could be rewritten as 1^2, 2^2, 3^2, 4^2, 5^2, and all these could be summed up by writing

$$u_r = r^2.$$

The terms of (b) are $\dfrac{1}{1+1}$, $\dfrac{2}{2+1}$, $\dfrac{3}{3+1}$, $\dfrac{4}{4+1}$, $\dfrac{5}{5+1}$, so $u_r = \dfrac{r}{r+1}$.

In (c), (d) and (e) you would probably expect that there is a formula, but it is not so easy to find it. What is more obvious is how to get each term from the one before. For example, in (c) the terms go down by 2 at each step, so that $u_2 = u_1 - 2$, $u_3 = u_2 - 2$, $u_4 = u_3 - 2$, and so on. These can be summarised by the single equation

$$u_{r+1} = u_r - 2.$$

The terms in (d) are multiplied by 1.1 at each step, so the rule is

$$u_{r+1} = 1.1u_r.$$

Unfortunately, there are many other sequences which satisfy an equation like $u_{r+1} = u_r - 2$. Other examples are $10, 8, 6, 4, 2, ...$ and $-2, -4, -6, -8, -10, ...$

The definition is not complete until you know the first term. So to complete the
definitions of the sequences (c) and (d) you have to write

(c) $u_1 = 99$ and $u_{r+1} = u_r - 2$,

(d) $u_1 = 1$ and $u_{r+1} = 1.1u_r$.

Definitions like this are called **inductive definitions**.

The sequence (e) originates from geometry. It gives the greatest number of regions into
which a plane can be split by different numbers of circles. (Try drawing your own
diagrams with 1, 2, 3, 4, ... circles.) This sequence is developed as $u_2 = u_1 + 2$,
$u_3 = u_2 + 4$, $u_4 = u_3 + 6$, and so on. Since the increments 2, 4, 6, ... are themselves
given by the formula $2r$, this can be summarised by the inductive definition

$u_1 = 2$ and $u_{r+1} = u_r + 2r$.

For (f) you may have given the next three terms as 1, 6, 1 (expecting the even-
numbered terms all to be 1, and the odd terms to go up by 1 at each step). In fact this
sequence had a quite different origin, as the first five digits of π in decimal form! With
this meaning, the next three terms would be 9, 2, 6.

There is an important point here, that a sequence can never be uniquely defined by
giving just the first few terms. Try, for example, working out the first eight terms of the
sequence defined by

$u_r = r^2 + (r-1)(r-2)(r-3)(r-4)(r-5)$.

You will find that the first five terms are the same as those given in (a), but the next
three are probably very different from your original conjecture.

A sequence can only be described unambiguously by giving a formula, an inductive
definition in terms of a general natural number r, or some other general rule.

3.2   What is a sequence?

In the last chapter you met the symbols $\mathbb{R}$ for the set of real numbers, and $\mathbb{Z}$ for the set
of integers. Another useful symbol is $\mathbb{N}$, for the set of natural numbers.

There is not complete agreement amongst mathematicians whether the natural numbers
include zero, but you need not worry about this. If $\mathbb{N}$ stands for the set $\{0, 1, 2, 3, ...\}$,
then you can think of a sequence as a function whose domain is $\mathbb{N}$, or a consecutive
subset of $\mathbb{N}$. The phrase 'consecutive subset' allows you to start the sequence either at
u_0 or u_1, and also to choose whether to continue it indefinitely or only for a finite
number of terms. The sequence (a) above could then be described in full as

$u_r = r^2$ where $r \in \mathbb{N}$ and $r \geqslant 1$.

The reason for using u_r rather than the usual function notation $f(r)$ for the terms of a
sequence is simply one of convenience.

An important difference between $\mathbb{N}$ and $\mathbb{R}$ is that, for every natural number r, there is a 'next number'. This is what makes it possible to use an inductive definition to define a sequence. There is no comparable way of defining a function $f(x)$ where $x \in \mathbb{R}$, because there is no such thing as 'the next real number'.

Exercise 3A

1 Write down the first five terms of the sequences with the following definitions.

(a) $u_1 = 7$, $u_{r+1} = u_r + 7$ (b) $u_1 = 13$, $u_{r+1} = u_r - 5$

(c) $u_1 = 4$, $u_{r+1} = 3u_r$ (d) $u_1 = 6$, $u_{r+1} = \frac{1}{2}u_r$

(e) $u_1 = 2$, $u_{r+1} = 3u_r + 1$ (f) $u_1 = 1$, $u_{r+1} = u_r^2 + 3$

2 Suggest inductive definitions which would produce the following sequences.

(a) 2 4 6 8 10 ...   (b) 11 9 7 5 3 ...

(c) 2 6 10 14 18 ...   (d) 2 6 18 54 162 ...

(e) $\frac{1}{3}$ $\frac{1}{9}$ $\frac{1}{27}$ $\frac{1}{81}$ ...   (f) $\frac{1}{2}a$ $\frac{1}{4}a$ $\frac{1}{8}a$ $\frac{1}{16}a$ ...

(g) $b - 2c$ $b - c$ b $b + c$ ...   (h) 1 -1 1 -1 1 ...

(i) $\frac{p}{q^3}$ $\frac{p}{q^2}$ $\frac{p}{q}$ ...   (j) $\frac{a^3}{b^2}$ $\frac{a^2}{b}$ a b ...

(k) x^3 $5x^2$ $25x$ ...   (l) 1 $1 + x$ $(1+x)^2$ $(1+x)^3$ ...

3 Write down the first five terms of each sequence and give an inductive definition for it.

(a) $u_r = 2r + 3$ (b) $u_r = r^2$ (c) $u_r = \frac{1}{2}r(r + 1)$

(d) $u_r = \frac{1}{6}r(r+1)(2r+1)$ (e) $u_r = 2 \times 3^r$ (f) $u_r = 3 \times 5^{r-1}$

4 For each of the following sequences give a possible formula for the rth term.

(a) 9 8 7 6 ...   (b) 6 18 54 162 ...

(c) 4 7 12 19 ...   (d) 4 12 24 40 60 ...

(e) $\frac{1}{4}$ $\frac{3}{5}$ $\frac{5}{6}$ $\frac{7}{7}$ ...   (f) $\frac{2}{2}$ $\frac{5}{4}$ $\frac{10}{8}$ $\frac{17}{16}$ ...

3.3 The triangle number sequence

The numbers of crosses in the triangular patterns in Fig. 3.1 are called triangle numbers. If t_r denotes the rth triangle number, then you can see by counting the numbers of crosses in successive rows that

$$t_1 = 1, \quad t_2 = 1 + 2 = 3, \quad t_3 = 1 + 2 + 3 = 6,$$

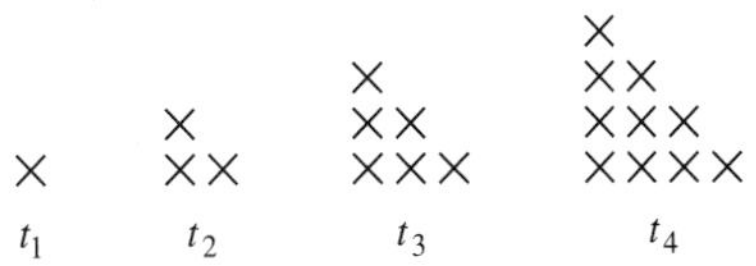

and in general $t_r = 1 + 2 + 3 + ... + r$, where the dots indicate that all the natural numbers between 3 and r have to be included in the addition.

Fig. 3.1

Fig. 3.2 shows a typical pattern of crosses forming a
triangle number t_r. (It is in fact drawn for $r = 9$, but
any other value of r could have been chosen.) An easy
way of finding a formula for t_r is to make a similar
pattern of 'noughts', and then to turn it upside down and
place it alongside the pattern of crosses, as in Fig. 3.3.
The noughts and crosses together then make a
rectangular pattern, $r + 1$ objects wide and r objects
high. So the total number of objects is $r(r + 1)$, half of
them crosses and half noughts. The number of crosses
alone is therefore

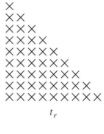

t_r

Fig. 3.2

$$t_r = \tfrac{1}{2} r(r + 1).$$

This shows that:

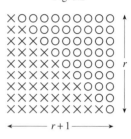

$r + 1$

Fig. 3.3

> The sum of all the natural numbers from 1 to r
> is $\tfrac{1}{2} r(r + 1)$.

You can put this argument into algebraic form. If you count the crosses from the top
downwards you get

$$t_r = \quad 1 \quad + \quad 2 \quad + \quad 3 \quad + \ldots + (r - 2) + (r - 1) + \quad r,$$

but if you count the noughts from the top downwards you get

$$t_r = \quad r \quad + (r - 1) + (r - 2) + \ldots + \quad 3 \quad + \quad 2 \quad + \quad 1.$$

Counting all the objects in the rectangle is equivalent to adding these two equations:

$$2t_r = (r + 1) + (r + 1) + (r + 1) + \ldots + (r + 1) + (r + 1) + (r + 1).$$

with one $(r + 1)$ bracket for each of the r rows. It follows that $2t_r = r(r + 1)$, so that

$$t_r = \tfrac{1}{2} r(r + 1).$$

It is also possible to give an inductive definition for the sequence t_r. Fig. 3.1 shows that
to get from any triangle number to the next you simply add an extra row of crosses
underneath. Thus $t_2 = t_1 + 2, t_3 = t_2 + 3, t_4 = t_3 + 4$, and in general

$$t_{r+1} = t_r + (r + 1).$$

You can complete this definition by specifying either $t_1 = 1$ or $t_0 = 0$. If you choose
$t_0 = 0$, then you can find t_1 by putting $r = 0$ in the general equation, as
$t_1 = t_0 + 1 = 0 + 1 = 1$. So you may as well define the triangle number sequence by

$$t_0 = 0 \quad \text{and} \quad t_{r+1} = t_r + (r + 1) \quad \text{where } r \in \mathbb{N}.$$

3.4 The factorial sequence

If, in the definition of t_r, you replace addition by multiplication, you get the factorial sequence

$$f_{r+1} = f_r \times (r+1) \quad \text{where } r \in \mathbb{N}.$$

There would be little point in defining f_0 to be 0 (think about why this is), so take f_0 to be 1. (This may seem strange, but you will see the reason in the next chapter.) You then get

$$f_1 = f_0 \times 1 = 1 \times 1 = 1, \quad f_2 = f_1 \times 2 = 1 \times 2 = 2, \quad f_3 = f_2 \times 3 = 2 \times 3 = 6,$$

and if you go on in this way you find that, for any $r \geq 1$,

$$f_r = 1 \times 2 \times 3 \times \ldots \times r.$$

This sequence is so important that it has its own special notation, $r!$, read as 'factorial r' or 'r factorial' (or often, colloquially, as 'r shriek').

> **Factorial r** is defined by $0! = 1$ and $(r+1)! = r! \times (r+1)$ where $r \in \mathbb{N}$.
>
> For $r \geq 1$, $r!$ is the product of all the natural numbers from 1 to r.

Many calculators have a special key labelled $[n!]$. For small values of n the display gives the exact value, but the numbers in the sequence increase so rapidly that from about $n = 14$ onwards only an approximate value in standard form can be displayed.

3.5 Pascal sequences

Another important type of sequence based on a multiplication rule is a Pascal sequence. You will find in the next chapter that these sequences feature in the expansion of expressions like $(x + y)^n$. A typical example has an inductive definition

$$p_0 = 1 \quad \text{and} \quad p_{r+1} = \frac{4-r}{r+1} p_r \quad \text{where } r \in \mathbb{N}.$$

Using the inductive definition for $r = 0, 1, 2, \ldots$ in turn produces the terms

$$p_1 = \tfrac{4}{1} p_0 = 4, \quad p_2 = \tfrac{3}{2} p_1 = 6, \quad p_3 = \tfrac{2}{3} p_2 = 4,$$
$$p_4 = \tfrac{1}{4} p_3 = 1, \quad p_5 = \tfrac{0}{5} p_4 = 0, \quad p_6 = \tfrac{(-1)}{6} p_5 = 0, \quad \text{and so on.}$$

You will see that at a certain stage the sequence has a zero term, and because it is formed by multiplication all the terms after that will be zero. So the complete sequence is

$$1, 4, 6, 4, 1, 0, 0, 0, 0, 0, \ldots.$$

This is only one of a family of Pascal sequences, and its terms also have a special notation, $\binom{4}{r}$. For example, $\binom{4}{0} = 1, \binom{4}{1} = 4, \binom{4}{2} = 6$, and so on. Other Pascal sequences have numbers different from 4 in the multiplying factor.

The general definition of a Pascal sequence, whose terms are denoted by $\binom{n}{r}$, is

$$\binom{n}{0} = 1 \quad \text{and} \quad \binom{n}{r+1} = \frac{n-r}{r+1}\binom{n}{r} \quad \text{where } r \in \mathbb{N}.$$

Check for yourself that the Pascal sequences for $n = 0, 1, 2, 3$ are

$$n = 0: \quad 1, \quad 0, \quad 0, \quad 0, \quad 0, \quad \dots$$
$$n = 1: \quad 1, \quad 1, \quad 0, \quad 0, \quad 0, \quad \dots$$
$$n = 2: \quad 1, \quad 2, \quad 1, \quad 0, \quad 0, \quad \dots$$
$$n = 3: \quad 1, \quad 3, \quad 3, \quad 1, \quad 0, \quad \dots$$

The complete pattern of Pascal sequences, without the trailing zeros, is called **Pascal's triangle**. The earliest record of its use was in China, but Blaise Pascal (a French mathematician of the 17th century, one of the originators of probability theory) was one of the first people in Europe to publish it. It is usually presented in isosceles form (Fig. 3.4), drawing attention to the symmetry of the sequence. But for its algebraic applications the format of Fig. 3.5 is often more convenient, since each column then corresponds to a particular value of r.

<pre>
            1   1
         1   1   1   1
       1   2   1   1   2   1
      1   3   3   1   1   3   3   1
    1   4   6   4   1   1   4   6   4   1
         Fig. 3.4   Fig. 3.5
</pre>

You may be surprised to notice that every number in the pattern in Fig. 3.4 except for the 1s is the sum of the two numbers most closely above it.

You have seen these numbers before: look back at sequence (d) in Section 3.1.

Exercise 3B

1 Using Fig. 3.3 as an example,

   (a) draw a pattern of dots to represent the rth triangle number t_r;

   (b) draw another pattern to represent t_{r-1};

   (c) combine these two patterns to show that $t_r + t_{r-1} = r^2$.

   Use the fact that $t_r = \frac{1}{2}r(r+1)$ to show the result in part (c) algebraically.

2 (a) Find an expression in terms of r for $t_r - t_{r-1}$ for all $r \geq 1$.

   (b) Use this result and that in Question 1 part (c) to show that $t_r^2 - t_{r-1}^2 = r^3$.

   (c) Use part (b) to write expressions in terms of triangle numbers for 1^3, 2^3, 3^3, ..., n^3. Hence show that $1^3 + 2^3 + 3^3 + \dots + n^3 = \frac{1}{4}n^2(n+1)^2$.

3 Without using a calculator, evaluate the following.

   (a) $7!$ 　　　　　(b) $\dfrac{8!}{3!}$ 　　　　　(c) $\dfrac{7!}{4! \times 3!}$

4 Write the following in terms of factorials.

(a) $8 \times 7 \times 6 \times 5$ (b) $9 \times 10 \times 11 \times 12$ (c) $n(n-1)(n-2)$

(d) $n(n^2-1)$ (e) $n(n+1)(n+2)(n+3)$ (f) $(n+6)(n+5)(n+4)$

(g) $8 \times 7!$ (h) $n \times (n-1)!$

5 Simplify

(a) $\dfrac{12!}{11!}$ (b) $23! - 22!$ (c) $\dfrac{(n+1)!}{n!}$ (d) $(n+1)! - n!$

6 Show that $\dfrac{(2n)!}{n!} = 2^n (1 \times 3 \times 5 \times \ldots \times (2n-1))$.

7 Use the inductive definition in Section 3.5 to find the Pascal sequences for

(a) $n = 5$,   (b) $n = 6$,   (c) $n = 8$.

8 Use the inductive definition for $\dbinom{n}{r}$ to show that $\dbinom{9}{6} = \dfrac{9 \times 8 \times 7}{1 \times 2 \times 3}$, and show that this can be written as $\dfrac{9!}{6! \times 3!}$.

Use a similar method to write the following in terms of factorials.

(a) $\dbinom{11}{4}$ (b) $\dbinom{11}{7}$ (c) $\dbinom{10}{5}$ (d) $\dbinom{12}{3}$ (e) $\dbinom{12}{9}$

9 The answers to Question 8 suggest a general result, that $\dbinom{n}{r} = \dfrac{n!}{r! \times (n-r)!}$. Assuming this to be true, show that $\dbinom{n}{r} = \dbinom{n}{n-r}$.

10 Show by direct calculation that

(a) $\dbinom{6}{3} + \dbinom{6}{4} = \dbinom{7}{4}$,   (b) $\dbinom{8}{4} + \dbinom{8}{5} = \dbinom{9}{5}$.

Write a general statement, involving n and r, suggested by these results.

11 The Pascal sequence for $n = 2$ is   1   2   1.

The sum of the terms in this sequence is $1 + 2 + 1 = 4$.

Investigate the sum of the terms in Pascal sequences for other values of n.

3.6 Arithmetic sequences

An **arithmetic sequence**, or **arithmetic progression**, is a sequence whose terms go up or down by constant steps. Sequence (c) in Section 3.1 is an example. The inductive definition for an arithmetic sequence has the form

$$u_1 = a, \quad u_{r+1} = u_r + d.$$

The number d is called the **common difference**.

For sequence (c) the first term $a = 99$, and the common difference $d = -2$.

Example 3.6.1

Sarah would like to give a sum of money to a charity each year for 10 years. She decides to give £100 in the first year, and to increase her contribution by £20 each year. How much does she give in the last year, and how much does the charity receive altogether?

Although she makes 10 contributions, there are only 9 increases. So in the last year she gives $£(100 + 9 \times 20) = £280$.

If the total amount the charity receives is $£S$, then

$$S = 100 + 120 + 140 + \ldots + 240 + 260 + 280.$$

With only ten numbers it would be easy enough to add these up, but you can also find the sum by a method similar to that used to find a formula for t_n. If you add up the numbers in reverse order, you get

$$S = 280 + 260 + 240 + \ldots + 140 + 120 + 100.$$

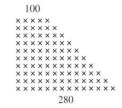

Fig. 3.6

Adding the two equations then gives

$$2S = 380 + 380 + 380 + \ldots + 380 + 380 + 380,$$

where the number 380 occurs 10 times. So

$$2S = 380 \times 10 = 3800, \text{ giving } S = 1900.$$

Over the ten years the charity receives £1900.

This calculation can be illustrated with diagrams similar to Figs. 3.2 and 3.3. Sarah's contributions are shown by Fig. 3.6, with the first year in the top row. (Each cross is worth £20.) In Fig. 3.7 a second copy, with noughts instead of crosses, is put alongside it, but turned upside down. There are then 10 rows, each with 19 crosses or noughts and worth £380.

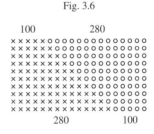

Fig. 3.7

Two features of Example 3.6.1 are typical of arithmetic progressions. First, they usually only continue for a finite number of terms. If this number is n, you could say that the domain of the sequence is $1 \leqslant r \leqslant n$, where $r \in \mathbb{N}$.

Secondly, it is often interesting to know the sum of all the terms. In this case, it is usual to describe the sequence as a **series**. In Example 3.6.1, the annual contributions

$$100, 120, 140, \ldots, 240, 260, 280$$

form an arithmetic sequence, but if they are to be added as

$$100 + 120 + 140 + \ldots + 240 + 260 + 280$$

they become an arithmetic series.

If the general arithmetic sequence

$$a, a+d, a+2d, a+3d, \dots$$

has n terms in all, then from the first term to the last there are $n-1$ steps of the common difference d. Denote the last term, u_n, by l. Then

$$l = a + (n-1)d.$$

From this equation you can calculate any one of the four quantities a, l, n, d if you know the other three.

Let S be the sum of the arithmetic series formed by adding these terms. Then it is possible to find a formula for S in terms of a, n and either d or l.

Method 1   This generalises the argument used in Example 3.6.1. The series can be written as

$$S = \quad a \quad +(a+d)+(a+2d)+\dots+(l-2d)+(l-d)+ \quad l.$$

Turning this back to front,

$$S = \quad l \quad +(l-d)+(l-2d)+\dots+(a+2d)+(a+l)+(a+l).$$

Adding these,

$$2S = (a+l)+(a+l)+ \ (a+l) \ +\dots+ \ (a+l) \ +(a+l)+(a+l),$$

where the bracket $(a+l)$ occurs n times. So

$$2S = n(a+l), \text{ which gives } S = \tfrac{1}{2}n(a+l).$$

Method 2   This uses the formula for triangle numbers found in Section 3.3. In the series

$$S = a+(a+d)+(a+2d)+\dots+\big(a+(n-1)d\big)$$

you can collect separately the terms involving a and those involving d:

$$S = (a+a+\dots+a)+\big(1+2+3+\dots+(n-1)\big)d.$$

In the first bracket a occurs n times. The second bracket is the sum of the natural numbers from 1 to $n-1$, or t_{n-1}; using the formula $t_r = \tfrac{1}{2}r(r+1)$ with $r = n-1$ gives this sum as

$$t_{n-1} = \tfrac{1}{2}(n-1)\big((n-1)+1\big) = \tfrac{1}{2}(n-1)n.$$

Therefore

$$S = na + \tfrac{1}{2}(n-1)nd = \tfrac{1}{2}n\big(2a+(n-1)d\big).$$

Since $l = a + (n-1)d$, this is the same answer as in Method 1.

Example 3.6.2

Find the sum of the first n odd natural numbers.

Method 1   The odd numbers $1, 3, 5, \ldots$ form an arithmetic series with first term $a = 1$ and common difference $d = 2$. So

$$S = \tfrac{1}{2}n(2a + (n-1)d) = \tfrac{1}{2}n(2 + (n-1)2) = \tfrac{1}{2}n(2n) = n^2.$$

Method 2   Take the natural numbers from 1 to $2n$, and remove the n even numbers $2, 4, 6, \ldots, 2n$. You are left with the first n odd numbers.

The sum of the numbers from 1 to $2n$ is t_r where $r = 2n$, that is

$$t_{2n} = \tfrac{1}{2}(2n)(2n+1) = n(2n+1).$$

The sum of the n even numbers is

$$2 + 4 + 6 + \ldots + (2n) = 2(1 + 2 + 3 + \ldots + n) = 2t_n = n(n+1).$$

So the sum of the first n odd numbers is

$$n(2n+1) - n(n+1) = n((2n+1) - (n+1)) = n(n) = n^2.$$

Method 3   Fig. 3.8 shows a square of n rows with n crosses in each row (drawn for $n = 7$). You can count the crosses in the square by adding the numbers in the 'channels' formed by the L-shaped lines, which gives

$$n^2 = 1 + 3 + 5 + \ldots \text{ (to } n \text{ terms)}.$$

Fig. 3.8

Example 3.6.3

A student reading a 426-page book finds that he reads faster as he gets into the subject. He reads 19 pages on the first day, and his rate of reading then goes up by 3 pages each day. How long does he take to finish the book?

You are given that $a = 19$, $d = 3$ and $S = 426$. Since $S = \tfrac{1}{2}n(2a + (n-1)d)$,

$$426 = \tfrac{1}{2}n(38 + (n-1)3),$$
$$852 = n(3n + 35),$$
$$3n^2 + 35n - 852 = 0.$$

Using the quadratic equation formula,

$$n = \frac{-35 \pm \sqrt{35^2 - 4 \times 3 \times (-852)}}{2 \times 3} = \frac{-35 \pm 107}{6}.$$

Since n must be positive, $n = \dfrac{-35 + 107}{6} = \dfrac{72}{6} = 12$. He will finish the book in 12 days.

Exercise 3C

1 Which of the following sequences are the first four terms of an arithmetic sequence? For those that are, write down the value of the common difference.

(a) 7 10 13 16 ...

(b) 3 5 9 15 ...

(c) 1 0.1 0.01 0.001 ...

(d) 4 2 0 -2 ...

(e) 2 -3 4 -5 ...

(f) $p-2q$ $p-q$ p $p+q$ ...

(g) $\frac{1}{2}a$ $\frac{1}{3}a$ $\frac{1}{4}a$ $\frac{1}{5}a$ ...

(h) x $2x$ $3x$ $4x$ ...

2 Write down (i) the sixth term, and (ii) an expression for the rth term, of the arithmetic sequences which begin as follows.

(a) 2 4 6 ...

(b) 17 20 23 ...

(c) 5 2 -1 ...

(d) 1.3 1.7 2.1 ...

(e) 1 $1\frac{1}{2}$ 2 ...

(f) 73 67 61 ...

(g) x $x+2$ $x+4$ ...

(h) $1-x$ 1 $1+x$ ...

3 In the following arithmetic progressions, the first three terms and the last term are given. Find the number of terms.

(a) 4 5 6 ... 17

(b) 3 9 15 ... 525

(c) 8 2 -4 ... -202

(d) $2\frac{1}{8}$ $3\frac{1}{4}$ $4\frac{3}{8}$ ... $13\frac{3}{8}$

(e) $3x$ $7x$ $11x$ ... $43x$

(f) -3 $-1\frac{1}{2}$ 0 ... 12

(g) $\frac{1}{6}$ $\frac{1}{3}$ $\frac{1}{2}$ ... $2\frac{2}{3}$

(h) $1-2x$ $1-x$ 1 ... $1+25x$

4 Find the sum of the given number of terms of the following arithmetic series.

(a) $2+5+8+...$ (20 terms)

(b) $4+11+18+...$ (15 terms)

(c) $8+5+2+...$ (12 terms)

(d) $\frac{1}{2}+1+1\frac{1}{2}+...$ (58 terms)

(e) $7+3+(-1)+...$ (25 terms)

(f) $1+3+5+...$ (999 terms)

(g) $a+5a+9a+...$ (40 terms)

(h) $-3p-6p-9p-...$ (100 terms)

5 Find the number of terms and the sum of each of the following arithmetic series.

(a) $5+7+9+...+111$

(b) $8+12+16+...+84$

(c) $7+13+19+...+277$

(d) $8+5+2+...+(-73)$

(e) $-14-10-6-...+94$

(f) $157+160+163+...+529$

(g) $10+20+30+...+10\,000$

(h) $1.8+1.2+0.6+...+(-34.2)$

6 In each of the following arithmetic sequences you are given two terms. Find the first term and the common difference.

(a) 4th term $=15$, 9th term $=35$

(b) 3rd term $=12$, 10th term $=47$

(c) 8th term $=3.5$, 13th term $=5.0$

(d) 5th term $=2$, 11th term $=-13$

(e) 12th term $=-8$, 20th term $=-32$

(f) 3rd term $=-3$, 7th term $=5$

(g) 2nd term $=2x$, 11th term $=-7x$

(h) 3rd term $=2p+7$, 7th term $=4p+19$

7 Find how many terms of the given arithmetic series must be taken to reach the given sum.

   (a) $3 + 7 + 11 + \ldots$, sum = 820   (b) $8 + 9 + 10 + \ldots$, sum = 162

   (c) $20 + 23 + 26 + \ldots$, sum = 680   (d) $27 + 23 + 19 + \ldots$, sum = -2040

   (e) $1.1 + 1.3 + 1.5 + \ldots$, sum = 1017.6   (f) $-11 - 4 + 3 + \ldots$, sum = 2338

8 A squirrel is collecting nuts. It collects 5 nuts on the first day of the month, 8 nuts on the second, 11 on the third and so on in arithmetic progression.

   (a) How many nuts will it collect on the 20th day?

   (b) After how many days will it have collected more than 1000 nuts?

9 Kathryn is given an interest-free loan to buy a car. She repays the loan in unequal monthly instalments; these start at £30 in the first month and increase by £2 each month after that. She makes 24 payments.

   (a) Find the amount of her final payment.

   (b) Find the amount of her loan.

10 (a) Find the sum of the natural numbers from 1 to 100 inclusive.

   (b) Find the sum of the natural numbers from 101 to 200 inclusive.

   (c) Find and simplify an expression for the sum of the natural numbers from $n+1$ to $2n$ inclusive.

11 An employee starts work on 1 January 2000 on an annual salary of £15,000. His pay scale, inflation apart, will give him an increase of £400 per annum on the first of January until 1 January 2015 inclusive. He remains on this salary until he retires on 31 December 2040. How much will he earn during his working life?

Miscellaneous exercise 3

1 A sequence is defined inductively by $u_{r+1} = 3u_r - 1$ and $u_0 = c$.

   (a) Find the first five terms of the sequence if (i) $c = 1$, (ii) $c = 2$, (iii) $c = 0$, (iv) $c = \frac{1}{2}$.

   (b) Show that, for each of the values of c in part (a), the terms of the sequence are given by the formula $u_r = \frac{1}{2} + b \times 3^r$ for some value of b.

   (c) Show that, if $u_r = \frac{1}{2} + b \times 3^r$ for some value of r, then $u_{r+1} = \frac{1}{2} + b \times 3^{r+1}$.

2 The sequence $u_1, u_2, u_3, \ldots$ is defined by

$$u_1 = 0, \quad u_{r+1} = (2 + u_r)^2.$$

Find the value of u_4.

3 The sequence $u_1, u_2, u_3, \ldots$, where u_1 is a given real number, is defined by

$$u_{n+1} = \sqrt{(4 - u_n)^2}.$$

   (a) Given that $u_1 = 1$, evaluate u_2, u_3 and u_4, and describe the behaviour of the sequence.

   (b) Given alternatively that $u_1 = 6$, describe the behaviour of the sequence.

   (c) For what value of u_1 will all the terms of the sequence be equal to each other?

(OCR, adapted)

4 The sequence $u_1, u_2, u_3, \ldots$, where u_1 is a given real number, is defined by $u_{n+1} = u_n{}^2 - 1$.

(a) Describe the behaviour of the sequence for each of the cases $u_1 = 0$, $u_1 = 1$ and $u_1 = 2$.

(b) Given that $u_2 = u_1$, find exactly the two possible values of u_1.

(c) Given that $u_3 = u_1$, show that $u_1{}^4 - 2u_1{}^2 - u_1 = 0$. (OCR)

5 The rth term of an arithmetic progression is $1 + 4r$. Find, in terms of n, the sum of the first n terms of the progression. (OCR)

6 The sum of the first two terms of an arithmetic progression is 18 and the sum of the first four terms is 52. Find the sum of the first eight terms. (OCR)

7 The sum of the first twenty terms of an arithmetic progression is 50, and the sum of the next twenty terms is -50. Find the sum of the first hundred terms of the progression. (OCR)

8 An arithmetic progression has first term a and common difference -1. The sum of the first n terms is equal to the sum of the first $3n$ terms. Express a in terms of n. (OCR)

9 Find the sum of the arithmetic progression $1, 4, 7, 10, 13, 16, \ldots, 1000$.

Every third term of the above progression is removed, i.e. $7, 16$, etc. Find the sum of the remaining terms. (OCR)

10 The sum of the first hundred terms of an arithmetic progression with first term a and common difference d is T. The sum of the first 50 odd-numbered terms, i.e. the first, third, fifth, $\ldots$, ninety-ninth, is $\frac{1}{2}T - 1000$. Find the value of d. (OCR)

11 In the sequence $1.0, 1.1, 1.2, \ldots, 99.9, 100.0$, each number after the first is 0.1 greater than the preceding number. Find

(a) how many numbers there are in the sequence,

(b) the sum of all the numbers in the sequence. (OCR)

12 The sequence $u_1, u_2, u_3, \ldots$ is defined by $u_n = 2n^2$.

(a) Write down the value of u_3.

(b) Express $u_{n+1} - u_n$ in terms of n, simplifying your answer.

(c) The differences between successive terms of the sequence form an arithmetic progression. For this arithmetic progression, state its first term and its common difference, and find the sum of its first 1000 terms. (OCR)

13 A small company producing children's toys plans an increase in output. The number of toys produced is to be increased by 8 each week until the weekly number produced reaches 1000. In week 1, the number to be produced is 280; in week 2, the number is 288; etc. Show that the weekly number produced will be 1000 in week 91.

From week 91 onwards, the number produced each week is to remain at 1000. Find the total number of toys to be produced over the first 104 weeks of the plan. (OCR)

14 In 1971 a newly-built flat was sold with a 999-year lease. The terms of the sale included a requirement to pay 'ground rent' yearly. The ground rent was set at £28 per year for the first 21 years of the lease. increasing by £14 to £42 per year for the next 21 years, and then increasing again by £14 at the end of each subsequent period of 21 years.

  (a) Find how many complete 21-year periods there would be if the lease ran for the full 999 years, and how many years there would be left over.

  (b) Find the total amount of ground rent that would be paid in all of the complete 21-year periods of the lease.   (OCR)

15 An arithmetic progression has first term a and common difference 10. The sum of the first n terms of the progression is $10\,000$. Express a in terms of n, and show that the nth term of the progression is

$$\frac{10\,000}{n} + 5(n-1).$$

Given that the nth term is less than 500, show that $n^2 - 101n + 2000 < 0$ and hence find the largest possible value of n.   (OCR)

16 Three sequences are defined, for $r \in \mathbb{N}$, by

  (a) $u_0 = 0$ and $u_{r+1} = u_r + (2r+1)$,

  (b) $u_0 = 0$, $u_1 = 1$ and $u_{r+1} = 2u_r - u_{r-1}$ for $r \geqslant 1$,

  (c) $u_0 = 1$, $u_1 = 2$ and $u_{r+1} = 3u_r - 2u_{r-1}$ for $r \geqslant 1$.

For each sequence calculate the first few terms, and suggest a formula for u_r. Check that the formula you have suggested does in fact satisfy all parts of the definition.

17 A sequence F_n is constructed from terms of Pascal sequences as follows:

$$F_0 = \binom{0}{0}, \; F_1 = \binom{1}{0} + \binom{0}{1}, \; F_2 = \binom{2}{0} + \binom{1}{1} + \binom{0}{2}, \text{ and in general}$$

$$F_n = \binom{n}{0} + \binom{n-1}{1} + \ldots + \binom{1}{n-1} + \binom{0}{n}$$

Show that terms of the sequence F_n can be calculated by adding up numbers in Fig. 3.5 along diagonal lines. Verify by calculation that, for small values of n, $F_{n+1} = F_n + F_{n-1}$. (This is called the 'Fibonacci sequence', after the man who introduced algebra from the Arabs to Italy in about the year 1200.)

Use the Pascal sequence property $\binom{n}{r} + \binom{n}{r+1} = \binom{n+1}{r+1}$ (see Miscellaneous exercise 4 Question 26) to explain why $F_3 + F_4 = F_5$ and $F_4 + F_5 = F_6$.

4 The binomial theorem

This chapter is about the expansion of $(x+y)^n$, where n is a positive integer (or zero). When you have completed it, you should

- be able to use Pascal's triangle to find the expansion of $(x+y)^n$ when n is small
- know how to calculate the coefficients in the expansion of $(x+y)^n$ when n is large
- be able to use the notation $\binom{n}{r}$ in the context of the binomial theorem.

4.1 Expanding $(x+y)^n$

The binomial theorem is about calculating $(x+y)^n$ quickly and easily. It is useful to start by looking at $(x+y)^n$ for $n=2,3$ and 4.

These expansions are:

$$(x+y)^2 = x(x+y)+y(x+y) = x^2 +2xy+y^2,$$

$$
\begin{aligned}
(x+y)^3 &= (x+y)(x+y)^2 = (x+y)\left(x^2 + 2xy + y^2\right)\\
&= x\left(x^2 +2xy+y^2\right)+y\left(x^2 +2xy+y^2\right)\\
&= x^3 \ + \ 2x^2y \ + \ xy^2 \\
&\quad \ \ + \ \ x^2y \ + \ 2xy^2 \ + \ y^3 \\
\hline
&= x^3 \ + \ 3x^2y \ + \ 3xy^2 \ + \ y^3,
\end{aligned}
$$

$$
\begin{aligned}
(x+y)^4 &= (x+y)(x+y)^3 = (x+y)\left(x^3 +3x^2y + 3xy^2 +y^3\right)\\
&= x\left(x^3 +3x^2y+3xy^2 +y^3\right)+y\left(x^3 +3x^2y+3xy^2 +y^3\right)\\
&= x^4 \ + \ 3x^3y \ + \ 3x^2y^2 \ + \ xy^3 \\
&\quad \ \ + \ \ x^3y \ + \ 3x^2y^2 \ + \ 3xy^3 \ + \ y^4 \\
\hline
&= x^4 \ + \ 4x^3y \ + \ 6x^2y^2 \ + \ 4xy^3 \ + \ y^4.
\end{aligned}
$$

You can summarise these results, including $(x+y)^1$, as follows. The coefficients are in bold type.

$$
\begin{aligned}
(x+y)^1 &= \mathbf{1}x \ + \mathbf{1}y\\
(x+y)^2 &= \mathbf{1}x^2 + \mathbf{2}xy \ +\mathbf{1}y^2\\
(x+y)^3 &= \mathbf{1}x^3 + \mathbf{3}x^2y+\mathbf{3}xy^2 \ +\mathbf{1}y^3\\
(x+y)^4 &= \mathbf{1}x^4 + \mathbf{4}x^3y+\mathbf{6}x^2y^2 +\mathbf{4}xy^3 +\mathbf{1}y^4
\end{aligned}
$$

Study these expansions carefully. Notice how the powers start from the left with x^n. The powers of x then successively reduce by 1, and the powers of y increase by 1 until reaching the term y^n.

Notice also that the coefficients form the pattern commonly known as Pascal's triangle, which you saw in Chapter 3 and which is shown again in Fig. 4.1.

In Pascal's triangle, you obtain the next row by starting with 1; you then add pairs of elements in the row above to get the entry positioned below and between them (as the arrows in Fig. 4.1 show); and you complete the row with a 1. This is identical to the way in which the two rows are added to give the final result in the expansions of $(x+y)^3$ and $(x+y)^4$ on the previous page.

Row 1				1	1	
Row 2			1	2	1	
Row 3		1	3	3	1	
Row 4	1	4	6	4	1	

Fig. 4.1

You should now be able to predict that the coefficients in the fifth row are

> 1   5   10   10   5   1

and that $(x+y)^5 = x^5 + 5x^4y + 10x^3y^2 + 10x^2y^3 + 5xy^4 + y^5$.

Example 4.1.1
Write down the expansion of $(1+y)^6$.

Using the next row of Pascal's triangle, continuing the pattern of powers and replacing x by 1,

$$(1+y)^6 = (1)^6 + 6(1)^5 y + 15(1)^4 y^2 + 20(1)^3 y^3 + 15(1)^2 y^4 + 6(1)y^5 + y^6$$
$$= 1 + 6y + 15y^2 + 20y^3 + 15y^4 + 6y^5 + y^6.$$

Example 4.1.2
Multiply out the brackets in the expression $(2x+3)^4$.

Use the expansion of $(x+y)^4$, with $(2x)$ replacing x and 3 replacing y. Then

$$(2x+3)^4 = (2x)^4 + 4 \times (2x)^3 \times 3 + 6 \times (2x)^2 \times 3^2 + 4 \times (2x) \times 3^3 + 3^4$$
$$= 16x^4 + 96x^3 + 216x^2 + 216x + 81.$$

Example 4.1.3
Expand $(x^2 + 2)^3$.

$$(x^2 + 2)^3 = (x^2)^3 + 3 \times (x^2)^2 \times 2 + 3 \times x^2 \times 2^2 + 2^3 = x^6 + 6x^4 + 12x^2 + 8.$$

Example 4.1.4
Find the coefficient of x^3 in the expansion of $(3x-4)^5$.

The term in x^3 comes third in the row with coefficients 1, 5, 10, ... So the term is

$$10 \times (3x)^3 \times (-4)^2 = 10 \times 27 \times 16x^3 = 4320x^3.$$

The required coefficient is therefore 4320.

Example 4.1.5

Expand $\left(1 + 2x + 3x^2\right)^3$.

To use the binomial expansion, you need to write $1 + 2x + 3x^2$ in a form with two terms rather than three. One way to do this is to consider $\left(1 + \left(2x + 3x^2\right)\right)^3$. Then

$$\left(1 + \left(2x + 3x^2\right)\right)^3 = 1^3 + 3 \times 1^2 \times \left(2x + 3x^2\right) + 3 \times 1 \times \left(2x + 3x^2\right)^2 + \left(2x + 3x^2\right)^3.$$

Now you can use the binomial theorem to expand the bracketed terms:

$$\left(1 + 2x + 3x^2\right)^3 = 1 + 3\left(2x + 3x^2\right) + 3\left((2x)^2 + 2 \times (2x) \times \left(3x^2\right) + \left(3x^2\right)^2\right)$$

$$+ \left((2x)^3 + 3 \times (2x)^2 \times \left(3x^2\right) + 3 \times (2x) \times \left(3x^2\right)^2 + \left(3x^2\right)^3\right)$$

$$= 1 + \left(6x + 9x^2\right) + \left(12x^2 + 36x^3 + 27x^4\right)$$

$$+ \left(8x^3 + 36x^4 + 54x^5 + 27x^6\right)$$

$$= 1 + 6x + 21x^2 + 44x^3 + 63x^4 + 54x^5 + 27x^6.$$

In this kind of detailed work, it is useful to check your answers. You could do this by expanding $\left(1 + 2x + 3x^2\right)^3$ *in the form* $\left((1 + 2x) + 3x^2\right)^3$ *to see if you get the same answer. Rather quicker is to give* x *a particular value,* $x = 1$*, for example. Then the left side is* $(1 + 2 + 3)^3 = 6^3 = 216$*; the right is* $1 + 6 + 21 + 44 + 63 + 54 + 27 = 216$*. Note that if the results are the same that it does not guarantee that the expansion is correct, but if they are different, it is certain that there is a mistake.*

Exercise 4A

1 Write down the expansion of each of the following.

(a) $(2x + y)^2$ (b) $(5x + 3y)^2$ (c) $(4 + 7p)^2$ (d) $(1 - 8t)^2$

(e) $\left(1 - 5x^2\right)^2$ (f) $\left(2 + x^3\right)^2$ (g) $\left(x^2 + y^3\right)^3$ (h) $\left(3x^2 + 2y^3\right)^3$

2 Write down the expansion of each of the following.

(a) $(x + 2)^3$ (b) $(2p + 3q)^3$ (c) $(1 - 4x)^3$ (d) $\left(1 - x^3\right)^3$

3 Find the coefficient of x in the expansion of

(a) $(3x + 7)^2$,   (b) $(2x + 5)^3$.

4 Find the coefficient of x^2 in the expansion of

(a) $(4x + 5)^3$,   (b) $(1 - 3x)^4$.

5 Expand each of the following expressions.

(a) $(1 + 2x)^5$ (b) $(p + 2q)^6$ (c) $(2m - 3n)^4$ (d) $\left(1 + \frac{1}{2}x\right)^4$

6 Find the coefficient of x^3 in the expansion of

(a) $(1 + 3x)^5$,   (b) $(2 - 5x)^4$.

7 Expand $\left(1 + x + 2x^2\right)^2$. Check your answer with a numerical substitution.

8 Write down the expansion of $(x+4)^3$ and hence expand $(x+1)(x+4)^3$.

9 Expand $(3x+2)^2(2x+3)^3$.

10 In the expansion of $(1+ax)^4$, the coefficient of x^3 is 1372. Find the constant a.

11 Expand $(x+y)^{11}$.

12 Find the coefficient of x^6y^6 in the expansion of $(2x+y)^{12}$.

4.2 The binomial theorem

The treatment given in Section 4.1 is fine for finding the coefficients in the expansion of $(x+y)^n$ where n is small, but it is hopelessly inefficient for finding the coefficient of $x^{11}y^4$ in the expansion of $(x+y)^{15}$. Just think of all those rows of Pascal's triangle which you would have to write out! What you need is a formula in terms of n and r for the coefficient of $x^{n-r}y^r$ in the expansion of $(x+y)^n$.

Fortunately, the nth row of Pascal's triangle is the nth Pascal sequence given in Section 3.5. It was shown there that

$$\binom{n}{0}=1, \quad \binom{n}{r+1}=\frac{n-r}{r+1}\binom{n}{r}, \quad \text{where } r \in \mathbb{N}.$$

In fact, you can write Pascal's triangle as

Row 1 $\qquad\qquad\qquad \binom{1}{0} \quad \binom{1}{1}$

Row 2 $\qquad\qquad \binom{2}{0} \quad \binom{2}{1} \quad \binom{2}{2}$

Row 3 $\qquad \binom{3}{0} \quad \binom{3}{1} \quad \binom{3}{2} \quad \binom{3}{3}$

Row 4 $\binom{4}{0} \quad \binom{4}{1} \quad \binom{4}{2} \quad \binom{4}{3} \quad \binom{4}{4}$

and so on.

This enables you to write down a neater form of the expansion of $(x+y)^n$.

> The **binomial theorem** states that
> $$(x+y)^n = \binom{n}{0}x^n + \binom{n}{1}x^{n-1}y + \binom{n}{2}x^{n-2}y^2 + \ldots + \binom{n}{n}y^n, \quad \text{where } n \in \mathbb{N}.$$

To calculate the coefficients, you can use the inductive formula given at the beginning of this section to generate a formula for $\binom{n}{r}$. For example, to calculate $\binom{4}{2}$, start by putting $n=4$. Then

$$\binom{4}{0}=1, \text{ so } \binom{4}{1}=\frac{4-0}{0+1}\binom{4}{0}=\frac{4}{1}\times 1=\frac{4}{1}, \text{ and } \binom{4}{2}=\frac{4-1}{1+1}\binom{4}{1}=\frac{3}{2}\times\frac{4}{1}=\frac{4\times 3}{1\times 2}.$$

In the general case,

$$\binom{n}{0} = 1, \quad \binom{n}{1} = \frac{n-0}{0+1} \times 1 = \frac{n}{1}, \quad \binom{n}{2} = \frac{n-1}{1+1}\binom{n}{1} = \frac{n-1}{2} \times \frac{n}{1} = \frac{n(n-1)}{1 \times 2}, \quad \dots$$

Continuing in this way, you find that $\binom{n}{r} = \dfrac{n(n-1)\dots(n-(r-1))}{1 \times 2 \times \dots \times r}$.

You can also write $\binom{n}{r}$ in the form

$$\binom{n}{r} = \frac{n(n-1)\dots(n-(r-1))}{1 \times 2 \times \dots \times r} \times \frac{(n-r) \times (n-r-1) \times \dots \times 2 \times 1}{(n-r) \times (n-r-1) \times \dots \times 2 \times 1} = \frac{n!}{r!(n-r)!}.$$

Notice that this formula works for $r = 0$ and $r = n$ as well as the values in between, since (from Section 3.4) $0! = 1$.

The **binomial coefficients** $\binom{n}{r}$ are given by

$$\binom{n}{r} = \frac{n(n-1)\dots(n-(r-1))}{1 \times 2 \times \dots \times r}, \quad \text{or} \quad \binom{n}{r} = \frac{n!}{r!(n-r)!}.$$

When you use the first formula to calculate any particular value of $\binom{n}{r}$, such as $\binom{10}{4}$ or $\binom{12}{7}$, it is helpful to remember that there are as many factors in the top line as there are in the bottom. So you can start by putting in the denominators, and then count down from 10 and 12 respectively, making sure that you have the same number of factors in the numerator as in the denominator.

$$\binom{10}{4} = \frac{10 \times 9 \times 8 \times 7}{1 \times 2 \times 3 \times 4} = 210, \quad \binom{12}{7} = \frac{12 \times 11 \times 10 \times 9 \times 8 \times 7 \times 6}{1 \times 2 \times 3 \times 4 \times 5 \times 6 \times 7} = 792.$$

Many calculators give you values of $\binom{n}{r}$, usually with a key labelled $[_nC_r]$. To find $\binom{10}{4}$, you would normally key in the sequence $[10, {}_nC_r, 4]$, but you may need to check your calculator manual for details.

Example 4.2.1
Calculate the coefficient of $x^{11}y^4$ in the expansion of $(x + y)^{15}$.

$$\text{The coefficient is } \binom{15}{4} = \frac{15 \times 14 \times 13 \times 12}{1 \times 2 \times 3 \times 4} = 1365.$$

There is one other step which is required before you can be sure that the values of $\binom{n}{r}$ are the values that you need for the binomial theorem. In Fig. 4.1 you saw that each term of Pascal's triangle, except for the ones at the end of each row, is obtained by adding the two terms immediately above it. So it should be true that

$$\binom{n+1}{r+1} = \binom{n}{r} + \binom{n}{r+1}.$$

For example:

$$\begin{aligned}
\binom{6}{3} + \binom{6}{4} &= \frac{6 \times 5 \times 4}{1 \times 2 \times 3} + \frac{6 \times 5 \times 4 \times 3}{1 \times 2 \times 3 \times 4} \\
&= \frac{6 \times 5 \times 4 \times 4 + 6 \times 5 \times 4 \times 3}{1 \times 2 \times 3 \times 4} \\
&= \frac{6 \times 5 \times 4}{1 \times 2 \times 3 \times 4} \times (4+3) \\
&= \frac{7 \times 6 \times 5 \times 4}{1 \times 2 \times 3 \times 4} \\
&= \binom{7}{4}.
\end{aligned}$$

The proof that $\binom{n+1}{r+1} = \binom{n}{r} + \binom{n}{r+1}$ is not easy. You may wish to accept the result and omit the proof, and jump to Example 4.2.2.

To prove this result, start from the right side.

$$\begin{aligned}
\binom{n}{r} + \binom{n}{r+1} &= \frac{n(n-1)\dots(n-(r-1))}{1 \times 2 \times \dots \times r} + \frac{n(n-1)\dots(n-r)}{1 \times 2 \times \dots \times r \times (r+1)} \\
&= \frac{n(n-1)\dots(n-(r-1)) \times (r+1) + n(n-1)\dots(n-r)}{1 \times 2 \times \dots \times r \times (r+1)} \\
&= \frac{n(n-1)\dots(n-(r-1))}{1 \times 2 \times \dots \times r \times (r+1)} \times \big((r+1)+(n-r)\big) \\
&= \frac{n(n-1)\dots(n-(r-1))}{1 \times 2 \times \dots \times r \times (r+1)} \times (n+1) \\
&= \frac{(n+1)n(n-1)\dots((n+1)-r)}{1 \times 2 \times \dots \times r \times (r+1)} \\
&= \binom{n+1}{r+1}.
\end{aligned}$$

This completes the chain of reasoning which connects Pascal's triangle with the binomial coefficients.

The following example is one in which the value of x is assumed to be small. When this is the case, say for $x = 0.1$, the successive powers of x decrease by a factor of 10 each time and become very small indeed, so higher powers can be neglected in approximations.

Example 4.2.2

Find the first four terms in the expansion of $(2-3x)^{10}$ in ascending powers of x. By putting $x = \frac{1}{100}$, find an approximation to 1.97^{10} correct to the nearest whole number.

$$(2+3x)^{10} = 2^{10} - \binom{10}{1} \times 2^9 \times (3x) + \binom{10}{2} \times 2^8 \times (3x)^2 - \binom{10}{3} \times 2^7 \times (3x)^3 + \dots$$

$$= 1024 - 10 \times 512 \times 3x + \frac{10 \times 9}{1 \times 2} \times 256 \times 9x^2 - \frac{10 \times 9 \times 8}{1 \times 2 \times 3} \times 128 \times 27x^3 + \dots$$

$$= 1024 - 15\,360x + 103\,680x^2 - 414\,720x^3 + \dots.$$

The first four terms are therefore $1024 - 15\,360x + 103\,680x^2 - 414\,720x^3$.

Putting $x = \frac{1}{100}$ gives

$$1.97^{10} \approx 1024 - 15\,360 \times \tfrac{1}{100} + 103\,680 \times \left(\tfrac{1}{100}\right)^2$$

$$- 414\,720 \times \left(\tfrac{1}{100}\right)^3 = 880.353\,28.$$

Therefore $1.97^{10} \approx 880$.

The next term is actually $\binom{10}{4} \times 2^6 \times (3x)^4 = 1\,088\,640x^4 = 0.010\,886\,4$ and the rest are very small indeed.

Exercise 4B

1 Find the value of each of the following.

(a) $\binom{7}{3}$ (b) $\binom{8}{6}$ (c) $\binom{9}{5}$ (d) $\binom{13}{4}$

(e) $\binom{6}{4}$ (f) $\binom{10}{2}$ (g) $\binom{11}{10}$ (h) $\binom{50}{2}$

2 Find the coefficient of x^3 in the expansion of each of the following.

(a) $(1+x)^5$ (b) $(1-x)^8$ (c) $(1+x)^{11}$ (d) $(1-x)^{16}$

3 Find the coefficient of x^5 in the expansion of each of the following.

(a) $(2+x)^7$ (b) $(3-x)^8$ (c) $(1+2x)^9$ (d) $\left(1-\tfrac{1}{2}x\right)^{12}$

4 Find the coefficient of $x^6 y^8$ in the expansion of each of the following.

(a) $(x+y)^{14}$ (b) $(2x+y)^{14}$ (c) $(3x-2y)^{14}$ (d) $\left(4x+\tfrac{1}{2}y\right)^{14}$

5 Find the first four terms in the expansion in ascending powers of x of the following.

(a) $(1+x)^{13}$ (b) $(1-x)^{15}$ (c) $(1+3x)^{10}$ (d) $(2-5x)^7$

6 Find the first three terms in the expansion in ascending powers of x of the following.

(a) $(1+x)^{22}$ (b) $(1-x)^{30}$ (c) $(1-4x)^{18}$ (d) $(1+6x)^{19}$

7   Find the first three terms in the expansion, in ascending powers of x, of $(1+2x)^8$. By substituting $x = 0.01$, find an approximation to 1.02^8.

8   Find the first three terms in the expansion, in ascending powers of x, of $(2+5x)^{12}$. By substituting a suitable value for x, find an approximation to 2.005^{12} correct to two decimal places.

9   Expand $(1+2x)^{16}$ up to and including the term in x^3. Deduce the coefficient of x^3 in the expansion of $(1+3x)(1+2x)^{16}$.

10 Expand $(1-3x)^{10}$ up to and including the term in x^2. Deduce the coefficient of x^2 in the expansion of $(1+3x)^2(1-3x)^{10}$.

11 Given that the coefficient of x in the expansion of $(1+ax)(1+5x)^{40}$ is 207, determine the value of a.

12 Simplify $(1-x)^8 + (1+x)^8$. Substitute a suitable value of x to find the exact value of $0.99^8 + 1.01^8$.

13 Given that the expansion of $(1+ax)^n$ begins $1+36x+576x^2$, find the values of a and n.

Miscellaneous exercise 4

1   Expand $(3+4x)^3$.

2   Find the first three terms in the expansion, in ascending powers of x, of
    (a) $(1+4x)^{10}$,   (b) $(1-2x)^{16}$.

3   Find the coefficient of a^3b^5 in the expansion of
    (a) $(3a-2b)^8$,   (b) $\left(5a+\tfrac{1}{2}b\right)^8$.

4   Expand $(3+5x)^7$ in ascending powers of x up to and including the term in x^2. By putting $x = 0.01$, find an approximation, correct to the nearest whole number, to 3.05^7.

5   Obtain the first four terms in the expansion of $\left(2+\tfrac{1}{4}x\right)^8$ in ascending powers of x. By substituting an appropriate value of x into this expansion, find the value of 2.0025^8 correct to three decimal places.   (OCR)

6   Find, in ascending powers of x, the first three terms in the expansion of $(2-3x)^8$. Use the expansion to find the value of 1.997^8 to the nearest whole number.   (OCR)

7   Expand $\left(x^2 + \dfrac{1}{x}\right)^3$, simplifying each of the terms.

8   Expand $\left(2x - \dfrac{3}{x^2}\right)^4$.

9   Expand and simplify $\left(x + \dfrac{1}{2x}\right)^6 + \left(x - \dfrac{1}{2x}\right)^6$.   (OCR)

10 Find the coefficient of x^2 in the expansion of $\left(x^4 + \dfrac{4}{x}\right)^3$.

11 Find the term independent of x in the expansion of $\left(2x + \dfrac{5}{x}\right)^6$.

12 Find the coefficient of y^4 in the expansion of $(1 + y)^{12}$. Deduce the coefficient of

    (a) y^4 in the expansion of $(1 + 3y)^{12}$;

    (b) y^8 in the expansion of $(1 - 2y^2)^{12}$;

    (c) $x^8 y^4$ in the expansion of $\left(x + \tfrac{1}{2} y\right)^{12}$.

13 Determine the coefficient of $p^4 q^7$ in the expansion of $(2p - q)(p + q)^{10}$.

14 Find the first three terms in the expansion of $(1 + 2x)^{20}$. By substitution of a suitable value of x in each case, find an approximation to

    (a) 1.002^{20} (b) 0.996^{20}

15 Write down the first three terms in the binomial expansion of $\left(2 - \dfrac{1}{2x^2}\right)^{10}$ in ascending

powers of x. Hence find the value of 1.995^{10} correct to three significant figures.   (OCR)

16 Two of the following expansions are correct and two are incorrect. Find the two expansions which are incorrect.

    A: $(3 + 4x)^5 = 243 + 1620x + 4320x^2 + 5760x^3 + 3840x^4 + 1024x^5$

    B: $(1 - 2x + 3x^2)^3 = 1 + 6x - 3x^2 + 28x^3 - 9x^4 + 54x^5 - 27x^6$

    C: $(1 - x)(1 + 4x)^4 = 1 + 15x + 80x^2 + 160x^3 - 256x^5$

    D: $(2x + y)^2 (3x + y)^3 = 108x^5 + 216x^4 y + 171x^3 y^2 + 67x^2 y^3 + 13xy^4 + y^6$

17 Find and simplify the term independent of x in the expansion of $\left(\dfrac{1}{2x} + x^3\right)^8$.   (OCR)

18 Find the term independent of x in the expansion of $\left(2x + \dfrac{1}{x^2}\right)^9$.

19 Evaluate the term which is independent of x in the expansion of $\left(x^2 - \dfrac{1}{2x^2}\right)^{16}$.   (OCR)

20 Find the coefficient of x^{-12} in the expansion of $\left(x^3 - \dfrac{1}{x}\right)^{24}$.   (OCR)

21 Expand $(1 + 3x + 4x^2)^4$ in ascending powers of x as far as the term in x^2. By substituting a suitable of x, find an approximation to 1.0304^4.

22 Expand and simplify $(3x + 5)^3 - (3x - 5)^3$.
Hence solve the equation $(3x + 5)^3 - (3x - 5)^3 = 730$.

23 Solve the equation $(7 - 6x)^3 + (7 + 6x)^3 = 1736$.

24 Find, in ascending powers of t, the first three terms in the expansions of

(a) $(1 + \alpha t)^5$ (b) $(1 - \beta t)^8$.

Hence find, in terms of α and β, the coefficient of t^2 in the expansion of $(1 + \alpha t)^5 (1 - \beta t)^8$.   (OCR)

25 (a) Show that

(i) $\binom{6}{4} = \binom{6}{2}$ (ii) $\binom{10}{3} = \binom{10}{7}$ (iii) $\binom{15}{12} = \binom{15}{3}$ (iv) $\binom{13}{6} = \binom{13}{7}$.

(b) State the possible values of x in each of the following.

(i) $\binom{11}{4} = \binom{11}{x}$ (ii) $\binom{16}{3} = \binom{16}{x}$ (iii) $\binom{20}{7} = \binom{20}{x}$ (iv) $\binom{45}{17} = \binom{45}{x}$

(c) Use the definition $\binom{n}{r} = \dfrac{n!}{r!(n-r)!}$ to prove that $\binom{n}{r} = \binom{n}{n-r}$.

26 The inductive property $\binom{n}{r+1} = \dfrac{n-r}{r+1}\binom{n}{r}$ was given in Section 3.5. Use this to prove the Pascal triangle property that $\binom{n}{r} + \binom{n}{r+1} = \binom{n+1}{r+1}$.

27 (a) Show that

(i) $4 \times \binom{6}{2} = 3 \times \binom{6}{3} = 6 \times \binom{5}{2}$ (ii) $3 \times \binom{7}{4} = 5 \times \binom{7}{5} = 7 \times \binom{6}{4}$

(b) State numbers a, b and c such that

(i) $a \times \binom{8}{5} = b \times \binom{8}{6} = c \times \binom{7}{5}$ (ii) $a \times \binom{9}{3} = b \times \binom{9}{4} = c \times \binom{8}{3}$

(c) Prove that $(n-r) \times \binom{n}{r} = (r+1) \times \binom{n}{r+1} = n \times \binom{n-1}{r}$.

28 Prove that $\binom{n}{r-1} + 2\binom{n}{r} + \binom{n}{r+1} = \binom{n+2}{r+1}$.

29 Find the value of 1.0003^{18} correct to fifteen decimal places.

30 (a) Expand $\left(2\sqrt{2} + \sqrt{3}\right)^4$ in the form $a + b\sqrt{6}$, where a and b are integers.

(b) Find the exact value of $\left(2\sqrt{2} + \sqrt{3}\right)^5$.

31 (a) Expand and simplify $\left(\sqrt{7} + \sqrt{5}\right)^4 + \left(\sqrt{7} - \sqrt{5}\right)^4$. By using the fact that $0 < \sqrt{7} - \sqrt{5} < 1$, state the consecutive integers between which $\left(\sqrt{7} + \sqrt{5}\right)^4$ lies.

(b) Without using a calculator, find the consecutive integers between which the value of $\left(\sqrt{3} + \sqrt{2}\right)^6$ lies.

32 Find an expression, in terms of n, for the coefficient of x in the expansion

$$(1 + 4x) + (1 + 4x)^2 + (1 + 4x)^3 + \ldots + (1 + 4x)^n.$$

33 Given that

$$a + b(1 + x)^3 + c(1 + 2x)^3 + d(1 + 3x)^3 = x^3$$

for all values of x, find the values of the constants a, b, c and d.

5 The trapezium rule

This chapter is about approximating to integrals. When you have completed it, you should

- be able to use the trapezium rule to estimate the value of a definite integral
- be able to use a sketch, in some cases, to determine whether the trapezium rule approximation is an overestimate or an underestimate.

5.1 The need for approximation

There are times when it is not possible to evaluate a definite integral directly, using the standard method,

$$\int_a^b f(x)\,dx = \left[I(x)\right]_a^b = I(b) - I(a),$$

where $I(x)$ is the simplest function for which $\dfrac{d}{dx}I(x) = f(x)$.

Two examples which you cannot integrate with your knowledge so far are $\displaystyle\int_0^1 \frac{1}{1+x^2}\,dx$ and $\displaystyle\int_0^1 \sqrt{1+x^3}\,dx$. You need to use another method for approximating to the integrals.

5.2 The trapezium rule: simple form

Suppose that you wish to find an estimate for the integral $\displaystyle\int_a^b f(x)\,dx$.

You know, from P1 Section 10.3, that the value of the definite integral $\displaystyle\int_a^b f(x)\,dx$ represents the shaded area in Fig. 5.1. The principle behind the trapezium rule is to approximate to this area by using the shaded trapezium in Fig. 5.2.

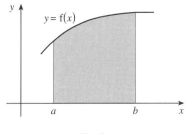
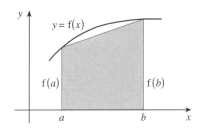

Fig. 5.1   Fig. 5.2

Since the area of the shaded trapezium is given by

$$\text{area of trapezium} = \tfrac{1}{2}\times(\text{sum of parallel sides})\times\text{distance between them},$$

$$\text{area of trapezium} = \tfrac{1}{2}\times(f(a)+f(b))\times(b-a).$$

So $\displaystyle\int_a^b f(x)\,dx \approx \tfrac{1}{2}(b-a)(f(a)+f(b))$.

This is the simplest form of the **trapezium rule**.

Example 5.2.1
Use the simplest form of the trapezium rule to find estimates for $\displaystyle\int_0^1 \frac{1}{1+x^2}\,dx$ and $\displaystyle\int_0^1 \sqrt{1+x^3}\,dx$.

$$\int_0^1 \frac{1}{1+x^2}\,dx \approx \tfrac{1}{2}(1-0)\left(\frac{1}{1+0^2}+\frac{1}{1+1^2}\right)=\tfrac{1}{2}\times 1\times\left(1+\tfrac{1}{2}\right)=0.75.$$

$$\int_0^1 \sqrt{1+x^3}\,dx \approx \tfrac{1}{2}(1-0)\left(\sqrt{1+1^3}+\sqrt{1+0^3}\right)=\tfrac{1}{2}\times 1\times\left(\sqrt{2}+1\right)\approx 1.21.$$

5.3   The trapezium rule: general form

If you said that the simple form of the trapezium rule is not very accurate, especially over a large interval on the x-axis, you would be correct.

You can improve the accuracy by dividing the large interval from a to b into several smaller ones, and then using the trapezium rule on each interval. The amount of work sounds horrendous but, with good notation and organisation, it is not too bad.

Divide the interval from a to b into n equal intervals, each of width h, so that $nh=b-a$.

Call the x-coordinate of the left side of the first interval x_0, so $x_0=a$, and then successively let $x_1=x_0+h$, $x_2=x_0+2h$ and so on until $x_{n-1}=x_0+(n-1)h$ and $x_n=x_0+nh=b$.

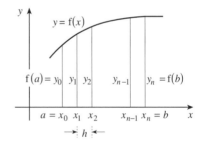

Fig. 5.3

To shorten the amount of writing, use the shorthand $y_0=f(x_0)$, $y_1=f(x_1)$ and so on, as in Fig. 5.3.

Then, using the simple form of the trapezium rule on each interval of width h in turn, you find that

$$\int_a^b f(x)\,dx \approx \tfrac{1}{2}h(y_0+y_1)+\tfrac{1}{2}h(y_1+y_2)+\tfrac{1}{2}h(y_2+y_3)+\ldots+\tfrac{1}{2}h(y_{n-1}+y_n)$$

$$=\tfrac{1}{2}h(y_0+y_1+y_1+y_2+y_2+y_3+\ldots+y_{n-2}+y_{n-1}+y_{n-1}+y_n)$$

$$=\tfrac{1}{2}h\{(y_0+y_n)+2(y_1+y_2+\ldots+y_{n-1})\}.$$

The trapezium rule with n intervals is sometimes called the trapezium rule with $n+1$ ordinates. (The term 'ordinate' means y-coordinate.)

> The **trapezium rule** with n intervals states that
>
> $$\int_a^b y\,dx \approx \tfrac{1}{2}h\{(y_0 + y_n) + 2(y_1 + y_2 + \ldots + y_{n-1})\}, \text{ where } h = \frac{b-a}{n}.$$

Example 5.3.1

Use the trapezium rule with five intervals to estimate $\int_0^1 \dfrac{1}{1+x^2}\,dx$, giving your answer correct to three decimal places.

The values of y_n in Table 5.4 are given correct to 5 decimal places.

n	x_n	y_n	Sums	Weight	Total
0	0	1			
5	1	0.5	1.5	$\times\,1 =$	1.5
1	0.2	0.961 54			
2	0.4	0.862 07			
3	0.6	0.735 29			
4	0.8	0.609 76	3.168 66	$\times\,2 =$	6.337 32
					7.837 32

Table 5.4

The factor $\tfrac{1}{2}h$ is $\tfrac{1}{2}\times 0.2 = 0.1$. Therefore the approximation to the integral is $0.1 \times 7.837\,32 = 0.783\,732$. Thus the five-interval approximation correct to three decimal places is 0.784.

The accurate value of $\int_0^1 \dfrac{1}{1+x^2}\,dx$ is $\tfrac{1}{4}\pi$, which correct to three decimal places is 0.785, so you can see that the five-interval version of the trapezium rule is a considerable improvement on the one-interval version in Example 5.2.1.

How you organise the table to give the value of $\{(y_0 + y_n) + 2(y_1 + y_2 + \ldots + y_{n-1})\}$ is up to you, and may well depend on the kind of software or calculator that you have. It is important, however, that you make clear how you reach your answer.

5.4 Accuracy of the trapezium rule

It is not easy with the mathematics that you know at present to give a quantitative approach to the possible error involved with the trapezium rule.

However, if a graph is bending downwards over the whole interval from a to b, as in Fig. 5.5, then you can be certain that the trapezium rule will give you an underestimate of the true area. If on the other hand, a graph is bending upwards over the whole interval from a to b, as in Fig. 5.6, then you can be certain that the trapezium rule will give you an overestimate of the true area.

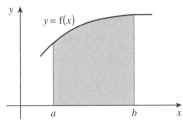

Fig. 5.5   Fig. 5.6

However, if the graph sometimes bends upwards and sometimes downwards over the interval from a to b, you cannot be sure whether your approximation to the integral is an overestimate or an underestimate.

Exercise 5

1 Use the simplest case of the trapezium rule (that is, one interval) to estimate the values of

(a) $\displaystyle\int_3^4 \sqrt{1+x}\,dx,$ (b) $\displaystyle\int_2^4 \frac{1}{x}\,dx.$

2 Use the trapezium rule with 3 intervals to estimate the value of $\displaystyle\int_0^3 \sqrt{1+x^2}\,dx.$

3 Use the trapezium rule with 3 ordinates (that is, 2 intervals) to estimate the value of $\displaystyle\int_1^3 \sqrt{1+\sqrt{x}}\,dx.$

4 Find approximations to the value of $\displaystyle\int_1^5 \frac{1}{x^2}\,dx$ by:

   (a) using the trapezium rule with 2 intervals,

   (b) using the trapezium rule with 4 intervals.

   (c) Evaluate the integral exactly and compare your answer with those found in parts (a) and (b).

5 The diagram shows the graph of $y = \dfrac{4}{\sqrt{x}}$.

Use the trapezium rule with 6 intervals to find an approximation to the area of the shaded region, and explain why the trapezium rule overestimates the true value.

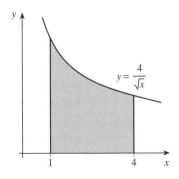

6 Use the trapezium rule with 5 intervals to estimate the value of $\int_0^1 \left(\frac{1}{10}x^2 + 1\right)dx$.
Draw the graph of $y = \frac{1}{10}x^2 + 1$ and explain why the trapezium rule gives an overestimate of the true value of the integral.

7 Draw the graph of $y = x^3 + 8$ and use it to explain why use of the trapezium rule with 4 intervals will give the exact value of $\int_{-2}^2 (x^3 + 8)dx$.

8 Find an approximation to $\int_1^2 \sqrt{x^2 + 4x}\, dx$ by using the trapezium rule with 4 intervals.

9 Find an approximation to $\int_0^4 \frac{x^2}{2^x}\, dx$ by using the trapezium rule with 8 intervals.

10 The diagram shows part of a circle with its centre at the origin. The curve has equation $y = \sqrt{25 - x^2}$.

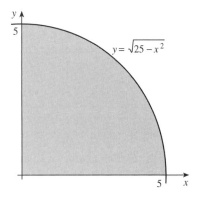

(a) Use the trapezium rule with 10 intervals to find an approximation to the area of the shaded region.

(b) Does the trapezium rule overestimate or underestimate the true area?

(c) Find the exact area of the shaded region.

(d) By comparing your answers to parts (a) and (c), obtain an estimate for π correct to 2 decimal places.

Miscellaneous exercise 5

1 Use the trapezium rule, with ordinates at $x = 1$, $x = 2$ and $x = 3$, to estimate the value of $\int_1^3 \sqrt{40 - x^3}\, dx$.   (OCR)

2 The diagram shows the region R bounded by the curve, $y = \sqrt{1 + x^3}$, the axes and the line $x = 2$. Use the trapezium rule with 4 intervals to obtain an approximation for the area of R, showing your working and giving your answer to a suitable degree of accuracy.

Explain, with the aid of a sketch, whether the approximation is an overestimate or an underestimate.   (OCR)

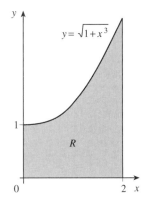

3   Use the trapezium rule with subdivisions at $x = 3$ and $x = 5$ to obtain an approximation to
    $\int_1^7 \dfrac{x^3}{1 + x^4}\,dx$, giving your answer correct to 3 places of decimals.   (OCR)

4   Use the trapezium rule with 5 intervals to estimate the value of $\int_0^{0.5} \sqrt{1 + x^2}\,dx$, showing
    your working. Give your answer correct to 2 decimal places.   (OCR)

5   The diagram shows the region R bounded by
    the axes, the curve $y = (x^2 + 1)^{-\frac{3}{2}}$ and the
    line $x = 1$. Use the trapezium rule, with
    ordinates at $x = 0$, $x = \frac{1}{2}$ and $x = 1$, to
    estimate the value of

    $$\int_0^1 (x^2 + 1)^{-\frac{3}{2}}\,dx,$$

    giving your answer correct to 2 significant
    figures.   (OCR)

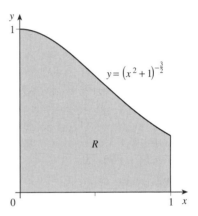

6   The diagram shows a sketch of $y = \sqrt{2 + x^3}$
    for values of x between -0.5 and 0.5.

    (a) Use the trapezium rule, with ordinates at
         $x = -0.5$, $x = 0$ and $x = 0.5$ to find an
         approximate value for $\int_{-0.5}^{0.5} \sqrt{2 + x^3}\,dx$.

    (b) Explain briefly, with reference to the
         diagram, why the trapezium rule can be
         expected to give a good approximation
         to the value of the integral in this case.
                                             (OCR)

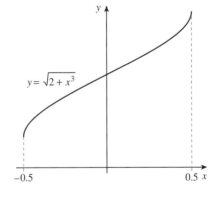

7   A certain function f is continuous and is such that
        $f(2.0) = 15$, $f(2.5) = 22$, $f(3.0) = 31$, $f(3.5) = 28$, $f(4.0) = 27$.

    Use the trapezium rule to find an approximation to $\int_2^4 f(x)\,dx$.

8   The speeds of an athlete on a training run were recorded at 30-second intervals:

Time after start (s)	0	30	60	90	120	150	180	210	240
Speed (m s^{-1})		3.0	4.6	4.8	5.1	5.4	5.2	4.9	4.6	3.8

The area under a speed–time graph represents the distance travelled. Use the trapezium rule
to estimate the distance covered by the athlete.

9 At a time t minutes after the start of a journey, the speed of a car travelling along a main road is v km h^{-1}. The table gives values of v every minute on the ten-minute journey.

t	0	1	2	3	4	5	6	7	8	9	10
v	0	31	46	42	54	57	73	70	68	48	0

Use the trapezium rule to estimate of the length of the ten-minute journey in kilometres.

10 A river is 18 metres wide in a certain region and its depth, d metres, at a point x metres from one side is given by the formula $d = \frac{1}{18}\sqrt{x(18-x)(18+x)}$.

(a) Produce a table showing the depths (correct to 3 decimal places where necessary) at $x = 0, 3, 6, 9, 12, 15$ and 18.

(b) Use the trapezium rule to estimate the cross-sectional area of the river in this region.

(c) Given that, in this region, the river is flowing at a uniform speed of 100 metres per minute, estimate the number of cubic metres of water passing per minute. (OCR)

11 The diagram shows the curve $y = 4^{-x}$.
Taking subdivisions at $x = 0.25, 0.5, 0.75$, find an approximation to the shaded area.

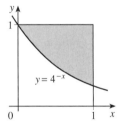

12 The left diagram shows the part of the curve $y = 2.5 - 2^{1-x^2}$ for which $-0.5 \leqslant x \leqslant 0.5$. The shaded region forms the cross-section of a straight concrete drainage channel, as shown in the right diagram. The units involved are metres.

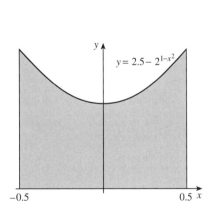 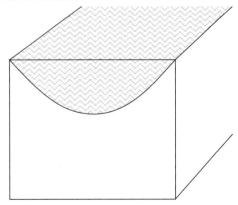

(a) Use the trapezium rule with 4 intervals to estimate the area of the shaded region.

(b) Estimate the volume of concrete in a 20-metre length of channel.

(c) Estimate the volume of water in the 20-metre length of channel when it is full.

(d) Of the estimates in parts (b) and (c), which is an overestimate and which is an underestimate?

13 The integral $\displaystyle\int_{36}^{64} \sqrt{x}\,dx$ is denoted by I.

    (a) Find the exact value of I.

    (b) Use the trapezium rule with two intervals to find an estimate for I, giving your answer in terms of $\sqrt{2}$.

    Use your two answers to deduce that $\sqrt{2} \approx \frac{149}{105}$.

14 It is given that $x-2$ is a factor of $f(x)$, where $f(x) = 2x^3 - 7x^2 + x + a$. Find the value of a and factorise $f(x)$ completely.

    Sketch the graph of $y = f(x)$. (You do not need to find the coordinates of the stationary points.)

    Use the trapezium rule, with ordinates $x = -1$, $x = 0$, $x = 1$ and $x = 2$ to find an approximation to $\displaystyle\int_{-1}^{2} f(x)\,dx$.

    Find the exact value of the integral and show that the trapezium rule gives a value that is in error by about 11%.   (OCR)

15 The trapezium rule, with 2 intervals of equal width, is to be used to find an approximate value for $\displaystyle\int_{1}^{2} \frac{1}{x^2}\,dx$. Explain, with the aid of a sketch, why the approximation will be greater than the exact value of the integral.

    Calculate the approximate value and the exact value, giving each answer correct to 3 decimal places.

    Another approximation to $\displaystyle\int_{1}^{2} \frac{1}{x^2}\,dx$ is to be calculated by using two trapezia of unequal width; the ordinates are at $x = 1$, $x = h$ and $x = 2$. Find, in terms of h, the total area, T, of these two trapezia.

    Find the value of h for which T is a minimum.

16 (a) Calculate the exact value of the integral $\displaystyle\int_{0}^{1} x^2\,dx$.

    (b) Find the trapezium rule approximations to this integral using 1, 2, 4 and 8 intervals. Call these A_1, A_2, A_4 and A_8.

    (c) For each of your answers in part (a), calculate the error E_i, where

$$E_i = \int_{0}^{1} x^2\,dx - A_i, \text{ for } i = 1, 2, 4 \text{ and } 8.$$

    (d) Look at your results for part (c), and guess the relationship between the error E_n and the number n of intervals taken.

    (e) How many intervals would you need to approximate to the integral to within 10^{-6}?

6 Extending differentiation and integration

This chapter is about differentiating a certain kind of composite function of the form $f(ax+b)$. When you have completed it, you should

- be able to differentiate composite functions of the form $(ax+b)^n$
- be able to integrate composite functions of the form $(ax+b)^n$.

You may want to leave out Section 6.3 on a first reading, and you will find that the exercises are independent of it. You will, however, need the results stated at the end of Section 6.1 and in Section 6.2 (and proved in Section 6.3) later, in Chapter 12.

6.1 Differentiating $(ax+b)^n$

To differentiate a function like $(2x+1)^3$, the only method available to you at present is to use the binomial theorem to multiply out the brackets, and then to differentiate term by term.

Example 6.1.1

Find $\dfrac{dy}{dx}$ for (a) $y=(2x+1)^3$, (b) $y=(1-3x)^4$.

(a) Expanding by the binomial theorem,

$$y = (2x)^3 + 3\times(2x)^2\times1 + 3\times(2x)\times1^2 + 1^3 = 8x^3 + 12x^2 + 6x + 1.$$

So $\dfrac{dy}{dx} = 24x^2 + 24x + 6.$

It is useful to express the result in factors, as $\dfrac{dy}{dx} = 6(4x^2 + 4x + 1) = 6(2x+1)^2.$

(b) Expanding by the binomial theorem,

$$y = 1^4 + 4\times1^3\times(-3x) + 6\times1^2\times(-3x)^2 + 4\times1\times(-3x)^3 + (-3x)^4$$
$$= 1 - 12x + 54x^2 - 108x^3 + 81x^4.$$

So $\dfrac{dy}{dx} = -12 + 108x - 324x^2 + 324x^3 = -12(1 - 9x + 27x^2 - 27x^3) = -12(1-3x)^3.$

Exercise 6A

In Question 1, see if you can predict what the result of the differentiation will be. If you can predict the result, then check by carrying out the differentiation, and factorising your result. If you can't, differentiate and simplify and look for a pattern in your answer.

1 Find $\dfrac{dy}{dx}$ for each of the following functions. In parts (d) and (e), a and b are constants.

(a) $(x+3)^2$ (b) $(2x-3)^2$ (c) $(1-3x)^3$ (d) $(ax+b)^3$

(e) $(b-ax)^3$ (f) $(1-x)^5$ (g) $(2x-3)^4$ (h) $(3-2x)^4$

2 Suppose that $y = (ax+b)^n$, where a and b are constants and n is a positive integer. Make a guess at a formula for $\dfrac{dy}{dx}$.

3 Use the formula you guessed in Question 2, after checking that it is correct, to differentiate each of the following functions, where a and b are constants.

(a) $(x+3)^{10}$ (b) $(2x-1)^5$ (c) $(1-4x)^7$ (d) $(3x-2)^5$

(e) $(4-2x)^6$ (f) $4(2+3x)^6$ (g) $(2x+5)^5$ (h) $(2x-3)^9$

In Exercise 6A, you were asked to predict how to differentiate a function of the form $(ax+b)^n$ where a and b are constants, and n is a positive integer. The result was

If $y = (ax+b)^n$, then $\dfrac{dy}{dx} = n(ax+b)^{n-1} \times a$.

Now assume that the same formula works for all n, including fractional and negative values. There is a proof in Section 6.3, but you can skip this on a first reading. The result, however, is important, and you must be able to use it confidently.

If a, b and n are constants, and $y = (ax+b)^n$, then $\dfrac{dy}{dx} = n(ax+b)^{n-1} \times a$.

Example 6.1.1

Find $\dfrac{dy}{dx}$ when   (a) $y = \sqrt{3x+2}$,   (b) $y = \dfrac{1}{1-2x}$.

(a) Writing $\sqrt{3x+2}$ in index form as $(3x+2)^{\frac{1}{2}}$ and using the result in the shaded box,

$$\frac{dy}{dx} = \tfrac{1}{2}(3x+2)^{-\frac{1}{2}} \times 3 = \tfrac{3}{2}\frac{1}{(3x+2)^{\frac{1}{2}}} = \frac{3}{2\sqrt{3x+2}}.$$

(b) In index form $y = (1-2x)^{-1}$, so $\dfrac{dy}{dx} = -1(1-2x)^{-2} \times (-2) = \dfrac{2}{(1-2x)^2}$.

Example 6.1.2

Find any stationary points on the graph $y = \sqrt{2x+1} + \dfrac{1}{\sqrt{2x+1}}$, and determine whether they are maxima, minima or neither.

$\sqrt{2x+1}$ is defined for $x \geqslant -\tfrac{1}{2}$, and $\dfrac{1}{\sqrt{2x+1}}$ for $x > -\tfrac{1}{2}$. So the largest possible domain is $x > -\tfrac{1}{2}$.

$y = (2x+1)^{\frac{1}{2}} + (2x+1)^{-\frac{1}{2}}$, so $\dfrac{dy}{dx} = \tfrac{1}{2}(2x+1)^{-\frac{1}{2}} \times 2 + \left(-\tfrac{1}{2}\right)(2x+1)^{-\frac{3}{2}} \times 2$, or

$\dfrac{dy}{dx} = (2x+1)^{-\frac{1}{2}} - (2x+1)^{-\frac{3}{2}}$, which can be written as

$$\frac{1}{(2x+1)^{\frac{1}{2}}} - \frac{1}{(2x+1)^{\frac{3}{2}}} = \frac{2x+1-1}{(2x+1)^{\frac{3}{2}}} = \frac{2x}{(2x+1)^{\frac{3}{2}}}.$$

Stationary points are those for which $\dfrac{dy}{dx} = 0$, which happens when $x = 0$.

Also $\dfrac{d^2y}{dx^2} = -\frac{1}{2}(2x+1)^{-\frac{3}{2}} \times 2 - \left(-\frac{3}{2}\right)(2x+1)^{-\frac{5}{2}} \times 2$

$\qquad = -(2x+1)^{-\frac{3}{2}} + 3(2x+1)^{-\frac{5}{2}}$.

When $x = 0$, $\dfrac{d^2y}{dx^2} = -(1)^{-\frac{3}{2}} + 3(1)^{-\frac{5}{2}} = 2 > 0$, so y has a minimum at $x = 0$.

A proof of the statement 'if $y = (ax+b)^n$, then $\dfrac{dy}{dx} = n(ax+b)^{n-1} \times a$' is given in Section 6.3 in the following form.

If a and b are constants, and if $\dfrac{d}{dx} f(x) = g(x)$,

then $\dfrac{d}{dx} f(ax+b) = ag(ax+b)$.

For the special case in this chapter, $f(x) = x^n$ and $g(x) = nx^{n-1}$. Then

$$\frac{d}{dx}(ax+b)^n = \frac{d}{dx} f(ax+b) = ag(ax+b) = an(ax+b)^{n-1}.$$

6.2 Integrating $(ax+b)^n$

You can also use the differentiation result in reverse for integration. For example, to integrate $(3x+1)^3$, you should recognise that it comes from differentiating $(3x+1)^4$.

A first guess at the integral $\displaystyle\int (3x+1)^3 \, dx$ is $(3x+1)^4$. If you differentiate $(3x+1)^4$, you find that you get $4(3x+1)^3 \times 3 = 12(3x+1)^3$. Therefore

$$\int (3x+1)^3 \, dx = \tfrac{1}{12}(3x+1)^4 + k.$$

You can formalise the guessing process by reversing the last result from Section 6.1.

$\displaystyle\int g(ax+b)\,dx = \frac{1}{a} f(ax+b) + k$ where $f(x)$ is the simplest integral of $g(x)$.

Applying this to the previous example, $g(x) = x^3$, $a = 3$ and $b = 1$. Then $f(x) = \frac{1}{4}x^4$, so

$$\int (3x+1)^3 \, dx = \int g(3x+1)\,dx = \tfrac{1}{3} f(3x+1) + k = \tfrac{1}{3} \times \tfrac{1}{4}(3x+1)^4 + k.$$

$$= \tfrac{1}{12}(3x+1)^4 + k.$$

Example 6.2.1

Find the integrals of   (a) $\sqrt{5-2x}$,   (b) $\dfrac{1}{(3-x)^2}$.

(a) **Method 1**   The first guess at $\displaystyle\int \sqrt{5-2x}\,dx = \int (5-2x)^{\frac{1}{2}}\,dx$ is $(5-2x)^{\frac{3}{2}}$.

Differentiating $(5-2x)^{\frac{3}{2}}$, you obtain $\frac{3}{2}(5-2x)^{\frac{1}{2}}\times(-2) = -3(5-2x)^{\frac{1}{2}}$. Therefore

$$\int (5-2x)^{\frac{1}{2}}\,dx = -\tfrac{1}{3}(5-2x)^{\frac{3}{2}} + k.$$

Method 2   Using the result in the shaded box, $g(x) = \sqrt{x} = x^{\frac{1}{2}}$, $a = -2$, $b = 5$,

so $f(x) = \dfrac{x^{\frac{3}{2}}}{{}^{3}\!/\!_{2}} = \tfrac{2}{3}x^{\frac{3}{2}}$, and $\displaystyle\int \sqrt{5-2x}\,dx = \tfrac{1}{-2}\times\tfrac{2}{3}(5-2x)^{\frac{3}{2}} + k = -\tfrac{1}{3}(5-2x)^{\frac{3}{2}} + k.$

(b) First write $\dfrac{1}{(3-x)^2}$ as $(3-x)^{-2}$. Then

$$\int \frac{1}{(3-x)^2}\,dx = \int (3-x)^{-2}\,dx = \tfrac{1}{-1}\times\tfrac{1}{-1}(3-x)^{-1} + k = \frac{1}{3-x} + k.$$

With practice you might find that you can write down the correct integral, but check your answer by differentiation, because it is easy to make a numerical mistake.

Example 6.2.2

Find the area between the curve $y = 16 - (2x+1)^4$
and the x-axis. (See Fig. 6.1.)

To find where the graph cuts the x-axis,
solve the equation $16 - (2x+1)^4 = 0$.
Thus $(2x+1)^4 = 16$, so $(2x+1) = 2$ or
$(2x+1) = -2$, leading to the limits of
integration, $x = \tfrac{1}{2}$ and $x = -\tfrac{3}{2}$.

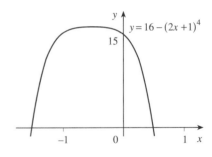

Fig. 6.1

The area is given by

$$\int_{-\frac{3}{2}}^{\frac{1}{2}} \left(16 - (2x+1)^4\right)dx = \left[16x - \tfrac{1}{10}(2x+1)^5\right]_{-\frac{3}{2}}^{\frac{1}{2}}$$

$$= \left(16\times\tfrac{1}{2} - \tfrac{1}{10}\left(2\times\tfrac{1}{2}+1\right)^5\right) - \left(16\times\left(-\tfrac{3}{2}\right) - \tfrac{1}{10}\left(2\times\left(-\tfrac{3}{2}\right)+1\right)^5\right)$$

$$= \left(8 - \tfrac{1}{10}\times 2^5\right) - \left(-24 - \tfrac{1}{10}\times(-2)^5\right)$$

$$= 4.8 - (-20.8) = 25.6.$$

The required area is then 25.6.

Exercise 6B

1 Find $\dfrac{dy}{dx}$ for each of the following.

   (a) $y=(4x+5)^5$
   (b) $y=(2x-7)^8$
   (c) $y=(2-x)^6$
   (d) $y=\left(\tfrac{1}{2}x+4\right)^4$

2 Find $\dfrac{dy}{dx}$ for each of the following.

   (a) $y=\dfrac{1}{3x+5}$
   (b) $y=\dfrac{1}{(4-x)^2}$
   (c) $y=\dfrac{1}{(2x+1)^3}$
   (d) $y=\dfrac{4}{(4x-1)^4}$

3 Find $\dfrac{dy}{dx}$ for each of the following.

   (a) $y=\sqrt{2x+3}$
   (b) $y=\sqrt[3]{6x-1}$
   (c) $y=\dfrac{1}{\sqrt{4x+7}}$
   (d) $y=5(3x-2)^{-\frac{2}{3}}$

4 Given that $y=(2x+1)^3+(2x-1)^3$, find the value of $\dfrac{dy}{dx}$ when $x=1$.

5 Find the coordinates of the point on the curve $y=(1-4x)^{\frac{3}{2}}$ at which the gradient is -30.

6 Find the equation of the tangent to the curve $y=\dfrac{1}{3x+1}$ at $\left(-1,-\tfrac{1}{2}\right)$.

7 Find the equation of the normal to the curve $y=\sqrt{6x+3}$ at the point for which $x=13$.

8 Integrate the following with respect to x.

   (a) $(2x+1)^6$
   (b) $(3x-5)^4$
   (c) $(1-7x)^3$
   (d) $\left(\tfrac{1}{2}x+1\right)^{10}$

9 Integrate the following with respect to x.

   (a) $(5x+2)^{-3}$
   (b) $2(1-3x)^{-2}$
   (c) $\dfrac{1}{(x+1)^5}$
   (d) $\dfrac{3}{2(4x+1)^4}$

10 Integrate the following with respect to x.

   (a) $\sqrt{10x+1}$
   (b) $\dfrac{1}{\sqrt{2x-1}}$
   (c) $\left(\tfrac{1}{2}x+2\right)^{\frac{2}{3}}$
   (d) $\dfrac{8}{\sqrt[4]{2+6x}}$

11 Evaluate the following integrals.

   (a) $\displaystyle\int_{1}^{5}(2x-1)^3\,dx$
   (b) $\displaystyle\int_{1}^{5}\sqrt{2x-1}\,dx$
   (c) $\displaystyle\int_{1}^{3}\dfrac{1}{(x+2)^2}\,dx$
   (d) $\displaystyle\int_{1}^{3}\dfrac{2}{(x+2)^3}\,dx$

12 Find the value of each of the following improper integrals.

   (a) $\displaystyle\int_{-2}^{2}\dfrac{1}{\sqrt{x+2}}\,dx$
   (b) $\displaystyle\int_{\frac{1}{2}}^{\frac{9}{2}}\dfrac{6}{\sqrt[3]{2x-1}}\,dx$

13 Find the value of each of the following infinite integrals.

   (a) $\displaystyle\int_{0}^{\infty}\dfrac{1}{(4x+1)^2}\,dx$
   (b) $\displaystyle\int_{-\infty}^{1}\dfrac{5}{(5-2x)^3}\,dx$

14 Find the area of each of the following shaded regions.

(a)
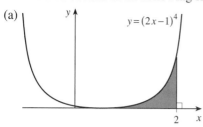

(b)
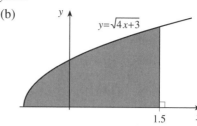

(c)
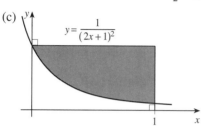

(d)
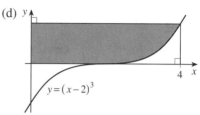

15 Given that $\displaystyle\int_{1.25}^{p} (4x-5)^4 \, \mathrm{d}x = 51.2$, find the value of p.

16 The curve $y = (ax+b)^4$ crosses the y-axis at $(0,16)$ and has gradient 160 there. Find the possible values of a and b.

17 Find the coordinates of the stationary point of the curve $y = \sqrt{2x+1} - \frac{1}{3}x + 7$, and determine whether the stationary point is a maximum or a minimum.

18 The diagram shows the curve $y = (2x-5)^4$. The point P has coordinates $(4,81)$ and the tangent to the curve at P meets the x-axis at Q. Find the area of the region (shaded in the diagram) enclosed between the curve, PQ and the x-axis.

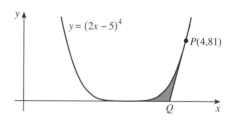

19 Find the area of the region enclosed between the curves $y = (x-2)^4$ and $y = (x-2)^3$.

6.3* Justifying the rule for differentiating $(ax+b)^n$

You may omit this section if you wish; a more general piece of theory will be developed in Section 13.2.

Suppose that you know how to differentiate $y = \mathrm{f}(x)$; call the result $\mathrm{g}(x)$, so $\dfrac{\mathrm{d}y}{\mathrm{d}x} = \mathrm{g}(x)$.

What can you deduce about the gradient of the graph of $\mathrm{f}(ax+b)$, where a and b are constants? For example, you know how to differentiate $y = \sqrt{x} = x^{\frac{1}{2}}$; how can you use this information to differentiate $y = (3x+1)^{\frac{1}{2}}$?

The argument is presented in two parts.

How does translation affect the gradient?

If $\dfrac{d}{dx}f(x) = g(x)$, what is $\dfrac{d}{dx}f(x-k)$?

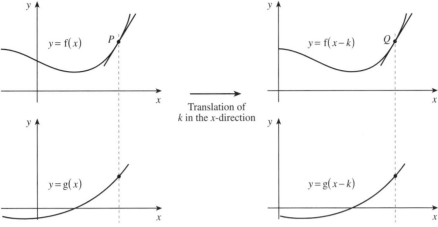

Fig. 6.2

The left side of Fig. 6.2 shows the relationship between the graphs of a function $f(x)$ and its derived function $g(x)$. (See P1 Section 8.4.) On the right, the graphs have been translated by k units in the direction of the positive x-axis, with corresponding points shown on each graph. The vertical dashed lines show that, because the gradients at P and Q have the same value, the graph of the gradient function is also translated by k units in the same direction. (See P1 Section 8.5.)

$$\text{If } \dfrac{d}{dx}f(x) = g(x), \text{ then } \dfrac{d}{dx}f(x-k) = g(x-k).$$

How does stretching affect the gradient?

Suppose first that a is positive. In P1 Section 8.6 you saw that 'replacing x by $\dfrac{x}{c}$ in the equation $y = f(x)$ produces a stretch of factor c in the x-direction'. If you replace c by $\dfrac{1}{a}$ you will see that the effect of replacing x by ax in the equation $y = f(x)$ is to stretch the graph by a factor of $\dfrac{1}{a}$ in the x-direction.

Fig. 6.3 shows the graphs of the functions $y = f(x)$ and $y = f(ax)$ with corresponding points P and Q marked on the each graph.

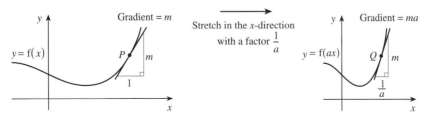

Fig. 6.3

To answer the question, 'What is the relation between the gradients at P and at Q?', consider what happens to the gradient of the tangent at P under the stretch with factor $\dfrac{1}{a}$. Suppose that the tangent at P has gradient m; a right-angled triangle with base 1 and height m has been drawn to illustrate this gradient. On the right, the figure has been stretched by a factor of $\dfrac{1}{a}$, that is, compressed by a factor of a, in the x-direction. The right-angled triangle now has a base of $\dfrac{1}{a}$, so the gradient of the new tangent is $\dfrac{m}{1/a} = am$. That is, the gradient of the tangent has been multiplied by a factor of a.

If a is negative, the transformation could be made up of two parts. The first part would be a reflection in the y-axis which would multiply the gradient by -1. The second would be a stretch of $\dfrac{1}{|a|}$. So the effect on the gradient would be to multiply it by $-|a|$; but, as a is negative, this is the same as multiplying by a.

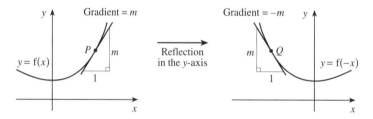

Fig. 6.4

Stretching a graph by a factor of $\dfrac{1}{a}$ in the x-direction multiplies the gradient at every point by a. So if $\dfrac{d}{dx}f(x) = g(x)$, then $\dfrac{d}{dx}f(ax) = ag(ax)$.

You can combine the results in the two shaded boxes above to find the result of differentiating $f(ax+b)$, by writing $f(ax+b)$ in the form $f\left(a\left(x+\dfrac{b}{a}\right)\right)$.

The result in the first shaded box says that

$$\text{if } \frac{d}{dx}f(x) = g(x), \quad \text{then } \frac{d}{dx}f\left(x+\frac{b}{a}\right) = g\left(x+\frac{b}{a}\right).$$

Using the result in the second shaded box then shows that

$$\frac{d}{dx}f\left(a\left(x+\frac{b}{a}\right)\right) = ag\left(a\left(x+\frac{b}{a}\right)\right) = ag(ax+b).$$

This is the result in the shaded box at the end of Section 6.1.

Miscellaneous exercise 6

1 Differentiate $(4x-1)^{20}$ with respect to x. (OCR)

2 Differentiate $\dfrac{1}{(3-4x)^2}$ with respect to x. (OCR)

3 Evaluate $\displaystyle\int_0^{\frac{2}{3}} (3x-2)^3 \, dx$. (OCR)

4 Find $\displaystyle\int_0^4 \sqrt{2x+1} \, dx$. (OCR)

5 Find the equation of the tangent to the curve $y=(4x+3)^5$ at the point $\left(-\tfrac{1}{2},1\right)$, giving your answer in the form $y=mx+c$. (OCR)

6 The diagram shows a sketch of the curve $y=\sqrt{4-x}$ and the line $y=2-\tfrac{1}{3}x$. The coordinates of the points A and B where the curve and line intersect are $(0,2)$ and $(3,1)$ respectively. Calculate the area of the region between the line and the curve (shaded in the diagram), giving your answer as an exact fraction. (OCR)

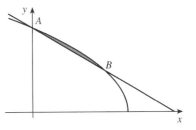

7 The diagram shows the curve $y=(2x-3)^3$.

   (a) Find the x-coordinates of the two points on the curve which have gradient 6.

   (b) The region shaded in the diagram is bounded by part of the curve and by the two axes. Find, by integration, the area of this region. (OCR)

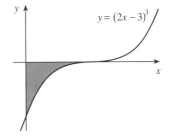

8 The diagram shows the curve with equation $y=\sqrt{4x+1}$ and the normal to the curve at the point A with coordinates $(6,5)$.

   (a) Show that the equation of the normal to the curve at A is $y=-\tfrac{5}{2}x+20$.

   (b) Find the area of the region (shaded in the diagram) which is enclosed by the curve, the normal and the x-axis. Give your answer as a fraction in its lowest terms. (OCR)

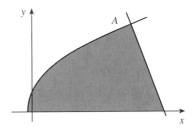

9 Find the equation of the tangent to the curve $y=\dfrac{50}{(2x-1)^2}$ at the point $(3,2)$, giving your answer in the form $ax+by+c=0$, where a, b and c are integers. (OCR)

7 Volume of revolution

This chapter is about using integration to find the volume of a particular kind of solid, called a solid of revolution. When you have completed it, you should

- be able to find a volume of revolution about either the x- or y-axis.

7.1 Volumes of revolution

Let O be the origin, and let OA be a line through the origin, as shown in Fig. 7.1. Consider the region between the line OA and the x-axis, shown shaded. If you rotate this region about the x-axis through $360°$, it sweeps out a solid cone, shown in Fig. 7.2. A solid shape constructed in this way is called a **solid of revolution**. The volume of a solid of revolution is sometimes called a **volume of revolution**.

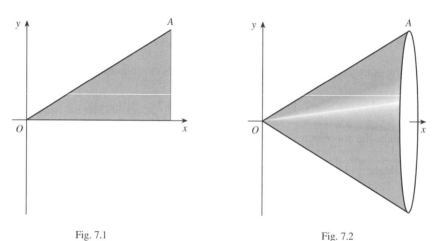

Fig. 7.1   Fig. 7.2

Calculating a volume of revolution is similar in many ways to calculating the area of a region under a curve, and can be illustrated by an example.

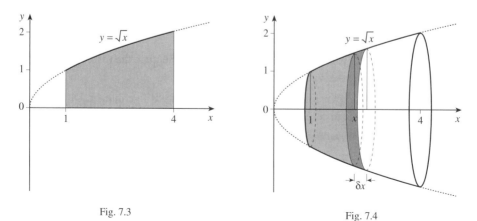

Fig. 7.3   Fig. 7.4

Suppose that the region between the graph of $y = \sqrt{x}$ and the x-axis from $x = 1$ to $x = 4$, shown in Fig. 7.3, is rotated about the x-axis to form the solid of revolution in Fig. 7.4.

The technique for calculating a volume of revolution is very similar to that for calculating area which you saw in P1 Section 10.2. The key is to begin by asking a more general question: what is the volume, V, of the solid of revolution from $x = 1$ as far as any value of x? This solid is shown by the light shading in Fig. 7.4.

Suppose that x is increased by δx. Since y and V are both functions of x, the corresponding increases in y and V can be written as δy and δV. The increase δV is shown by darker shading in Fig. 7.4. Examine this increase δV in the volume more closely. It is shown in more detail in the left diagram in Fig. 7.5.

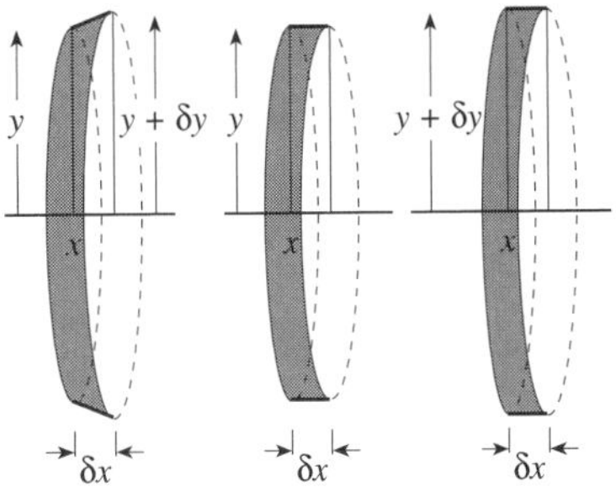

The increase δV in the volume is between the volumes of two disc-like cylinders, each of width δx and having radii y and $y + \delta y$. (These two cylinders are shown in the centre and right diagrams in Fig. 7.5.) So

$$\delta V \text{ is between } \pi y^2 \delta x \text{ and } \pi(y + \delta y)^2 \delta x$$

from which it follows that

Fig. 7.5

$$\frac{\delta V}{\delta x} \text{ is between } \pi y^2 \text{ and } \pi(y + \delta y)^2.$$

Now let δx tend to 0. From the definition in P1 Section 9.3, $\dfrac{\delta V}{\delta x}$ tends to the derivative $\dfrac{dV}{dx}$. Also, δy tends to 0, so that $y + \delta y$ tends to y. It follows that

$$\frac{dV}{dx} = \pi y^2.$$

So V is a function whose derivative is πy^2, and since $y = \sqrt{x}$, $\dfrac{dV}{dx} = \pi x$. Therefore

$$V = \tfrac{1}{2} \pi x^2 + k$$

for some number k.

Since the volume V is 0 when $x = 1$, $0 = \tfrac{1}{2}\pi \times 1^2 + k$, giving $k = -\tfrac{1}{2}\pi$. Thus

$$V = \tfrac{1}{2}\pi x^2 - \tfrac{1}{2}\pi.$$

To find the volume up to $x = 4$, substitute $x = 4$ in this expression for V. The volume is $\tfrac{1}{2}\pi \times 4^2 - \tfrac{1}{2}\pi = \tfrac{1}{2}\pi(16 - 1) = \tfrac{15}{2}\pi$.

You can shorten the last part of this work by noticing that you can use the integral notation introduced in P1 Section 10.3:

$$V = \int_1^4 \pi y^2 \, dx = \int_1^4 \pi x \, dx = \left[\tfrac{1}{2}\pi x^2\right]_1^4 = \tfrac{1}{2}\pi \times 16 - \tfrac{1}{2}\pi \times 1 = \tfrac{15}{2}\pi.$$

Notice that the argument used at the beginning of the example was completely general, and did not depend in any way on the equation of the original curve.

Notice that the answer has been given without a unit, because it is not usual to attach a unit to the variables x and y when graphs are drawn. But if in a particular situation x and y each denote numbers of units, then you should attach the corresponding unit to the value of V.

> When the region under the graph of $y = f(x)$ between $x = a$ and $x = b$ (where $a < b$) is rotated about the x-axis, the volume of the solid of revolution formed is
>
> $$\int_a^b \pi(f(x))^2\, dx, \quad \text{or} \quad \int_a^b \pi y^2\, dx.$$

Example 7.1.1
Find the volume generated when the region under the graph of $y = 1 + x^2$ between $x = -1$ and $x = 1$ is rotated through four right angles about the x-axis.

The phrase 'four right angles' is sometimes used in place of $360°$ for describing the rotation about the x-axis.

The required volume is V cubic units, where

$$V = \int_{-1}^{1} \pi y^2\, dx = \int_{-1}^{1} \pi\left(1 + x^2\right)^2 dx = \int_{-1}^{1} \pi\left(1 + 2x^2 + x^4\right) dx$$

$$= \left[\pi\left(x + \tfrac{2}{3}x^3 + \tfrac{1}{5}x^5\right)\right]_{-1}^{1}$$

$$= \pi\left\{\left(1 + \tfrac{2}{3} + \tfrac{1}{5}\right) - \left((-1) + \tfrac{2}{3}(-1)^3 + \tfrac{1}{5}(-1)^5\right)\right\} = \tfrac{56}{15}\pi.$$

The volume of the solid is $\tfrac{56}{15}\pi$.

It is usual to give the result as an exact multiple of π, unless you are asked for an answer correct to a given number of significant figures or decimal places.

You can also use the method to obtain the formula for the volume of a cone.

Example 7.1.2
Prove that the volume V of a cone with base radius r and height h is $V = \tfrac{1}{3}\pi r^2 h$.

The triangle which rotates to give the cone is shown in Fig. 7.6, where the 'height' has been drawn across the page. The gradient of

OA is $\dfrac{r}{h}$, so its equation is $y = \dfrac{r}{h}x$.

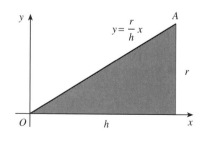

Fig. 7.6

Therefore, remembering that π, r and h are constants and do not depend on x,

$$V = \int_0^h \pi y^2 \, dx = \int_0^h \pi \left(\frac{r}{h} x\right)^2 dx = \int_0^h \pi \frac{r^2}{h^2} x^2 \, dx$$

$$= \pi \frac{r^2}{h^2} \int_0^h x^2 \, dx = \pi \frac{r^2}{h^2} \left[\tfrac{1}{3} x^3\right]_0^h = \pi \frac{r^2}{h^2} \times \tfrac{1}{3} h^3 = \tfrac{1}{3} \pi r^2 h.$$

7.2 Volumes of revolution about the y-axis

In Fig. 7.7, the region between the graph of $y = f(x)$ between $y = c$ and $y = d$ is rotated about the y-axis to give the solid shown in Fig. 7.8.

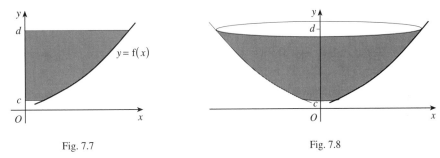

Fig. 7.7   Fig. 7.8

To find the volume of this solid of revolution about the y-axis, you can reverse the roles of x and y in the discussion in Section 7.1.

> When the graph of the region bounded by the graph of $y = f(x)$, the lines $y = c$ and $y = d$ and the y-axis is rotated about the y-axis, the volume of the solid of revolution formed is
>
> $$\int_c^d \pi x^2 \, dy.$$

You can only use this result if the inverse function $x = f^{-1}(y)$ is defined for $c \leqslant y \leqslant d$ (see Chapter 2). Remember that the limits in the integral are limits for y, not for x.

Example 7.2.1
Find the volume generated when the region bounded by $y = x^3$ and the y-axis between $y = 1$ to $y = 8$ is rotated through $360°$ about the y-axis.

Since the volume is given by $\int_1^8 \pi x^2 \, dy$, you need to express x^2 in terms of y.

The equation $y = x^3$ can be inverted to give $x = y^{\frac{1}{3}}$, so that $x^2 = y^{\frac{2}{3}}$. Then

$$V = \int_1^8 \pi y^{\frac{2}{3}} \, dy = \pi \left[\tfrac{3}{5} y^{\frac{5}{3}}\right]_1^8 = \pi \left(\tfrac{3}{5} \times 8^{\frac{5}{3}}\right) - \pi \left(\tfrac{3}{5} \times 1^{\frac{5}{3}}\right)$$

$$= \pi \left(\tfrac{3}{5} \times 32\right) - \pi \left(\tfrac{3}{5} \times 1\right) = \tfrac{93}{5} \pi.$$

The required volume is $\tfrac{93}{5} \pi$.

Exercise 7

In all the questions in this exercise, leave your answers as multiples of π.

1 Find the volume generated when the region under the graph of $y = f(x)$ between $x = a$ and $x = b$ is rotated through $360°$ about the x-axis.

(a) $f(x) = x; \quad a = 3, b = 5$

(b) $f(x) = x^2; \quad a = 2, b = 5$

(c) $f(x) = x^3; \quad a = 2, b = 6$

(d) $f(x) = \dfrac{1}{x}; \quad a = 1, b = 4$

2 Find the volume formed when the region under the graph of $y = f(x)$ between $x = a$ and $x = b$ is rotated through $360°$ about the x-axis.

(a) $f(x) = x + 3; \quad a = 3, b = 9$

(b) $f(x) = x^2 + 1; \quad a = 2, b = 5$

(c) $f(x) = \sqrt{x + 1}; \quad a = 0, b = 3$

(d) $f(x) = x(x - 2); \quad a = 0, b = 2$

3 Find the volume generated when the region bounded by the graph of $y = f(x)$, the y-axis and the lines $y = c$ and $y = d$ is rotated about the y-axis to form a solid of revolution.

(a) $f(x) = x^2; \quad c = 1, d = 3$

(b) $f(x) = x + 1; \quad c = 1, d = 4$

(c) $f(x) = \sqrt{x}; \quad c = 2, d = 7$

(d) $f(x) = \dfrac{1}{x}; \quad c = 2, d = 5$

(e) $f(x) = \sqrt{9 - x}; \quad c = 0, d = 3$

(f) $f(x) = x^2 + 1; \quad c = 1, d = 4$

(g) $f(x) = x^{\frac{2}{3}}; \quad c = 1, d = 5$

(h) $f(x) = \dfrac{1}{x} + 2; \quad c = 3, d = 5$

4 In each case the region enclosed between the following curves and the x-axis is rotated through $360°$ about the x-axis. Find the volume of the solid generated.

(a) $y = (x + 1)(x - 3)$

(b) $y = 1 - x^2$

(c) $y = x^2 - 5x + 6$

(d) $y = x^2 - 3x$

5 The region enclosed between the graphs of $y = x$ and $y = x^2$ is denoted by R. Find the volume generated when R is rotated through $360°$ about

(a) the x-axis,

(b) the y-axis.

6 The region enclosed between the graphs of $y = 4x$ and $y = x^2$ is denoted by R. Find the volume generated when R is rotated through $360°$ about

(a) the x-axis,

(b) the y-axis.

7 The region enclosed between the graphs of $y = \sqrt{x}$ and $y = x^2$ is denoted by R. Find the volume generated when R is rotated through $360°$ about

(a) the x-axis,

(b) the y-axis.

8 A glass bowl is formed by rotating about the y-axis the region between the graphs of $y = x^2$ and $y = x^3$. Find the volume of glass in the bowl.

9 The region enclosed by both axes, the line $x = 2$ and the curve $y = \frac{1}{8}x^2 + 2$ is rotated about the y-axis to form a solid. Find the volume of this solid.

Miscellaneous exercise 7

1 The region bounded by the curve $y = x^2 + 1$, the x-axis, the y-axis and the line $x = 2$ is rotated completely about the x-axis. Find, in terms of π, the volume of the solid formed.

(OCR)

2 Explain why the coordinates (x, y) of any point on a circle, centre O, radius a satisfy the equation $x^2 + y^2 = a^2$.

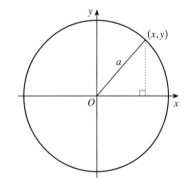

The semicircle above the x-axis is rotated about the x-axis through $360°$ to form a sphere of radius a. Explain why the volume V of this sphere is given by

$$V = 2\pi \int_0^a \left(a^2 - x^2\right) dx.$$

Hence show that $V = \frac{4}{3}\pi a^3$.

3 The ellipse with equation $\dfrac{x^2}{a^2} + \dfrac{y^2}{b^2} = 1$, shown in the diagram, has semi-axes a and b.

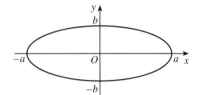

The ellipse is rotated about the x-axis to form an 'ellipsoid'. Find the volume of this ellipsoid.

Deduce the volume of the ellipsoid if, instead, the ellipse had been rotated about the y-axis.

4 The diagram shows the curve $y = x^{-\frac{2}{3}}$.

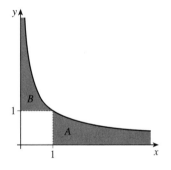

(a) Show that the shaded area A is infinite.

(b) Find the shaded area B.

(c) Area A is rotated through $360°$ about the x-axis. Find the volume generated.

(d) Area B is rotated through $360°$ about the y-axis. Find the volume generated.

5 Investigate the equivalent areas and volumes to those in Question 4 for the equations
  (i) $y = x^{-\frac{3}{5}}$, (ii) $y = x^{-\frac{1}{4}}$.

6 Sketch the curve $y = 9 - x^2$, stating the coordinates of the turning point and of the intersections with the axes.

The finite region bounded by the curve and the x-axis is denoted by R.

(a) Find the area of R and hence or otherwise find $\displaystyle\int_0^9 \sqrt{9 - y}\, dy$.

(b) Find the volume of the solid of revolution obtained when R is rotated through $360°$ about the x-axis.

(c) Find the volume of the solid of revolution obtained when R is rotated through $360°$ about the y-axis.

7 The region R is bounded by the part of the curve $y = (x-2)^{\frac{3}{2}}$ for which $2 \leqslant x \leqslant 4$, the x-axis, and the line $x = 4$. Find, in terms of π, the volume of the solid obtained when R is rotated through four right angles about the x-axis.   (OCR)

8 The diagram shows the region R, which is bounded by the axes and the part of the curve $y^2 = 4a(a-x)$ lying in the first quadrant. Find, in terms of a,

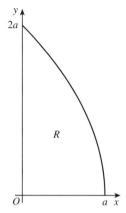

(a) the area of R,

(b) the volume, V_x, of the solid formed when R is rotated completely about the x-axis.

The volume of the solid formed when R is rotated completely about the y-axis is V_y. Show that $V_y = \frac{8}{15}V_x$.

The region S, lying in the first quadrant, is bounded by the curve $y^2 = 4a(a-x)$ and the lines $y = a$ and $y = 2a$. Find, in terms of a, the volume of the solid formed when S is rotated completely about the y-axis.   (OCR, adapted)

Revision exercise 3

1 Find the factors of the polynomial $x^3 - x^2 - 14x + 24$.

2 The region R is bounded by the x-axis, the line $x = 16$ and the curve with equation
$y = 6 - \sqrt{x}$, where $0 \leqslant x \leqslant 36$. Find, in terms of π, the volume of the solid generated
when R is rotated through one revolution about the x-axis. (OCR, adapted)

3 The function $x \mapsto \dfrac{1-x}{1+2x}$, $x \in \mathbb{R}$, $x \neq -\frac{1}{2}$ has an inverse. Find the inverse function, giving
your answer in similar language to the original.

4 The nth term of a series is $\frac{1}{2}(2n - 1)$. Write down the $(n+1)$th term.

   (a) Prove that the series is an arithmetic progression.

   (b) Find, algebraically, the value of n for which the sum to n terms is 200. (OCR)

5 (a) Determine the first three terms in the binomial expansion of $\left(x - \dfrac{1}{x} \right)^8$.

   (b) Write down the constant term in the binomial expansion of $\left(2x + \dfrac{3}{x} \right)^4$. (OCR)

6 Sketch the curve $y = 2x + \dfrac{1}{x}$ for positive values of x. Let R be the region bounded by the
curve, the x-axis, and the lines $x = 1$ and $x = 4$. Use the trapezium rule, with intervals of
width 0.5, to find an approximate value of the area of R, giving your answer correct to
four significant figures.

7 Differentiate $y = \dfrac{1}{\sqrt{2x + 3}}$ with respect to x. Draw a sketch of the curve.

8 The polynomial $P(x)$ is defined by: $P(x) = 2x^3 - 7x^2 + 2x + 3$.

   (a) Show that $x + 2$ is not a factor of $P(x)$.

   (b) Show that $P(x)$ has a factor of $2x + 1$.

   (c) Express $P(x)$ as the product of three linear factors. (OCR)

9 (a) The function f is defined by $f(x) = x^2 - 2x - 1$ for the domain $-2 \leqslant x \leqslant 5$. Write
   $f(x)$ in completed square form. Hence find the range of f. Explain why f does not
   have an inverse.

   (b) A function g is defined by $g(x) = 2x^2 - 4x - 3$. Write down a domain for g such that
   g^{-1} exists. (OCR, adapted)

10 The tenth term of an arithmetic progression is 125 and the sum of the first ten terms is
260.

   (a) Show that the first term in the progression is -73.

   (b) Find the common difference. (OCR)

11 The binomial expansion of $(1 + ax)^n$, where n is a positive integer, has six terms.

(a) Write down the value of n.

The coefficient of the x^3 term is $\frac{5}{4}$.

(b) Find a.   (OCR)

12 A region R is bounded by part of the curve with equation $y = \sqrt{64 - x^3}$, the positive x-axis and the positive y-axis. Use the trapezium rule with four intervals to approximate to the area of R, giving your answer correct to one decimal place.

13 Calculate the area of the region in the first quadrant bounded by the curve with equation $y = \sqrt{9 - x}$ and the axes.

14 The function f is defined for the domain $x \geqslant 0$ by $f : \mapsto 4 - x^2$.

(a) Sketch the graph of f and state the range of f.

(b) Describe a simple transformation whereby the graph of $y = f(x)$ may be obtained from the graph of $y = x^2$ for $x \geqslant 0$.

(c) The inverse of f is denoted by f^{-1}. Find an expression for $f^{-1}(x)$ and state the domain of f^{-1}.

(d) Show, by reference to a sketch, or otherwise, that the solution to the equation $f(x) = f^{-1}(x)$ can be obtained from the quadratic equation $x^2 + x - 4 = 0$. Determine the solution of $f(x) = f^{-1}(x)$, giving your value to two decimal places.

15 (a) Draw a sketch of the part of the curve $y = \dfrac{1}{\sqrt{x}}$ from $x = 1$ to $x = 4$.

(b) Calculate the area of the region R bounded by the curve, the x-axis and the lines $x = 1$ and $x = 4$.

(c) The region R is rotated through $360°$ about the x-axis to form a solid of revolution. Use the trapezium rule with 12 intervals to find an approximation to the volume of this solid. Give your answer correct to 3 significant figures.

16 Find the coefficient of $\dfrac{1}{x^4}$ in the binomial expansion of $\left(1 + \dfrac{3}{x}\right)^6$.

17 A polynomial $P(x)$ is the product of $\left(x^3 + ax^2 - x - 2\right)$ and $x - b$.

(a) The coefficients of x^3 and x in $P(x)$ are zero. Find the values of a and b.

(b) Hence factorise $P(x)$ completely and find the roots of the equation $P(x) = 0$.   (OCR)

18 An arithmetic progression has first term 3 and common difference 0.8. The sum of the first n terms of this arithmetic progression is 231. Find the value of n.

19 You are given that the area of the region between the curve with equation $y = \dfrac{1}{x}$ and the x-axis between $x = 1$ and $x = 2$ is 0.693 correct to 3 decimal places. By using the trapezium rule, find an approximation to the number k such that the area between the curve and the x-axis between $x = 1$ and $x = k$ is 1.

8 The logic of mathematics

This chapter analyses the kinds of argument that are used in mathematics. When you have completed it, you should

- be able to use the symbols $\Rightarrow$ and $\Leftrightarrow$ correctly, especially in solving equations
- understand how results can be proved by deduction or by indirect methods
- understand the relation between a theorem and its converse
- know that you can disprove an incorrect conjecture by finding a counterexample
- be able to distinguish necessary and sufficient conditions.

The first section, about the use of the signs $\Rightarrow$ and $\Leftrightarrow$ should be read by all who are taking the course. It is important also to work Exercise 8A.

The remainder of this chapter is optional, but it is useful for those who are continuing to study mathematics after having worked through this book.

8.1 Implication

It is extremely useful to have a way of shortening the argument 'If A, then B', where A and B are mathematical statements. Examples of such arguments with statements A and B might be

'If $x = 5$, then $x^2 = 25$', and

'If XYZ is a triangle and angle $X = 90°$, then $XY^2 + XZ^2 = YZ^2$'.

These statements can be rewritten using the symbol $\Rightarrow$ as

$$x = 5 \quad \Rightarrow \quad x^2 = 25,$$

$$XYZ \text{ is a triangle and } X = 90° \quad \Rightarrow \quad XY^2 + XZ^2 = YZ^2$$

The $\Rightarrow$ sign is read as 'implies'. If the statement on the left is true, then the statement on the right is true.

Notice that if the statement on the left is not true, nothing is said about the statement on the right. The use of $\Rightarrow$ in the statement $0 = 1 \Rightarrow 1 = 2$ is perfectly correct. If the statement on the left is true, the statement on the right follows logically. This is not a particularly helpful piece of deduction, because $0 = 1$ is false!

If you link several statements together by a chain of implications, as

$$A \Rightarrow B \Rightarrow C \Rightarrow \dots \Rightarrow K,$$

then you can deduce that $A \Rightarrow K$. In this way you can sometimes prove a whole theorem through a number of small steps.

Sometimes the sign is reversed, as $\Leftarrow$, which is read as 'is implied by'. So $A \Rightarrow B$ can also be written as $B \Leftarrow A$.

It sometimes happens that $A \Rightarrow B$ and $A \Leftarrow B$. You can then combine $\Rightarrow$ and $\Leftarrow$, to write

$$A \quad \Leftrightarrow \quad B$$

where the symbol $\Leftrightarrow$ means 'implies and is implied by'. This means that the two statements are completely equivalent; if either one is known to be true, so is the other. So $\Leftrightarrow$ is often read as 'is logically equivalent to'.

For example, when doing algebra, you can add the same number to both sides of an equation, so that

$$x = y \quad \Rightarrow \quad x + z = y + z.$$

It is also true that

$$x = y \quad \Leftarrow \quad x + z = y + z, \quad \text{or} \quad x + z = y + z \quad \Rightarrow \quad x = y.$$

So you can write

$$x = y \quad \Leftrightarrow \quad x + z = y + z.$$

But there are some important algebraic steps which cannot be reversed in this way. For example, the step

$$x = y \quad \Rightarrow \quad xz = yz$$

is valid, but it is not true that

$$x = y \quad \Leftarrow \quad xz = yz, \quad \text{or} \quad xz = yz \quad \Rightarrow \quad x = y,$$

since z could be zero, and then x and y need not be equal.

Another non-reversible step is squaring both sides of an equation. You can write

$$x = y \quad \Rightarrow \quad x^2 = y^2, \quad \text{but not} \quad x = y \quad \Leftarrow \quad x^2 = y^2.$$

The correct reverse implication is

$$x^2 = y^2 \quad \Rightarrow \quad x^2 - y^2 = 0 \quad \Rightarrow \quad (x - y)(x + y) = 0$$
$$\Rightarrow \quad \text{either } x - y = 0 \text{ or } x + y = 0$$
$$\Rightarrow \quad \text{either } x = y \text{ or } x = -y.$$

These points are important when you solve equations. It is very tempting to join up the steps in a solution with $\Leftrightarrow$ signs without thinking. But you can easily reach a wrong conclusion if one of the implications is not reversible.

Example 8.1.1

Solve the equation $\sqrt{2x+1} = \sqrt{x} - 5$.

$$\sqrt{2x+1} = \sqrt{x} - 5 \quad \Rightarrow \quad 2x+1 = \left(\sqrt{x}-5\right)^2$$
$$\Leftrightarrow \quad 2x+1 = x - 10\sqrt{x} + 25$$
$$\Leftrightarrow \quad 10\sqrt{x} = 24 - x$$
$$\Rightarrow \quad 100x = (24-x)^2$$
$$\Leftrightarrow \quad 100x = 576 - 48x + x^2$$
$$\Leftrightarrow \quad x^2 - 148x + 576 = 0$$
$$\Leftrightarrow \quad (x-4)(x-144) = 0$$
$$\Leftrightarrow \quad \text{either } x = 4 \text{ or } x = 144.$$

But in fact, neither $x = 4$ nor $x = 144$ satisfies the equation. With $x = 4$ the left side is $\sqrt{9} = 3$, and the right side is $\sqrt{4} - 5 = -3$. With $x = 144$ the left side is $\sqrt{289} = 17$, and the right side is $\sqrt{144} - 5 = 7$. It follows that the equation has no solution.

The point is that solving equations is a two-way process. You need to show both that

If x satisfies the equation, then x would have certain values

and that

If x has one of these values, then it satisfies the equation.

With a simple equation such as

$$2x + 3 = 7 - 3x \quad \Leftrightarrow \quad 3x + 2x = 7 - 3 \quad \Leftrightarrow \quad x = 0.8,$$

all the steps are equivalence steps, so that both parts of the solution are included in the single chain of reasoning. (But it is still a good idea to check that $x = 0.8$ does satisfy the original equation, to make sure you haven't made a mistake.)

But in Example 8.1.1 above there are two non-reversible steps,

(a) $\sqrt{2x+1} = \sqrt{x} - 5 \quad \Rightarrow \quad 2x+1 = \left(\sqrt{x}-5\right)^2$

and (b) $10\sqrt{x} = 24 - x \quad \Rightarrow \quad 100x = (24-x)^2$.

You can easily check that when $x = 4$ the equation on the right of (a) is satisfied, but the equation on the left is not; and when $x = 144$ the equation on the right of (b) is satisfied, but the equation on the left is not.

There are actually four different equations,

(i) $\sqrt{2x+1} = \sqrt{x} - 5$ (ii) $-\sqrt{2x+1} = \sqrt{x} - 5$

(iii) $\sqrt{2x+1} = -\sqrt{x} - 5$ (iv) $-\sqrt{2x+1} = -\sqrt{x} - 5$

all of which after two squarings lead to $100x = (24-x)^2$, and thence to $x = 4$ or $x = 144$. Equation (ii) has $x = 4$ as a root; (iv) has $x = 144$; and (i) and (iii) have no solution.

Example 8.1.2

Solve the simultaneous equations $2x - 5y = 3, 10y - 4x = -5$.

$$2x - 5y = 3 \text{ and } 10y - 4x = -5 \quad \Rightarrow \quad 2(2x - 5y) + (10y - 4x) = 2 \times 3 + (-5)$$
$$\Rightarrow \quad 4x - 10y + 10y - 4x = 6 - 5$$
$$\Rightarrow \quad 0 = 1.$$

This is *not* a 'proof' that $0 = 1$. It would have been wrong to write down a sequence of equations ending with the statement 'Therefore $0 = 1$'. The advantage of the $\Rightarrow$ notation is that nowhere in the chain of reasoning is it asserted that any of the statements are true; only that *if* the first statement is true, then so is the last.

The correct interpretation of this example is that if there were numbers x and y such that $2x - 5y = 3$ and $10y - 4x = -5$, then 0 would equal 1. Since you know that 0 does not equal 1, the conclusion is that there are no numbers x and y satisfying these simultaneous equations. That is, the equations have no solution. This is an example of proof by contradiction; you will find more about this kind of proof in Section 8.4.

Solving equations is an act of faith. You begin by assuming that there is a solution, and use the rules of algebra to find out what it must be. If you end up with an answer (or answers), you must check that it does (or they do) satisfy the equation. You do this either by making sure that all the steps can be joined by $\Leftrightarrow$ and not just $\Rightarrow$, or by direct substitution. If you end up with a false statement, then the equation has no solution.

Example 8.1.3

Find the regions of the (x, y)-plane which satisfy the inequality $xy < y$.

You can rewrite the inequality as $xy - y < 0$, or $y(x - 1) < 0$.

Method 1   As the product of y and $(x - 1)$ is negative, one of them must be negative, and the other must be positive. So

$$y(x - 1) < 0 \quad \Rightarrow \quad (y < 0 \quad \text{and} \quad (x - 1) > 0) \quad \text{or} \quad (y > 0 \quad \text{and} \quad (x - 1) < 0)$$
$$\Rightarrow \quad (y < 0 \quad \text{and} \quad x > 1) \quad \text{or} \quad (y > 0 \quad \text{and} \quad x < 1).$$

Method 2   Suppose first that $y > 0$. Then, since y is positive, you can divide the inequality by y without changing the direction of the inequality sign. So

$$y > 0 \quad \text{and} \quad xy < y \quad \Rightarrow \quad x < 1,$$

and one solution is $y > 0$ and $x < 1$.

Now suppose that $y < 0$. Then, since y is negative, when you divide the inequality by y you must change the direction of the inequality sign. So

$$y < 0 \quad \text{and} \quad xy < y \quad \Rightarrow \quad x > 1,$$

and another solution is $y < 0$ and $x > 1$.

Finally, if $y = 0$, there is no solution.

<hr>

Exercise 8A

1 At which points in the following arguments can $\Rightarrow$ be replaced by $\Leftrightarrow$?

(a) $\dfrac{4}{x^2} = \dfrac{2}{x} \Rightarrow 4x = 2x^2 \Rightarrow 2x^2 - 4x = 0 \Rightarrow 2x(x-2) = 0 \Rightarrow x = 0$ or 2.

(b) $\dfrac{1}{x} = \dfrac{1}{2x+1} \Rightarrow 2x + 1 = x \Rightarrow x = -1$.

(c) $x + \sqrt{x} = 0 \Rightarrow x = -\sqrt{x} \Rightarrow x^2 > \left(-\sqrt{x}\right)^2 \Rightarrow x^2 = x$

$\Rightarrow x(x-1) = 0 \Rightarrow x = 0$ or 1.

In each case amend the argument to produce a correct solution to the original statement.

2 Solve, where possible, the following equations, using the symbols $\Rightarrow$ and $\Leftrightarrow$.

(a) $\sqrt{x} + \sqrt{10 - x} = 4$ (b) $\sqrt{2x - 1} + \sqrt{x - 1} = 5$

(c) $\sqrt{x+4} = \sqrt{3x+1} + 1$ (d) $\sqrt{x-4} - \sqrt{x+4} = 8$

3 At which stages in the following arguments can $\Rightarrow$ be replaced by $\Leftrightarrow$?

(a) $\left.\begin{array}{r} x - 2y = 4 \\ -2x + 4y = 8 \end{array}\right\} \Rightarrow \left.\begin{array}{r} x - 2y = 4 \\ 0 = 0 \end{array}\right\} \Rightarrow x - 2y = 4$

(b) $\left.\begin{array}{r} x - 2y = 4 \\ -2x + 5y = 9 \end{array}\right\} \Rightarrow \left.\begin{array}{r} x - 2y = 4 \\ y = 17 \end{array}\right\} \Rightarrow \left.\begin{array}{r} x = 38 \\ y = 17 \end{array}\right\}$

(c) $\left.\begin{array}{r} x - 2y = 4 \\ -2x + 4y = 9 \end{array}\right\} \Rightarrow \left.\begin{array}{r} x - 2y = 4 \\ 0 = 1 \end{array}\right\}$

4 Solve the following inequalities, using the symbols $\Rightarrow$ and $\Leftrightarrow$.

(a) $x^2 < x$ (b) $x^2 \leqslant xy$ (c) $x^2 \leqslant x^3$ (d) $x^2 \leqslant y^2$

8.2* Deduction

Mathematics faces two ways. In one direction it develops techniques which provide tools for science and technology. In the other it builds up a theoretical structure from the foundations by logical argument. This structure justifies the use of the techniques.

The simplest kind of argument used in mathematics is deduction, in which you build from one set of known facts to the next, step by step. It takes the form:

> $A, B, C, \ldots$ are already known.
>
> $A, B, C, \ldots$ taken together imply K.
>
> Therefore K.

The known facts themselves $(A, B, C, \ldots, K)$ are **theorems**. You already know many theorems; some of them have names such as 'Pythagoras' theorem', 'the remainder theorem', and so on. A theorem is a general statement which has already been proved.

(Until it is proved it is called a 'conjecture'.) For example, $5 + 17 = 22$ would not be called a theorem, because it is just a special case. But it is an illustration of the theorem:

The sum of an even number of odd numbers is an even number.

This theorem could then be used in proving other theorems.

Example 8.2.1

Prove that the product of any six consecutive natural numbers is divisible by $6!$.

This proof is based on the theorem that, in any row of r consecutive natural numbers, one is divisible by r.

In any row of six consecutive natural numbers, three are even. Also, every fourth number is divisible by 4, so that the row includes at least one of these. The product is therefore divisible by $2 \times 2 \times 4 = 2^4$.

Also, the row includes two multiples of 3 and one multiple of 5, so the product is divisible by $3^2 \times 5$.

The product is therefore divisible by $2^4 \times 3^2 \times 5 = 720$, which is $6!$.

In Section 4.2 it was shown that the binomial coefficient $\binom{n}{6}$ is equal to $\dfrac{n(n-1)(n-2)(n-3)(n-4)(n-5)}{6!}$. If n is a natural number greater than 5, the top line is the product of six consecutive natural numbers. Example 8.2.1 then proves that $\binom{n}{6}$ is a natural number.

You can use similar reasoning with $2, 3, 4, 5$ or 7 in place of 6. This suggests a conjecture:

For any natural numbers n and r with $r \leqslant n$, $\binom{n}{r}$ is a natural number.

In Example 8.4.3 this conjecture will be proved by a different method for all values of r, and will then become a theorem.

Notice the use of the word 'therefore' in Example 8.2.1. This means that the statement can be made with confidence, since it is based on deduction from something already known to be true. In mathematical arguments it is sometimes replaced at the start of a sentence by the symbol '$\therefore$'.

Example 8.2.2

A set of n positive real numbers is denoted by $a, b, c, d, \ldots, k$. Two kinds of average used by statisticians are the **arithmetic mean** $A = \dfrac{a + b + c + d + \ldots + k}{n}$ and the **geometric mean** $G = (abcd \ldots k)^{\frac{1}{n}}$. Show that $A \geqslant G$ for   (a) $n = 2$,   (b) $n = 4$,   (c) $n = 3$.

(a) If x is any real number, $x^2 \geqslant 0$. Therefore $\left(a^{\frac{1}{2}} - b^{\frac{1}{2}}\right)^2 \geqslant 0$.

$$\left(a^{\frac{1}{2}}-b^{\frac{1}{2}}\right)^2 \geqslant 0 \quad \Rightarrow \quad \left(a^{\frac{1}{2}}\right)^2 - 2a^{\frac{1}{2}}b^{\frac{1}{2}} + \left(b^{\frac{1}{2}}\right)^2 \geqslant 0$$

$$\Rightarrow \quad a+b \geqslant 2a^{\frac{1}{2}}b^{\frac{1}{2}}.$$

Therefore $\dfrac{a+b}{2} \geqslant (ab)^{\frac{1}{2}}$, which means that $A \geqslant G$ for $n=2$.

(b) $\frac{1}{4}(a+b+c+d) = \frac{1}{2}\left(\frac{1}{2}(a+b) + \frac{1}{2}(c+d)\right) \geqslant \frac{1}{2}\left((ab)^{\frac{1}{2}} + (cd)^{\frac{1}{2}}\right)$ using (a)

$$\geqslant \left((ab)^{\frac{1}{2}}(cd)^{\frac{1}{2}}\right)^{\frac{1}{2}}$$ using (a) again

$$= (abcd)^{\frac{1}{4}}.$$

Therefore $A \geqslant G$ for $n=4$.

(c) In the result of (b) let $d = \frac{1}{3}(a+b+c)$. Then

$$\frac{1}{4}(a+b+c+d) = \frac{1}{4}\left(a+b+c+\frac{1}{3}(a+b+c)\right) = \frac{1}{4}\left(\frac{4}{3}(a+b+c)\right) = \frac{1}{3}(a+b+c).$$

Raising both sides of the result of (b) to the power 4 gives

$$\left(\frac{1}{4}(a+b+c+d)\right)^4 \geqslant abcd,$$

so $\left(\frac{1}{3}(a+b+c)\right)^4 \geqslant abc \times \frac{1}{3}(a+b+c).$

Dividing both sides by $\frac{1}{3}(a+b+c)$,

$$\left(\frac{1}{3}(a+b+c)\right)^3 \geqslant abc.$$

∴ $\frac{1}{3}(a+b+c) \geqslant (abc)^{\frac{1}{3}}$, which means that $A \geqslant G$ for $n=3$.

Notice that, having proved (a), you use (a) to prove (b), and then use (b) to prove (c).

This technique can be extended to prove that $A \geqslant G$ for any value of n. For example, if $n=13$ you can use the method of (b) to prove the result for $n=8$ and then $n=16$, and then use the method of (c) to reduce the value of n by one at a time from 16 to 15, 15 to 14 and finally 14 to 13.

The result $A \geqslant G$ then becomes a theorem which is true for any natural number n. It is sometimes called 'the theorem of the means'.

Example 8.2.3
If $sx-t$ is a factor of the polynomial $p(x) = ax^n + bx^{n-1} + \ldots + jx + k$, where a, b, … , j, k are integers and s, t are (non-zero) integers with no common factor, and if a and k are non-zero, then s divides a and t divides k.

This result was stated without proof in Section 1.5.

Since $p(x) = (sx-t)q(x)$, where $q(x)$ is another polynomial, $p\!\left(\dfrac{t}{s}\right) = 0$. That is,

$$a\left(\frac{t}{s}\right)^n + b\left(\frac{t}{s}\right)^{n-1} + \ldots + j\left(\frac{t}{s}\right) + k = 0.$$

Multiplying this equation by s^n and then rearranging,

$$at^n + bt^{n-1}s + \ldots + jts^{n-1} + ks^n = 0,$$
$$at^n = -s\left(bt^{n-1} + \ldots + jts^{n-2} + ks^{n-1}\right).$$

As neither a nor s is zero, neither side is zero. The right side has s as a factor, so s is a factor of the left side, at^n. Since s and t^n have no common factors, s divides a.

A different rearrangement of the equation is

$$ks^n = -t\left(at^{n-1} + bt^{n-2}s + \ldots + jt^{n-1}\right).$$

The same argument as above, with various letters changed, leads to the conclusion that t divides k. (Try writing this out for yourself.)

You should notice two points about this proof. First, it is built on a number of other theorems, which would have to be proved first. Apart from the definition of a factor and some basic laws of algebra, there is the result that, since t^n and s have no common factor,

s divides at^n $\Rightarrow$ s divides a.

Secondly, notice the care that is needed over apparently minor details. For example, the facts that s and t are non-zero and have no common factor play an important part in the proof.

Exercise 8B*

1 An even number is a number of the form $2n$ where $n \in \mathbb{N}$, and an odd number is a number of the form $2m+1$ where $m \in \mathbb{N}$. Prove that

   (a) the sum of two consecutive numbers is odd,

   (b) the sum of two even numbers is even,

   (c) the product of two odd numbers is odd,

   (d) the sum of an odd number of odd numbers is odd,

   (e) a number plus its square is always even.

2 Prove that:

   (a) When a square natural number is divided by 4, the remainder is either 0 or 1.

   (b) If the sum of two square natural numbers is divided by 4, the remainder cannot be 3.

   (c) If a right-angled triangle has sides whose lengths are natural numbers with no common factors, the hypotenuse cannot be even.

3 Prove that:

   (a) When a square natural number is divided by 5, the remainder is 0, 1 or 4.

   (b) When the sum of two square natural numbers is divided by 5, the remainder can be any one of 0, 1, 2, 3 or 4.

4 Prove that if a and b are two natural numbers which have lowest common multiple l and highest common factor h, then $ab = lh$.

5 (a) Prove that the sum of any five consecutive integers is divisible by 5.

    (b) Prove that the sum of any six consecutive integers is divisible by 3 but not by 6.

    (c) Generalise the results of parts (a) and (b), and prove your statement.

8.3* Converses

Many theorems can be expressed in the form:

    If A, then B.

For example, when you solve polynomial equations by factors you use the theorem

    If $x - t$ is a factor of $\mathrm{p}(x)$, then $\mathrm{p}(t) = 0$.

Here A stands for the statement '$x - t$ is a factor of $\mathrm{p}(x)$', and B for the statement '$\mathrm{p}(t) = 0$'.

In this case, the two statements A and B can be interchanged:

    If $\mathrm{p}(t) = 0$, then $x - t$ is a factor of $\mathrm{p}(x)$.

This is called the **converse**. For this theorem the converse is also true; you should recognise it as the factor theorem (see Section 1.5).

Example 8.3.1
State and prove the converse of Pythagoras' theorem.

    Pythagoras' theorem states:

        In a triangle ABC, if angle A is a right angle, then $a^2 = b^2 + c^2$.

    The converse is therefore:

        In a triangle ABC, if $a^2 = b^2 + c^2$, then angle A is a right angle.

    It was shown in P1 Section 11.6 that the cosine formula for any triangle,

$$a^2 = b^2 + c^2 - 2bc \cos A,$$

    can be proved from the formula for the distance between two points, which itself depends on Pythagoras' theorem.

    If $a^2 + b^2 = c^2$, it follows from the cosine formula that $2bc \cos A = 0$. Since neither b nor c is 0, $\cos A$ must be 0, so A is a right angle.

An example of a converse which is **not** true is the theorem in Example 8.2.3. The converse of 'if $sx - t$ is a factor of $ax^n + \ldots + k$, then s divides a and t divides k' would be the (false) statement

    If s divides a and t divides k, then $sx - t$ is a factor of $ax^n + \ldots + k$.

The simplest way of showing that this is not true is to find a **counterexample**, that is a *single* example for which the statement is false. If you can find a polynomial $p(x)$ and a linear expression $sx - t$ such that s divides a and t divides k but $sx - t$ is not a factor of $p(x)$, then the converse cannot be true. One possibility is to take $sx - t$ as $2x - 3$, and $p(x)$ as $4x^2 - 81$. You can see that 2 divides 4, and 3 divides 81; but the factors of $p(x)$ are $2x - 9$ and $2x + 9$, neither of which is $2x - 3$.

Notice that you only need one counterexample to prove that a conjecture is not true.

8.4* Proof by contradiction

Sometimes it is not possible to find a way of proving a theorem by deduction, and a more roundabout method of proof has to be used.

A typical form for such an argument is:

> $A, B, C, \ldots$ are already known to be true.
>
> If K were not true, one of $A, B, C, \ldots$ would not be true.
>
> Therefore K.

That is, you look at what you want to prove, and investigate the effect of assuming the opposite. If this leads you to a contradiction, then it follows that the conclusion is true. This technique is known as **proof by contradiction**.

Example 8.4.1
(a) Prove that the cube of an odd number is odd.
(b) Prove that, if the cube of a natural number is odd, the number itself is odd.

(a) This can be proved deductively. Any odd number can be written as $2m + 1$, where $m \in \mathbb{N}$. By the binomial theorem,

$$(2m + 1)^3 = (2m)^3 + 3(2m)^2 + 3(2m) + 1$$
$$= 8m^3 + 12m^2 + 6m + 1$$
$$= 2(4m^3 + 6m^2 + 3m) + 1.$$

Since $m \in \mathbb{N}$, $4m^3 + 6m^2 + 3m \in \mathbb{N}$, so that $(2m + 1)^3$ can be written as $2k + 1$, where $k \in \mathbb{N}$. Therefore $(2m + 1)^3$ is an odd number.

(b) The argument in (a) cannot be reversed, so an indirect approach is used. Let n be a natural number whose cube is odd. Then, if n were not odd, it would be even, so you could write n as $2m$, where $m \in \mathbb{N}$. But

$$n = 2m \implies n^3 = 8m^3 = 2(4m^3),$$
$$\implies n^3 = 2k, \text{ where } k = 4m^3.$$

So if n were even, n^3 would be even, which contradicts the definition of n. It follows that n is not even, so n is odd.

Example 8.4.2

Prove that if $2^x = 10$, then x is an irrational number.

If x were not irrational, it would be rational. That is, one could write x as $\dfrac{p}{q}$, where p and q are integers and $q \neq 0$. Then

$$2^x = 10 \quad \Rightarrow \quad 2^{\frac{p}{q}} = 10 \quad \Rightarrow \quad 2^p = 10^q \quad \Rightarrow \quad 2^p = 2^q 5^q \quad \Rightarrow \quad 2^{p-q} = 5^q.$$

In the last equation the left side is a power of 2 and the right side is a power of 5. Since 2 and 5 are both prime numbers, this is only possible if the indices are zero, which means $p - q = 0$ and $q = 0$. But if $q = 0$, $\dfrac{p}{q}$ is not defined. So x is not a rational number.

It follows that x is an irrational number.

You will learn in Section 11.2 that the number x is denoted by $\log_2 10$. The result of this Example can then be stated as '$\log_2 10$ is an irrational number'.

Example 8.4.3

Prove that the binomial coefficients $\dbinom{n}{r}$, where n and r are natural numbers with $0 < r < n$, are all integers.

This proof depends on the method of calculating binomial coefficients described in Section 4.1, building up Pascal's triangle row by row by adding pairs of coefficients from the row above.

The coefficients $\dbinom{n}{0}$ and $\dbinom{n}{n}$ at the ends of each row are always 1; the coefficients with $0 < r < n$ will be called 'interior coefficients'.

Suppose that somewhere in Pascal's triangle there is an interior coefficient $\dbinom{n}{r}$ which is not an integer. Since this is found by adding two of the coefficients from the row above, there must be at least one coefficient in the row above which is not an integer, and this must again be an interior coefficient.

Now you can repeat the argument, and deduce that there must be an interior coefficient in the row above that which is not an integer. And so on, until you get to the top row in the triangle which has an interior coefficient, and deduce that $\dbinom{2}{1}$ is not an integer.

But you know that $\dbinom{2}{1} = 2$, which is an integer. So you have a contradiction. It follows that there is no interior coefficient $\dbinom{n}{r}$ which is not an integer; that is, all the coefficients are integers.

Notice that in the first example the contradiction is with the data, that n^3 is an odd number. In the second, it is with a known property of natural numbers. In the third, it is with the known particular value of $\binom{n}{r}$ when $n = 2$ and $r = 1$. But however the contradiction is established, the logic is essentially the same.

Exercise 8C*

1 State the converse of each of the following. If the converse is true, prove it; if not, give a counterexample.

(a) The square of an odd number is odd.

(b) The product of two odd numbers is odd.

(c) The product of two even numbers is even.

(d) The product of two prime numbers is not prime.

(e) The sum of two odd numbers is even.

(f) The sum of an even number and an odd number is odd.

2 State the converses of the following, and give counterexamples to prove that these converses are false.

(a) For any numbers m and c, the set of points (x, y) which satisfy $y = mx + c$ lie on a straight line.

(b) Any straight line has an equation of the form $ax + by + c = 0$ for some numbers a, b and c.

3 Suppose that $\sqrt{2}$ can be written as a rational number $\dfrac{p}{q}$, where p and q are natural numbers with no common factor.

(a) Deduce that p is even.

(b) Deduce that q is even.

(c) Deduce that p and q have a common factor.

What conclusion can you draw from this sequence of deductions?

4 Explain why, with suitable changes, the argument in Question 3 can be applied to $\sqrt[3]{2}$, $\sqrt{3}$ and $\sqrt{5}$, but not to $\sqrt{4}$.

5 Here are three theorems about a circle. In each case, write down the converse, and if the converse is true, prove it.

(a) The angle in a semicircle is a right angle.

(b) The perpendicular from the centre to a chord bisects the chord.

(c) The tangent at a point on the circle is perpendicular to the radius.

6 Prove that, if a and b are positive integers with highest common factor h, and if $c = a + b$, then h is the highest common factor of a and c.

7 Use proof by contradiction to prove that there are no positive integers a and b such that $a^2 - b^2$ is equal to 6.

8.5* Necessary and sufficient conditions

'Necessary' and 'sufficient' are two words sometimes used in describing implication. If $A \Rightarrow B$, you can say that

A is a sufficient condition for B.

For example,

Divisibility by 6 is a sufficient condition for divisibility by 3

is another way of saying

If $n \in \mathbb{N}$, n is divisible by $6 \Rightarrow n$ is divisible by 3.

If A and B are interchanged so that $B \Rightarrow A$, or $A \Leftarrow B$, you can say that

A is a necessary condition for B.

You can think of this as

B can't be true unless A is true.

For example,

Divisibility by 3 is a necessary condition for divisibility by 6.

That is,

A number can't be divisible by 6 unless it is divisible by 3.

Example 8.5.1
Make sentences using the words 'necessary' and 'sufficient' connecting rectangles and parallelograms.

Rectangles are special cases of parallelograms, so

F is a rectangle $\quad \Rightarrow \quad F$ is a parallelogram.

Therefore

To be a rectangle is a sufficient condition for being a parallelogram,

and   For a figure to be a rectangle it is necessary for it to be a parallelogram.

Example 8.5.2
For a smooth function $f(x)$ to have a maximum at $x = q$, is it sufficient that $f'(q) = 0$?

If $f'(q) = 0$ were a sufficient condition for $f(x)$ to have a maximum at $x = q$, this could be written formally as

$f'(q) = 0 \quad \Rightarrow \quad f(x)$ has a maximum at $x = q$.

This is not true. Suitable counterexamples are $f(x) = x^2$ (which has a minimum at $x = 0$) and $f(x) = x^3$ (which has a point of inflexion at $x = 0$).

A correct implication, for a smooth function, is

f(x) has a maximum at $x = q \implies f'(q) = 0$.

So a correct statement would be that, for a smooth function f(x) to have a maximum at $x = q$, it is necessary that $f'(q) = 0$.

Exercise 8D*

1   Prove that the product of two integers a and b is even if, and only if, at least one of a and b is even.

2   A student finding the point of intersection of the lines $x + 2y = 5$ and $y - x = 1$ writes:

$$x + 2y = 5 \text{ and } y - x = 1 \implies (x + 2y) + (y - x) = 5 + 1$$
$$\implies 3y = 6$$
$$\implies y = 2$$
$$\implies x + 4 = 5$$
$$\implies x = 1.$$

The point of intersection is therefore $(1, 2)$.

Criticise this argument and give a correct version.

3   Insert the words 'necessary' (N), sufficient (S), or 'necessary and sufficient' (N&S) in place of the dots to make the following statements true.

(a)   A ...... condition for AB to be the largest side of a triangle ABC is that the angle at C is obtuse.

(b)   A ...... condition for two triangles to have the same area is that their bases and their heights are equal.

(c)   A ...... condition for a quadrilateral to be a kite is that its diagonals are perpendicular.

(d)   A ...... condition that $a > b \implies a^2 > b^2$ is that a and b are positive.

(e)   A ...... condition that $a > b \implies a^2 > b^2$ is that $a + b$ is positive.

(f)   A ...... condition that the polynomial equation $p(x) = 0$ has a root between a and b is that $p(a)p(b) < 0$.

(g)   A ...... condition that the polynomial equation $p(x) = 0$ has exactly one (simple) root between a and b is that $p(a)p(b) < 0$.

Miscellaneous exercise 8*

1   The numbers a and b are integers.

(a)   Prove that if $a - b$ is even, then $a + b$ is even.

(b)   Prove that if $a - b$ is divisible by 3, then $a + 2b$ is also divisible by 3.

(b)   Prove that if $a^2 - b^2$ is even, then 4 divides $a^2 - b^2$,

2   Prove that, if f is a decreasing function with domain and range $\mathbb{R}$, and if f has an inverse f^{-1}, then f^{-1} is also a decreasing function.

3 The number 321 has digits 3, 2 and 1 and has a value of $3 \times 100 + 2 \times 10 + 1$. Similarly the number abc, with digits a, b and c has value $100a + 10b + c$.

    (a) Prove that 3 divides the two-digit number ab if and only if 3 divides $a + b$.

    (b) Prove that 9 divides $a_0 a_1 \ldots a_n$ if and only if 9 divides $a_0 + a_1 + \ldots + a_n$.

    (c) Find and prove a divisibility test for dividing $a_0 a_1 \ldots a_n$ by 11.

4 Consider the number N, where $N = (1 \times 2 \times 3 \times \ldots \times p) + 1$, and p is prime.

    (a) Prove that N is not divisible by any integer up to and including p.

    (b) Deduce that either N is prime or it is divisible by a prime number greater than p.

    (c) Deduce that there is no greatest prime number.

5 (a) Prove that, if the square of the sum of two numbers is equal to twice the sum of their squares, then the two numbers are equal.

    (b) Prove that the square of the sum of two unequal positive numbers is less than twice the sum of their squares.

    (c) Prove that the square of the sum of any four unequal positive numbers is less than four times the sum of their squares.

    (d) Prove that the sum of any three unequal positive numbers is less than three times the sum of their squares.

6 State the two theorems that you need to deduce that, if a cuboid has edges of lengths a, b and c, and an internal diagonal of length d, then $d^2 = a^2 + b^2 + c^2$.

7 Investigate whether each of the following is true or false.

    (a) If n is a prime number, all the binomial coefficients $\binom{n}{r}$ for $1 \leqslant r \leqslant n - 1$ are divisible by n.

    (b) If n is a natural number, all the binomial coefficients $\binom{n}{r}$ for $1 \leqslant r \leqslant n - 1$ have a common factor.

    (c) A necessary and sufficient condition for a natural number n to be prime is that all the binomial coefficients $\binom{n}{r}$ for $1 \leqslant r \leqslant n - 1$ have a common factor.

8 The diagram shows a set of four playing cards, two face down and two face up. You are told by someone that every card with a diamond pattern on the back, as in Card 3, is a club.

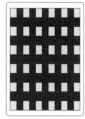

    Card 1   Card 2   Card 3   Card 4

Which cards do you need to turn over in order to verify the truth of this statement?

9 The modulus function

This chapter introduces the modulus function, written as $|x|$. When you have completed it, you should

- know the definition of modulus, and recognise $|x|$ as a function
- know how to draw graphs of functions involving modulus
- know how to use modulus algebraically and geometrically
- be able to solve simple equations and inequalities involving modulus.

9.1 The modulus function and its graph

You met the modulus notation briefly in P1 Section 8.3, and have used it from time to time since then. Since $|x|$ is defined for all real numbers x, it is another example of a function of x. Its domain is $\mathbb{R}$, and its range is $\mathbb{R}, y \geqslant 0$.

> The **modulus** of x, denoted by $|x|$, is defined by
>
> $|x| = x \qquad$ if $x \geqslant 0$,
>
> $|x| = -x \qquad$ if $x < 0$.

On some calculators the modulus function is $\mod x$; on others it is $\operatorname{abs} x$, short for 'the absolute value of x'. This book always uses the notation $|x|$.

Fig. 9.1 shows the graph of $y = |x|$. The graph has a 'V' shape, with both branches making an angle of $45°$ with the x-axis, provided that the scales are the same on both axes.

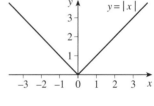

Fig. 9.1

9.2 Graphs of functions involving modulus

Suppose that you want to draw the graph of $y = |x-2|$. You can do this directly from the definition of modulus. When $x \geqslant 2$, $x - 2 \geqslant 0$, so $|x-2| = x-2$. For these values of x, the graphs of $y = |x-2|$ and $y = x-2$ are the same.

When $x < 2$, $x - 2 < 0$, so $|x-2| = -(x-2) = 2-x$. So for these values of x, the graph of $y = |x-2|$ is the same as the graph of $y = 2-x$.

Another way of dealing with the case $x < 2$ is to note that the graph of $y = -(x-2)$ is the reflection of $y = x-2$ in the x-axis. (See P1 Section 8.7.) So you can draw the graph of $y = |x-2|$ by first drawing the graph of $y = x-2$ and then reflecting in the x-axis that part of the line which is below the x-axis. This is illustrated in Fig. 9.2.

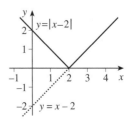

Fig. 9.2

This method can always be used to get the graph of $y=|f(x)|$ from the graph of $y=f(x)$. In the definition of $|x|$ in the shaded box, you can write any expression in place of x. So, replacing x by $f(x)$,

$$|f(x)|=f(x) \text{ if } f(x)\geqslant 0, \quad \text{and} \quad |f(x)|=-f(x) \text{ if } f(x)<0.$$

It follows that, for the parts of the graph $y=f(x)$ which are on or above the x-axis, the graphs of $y=f(x)$ and $y=|f(x)|$ coincide. But for the parts of $y=f(x)$ below the x-axis, $y=|f(x)|=-f(x)$ is obtained from $y=f(x)$ by reflection in the x-axis.

A nice way of showing this is to draw the graph of $y=f(x)$ on a transparent sheet. You can then get the graph of $y=|f(x)|$ by folding the sheet along the x-axis so that the negative part of the sheet lies on top of the positive part.

Example 9.2.1

Sketch the graphs of   (a) $y=|2x-3|$,   (b) $y=|(x-1)(x-3)|$.

Figs. 9.3 and 9.4 show the graphs of (a) $y=2x-3$ and (b) $y=(x-1)(x-3)$ with the part below the x-axis (drawn dotted) reflected in the x-axis to give the graphs required.

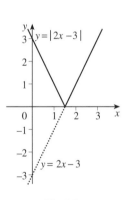

Fig. 9.3

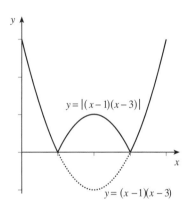

Fig. 9.4

Graphs which involve the modulus function are likely to have sharp corners. If you can, show the graphs in Example 9.2.1 on a graphic calculator.

Example 9.2.2

Sketch the graph of $y=|x-2|+|1-x|$.

With two moduli involved it is usually best to go back to the definition of modulus. For $|x-2|$ you have to consider $x-2\geqslant 0$ and $x-2<0$ separately, and for $|1-x|$ you have to consider $1-x\geqslant 0$ and $1-x<0$. So altogether there are three intervals to investigate: $x\leqslant 1$, $1<x<2$ and $x\geqslant 2$.

When $x\leqslant 1$, $|x-2|=-(x-2)$ and $|1-x|=1-x$, so $y=-x+2+1-x=3-2x$.
When $1<x<2$, $|x-2|=-(x-2)$ and $|1-x|=-(1-x)$, so $y=-x+2-1+x=1$.
When $x\geqslant 2$, $|x-2|=x-2$ and $|1-x|=-(1-x)$, so $y=x-2-1+x=2x-3$.

The graph is therefore in three parts, as shown in Fig. 9.5.

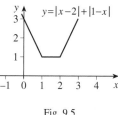

You may sometimes also want to get the graph of $y = f(|x|)$ from the graph of $y = f(x)$. From the definition, $f(|x|)$ is the same as $f(x)$ when $x \geqslant 0$, but $f(|x|) = f(-x)$ when $x < 0$. So the graph of $y = f(|x|)$ is the same as the graph of $y = f(x)$ to the right of the y-axis, but to the left of the y-axis it is the reflection in the y-axis of $y = f(x)$ for $x > 0$. (See P1 Section 8.7.)

Fig. 9.5

Example 9.2.3

Sketch the graph of $y = \sin|x|°$.

To the right of the y-axis the graph is the same as the graph of $y = \sin x°$. The graph is completed for $x < 0$ by reflecting the graph of $y = \sin x°$ to the right of the y-axis $(x > 0)$ in the y-axis, to get Fig. 9.6.

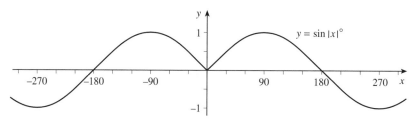

Fig. 9.6

9.3 Some algebraic properties

Let a and b be two real numbers. Since $|a|$ is always equal to either $-a$ or a, it follows that a is always equal to $-|a|$ or $|a|$. Similarly, b is always equal to $-|b|$ or $|b|$. So $a \times b$ is always equal to $|a| \times |b|$ or $-|a| \times |b|$. And since $|a| \times |b|$ is positive or zero, you can deduce that $|a \times b| = |a| \times |b|$.

A similar argument holds for division.

If a and b are real numbers,

$$|a \times b| = |a| \times |b| \quad \text{and} \quad \left|\frac{a}{b}\right| = \frac{|a|}{|b|} \quad \text{(provided that } b \neq 0\text{)}.$$

Example 9.3.1

Show that   (a) $|4x + 6| = 2 \times |2x + 3|$,   (b) $|3 - x| = |x - 3|$.

(a) $|4x + 6| = |2(2x + 3)| = |2| \times |2x + 3| = 2 \times |2x + 3|$.

(b) $|3 - x| = |(-1) \times (x - 3)| = |-1| \times |x - 3| = 1 \times |x - 3| = |x - 3|$.

But beware! Similar rules don't hold for addition and subtraction. For example, if $a = 2$ and $b = -3$, $|a+b| = |2 + (-3)| = |-1| = 1$, but $|a| + |b| = 2 + 3 = 5$. So, for these values of a and b, $|a+b|$ does not equal $|a| + |b|$. See Exercise 9A Question 5.

9.4 Modulus on the number line

Some results about modulus can be illustrated by the distance between points on a number line. Let A and B be two points on a line with coordinates a and b (which can be positive, negative or zero) relative to an origin O, as in Fig. 9.7. Then the distance AB is given by $b - a$ if $b \geqslant a$, or $b - a \geqslant 0$; and by $a - b$, which is $-(b - a)$, if $b < a$, or $b - a < 0$. You will recognise this as the definition of $|b - a|$.

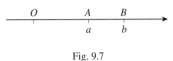

Fig. 9.7

> The distance between points on the number line with coordinates a and b is $|b - a|$.

As a special case, if a point X has coordinate x, then $|x|$ is the distance of X from the origin.

Example 9.4.1
What can you deduce about x if you know that (a) $|x| = 3$,   (b) $|x| \leqslant 3$?

(a) If $|x| = 3$, X is a point 3 units from O. This happens if, and only if, $x = 3$ or $x = -3$. So

$$|x| = 3 \quad \Leftrightarrow \quad x = 3 \text{ or } x = -3.$$

(b) If $|x| \leqslant 3$, X is less than or equal to 3 units from O. This happens if, and only if, x is between -3 and 3 (inclusive). So

$$|x| \leqslant 3 \quad \Leftrightarrow \quad -3 \leqslant x \leqslant 3.$$

You can prove the result in part (b) of Example 9.4.1 more formally from the definition of $|x|$. If $|x| \leqslant 3$, then either $x \geqslant 0$ and $x = |x| \leqslant 3$, so $0 \leqslant x \leqslant 3$; or $x < 0$ and $x = -|x| \geqslant -3$, so $-3 \leqslant x < 0$. In either case, $-3 \leqslant x \leqslant 3$.

The converse is also true. For if you know that $-3 \leqslant x \leqslant 3$, you have $-3 \leqslant x$ and $x \leqslant 3$. This is the same as $-x \leqslant 3$ and $x \leqslant 3$. Since $|x|$ is equal to either $-x$ or x, it follows that $|x| \leqslant 3$.

Putting the two results together gives

$$|x| \leqslant 3 \quad \Leftrightarrow \quad -3 \leqslant x \leqslant 3.$$

You can use the same argument to show that if $a > 0$, $|x| \leqslant a \quad \Leftrightarrow \quad -a \leqslant x \leqslant a$.

Notice that if $a = 0$, then $|x| \leq a$ means that $|x| \leq 0$, so $x = 0$, and $-a \leq x \leq a$ means that $-0 \leq x \leq 0$, so $x = 0$. Combining this result with the previous one gives:

> If $a \geq 0$, $\quad |x| \leq a \iff -a \leq x \leq a$.

Taking this a little further, you can deduce a useful generalisation about the inequality $|x - k| \leq a$. Let $X = x - k$, so that $|X| \leq a$. Then $-a \leq X \leq a$, so $-a \leq x - k \leq a$ and $k - a \leq x \leq k + a$.

Working in reverse, if $k - a \leq x \leq k + a$, then $-a \leq x - k \leq a$ and $-a \leq X \leq a$, so $|X| \leq a$, or $|x - k| \leq a$.

This has proved that:

> If $a \geq 0$, $\quad |x - k| \leq a \iff k - a \leq x \leq k + a$.

This inequality is involved when you give a number correct to a certain number of decimal places. For example, to say that $x = 3.87$ 'correct to two decimal places' is in effect saying that $|x - 3.87| \leq 0.005$. However, $|x - 3.87| \leq 0.005$ is equivalent to

$$3.87 - 0.005 \leq x \leq 3.87 + 0.005,$$

or

$$3.865 \leq x \leq 3.875.$$

This is illustrated in Fig. 9.8.

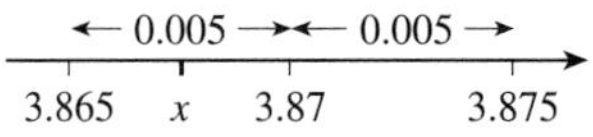

Fig. 9.8

Exercise 9A

1 Sketch the following graphs.

(a) $y = |x + 3|$

(b) $y = |3x - 1|$

(c) $y = |x - 5|$

(d) $y = |3 - 2x|$

(e) $y = 2|x + 1|$

(f) $y = 3|x - 2|$

(g) $y = -2|2x - 1|$

(h) $y = 3|2 - 3x|$

(i) $y = |x + 4| + |3 - x|$

(j) $y = |6 - x| + |1 + x|$

(k) $y = |x - 2| + |2x - 1|$

(l) $y = 2|x - 1| - |2x + 3|$

2 Draw sketches of each of the following sets of graphs.

(a) $y = x^2 - 2$ and $y = |x^2 - 2|$

(b) $y = \sin x°$ and $y = |\sin x°|$

(c) $y = (x - 1)(x - 2)(x - 3)$ and $y = |(x - 1)(x - 2)(x - 3)|$

(d) $y = \cos 2x°$ and $y = |\cos 2x°|$ and $y = \cos|2x|°$

(e) $y = |x - 2|$ and $y = ||x| - 2|$

3   Write the given inequalities in an equivalent form of the type $a < x < b$ or $a \leqslant x \leqslant b$.

   (a) $|x-3|<1$ (b) $|x+2|\leqslant 0.1$ (c) $|2x-3|\leqslant 0.001$ (d) $|4x-3|\leqslant 8$

4   Rewrite the given inequalities using modulus notation.

   (a) $1\leqslant x\leqslant 2$ (b) $-1<x<3$ (c) $-3.8\leqslant x\leqslant -3.5$ (d) $2.3<x<3.4$

5   Investigate the value of $|a+b|$ for various positive and negative choices for the real numbers a and b, and make a conjecture about the largest possible value for $|a+b|$.

   See also if you can make a conjecture about the smallest possible value of $|a+b|$.

6   Construct an argument like that on page 280 to show that $\left|\dfrac{a}{b}\right| = \dfrac{|a|}{|b|}$, provided that $b \neq 0$.

9.5   Equations involving modulus

You can now use the results of the preceding sections to solve equations which involve the modulus function.

In the examples which follow, several methods are used.

- Method 1 is graphical.
- Method 2 uses the definition of modulus.
- Method 3 uses the idea that $|x-a|$ is the distance of x from a.

Not all the methods are used for every example.

Example 9.5.1
Solve the equation $|x-2|=3$.

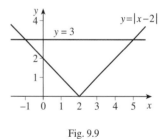

Fig. 9.9

Method 1   From the graphs of $y=|x-2|$ and $y=3$ in Fig. 9.9, the solution is $x=-1$ or $x=5$.

Method 2 $|x-2|=3$ means that $x-2=3$ or $-(x-2)=3$. Thus the solution is $x=5$ or $x=-1$.

Method 3 $|x-2|$ is the distance of x from 2. If this distance is 3, then, thinking geometrically, $x=2+3=5$ or $x=2-3=-1$.

Example 9.5.2
Solve the equation $|x-2|=|2x-1|$.

Method 2   Either $x-2=2x-1,$ giving $x=-1$

         or $x-2=-(2x-1),$ giving $x=1.$

The solution is $x=-1$ or $x=1$.

Method 3   Since $|2x-1|=\left|2\left(x-\tfrac{1}{2}\right)\right|=|2|\times\left|x-\tfrac{1}{2}\right|$, the equation can be written as $|x-2|=2\times\left|x-\tfrac{1}{2}\right|$. This means that you want the points x on the number line such that the distance of x from 2 is twice the distance of x from $\frac{1}{2}$ (see Fig. 9.10). It is easy to see that, if x is between $\frac{1}{2}$ and 2 then $x = 1$; and if x is to the left of $\frac{1}{2}$, then $x = -1$.

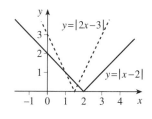

Fig. 9.10

9.6 Inequalities involving modulus

In the examples which follow, a variety of methods for solving inequalities is given.

- Method 1 is graphical.
- Method 2 uses the definition of modulus.
- Method 3 uses the result 'If $a \geqslant 0$, $\;|x| \leqslant a \;\Leftrightarrow\; -a \leqslant x \leqslant a$'.

Not all the methods are used for each example.

Example 9.6.1

Solve the inequality $|x - 2| < 3$.

Method 2   From the definition of modulus, either $x < 2$ and $-(x-2) < 3$, or $x \geqslant 2$ and $x - 2 < 3$. The first of these gives $x < 2$ and $-x < 1$, which together give $-1 < x < 2$; the second gives $x \geqslant 2$ and $x < 3 + 2$, which together give $2 \leqslant x < 5$. Therefore $-1 < x < 5$.

Method 3   From the result 'If $a \geqslant 0$, the inequalities $|x - k| \leqslant a$ and $k - a \leqslant x \leqslant k + a$ are equivalent', the solution is $2 - 3 < x < 2 + 3$, which is $-1 < x < 5$.

Example 9.6.2

Solve the inequality $|x - 2| \geqslant |2x - 3|$.

Method 1   Consider the graphs of $y = |x - 2|$ and $y = |2x - 3|$. These were drawn in Figs. 9.2 and 9.3. They are reproduced together in Fig. 9.11; the graph of $y = |2x - 3|$ is shown with a dashed line.

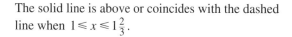

Fig. 9.11

The solid line is above or coincides with the dashed line when $1 \leqslant x \leqslant 1\frac{2}{3}$.

Method 2   In the definition of $|x - 2|$ you have to separate the cases $x < 2$ and $x \geqslant 2$; and in $|2x - 3|$ you have to separate $x < 1\frac{1}{2}$ and $x \geqslant 1\frac{1}{2}$. So it is necessary to consider the cases $x < 1\frac{1}{2}$, $1\frac{1}{2} \leqslant x < 2$ and $x \geqslant 2$.

When $x < 1\frac{1}{2}$, $|x - 2| = -(x - 2)$ and $|2x - 3| = -(2x - 3)$, so $-x + 2 \geqslant -2x + 3$, giving $x \geqslant 1$. So the inequality is satisfied when $1 \leqslant x < 1\frac{1}{2}$.

When $1\frac{1}{2} \leqslant x < 2$, $|x - 2| = -(x - 2)$ and $|2x - 3| = 2x - 3$, so $-x + 2 \geqslant 2x - 3$, giving $x \leqslant 1\frac{2}{3}$. So the inequality is satisfied when $1\frac{1}{2} \leqslant x \leqslant 1\frac{2}{3}$.

When $x \geqslant 2$, $|x - 2| = x - 2$ and $|2x - 3| = 2x - 3$, so $x - 2 \geqslant 2x - 3$, giving $x \leqslant 1$. This is inconsistent with $x \geqslant 2$.

Since the inequality is satisfied when $1 \leqslant x < 1\frac{1}{2}$ and when $1\frac{1}{2} \leqslant x \leqslant 1\frac{2}{3}$, the complete solution is $1 \leqslant x \leqslant 1\frac{2}{3}$.

Example 9.6.3

Solve the inequality $|x-2| \geqslant 2x+1$.

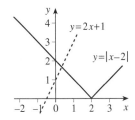

Fig. 9.12

Method 1   Consider the graphs of $y = |x-2|$ and $y = 2x+1$, shown in Fig. 9.12.

The solid line is above or on the dashed line when $x \leqslant \frac{1}{3}$.

Method 2   If $x < 2$, then $|x-2| = 2-x$, so $2-x \geqslant 2x+1$, giving $x \leqslant \frac{1}{3}$. So the inequality is satisfied when $x \leqslant \frac{1}{3}$.

If $x \geqslant 2$, then $|x-2| = x-2$, so $x-2 \geqslant 2x+1$, giving $x \leqslant -3$. This is inconsistent with $x \geqslant 2$.

So the complete solution is $x \leqslant \frac{1}{3}$.

9.7   Squares, square roots and moduli

You know that, if x is any real number, then $x^2 \geqslant 0$. It follows that $|x^2| = x^2$. Also, from the rule $|a \times b| = |a| \times |b|$, $|x^2| = |x| \times |x| = |x|^2$.

> If x is any real number, $|x^2| = |x|^2 = x^2$.

Now since $|x|^2 = x^2$, and $|x|$ is positive or zero, it follows that $|x|$ is the square root of x^2. You can show this by evaluating the composite function

$$x \;\; \rightarrow \;\; [\text{ square }] \;\; \rightarrow \;\; x^2 \;\; \rightarrow \;\; [\sqrt{}\,] \;\; \rightarrow \;\; \sqrt{x^2}$$

on your calculator with various inputs for x, positive or negative. If you put $x = 3$, say, then you will get the display sequence $3, 9, 3$. But if you put $x = -3$, you will get $-3, 9, 3$, because $\sqrt{}$ always gives the positive square root. That is, $\sqrt{x^2}$ is equal to x when $x \geqslant 0$, but equal to $-x$ when $x < 0$. This is just the definition of $|x|$. It follows that

> If x is any real number, $\sqrt{x^2} = |x|$.

Verify this by displaying the graphs of $y = \sqrt{x^2}$ and $y = |x|$ on a graphic calculator.

Example 9.7.1

Find the distance between the points with coordinates (a, k) and (b, k).

Method 1   Both points have the same y-coordinate, so the distance is the same as the distance between points with coordinates a and b on the number line, which is $|b-a|$.

Method 2   By the formula for the distance between two points in P1 Section 1.1, the distance is

$$\sqrt{(b-a)^2 + (k-k)^2} = \sqrt{(b-a)^2 + 0} = \sqrt{(b-a)^2} = |b-a|,$$

using $\sqrt{x^2} = |x|$ with $x = b - a$.

Useful results connecting squares with moduli can be got from the identity

$$x^2 - a^2 \equiv |x|^2 - |a|^2 \equiv (|x| - |a|)(|x| + |a|).$$

Suppose first that $a \neq 0$. Then $|a| > 0$, so $|x| + |a| > 0$. It then follows that

$$x^2 - a^2 = 0 \iff |x| - |a| = 0,$$
$$x^2 - a^2 > 0 \iff |x| - |a| > 0,$$
$$x^2 - a^2 < 0 \iff |x| - |a| < 0.$$

You can easily check that the first two of these are also true when $a = 0$; but the third is impossible if $a = 0$, since it gives $x^2 < 0$, which can never occur for any real number x.

$$|x| = |a| \iff x^2 = a^2,$$

$$|x| > |a| \iff x^2 > a^2, \quad \text{and}$$

$$\text{if } a \neq 0, \quad |x| < |a| \iff x^2 < a^2.$$

These relations are sometimes useful in solving equations and inequalities. They are effective because, although squaring is involved, the two sides are logically equivalent. The usual warning that squaring may introduce extra roots which don't satisfy the original equation (see the commentary on Example 8.1.1) doesn't apply.

Example 9.7.2 (see Example 9.5.2)
Solve the equation $|x - 2| = |2x - 1|$.

$$
\begin{aligned}
|x - 2| = |2x - 1| &\iff (x-2)^2 = (2x-1)^2 \\
&\iff x^2 - 4x + 4 = 4x^2 - 4x + 1 \\
&\iff 3x^2 - 3 = 0 \\
&\iff 3(x+1)(x-1) = 0 \\
&\iff x = -1 \quad \text{or} \quad x = 1.
\end{aligned}
$$

Example 9.7.3 (see Example 9.6.2)
Solve the inequality $|x - 2| \geq |2x - 3|$.

$$|x-2| \geqslant |2x-3| \quad \Leftrightarrow \quad (x-2)^2 \geqslant (2x-3)^2$$
$$\Leftrightarrow \quad x^2 - 4x + 4 \geqslant 4x^2 - 12x + 9$$
$$\Leftrightarrow \quad 3x^2 - 8x + 5 \leqslant 0$$
$$\Leftrightarrow \quad (x-1)(3x-5) \leqslant 0$$
$$\Leftrightarrow \quad 1 \leqslant x \leqslant 1\tfrac{2}{3}.$$

This method is very quick when it works, but there is a drawback. It can only be used for a very specific type of equation or inequality. It is easy to fall into the trap of assuming it can be applied to equations and inequalities of forms other than $|f(x)| = |g(x)|$ or $|f(x)| < |g(x)|$, which can have disastrous consequences.

Example 9.7.4

Solve the equation $|x-2| + |1-x| = 0$.

It is obvious from the answer to Example 9.2.2 that this equation has no solution.

False solution

$$|x-2| + |1-x| = 0 \quad \Leftrightarrow \quad |x-2| = -|1-x|$$
$$\Leftrightarrow (!) \quad (x-2)^2 = (1-x)^2$$
$$\Leftrightarrow \quad x^2 - 4x + 4 = 1 - 2x + x^2$$
$$\Leftrightarrow \quad 2x = 3$$
$$\Leftrightarrow \quad x = 1\tfrac{1}{2}.$$

There is no justification for the step marked (!). The previous line has the form $|x| = -|a|$, not $|x| = |a|$, so the result in the shaded box can't be used.

Exercise 9B

1 Solve the following equations, using at least two methods for each case.

(a) $|x+2| = 5$ (b) $|x-1| = 7$

(c) $|2x-3| = 3$ (d) $|3x+1| = 10$

(e) $|x+1| = |2x-3|$ (f) $|x-3| = |3x+1|$

(g) $|2x+1| = |3x+9|$ (h) $|5x+1| = |11-2x|$

2 Solve the following inequalities, using at least two methods for each case.

(a) $|x+2| < 1$ (b) $|x-3| > 5$

(c) $|2x+7| \leqslant 3$ (d) $|3x+2| \geqslant 8$

(e) $|x+2| < |3x+1|$ (f) $|2x+5| > |x+2|$

(g) $|x| > |2x-3|$ (h) $|4x+1| \leqslant |4x-1|$

3 Solve the equations

(a) $|x+1|+|1-x|=2,$ (b) $|x+1|-|1-x|=2,$ (c) $-|x+1|+|1-x|=2.$

4 Solve the equations

(a) $|x|=|1-x|+1,$ (b) $|x-1|=|x|+1,$ (c) $|x-1|+|x|=1.$

5 Are the following statements true or false? Give a counterexample where appropriate.

(a) The graph of $y=|f(x)|$ never has negative values for y.

(b) The graph of $y=f(|x|)$ never has negative values for y.

Miscellaneous exercise 9

1 Solve the inequality $|x+1|<|x-2|.$ (OCR)

2 Find the greatest and least values of x satisfying the inequality $|2x-1|\leqslant 5.$ (OCR)

3 Sketch, on a single diagram, the graphs of $x+2y=6$ and $y=|x+2|.$ Hence, or otherwise, solve the inequality $|x+2|<\frac{1}{2}(6-x).$ (OCR)

4 Solve the equation $|x|=|2x+1|.$ (OCR)

5 Sketch the graph of $y=|x+2|$ and hence, or otherwise, solve the inequality $|x+2|>2x+1.$ (OCR)

6 Solve the equation $4|x|=|x-1|.$
On the same diagram sketch the graphs of $y=4|x|$ and $y=|x-1|,$ and hence, or otherwise, solve the inequality $4|x|>|x-1|.$

7 Sketch, on separate diagrams, the graphs of $y=|x|,$ $y=|x-3|$ and $y=|x-3|+|x+3|.$ Find the solution set of the equation $|x-3|+|x+3|=6.$ (OCR)

8 The functions f and g are defined on the set of real numbers as follows:

$f:x\mapsto|2\sin x°|,$ $g:x\mapsto\sin|2x°|.$

(a) (i) Make clearly labelled sketches of the graphs of $y=f(x)$ and $y=g(x)$ in the interval $-270\leqslant x\leqslant 270.$

(ii) State the range of each function.

(b) Decide whether or not each function is periodic and, if so, state its period.   (OCR)

9 Solve the inequality $|x|<4|x-3|.$

10 Rewrite the function $k(x)$ defined by $k(x)=|x+3|+|4-x|$ for the following three cases, without using the modulus in your answer.

(a) $x>4$ (b) $-3\leqslant x\leqslant 4$ (c) $x<-3$

11 Solve the equations   (a) $x+|2x-1|=3,$ (b) $3+|2x-1|=x.$

12 Sketch the graph of $y = |2x - 3| + |5 - x|$.

(a) Calculate the y-coordinate of the point where the graph cuts the y-axis.

(b) Determine the gradient of the graph where $x < -5$.   (OCR, adapted)

13 A graph has equation $y = x + |2x - 1|$. Express y as a linear function of x (that is, in the form $y = mx + c$ for constants m and c) in each of the following intervals for x.

(a) $x > \frac{1}{2}$,   (b) $x < \frac{1}{2}$.   (OCR)

14 Draw sketches of the graphs of the following functions.

(a) $y = \sin 3x°$ (b) $y = |\sin 3x°|$ (c) $y = \sin |3x|°$

15* Solve the following inequalities.

(a) $\dfrac{x+1}{x-1} < 4$ (b) $\dfrac{|x|+1}{|x|-1} < 4$ (c) $\left|\dfrac{x+1}{x-1}\right| < 4$ (OCR)

10 Geometric sequences and exponential growth

This chapter introduces another type of sequence, which has applications in both discrete and continuous forms. When you have completed it, you should

- recognise geometric sequences and be able to do calculations on them
- know and be able to obtain the formula for the sum of a geometric series
- know the condition for a geometric series to converge, and how to find its limiting sum
- understand the essential features of exponential growth and decay
- be able to do calculations on continuous exponential growth and decay
- appreciate the uniformity of the exponential growth graph.

10.1 Geometric sequences

In Chapter 3 you met arithmetic sequences, in which to get from one term to the next you add a constant. A sequence in which to get from one term to the next you multiply by a constant, is called a geometric sequence.

> A **geometric sequence**, or **geometric progression**, is a sequence defined by $u_1 = a$ and $u_{i+1} = ru_i$, where $i \in \mathbb{N}$ and $r \neq 0$ or 1.
>
> The constant r is called the **common ratio** of the sequence.

You should notice two points about this definition. First, since the letter r is conventionally used for the common ratio, a different letter, i, is used for the suffixes.

Secondly, the ratios 0 and 1 are excluded. If you put $r = 0$ in the definition you get the sequence $a, 0, 0, 0, \ldots$; if you put $r = 1$ you get $a, a, a, a, \ldots$. Neither is very interesting, and some of the properties of geometric sequences break down if $r = 0$ or 1. However, r can be negative; in that case the terms are alternately positive and negative.

It is easy to give a formula for the ith term. To get from u_1 to u_i you multiply by the common ratio $i - 1$ times, so $u_i = r^{i-1} \times u_1$, which gives $u_i = ar^{i-1}$.

Example 10.1.1

A geometric sequence has first term $u_1 = 1$ and common ratio 1.1. Which is the first term greater than   (a) 2,   (b) 5,   (c) 10,   (d) 1000?

On many calculators you can keep multiplying by 1.1 by repeatedly pressing a single key. This makes it easy to display successive terms of a geometric sequence.

(a) This can easily be done experimentally, counting how many times you press the key until the display exceeds 2. You should find that after 8 presses you get $2.143\,588\,81$, which is 1.1^8. The ith term of the sequence is $u_i = 1 \times 1.1^{i-1}$, so this is first greater than 2 when $i - 1 = 8$, or $i = 9$.

(b) Go on pressing the key. After another 8 presses you should reach $(2.143\,588\,81)^2$, which is certainly greater than 4, so you will reach 5 quite soon. In fact it turns out that 1.1^{15} is already greater than 4, and two more presses take you to $1.1^{17} = 5.054\ldots$. So $u_{18} = 1 \times 1.1^{17}$ is the first term greater than 5.

(c) Since $1.1^8 > 2$ and $1.1^{17} > 5$, it is certainly true that $1.1^{25} = 1.1^8 \times 1.1^{17}$ is greater than 10. Rather than continuing to multiply, you can just use the power key to find $1.1^{25} = 10.834\ldots$. But you must check that 1.1^{24} is not already greater than 10. In fact it isn't, since $1.1^{24} = 9.849\ldots$. So the first term greater than 10 is $u_{26} = 1 \times 1.1^{26-1}$.

(d) Since $1.1^{24} < 10$ and $1 \times 1.1^{25} > 10$, you can cube both sides to find that $1.1^{72} = \left(1.1^{24}\right)^3 < 1000$ and $1.1^{75} = \left(1.1^{25}\right)^3 > 1000$. So you only need to check 1.1^{73} and 1.1^{74}. Using the power key, $1.1^{73} = 1051.1\ldots$. So the first term greater than 1000 is $u_{74} = 1.1^{74-1}$.

The first terms greater than 2, 5, 10 and 1000 are u_9, u_{18}, u_{26} and u_{74}.

You can see from this example that, even with a common ratio only slightly greater than 1, the terms of a geometric sequence get big quite quickly.

10.2 Summing geometric series

Geometric sequences have many applications in finance, biology, mechanics and probability, and you often need to find the sum of all the terms. In this context it is usual to call the sequence a **geometric series**.

The method used in Chapter 3 to find the sum of an arithmetic series does not work for geometric series. You can see this by taking a simple geometric series like $1+2+4+8+16$ and placing an upside-down copy next to it, as in Fig. 10.1. When you did this with arithmetic series the two sets of crosses and noughts made a perfect join (see Fig. 3.7), so they could easily be counted; but for the geometric series there is a gap in the middle.

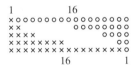

Fig. 10.1

For geometric series a different method is used. If you multiply the equation $S = 1+2+4+8+16$ by 2, then you get $2S = 2+4+8+16+32$. Notice that the right sides in these two equations have the terms $2+4+8+16$ in common; the sum of these terms is equal to $S-1$ from the first equation and $2S-32$ from the second. So

$$S-1 = 2S-32, \text{ giving } S = 31.$$

You can use this method to find the sum of any geometric series. Let S be the sum of the first n terms of the series. Then

$$S = a + ar + ar^2 + \ldots + ar^{n-2} + ar^{n-1}.$$

If you multiply this equation by r, you get

$$Sr = ar + ar^2 + ar^3 + \ldots + ar^{n-1} + ar^n.$$

The right sides in these two equations have the terms $ar + ar^2 + \ldots + ar^{n-2} + ar^{n-1}$ in common; so

$$S - a = ar + ar^2 + \ldots + ar^{n-2} + ar^{n-1} = Sr - ar^n,$$

which gives

$$S(1-r) = a(1 - r^n), \quad \text{or} \quad S = \frac{a(1 - r^n)}{1 - r}.$$

The sum of the geometric series $a + ar + ar^2 + \ldots + ar^{n-1}$, with n terms, is

$$\frac{a(1 - r^n)}{1 - r}.$$

You should notice that it has nowhere been assumed that r is positive. The formula is valid whether r is positive or negative. When $r > 1$, some people prefer to avoid fractions with negative numerator and denominator by using the result in the alternative form

$$S = \frac{a(r^n - 1)}{r - 1}.$$

Example 10.2.1

A child lives 200 metres from school. He walks 60 metres in the first minute, and in each subsequent minute he walks 75% of the distance he walked in the previous minute. Show that he takes between 6 and 7 minutes to get to school.

The distances walked in the first, second, third, $\ldots$, nth minutes are 60 m, 60×0.75 m, 60×0.75^2 m, $\ldots$, $60 \times 0.75^{n-1}$ m. In the first n minutes the child walks S_n metres, where

$$S_n = 60 + 60 \times 0.75^1 + 60 \times 0.75^2 + \ldots + 60 \times 0.75^{n-1}$$

$$= \frac{60(1 - 0.75^n)}{1 - 0.75} = \frac{60(1 - 0.75^n)}{0.25} = 240(1 - 0.75^n).$$

From this formula you can calculate that

$$S_6 = 240(1 - 0.75^6) = 240(1 - 0.177\ldots) = 197.2\ldots, \text{ and}$$

$$S_7 = 240(1 - 0.75^7) = 240(1 - 0.133\ldots) = 207.9\ldots.$$

So he has not reached school after 6 minutes, but (if he had gone on walking) he would have gone more than 200 m in 7 minutes. That is, he takes between 6 and 7 minutes to walk to school.

Example 10.2.2

Find a simple expression for the sum $p^6 - p^5 q + p^4 q^2 - p^3 q^3 + p^2 q^4 - pq^5 + q^6$.

This is a geometric series of 7 terms, with first term p^6 and common ratio $-\dfrac{q}{p}$. Its sum is therefore

$$\frac{p^6\left(1-(-q/p)^7\right)}{1-(-q/p)} = \frac{p^6\left(1-\left(-q^7/p^7\right)\right)}{1+q/p} = \frac{p^7\left(1+q^7/p^7\right)}{p(1+q/p)} = \frac{p^7+q^7}{p+q}.$$

Another way of writing the result of this example is

$$p^7 + q^7 = (p+q)\left(p^6 - p^5 q + p^4 q^2 - p^3 q^3 + p^2 q^4 - pq^5 + q^6\right).$$

You can use a similar method for any odd number n to express $p^n + q^n$ as the product of $p+q$ and another factor.

Exercise 10A

1 For each of the following geometric sequences find the common ratio and the next two terms.

(a) $3, 6, 12, \ldots$ (b) $2, 8, 32, \ldots$ (c) $32, 16, 8, \ldots$

(d) $2, -6, 18, -54, \ldots$ (e) $1.1, 1.21, 1.331, \ldots$ (f) $x^2, x, 1, \ldots$

2 Find an expression for the nth term of each of the following geometric sequences.

(a) $2, 6, 18, \ldots$ (b) $10, 5, 2.5, \ldots$ (c) $1, -2, 4, \ldots$

(d) $81, 27, 9, \ldots$ (e) $x, x^2, x^3, \ldots$ (f) $pq^2, q^3, p^{-1}q^4, \ldots$

3 Find the number of terms in each of these geometric progressions.

(a) $2, 4, 8, \ldots, 2048$ (b) $1, -3, 9, \ldots, 531\,441$

(c) $2, 6, 18, \ldots, 1458$ (d) $5, -10, 20, \ldots, -40\,960$

(e) $16, 12, 9, \ldots, 3.796\,875$ (f) $x^{-6}, x^{-2}, x^2, \ldots, x^{42}$

4 Find the common ratio and the first term in the geometric progressions where

(a) the 2nd term is 4 and the 5th term is 108,

(b) the 3rd term is 6 and the 7th term is 96,

(c) the 4th term 19683 and the 9th term is 81,

(d) the 3rd term is 8 and the 9th term is 64,

(e) the nth term is 16807 and the $(n+4)$th term is 40\,353\,607.

5 Find the sum, for the given number of terms, of each of the following geometric series. Give decimal answers, correct to 4 places.

(a) $2+6+18+\ldots$ 10 terms   (b) $2-6+18+\ldots$ 10 terms

(c) $1+\frac{1}{2}+\frac{1}{4}+\ldots$ 8 terms   (d) $1-\frac{1}{2}+\frac{1}{4}+\ldots$ 8 terms

(e) $3+6+12+\ldots$ 12 terms   (f) $12-4+\frac{4}{3}+\ldots$ 10 terms

(g) $x+x^2+x^3+\ldots$ n terms   (h) $x-x^2+x^3+\ldots$ n terms

(i) $x+\dfrac{1}{x}+\dfrac{1}{x^3}+\ldots$ n terms   (j) $1-\dfrac{1}{x^2}+\dfrac{1}{x^4}+\ldots$ n terms

6 Use the method in Section 10.2 to find the sum of each of the following geometric series. Give numerical answers as rational numbers.

(a) $1 + 2 + 4 + \ldots + 1024$

(b) $1 - 2 + 4 - \ldots + 1024$

(c) $3 + 12 + 48 + \ldots + 196\,608$

(d) $1 + \frac{1}{2} + \frac{1}{4} + \ldots + \frac{1}{512}$

(e) $1 - \frac{1}{3} + \frac{1}{9} + \ldots - \frac{1}{19\,683}$

(f) $10 + 5 + 2.5 + \ldots + 0.156\,25$

(g) $\frac{1}{4} + \frac{1}{16} + \frac{1}{64} + \ldots + \frac{1}{1024}$

(h) $1 + \frac{1}{2} + \frac{1}{4} + \ldots + \frac{1}{2^n}$

(i) $16 + 4 + 1 + \ldots + \frac{1}{2^{2n}}$

(j) $81 - 27 + 9 + \ldots + \frac{1}{(-3)^n}$

7 A well known story concerns the inventor of the game of chess. As a reward for inventing the game it is rumoured that he was asked to choose his own prize. He asked for 1 grain of rice to be placed on the first square of the board, 2 grains on the second square, 4 grains on the third square and so on in geometric progression until all 64 squares had been covered. Calculate the total number of grains of rice he would have received. Give your answer in standard form!

8 A problem similar to that of Question 7 is posed by the child who negotiates a pocket money deal of 1p on 1 February, 2p on 2 February, 4p on 3 February and so on for 28 days. How much should the child receive in total during February?

9 If x, y and z are the first three terms of a geometric sequence, show that x^2, y^2 and z^2 form another geometric sequence.

10 Different numbers x, y and z are the first three terms of a geometric progression with common ratio r, and also the first, second and fourth terms of an arithmetic progression.

(a) Find the value of r.

(b) Find which term of the arithmetic progression will next be equal to a term of the geometric progression.

11 Different numbers x, y and z are the first three terms of a geometric progression with common ratio r and also the first, second and fifth terms of an arithmetic progression.

(a) Find the value of r.

(b) Find which term of the arithmetic progression will next be equal to a term of the geometric progression.

12* Consider the geometric progression

$$q^{n-1} + q^{n-2}p + q^{n-3}p^2 + \ldots + qp^{n-2} + p^{n-1}.$$

(a) Find the common ratio and the number of terms.

(b) Show that the sum of the series is equal to $\dfrac{q^n - p^n}{q - p}$.

(c) By considering the limit as $q \to p$ deduce expressions for $f'(p)$ in the cases
(i) $f(x) = x^n$, (ii) $f(x) = x^{-n}$, for all positive integers n.

10.3 Convergent sequences

Take any sequence, such as the sequence of triangle numbers $t_1 = 1$, $t_2 = 3$, $t_3 = 6$, ... (see Section 3.3). Form a new sequence whose terms are the sums of successive triangle numbers:

$$S_1 = t_1 = 1, \quad S_2 = t_1 + t_2 = 1 + 3 = 4, \quad S_3 = t_1 + t_2 + t_3 = 1 + 3 + 6 = 10, \text{ and so on.}$$

This is called the sum sequence of the original sequence.

Notice that $S_2 = S_1 + t_2$, $S_3 = S_2 + t_3$, ... This property can be used to give an inductive definition for the sum sequence:

> For a given sequence u_i, the **sum sequence** $S_i = u_1 + ... + u_i$ is defined by $S_1 = u_1$ and $S_{i+1} = S_i + u_{i+1}$.

(If the original sequence begins with u_0 rather than u_1, the equation $S_1 = u_1$ in the definition is replaced by $S_0 = u_0$.)

Geometric sequences have especially important sum sequences. Here are four examples, each with first term $a = 1$:

(a) $r = 3$

u_i	1	3	9	27	81	243	729	...
S_i	1	4	13	40	121	364	1093	...

Table 10.2

(b) $r = 0.2$

u_i	1	0.2	0.04	0.008	0.001 6	0.000 32	0.000 064	...
S_i	1	1.2	1.24	1.248	1.249 6	1.249 92	1.249 984	...

Table 10.3

(c) $r = -0.2$

u_i	1	−0.2	0.04	−0.008	0.001 6	−0.000 32	0.000 064	...
S_i	1	0.8	0.84	0.832	0.833 6	0.833 28	0.833 344	...

Table 10.4

(d) $r = -3$

u_i	1	−3	9	−27	81	−243	729	...
S_i	1	−2	7	−20	61	−182	547	...

Table 10.5

The sum sequences for (b) and (c) are quite different from the others. You would guess that in (b) the values of S_i are getting close to 1.25, but never reach it. This can be proved, since the formula for the sum of the first n values of u_i gives, with $a = 1$ and $r = 0.2$,

$$\frac{1 - 0.2^n}{1 - 0.2} = \frac{1 - 0.2^n}{0.8} = 1.25\left(1 - 0.2^n\right).$$

Now you can make 0.2^n as small as you like by taking n large enough, so that the expression in brackets approaches 1 as n increases indefinitely, though it never equals 1. You can say that the sum tends to the limit 1.25 as n tends to infinity.

It seems that the sum in (c) tends to $0.833\,33\ldots$ (the recurring decimal for $\frac{5}{6}$) as n tends to infinity, but here the values are alternately above and below the limiting value. This is because the formula for the sum is

$$\frac{1 - (-0.2)^n}{1 - (-0.2)} = \frac{1 - (-0.2)^n}{1.2} = \frac{5}{6}\left(1 - (-0.2)^n\right).$$

In this formula the expression $(-0.2)^n$ is alternately positive and negative, so $1 - (-0.2)^n$ alternates above and below 1.

The other two sequences, for which the sum formulae are (a) $\frac{1}{2}\left(3^n - 1\right)$ and (d) $\frac{1}{4}\left(1 - (-3)^n\right)$, do not tend to a limit. The sum (a) can be made as large as you like by taking n large enough; it is said to **diverge to infinity** as n tends to infinity. The sum (d) can also be made as large as you like; the sum sequence is said to **oscillate infinitely**.

It is the expression r^n in the sum formula $\dfrac{a\left(1 - r^n\right)}{1 - r}$ which determines whether or not the sum tends to a limit. If $|r| > 1$, then $|r^n|$ increases indefinitely; but if $|r| < 1$, then $|r^n|$ tends to 0 and the sum tends to the value $\dfrac{a(1 - 0)}{1 - r} = \dfrac{a}{1 - r}$. Even if r is very close to 1, r^n becomes very small if n is large enough; for example, if $r = 0.9999$ and $n = 1\,000\,000$, then $r^n \approx 3.70 \times 10^{-44}$.

> If $|r| < 1$, the sum of the geometric series with first term a and common
> ratio r tends to the limit $S_\infty = \dfrac{a}{1 - r}$ as the number of terms tends to infinity.
>
> The infinite geometric series is then said to be **convergent**.
>
> S_∞ is called the **sum to infinity** of the series.

Example 10.3.1
Express the recurring decimal $0.296\,296\,296\ldots$ as a fraction.

The decimal can be written as

$$0.296 + 0.000\ 296 + 0.000\ 000\ 296 + \ldots$$
$$= 0.296 + 0.296 \times 0.001 + 0.296 \times (0.001)^2 + \ldots,$$

which is a geometric series with $a = 0.296$ and $r = 0.001$. Since $|r| < 1$, the series is convergent with limiting sum $\dfrac{0.296}{1 - 0.001} = \dfrac{296}{999}$.

Since $296 = 8 \times 37$ and $999 = 27 \times 37$, this fraction in its simplest form is $\frac{8}{27}$.

Example 10.3.2

A beetle starts at a point O on the floor. It walks 1 m east, then $\frac{1}{2}$ m west, then $\frac{1}{4}$ m east, and so on, halving the distance at each change of direction. How far from O does it end up?

The final distance from O is $1 - \frac{1}{2} + \frac{1}{4} - \frac{1}{8} + \ldots$, which is a geometric series with common ratio $-\frac{1}{2}$. Since $\left| -\frac{1}{2} \right| < 1$, the series converges to a limit

$$\frac{1}{1 - (-\frac{1}{2})} = \frac{1}{\frac{3}{2}} = \frac{2}{3}.$$

The beetle ends up $\frac{2}{3}$ m from O.

Notice that a point of trisection was obtained as the limit of a process of repeated halving.

Exercise 10B

1 Find the sum to infinity of the following geometric series. Give your answers to parts (a) to (j) as whole numbers, fractions or exact decimals.

(a) $1 + \frac{1}{2} + \frac{1}{4} + \ldots$

(b) $1 + \frac{1}{3} + \frac{1}{9} + \ldots$

(c) $\frac{1}{5} + \frac{1}{25} + \frac{1}{125} + \ldots$

(d) $0.1 + 0.01 + 0.001 + \ldots$

(e) $1 - \frac{1}{3} + \frac{1}{9} - \ldots$

(f) $0.2 - 0.04 + 0.008 - \ldots$

(g) $\frac{3}{2} + \frac{3}{4} + \frac{3}{8} + \ldots$

(h) $\frac{1}{2} - \frac{1}{4} + \frac{1}{8} - \ldots$

(i) $10 - 5 + 2.5 -$

(j) $50 + 10 + 2 +$

(k) $x + x^2 + x^3 + \ldots$, where $-1 < x < 1$

(l) $1 - x^2 + x^4 - \ldots$, where $x^2 < 1$

(m) $1 + x^{-1} + x^{-2} + \ldots$, where $|x| > 1$

(n) $x^2 - x + 1 - \ldots$, where $|x| > 1$

2 Express each of the following recurring decimals as exact fractions.

(a) $0.363636\ldots$

(b) $0.123123123\ldots$

(c) $0.555\ldots$

(d) $0.471471471\ldots$

(e) $0.142857142857142857\ldots$

(f) $0.285714285714285714\ldots$

(g) $0.714285714285714285\ldots$

(h) $0.857142857142857142\ldots$

3 Find the common ratio of a geometric series which has a first term of 5 and a sum to infinity of 6.

4   Find the common ratio of a geometric series which has a first term of 11 and a sum to infinity of 6.

5   Find the first term of a geometric series which has a common ratio of $\frac{3}{4}$ and a sum to infinity of 12.

6   Find the first term of a geometric series which has a common ratio of $-\frac{3}{5}$ and a sum to infinity of 12.

7   In Example 10.3.2 a beetle starts at a point O on the floor. It walks 1 m east, then $\frac{1}{2}$ m west, then $\frac{1}{4}$ m east and so on. It finished $\frac{2}{3}$ m to the east of O. How far did it actually walk?

8   A beetle starts at a point O on the floor and walks 0.6 m east, then 0.36 m west, 0.216 m east and so on. Find its final position and how far it actually walks.

9   A 'supa-ball' is thrown upwards from ground level. It hits the ground after 2 seconds and continues to bounce. The time it is in the air for a particular bounce is always 0.8 of the time for the previous bounce. How long does it take for the ball to stop bouncing?

10 A 'supa-ball' is dropped from a height of 1 metre onto a level table. It always rises to a height equal to 0.9 of the height from which it was dropped. How far does it travel in total until it stops bouncing?

11 A frog sits at one end of a table which is 2 m long. In its first jump the frog goes a distance of 1 m along the table, with its second jump $\frac{1}{2}$ m, with its third jump $\frac{1}{4}$ m and so on.

    (a) What is the frog's final position?

    (b) After how many jumps will the frog be within 1 cm of the far end of the table?

10.4 Exponential growth and decay

Many everyday situations are described by geometric sequences. Of the next two examples, the first has a common ratio greater than 1, and the second has a common ratio between 0 and 1.

Example 10.4.1

A person invests £1000 in a building society account which pays interest of 6% annually. Calculate the amount in the account over the next 8 years.

> The interest in any year is 0.06 times the amount in the account at the beginning of the year. This is added on to the sum of money already in the account. The amount at the end of each year, after interest has been added, is 1.06 times the amount at the beginning of the year. So
>
> Amount after 1 year = £1000 × 1.06 = £1060
>
> Amount after 2 years = £1060 × 1.06 = £1124
>
> Amount after 3 years = £1124 × 1.06 = £1191, and so on.

Continuing in this way, you get the amounts shown in Table 10.6, to the nearest whole number of pounds.

Number of years	0	1	2	3	4	5	6	7	8
Amount (£)	1000	1060	1124	1191	1262	1338	1419	1504	1594

Table 10.6

You can see these values in Fig. 10.7.

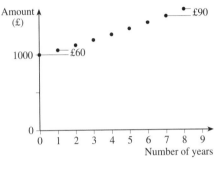

Notice that in the first year the interest is £60, but in the eighth year it is £90. This is because the amount on which the 6% is calculated has gone up from £1000 to £1504. This is characteristic of **exponential growth**, in which the increase is proportional to the current amount. As the amount goes up, the increase goes up.

Fig. 10.7

Example 10.4.2

A car cost £15,000 when new, and each year its value decreases by 20%. Find its value on the first five anniversaries of its purchase.

The value at the end of each year is 0.8 times its value a year earlier. The results of this calculation are given in Table 10.8.

Number of years	0	1	2	3	4	5
Value (£)	15 000	12 000	9600	7680	6144	4915

Table 10.8

These values are shown in the graph in Fig. 10.9.

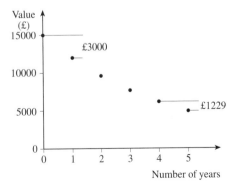

The value goes down by £3000 in the first year, but by only £1229 in the fifth year, because by then the 20% is calculated on only £6144 rather than £15,000. This is characteristic of **exponential decay**, in which the decrease is proportional to the current value. Notice that, if the 20% rule continues, the value never becomes zero however long you keep the car.

Fig. 10.9

Notice that in both these examples it is more natural to think of the first term of the sequence as u_0 rather than u_1, so that $£u_i$ is the amount in the account, or the value of the car, after i years. The sequence in Example 10.4.1 has

$$u_0 = 1000 \quad \text{and} \quad u_{i+1} = 1.06u_i \quad \text{for } 0 \leqslant i \leqslant 7.$$

From this you can deduce that $u_1 = 1000 \times 1.06$, $u_2 = 1000 \times 1.06^2$, and more generally $u_i = 1000 \times 1.06^i$. The sequence in Example 10.4.2 has

$$u_0 = 15\,000 \quad \text{and} \quad u_{i+1} = 0.8u_i \quad \text{for } 0 \leqslant i \leqslant 4.$$

In this case $u_1 = 15\,000 \times 0.8$, $u_2 = 15\,000 \times 0.8^2$ and $u_i = 15\,000 \times 0.8^i$.

These are both examples of exponential sequences. (The word 'exponential' comes from 'exponent', which is another word for index. The reason for the name is that the variable i appears in the exponent of the formula for u_i.) An exponential sequence is a special kind of geometric sequence, in which a and r are both positive. If the first term is denoted by u_0, the sequence can be defined inductively by

$$u_0 = a \quad \text{and} \quad u_{i+1} = ru_i,$$

or by the formula

$$u_i = ar^i.$$

If $r > 1$ the sequence represents exponential growth; if $0 < r < 1$ it represents exponential decay.

It may or may not be useful to find the sum of the terms of an exponential sequence. In Example 10.4.2 there would be no point in adding up the year-end values of the car. But many investment calculations (such as for pensions and mortgages) require the terms of an exponential sequence to be added up. This is illustrated by the next example.

Example 10.4.3

Sharon's grandparents put £1000 into a building society account for her on each birthday from her 10th to her 18th. The account pays interest at 6% for each complete year that the money is invested. How much money is in the account on the day after her 18th birthday?

Start with the most recent deposit. The £1000 on her 18th birthday has not earned any interest. The £1000 on her 17th birthday has earned interest for one year, so is now worth $£1000 \times 1.06 = £1060$. Similarly, the £1000 on her 16th birthday is worth $£1000 \times 1.06^2 = £1124$, and so on. So the total amount is now $£S$, where

$$S = 1000 + 1000 \times 1.06 + 1000 \times 1.06^2 + \ldots + 1000 \times 1.06^8.$$

Method 1   The terms of this series are just the amounts calculated in Example 10.4.1. The sum of the nine entries in Table 10.6 is 11 492.

Method 2   The sum is a geometric series with $a = 1000$, $r = 1.06$ and $n = 9$. Using the general formula,

$$S = \frac{a(r^n - 1)}{r - 1} = \frac{1000(1.06^9 - 1)}{1.06 - 1} = 11\,491.32.$$

There is a small discrepancy between the two answers, because the amounts in Table 10.6 were rounded to the nearest pound. The amount in the account just after Sharon's 18th birthday is £11,491.32.

10.5 Continuous exponential growth

Exponential growth doesn't only occur in situations which increase by discrete steps. Rampant inflation, a nuclear chain reaction, the spread of an epidemic or the growth of cells are phenomena which take place in continuous time, and they need to be described by functions having the real numbers rather than the natural numbers for their domain.

For continuous exponential growth, the equation $u_i = ar^i$, where $i \in \mathbb{N}$, is replaced by

$$f(x) = ab^x, \quad \text{where } x \in \mathbb{R} \text{ and } x > 0.$$

In this equation a stands for the initial value when $x = 0$, and b is a constant which indicates how fast the quantity is growing. (The idea of a 'common ratio' no longer applies in the continuous case, so a different letter is used.) In many applications the variable x represents time. The graph of $f(x)$ is shown in Fig. 10.10.

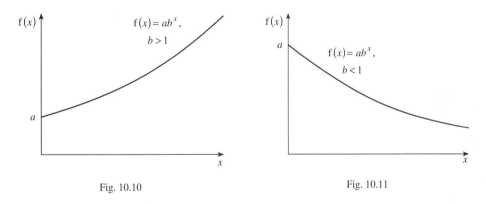

Fig. 10.10   Fig. 10.11

For exponential growth b has to be greater than 1. If $0 < b < 1$ the graph takes the form of Fig. 10.11; for large values of x the graph gets closer to the x-axis but never reaches it. This then represents exponential decay. Examples of this are the amount of radioactive uranium in a lump of ore, and the concentration of an antibiotic in the blood stream.

Example 10.5.1

The population of the USA grew exponentially from the end of the War of Independence until the Civil War. It increased from 3.9 million at the 1790 census to 31.4 million in 1860. What would the population have been in 1990 if it had continued to grow at this rate?

If the population x years after 1790 is P million, and if the growth were exactly exponential, then P and x would be related by an equation of the form

$$P = 3.9b^x,$$

where $P = 31.4$ when $x = 70$. The constant b therefore satisfies the equation

$$31.4 = 3.9b^{70}, \text{ so } b = \left(\frac{31.4}{3.9}\right)^{\frac{1}{70}} = 1.030....$$

At this rate the population in 1990 would have grown to about $3.9 \times 1.030...^{200}$ million, which is between 1.5 and 1.6 billion.

You can shorten this calculation as follows. In 70 years, the population multiplied by $\frac{31.4}{3.9}$. In 200 years, it therefore multiplied by $\left(\frac{31.4}{3.9}\right)^{\frac{200}{70}}$. The 1990 population can then be calculated as $3.9 \times \left(\frac{31.4}{3.9}\right)^{\frac{200}{70}}$ million, without working out b as an intermediate step.

Example 10.5.2

Carbon dating in archaeology is based on the decay of the isotope carbon-14, which has a half-life of 5715 years. By what percentage does carbon-14 decay in 100 years?

The half-life of a radioactive isotope is the time it would take half of any sample of the isotope to decay. After t years one unit of carbon-14 is reduced to b^t units, where

$$b^{5715} = 0.5 \qquad \text{(since 0.5 units are left after 5715 years)}$$

so $b = 0.5^{\frac{1}{5715}} = 0.999\,878\,721$.

When $t = 100$ the quantity left is $b^{100} \approx 0.988$ units, a reduction of 0.012 units, or 1.2%.

10.6* Transformations of the growth graph

The sum of a geometric series was found in Section 10.2 by multiplying each term by r. The effect of this was to produce a new series, which ran from the second term to the $(n+1)$th term of the original series. That is, the multiplication simply pushed the sequence along by one term.

A similar result holds for continuous exponential growth or decay. Fig. 10.12 shows part of the graph of $y = ab^x$ over an interval $p < x < q$. If you apply a translation of k in the x-direction to any graph $y = f(x)$, the equation of the translated graph is $y = f(x - k)$. In this case, the equation is

$$y = ab^{x-k},$$

and you can use the laws of indices to write this as

$$y = ab^{x-k} = \left(ab^{-k}\right)b^x.$$

The translated graph covers the interval $p + k < x < q + k$.

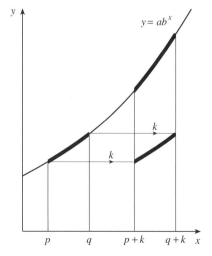

Fig. 10.12

If you now apply a stretch of factor b^k in the y-direction, you get a graph with equation

$$y = b^k \left(ab^{-k}\right)b^x = ab^{k-k}b^x = ab^x.$$

So the combination of the translation and the stretch takes the graph back to itself, but over the interval $p + k < x < q + k$ rather than $p < x < q$. This means that there is a special uniformity about the exponential growth function. If you are given a part of its graph, you can construct the whole graph by means of translations and stretches.

Exercise 10C

1 Trudy puts £500 into a building society account on the first day of January each year from 2000 to 2010 inclusive. The account pays interest at 5% for each complete year of investment. How much money will there be in the account on 1 January 2010?

2 Jayesh invests £100 in a building society on the first day of each month for one complete year. The account pays interest at $\frac{1}{2}$% for each complete month. How much does Jayesh have invested at the end of the year (but before making a thirteenth payment)?

3 Charles borrows £6000 for a new car. Compound interest is charged on the loan at a rate of 2% per month. Charles has to pay off the loan with 24 equal monthly payments. Calculate the value of each monthly payment.

4 Brenda invests £100 per month for a complete year, with interest added every month at the rate of $\frac{1}{2}$% per month at the end of the month. How much would she have had to invest at the beginning of the year to have the same total amount after the complete year?

5 Janet takes out a 25 year mortgage of £40,000 to buy her house. Compound interest is charged on the loan at a rate of 8% per annum. She has to pay off the mortgage with 25 equal payments, the first of which is to be one year after the loan is taken out. Continue the following argument to calculate the value of each annual payment.

   •   After 1 year she owes $£\left(40\,000 \times 1.08\right)$ (loan plus interest) less the payment. made $£P$, that is, she owes $£\left(40\,000 \times 1.08 - P\right)$.
   •   After 2 years she owes $£\left(\left(40\,000 \times 1.08 - P\right) \times 1.08 - P\right)$.
   •   After 3 years she owes $£\left(\left(\left(40\,000 \times 1.08 - P\right) \times 1.08 - P\right) \times 1.08 - P\right)$.

   At the end of the 25 years this (continued) expression must be zero. Form an equation in P and solve it.

6 The population of Camford is increasing at a rate of 6% each year. On 1 January 1990 it was $35\,200$. What was its population on

   (a) 1 January 2000,   (b) 1 July 1990,   (c) 1 January 1980?

7 The population of the United Kingdom in 1971 was 5.5615×10^7; by 1992 it was estimated to be 5.7384×10^7. Assuming a steady exponential growth estimate the population in

   (a) 2003,   (b) 1981.

8 The population of Blighton is decreasing steadily at a rate of 4% each year. The population in 1998 was $21\,000$. Estimate the population in

    (a) 2002,   (b) 1990.

9 A man of mass 90 kg plans to diet and to reduce his mass to 72 kg in four weeks by a constant percentage reduction each day.

    (a) What should his mass be 1 week after starting his diet?

    (b) He forgets to stop after 4 weeks. Estimate his mass 1 week later.

10 A savings account is opened with a single payment of £2000. It attracts compound interest at a constant rate of 0.5% per month.

    (a) Find the amount in the account after two complete years.

    (b) Find, by trial, after how many months the value of the investment will have doubled.

11 A radioactive substance decays at a rate of 12% per hour.

    (a) Find, by trial, after how many hours half of the radioactive material will be left.

    (b) How many hours earlier did it have twice the current amount of radioactive material?

12 The Bank of Utopia offers an interest rate of 100% per annum with various options as to how the interest may be added. Gordon invests £1000 and considers the following options.

Option A   Interest added annually at the end of the year.

Option B   Interest of 50% credited at the end of each half-year.

Option C, D, E, ...   The Bank is willing to add interest as often as required, subject to (interest rate) $\times$ (number of credits per year) $= 100$.

Investigate to find the maximum possible amount in Gordon's account after one year.

13 The points P and Q on the graph of $y = 3 \times 2^x$ have x-coordinates 3 and 4 respectively.

    (a) The images of P and Q after a translation of 5 units in the x-direction are P' and Q'. Write down the coordinates of P' and Q'.

    P'' and Q'' are the images of P' and Q' after a stretch of factor 2^5 in the y-direction.

    (b) Find the coordinates of P'' and Q''.

    (c) Show that P'' and Q'' both lie on the graph of $y = 3 \times 2^x$.

Miscellaneous exercise 10

1 In a geometric progression, the fifth term is 100 and the seventh term is 400. Find the first term.

2 A geometric series has first term a and common ratio $\dfrac{1}{\sqrt{2}}$. Show that the sum to infinity of the series is $a\left(2 + \sqrt{2}\right)$.   (Hint: $\left(\sqrt{2} - 1\right)\left(\sqrt{2} + 1\right) = 1$.)

3 The nth term of a sequence is ar^{n-1}, where a and r are constants. The first term is 3 and the second term is $-\frac{3}{4}$. Find the values of a and r.

Hence find the sum of the first n terms of the sequence.

4   Evaluate, correct to the nearest whole number,

$$0.99 + 0.99^2 + 0.99^3 + \ldots + 0.99^{99}.$$

5   Find the sum of the infinite series $\dfrac{1}{10^3} + \dfrac{1}{10^6} + \dfrac{1}{10^9} + \ldots$, expressing your answer as a fraction in its lowest terms.

Hence express the infinite recurring decimal $0.108\,108\,108\ldots$ as a fraction in its lowest terms.

6   A geometric series has first term 1 and common ratio r. Given that the sum to infinity of the series is 5, find the value of r.

Find the least value of n for which the sum of the first n terms of the series exceeds 4.9.

7   In a geometric series, the first term is 12 and the fourth term is $-\frac{3}{2}$. Find the sum, S_n, of the first n terms of the series.

Find the sum to infinity, S_∞, of the series and the least value of n for which the magnitude of the difference between S_n and S_∞ is less than 0.001.

8   A geometric series has non-zero first term a and common ratio r, where $0 < r < 1$. Given that the sum of the first 8 terms of the series is equal to half the sum to infinity, find the value of r, correct to 3 decimal places. Given also that the 17th term of the series is 10, find a.

9   An athlete plans a training schedule which involves running 20 km in the first week of training; in each subsequent week the distance is to be increased by 10% over the previous week. Write down an expression for the distance to be covered in the nth week according to this schedule, and find in which week the athlete would first cover more than 100 km.

10 At the beginning of 1990, an investor decided to invest £6000 in a Personal Equity Plan (PEP), believing that the value of the investment should increase, on average, by 6% each year. Show that, if this percentage rate of increase was in fact maintained for 10 years, the value of the investment will be about £10,745.

The investor added a further £6000 to the PEP at the beginning of each year between 1991 and 1995 inclusive. Assuming that the 6% annual rate of increase continues to apply, show that the total value, in £, of the PEP at the beginning of the year 2000 may be written as $6000(1.06^5 + 1.06^6 + \ldots + 1.06^{10})$ and evaluate this, correct to the nearest £.

11 A post is being driven into the ground by a mechanical hammer. The distance it is driven by the first blow is 8 cm. Subsequently, the distance it is driven by each blow is $\frac{9}{10}$ of the distance it was driven by the previous blow.

(a) The post is to be driven a total distance of at least 70 cm into the ground. Find the smallest number of blows needed.

(b) Explain why the post can never be driven a total distance of more than 80 cm into the ground.

12 When a table-tennis ball is dropped vertically on to a table, the time interval between any particular bounce and the next bounce is 90% of the time interval between that particular bounce and the preceding bounce. The interval between the first and second bounces is 2 seconds. Given that the interval between the nth bounce and the $(n+1)$th bounce is the first such interval less than 0.02 seconds, find n. Also find the total time from the first bounce to the nth bounce, giving three significant figures in your answer.

13 A £100 investment in the 41st Issue of National Savings Certificates is worth £130.08 after 5 years. Is the Department for National Savings justified in saying that the investment grows at an annual rate of 5.4%? Carry out an appropriate calculation to justify your answer.   (OCR)

14 A geometric series G has positive first term a, common ratio r and sum to infinity S. The sum to infinity of the even-numbered terms of G (the second, fourth, sixth, … terms) is $-\frac{1}{2}S$. Find the value of r.

(a) Given that the third term of G is 2, show that the sum to infinity of the odd-numbered terms of G (the first, third, fifth, … terms) is $\frac{81}{4}$.

(b) In another geometric series H, each term is the modulus of the corresponding term of G. Show that the sum to infinity of H is $2S$.

15 An infinite geometric series has first term a and sum to infinity b, where $b \neq 0$. Prove that a lies between 0 and $2b$.

16 The sum of the infinite geometric series $1 + r + r^2 + \dots$ is k times the sum of the series $1 - r + r^2 - \dots$, where $k > 0$. Express r in terms of k.

11 Exponential and logarithmic functions

This chapter investigates more closely the function b^x which appears in the equation for exponential growth, and its inverse $\log_b x$. When you have completed it, you should

- know the principal features of exponential functions and their graphs
- know the definition and properties of logarithmic functions
- be able to switch between the exponential and logarithmic forms of an equation
- understand the idea and possible uses of a logarithmic scale
- be familiar with logarithms to the special bases e and 10, and the relation between them
- be able to solve equations and inequalities with the unknown in the index.

11.1 Exponential functions

In the equation $y = ab^x$ for exponential growth the constant a simply sets a scale on the y-axis. The essential features of the relationship can be studied in the function

$$f(x) = b^x, \text{ where } x \in \mathbb{R}.$$

A function of this form is called an **exponential function**, because the variable x appears in the exponent (another word for the index).

This definition needs some points of explanation. First, note that it makes sense only if b is positive. To see this, note that, for some values of x, b^x has no meaning for negative b; for example, $b^{\frac{1}{2}} = \sqrt{b}$. Secondly, if $b = 1$, b^x has the constant value 1. So the definition of an exponential function applies only if $b > 0$, $b \neq 1$. With this restriction, the values of b^x are always positive.

However, there is no need to restrict x to positive values. Since $b^0 = 1$, the graphs of all exponential functions contain the point $(0,1)$. Notice also that

$$b^{-x} = \frac{1}{b^x} = \left(\frac{1}{b}\right)^x.$$

Therefore if b^x is greater than 1 then b^{-x} lies between 0 and 1. A further consequence of this relationship is that the reflection in the y-axis of the graph of $y = b^x$ is $y = \left(\frac{1}{b}\right)^x$.

These points are illustrated in Fig. 11.1, which shows the graph of exponential functions for several values of b. Note that the functions are increasing if $b > 1$, and decreasing if $0 < b < 1$.

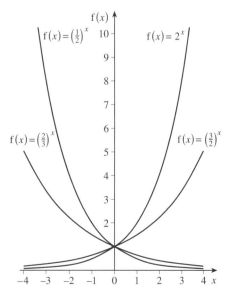

Fig. 11.1

Lastly, you should notice that up to now the expression b^x has only been defined when x is a positive or negative fraction (that is, x is rational). So the definition has to be extended to all of $\mathbb{R}$ by filling in the gaps where x is irrational.

As an example, suppose that you want to give a meaning to 2^π. Now π is an irrational number ($3.141\,592\,65\ldots$), but you can find pairs of rational numbers very close together such that π lies between them. For example, since $3.141\,592\,6 < \pi < 3.141\,592\,7$, 2^π ought to lie between $2^{\frac{31415926}{10000000}}$ and $2^{\frac{31415927}{10000000}}$, that is between $8.824\,977\,499\ldots$ and $8.824\,978\,11\ldots$; so $2^\pi = 8.824\,98$ correct to 5 decimal places. If you want to find 2^π to a greater degree of accuracy, you can sandwich π between a pair of rational numbers which are even closer together.

You could, if you wished, define 2^π as the limit, as n tends to infinity, of a sequence 2^{u_r}, where u_r is a sequence of numbers which tends to π. It can be proved that this definition is unique, and that values of 2^x defined in this way obey the rules for working with indices given in P1 Section 7.1.

11.2 Logarithmic functions

The graphs in Fig. 11.1 show that the exponential function $x \mapsto b^x$ has for its natural domain the set of all real numbers, and the corresponding range is the positive real numbers. The function is increasing if $b > 1$, and decreasing if $b < 1$; in either case it is one–one.

It follows that this function has an inverse whose domain is the set of positive real numbers and whose range is all real numbers. This inverse function is called the **logarithm to base b**, and is denoted by $\log_b$.

$$y = b^x \iff x = \log_b y, \text{ where } x \in \mathbb{R},\ y \in \mathbb{R},\ y > 0.$$

To draw the graph of $y = \log_b x$ you can use the general result proved in Section 2.7, that the graphs of $y = f(x)$ and $y = f^{-1}(x)$ are reflections of each other in the line $y = x$. This is illustrated in Fig. 11.2, which shows graphs of $y = b^x$ and $y = \log_b x$ using the same axes.

The figure is drawn for $b = 3$, and it is typical of the graphs for any base $b > 1$. The definition of $\log_b$ is still valid if $0 < b < 1$, in which case the graphs have a different form; but this is not important, since in practice logarithms are rarely used with bases less than 1.

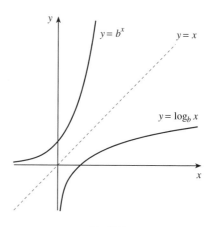

Fig. 11.2

Notice that, since the point $(0,1)$ lies on $y = b^x$, its reflection $(1,0)$ lies on $y = \log_b x$ for every base b. That is:

$\log_b 1 = 0$.

Other points on $y = b^x$ are $(1, b)$, $\left(2, b^2\right)$ and $\left(-1, \dfrac{1}{b}\right)$, so that other points on $y = \log_b x$ are $(b, 1)$, $\left(b^2, 2\right)$ and $\left(\dfrac{1}{b}, -1\right)$. That is,

$$\log_b(b) = 1, \quad \log_b\left(b^2\right) = 2 \quad \text{and} \quad \log_b\left(\dfrac{1}{b}\right) = -1.$$

These are important special cases of:

For any n, $\log_b b^n = n$.

This is simply an application of the general result given in Section 2.5, that $f^{-1}f$ is the identity function. With $f : x \mapsto b^x$ and $f^{-1} : x \mapsto \log_b x$, it follows that

$f^{-1}f : x \mapsto \log_b b^x$ is the identity function.

Example 11.2.1
Find (a) $\log_3 81$, (b) $\log_{81} 3$, (c) $\log_3\left(\dfrac{1}{81}\right)$, (d) $\log_{\frac{1}{3}} 81$.

(a) Since $81 = 3^4$, $\log_3 81 = 4$.

(b) $3 = 81^{\frac{1}{4}}$, so $\log_{81} 3 = \frac{1}{4}$.

(c) $\frac{1}{81} = 3^{-4}$, so $\log_3\left(\dfrac{1}{81}\right) = -4$.

(d) $81 = \dfrac{1}{(1/3)^4} = \left(\frac{1}{3}\right)^{-4}$, so $\log_{\frac{1}{3}} 81 = -4$.

11.3 Properties of logarithms

It was shown in P1 Section 7.1 that expressions involving indices could be simplified by applying a number of rules, including the multiplication and division rules, and the power-on-power rule. There are corresponding rules for logarithms, which can be deduced from the index rules by using the equivalence

$$\log_b x = y \quad \Leftrightarrow \quad x = b^y.$$

In listing these rules, which hold for logarithms to any base b, the notation $\log_b x$ has been simplified to $\log x$.

The power rule:	$\log x^n = n \log x$
The nth root rule:	$\log \sqrt[n]{x} = \dfrac{1}{n} \log x$
The multiplication rule:	$\log(pq) = \log p + \log q$
The division rule:	$\log\left(\dfrac{p}{q}\right) = \log p - \log q$

You can write out the proofs concisely by using the implies sign ($\Rightarrow$).

The power rule

$$\log x = r \ \Rightarrow \ x = b^r \ \Rightarrow \ x^n = \left(b^r\right)^n \ \Rightarrow \ x^n = b^{rn}$$

$$\Rightarrow \ \log x^n = rn = n \log x.$$

In this proof n can be any real number. The rule is often used with integer n, but this is not necessary.

The nth root rule

This is the same as the power rule, since the nth root of x is $x^{\frac{1}{n}}$.

The multiplication rule

$$\log p = r \text{ and } \log q = s \ \Rightarrow \ p = b^r \text{ and } q = b^s$$

$$\Rightarrow \ pq = b^r b^s = b^{r+s}$$

$$\Rightarrow \ \log(pq) = r + s = \log p + \log q.$$

The division rule

The proof is the same as for the multiplication rule, but with division in place of multiplication and subtraction in place of addition.

Example 11.3.1

If $\log 2 = r$ and $\log 3 = s$, express in terms of r and s (a) $\log 16$,   (b) $\log 18$,   (c) $\log 13.5$.

(a) $\log 16 = \log 2^4 = 4 \log 2 = 4r$.

(b) $\log 18 = \log\left(2 \times 3^2\right) = \log 2 + \log 3^2 = \log 2 + 2 \log 3 = r + 2s$.

(c) $\log 13.5 = \log \dfrac{3^3}{2} = \log 3^3 - \log 2 = 3 \log 3 - \log 2 = 3s - r$.

Example 11.3.2

Find the connection between $\log_b c$ and $\log_c b$.

$$\log_b c = x \ \Leftrightarrow \ c = b^x \ \Leftrightarrow \ c^{\frac{1}{x}} = \left(b^x\right)^{\frac{1}{x}} = b^1 \ \Leftrightarrow \ b = c^{\frac{1}{x}} \ \Leftrightarrow \ \log_c b = \frac{1}{x}.$$

Therefore $\log_c b = \dfrac{1}{\log_b c}$.

Historically logarithms were important because for many years, before calculators and computers were available, they provided the most useful form of calculating aid. With a table of logarithms students would, for example, find the cube root of 100 by looking up the value of $\log 100$ and dividing it by 3. By the nth root rule, this gave $\log \sqrt[3]{100}$, and the cube root could then be obtained from a table of the inverse function.

You could simulate this process on your calculator by keying in $[100, \log, \div, 3, =, 10^x]$, giving successive displays 100, 2, $0.666\,666\,6\ldots$ and the answer $4.641\,588\,83\ldots$ But of course you don't need to do this, since you have a special key for working out roots directly.

Exercise 11A

1 Write each of the following in the form $y = b^x$.

   (a) $\log_2 8 = 3$ (b) $\log_3 81 = 4$ (c) $\log_5 0.04 = -2$

   (d) $\log_7 x = 4$ (e) $\log_x 5 = t$ (f) $\log_p q = r$

2 Write each of the following in the form $x = \log_b y$.

   (a) $2^3 = 8$ (b) $3^6 = 729$ (c) $4^{-3} = \frac{1}{64}$

   (d) $a^8 = 20$ (e) $h^9 = g$ (f) $m^n = p$

3 Evaluate the following.

   (a) $\log_2 16$ (b) $\log_4 16$ (c) $\log_7 \frac{1}{49}$

   (d) $\log_4 1$ (e) $\log_5 5$ (f) $\log_{27} \frac{1}{3}$

   (g) $\log_{16} 8$ (h) $\log_2 2\sqrt{2}$ (i) $\log_{\sqrt{2}} 8\sqrt{2}$

4 Find the value of y in each of the following.

   (a) $\log_y 49 = 2$ (b) $\log_4 y = -3$ (c) $\log_3 81 = y$

   (d) $\log_{10} y = -1$ (e) $\log_2 y = 2.5$ (f) $\log_y 1296 = 4$

   (g) $\log_{\frac{1}{2}} y = 8$ (h) $\log_{\frac{1}{2}} 1024 = y$ (i) $\log_y 27 = -6$

5 Write each of the following in terms of $\log p$, $\log q$ and $\log r$. The logarithms have base 10.

   (a) $\log pqr$ (b) $\log pq^2 r^3$ (c) $\log 100 pr^5$

   (d) $\log \sqrt{\dfrac{p}{q^2 r}}$ (e) $\log \dfrac{pq}{r^2}$ (f) $\log \dfrac{1}{pqr}$

   (g) $\log \dfrac{p}{\sqrt{r}}$ (h) $\log \dfrac{qr^7 p}{10}$ (i) $\log \sqrt{\dfrac{10 p^{10} r}{q}}$

6 Express as a single logarithm, simplifying where possible. (All the logarithms are to base 10, so, for example, an answer of $\log 100$ simplifies to 2.)

   (a) $2\log 5 + \log 4$ (b) $2\log 2 + \log 150 - \log 6000$

   (c) $3\log 5 + 5\log 3$ (d) $2\log 4 - 4\log 2$

   (e) $\log 24 - \frac{1}{2}\log 9 + \log 125$ (f) $3\log 2 + 3\log 5 - \log 10^6$

   (g) $\frac{1}{2}\log 16 + \frac{1}{3}\log 8$ (h) $\log 64 - 2\log 4 + 5\log 2 - \log 2^7$

7 If $\log 3 = p$, $\log 5 = q$ and $\log 10 = r$, express the following in terms of p, q and r. (All the logarithms are to the same unspecified base.)

(a) $\log 2$ (b) $\log 45$ (c) $\log \sqrt{90}$

(d) $\log 0.2$ (e) $\log 750$ (f) $\log 60$

(g) $\log \frac{1}{6}$ (h) $\log 4.05$ (i) $\log 0.15$

11.4 Special bases

Although the base of the logarithm function can be any real positive number except 1, in practice only two bases are in common use. One is a number denoted by e, for which the logarithm function has a number of special properties; these are explored in the next chapter. Values of this function can be found using the key on your calculator labelled [LN].

The other base is 10, which is important because our system of writing numbers is based on powers of 10. On your calculator the key labelled [LOG] gives logarithms to base 10. In Sections 11.4 to 11.6 the symbol $\log$, with no base specified, will stand for $\log_{10}$.

When logarithms were used to do calculations, the table gave $\log x$ only for values of x between 1 and 10. So to find $\log 3456$, you would use the rules in Section 11.3 to write

$$\log 3456 = \log(3.456 \times 10^3) = \log 3.456 + \log 10^3 = \log 3.456 + 3.$$

The tables gave $\log 3.456$ as 0.5386 (correct to 4 decimal places), so $\log 3456$ is 3.5386. Notice that the number 3 before the decimal point is the same as the index when 3456 is written in standard form.

Logarithms to base 10 are sometimes useful in constructing logarithmic scales. As an example, suppose that you want to make a diagram to show the populations of countries which belong to the United Nations. In 1999 the largest of these was China, with about 1.2 billion people, and the smallest was San Marino, with 25 000. If you represented the population of China by a line of length 12 cm, then the USA would have length 2.6 cm, the UK just under 6 mm, and the line for San Marino would be only 0.0025 mm long!

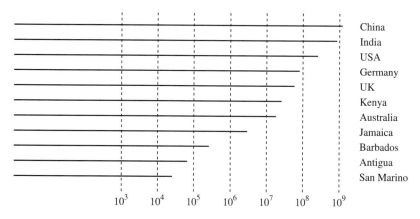

Fig. 11.3

Fig. 11.3 is an alternative way of showing the data, in which a country with population P is shown by a line of length $\log P$ cm. China now has a length of just over 9 cm, and San Marino a length of between 4 and 5 cm. You have to understand the diagram in a different way; an extra cm in length implies a population 10 times as large, rather than 100 million larger. But the countries are still placed in the correct order, and the population of any country can be found as 10^x where x is the length of its line in centimetres.

11.5 Equations and inequalities

You know that $\log_2 2 = 1$ and $\log_2 4 = 2$, but how can you find $\log_2 3$?

Suppose that $\log_2 3 = x$. Then from the definition,

$$2^x = 3.$$

So the problem is to solve an equation where the unknown appears in the index. The trick is to use logarithms and to write the equation as

$$\log 2^x = \log 3.$$

This is often described as 'taking logarithms of both sides of the equation'. You can now use the power rule to write this as

$$x \log 2 = \log 3.$$

Using the 'log' key on the calculator, this is

$$x \times 0.301\ldots \approx 0.477\ldots,$$

which gives $x = \log_2 3 = \dfrac{0.477\ldots}{0.301\ldots} = 1.58$, correct to 3 significant figures.

This type of equation arises in various applications.

Example 11.5.1

Iodine-131 is a radioactive isotope used in treatment of the thyroid gland. It decays so that, after t days, 1 unit of the isotope is reduced to 0.9174^t units. How many days does it take for the amount to fall to less than 0.1 units?

This requires solution of the inequality $0.9174^t < 0.1$. Since $\log$ is an increasing function, taking logarithms gives

$$\log\!\left(0.9174^t\right) < \log 0.1 \quad \Rightarrow \quad t \log 0.9174 < \log 0.1.$$

Now beware! The value of $\log 0.9174$ is negative, so that when you divide both sides by $\log 0.9174$ you must change the direction of the inequality:

$$t > \frac{\log 0.1}{\log 0.9174} = 26.708\ldots$$

The amount of iodine-131 will fall to less than 0.1 units after about 26.7 days.

Example 11.5.2

How many terms of the geometric series $1 + 1.01 + 1.01^2 + 1.01^3 + \ldots$ must be taken to give a sum greater than 1 million?

The sum of n terms of the series is given by the formula

$$\frac{1.01^n - 1}{1.01 - 1} = 100(1.01^n - 1).$$

The problem is to find the smallest value of n for which

$$\frac{1.01^n - 1}{1.01 - 1} = 100(1.01^n - 1) > 1\,000\,000, \text{ which gives } 1.01^n > 10\,001.$$

Taking logarithms of both sides,

$$\log 1.01^n > \log 10\,001, \text{ so } n \log 1.01 > \log 10\,001.$$

Since $\log 1.01$ is positive,

$$n > \frac{\log 10\,001}{\log 1.01} = 925.6\ldots.$$

The smallest integer n satisfying this inequality is 926.

11.6 Graphs of exponential growth

The technique of taking logarithms is often useful when you are dealing with economic, social or scientific data which you think might exhibit exponential growth or decay.

Suppose that a quantity y is growing exponentially, so that its value at time t is given by

$$y = ab^t,$$

where a and b are constants. Taking logarithms of both sides of this equation,

$$\log y = \log(ab^t) = \log a + \log b^t = \log a + t \log b.$$

The expression on the right increases linearly with t. So if $\log y$ is plotted against t, the graph would be a straight line with gradient $\log b$ and intercept $\log a$.

Example 11.6.1

If $\log y = 0.322 - 0.531t$, express y in terms of t.

Equating the right side to $\log a + t \log b$, $\log a = 0.322$ and $\log b = -0.531$. So $a = 10^{0.322} = 2.10$ and $b = 10^{-0.531} = 0.294$ (both to 3 significant figures). The equation for y is therefore

$$y = 2.10 \times 0.294^t.$$

An alternative way of writing this calculation is based on the property that if $\log y = x$ then $y = 10^x$, so $y = 10^{\log y}$. Therefore

$$y = 10^{\log y} = 10^{0.322 - 0.531t} = 10^{0.322} \times \left(10^{-0.531}\right)^t = 2.10 \times 0.294^t.$$

Example 11.6.2

An investment company claims that the price of its shares has grown exponentially over the past six years, and supports its claim with Fig. 11.4. Is this claim justified?

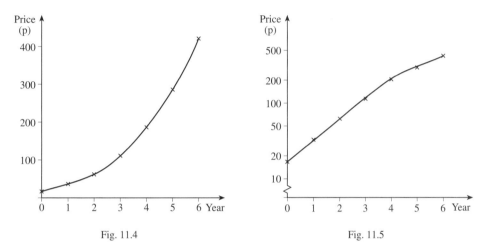

Fig. 11.4   Fig. 11.5

If the graph is drawn with the price shown on a logarithmic scale, you get Fig. 11.5. If the claim were true, this graph should be a straight line. This seems approximately true for the first three years, but more recently the graph has begun to bend downwards, suggesting that the early promise of exponential growth has not been sustained.

11.7* A relation between logarithmic functions

The equation $2^x = 3$ in Section 11.5 was solved using logarithms to base 10, but the steps leading to

$$x = \frac{\log_b 3}{\log_b 2}$$

could have been made with any base b. For example, you could choose base e, using the $\ln$ key on the calculator to give

$$x = \frac{\ln 3}{\ln 2} = \frac{1.098...}{0.693...} = 1.58, \text{ correct to 3 significant figures.}$$

The answer is the same, because logarithms to different bases are proportional to each other. If b and c are two different bases, then $\log_c x$ is a constant multiple of $\log_b x$ as x varies.

To prove this, let $\log_b x = y$. Then

$$\log_b x = y \iff x = b^y \iff \log_c x = \log_c b^y$$
$$\iff \log_c x = y \log_c b \qquad \text{by the power rule}$$
$$\iff \log_c x = \log_b x \log_c b.$$

So to get $\log_c x$ from $\log_b x$ you simply multiply by the constant $\log_c b$. From Example 11.3.2, $\log_c b$ is equal to $\dfrac{1}{\log_b c}$, so you can write the rule in the alternative form

$$\log_c x = \frac{\log_b x}{\log_b c}.$$

If b and c are taken as e and 10 respectively, then

$$\log_{10} x = \frac{\ln x}{\ln 10}.$$

This explains why $\dfrac{\ln 3}{\ln 2}$ and $\dfrac{\log_{10} 3}{\log_{10} 2}$ give the same answer for the value of $\log_2 3$.

Fig. 11.6 gives the graphs of $y = \log_{10} x$ and $y = \ln x$. The equation

$$\ln x = \ln 10 \times \log_{10} x$$

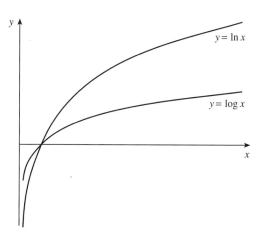

Fig. 11.6

shows that you can obtain the $\ln x$ graph from $\log_{10} x$ by a stretch of factor $\ln 10 = 2.303\,585\,8\ldots$ in the y-direction. More generally, the graph of $\log_c x$ can be obtained from $\log_b x$ by a stretch of factor $\log_c b$.

So all logarithmic functions are essentially the same apart from a scale factor.

Exercise 11B

1 Solve the following equations, giving your answers correct to 3 significant figures.

(a) $3^x = 5$

(b) $7^x = 21$

(c) $6^{2x} = 60$

(d) $5^{2x-1} = 10$

(e) $4^{\frac{1}{2}x} = 12$

(f) $2^{x+1} = 3^x$

(g) $\left(\frac{1}{2}\right)^{3x+2} = 25$

(h) $2^x \times 2^{x+1} = 128$

(i) $\left(\frac{1}{4}\right)^{2x-1} = 7$

2 Solve the following inequalities, giving your answers correct to 3 significant figures.

(a) $3^x > 8$

(b) $5^x < 10$

(c) $7^{2x+5} \leqslant 24$

(d) $0.5^x < 0.001$

(e) $0.4^x < 0.0004$

(f) $0.2^x > 25$

(g) $4^x \times 4^{3-2x} \leqslant 1024$

(h) $0.8^{2x+5} \geqslant 4$

(i) $0.8^{1-3x} \geqslant 10$

3 How many terms of the geometric series $1+2+4+8+\dots$ must be taken for the sum to exceed 10^{11}?

4 How many terms of the geometric series $2+6+18+54+\dots$ must be taken for the sum to exceed 3 million?

5 How many terms of the geometric series $1+\frac{1}{2}+\frac{1}{4}+\frac{1}{8}+\dots$ must be taken for its sum to differ from 2 by less than 10^{-8}?

6 How many terms of the geometric series $2+\frac{1}{3}+\frac{1}{18}+\frac{1}{108}+\dots$ must be taken for its sum to differ from its sum to infinity by less than 10^{-5}?

7 A radioactive isotope decays so that after t days an amount 0.82^t units remains. How many days does it take for the amount to fall to less than 0.15 units?

8 To say that a radioactive isotope has a half-life of 6 days means that 1 unit of isotope is reduced to $\frac{1}{2}$ unit in 6 days. So if the daily decay rate is given by r, then $r^6 = 0.5$.

   (a) For this isotope, find r.

   (b) How long will it take for the amount to fall to 0.25 units?

   (c) How long will it take for the amount to fall to 0.1 units?

9 A biological culture contains 500 000 bacteria at 12 noon on Monday. The culture increases by 10% every hour. At what time will the culture exceed 4 million bacteria?

10 A dangerous radioactive substance has a half-life of 90 years. It will be deemed safe when its activity is down to 0.05 of its initial value. How long will it be before it is deemed safe?

11 Jack is saving for a new car which will cost £14,500. He saves by putting £200 a month into a savings account which gives 0.1% interest per month. After how many months will he be able to buy his car? Assume it does not increase in price!

12 Finding $\log_3 10$ is equivalent to solving the equation $x = \log_3 10$, which itself is equivalent to solving $3^x = 10$. Find the following logarithms by forming and solving the appropriate equation. Give your answers correct to 3 significant figures.

   (a) $\log_4 12$ (b) $\log_7 100$ (c) $\log_8 2.75$

   (d) $\log_{\frac{1}{2}} 250$ (e) $\log_3 \pi$ (f) $\log_{\frac{1}{4}} 0.04$

13 Find the following logarithms directly by using the formula $\log_c x = \dfrac{\log_b x}{\log_b c}$. Give your answers correct to 3 significant figures.

   (a) $\log_5 17$ (b) $\log_9 4.5$ (c) $\log_{0.5} 5$

14 (a) If $\log_{10} y = 0.4 + 0.6x$, express y in terms of x.

   (b) If $\log_{10} y = 12 - 3x$, express y in terms of x.

   (c) If $\log_{10} y = 0.7 + 1.7x$, express y in terms of x.

   (d) If $\log_{10} y = 0.7 + 2\log_{10} x$, express y in terms of x.

   (e) If $\log_{10} y = -0.5 - 5\log_{10} x$, express y in terms of x.

15 (a) If $y = ab^x$, express $\log y$ in terms of x. Show that in this case the graph of $\log y$ plotted against x will be a straight line and state its gradient and intercept.

(b) If $y = ax^b$, express $\log y$ in terms of $\log x$. Show that in this case the graph of $\log y$ plotted against $\log x$ will be a straight line and state its gradient and intercept.

In Questions 16 and 17 use either logarithmic graph paper or standard graph paper together with the results you have obtained in Question 15.

16 The table shows the mean relative distance X of some of the planets from the Earth and the time T years taken for one revolution round the sun. By drawing an appropriate graph show that there is an approximate law of the form $T = aX^n$, stating the values of a and n.

	Mercury	Venus	Earth	Mars	Saturn
X	0.39	0.72	1.00	1.52	9.54
T	0.24	0.62	1.00	1.88	29.5

17 Jack takes out a fixed rate savings bond. This means he makes one payment and leaves his money for a fixed number of years. The value of his bond, £B, is given by the formula $B = Ax^n$ where A is the original investment and n is the number of complete years since he opened the account. The table gives some values of B and n. By plotting a suitable graph find the initial value of Jack's investment and the rate of interest he is receiving.

n	2	3	4	5	6
B	982	1056	1220	1516	1752

Miscellaneous exercise 11

1 Solve each of the following equations to find x in terms of a where $a > 0$ and $a \neq 100$.

(a) $a^x = 10^{2x+1}$ (b) $2\log(2x) = 1 + \log a$ (OCR, adapted)

2 Solve the equation $3^{2x} = 4^{2-x}$, giving your answer to three significant figures.   (OCR)

3 The function f is given by $f : x \mapsto \log(1 + x)$, where $x \in \mathbb{R}$ and $x > -1$. Express the definition of f^{-1} in a similar form.   (OCR, adapted)

4 Find the root of the equation $10^{2-2x} = 2 \times 10^{-x}$ giving your answer exactly in terms of logarithms.   (OCR, adapted)

5 Given the simultaneous equations

$2^x = 3^y$,
$x + y = 1$,

show that $x = \dfrac{\log 3}{\log 6}$.   (OCR, adapted)

6   Express $\log\left(2\sqrt{10}\right) - \frac{1}{3}\log 0.8 - \log\left(\frac{10}{3}\right)$ in the form $c + \log d$ where c and d are rational numbers and the logarithms are to base 10. (OCR, adapted)

7* Prove that $\log_b a \times \log_c b \times \log_a c = 1$, where a, b and c are positive numbers.

8   Prove that $\log\left(\dfrac{p}{q}\right) + \log\left(\dfrac{q}{r}\right) + \log\left(\dfrac{r}{p}\right) = 0$.

9   If a, b and c are positive numbers in geometric progression, show that $\log a$, $\log b$ and $\log c$ are in arithmetic progression.

10* If $\log_r p = q$ and $\log_q r = p$, prove that $\log_q p = pq$.

11 Express $\log_2(x + 2) - \log_2 x$ as a single logarithm.
    Hence solve the equation $\log_2(x + 2) - \log_2 x = 3$.

12 The strength of a radioactive source is said to 'decay exponentially'. Explain briefly what is meant by exponential decay, and illustrate your answer by means of a sketch-graph.

    After t years the strength S of a particular radioactive source, in appropriate units, is given by $S = 10000 \times 3^{-0.0014t}$. State the value of S when $t = 0$, and find the value of t when the source has decayed to one-half of its initial strength, giving your answer correct to 3 significant figures. (OCR, adapted)

12 Differentiating exponentials and logarithms

This chapter deals with exponentials and logarithms as functions which can be differentiated and integrated. When you have completed it, you should

- understand how to find the derivative of b^x from the definition
- understand the reason for selecting e as the exponential base
- know the derivative and integral of e^x
- know the derivative of $\ln x$, and how to obtain it
- know the integral of $\dfrac{1}{x}$, and be able to use it for both positive and negative x
- be able to use the extended methods from Chapter 6 to broaden the range of such functions that you can differentiate and integrate.

12.1 Differentiating exponential functions

One of the characteristics of exponential growth is that a quantity increases at a rate proportional to its current value. For continuous exponential growth, this rate of growth is measured by the derivative.

It will be simplest to begin with a particular value $b = 2$, and to consider $f(x) = 2^x$.

To find the derivative of this function you can use the definition given in P1 Section 5.6,

$$f'(x) = \lim_{h \to 0} \frac{f(x+h) - f(x)}{h}.$$

For this function, as illustrated in Fig. 12.1,

$$f(x+h) - f(x) = 2^{x+h} - 2^x = 2^x 2^h - 2^x$$
$$= 2^x (2^h - 1).$$

So the definition becomes

$$f'(x) = \lim_{h \to 0} \frac{2^x (2^h - 1)}{h}.$$

Since 2^x does not involve h, you can write

$$f'(x) = 2^x \lim_{h \to 0} \frac{2^h - 1}{h}.$$

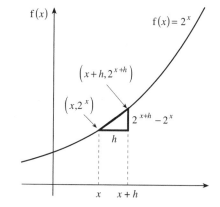

Fig. 12.1

This shows that $f'(x)$ is the product of two factors: 2^x, which is independent of h, and a limit expression which is independent of x.

This limit expression is in fact the gradient of the tangent at the point $(0,1)$. This is because $\dfrac{2^h - 1}{h}$ is the gradient of the chord joining $(0,1)$ to $(h, 2^h)$, and as h tends to 0 this chord tends to the tangent. So

$$f'(x) = 2^x \times \text{gradient of the tangent at } (0,1) = 2^x \times f'(0);$$

and since 2^x is $f(x)$, this can be written as

$$f'(x) = f(x) \times f'(0).$$

This confirms that the rate of growth of $f(x)$ is proportional to its current value.

The next step is to evaluate the limiting value $f'(0)$. You can do this by calculating $\dfrac{2^h - 1}{h}$ for some small values of h, and setting out the results as in Table 12.2.

h	1	0.1	0.01	0.001	0.000 1
$\dfrac{2^h - 1}{h}$	1	0.717 73	0.695 56	0.693 39	0.693 17

Table 12.2

These are the gradients of chords to the right of $(0,1)$, which you would expect to be greater than the gradient of the tangent. For chords to the left you can take h to be negative, as in Table 12.3.

h	-1	-0.1	-0.01	-0.001	$-0.000 1$
$\dfrac{2^h - 1}{h}$	0.5	0.669 67	0.690 75	0.692 91	0.693 12

Table 12.3

It follows that, for the function $f(x) = 2^x$, the derived function is

$$f'(x) = \text{constant} \times 2^x, \text{ where the constant is } f'(0) = 0.6931\ldots.$$

The method of finding the derivative for any other exponential function b^x is exactly the same. The only difference is that the numerical value of the constant $f'(0)$ is different for different values of the base b.

> For the general exponential function $f(x) = b^x$, where $b > 0$ and $b \neq 1$, the derived function is $f'(x) = \text{constant} \times b^x$, where the value of the constant, which depends on the base b, is equal to $f'(0)$.

Example 12.1.1
Show that, for any exponential function, the graph of $y = b^x$ bends upwards.

If $y = b^x$, $\dfrac{dy}{dx} = f'(0)b^x$ and $\dfrac{d^2y}{dx^2} = (f'(0))^2 b^x$. Since $b \neq 1$, $f'(0)$ is not zero, so $(f'(0))^2 > 0$. Also, for all x, $b^x > 0$.

Therefore $\dfrac{d^2 y}{dx^2} > 0$ for all x, so the graph bends upwards.

If you look back to Fig. 11.1, you can see that $f'(0)$ is positive for $b > 1$ and negative for $0 < b < 1$, but in either case the graph bends upwards throughout its length.

12.2 The number e

If you carry out the limit calculation $\displaystyle\lim_{h \to 0} \dfrac{b^h - 1}{h}$ for values of b other than 2, you get values for the constant $f'(0)$ like those in Table 12.4 below. Since the values of $f'(0)$ depend on b, they have been denoted by $L(b)$.

b	2	3	4	5	6	8	9	10
$L(b)$	0.693 1	1.098 6	1.386 3	1.609 4	1.791 8	2.079 4	2.197 2	2.302 6

Table 12.4

Before reading on, you should work out one or two of these for yourself. If you are working in a group, you could share the work and verify the whole table. It is also interesting to find $L(b)$ for a few values of b less than 1, such as 0.1, 0.2, 0.25 and 0.5. Look at the answers and keep a record of anything you notice for future reference.

None of these limits works out to a nice recognisable number; in fact they are all irrational numbers. But Table 12.4 shows that between 2 and 3 there should be a number for which $L(b)$ is 1. This is the number denoted by the letter e, and it turns out to be one of the most important numbers in mathematics.

You can find the value of e more precisely by decimal search. For example, the limit calculation shows that $L(2.71) = 0.9969\ldots$, which is too small, and $L(2.72) = 1.0006\ldots$, which is too large, so $2.71 < e < 2.72$. However, this is a rather tedious process, and you will find later on that there are far more efficient ways of calculating e to many decimal places.

Note that $L(e) = 1$, and that $L(b)$ is the symbol used for the constant $f'(0)$ in the statement

$$f(x) = b^x \quad \Rightarrow \quad f'(x) = f'(0)b^x.$$

This means that, if $f(x) = e^x$ then $f'(0) = 1$, so

$$f(x) = e^x \quad \Rightarrow \quad f'(x) = e^x.$$

It is this property that makes e^x so much more important than all the other exponential functions. It can be described as the 'natural' exponential function, but usually it is called 'the exponential function' (to distinguish it from b^x for any other value of b, which is simply 'an exponential function').

The function e^x is sometimes written as $\exp x$, so that the symbol 'exp' strictly stands for the function itself, rather than the output of the function. Thus, in formal function notation,

$$\exp : x \mapsto e^x.$$

For the (natural) exponential function e^x, or $\exp x$,

$$\frac{d}{dx} e^x = e^x.$$

Many calculators have a special key labelled [EXP] or $[e^x]$, for finding values of this function. If you want to know the numerical value of e, you can use this key with an input of 1, so that the output is $e^1 = e$. This gives $e = 2.718\,281\,828....$ (But do not assume that this is a recurring decimal; e is in fact an irrational number, and the single repetition of the digits 1828 is a curious accident.)

Example 12.2.1
Find the equations of the tangents to the graph $y = e^x$ at the points   (a) $(0,1)$,   (b) $(1,e)$.

(a) Since $\dfrac{dy}{dx} = e^x$, the gradient at $(0,1)$ is $e^0 = 1$. The equation of the tangent is therefore $y - 1 = 1(x - 0)$, which you can simplify to $y = x + 1$.

(b) The gradient at $(1,e)$ is $e^1 = e$. The equation of the tangent is
$y - e = e(x - 1)$, which you can simplify to $y = ex$.

It is interesting that the tangent at $(1,e)$ passes through the origin. You can demonstrate this nicely with a graphic calculator.

Example 12.2.2
Find   (a) $\dfrac{d}{dx}\left(e^{2x}\right)$,   (b) $\dfrac{d}{dx}\left(e^{-3x}\right)$,   (c) $\dfrac{d}{dx}\left(e^{2+x}\right)$.

These are all of the form $\dfrac{d}{dx}(f(ax + b))$, with $f(x) = e^x$. It was shown in

Section 6.1 that the derivative is $ag(ax + b)$, where $g(x) = f'(x)$. In this case
$g(x) = e^x$. The answers are therefore   (a) $2e^{2x}$,   (b) $-3e^{-3x}$,   (c) e^{2+x}.

For (c) you could write e^{2+x} as $e^2 e^x$. Since e^2 is constant, the derivative is $e^2 e^x$, or e^{2+x}.

Example 12.2.3
Find the area under the graph of $y = e^{2x}$ from $x = 0$ to $x = 1$.

$\displaystyle\int e^{2x}\,dx$ is of the form $\displaystyle\int g(ax + b)\,dx$, with $g(x) = e^x$. The indefinite integral

is therefore $\dfrac{1}{a} f(ax + b) + k$, where $f(x)$ is the simplest integral of $g(x)$. In this

case, $f(x) = e^x$, so that

$$\int e^{2x}\,dx = \tfrac{1}{2} e^{2x} + k.$$

The area under the graph is therefore $\displaystyle\int_0^1 e^{2x}\,dx = \left[\tfrac{1}{2}e^{2x}\right]_0^1 = \tfrac{1}{2}e^2 - \tfrac{1}{2}e^0 = \tfrac{1}{2}\left(e^2 - 1\right).$

<hr>

Exercise 12A

1 Differentiate each of the following functions with respect to x.

(a) e^{3x}

(b) e^{-x}

(c) $3e^{2x}$

(d) $-4e^{-4x}$

(e) e^{3x+4}

(f) e^{3-2x}

(g) e^{1-x}

(h) $3e \times e^{2+4x}$

2 Find, in terms of e, the gradients of the tangents to the following curves for the given values of x.

(a) $y = 3e^x$, where $x = 2$

(b) $y = 2e^{-x}$, where $x = -1$

(c) $y = x - e^{2x}$, where $x = 0$

(d) $y = e^{6-2x}$, where $x = 3$

3 Find the equations of the tangents to the given curves for the given values of x.

(a) $y = e^x$, where $x = -1$

(b) $y = 2x - e^{-x}$, where $x = 0$

(c) $y = x^2 + 2e^{2x}$, where $x = 2$

(d) $y = e^{-2x}$, where $x = \ln 2$

4 Find any stationary points of the graph of $y = 2 - e^x$, and determine whether they are maxima or minima.

5 Find the indefinite integrals of the following.

(a) $\displaystyle\int e^{3x}\,dx$

(b) $\displaystyle\int e^{-x}\,dx$

(c) $\displaystyle\int 3e^{2x}\,dx$

(d) $\displaystyle\int -4e^{-4x}\,dx$

(e) $\displaystyle\int e^{3x+4}\,dx$

(f) $\displaystyle\int e^{3-2x}\,dx$

(g) $\displaystyle\int e^{1-x}\,dx$

(h) $\displaystyle\int 3e \times e^{2+4x}\,dx$

6 Find the values of each of the following definite integrals in terms of e, or give their exact values.

(a) $\displaystyle\int_{1}^{2} e^{2x}\,dx$

(b) $\displaystyle\int_{-1}^{1} e^{-x}\,dx$

(c) $\displaystyle\int_{-2}^{0} 2e^{1-2x}\,dx$

(d) $\displaystyle\int_{4}^{5} 2e^{2x}\,dx$

(e) $\displaystyle\int_{\ln 3}^{\ln 9} e^x\,dx$

(f) $\displaystyle\int_{0}^{\ln 2} 2e^{1-2x}\,dx$

(g) $\displaystyle\int_{0}^{1} e^{x\ln 2}\,dx$

(h) $\displaystyle\int_{-3}^{9} e^{x\ln 3}\,dx$

7 Find the area bounded by the graph of $y = e^{2x}$, the axes and the line $x = 2$.

8 Find $\displaystyle\int_{0}^{N} e^{-x}\,dx$. Deduce the value of $\displaystyle\int_{0}^{\infty} e^{-x}\,dx$.

9 When you apply the trapezium rule with one interval to approximate the area under the graph of $y = e^x$ for $0 \leqslant x \leqslant 1$, would you expect to get an overestimate or an underestimate? Show that this approximation to the exact area leads to $e \approx 3$.

<hr>

12.3 The natural logarithm

The inverse function of the (natural) exponential function $\exp$ is the logarithmic function $\log_e$. You know from the last chapter that this is denoted by $\ln$. It is called the **natural logarithm**.

$y = e^x = \exp x \iff x = \log_e y = \ln y$ for $x \in \mathbb{R}$, $y \in \mathbb{R}$, $y > 0$.

$\ln 1 = 0$, $\ln e = 1$, $\ln e^n = n$ for any n.

The most important property of the natural logarithm is the derivative of $\ln x$. This can be deduced from the result $\dfrac{d}{dx} e^x = e^x$ in Section 12.2, but first we need a result from coordinate geometry.

Mini-theorem If a line with gradient m (where $m \neq 0$) is reflected in the line $y = x$, the gradient of the reflected line is $\dfrac{1}{m}$.

> **Proof** The proof is much like that of the perpendicular line property given in P1 Section 1.9. Fig. 12.5 shows the line of gradient m with a 'gradient triangle' ABC. Its reflection in $y = x$ is the triangle DEF. Completing the rectangle $DEFG$, DGF is a gradient triangle for the reflected line. $GF = DE = AB = 1$ and
>
> $DG = EF = BC = m$, so the gradient of the reflected line is $\dfrac{GF}{DG} = \dfrac{1}{m}$.

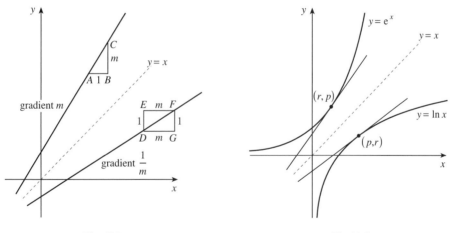

Fig. 12.5   Fig. 12.6

Now consider the graphs of $y = \ln x$ and $y = e^x$ in Fig. 12.6. Since these are graphs of inverse functions, they are reflections of each other in the line $y = x$. The reflection of the tangent at the point (p, r) on $y = \ln x$ is the tangent at the point (r, p) on $y = e^x$, where $p = e^r$.

Since $\dfrac{d}{dx} e^x = e^x$, the gradient of the tangent at (r, p) is $e^r = p$. It follows that the gradient of the tangent to $y = \ln x$ at (p, r) is $\dfrac{1}{p}$. Since this holds for any point (p, r) on $y = \ln x$, it follows that:

For $x > 0$, $\dfrac{d}{dx} \ln x = \dfrac{1}{x}$.

Example 12.3.1

Find the minimum value of the function $f(x) = 2x - \ln x$.

The natural domain of $f(x)$ is $x > 0$. Since $f'(x) = 2 - \dfrac{1}{x}$, $f'(x) = 0$ when $x = \tfrac{1}{2}$.

Also $f''(x) = \dfrac{1}{x^2}$, so $f''(\tfrac{1}{2}) = 4 > 0$. So the function has a minimum when $x = \tfrac{1}{2}$.

The minimum value is $f(\tfrac{1}{2}) = 1 - \ln \tfrac{1}{2}$. Since $\ln \tfrac{1}{2} = \ln 2^{-1} = -\ln 2$, it is simpler to write the minimum value as $1 + \ln 2$.

Unless you specifically need a numerical answer, it is better to leave it as $1 + \ln 2$, which is exact, than to use a calculator to convert it into decimal form.

Example 12.3.2

Find   (a) $\dfrac{d}{dx} \ln(3x + 1)$,   (b) $\dfrac{d}{dx} \ln 3x$,   (c) $\dfrac{d}{dx} \ln x^3$.

(a) This is of the form $f(ax + b)$, with $f(x) = \ln x$, so the derivative is

$$3 \times \frac{1}{3x + 1} = \frac{3}{3x + 1}.$$

(b) You have a choice of method. You can find the derivative as in (a), as $3 \times \dfrac{1}{3x} = \dfrac{1}{x}$. Or you can note that $\ln 3x = \ln 3 + \ln x$, so that $\dfrac{d}{dx} \ln 3x = \dfrac{d}{dx} \ln x = \dfrac{1}{x}$, since $\ln 3$ is constant.

(c) Begin by writing $\ln x^3$ as $3 \ln x$. Then $\dfrac{d}{dx} \ln x^3 = \dfrac{d}{dx}(3 \ln x) = 3 \times \dfrac{1}{x} = \dfrac{3}{x}$.

Exercise 12B

1 Differentiate each of the following functions with respect to x.

(a) $\ln 2x$ (b) $\ln(2x - 1)$ (c) $\ln(1 - 2x)$ (d) $\ln x^2$

(e) $\ln(a + bx)$ (f) $\ln \dfrac{1}{x}$ (g) $\ln \dfrac{1}{3x + 1}$ (h) $\ln \dfrac{2x + 1}{3x - 1}$

(i) $3 \ln x^{-2}$ (j) $\ln(x(x + 1))$ (k) $\ln(x^2(x - 1))$ (l) $\ln(x^2 + x - 2)$

2 Find the equations of the tangents to the following graphs for the given values of x.

(a) $y = \ln x$, where $x = \tfrac{1}{2}$ (b) $y = \ln 2x$, where $x = \tfrac{1}{2}$

(c) $y = \ln(-x)$, where $x = -\tfrac{1}{3}$ (d) $y = \ln 3x$, where $x = e$

3 Find any stationary values of the following curves and determine whether they are maxima or minima. Sketch the curves.

(a) $y = x - \ln x$ (b) $y = \tfrac{1}{2}x^2 - \ln 2x$

(c) $y = x^2 - \ln x^2$ (d) $y = x^n - \ln x^n$ for $n \geqslant 1$

4   Prove that the tangent at the point where $x = e$ to the curve with equation $y = \ln x$ passes through the origin.

5   Find the equation of the normal at $x = 2$ to the curve with equation $y = \ln(2x - 3)$.

6   Let $f(x) = \ln(x - 2) + \ln(x - 6)$. Write down the natural domain of $f(x)$.

Find $f'(x)$ and hence find the intervals for which $f'(x)$ is   (a) positive,   (b) negative.

Without using a calculator, draw a sketch of the curve.

7   Repeat Question 6 for the functions
   (i) $f(x) = \ln(x - 2) + \ln(6 - x)$,   (ii) $f(x) = \ln(2 - x) + \ln(x - 6)$.

12.4 The reciprocal integral

Now that you know that $\dfrac{d}{dx} \ln x = \dfrac{1}{x}$, you also know a new result about integration:

For $x > 0$, $\displaystyle\int \frac{1}{x}\,dx = \ln x + k$.

This is an important step forward. You may recall that in P1 Section 10.1, when giving the indefinite integral $\displaystyle\int x^n\,dx = \frac{1}{n+1} x^{n+1} + k$, a special exception had to be made for the case $n = -1$. You can now see why: $\displaystyle\int \frac{1}{x}\,dx$ is an entirely different kind of function, the natural logarithm.

Example 12.4.1

Find the area under the graph of $y = \dfrac{1}{x}$ from $x = 2$ to $x = 4$.

Before working out the exact answer, notice from Fig. 12.7 that the area should be less than the area of the trapezium formed by joining $(2, 0.5)$ and $(4, 0.25)$ with a chord. This area is

$$\tfrac{1}{2} \times 2 \times (0.5 + 0.25) = 0.75.$$

The exact area is given by the integral

$$\int_2^4 \frac{1}{x}\,dx = [\ln x]_2^4 = \ln 4 - \ln 2$$

$$= \ln \tfrac{4}{2} = \ln 2.$$

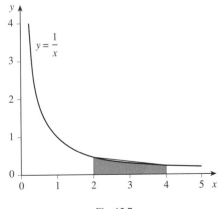

Fig. 12.7

The calculator gives this as $0.693\,14\ldots$, which is less than 0.75, as expected.

Example 12.4.2

Find the indefinite integral $\int \dfrac{1}{3x-1}\,dx$.

This is of the form $\int g(ax+b)\,dx$, so the integral is $\dfrac{1}{a}f(ax+b)+k$, where $f(x)$ is the simplest integral of $g(x)$. Here, $g(x)$ is $\dfrac{1}{x}$, so $f(x)=\ln x$. Therefore

$$\int \frac{1}{3x-1}\,dx = \frac{1}{3}\ln(3x-1)+k.$$

Note that this integral is only valid if $x>\tfrac{1}{3}$, since $\ln(3x-1)$ only exists if $3x-1>0$.

Exercise 12C

1 Carry out the following indefinite integrations, and state the values of x for which your answer is valid.

(a) $\displaystyle\int \frac{1}{2x}\,dx$ (b) $\displaystyle\int \frac{1}{x-1}\,dx$ (c) $\displaystyle\int \frac{1}{1-x}\,dx$ (d) $\displaystyle\int \frac{1}{4x+3}\,dx$

(e) $\displaystyle\int \frac{4}{1-2x}\,dx$ (f) $\displaystyle\int \frac{4}{1+2x}\,dx$ (g) $\displaystyle\int \frac{4}{-1-2x}\,dx$ (h) $\displaystyle\int \frac{4}{2x-1}\,dx$

2 Calculate the area under the graph of $y=\dfrac{1}{x}$ from

(a) $x=3$ to $x=6$ (b) $x=4$ to $x=8$

(c) $x=\tfrac{1}{2}$ to $x=1$ (d) $x=a$ to $x=2a,\quad a>0$

3 Calculate the areas under the following graphs.

(a) $y=\dfrac{1}{x+2}$ from $x=-1$ to $x=0$ (b) $y=\dfrac{1}{2x-1}$ from $x=2$ to $x=5$

(c) $y=\dfrac{2}{3x-5}$ from $x=4$ to $x=6$ (d) $y=\dfrac{e}{ex-7}$ from $x=4$ to $x=5$

(e) $y=\dfrac{1}{-x-1}$ from $x=-3$ to $x=-2$ (f) $y=2+\dfrac{1}{x-1}$ from $x=2$ to $x=6$

4 Draw a sketch of $y=\dfrac{2}{x+1}$, and use your sketch to make a rough estimate of the area under the graph between $x=3$ and $x=5$. Compare your answer with the exact answer.

5 Use the trapezium rule with three ordinates to find an approximation to the area under the graph of $y=\dfrac{6}{3x+4}$ between $x=3$ and $x=5$, indicating whether the approximation is an overestimate or an underestimate. Compare your answer with the exact area.

6 The region under the curve with equation $y=\dfrac{1}{\sqrt{x}}$ is rotated through 4 right angles about the x-axis to form a solid. Find the volume of the solid between $x=2$ and $x=5$.

7 The region under the curve with equation $y = \dfrac{1}{\sqrt{2x-1}}$ is rotated through 4 right angles

about the x-axis to form a solid. Find the volume of the solid between $x = 3$ and $x = 8$.

8 Given that $\dfrac{dy}{dx} = \dfrac{3}{2x+1}$ and that the graph of y against x passes through the point $(1,0)$,

find y in terms of x.

9 A curve has the property that $\dfrac{dy}{dx} = \dfrac{8}{4x-3}$, and it passes through $(1,2)$. Find its equation.

10 The graph of $y = \dfrac{1}{x^2}$ between $x = 1$ and $x = 2$ is rotated about the y-axis. Find the volume

of the solid formed.

12.5 Extending the reciprocal integral

For a first reading of this chapter you may prefer to skip ahead to Miscellaneous exercise 12.

You will have noticed that the statements of $\dfrac{d}{dx}\ln x = \dfrac{1}{x}$ and $\displaystyle\int \dfrac{1}{x}\,dx = \ln x$ both

contain the condition 'for $x > 0$'. In the case of the derivative the reason is obvious,

since $\ln x$ is only defined for $x > 0$. But no such restriction applies to the function $\dfrac{1}{x}$.

This then raises the question, what is $\displaystyle\int \dfrac{1}{x}\,dx$ when $x < 0$?

A good guess might be that it is $\ln(-x)$. This has a meaning if x is negative, and you

can differentiate it as a special case of $\dfrac{d}{dx}f(ax+b)$ with $a = -1$, $b = 0$ and $f(x) = \ln x$.
This gives

$$\frac{d}{dx}\ln(-x) = -\frac{1}{(-x)} = \frac{1}{x}, \text{ as required.}$$

So the full statement of the reciprocal integral is:

$$\int \frac{1}{x}\,dx = \begin{cases} \ln x + k, & \text{if } x > 0, \\ \ln(-x) + k, & \text{if } x < 0. \end{cases}$$

Notice that the possibility $x = 0$ is still excluded. You should expect this, as 0 is not in the

domain of the function $\dfrac{1}{x}$. Using the function $|x|$, the result can also be stated in the form

$$\text{For } x \neq 0, \int \frac{1}{x}\,dx = \ln|x| + k.$$

The function $|x|$ is an even function, with a graph symmetrical about the y-axis. It follows that the graph of $\ln|x|$ is symmetrical about the y-axis; it is shown in Fig. 12.8. For positive x it is the same as that of $\ln x$; for negative x, this is reflected in the y-axis.

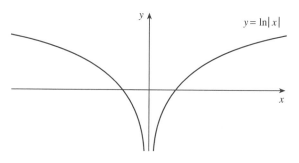

Fig. 12.8

You can see that the gradient of the graph is positive for $x > 0$ and negative for $x < 0$, which is as you would expect since $\dfrac{d}{dx}\ln|x| = \dfrac{1}{x}$.

Example 12.5.1

The graphs of $y = \dfrac{2}{x-2}$ and $y = -x-1$ intersect where $x = 0$ and $x = 1$. Find the area of the region between them.

You can check from a graphic calculator that the curve lies above the line, so that the area is

$$\int_0^1\left(\frac{2}{x-2}-(-x-1)\right)dx = \int_0^1\left(\frac{2}{x-2}+x+1\right)dx .$$

The trap which you have to avoid is writing the integral of $\dfrac{2}{x-2}$ as $2\ln(x-2)$. Over the interval $0 < x < 1$, $x-2$ is negative, so $\ln(x-2)$ has no meaning.

There are two ways of avoiding this. One is to write $\dfrac{2}{x-2}$ as $\dfrac{-2}{2-x}$. The integral of $\dfrac{1}{2-x}$ is $-\ln(2-x)$, so the integral of $\dfrac{-2}{2-x}$ is $2\ln(2-x)$. The area is then

$$\left[2\ln(2-x)+\tfrac{1}{2}x^2+x\right]_0^1 = \left(2\ln 1+\tfrac{1}{2}+1\right)-(2\ln 2)$$
$$= \tfrac{3}{2}-2\ln 2.$$

The alternative is to use the modulus form of the integral, and to find the area as

$$\left[2\ln|x-2|+\tfrac{1}{2}x^2+x\right]_0^1 = \left(2\ln|-1|+\tfrac{1}{2}+1\right)-(2\ln|-2|)$$
$$= \tfrac{3}{2}-2\ln 2.$$

You might think from this example that the modulus method has the edge. But it has to be used intelligently, as the following 'bogus' example shows.

Example 12.5.2

Find the area under the graph of $y = \dfrac{1}{x}$ from $x = -2$ to $x = +4$.

False solution

$$\int_{-2}^{4} \frac{1}{x} \, dx = \left[\ln |x| \right]_{-2}^{4} = \ln|4| - \ln|-2| = \ln 4 - \ln 2$$

$$= \ln \tfrac{4}{2} = \ln 2.$$

You only have to draw the graph of $y = \dfrac{1}{x}$ to see that there is a problem here. The area does not exist for either of the intervals $-2 < x < 0$ and $0 < x < 4$, so it certainly cannot exist for $-2 < x < 4$. The interval of integration contains $x = 0$, for which the rule $\dfrac{d}{dx} \ln|x| = \dfrac{1}{x}$ breaks down.

12.6*The derivative of b^x

In Section 12.2 the derivative of b^x was found in the form

$$\frac{d}{dx} b^x = L(b) b^x,$$

where $L(b)$ is a constant whose value depends on b.

It is now possible to find this constant. As exp and ln are inverse functions, the composite function 'exp ln' is an identity function, with domain the positive real numbers. Therefore

$$e^{\ln b} = b.$$

Raising both sides to the power x gives

$$b^x = \left(e^{\ln b} \right)^x = e^{x \ln b},$$

by the power-on-power rule. This is of the form e^{ax}, where a is constant, so

$$\frac{d}{dx} b^x = \frac{d}{dx} \left(e^{x \ln b} \right) = (\ln b) \, e^{x \ln b} = (\ln b) \, b^x.$$

Comparing this with the earlier form of the derivative, you find that

$$L(b) = \ln b.$$

You can check this by using your calculator to compare the values of $L(b)$ in Table 12.4 in Section 12.2 with the corresponding values of $\ln b$. Notice also that Table 12.4 gives a number of examples of the rules for logarithms listed on page 310. For example,

$$L(4) = 2L(2), \quad L(6) = L(2) + L(3), \quad L(8) = 3L(2),$$
$$L(9) = 2L(3), \quad L(10) = L(2) + L(5).$$

The reason for this is now clear.

12.7*How fast is exponential growth?

The graph of $y = e^x$ bends upwards throughout its length, so that it always lies above its tangents. The tangent at $(0,1)$ is $y = x+1$ (see Example 12.2.1), so, for all x other than 0, $e^x > x+1$.

This section uses the inequality $e^x > x$ (this obviously follows from $e^x > x+1$).

When x is positive, the expressions on both sides are positive. You can square to obtain

$$\left(e^x\right)^2 > x^2, \text{ or } e^{2x} > x^2.$$

Replacing $2x$ by u (which is always positive),

$$e^u > \left(\tfrac{1}{2}u\right)^2 = \tfrac{1}{4}u^2, \text{ or } \frac{u}{e^u} < \frac{4}{u}.$$

Since also $\dfrac{u}{e^u} > 0$, it follows that for $u > 0$, $0 < \dfrac{u}{e^u} < \dfrac{4}{u}$.

The main interest of this result lies in its consequences as $u \to \infty$. Then $\dfrac{u}{e^u}$ is sandwiched between 0 and $\dfrac{4}{u}$, which tends to 0. It follows that

$$\lim_{u \to \infty} \frac{u}{e^u} = 0.$$

This result may not surprise you; even with $u = 10$, $\dfrac{u}{e^u}$ is as small as 4.54×10^{-4}. But further transformations produce a more remarkable result. Since $\dfrac{u}{e^u}$ tends to 0, so does

$$\left(\frac{u}{e^u}\right)^n = \frac{u^n}{e^{nu}} \text{ for any positive power } n. \text{ Replacing } nu \text{ by } t, \text{ this expression becomes}$$

$$\frac{(t/n)^n}{e^t}, \text{ or } \frac{t^n/e^t}{n^n}.$$

Now n^n is simply a constant, so it cannot affect the limit:

$$\lim_{t \to \infty}\left(\frac{t^n}{e^t}\right) = \lim_{t \to \infty}\left(n^n\left(\frac{(t/n)^n}{e^t}\right)\right) = n^n \lim_{u \to \infty}\left(\frac{u^n}{e^{nu}}\right) = 0.$$

> For any positive number n, as $t \to \infty$, $\dfrac{t^n}{e^t} \to 0$.

If you draw the graph of $f(t) = t^n$ for a large value of n, you will see that, beyond the point $(1,1)$, it climbs very steeply. But this result shows that eventually the graph of e^t overtakes it. You can say that, although e^t and t^n tend to infinity, e^t tends to infinity faster than any power of t: 'exponentials beat powers'.

Take for example $n = 20$. When $t = 2$, $t^{20} = 1.04... \times 10^6$ is much greater than $e^2 = 7.3...$. But by $t = 100$, $t^{20} = 10^{40}$ has been overtaken by $e^{100} = 2.68... \times 10^{43}$.

━━━━━━━━━━━━━━━━━━━ **Exercise 12D** ━━━━━━━━━━━━━━━━━━━

1 Calculate the following.

(a) $\displaystyle\int_{-6}^{-3} \frac{1}{x+2}\,dx$

(b) $\displaystyle\int_{-1}^{0} \frac{1}{2x-1}\,dx$

(c) $\displaystyle\int_{-1}^{0} \frac{2}{3x-5}\,dx$

(d) $\displaystyle\int_{1}^{2} \frac{e}{ex-7}\,dx$

(e) $\displaystyle\int_{2}^{4} \frac{1}{-x-1}\,dx$

(f) $\displaystyle\int_{-1}^{0} \left(2+\frac{1}{x-1}\right)dx$

2 Calculate the value of $y = \ln|2x-3|$ for $x=-2$, and find $\dfrac{dy}{dx}$ when $x=-2$. Sketch the graph of $y = \ln|2x-3|$.

3* Find the derivatives with respect to x of 2^x, 3^x, 10^x and $\left(\frac{1}{2}\right)^x$.

4* Use a calculator to find a number a for which $e^x > x^5$ for all $x > a$.

5* (a) Use a calculator to draw sketches of the graphs of $y = \dfrac{\ln x}{x^2}$, $y = \dfrac{\ln x}{x^{\frac{1}{2}}}$ and $y = \dfrac{\ln x}{x^{\frac{1}{10}}}$ for

large values of x. Make a conjecture about the behaviour of these graphs as $x \to \infty$.

(b) Let $y = \dfrac{\ln x}{x^n}$, where $n > 0$. By writing $x^n = t^2$, show that $\displaystyle\lim_{x\to\infty} \frac{\ln x}{x^n} = \frac{2}{n}\lim_{t\to\infty} \frac{\ln t}{t^2}$.

(c) Consider $\dfrac{\ln t}{t^2}$. Justify each of the steps in the following argument.

For $t \geqslant 1$, $0 \leqslant \dfrac{1}{t^2}\ln t = \dfrac{1}{t^2}\displaystyle\int_{1}^{t} \frac{1}{z}\,dz \leqslant \dfrac{1}{t^2}\displaystyle\int_{1}^{t} 1\,dz = \dfrac{t-1}{t^2}$. Therefore, as $t \to \infty$, $\dfrac{\ln t}{t^2} \to 0$.

Therefore $\dfrac{2}{n}\displaystyle\lim_{t\to\infty} \frac{\ln t}{t^2} = 0$, so $\displaystyle\lim_{x\to\infty} \frac{\ln x}{x^n} = 0$. Thus 'powers beat logarithms'.

6* Draw graphs to conjecture the behaviour of graphs of the form $y = x^n \ln x$ for small positive values of x. By writing $x = \dfrac{1}{t}$ in the result of Question 5 part (c), deduce that $\displaystyle\lim_{x\to 0} x^n \ln x = 0$.

━━━━━━━━━━━━━━━━━━━ **Miscellaneous exercise 12** ━━━━━━━━━━━━━━━━━━━

1 Differentiate each of the following expressions with respect to x.

(a) $\ln(3x-4)$

(b) $\ln(4-3x)$

(c) $e^x \times e^{2x}$

(d) $e^x \div e^{2x}$

(e) $\ln\dfrac{2-x}{3-x}$

(f) $\ln(3-2x)^3$

2 Use the trapezium rule to show that $\frac{3}{4}$ and $\frac{17}{24}$ are approximations to $\ln 2$. Determine whether they are overestimates or underestimates, and justify your answers.

3 Find the coordinates of the points of intersection of $y = \dfrac{4}{x}$ and $2x+y=9$. Sketch both graphs for values of x such that $x>0$. Calculate the area between the graphs.

4 A curve is given by the equation $y = \frac{2}{3}e^x + \frac{1}{3}e^{-2x}$.

   (a) Evaluate a definite integral to find the area between the curve, the x-axis and the lines $x = 0$ and $x = 1$, showing your working.

   (b) Use calculus to determine whether the turning point at the point where $x = 0$ is a maximum or a minimum.   (OCR, adapted)

5 Find $\int \left(2 + e^{-x}\right) dx$.   (OCR)

6 The equation of a curve is $y = 2x^2 - \ln x$, where $x > 0$. Find by differentiation the x-coordinate of the stationary point on the curve, and determine whether this point is a maximum point or a minimum point.   (OCR)

7 Show that $\int_0^1 \left(e^x - e^{-x}\right) dx = \frac{(e-1)^2}{e}$.   (OCR)

8 Using differentiation, find the equation of the tangent to the curve $y = 4 + \ln(x+1)$ at the point where $x = 0$.   (OCR)

9 The equation of a curve is $y = \ln(2x)$. Find the equation of the normal at the point $\left(\frac{1}{2}, 0\right)$, giving your answer in the form $y = mx + c$.   (OCR)

10 (a) Express $\dfrac{x-7}{(x-4)(x-1)} + \dfrac{1}{x-4}$ as a single fraction.

   (b) Use a calculator to draw a sketch of $y = \dfrac{x-7}{(x-4)(x-1)}$, and calculate the area under the graph between $x = 2$ and $x = 3$.

11 (a) Show that e^x is an increasing function of x for all x. Deduce that $e^x \geq 1$ for $x \geq 0$.

   (b) By finding the area under the graphs of $y = e^x$ and $y = 1$ between 0 and X, where $X \geq 0$, deduce that $e^X \geq 1 + X$ for $X \geq 0$, and that $y = e^X \geq 1 + X + \frac{1}{2}x^2$ for $X \geq 0$.

12 (a) Find the stationary value of $y = \ln x - x$, and deduce that $\ln x \leq x - 1$ for $x > 0$ with equality only when $x = 1$.

   (b) Find the stationary value of $\ln x + \frac{1}{x}$, and deduce that $\dfrac{x-1}{x} \leq \ln x$ for $x > 0$ with equality only when $x = 1$.

   (c) By putting $x = \dfrac{y}{z}$ where $0 < y < z$, deduce Napier's inequality, $\dfrac{1}{z} < \dfrac{\ln z - \ln y}{z - y} < \dfrac{1}{y}$.

13 The diagram shows sketches of the graphs of $y = 2 - e^{-x}$ and $y = x$. These graphs intersect at $x = a$ where $a > 0$.

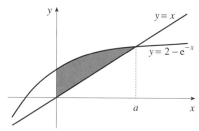

   (a) Write down an equation satisfied by a. (Do not attempt to solve the equation.)

   (b) Write down an integral which is equal to the area of the shaded region.

   (c) Use integration to show that the area is equal to $1 + a - \frac{1}{2}a^2$.   (OCR, adapted)

14 Use your graphic calculator to draw a sketch of the curve $y = e^{-2x} - 3x$. The curve crosses the x-axis at $A(a,0)$ and the y-axis at $B(0,1)$. O is the origin.

(a) Write down an equation satisfied by a.

(b) Show that the tangent at A meets the y-axis at the point whose y-coordinate is $2ae^{-2a} + 3a$.

(c) Show that $\dfrac{d^2 y}{dx^2} > 0$, and using the results from parts (a) and (b), deduce that $6a^2 + 3a < 1$.

(d) Find, in terms of a, the area of the region bounded by the curve and the line segments OA and OB.

(e) By comparing this area with the area of the triangle OAB, show that $3a^2 + 4a > 1$. Hence show that $\frac{1}{3}\sqrt{7} - \frac{2}{3} < a < \frac{1}{12}\sqrt{33} - \frac{1}{4}$.   (OCR, adapted)

15 Find the exact value of $\displaystyle\int_0^\infty e^{1-2x}\, dx$.

16 The graph of $y = e^x$ can be transformed to that of $y = e^{x+1}$ either by means of a stretch or by means of a translation. State the scale factor and the directions of the stretch and the magnitude and direction of the translation.

Describe the transformation which maps the graph of $y = e^x$ onto the graph of $y = \ln x$.

(OCR)

17 The number of bacteria present in a culture at time t hours after the beginning of an experiment is denoted by N. The relation between N and t is modelled by $N = 100e^{\frac{3}{2}t}$.

(a) After how many hours will the number of bacteria be 9000?

(b) At what rate per hour will the number of bacteria be increasing when $t = 6$?   (OCR)

13 The chain rule

This chapter is about differentiating more general composite functions than those in Chapter 6. When you have completed it, you should

- be able to differentiate composite functions
- be able to apply differentiation to rates of change, and to related rates of change.

You can omit Section 13.2 on a first reading. The exercises are independent of it.

13.1 The chain rule: an informal treatment

When you differentiate $(ax + b)^n$ by using the methods of Section 6.1, you are actually differentiating the composite function

$$x \rightarrow [\ \times, a, +, b, =\ ] \rightarrow ax + b \rightarrow [\ \text{raise to power } n\ ] \rightarrow (ax + b)^n.$$

It is now time to generalise to composite functions such as $\ln(x^2 + 1)$, shown by

$$x \rightarrow [\ \text{square}, +, 1, =\ ] \rightarrow x^2 + 1 \rightarrow [\ \ln\ ] \rightarrow \ln(x^2 + 1).$$

However, it is worth beginning with an easier example.

Example 13.1.1
Find the derivative of the composite function
$$x \rightarrow [\ \times, a, +, b, =\ ] \rightarrow ax + b \rightarrow [\ \times, c, +, d, =\ ] \rightarrow c(ax + b) + d.$$

If you let $y = c(ax + b) + d$, then

$$\frac{dy}{dx} = \frac{d}{dx}(c(ax + b) + d) = \frac{d}{dx}(cax + cb + d) = ca.$$

However, if you let u stand for the intermediate output $ax + b$, then $y = cu + d$.
So $\dfrac{dy}{du} = c$ and $\dfrac{du}{dx} = a$, and $\dfrac{dy}{dx} = ca$. That is, $\dfrac{dy}{dx} = \dfrac{dy}{du} \times \dfrac{du}{dx}$.

You can think of this another way, by thinking about rates of change. Recall that:

- $\dfrac{dy}{dx}$ is the rate at which y changes with respect to x

- $\dfrac{dy}{du}$ is the rate at which y changes with respect to u

- $\dfrac{du}{dx}$ is the rate at which u changes with respect to x.

The equation $\dfrac{dy}{du} = c$ means that y is changing c times as fast as u; similarly u is changing a times as fast as x. It is natural to think that if y is changing c times as fast as u, and u is changing a times as fast as x, then y is changing $c \times a$ times as fast as x. Thus, again,

$$\frac{dy}{dx} = \frac{dy}{du} \times \frac{du}{dx}.$$

Example 13.1.2

Find $\dfrac{dy}{dx}$ when $y = \left(1 + x^2\right)^3$.

So far there has been no alternative to expanding by the binomial theorem. You have had to write

$$y = \left(1 + x^2\right)^3 = 1 + 3x^2 + 3x^4 + x^6.$$

$$\frac{dy}{dx} = 6x + 12x^3 + 6x^5 = 6x\left(1 + 2x^2 + x^4\right)$$

$$= 6x\left(1 + x^2\right)^2.$$

But now the relation $\dfrac{dy}{dx} = \dfrac{dy}{du} \times \dfrac{du}{dx}$ suggests another approach. If you substitute $u = 1 + x^2$, so that $y = u^3$, then

$$\frac{dy}{du} = 3u^2 = 3\left(1 + x^2\right)^2 \text{ and } \frac{du}{dx} = 2x.$$

So $\dfrac{dy}{du} \times \dfrac{du}{dx} = 3\left(1 + x^2\right)^2 \times 2x = 6x\left(1 + x^2\right)^2.$

So once again $\dfrac{dy}{dx} = \dfrac{dy}{du} \times \dfrac{du}{dx}.$

Assume now that this result, known as the chain rule, holds in all cases. It is also sometimes called the 'composite function' rule, or the 'function of a function' rule.

The chain rule is extremely easy to remember because the term du *appears to cancel, but bear in mind that this is simply a helpful feature of the notation. Cancellation has no meaning in this context, but you can take full advantage of the notation.*

The chain rule

If $y = g(f(x))$, and $u = f(x)$ so that $y = g(u)$, then $\dfrac{dy}{dx} = \dfrac{dy}{du} \times \dfrac{du}{dx}.$

A proof is given in Section 13.2, but you can omit the proof on a first reading.

Example 13.1.3

Differentiate $y = (2x + 1)^{\frac{1}{2}}$ with respect to x.

Substitute $u = 2x + 1$, so that $y = u^{\frac{1}{2}}$. Then $\dfrac{dy}{du} = \frac{1}{2}u^{-\frac{1}{2}} = \frac{1}{2}(2x + 1)^{-\frac{1}{2}}$ and $\dfrac{du}{dx} = 2$.

As $\dfrac{dy}{dx} = \dfrac{dy}{du} \times \dfrac{du}{dx}, \dfrac{dy}{dx} = \frac{1}{2}(2x + 1)^{-\frac{1}{2}} \times 2 = (2x + 1)^{-\frac{1}{2}} = \dfrac{1}{\sqrt{2x + 1}}.$

Example 13.1.4

Find $\dfrac{dy}{dx}$ when   (a) $y = \ln(1 + x^2)$,   (b) $y = e^{-x^2}$,   (c) $y = \sqrt{1 - x^2}$.

(a) Substitute $u = 1 + x^2$, so $y = \ln u$. Then $\dfrac{dy}{du} = \dfrac{1}{u} = \dfrac{1}{1 + x^2}$ and $\dfrac{du}{dx} = 2x$.

So $\dfrac{dy}{dx} = \dfrac{dy}{du} \times \dfrac{du}{dx} = \dfrac{1}{1 + x^2} \times 2x = \dfrac{2x}{1 + x^2}$.

(b) Substitute $u = -x^2$, so $y = e^u$. Then $\dfrac{dy}{du} = e^u = e^{-x^2}$ and $\dfrac{du}{dx} = -2x$.

So $\dfrac{dy}{dx} = \dfrac{dy}{du} \times \dfrac{du}{dx} = e^{-x^2} \times (-2x) = -2xe^{-x^2}$.

(c) Substitute $u = 1 - x^2$, so $y = \sqrt{u} = u^{\frac{1}{2}}$. Then $\dfrac{dy}{du} = \dfrac{1}{2} u^{-\frac{1}{2}} = \dfrac{1}{2\sqrt{u}} = \dfrac{1}{2\sqrt{1 - x^2}}$

and $\dfrac{du}{dx} = -2x$. So $\dfrac{dy}{dx} = \dfrac{dy}{du} \times \dfrac{du}{dx} = \dfrac{1}{2\sqrt{1 - x^2}} \times (-2x) = \dfrac{-x}{\sqrt{1 - x^2}}$.

Exercise 13A

1 Use the substitution $u = 5x + 3$ to differentiate

    (a) $y = (5x + 3)^6$,   (b) $y = (5x + 3)^{\frac{1}{2}}$,   (c) $y = \ln(5x + 3)$,

    with respect to x.

2 Use the substitution $u = 1 - 4x$ to differentiate

    (a) $y = (1 - 4x)^5$,   (b) $y = (1 - 4x)^{-3}$,   (c) $y = e^{1 - 4x}$,

    with respect to x.

3 Use the substitution $u = 1 + x^3$ to differentiate

    (a) $y = (1 + x^3)^5$,   (b) $y = (1 + x^3)^{-4}$,   (c) $y = \ln(1 + x^3)$,

    with respect to x.

4 Use the substitution $u = 2x^2 + 3$ to differentiate

    (a) $y = (2x^2 + 3)^6$,   (b) $y = \dfrac{1}{2x^2 + 3}$,   (c) $y = \dfrac{1}{\sqrt{2x^2 + 3}}$,

    with respect to x.

5 Differentiate $y = (3x^4 + 2)^2$ with respect to x by using the chain rule. Confirm your answer by expanding $(3x^4 + 2)^2$ and then differentiating.

6 Differentiate $y = (2x^3 + 1)^3$ with respect to x.

    (a)   by using the binomial theorem to expand $y = (2x^3 + 1)^3$ and then differentiating term by term,

    (b)   by using the chain rule.

    Check that your answers are the same.

7 Use appropriate substitutions to differentiate

(a) $y = (x^5 + 1)^4$,   (b) $y = (2x^3 - 1)^8$,   (c) $y = (e^{2x} + 3)^6$,   (d) $y = (\sqrt{x} - 1)^5$,

with respect to x.

8 Differentiate the following with respect to x; try to do this without writing down the substitutions.

(a) $y = (x^2 + 6)^4$ (b) $y = (5x^3 + 4)^3$ (c) $y = (x^4 - 8)^7$ (d) $y = (2 - x^9)^5$

9 Differentiate the following with respect to x.

(a) $y = \sqrt{4x + 3}$ (b) $y = (x^2 + 4)^6$ (c) $y = (6x^3 - 5)^{-2}$ (d) $y = (5 - x^3)^{-1}$

10 Differentiate the following with respect to x.

(a) $y = (\ln x + 1)^6$ (b) $y = \left(\dfrac{1}{x} + 2\right)^4$ (c) $y = \frac{1}{2}\ln(2 + x^4)$ (d) $y = 3(e^{-x} + 1)^5$

11 Given that $f(x) = \dfrac{1}{1 + x^2}$, find   (a) f$'(2)$,   (b) the value of x such that f$'(x) = 0$.

12 Given that $y = \sqrt[4]{x^3 + 8}$, find the value of $\dfrac{dy}{dx}$ when $x = 2$.

13 Given that $y = \dfrac{5}{1 + e^{3x}}$, find the value of $\dfrac{dy}{dx}$ when $x = 0$.

14 Differentiate with respect to x.

(a) $y = (x^2 + 3x + 1)^6$,   (b) $y = \ln(x^3 + 4x)$,   (c) $y = \dfrac{1}{(x^2 + 5x)^3}$,   (d) $y = 2e^{x^2 + x + 1}$.

15 Find the equation of the tangent to the curve $y = (x^2 - 5)^3$ at the point $(2, -1)$.

16 Find the equation of the tangent to the curve $y = \dfrac{1}{\sqrt{x - 1}}$ at the point $(4, 1)$.

17 Find the equation of the normal to the curve $y = \dfrac{8}{1 - x^3}$ at the point $(-1, 4)$.

18 Use the substitutions $u = x^2 - 1$ and $v = \sqrt{u} + 1$ with the chain rule in the form

$\dfrac{dy}{dx} = \dfrac{dy}{dv} \times \dfrac{dv}{du} \times \dfrac{du}{dx}$ to differentiate $y = (\sqrt{x^2 - 1} + 1)^6$.

19 Use two substitutions to find $\dfrac{d}{dx}(e^{\sqrt{1 - x^2}})$.

20 A curve has equation $y = (x^2 + 1)^4 + 2(x^2 + 1)^3$. Show that $\dfrac{dy}{dx} = 4x(x^2 + 1)^2(2x^2 + 5)$ and

hence show that the curve has just one stationary point. State the coordinates of the stationary point and, by considering the gradient of the curve either side of the stationary point, determine its nature.

13.2*Deriving the chain rule

You may omit this section if you wish.

In P1 Section 9.3 you met $\dfrac{dy}{dx}$ as $\dfrac{dy}{dx} = \lim\limits_{\delta x \to 0} \dfrac{\delta y}{\delta x}$.

Similarly, simply by changing the letters in the definition,

$$\frac{dy}{du} = \lim_{\delta u \to 0} \frac{\delta y}{\delta u} \text{ and } \frac{du}{dx} = \lim_{\delta x \to 0} \frac{\delta u}{\delta x}.$$

Now, in these expressions, when y is a function of u, where u is a function of x, then as x changes u changes and so y changes.

Take a particular value of x, and increase x by δx with a corresponding increase of δu in the value of u, which, in turn, increases the value of y by δy. Then

$$\frac{\delta y}{\delta x} = \frac{\delta y}{\delta u} \times \frac{\delta u}{\delta x}$$

because δy, δu and δx are numbers which you can cancel, assuming that $\delta u \neq 0$.

To find $\dfrac{dy}{dx}$, you must take the limit as $\delta x \to 0$, so

$$\frac{dy}{dx} = \lim_{\delta x \to 0} \frac{\delta y}{\delta x} = \lim_{\delta x \to 0} \left(\frac{\delta y}{\delta u} \times \frac{\delta u}{\delta x} \right).$$

Assuming that as $\delta x \to 0$, $\delta u \to 0$ and that $\lim\limits_{\delta x \to 0} \left(\dfrac{\delta y}{\delta u} \times \dfrac{\delta u}{\delta x} \right) = \lim\limits_{\delta x \to 0} \left(\dfrac{\delta y}{\delta u} \right) \times \lim\limits_{\delta x \to 0} \left(\dfrac{\delta u}{\delta x} \right)$, it follows that

$$\frac{dy}{dx} = \lim_{\delta x \to 0} \frac{\delta y}{\delta x} = \lim_{\delta x \to 0} \left(\frac{\delta y}{\delta u} \times \frac{\delta u}{\delta x} \right)$$

$$= \lim_{\delta x \to 0} \left(\frac{\delta y}{\delta u} \right) \times \lim_{\delta x \to 0} \left(\frac{\delta u}{\delta x} \right) = \lim_{\delta u \to 0} \left(\frac{\delta y}{\delta u} \right) \times \lim_{\delta x \to 0} \left(\frac{\delta u}{\delta x} \right)$$

$$= \frac{dy}{du} \times \frac{du}{dx}.$$

This result, $\dfrac{dy}{dx} = \dfrac{dy}{du} \times \dfrac{du}{dx}$, is the chain rule for differentiating composite functions.

Note that the results in Section 6.1 are particular cases of the chain rule since, if $u = ax + b$, $\dfrac{du}{dx} = a$.

13.3 An application of the chain rule

The chain rule enables you to extend the rule $\dfrac{d}{dx} x^n = nx^{n-1}$ to all real values of n.

Note that, since P1 Section 7.5, you have been assuming this result for rational values of n without proof.

The proof which follows applies only when $x > 0$, but it can be extended to negative values of x provided that x^n still has a meaning when $x < 0$. (See Miscellaneous exercise 13 Question 19.)

Begin by writing x^n in the unusual form $x = e^{\ln x}$. Then you can write $x^n = \left(e^{\ln x}\right)^n = e^{n \ln x}$. Letting $u = n \ln x$ and differentiating,

$$\frac{d}{dx}\left(e^u\right) = e^u \times \frac{du}{dx} = e^{n \ln x} \times \frac{n}{x} = x^n \times \frac{n}{x} = nx^{n-1}.$$

13.4 Related rates of change

You frequently need to be able to calculate the rate at which one quantity varies with another when one of them is time. In P1 Section 9.3 it was shown that if r is some quantity, then the rate of change of r with respect to time t is $\dfrac{dr}{dt}$.

But suppose that r is the radius of a spherical balloon, and you know how fast the volume V of the balloon is increasing. How can you find out how fast the radius is increasing?

The situation here is best described by a problem.

Example 13.4.1

Suppose that a spherical balloon is being inflated at a constant rate of $5 \text{ m}^3 \text{ s}^{-1}$. At a particular moment, the radius of the balloon is 4 metres. Find how fast the radius of the balloon is increasing at that instant.

First translate the information into a mathematical form.

Let $V \text{ m}^3$ be the volume of the balloon, and let r metres be its radius. Let t seconds be the time for which the balloon has been inflating. Then you are given that $\dfrac{dV}{dt} = 5$ and $r = 4$, and you are asked to find $\dfrac{dr}{dt}$ at that moment.

Your other piece of information is that the balloon is spherical, so that $V = \frac{4}{3}\pi r^3$.

The key to solving the problem is to use the chain rule in the form

$$\frac{dV}{dt} = \frac{dV}{dr} \times \frac{dr}{dt}.$$

You can now use $\dfrac{dV}{dr} = 4\pi r^2$. Substituting the various values into the chain rule formula gives

$$5 = \left(4\pi \times 4^2\right) \times \frac{dr}{dt}.$$

Therefore, rearranging this equation, you find that $\dfrac{dr}{dt} = \dfrac{5}{64\pi}$, so the radius is increasing at $\dfrac{5}{64\pi} \text{ m s}^{-1}$.

In practice you do not need to write down so much detail. Here is another example.

Example 13.4.2

The surface area of a cube is increasing at a constant rate of $24 \text{ cm}^2 \text{ s}^{-1}$. Find the rate at which its volume is increasing at the moment when the volume is 216 cm^3.

Let the side of the cube be x cm at time t seconds, let the surface area be $S \text{ cm}^2$ and let the volume be $V \text{ cm}^3$.

Then $S = 6x^2$, $V = x^3$ and $\dfrac{\mathrm{d}S}{\mathrm{d}t} = 24$, and you need to find $\dfrac{\mathrm{d}V}{\mathrm{d}t}$ when $V = 216$,

which is when $x^3 = 216$, or $x = 6$.

If you know S and want to find V you would need to go via x. Similarly, when you know $\dfrac{\mathrm{d}S}{\mathrm{d}t}$ and want to find $\dfrac{\mathrm{d}V}{\mathrm{d}t}$ you should expect to go via $\dfrac{\mathrm{d}x}{\mathrm{d}t}$.

From the chain rule, $\dfrac{\mathrm{d}V}{\mathrm{d}t} = \dfrac{\mathrm{d}V}{\mathrm{d}x} \times \dfrac{\mathrm{d}x}{\mathrm{d}t} = 3x^2 \dfrac{\mathrm{d}x}{\mathrm{d}t}$, so, when $x = 6$, $\dfrac{\mathrm{d}V}{\mathrm{d}t} = 108 \dfrac{\mathrm{d}x}{\mathrm{d}t}$.

But $\dfrac{\mathrm{d}S}{\mathrm{d}t} = \dfrac{\mathrm{d}S}{\mathrm{d}x} \times \dfrac{\mathrm{d}x}{\mathrm{d}t} = 12x \dfrac{\mathrm{d}x}{\mathrm{d}t}$, so $24 = (12 \times 6) \times \dfrac{\mathrm{d}x}{\mathrm{d}t}$, giving $\dfrac{\mathrm{d}x}{\mathrm{d}t} = \frac{1}{3}$. Substituting

this in the equation $\dfrac{\mathrm{d}V}{\mathrm{d}t} = 108 \dfrac{\mathrm{d}x}{\mathrm{d}t}$ gives $\dfrac{\mathrm{d}V}{\mathrm{d}t} = 108 \times \frac{1}{3} = 36$.

Therefore the volume is increasing at a rate of $36 \text{ cm}^3 \text{ s}^{-1}$.

Exercise 13B

1   The number of bacteria present in a culture at time t hours after the beginning of an experiment is denoted by N. The relation between N and t is modelled by $N = \mathrm{e}^{\frac{3}{2}t}$. At what rate per hour will the number of bacteria be increasing when $t = 6$?   (OCR)

2   A metal bar is heated to a certain temperature and then the heat source is removed. At time t minutes after the heat source is removed, the temperature, θ degrees Celsius, of the metal bar is given by $\theta = 280\mathrm{e}^{-0.02t}$. At what rate is the temperature decreasing 100 minutes after the removal of the heat source?   (OCR)

3   The length of the side of a square is increasing at a constant rate of 1.2 cm s^{-1}. At the moment when the length of the side is 10 cm, find

   (a) the rate of increase of the perimeter,

   (b) the rate of increase of the area.

4   The length of the edge of a cube is increasing at a constant rate of 0.5 mm s^{-1}. At the moment when the length of the edge is 40 mm, find

   (a) the rate of increase of the surface area,

   (b) the rate of increase of the volume.

5   A circular stain is spreading so that its radius is increasing at a constant rate of 3 mm s^{-1}. Find the rate at which the area is increasing when the radius is 50 mm.

6 A water tank has a rectangular base 1.5 m by 1.2 m. The sides are vertical and water is being added to the tank at a constant rate of 0.45 m³ per minute. At what rate is the depth of water in the tank increasing?

7 Air is being lost from a spherical balloon at a constant rate of 0.6 m³ s⁻¹. Find the rate at which the radius is decreasing at a instant when the radius is 2.5 m.

8 The volume of a spherical balloon is increasing at a constant rate of 0.25 m³ s⁻¹. Find the rate at which the radius is increasing at a instant when the volume is 10 m³.

9 A funnel has a circular top of diameter 20 cm and a height of 30 cm. When the depth of liquid in the funnel is 15 cm, the liquid is dripping from the funnel at a rate of 0.2 cm³ s⁻¹. At what rate is the depth of the liquid in the funnel decreasing at this instant?

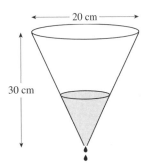

Miscellaneous exercise 13

1 Differentiate $2(x^4 + 3)^5$ with respect to x.

2 Find the equation of the tangent to the curve $y = (x^2 - 5)^6$ at the point $(2, 1)$.

3 Given that $y = \sqrt{x^3 + 1}$, show that $\dfrac{dy}{dx} > 0$ for all $x > -1$.

4 Given that $y = \dfrac{1}{2x - 1} + \dfrac{1}{(2x - 1)^2}$, find the exact value of $\dfrac{dy}{dx}$ when $x = 2$.

5 Find the coordinates of the stationary point of the curve with equation $y = \dfrac{1}{x^2 + 4}$.

6 Find the equation of the normal to the curve $y = \sqrt{2x^2 + 1}$ at the point $(2, 3)$.

7 The radius of a circular disc is increasing at a constant rate of 0.003 cm s⁻¹. Find the rate at which the area is increasing when the radius is 20 cm.   (OCR)

8 A viscous liquid is poured on to a flat surface. It forms a circular patch whose area grows at a steady rate of 5 cm² s⁻¹. Find, in terms of π,

(a) the radius of the patch 20 seconds after pouring has commenced,

(b) the rate of increase of the radius at this instant.   (OCR)

9 The formulae for the volume of a sphere of radius r and for its surface area are $V = \frac{4}{3}\pi r^3$ and $A = 4\pi r^2$ respectively. Given that, when $r = 5$ m, V is increasing at a rate of 10 m³ s⁻¹, find the rate of increase of A at this instant.   (OCR)

10 Differentiate with respect to x (a) $\sqrt{x + \dfrac{1}{x}}$,   (b) $\ln(1 + \sqrt{4x})$.   (OCR)

11 Using differentiation, find the equation of the tangent at the point $(2,1)$ on the curve with equation $y = \sqrt{x^2 - 3}$.   (OCR)

12 Differentiate with respect to t (a) $\dfrac{1}{\left(3t^2 + 5\right)^2}$,   (b) $\ln\left(\dfrac{4}{t^2}\right)$.   (OCR)

13 Find the coordinates of the stationary point of the curve $y = \ln(x^2 - 6x + 10)$ and show that this stationary point is a minimum.

14 (a) Curve C_1 has equation $y = \sqrt{4x - x^2}$. Find $\dfrac{dy}{dx}$ and hence find the coordinates of the stationary point.

    (b) Show that the curve C_2 with equation $y = \sqrt{x^2 - 4x}$ has no stationary point.

15 If a hemispherical bowl of radius 6 cm contains water to a depth of x cm, the volume of the water is $\frac{1}{3}\pi x^2(18 - x)$. Water is poured into the bowl at a rate of 3 cm^3 s^{-1}. Find the rate at which the water level is rising when the depth is 2 cm.

16 An underground oil storage tank $ABCDEFGH$ is part of a square pyramid, as shown in the diagram. The complete pyramid has a square base of side 12 m and height 18 m. The tank has depth 12 m.

When the depth of oil in the tank is h metres, show that the volume V m^3 is given by $V = \frac{4}{27}(h + 6)^3 - 32$.

Oil is being added to the tank at the constant rate of 4.5 m^3 s^{-1}. At the moment when the depth of oil is 8 m, find the rate at which the depth is increasing.

17 Find the coordinates of the three stationary points of the curve $y = e^{x^2\left(x^2 - 18\right)}$.

18 A curve has equation $y = \left(x^2 - 1\right)^3 - 3\left(x^2 - 1\right)^2$. Find the coordinates of the stationary points and determine whether each is a minimum or a maximum. Sketch the curve.

19* The expression x^n only has a meaning when $x < 0$ if n is a rational number $\dfrac{p}{q}$ and q is an odd integer.

Make the substitution $u = -x$ so that, when $x < 0$, $u > 0$.

    (a) Show that, if $x < 0$ and q is odd, then $x^{\frac{p}{q}} = -u^{\frac{p}{q}}$ if p is odd,

    and $x^{\frac{p}{q}} = u^{\frac{p}{q}}$ if p is even.

    (b) Use the chain rule and the result in Section 13.3 to show that, if p is odd, then

$$\frac{d}{dx}\left(x^{\frac{p}{q}}\right) = \frac{p}{q}u^{\frac{p-q}{q}} = \frac{p}{q}x^{\frac{p}{q}-1}; \text{ and that, if } p \text{ is even, } \frac{d}{dx}\left(x^{\frac{p}{q}}\right) = -\frac{p}{q}u^{\frac{p-q}{q}} = \frac{p}{q}x^{\frac{p}{q}-1}.$$

    (c) Deduce that, for all the values of n for which x^n has a meaning when x is negative,

$$\frac{d}{dx}\left(x^n\right) = nx^{n-1} \text{ for } x < 0.$$

14 Solving equations numerically

This chapter is about numerical methods for equations which cannot be solved exactly. When you have completed it, you should

- be able to use the sign-change rule to find approximate solutions by decimal search
- know how to use a chord approximation to improve the efficiency of decimal search
- be able to use an iterative method to produce a sequence which converges to a root
- understand that the choice of iterative method affects whether a sequence converges or not, and know what determines its behaviour
- appreciate that it is possible to modify an iterative method to speed up convergence
- appreciate that decisions about choice of method may depend on what sort of calculator or computer software you are using.

How you use this chapter will depend on what calculating aids you have available. It has been written to emphasise the underlying mathematical principles, so that you can follow the procedures with a simple calculator. But if you have a programmable or graphic calculator, if you like to write your own computer programs, or if you have access to a spreadsheet, you will be able to carry out some of the calculations far more quickly.

14.1 Some basic principles

In mathematical problems the final step is often to solve an equation. If this is a linear or a quadratic equation, or if it is an equation which can be reduced to one of these forms, then you have a method for solving it. But for equations of any other form you usually have to resort to some kind of solution by successive approximation, either numerical or algebraic.

Any equation in x can be rearranged so that it takes the form $f(x) = 0$. A value of x for which $f(x)$ takes the value 0 is called a **root** of the equation. The **solution** of the equation is the set of all the roots.

A useful way of representing the solution of $f(x) = 0$ is to draw the graph of $y = f(x)$. The roots are the x-coordinates of the points of the graph on the x-axis.

This leads at once to a result which is very useful for locating roots.

> **The sign-change rule**
> If the function $f(x)$ is continuous in an interval $p \leqslant x \leqslant q$ of its domain, and if $f(p)$ and $f(q)$ have opposite signs, then there is at least one root of $f(x) = 0$ between p and q.

This is illustrated in Fig. 14.1. The condition that $f(x)$ is continuous means that the graph cannot jump across the x-axis without meeting it.

The words 'at least one' are important. Fig. 14.2 shows that there may be more than one root between p and q.

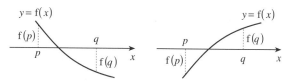

Fig. 14.1

When you have an equation to solve, it usually helps to begin by finding the shape of the graph of $y = f(x)$. Suppose that you want to solve the cubic equation

$$x^3 - 3x - 5 = 0.$$

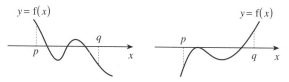

Fig. 14.2

Writing $f(x) = x^3 - 3x - 5$, you can find

$$f'(x) = 3x^2 - 3 = 3(x+1)(x-1) \text{ and } f''(x) = 6x.$$

It follows that $f(x)$ has a maximum where $x = -1$ and a minimum where $x = 1$. The coordinates of the maximum and minimum points are $(-1, -3)$ and $(1, -7)$. From this you can draw a sketch of the graph, as in Fig. 14.3.

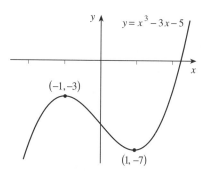

The graph shows that this equation has only one root, and that it is greater than 1. Also, $f(x)$ is negative for values of x below the root, and positive above the root. This suggests where to start looking for it.

Fig. 14.3

14.2 Decimal search

This section describes how you can use the sign-change rule to find a sequence of approximations to the root, improving the accuracy by one decimal place at a time.

Continuing with the equation $x^3 - 3x - 5 = 0$, the graph suggests calculating $f(2) = -3$ and $f(3) = 13$. It follows that the root is between 2 and 3.

You could now start calculating $f(2.1), f(2.2), \ldots$ until you reach a value of x for which $f(x)$ is positive. But it is worth spending a moment to ask if this is a sensible strategy. Fig. 14.4 is a sketch of the graph of $f(x)$ between $x = 2$ and $x = 3$. Since $AP = 3$ is about $\frac{1}{4}$ of $BQ = 13$, you might guess that X is about $\frac{1}{5}$ of the distance from P to Q. So it might be best to begin by calculating $f(2.2) = -0.952$. Since this is negative, go on to calculate $f(2.3) = 0.267$.

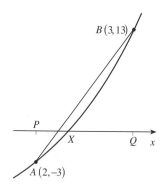

There is no need to go further. Since $f(2.2)$ is negative and $f(2.3)$ is positive, the root is between 2.2 and 2.3.

Fig. 14.4

If you use a graphic calculator, the equivalent procedure would be to zoom in on the interval $2 \leqslant x \leqslant 3$. You will then see that the graph cuts the x-axis between 2.2 and 2.3.

The process is now repeated to get the second decimal place. Since $|f(2.2)| = 0.952$ is about 4 times $|f(2.3)| = 0.267$, the root is probably about $\frac{4}{5}$ of the distance from 2.2 to 2.3, so begin by calculating $f(2.28) = 0.012\ldots$. Since this is positive, 2.28 is too large, so try calculating $f(2.27) = -0.112\ldots$. This is negative, so the root is between 2.27 and 2.28.

With a graphic calculator you would zoom in on the interval $2.2 \leqslant x \leqslant 2.3$, and see that the graph cuts the x-axis between 2.27 and 2.28.

To make sure you know what to do, continue the calculation for yourself to the third decimal place. You will find that $f(2.279)$ is negative, and you know that $f(2.280)$ is positive, so the root is between 2.279 and 2.280.

Notice that, if you wanted to find the root correct to 3 decimal places, you would need to know whether it is closer to 2.279 or to 2.280, so you would need to find $f(2.2795)$, which is $0.006\,05\ldots$. Since this is positive, and $f(2.279)$ is negative, the root lies between 2.279 and 2.2795. That is, its value is 2.279 correct to 3 decimal places.

What you are finding by this method are the terms in two sequences; one sequence of numbers above the root

$$a_0 = 3, \quad a_1 = 2.3, \quad a_2 = 2.28, \quad a_3 = 2.280, \quad \ldots,$$

and one sequence of numbers below the root

$$b_0 = 2, \quad b_1 = 2.2, \quad b_2 = 2.27, \quad b_3 = 2.279, \quad \ldots.$$

Both sequences converge on the root as a limit; the difference between a_r and b_r is 10^{-r}, which tends to 0 as r increases.

Example 14.2.1
Solve the equation $x\,e^x = 1$.

Begin by investigating the equation graphically, using the idea that a root of an equation $f(x) = g(x)$ is the x-coordinate of a point of intersection of the graphs of $y = f(x)$ and $y = g(x)$. Fig. 14.5 on the next page shows four different ways of doing this, based on the equation as stated and the three rearrangements

$$e^x = \frac{1}{x}, \quad x = e^{-x}, \quad x = -\ln x.$$

All the graphs show that there is just one root, but the third graph is probably the most informative. The tangent to $y = -x$ at $(0,1)$ has gradient -1, and so meets $y = x$ at $\left(\frac{1}{2}, \frac{1}{2}\right)$. This shows that the root is slightly greater than 0.5.

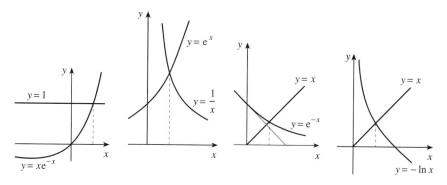

Fig. 14.5

To use the sign-change method you need to write the equation as $f(x) = 0$. There are again several possibilities:

$$x e^x - 1 = 0, \quad e^x - \frac{1}{x} = 0, \quad x - e^{-x} = 0, \quad x + \ln x = 0.$$

If you have a calculator with graphics or programming facilities it makes little difference which you use. But with a basic calculator it pays to use the form whose calculation involves the fewest key steps. This is probably the last, so take $f(x) = x + \ln x$.

The calculation then proceeds as follows.

$$f(0.5) = -0.193\ldots, \quad f(0.6) = 0.089\ldots.$$

The root is between 0.5 and 0.6. Since $|f(0.5)|$ is about 2 times $|f(0.6)|$, the root is probably about $\frac{2}{3}$ of the distance from 0.5 to 0.6, which is about 0.57. So calculate

$$f(0.57) = 0.0078\ldots \qquad (0.57 \text{ is too large}),$$
$$f(0.56) = -0.0198\ldots.$$

The root is between 0.56 and 0.57, and $|f(0.56)|$ is between 2 and 3 times $|f(0.57)|$. This suggests that the root is between $\frac{2}{3}$ and $\frac{3}{4}$ of the distance from 0.56 to 0.57, which is about 0.567. So calculate

$$f(0.567) = -0.000\,39\ldots \qquad (0.567 \text{ is too small}),$$
$$f(0.568) = 0.002\,36\ldots.$$

The root therefore lies between 0.567 and 0.568.

Notice that in the calculation to find where the chord cuts the axis, only a small number of decimal figures has been used. There is no point in doing this calculation very accurately; its only purpose is to decide where to begin the next step of the search, and for that you only need to work to 1 *significant figure.*

▓▓▓▓▓▓▓▓▓▓▓▓▓▓▓▓▓▓▓▓▓▓ **Exercise 14A** ▓▓▓▓▓▓▓▓▓▓▓▓▓▓▓▓▓▓▓▓▓▓

1 Show that there is a root of the equation $2x^3 - 3x^2 - 2x + 5 = 0$ between -1.5 and -1.

2 The equation $e^{-x} - x + 2 = 0$ has one root, α. Find an integer N such that $N < \alpha < N+1$.

3 Given $f(x) = 3x + 13 - e^x$, evaluate $f(3)$ and $f(4)$, correct to three significant figures. Explain the significance of the answers in relation to the equation $3x + 7 = e^x$.

4 For each of parts (a) to (f),
   (i) use the sign-change rule to determine the integer N such that the equation $f(x) = 0$ has a root in the interval $N < x < N+1$;

   (ii) use decimal search to find each root correct to two decimal places.

   (a) $f(x) = x^5 - 5x + 6$ (b) $f(x) = x + \sqrt{x^3 + 1} - 7$ (c) $f(x) = e^x - \dfrac{5}{x}$

   (d) $f(x) = 1000 - e^x \ln x$ (e) $f(x) = \ln(x^2 + 1) - 12 - x$ (f) $f(x) = x^5 + x^3 - 1999$

5 The function $f(x)$ is such that $f(a)f(b) < 0$ for real constants a and b with $a < b$, yet $f(x) = 0$ for no value of x such that $a < x < b$. Explain the feature of the function which allows this situation to arise, and illustrate your answer with a suitable example.

14.3 Finding roots by iteration

Example 14.3.1
Find the terms of the sequence defined by the inductive definition $x_0 = 0, \quad x_{r+1} = e^{-x_r}$.

In the calculation all the available figures have been retained in the calculator, but the answers are tabulated correct to 5 decimal places.

r	x_r	r	x_r	r	x_r
0	0	9	0.571 14	18	0.567 12
1	1	10	0.564 88	19	0.567 16
2	0.367 88	11	0.568 43	20	0.567 14
3	0.692 20	12	0.566 41	21	0.567 15
4	0.500 47	13	0.567 56	22	0.567 14
5	0.606 24	14	0.566 91	23	0.567 14
6	0.545 40	15	0.567 28	24	0.567 14
7	0.579 61	16	0.567 07	...	...
8	0.560 12	17	0.567 19	...	...

Table 14.6

From $r = 22$ onwards it seems that the values correct to 5 decimal places are all $0.567\,14$. This is especially convincing in this example, since you can notice that the terms are alternately below and above $0.567\,14$; so once you have two successive terms with this value, the same value will continue indefinitely. (You met a similar sequence in Section 10.3. The sum sequence for a geometric series with common ratio -0.2 had terms alternately above and below $0.8333\ldots$.)

Notice also that the limit towards which these terms are converging appears to be the same (to the accuracy available) as the root of the equation $x = e^{-x}$ found in Example 14.2.1. This is an example of a process called **iteration**, which can often be used to solve equations of the form $x = F(x)$.

> If the sequence given by the inductive definition $x_{r+1} = F(x_r)$, with some initial value x_0, converges to a limit l, then l is a root of the equation $x = F(x)$.

It is quite easy to see why. Since the sequence is given to be convergent, the left side x_{r+1} tends to l as $r \to \infty$, and the right side $F(x_r)$ tends to $F(l)$. (To be sure of this, the function $F(x)$ must be continuous.)

So $l = F(l)$; that is, l is a root of $x = F(x)$.

For another illustration take the equation $x^3 - 3x - 5 = 0$, for which the root was found earlier by the sign-change method. This can be rearranged as

$$x^3 = 3x + 5, \text{ or } x = \sqrt[3]{3x + 5}.$$

This is of the form $x = F(x)$, so you can try to find the root by iteration, using a sequence defined by

$$x_{r+1} = \sqrt[3]{3x_r + 5}.$$

Fig. 14.3 suggests that the root is close to 2, so take $x_0 = 2$. Successive terms, correct to 5 decimal places, are then as in Table 14.7.

r	x_r	r	x_r	r	x_r
0	2	4	2.278 62	8	2.279 02
1	2.223 98	5	2.278 94	9	2.279 02
2	2.268 37	6	2.279 00	…	…
3	2.276 97	7	2.279 02	…	…

Table 14.7

This suggests that the limit is $2.279\,02$, but this time you cannot be quite sure. Since the terms get steadily larger, rather than being alternately too large and too small, it is just possible that if you go on longer there might be another change in the final digit. So for a final check go back to the sign-change method. Writing $f(x) = x^3 - 3x - 5$, calculate $f(2.279\,015) = -0.000\,047\ldots$ and $f(2.279\,025) = 0.000\,078\ldots$. This shows that the root is indeed $2.279\,02$ correct to 5 decimal places.

At each step of this iteration you have to use the key sequence $\times, 3, +, 5, =, \sqrt[3]{\ }$ to get from one term to the next. If you have a calculator with an [ANS] key, or if you set the process up as a small computer program or a spreadsheet, you can get the answer much more quickly.

14.4 Iterations which go wrong

There is more than one way of rearranging an equation $f(x) = 0$ as $x = F(x)$. For example, $x^3 - 3x - 5 = 0$ could be written as

$$3x = x^3 - 5, \quad \text{or} \quad x = \tfrac{1}{3}(x^3 - 5).$$

But if you perform the iteration

$$x_{r+1} = \tfrac{1}{3}(x_r^{\,3} - 5), \text{ with } x_0 = 2,$$

the first few terms are

$$2, 1, -1.333\,33, -2.456\,79, -6.609\,58, -97.916\,54, \ldots.$$

Clearly this is never going to converge to a limit.

The same can happen with the equation $xe^x = 1$. If, instead of constructing an iteration from $x = e^{-x}$, you write it as

$$\ln x = -x, \text{ or } x = -\ln x,$$

then the corresponding iteration is

$$x_{r+1} = -\ln x_r.$$

You can't start with $x_0 = 0$ this time, so take x_0 to be 0.5. Then you get

$$0.5, \ 0.693\,15, \ 0.366\,51, \ 1.003\,72, \ -0.003\,71, \ \text{ERROR!}$$

The terms are alternately above and below the root, as they were in Example 14.3.1, but they get further away from it each time until you eventually get a term which is outside the domain of $\ln x$.

So if you have an equation $f(x) = 0$, and rearrange it as $x = F(x)$, then the sequence $x_{r+1} = F(x_r)$ may or may not converge to a limit. If it does, then the limit is a root of the equation. If not, you should try rearranging the equation another way.

Exercise 14B

1   For each of parts (a) to (c), find three possible rearrangements of the equation $f(x) = 0$ into the form $x = F(x)$.

(a) $f(x) = x^5 - 5x + 6$ (b) $f(x) = e^x - \dfrac{5}{x}$ (c) $f(x) = x^5 + x^3 - 1999$

2 Each of parts (a) to (c) defines a sequence by an iteration of the form $x_{r+1} = F(x_r)$.

   (i) Rearrange the equation $x = F(x)$ into the form $f(x) = 0$, where f is a polynomial function.

   (ii) Use the iteration, with the given initial approximation x_0, to find the terms of the sequence $x_0, x_1, \ldots$ as far as x_5.

   (iii) Describe the behaviour of the sequence.

   (iv) If the sequence converges, investigate whether x_5 is an approximate root of $f(x) = 0$.

   (a) $x_0 = 0, x_{r+1} = \sqrt[11]{x_r^7 - 6}$ (b) $x_0 = 3, x_{r+1} = \left(\dfrac{17 - x_r^2}{x_r}\right)^2$ (c) $x_0 = 7, x_{r+1} = \sqrt[3]{500 + \dfrac{10}{x_r}}$

3 Show that the equation $x^5 + x - 19 = 0$ can be arranged into the form $x = \sqrt[3]{\dfrac{19 - x}{x^2}}$ and that the equation has a root α between $x = 1$ and $x = 2$.

   Use an iteration based on this arrangement, with initial approximation $x_0 = 2$, to find the values of $x_1, x_2, \ldots, x_6$. Investigate whether this sequence is converging to α.

4 (a) Show that the equation $x^2 + 2x - e^x = 0$ has a root in the interval $2 < x < 3$.

   (b) Use an iterative method based on the re-arrangement $x = \sqrt{e^x - 2x}$, with initial approximation $x_0 = 2$, to find the value of x_{10} to four decimal places. Describe what is happening to the terms of this sequence of approximations.

5 Show that the equation $e^x = x^3 - 2$ can be arranged into the form $x = \ln(x^3 - 2)$. Show also that it has a root between 2 and 3.

   Use the iteration $x_{r+1} = \ln(x_r^3 - 2)$, commencing with $x_0 = 2$ as an initial approximation to the root, to show that this arrangement is not a suitable one for finding this root.

   Find an alternative arrangement of $e^x = x^3 - 2$ which can be used to find this root, and use it to calculate the root correct to two decimal places.

6 (a) Determine the value of the positive integer N such that the equation $12 - x - \ln x = 0$ has a root α such that $N < \alpha < N + 1$.

   (b) Define the sequence $x_0, x_1, \ldots$ of approximations to α iteratively by $x_0 = N + \frac{1}{2}$, $x_{r+1} = 12 - \ln x_r$.

   Find the number of steps required before two consecutive terms of this sequence are the same when rounded to 4 significant figures. Show that this common value is equal to α to this degree of accuracy.

14.5*Choosing convergent iterations

The rest of this chapter is about how to rearrange an equation to ensure that the iterative sequence converges. You may if you like omit it and go on to Miscellaneous exercise 14. The issue of convergence will be explored in more detail in module P5.

The solution of $x = F(x)$ can be represented graphically by the intersection of the graph of $y = F(x)$ with the line $y = x$. Fig. 14.8 shows this for the equations in the last two sections, each with two alternative forms.

(a) $xe^x = 1$ (b) $x^3 - 3x - 5 = 0$

(i) $x = e^{-x}$ (ii) $x = -\ln x$ (i) $x = \sqrt[3]{3x+5}$ (ii) $x = \dfrac{x^3 - 5}{3}$

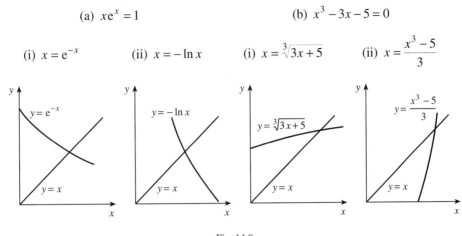

Fig. 14.8

In both cases the sequence converged in version (i), but not in version (ii).

Inspection of the graphs suggests that it is the gradient of the graph of $y = F(x)$ at or near the root which governs the nature of the iteration.

In (a)(i) the gradient is negative, but numerically quite small (about -0.5). The sequence converges, though quite slowly; it takes 22 steps to reach the root correct to 5 decimal places. The terms alternate above and below the root.

In (a)(ii) the gradient is negative, but numerically much larger (about -2). The sequence does not converge, but the terms again alternate above and below the root.

In (b)(i) the gradient is positive, and numerically small (about 0.2). The sequence converges quite fast, taking only 7 steps to reach the root correct to 5 decimal places. The terms get steadily larger, approaching the root from below.

In (b)(ii) the gradient is positive and numerically large (about 5). The sequence does not converge, and the terms get steadily smaller.

This points to the following conclusions, which are generally true. You can test these further for yourself from the sequences which you produced in Exercise 14B.

- If the equation $x = F(x)$ has a root, then a sequence defined by $x_{r+1} = F(x_r)$ with a starting value close to the root will converge if the gradient of the graph of $y = F(x)$ at and around the root is not too large (roughly between -1 and 1).
- The smaller the modulus of the gradient, the fewer steps will be needed to reach the root to a given accuracy.
- If the gradient is negative the terms will be alternately above and below the root; if it is positive, the terms will approach the root steadily from one side.

There is one further point to notice about these examples. The pairs of functions used for $F(x)$ are in fact inverses.

(a) $x \rightarrow [\ +/-\ ] \rightarrow [\ \exp\ ] \rightarrow$ has output e^{-x},

   $\leftarrow [\ +/-\ ] \leftarrow [\ \ln\ ] \leftarrow x$ (read right to left) has output $-\ln x$

(b) $x \rightarrow [\ \times 3\ ] \rightarrow [\ +5\ ] \rightarrow [\ \sqrt[3]{\ }\ ] \rightarrow$ has output $\sqrt[3]{3x+5}$,

   $\leftarrow [\ \div 3\ ] \leftarrow [\ -5\ ] \leftarrow [\ (\ )^3\ ] \leftarrow x$ has output $\frac{1}{3}(x^3-5)$.

Their graphs are therefore reflections of each other in the line $y = x$. This is why, if the gradient of one graph is numerically small, the gradient of the other is large. This leads to a useful rule for deciding how to rearrange an equation.

> If the function F is one–one, and if $x = F(x)$ has a root, then usually one of the sequences $x_{r+1} = F(x_r)$ and $x_{r+1} = F^{-1}(x_r)$ converges to the root, but the other does not.

Example 14.5.1

Show that the equation $x^3 - 3x - 1 = 0$ has three roots, and find them correct to 4 decimal places.

The graph of $y = x^3 - 3x - 1$ is shown in Fig. 14.9. It is in fact the graph in Fig. 14.3 translated by $+4$ in the y-direction. You can see that it cuts the x-axis in three places: between -2 and -1, -1 and 0, and 1 and 2.

You could use iterations based on a rearrangement $x = F(x)$, where $F(x)$ is either $\frac{1}{3}(x^3 - 1)$ or $\sqrt[3]{3x+1}$. These are illustrated in Fig. 14.10; again, they are inverse functions. To get a small gradient at the intersection, you should use $F(x) = \sqrt[3]{3x+1}$

for the first and last of the roots, and $F(x) = \frac{1}{3}(x^3 - 1)$ for the middle root.

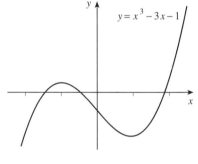

Fig. 14.9

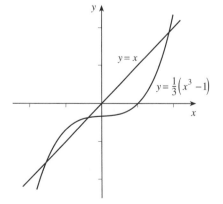
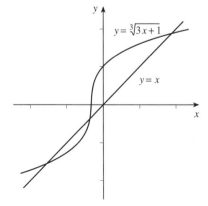

Fig. 14.10

You can check for yourself that:

$x_{r+1} = \sqrt[3]{3x_r + 1}$ with $x_0 = -2$ reaches the root -1.5321 in 11 steps,

$x_{r+1} = \frac{1}{3}\left(x_r^3 - 1\right)$ with $x_0 = 0$ reaches the root -0.3473 in 4 steps,

$x_{r+1} = \sqrt[3]{3x_r + 1}$ with $x_0 = 2$ reaches the root 1.8794 in 6 steps.

The next example shows a trick which you can use to reduce the number of steps needed to reach the root, or even to produce a convergent iteration from one which does not converge.

Example 14.5.2
For each of the equations   (a) $x = e^{-x}$,   (b) $x = -\ln x$,   add an extra term kx to both sides, and choose k so that, near the root, the function on the right has a small gradient. Use this to produce a sequence which converges rapidly to the root.

(a) Write $kx + x = kx + e^{-x}$. You saw earlier that near the root the graph of e^{-x} has a gradient of about -0.5, so $kx + e^{-x}$ has a gradient of about $k - 0.5$. To make this small, choose $k = 0.5$. Then the equation becomes

$$1.5x = 0.5x + e^{-x}, \quad \text{or} \quad x = \frac{1}{3}\left(x + 2e^{-x}\right).$$

The iteration $x_{r+1} = \frac{1}{3}\left(x_r + 2e^{-x_r}\right)$ with $x_0 = 1$ reaches the root $0.567\,14$, correct to 5 decimal places, in 4 steps. (In Example 14.3.1 it took 22 steps of the iteration $x_{r+1} = e^{-x_r}$ to achieve the same accuracy.)

(b) Write $kx + x = kx - \ln x$. Near the root the graph of $-\ln x$ has a gradient of about -2, so $kx - \ln x$ has a gradient of about $k - 2$. Choose $k = 2$, so that the equation becomes

$$3x = 2x - \ln x, \text{ or } x = \frac{1}{3}(2x - \ln x).$$

The iteration $x_{r+1} = \frac{1}{3}(2x_r - \ln x_r)$ with $x_0 = 1$ reaches the root in 6 steps.
(You saw in Section 14.4 that the iteration $x_{r+1} = -\ln x_r$ does not even converge.)

Exercise 14C*

1   In parts (a) to (f), use a graphic calculator to display the graph of $y = F(x)$, and hence decide whether the iteration $x_{r+1} = F(x_r)$, with initial approximation x_0, is suitable for finding the root of the equation $x = F(x)$ near to $x = x_0$.

Where the process leads to a convergent sequence of approximations to the required root, find this root. Where the process is unsuitable, find $F^{-1}(x)$ and use it to find the root.

In parts (a) to (c) give your answers correct to 3 decimal places; in parts (d) to (f) give your answers correct to 4 decimal places.

(a) $F(x) = \dfrac{3}{x} - 1, x_0 = 1$

(b) $F(x) = 5 - e^{3x}, x_0 = 0$

(c) $F(x) = \sqrt[3]{17 - x^2}, x_0 = 3$

(d) $F(x) = 30 - \frac{1}{10}x^6, x_0 = -2$

(e) $F(x) = 8 + \ln(x^2 + 7), x_0 = 10$

(f) $F(x) = \dfrac{3}{20 - x^2}, x_0 = 4$

2 In each of parts (a) to (d) find a constant k for which

$$kx_{r+1} + x_{r+1} = kx_r + F(x_r)$$

is a better form than $x_{r+1} = F(x_r)$ to use to find the root of the equation $x = F(x)$ near x_0. In each case, find this root correct to 4 significant figures.

(a) $F(x) = 2 - 5\ln x$, $x_0 = 1$ (b) $F(x) = x^2 + 6\ln x - 50$, $x_0 = 6$

(c) $F(x) = \frac{1}{48}(x^4 - x^7 - 192)$, $x_0 = -2$ (d) $F(x) = x\ln x - e^{-x} - 20$, $x_0 = 12$

Miscellaneous exercise 14

1 Given that $f(x) = 2^x + 3^x$, evaluate $f(1)$ and $f(2)$. Using these values,

(a) state what this tells you about the root of the equation $f(x) = 10$,

(b) suggest a suitable initial approximation to this root.

2 Find the positive integer N such that $40e^{-x} = x^2$ has a root between N and $N+1$.

3 Show that there exists a root, $x = \alpha$, of the equation $x^3 - 6x + 3 = 0$ such that $2 < \alpha < 3$. Use decimal search to find this root correct to two decimal places.

4 Show that the equation $2x - \ln(x^2 + 2) = 0$ has a root in the interval $0.3 < x < 0.4$. Use decimal search to find an interval of width 0.001 in which this root lies.

5 The equation $e^x = 50\sqrt{2x-1}$ has two positive real roots. Use decimal search to find the larger root correct to one decimal place.

6 (a) On the same diagram, sketch the graphs of $y = 2^{-x}$ and $y = x^2$.

(b) One of the points of intersection of these graphs has a positive x-coordinate. Find this x-coordinate correct to 2 decimal places and give a brief indication of your method.

(OCR)

7 (a) On a single diagram, sketch the graphs of $y = \tan x°$ and $y = 4\cos x° - 3$ for $0 \leqslant x \leqslant 180$. Deduce the number of solutions of the equation $f(x) = 0$ which exist for $0 \leqslant x \leqslant 180$, where $f(x) = 3 + \tan x° - 4\cos x°$.

(b) By evaluating $f(x)$ for suitably chosen values of x, show that a root of the equation $f(x) = 0$ occurs at $x = 28$ (correct to the nearest integer).

8 Show that there is a root α of the equation $2\sin x° - \cos x° + 1 = 0$ such that $230 < \alpha < 240$. Use a decimal search method to determine this root to the nearest 0.1.

9 The points A and B have coordinates $(0, -2)$ and $(-30, 0)$ respectively.

(a) Find an equation of the line which passes through A and B.

The function f is defined by $f(x) = 1 + \tan x°$, $-90 < x < 90$.

(b) Explain why there is just one point where the line in (a) meets the graph of $y = f(x)$.

(c) Use an appropriate method to find the value of the integer N such that the value of the x-coordinate of the point where the graph of $y = f(x)$ meets the line of part (a) satisfies $N < x < N+1$.

(OCR, adapted)

10 Find, correct to two decimal places, the x-coordinate of the turning point on the curve with equation $y = x^3 - 50x + 7e^x$, $x \geqslant 0$.

11 The region, R, of the plane enclosed by the axes, the curve $y = e^x + 4$ and the line $x = 2$ has area A. Find, correct to four significant figures, the value of m, $0 < m < 2$, such that the portion of R between the y-axis and the line $x = m$ has area $\frac{1}{2}A$.

12 Show that the equation $3.5x = 1.6^x$ has a real solution between 6 and 7. By rearranging the equation into the form $x = a + b \ln x$, determine this root correct to two decimal places.

13 (a) Given that $f(x) = e^{2x} - 6x$, evaluate $f(0)$ and $f(1)$, giving each answer correct to three decimal places. Explain how the equation $f(x) = 0$ could still have a root in the interval $0 < x < 1$ even though $f(0)f(1) > 0$.

  (b) Rewrite the equation $f(x) = 0$ in the form $x = F(x)$, for some suitable function F. Taking $x_0 = 0.5$ as an initial approximation, use an iterative method to determine one of the roots of this equation correct to three decimal places. How could you demonstrate that this root has the required degree of accuracy?

  (c) Deduce the value, to two decimal places, of one of the roots of the equation $e^x - 3x = 0$.

14 (a) Show that the equation $x^3 - 3x^2 - 1 = 0$ has a root α between $x = 3$ and $x = 4$.

  (b) The iterative formula $x_{r+1} = 3 + \dfrac{1}{x_r^2}$ is used to calculate a sequence of approximations to this root. Taking $x_0 = 3$ as an initial approximation to α, determine the values of x_1, x_2, x_3 and x_4 correct to 5 decimal places. State the value of α to 3 decimal places and justify this degree of accuracy.

15* (a) Show that the equation $x + \ln x - 4 = 0$ has a root α in the interval $2 < x < 3$.

  (b) Find which of the two iterative forms $x_{r+1} = e^{4-x_r}$ and $x_{r+1} = \ln(4 - x_r)$
  is more likely to give a convergent sequence of approximations to α, giving a reason for your answer. Use your chosen form to determine α correct to two decimal places.

16* (a) Find the positive integer N such that the equation $(t - 1)\ln 4 = \ln(9t)$ has a solution $t = r$ in the interval $N < t < N + 1$.

  (b) Write down two possible rearrangements of this equation in the form $t = F(t)$ and $t = F^{-1}(t)$. Show which of these two arrangements is more suitable for using iteratively to determine an approximation to r to three decimal places, and find such an approximation.

17* (a) Use a graphic calculator to display the graph of $y = F(x)$, where $F(x) = 3x^2 + 20 - e^{-x}$.

  (b) The equation $x = F(x)$ has a single root α. Find the integer N such that $N < \alpha < N + 1$.

  (c) By adding a term kx to both sides of $x = F(x)$, where k is a suitably chosen integer, determine α correct to four decimal places.

18* (a) Find the coordinates of the points of intersection of the graphs with equations

$y = x$ and $y = g(x)$, where $g(x) = \dfrac{5}{x}$.

(b) Show that the iterative process defined by $x_0 = 2$, $x_{r+1} = g(x_r)$ can't be used to find good approximations to the positive root of the equation $x = \dfrac{5}{x}$.

(c) Describe why the use of the inverse function $g^{-1}(x)$ is also inappropriate in this case.

(d) Use a graph to explain why the iterative process defined by

$$x_0 = 2,\ x_{r+1} = \frac{1}{2}\left(x_r + \frac{5}{x_r}\right)$$

leads to a convergent sequence of approximations to this root. Find this root correct to six decimal places.

19* (a) Use a graph to show that the equation $f(x) = 0$, where $f(x) = x - 10 - 30\cos x°$, has only one root. Denote this root by α.

(b) Find two numbers, a_0 and b_0, such that $b_0 - a_0 = 10$ and $a_0 < \alpha < b_0$.

(c) Evaluate $f(m)$, where $m = \frac{1}{2}(a_0 + b_0)$. Determine whether $a_0 < \alpha < m$ or $m < \alpha < b_0$. Hence write down two numbers, a_1 and b_1, such that $b_1 - a_1 = 5$ and $a_1 < \alpha < b_1$.

(d) Use a method similar to part (c) to find two numbers, a_2 and b_2, such that $b_2 - a_2 = 2.5$ and $a_2 < \alpha < b_2$.

(e) Continuing this way, find two sequences, a_r and b_r, such that $b_r - a_r = 10 \times 2^{-r}$ and $a_r < \alpha < b_r$. Go on until you find two numbers of the sequence which enable you to write down the value of α correct to 1 decimal place. (This is called the 'bisection method'.)

20 Given the one–one function $F(x)$, explain why roots of the equation $F(x) = F^{-1}(x)$ are also roots of the equation $x = F(x)$.

Use this to solve the equations

(a) $x^3 - 1 = \sqrt[3]{1 + x}$,   (b) $\frac{1}{10}e^x = \ln(10x)$.

15 Radians

This chapter introduces radians, an alternative to degrees for measuring angles. When you have completed it, you should

- know how to convert from degrees to radians and vice versa
- be able to use the formula $r\theta$ for the length of a circular arc, and $\frac{1}{2}r^2\theta$ for the area of a circular sector.

15.1 Radians

Suppose that you were meeting angles for the first time, and that you were asked to suggest a unit for measuring them. It seems highly unlikely that you would suggest the degree. The full circle or the right angle both seem more natural than the degree, which was invented by the Babylonians in ancient times.

However, the unit used in modern mathematics is the radian, illustrated in Fig. 15.1. This is particularly useful in differentiating trigonometric functions, as you will see if you go on to module P3.

In a circle of radius 1 unit, radii joining the centre O to the ends of an arc of length 1 unit form an angle called **1 radian**. The abbreviation for radian is **rad**.

You can see immediately from this definition that there are 2π radians in $360°$. This leads to the following conversion factor for radians to degrees:

$\pi \text{ rad} = 180°.$

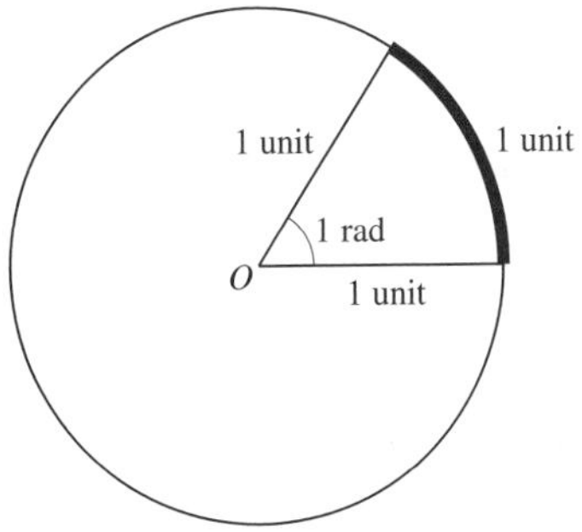

Fig. 15.1

You could calculate that 1 radian is equal to $57.296°$, but no one uses this conversion. It is simplest to remember that $\pi \text{ rad} = 180°$, and use this to convert between radians and degrees.

You might find on your calculator another unit for angle called the 'grad'; there are 100 grads to the right angle. Grads will not be used in this course.

Example 15.1.1
Convert $40°$ to radians, leaving your answer as a multiple of π.

Since $40°$ is $\frac{2}{9}$ of $180°$, $40° = \frac{2}{9}\pi \text{ rad}$.

It is worthwhile learning a few common conversions, so that you can think in both radians and degrees. For example, you should know and recognise the following conversions:

$180° = \pi \text{ rad}, \quad 90° = \frac{1}{2}\pi \text{ rad}, \quad 45° = \frac{1}{4}\pi \text{ rad}, \quad 30° = \frac{1}{6}\pi \text{ rad}, \quad 60° = \frac{1}{3}\pi \text{ rad}.$

15.2 Length of arc and area of sector

Fig. 15.2 shows a circular sector, centre O and radius r, which subtends an angle θ rad at its centre. You can calculate the length of the circular arc by noticing that the length of the arc is the fraction $\dfrac{\theta}{2\pi}$ of the length $2\pi r$ of the circumference of the circle.

Let s be the arc length. Then

$$s = \frac{\theta}{2\pi} \times 2\pi r = r\theta.$$

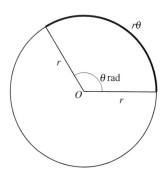

Fig. 15.2

You can use a similar argument to calculate the area of a sector.

The circular sector, centre O and radius r, shown shaded in Fig. 15.3, forms an angle θ rad at its centre.

The area of the circular sector is the fraction $\dfrac{\theta}{2\pi}$ of the area πr^2 of the area of the circle.

Let A be the required area. Then

$$A = \frac{\theta}{2\pi} \times \pi r^2 = \tfrac{1}{2} r^2 \theta.$$

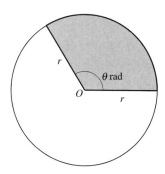

Fig. 15.3

> The length of a circular arc with radius r and angle θ rad is $s = r\theta$.
>
> The area of a circular sector with radius r and angle θ rad is $A = \tfrac{1}{2} r^2 \theta$.

Notice that no units are given in the shaded formulae above. The units are the appropriate units associated with the length; for instance, length in m *and area in* m^2.

Example 15.2.1

Find the perimeter and the area of the segment cut off by a chord PQ of length 8 cm from a circle centre O and radius 6 cm. Give your answers correct to 3 significant figures.

In problems of this type, it is helpful to start by thinking about the complete sector OPQ, rather than just the shaded segment of Fig. 15.4.

The perimeter of the segment consists of two parts, the straight part of length 8 cm, and the curved part; to calculate the curved part you need to know the angle POQ.

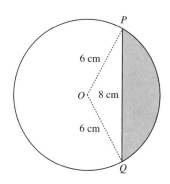

Fig. 15.4

Call this angle 2θ. As triangle POQ is isosceles, a perpendicular drawn from O to PQ bisects both PQ and angle POQ.

$$\sin\theta = \tfrac{4}{6} = 0.666\ldots, \text{ so } \theta = 0.7297\ldots.$$

Make sure that your calculator is in radian mode.

Then the perimeter d cm is given by $d = 8 + 6 \times 2(0.7297\ldots) = 16.756\ldots$; the perimeter is 16.8 cm, to 3 significant figures.

To find the area of the segment, you need to find the area of the sector OPQ, and then subtract the area of the triangle OPQ. Using the formula $\tfrac{1}{2}bc\sin A$ for the area of a triangle, the area of the triangle POQ is given by $\tfrac{1}{2}r^2 \sin(2\theta)$. Thus the area in cm^2 of the shaded region is

$$\tfrac{1}{2}r^2(2\theta) - \tfrac{1}{2}r^2\sin(2\theta) = \tfrac{1}{2}\times 6^2 \times (2\times 0.7297\ldots) - \tfrac{1}{2}\times 6^2 \times \sin(2\times 0.7297\ldots)$$
$$= 8.381\ldots.$$

The area is 8.38 cm^2, correct to 3 significant figures.

It is worthwhile using your calculator to store the value of θ to use in the calculations. If you round θ to 3 significant figures and use the rounded value, you are liable to introduce errors.

In the course of Example 15.2.1, the notations $\sin\theta = \tfrac{4}{6} = 0.666\ldots$, $\sin(2\theta)$ and $\sin(2\times 0.7297\ldots)$ were used, without any indication that the angles were in radians. The convention is that when you see '$\sin 12$', you should read it as the sine of 12 radians. If it were the sine of $12°$ it would be written $\sin 12°$.

Example 15.2.2

A chord of a circle which subtends an angle of θ at the centre of the circle cuts off a segment equal in area to $\tfrac{1}{3}$ of the area of the whole circle.

(a) Show that $\theta - \sin\theta = \tfrac{2}{3}\pi$.

(b) Use an iterative method to find θ correct to 2 decimal places.

(a) Let r cm be the radius of the circle. Using a method similar to the one in Example 15.2.1, the area of the segment is

$$\tfrac{1}{2}r^2\theta - \tfrac{1}{2}r^2\sin\theta.$$

This is $\tfrac{1}{3}$ of the area of the whole circle if

$$\tfrac{1}{2}r^2\theta - \tfrac{1}{2}r^2\sin\theta = \tfrac{1}{3}\pi r^2.$$

Multiplying by 2 and dividing by r^2 you find

$$\theta - \sin\theta = \tfrac{2}{3}\pi.$$

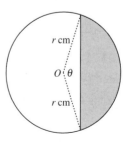

Fig. 15.5

(b) Use the iterative formula $\theta_{r+1} = \frac{2}{3}\pi + \sin\theta_r$, starting with $\theta_0 = \pi$. Convergence is slow, but if you use your calculator efficiently you find within a few seconds that $\theta = 2.61$ (to 3 significant figures).

Exercise 15

1 Write each of the following angles in radians, leaving your answer as a multiple of π.

   (a) 90°   (b) 135°   (c) 45°   (d) 30°

   (e) 72°   (f) 18°   (g) 120°   (h) $22\frac{1}{2}°$

   (i) 720°   (j) 600°   (k) 270°   (l) 1°

2 Each of the following is an angle in radians. Without using a calculator change these to degrees.

   (a) $\frac{1}{3}\pi$ (b) $\frac{1}{20}\pi$ (c) $\frac{1}{5}\pi$ (d) $\frac{1}{8}\pi$

   (e) $\frac{1}{9}\pi$ (f) $\frac{2}{3}\pi$ (g) $\frac{5}{8}\pi$ (h) $\frac{3}{5}\pi$

   (i) $\frac{1}{45}\pi$ (j) 6π (k) $-\frac{1}{2}\pi$ (l) $\frac{5}{18}\pi$

3 Without the use of a calculator write down the exact values of the following.

   (a) $\sin\frac{1}{3}\pi$ (b) $\cos\frac{1}{4}\pi$ (c) $\tan\frac{1}{6}\pi$ (d) $\cos\frac{3}{2}\pi$

   (e) $\sin\frac{7}{4}\pi$ (f) $\cos\frac{7}{6}\pi$ (g) $\tan\frac{5}{3}\pi$ (h) $\sin^2\frac{2}{3}\pi$

4 The following questions refer to the diagram, where

   r = radius of circle (in cm),

   s = arc length (in cm),

   A = area of sector (in cm^2),

   θ = angle subtended at centre (in radians).

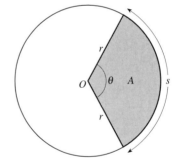

   (a) $r = 7, \theta = 1.2$. Find s and A.

   (b) $r = 3.5$, $\theta = 2.1$. Find s and A.

   (c) $s = 12$, $r = 8$. Find θ and A.

   (d) $s = 14$, $\theta = 0.7$. Find r and A.

   (e) $A = 30$, $r = 5$. Find θ and s.   (f) $A = 24$, $r = 6$. Find s.

   (g) $A = 64$, $s = 16$. Find r and θ.   (h) $A = 30$, $s = 10$. Find θ.

5 Find the area of the shaded segment in each of the following cases.

   (a) $r = 5$ cm, $\theta = \frac{1}{3}\pi$

   (b) $r = 3.1$ cm, $\theta = \frac{2}{5}\pi$

   (c) $r = 28$ cm, $\theta = \frac{5}{6}\pi$

   (d) $r = 6$ cm, $s = 9$ cm

   (e) $r = 9.5$ cm, $s = 4$ cm

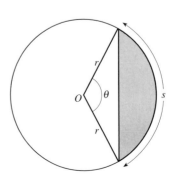

6 Find the area of the segment cut off by a chord of length 10 cm from a circle radius 13 cm.

7 Find the perimeter of the segment cut off by a chord of length 14 cm from a circle radius 25 cm.

8 A chord of a circle which subtends an angle of θ at the centre cuts off a segment equal in area to $\frac{1}{4}$ of the whole circle.

(a) Show that $\theta - \sin\theta = \frac{1}{2}\pi$.

(b) Use either an iterative method or decimal search to find the value of θ correct to 3 significant figures.

9 A chord of a circle which subtends an angle of θ at the centre cuts off a segment equal in area to $\frac{3}{8}$ of the whole circle.

Use a numerical method to find the value of θ correct to 3 significant figures.

10 Two circles of radii 5 cm and 12 cm are drawn, partly overlapping. Their centres are 13 cm apart. Find the area common to the two circles.

11 An eclipse of the sun is said to be 10% total when 90% of the area of the sun's disc is visible behind the disc of the moon.

A child models this with two discs, each of radius r cm, as shown.

(a) Calculate, in terms of r, the distance between the centres of the two discs.

(b) Calculate also the distance between the centres when the eclipse is 80% total.

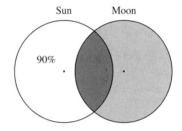

12 The diagram shows two intersecting circles of radius 6 cm and 4 cm with centres 7 cm apart. Find the perimeter and area of the region common to both circles.

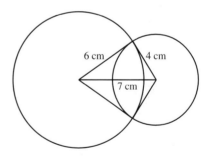

<hr />

Miscellaneous exercise 15

1 The diagram shows a sector of a circle with centre θ and radius 6 cm. Angle $POQ = 0.6$ radians. Calculate the length of arc PQ and the area of sector POQ.　　(OCR)

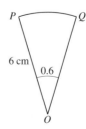

2   A sector OAB of a circle, of radius a and centre O, has $\angle OAB = \theta$ radians. Given that the area of the sector OAB is twice the square of the length of the arc AB, find θ.   (OCR)

3   The diagram shows a sector of a circle, with centre O and radius r. The length of the arc is equal to half the perimeter of the sector. Find the area of the sector in terms of r.   (OCR)

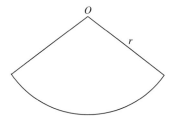

4   The diagram shows two circles, with centres A and B, intersecting at C and D in such a way that the centre of each lies on the circumference of the other. The radius of each circle is 1 unit. Write down the size of angle CAD and calculate the area of the shaded region (bounded by the arc CBD and the straight line CD). Hence show that the area of the region common to the interiors of the two circles is approximately 39% of the area of one circle.   (OCR)

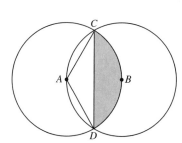

5   In the diagram, ABC is an arc of a circle with centre O and radius 5 cm. The lines AD and CD are tangents to the circle at A and C respectively. Angle $AOC = \frac{2}{3}\pi$ radians. Calculate the area of the region enclosed by AD, DC and the arc ABC, giving your answer correct to 2 significant figures.   (OCR)

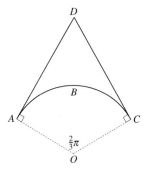

6   The diagram shows a circle with centre O and radius r, and a chord AB which subtends an angle θ radians at O. Express the area of the shaded segment bounded by the chord AB in terms of r and θ.

Given that the area of this segment is one-third of the area of triangle OAB, show that $3\theta - 4\sin\theta = 0$.

Find the positive value of θ satisfying $3\theta - 4\sin\theta = 0$ to within 0.1 radians, by tabulating values of $3\theta - 4\sin\theta$ and looking for a sign change, or otherwise.   (OCR)

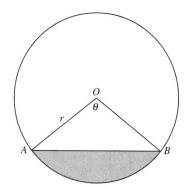

7 The diagram shows two circles, with centres A and B, which touch at C. The radius of each circle is r. The points D and E, one on each circle, are such that DE is parallel to the line ACB. Each of the angles DAC and EBC is θ radians, where $0 < \theta < \pi$. Express the length of DE in terms of r and θ.

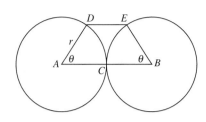

The length of DE is equal to the length of each of the minor arcs CD and CE.

(a) Show that $\theta + 2\cos\theta - 2 = 0$.

(b) Sketch the graph of $y = \cos\theta$ for $0 < \theta < \frac{1}{2}\pi$. By drawing on your graph a suitable straight line, the equation of which must be stated, show that the equation $\theta + 2\cos\theta - 2 = 0$ has exactly one root in the interval $0 < \theta < \frac{1}{2}\pi$.

Verify by calculation that θ lies between 1.10 and 1.11.   (OCR)

8 The diagram shows an arc ABC of a circle with centre O and radius r, and the chord AC. The length of the arc ABC is s, and angle $AOC = \theta$ rad. Express θ in terms of r and s, and deduce that the area of triangle AOC may be expressed as

$$\tfrac{1}{2}r^2 \sin\left(2\pi - \frac{s}{r}\right).$$

Show, by a graphical argument based on a sketch of $y = \sin x$, or otherwise, that $\sin(2\pi - \alpha) = -\sin\alpha$, where α is any angle measured in radians.

Given that the area of triangle AOC is equal to one fifth of the area of the major sector $OABC$, show that $\dfrac{s}{r} + 5\sin\left(\dfrac{s}{r}\right) = 0$.

9 The diagram shows a sector of a circle with centre O and radius r, and a chord AB which subtends an angle θ radians at O, where $0 < \theta < \pi$.

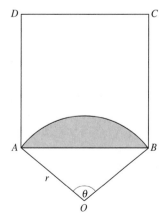

A square $ABCD$ is drawn, as shown in the diagram. It is given that the area of the shaded segment is exactly one-eighth of the area of the square. Show that

$$2\theta - 2\sin\theta + \cos\theta - 1 = 0.$$

Hence show that θ lies between 1 and 2, and find θ correct to 1 decimal place.

Revision exercise 4

1 You are given that the equation $f(x) = 0$ has a solution at $x = 3$. Using this information, write down as many solutions as you can to each of the following equations.

(a) $2f(x+5) = 0$ (b) $f(3x) = 0$

(c) $|f(x)| = 0$ (d) $f(|x|) = 0$ (OCR)

2 A teacher received a salary of £12,800 in his first full year of teaching. He models his future salary by assuming it to increase by a constant amount of £950 each year up to a maximum of £20,400.

(a) How much will he earn in his fifth year of teaching?

(b) In which year does he first receive the maximum salary?

(c) Determine expressions for the total amount he will have received by the end of his nth year of teaching, stating clearly for which values of n each is valid.

His twin sister chose accountancy as her profession. She started her career in the same year as he did. Her first year's salary was £13,500, and she can expect her salary to increase at a constant rate of 5% each year.

(d) Select an appropriate mathematical model and use this to determine her annual salary in her nth year as an accountant.

(e) Show that she earns less than he in their 4th year of working.

(f) Which is the first year after that in which he earns less than she?   (OCR)

3 Differentiate each of the following functions with respect to x.

(a) $\left(x^3 + 2x - 1\right)^3$ (b) e^{3x-1} (c) $\ln\left(x^2 - 1\right)$ (d) $\sqrt{\dfrac{1}{x^2 + 1}}$

4 A spherical star is collapsing in size, while remaining spherical. When its radius is one million kilometres, the radius is decreasing at the rate 500 km s^{-1}. Use calculus to find

(a) the rate of decrease of its volume,   (b) the rate of decrease of its surface area.

5 The region R is bounded by the x-axis, the y-axis, part of the curve with equation $y = e^{2x}$ and part of the straight line with equation $x = 3$.

Calculate, giving your answers in exact form,

(a) the area of R,

(b) the volume of the solid of revolution generated when R is rotated through 4 right angles about the x-axis.

6 (a) A geometric progression has first term 3 and common ratio 0.8. Find the sum of the first twelve terms of this geometric progression, giving your answer correct to two decimal places. Write down the sum to infinity of the geometric progression.

(b) An arithmetic progression has first term 3 and common difference 0.8. The sum to n terms of this progression is 231. Find the value of n.   (OCR)

7 Use an approximate method to find all the roots of the cubic equation
$x^3 - 2x^2 - 2x + 2 = 0$, giving your answers correct to 2 decimal places.

8 The region R, bounded by the curve

$y = 2x + \dfrac{1}{x^2}$, the x-axis and the lines

$x = 1$ and $x = k$ is shaded in the figure.

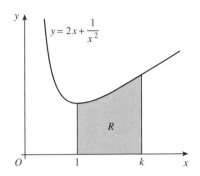

(a) Use integration to calculate the area of
the region R when $k = 2$.

For a different value of k, the area of R is
10 square units.

(b) Show that k satisfies the equation
$k^3 - 10k - 1 = 0$, and use a numerical
method to find the value of k correct
to 3 significant figures.

(OCR, adapted)

9 The number of bacteria in a culture increases exponentially with time. When observation
started there were 1000 bacteria, and five hours later there were 10 000 bacteria. Find,
correct to 3 significant figures,

(a) when there were 5000 bacteria,

(b) when the number of bacteria would exceed one million,

(c) how may bacteria there would be 12 hours after the first observation.

10 (a) Let $y = e^{3x^2 - 6x}$. Find $\dfrac{dy}{dx}$.

(b) Find the coordinates of the stationary point on the curve $y = e^{3x^2 - 6x}$, and decide
whether it is a maximum or a minimum.

(c) Find the equation of the normal to the curve $y = e^{3x^2 - 6x}$ at the point where $x = 2$.

11 A coin is made by starting with an equilateral
triangle ABC of side 2 cm. With centre A an arc
of a circle is drawn joining B to C. Similar arcs
join C to A and A to B.

Find, exactly, the perimeter of the coin and the
area of one of its faces.

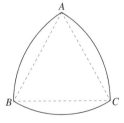

12 (a) Find the gradient m of the line segment joining
the points A and B with x-coordinates 0 and
1 respectively on the graph of $y = e^x$.

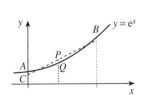

With this value of m, the line $y = mx + c$ is drawn
to meet the y-axis at C and intersect the graph of
$y = e^x$ twice between A and B, as shown in the
diagram. A line parallel to the y-axis between the points of intersection of the straight line
and the curve meets the straight line at P and the curve at Q.

(b) Find the value of c which makes the maximum value of $|PQ|$ equal to the value of
the distance $|AC|$.

Mock examination 1 for P2

Time 1 hour 20 minutes

Answer all the questions.
Graphic calculators are allowed.

1 Solve the inequality $2^x > 3$, giving your answer in an exact form using logarithms. [2]

2 Solve exactly the equation $|x-2| = |3-2x|$. [4]

3 Use the remainder theorem to find the remainder when x^3 is divided by $x-2$. [2]

  Find the quotient when x^3 is divided by $x-2$. [3]

4 A solid is made by rotating the part of the curve with equation $y = (3x-1)^{\frac{3}{2}}$ from $x = \frac{1}{3}$ to $x = k$, where $k > \frac{1}{3}$, through four right angles about the x-axis. Find the volume of the solid, giving your answer in terms of π and k. [5]

  Given that the volume of the solid is 100 units^3, find the value of k, giving your answer correct to two decimal places. [2]

5 The first three terms of a geometric progression are equal to the first, second and sixth terms respectively of an arithmetic progression. The terms are not all equal, and the first term of each progression is denoted by a. Prove that the common ratio of the geometric progression is 4, and find the common difference of the arithmetic progression in terms of a. [5]

  Find in terms of a the sum of the first 20 terms of each progression. [3]

6 The functions f and g are defined by
$$f:x \mapsto \frac{1}{x+1}, \quad -1 < x \leqslant 2,$$

$$g:x \mapsto 2x-1, \quad x \in \mathbb{R}.$$

  (i) Using a graphical method, or otherwise, find the range of f. [1]

  (ii) Calculate gf(1). [1]

  (iii) Find an expression in terms of x for $g^{-1}(x)$. [2]

  (iv) Solve for x the equation $3g(x) = 5gf(x)$. [4]

7   A circle with centre O has radius r cm. A sector of the circle, which has an angle of θ radians at O, has a perimeter of 6 cm. Show that $\theta = \dfrac{6}{r} - 2$.   [2]

Show that the area of the sector is a maximum, and not a minimum, when $r = \frac{3}{2}$, and calculate the corresponding value of θ.   [6]

8   The amount, q units, of radioactivity present in a substance is given at time t seconds by the equation

$$q = 10e^{-\frac{1}{100}t}.$$

Calculate
(i)   the amount of radioactivity present when $t = 5$,

(ii)   the rate of decay of q when $t = 5$.   [5]

Find the value of t when the amount of radioactivity has halved from its value when $t = 0$.   [4]

9   Use the trapezium rule with two intervals to approximate the area of the region bounded by the graph of $y = e^x$, the y-axis, the x-axis and the line $x = 1$. Give your answer in the form

$$\text{area} \approx a + b\sqrt{e} + ce,$$

where a, b and c are fractions to be determined. State, with a reason, whether the approximation is an overestimate or an underestimate.   [4]

Calculate the exact value of the area, and hence show that $e \approx \dfrac{25}{9}$.   [5]

Mock examination 2 for P2

Time 1 hour 20 minutes

Answer all the questions.
Graphic calculators are allowed.

1   Express $\ln 12 - \ln 3 + \ln 9 + 1$ as a single logarithm. [3]

2   Use the binomial theorem to expand $(3x+2)^4$ in powers of x. [3]

3   The figure shows the graph of $y = f(x)$ defined for $-5 \leqslant x \leqslant 5$.

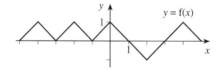

   (i)   Sketch the graph of $y = |f(x)|$. [2]

   (ii) Sketch the graph of $y = f(|x|)$. [2]

4   When the polynomial $x^3 + Ax^2 - 3x + B$, where A and B are constants, is divided by $x - 1$, the remainder is 5, and when it is divided by $x + 2$ the remainder is 11. Find the constants A and B. [5]

5   A sequence is defined for $n \geqslant 3$ by

$$t_{n+1} = 2t_n - t_{n-1},$$

   where $t_1 = 1$ and $t_2 = 2$. Calculate t_3, t_4 and t_5. [2]

   Show that the equation above may be written in the form $t_{n+1} - t_n = t_n - t_{n-1}$. Deduce, in terms of a, b and n, the value of t_n when $n \geqslant 3$ for the sequence for which $t_1 = a$ and $t_2 = b$. [4]

6   Show that the equation $x^3 - 3x - 10 = 0$ has a root between $x = 2$ and $x = 3$. [2]

   Find an approximation to this root by starting with $x = 2$ and using an iteration based on the equation in the form

$$x = (3x+10)^{\frac{1}{3}},$$

   giving your answer correct to 3 decimal places. [3]

   Show that your answer is actually correct to 3 decimal places. [2]

7

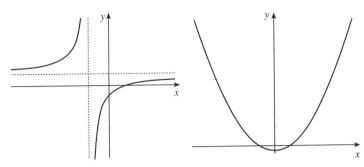

The diagram shows the graphs for two functions f and g defined by

$$f:x \mapsto \frac{3x-1}{3x+1}, \qquad x \in \mathbb{R}, x \neq -\tfrac{1}{3},$$

$$g:x \mapsto 3x^2 - 1, \qquad x \in \mathbb{R}.$$

(i)   Find the range of each of these functions.   [2]

(ii) One of these functions does not have an inverse. Identify this function, and give a clear reason why it does not have an inverse.   [3]

(iii) Find the inverse of the other function, expressing your answer in a form similar to that given in the definition of the function.   [4]

8 (i)   Differentiate e^{-x^2} with respect to x.   [2]

(ii) Calculate the value of the definite integral $\displaystyle\int_{4}^{12} \frac{1}{2x+1}\,dx$, giving your answer in an exact form, and simplifying it as much as possible.   [4]

9 Two circles of radii $3\,\text{cm}$ and $4\,\text{cm}$ have their centres $5\,\text{cm}$ apart. Calculate the perimeter and the area of the overlapping region, giving your answers correct to 3 significant figures.   [9]

10 A solid sphere of radius $5\,\text{cm}$ is formed by rotating the region under the semicircle $y = \sqrt{25 - x^2}$ through 4 right angles about the x-axis. The units on both axes are centimetres.

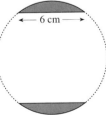

A hole of length $6\,\text{cm}$ is drilled symmetrically through the sphere, as shown in the diagram, leaving an object (shown shaded) with a hole in it. Calculate, in terms of π, the volume of the object remaining.   [8]

Answers to P1

1 Coordinates, points and lines

Exercise 1A (page 8)

1. (a) 13   (b) 5
   (c) $\sqrt{50}$ (d) $\sqrt{52}$
   (e) $17a$ (f) $\sqrt{20}$
   (g) 23   (h) $9a$
   (i) $\sqrt{2(p-q)^2}$ (j) $\sqrt{50q^2}$

5. (a) $(4,13)$ (b) $(1,8)$
   (c) $\left(-\frac{1}{2},-4\frac{1}{2}\right)$ (d) $\left(-5\frac{1}{2},4\frac{1}{2}\right)$
   (e) $(2p+3,2p-3)$ (f) $(p+4,-2)$
   (g) $(3p,3q)$ (h) $(a+3,b+1)$

6. $(2,3)$

7. $(7,10)$

9. A

10. (a) 2   (b) -3
    (c) $\frac{1}{2}$ (d) $-\frac{3}{4}$
    (e) -2 (f) -1
    (g) $(p-3)/(q-1)$ (h) 0

11. $\frac{1}{2}$, $\frac{1}{2}$; points are collinear

12. $\dfrac{y}{x-3}$, $\dfrac{6-y}{5-x}$

13. 5

14. (a) M is $\left(\frac{1}{2},-1\frac{1}{2}\right)$, N is $\left(1\frac{1}{2},4\right)$

15. (a) $MN=5$, $BC=10$

16. (a) Gradients PQ and RS both -1, QR and SP both $\frac{3}{5}$
    (b) Parallelogram

17. (d) Rhombus

18. (d) Rectangle

19. (a) Gradients PQ and RS are both $-\frac{1}{3}$, QR is 4 and SP is $\frac{3}{4}$
    (b) Trapezium

21. (a) $DE=DG=\sqrt{10}$, $EF=FG=\sqrt{40}$
    (b) Kite

22. (a) M is $(6,1)$ (c) N is $\left(8,5\frac{1}{2}\right)$

Exercise 1B (page 13)

1. (a) Yes   (b) No
   (c) Yes   (d) No
   (e) Yes   (f) No
   (g) Yes   (h) Yes

2. (a) $y=5x-7$ (b) $y=-3x+1$
   (c) $2y=x+8$ (d) $8y=-3x+2$
   (e) $y=-3x$ (f) $y=8$
   (g) $4y=-3x-19$ (h) $2y=x+3$
   (i) $8y=3x+1$ (j) $2y=-x+11$
   (k) $y=-2x+3$ (l) $y=3x+1$
   (m) $y=7x-4$ (n) $y=-x+2$
   (o) $8y=-5x-1$ (p) $5y=-3x+9$
   (q) $y=7x-7d$ (r) $y=mx+4$
   (s) $y=3x+c$ (t) $y=mx-mc$

3. (a) $y=3x+1$ (b) $y=2x-3$
   (c) $2x+3y-12=0$ (d) $x-3=0$
   (e) $3x-5y-45=0$ (f) $3x+y-8=0$
   (g) $y=-3$ (h) $x+3y-2=0$
   (i) $5x+3y+14=0$ (j) $2x+7y+11=0$
   (k) $x+3=0$ (l) $x+y+1=0$
   (m) $y=3x+1$ (n) $5x+3y+13=0$
   (o) $3x+5y=0$ (p) $qx-py=0$
   (q) $x+3y-p-3q=0$ (r) $x-p=0$
   (s) $x-y-p+q=0$ (t) $qx+py-pq=0$

4. (a) -2 (b) $\frac{3}{4}$ (c) $-2\frac{1}{2}$
   (d) 0   (e) $1\frac{1}{2}$ (f) Undefined
   (g) -1 (h) 3   (i) $-\frac{1}{2}$
   (j) $2\frac{1}{3}$ (k) m (l) $-p/q$

5. $y=\frac{1}{2}x+2$

6. $y+2x=5$

7. $3x+8y=19$

8. $x+y=12$

9. $y=7$

10. $y=mx-md$

11. (a) $(7,3)$ (b) $(2,7)$
    (c) $\left(-\frac{1}{4},-\frac{7}{8}\right)$ (d) $(-3,-1)$
    (e) $(2,4)$ (f) $(6,5)$
    (g) No intersection   (h) $(2,-1)$
    (i) Same lines
    (j) $(c/a(1+2b), 2c/(1+2b))$
    (k) $((d-c)/2m, (c+d)/2)$
    (l) $(1/(a-b), 1/(a-b))$

Exercise 1C (page 16)

1. (a) $-\frac{1}{2}$ (b) $\frac{1}{3}$ (c) $-1\frac{1}{3}$
   (d) $1\frac{1}{5}$ (e) 1   (f) $-\frac{4}{7}$
   (g) m (h) $-1/m$ (i) $-q/p$
   (j) Undefined   (k) $1/m$ (l) $(c-b)/a$

2. (a) $x+4y=14$ (b) $y=2x+7$
   (c) $x-5y=27$ (d) $x=7$
   (e) $3x-2y=-11$ (f) $5x+3y=29$
   (g) $y+3=0$ (h) $x+2y=6$
   (i) $x+my=0$ (j) $x+my=a+mb$
   (k) $nx+y=d+nc$ (l) $bx-ay=2a-b$

3 $x + 3y = 13, (1, 4)$

4 $3x + 2y = 5, (3, -2)$

5 $x + 2y = 8$

6   (a)   (i) $x = 8$ (ii) $x - 2y = 2$ (b) $(8, 3)$

Miscellaneous exercise 1 (page 17)

2 $(2, -1)$

3   (b) $(3.6, 0)$

4   (a) $3x - y = 9$ (b) $(3, 0)$ and $(5, 6)$

6   (a) $4x - 3y = 13$ (b) $(4, 1)$ (c) 5

7   Area $= 78$

8 $(0, 0), (12, 12)$ and $(14, 4)$

9 $2x + 7y = 23$

10 $3x - 4y = 1$

11 $\left(3\tfrac{1}{2}, 4\right), (4, 3)$

12   (a) $x + 3y = 9$ (b) $(0.9, 2.7)$

     (c) $\sqrt{0.9}$

14 $3x + 5y - 4 = 0, \left(1\tfrac{1}{3}, 0\right)$

15 $\left(3\tfrac{1}{2}, -1\tfrac{1}{2}\right), -7, x - 7y - 14 = 0$

16   (a) $(-3, 0), (0, 1.5)$ (b) $x - 2y + 3 = 0$

     (c) $(1.8, 2.4)$

17 $x - 2y - 8 = 0, (2, -3), \sqrt{80}$

19 25

20   (a) $x + y = 1$ (b) $(2, -1), (0, 1)$

21 $y = 2, 3x + 4y = 18, y = 3x - 8$

22   Draw gradient triangles for both lines. Because $1/(-m_2) = m_1/1$, one triangle is similar to the other, but rotated through 90°.

2 Surds

Exercise 2 (page 21)

1   (a) 3 (b) 10

     (c) 16 (d) 4

     (e) 8 (f) 6

     (g) 15 (h) 30

     (i) 72 (j) 60

     (k) 28 (l) 27

     (m) 5 (n) 48

     (o) 256 (p) 5

2   (a) $3\sqrt{2}$ (b) $2\sqrt{5}$

     (c) $2\sqrt{6}$ (d) $4\sqrt{2}$

     (e) $2\sqrt{10}$ (f) $3\sqrt{5}$

     (g) $4\sqrt{3}$ (h) $5\sqrt{2}$

     (i) $3\sqrt{6}$ (j) $6\sqrt{2}$

     (k) $3\sqrt{15}$ (l) $15\sqrt{3}$

3   (a) $5\sqrt{2}$ (b) $3\sqrt{3}$

     (c) $\sqrt{5}$ (d) $2\sqrt{2}$

     (e) 0 (f) $6\sqrt{3}$

     (g) $6\sqrt{11}$ (h) $12\sqrt{2}$

     (i) $13\sqrt{5}$ (j) $\sqrt{13}$

     (k) $30\sqrt{5}$ (l) $6\sqrt{6} - \sqrt{3}$

4   (a) 2 (b) 3

     (c) 2 (d) 5

     (e) 5 (f) 3

     (g) $\tfrac{1}{4}$ (h) $\tfrac{1}{2}$

5   (a) $\sqrt{3}/3$ (b) $\sqrt{5}/5$

     (c) $2\sqrt{2}$ (d) $\sqrt{6}$

     (e) $\sqrt{11}$ (f) $\sqrt{2}/2$

     (g) $4\sqrt{3}$ (h) $2\sqrt{7}$

     (i) $\sqrt{3}$ (j) $\sqrt{3}/3$

     (k) $\sqrt{15}$ (l) $4\sqrt{30}/5$

     (m) $7\sqrt{6}/6$ (n) $2\sqrt{6}/3$

     (o) $3\sqrt{6}/2$ (p) $\sqrt{6}/9$

6   (a) $7\sqrt{3}$ (b) $4\sqrt{3}$

     (c) $\sqrt{3}$ (d) $\sqrt{3}$

     (e) $12\sqrt{3}$ (f) $-5\sqrt{3}$

7   (a) $20\sqrt{2}$ cm^2 (b) $3\sqrt{10}$ cm

8   (a) $x = 5\sqrt{2}$ (b) $y = -4\sqrt{2}$

     (c) $z = 3\sqrt{2}$

9   (a) $2\sqrt[3]{3}$ (b) $4\sqrt[3]{3}$

     (c) $3\sqrt[3]{3}$ (d) $5\sqrt[3]{3}$

10   (a) $4\sqrt{13}$ cm   (b) $5\sqrt{11}$ cm

     (c) $2\sqrt{15}$ cm   (d) $3\sqrt{5}$ cm

11   (a) $10.198\ 039\ 027\ 2$

     (b) $25.495\ 097\ 568\ 0$

     (c) $2.549\ 509\ 756\ 8$

12 $x = 3\sqrt{5}, y = 4$

13   (a) 1 (b) 1

     (c) 4 (d) 7

     (e) 46 (f) 5

     (g) 107 (h) -3

14   (a) $\sqrt{3} + 1$ (b) $\sqrt{5} - 1$

     (c) $\sqrt{6} + \sqrt{2}$ (d) $2\sqrt{7} - \sqrt{3}$

     (e) $\sqrt{11} - \sqrt{10}$ (f) $3\sqrt{5} + 2\sqrt{6}$

16   (a) $2 + \sqrt{3}$ (b) $\left(3\sqrt{5} + 5\right)/20$

     (c) $4\sqrt{2} - 2\sqrt{6}$

Miscellaneous exercise 2 (page 23)

1   (a) $11 + \sqrt{2}$ (b) 29

     (c) $10 - 4\sqrt{5}$ (d) $128\sqrt{2}$

2   (a) $4\sqrt{3}$ (b) $\sqrt{7}$

     (c) $111\sqrt{10}$ (d) $3\sqrt[3]{2}$

3   (a) $3\sqrt{3}/2$ (b) $\sqrt{5}/25$

     (c) $\sqrt{2}/3$ (d) $2\sqrt{30}/15$

4   (a) $\sqrt{2}$ (b) $4\sqrt{5}$

     (c) $-2 + \sqrt{2}/2$ (d) $4\sqrt{3}$

5 $5\sqrt{7}/7$

7 (a) 14 cm^2

8 $3\sqrt{7}$ cm

9 $x = 3\sqrt{2} + 4, y = 5\sqrt{2} - 7$

10 $2\sqrt{10}, (3,0)$

11 (a) $x + 2y = 8$ (c) $\sqrt{5}$ or $-\sqrt{5}$

    (d) $t = -\frac{1}{5}, \ 8\sqrt{5}/5$

12 $a = 2\sqrt{10}, b = 6\sqrt{10}$

13 Either $3\sqrt{2}$ and $9\sqrt{2}/2$ or $3\sqrt{5}$ and $9\sqrt{5}/5$; 27

3 Some important graphs

Exercise 3A (page 28)

1 (a) 11   (b) 5   (c) −3   (d) 0

2 (a) 50   (b) 5   (c) 29   (d) 29

3 (a) 15   (b) $5\frac{1}{4}$ (c) 0   (d) 0

4 (a) 17   (b) 9   (d) 33

6 4

7 (a) and (c) are odd; (b) is even.

8 $a = 5, b = -3$

Exercise 3B (page 29)

11 (c)

12 (a)

Exercise 3C (page 31)

1 (a) $(3,14)$ (b) $(1,3), (4,3)$

   (c) $(-4,8), (2,8)$ (d) $(-3,-3), \left(\frac{1}{2},-3\right)$

2 (a) $(1,2), (3,4),$ (b) $(-4,-5), (3,9)$

   (c) $\left(-1\frac{1}{2}, 6\frac{1}{2}\right), (2,17)$ (d) $(-2,-7), (2,9)$

   (e) $\left(-\frac{1}{3}, 2\right), \left(2\frac{1}{2}, -6\frac{1}{2}\right)$

3 (a) $(2,6)$ (b) $(-3,-1)$

4 (a) $(0,0), (2,2)$ (b) $(1,0)$

5 (a) $(-4,14)$ (b) $(-6,24), (-2,12)$

6 (a) $(-1,4), (3,8)$ (b) $(1,6)$

7 (a) $(5,51)$ (b) $(-2,3)$ (c) $(0,1)$

8 (a) $\left(-1,\frac{1}{2}\right), \left(1,\frac{1}{2}\right)$ (b) $(1,9), (2,18)$

   (c) $(-3,1), (-2,3)$ (d) $(-1,-5), (2,19)$

   (e) $(-3,65), (2.4, 7.76)$

   (f) $(0,0), (8,80)$

Exercise 3D (page 34)

4 (a) $y = x^2 - 7x + 10$ (b) $y = x^2 + 17x + 70$

   (c) $y = x^2 + 2x - 15$ (d) $y = x^2 - 2x - 15$

6 (a) $y = 3x^2 - 18x + 15$

   (b) $y = 4x^2 - 20x - 56$

   (c) $y = -\frac{1}{2}x^2 - 4x - 6$

   (d) $y = -4x^2 - 4x + 24$

   (e) $y = 5x^2 + 15x - 350$

8 (a) A, B, G, H   (b) B, D, F   (c) F, G, H

   (d) D   (e) G   (f) I

   (g) B, E   (h) A, C, E

Miscellaneous exercise 3 (page 36)

1 (a) $45, -\frac{1}{2}, -39$ (b) 2

   (c) $\frac{2}{3}$ (d) 37

2 $-1, 4$

3 9

4 $\left(\frac{1}{2}, 1\frac{3}{4}\right), (4,-7)$

5 $\left(-2\frac{1}{2}, -2\right), (2,7)$

6 $(1,-1)$

7 $(2,0)$

9 $a = 2, b = -7, c = 6$

10 $\left(-\frac{3}{4}, 6\right)$

12 6

13 $(0,108)$

14 $p = 35, q = -\frac{1}{2}$ or 4

15 $(3,33)$

17 $c = 2, k = 14, (3,2)$

18 2

19 $p = q = 13$

20 -25

21 $\left(\sqrt{3}, -5\sqrt{3}\right), \left(-\sqrt{3}, 5\sqrt{3}\right)$

22 $\left(2 + \sqrt{2}, 13 + 6\sqrt{2}\right)$

23 (a) 2   (b) 0   (c) 1

4 Quadratics

Exercise 4A (page 41)

1 (a) (i) $(2,3)$ (ii) $x = 2$

   (b) (i) $(5,-4)$ (ii) $x = 5$

   (c) (i) $(-3,-7)$ (ii) $x = -3$

   (d) (i) $\left(\frac{3}{2}, 1\right)$ (ii) $x = \frac{3}{2}$

   (e) (i) $\left(-\frac{3}{5}, 2\right)$ (ii) $x = -\frac{3}{5}$

   (f) (i) $\left(-\frac{7}{3}, -4\right)$ (ii) $x = -\frac{7}{3}$

   (g) (i) $(3,c)$ (ii) $x = 3$

   (h) (i) (p,q) (ii) $x = p$

   (i) (i) $(-b/a, c)$ (ii) $x = -b/a$

2 (a) (i) -1 (ii) -2 (b) (i) 2 (ii) 1

   (c) (i) 5 (ii) -3 (d) (i) -7 (ii) $-\frac{1}{2}$

   (e) (i) 3 (ii) 4   (f) (i) q (ii) $-p$

   (g) (i) $-q$ (ii) p (h) (i) r (ii) t

   (i) (i) c (ii) $-b/a$

3 (a) $3 \pm \sqrt{3}$ (b) $0, -4$

   (c) $-3 \pm \sqrt{10}/2$ (d) $\left(7 \pm 2\sqrt{2}\right)/3$

   (e) $-p \pm \sqrt{q}$ (f) $-b \pm \sqrt{c/a}$

4 (a) $(x+1)^2+1$ (b) $(x-4)^2-19$

    (c) $\left(x+1\frac{1}{2}\right)^2-9\frac{1}{4}$ (d) $(x-3)^2-4$

    (e) $(x+7)^2$ (f) $2(x+3)^2-23$

    (g) $3(x-2)^2-9$ (h) $11-4(x+1)^2$

    (i) $2\left(x+1\frac{1}{4}\right)^2-6\frac{1}{8}$

5 (a) $(x-7)(x+5)$ (b) $(x-22)(x+8)$

    (c) $(x+24)(x-18)$ (d) $(3x+2)(2x-3)$

    (e) $(2+7x)(7-2x)$ (f) $(4x+3)(3x-2)$

6 (a) 3 when $x=2$ (b) $2\frac{3}{4}$ when $x=1\frac{1}{2}$

    (c) 13 when $x=3$ (d) $-1\frac{1}{8}$ when $x=1\frac{1}{4}$

    (e) $-4\frac{1}{3}$ when $x=-\frac{1}{3}$ (f) $7\frac{1}{12}$ when $x=-1\frac{1}{6}$

7 (a) (i) $(2,2)$ (ii) $x=2$

    (b) (i) $(-3,-11)$ (ii) $x=-3$

    (c) (i) $(-5,32)$ (ii) $x=-5$

    (d) (i) $\left(-1\frac{1}{2},-1\frac{1}{4}\right)$ (ii) $x=-1\frac{1}{2}$

    (e) (i) $\left(1\frac{3}{4},-4\frac{1}{8}\right)$ (ii) $x=1\frac{3}{4}$

    (f) (i) $(2,-7)$ (ii) $x=2$

Exercise 4B (page 44)

1 (a) $\frac{1}{2}\left(-3\pm\sqrt{29}\right)$ (b) $2\pm\sqrt{11}$

    (c) -3 (repeated)   (d) $\frac{1}{2}\left(-5\pm\sqrt{17}\right)$

    (e) No solution   (f) $\frac{1}{6}\left(5\pm\sqrt{97}\right)$

    (g) -3 and $-\frac{1}{2}$ (h) $\frac{1}{2}\left(-3\pm\sqrt{41}\right)$

    (i) $\frac{1}{6}\left(2\pm\sqrt{34}\right)$

2 (a) 2 (b) 1 (c) 0 (d) 0

    (e) 2 (f) 2 (g) 1 (h) 2

    (i) 2 (j) 2

3 (a) $-\frac{9}{4}$ (b) $-\frac{25}{32}$ (c) 81

    (d) $\pm2\sqrt{6}$ (e) $\pm4\sqrt{6}$ (f) $p^2/4q$

4 (a) $k<\frac{9}{4}$ (b) $k=\frac{49}{4}$

    (c) $k>\frac{9}{20}$ (d) $k>-\frac{25}{12}$

    (e) $k=\frac{4}{3}$ (f) $k>\frac{25}{28}$

    (g) $k>4$ or $k<-4$ (h) $-6<k<6$

5 (a) 2 (b) 0 (c) 1 (d) 0

    (e) 2 (f) 2 (g) 0 (h) 0

    (i) 1

6 Intersects x-axis twice, faces up.

7 Intersects x-axis twice, faces down.

Exercise 4C (page 47)

1 (a) $x=3, y=4$ or $x=-4, y=-3$

    (b) $x=3, y=4$ or $x=4, y=3$

    (c) $x=5, y=2$ or $x=-1, y=-4$

    (d) $x=3, y=-1$

    (e) $x=0, y=5$ or $x=4, y=-3$

    (f) $x=1, y=0$ or $x=\frac{1}{2}, y=\frac{1}{2}$

    (g) $x=0, y=7$

    (h) $x=3, y=-2$ or $x=\frac{1}{7}, y=-10\frac{4}{7}$

2 (a) $(2,5)$ and $(1,3)$

    (b) $(1,5)$ and $(-2.2,-4.6)$

    (c) $(3,4)$ and $(-1,-4)$

    (d) $(1,1)$ and $\left(-4,3\frac{1}{2}\right)$

    (e) $(4,3)$

    (f) $(2,-1)$ and $\left(-\frac{7}{8},4\frac{3}{4}\right)$

    (g) $(5,-2)$ and $(27,42)$

    (h) $\left(\frac{1}{2},-1\right)$ and $\left(-1\frac{5}{8},-1\frac{17}{20}\right)$

3 (a) 2 (b) 0 (c) 2

    (d) 1 (e) 0 (f) 1

4 (a) $\pm1,\pm2$ (b) $\pm1,\pm3$ (c) ±2

    (d) $\pm\sqrt{6}$ (e) $-1,2$ (f) $\sqrt[3]{3},-\sqrt[3]{4}$

5 (a) 16 (b) $25,9$ (c) 49

    (d) 25 (e) $-8,27$ (f) $-1,64$

6 (a) $-2,5$ (b) $-6,1$ (c) $-3,\frac{1}{2}$

    (d) $-4,3$ (e) 36 (f) 9

    (g) $1,-\frac{8}{3}$ (h) $-7,2$ (i) $5,-\frac{11}{3}$

    (j) $\frac{1}{2},-\frac{4}{11}$ (k) ±2 (l) ±1

Miscellaneous exercise 4 (page 48)

1 $x=3, y=-1$ or $x=-\frac{1}{3}, y=\frac{7}{3}$

2 $a=5, b=-8$. Least value is -8 when $x=5$.

3 $x=2, y=-1$ or $x=-\frac{5}{4}, y=\frac{11}{2}$

4 8 and -8

5 (a) $2\sqrt{3}, 4\sqrt{3}$ (b) $\pm1.86, \pm2.63$

7 $(3x-6)^2+16$. Takes values $\geqslant16$.

8 $(-1.64,6.63), (0.24,-1.67)$

9 (a) $(3x+2)^2+3$ (b) $0<f(x)\leqslant\frac{1}{3}$

10 ±0.991 and ±0.131

11 $a=3, b=-\frac{5}{6}, c=-\frac{13}{12}$.

    Minimum is $\left(\frac{5}{6},-\frac{13}{12}\right)$.

12 $(1,6)$ and $(2,3)$

13 (a) $\left(b/a,c-b^2/a\right)$ (b) $c=b(b+1)/a$

14 (b) (i) Line is tangent to curve.

          (ii) Line and curve do not intersect.

16 (a) $2\sqrt{5}/5$ (b) $4\sqrt{5}/5$ (c) 1

18 (a) $2\sqrt{5}$ m

    (b) $8\sqrt{5}$ m

    (c) They collide!

5 Differentiation

Exercise 5A (page 53)

1 $y=3x-2$

2 (a) 2.001 (b) 1.9999

    (c) 4.002 (d) 3.999

    (e) $6.000\,001$ (f) $5.999\,99$

Exercise 5B (page 55)

1. (a) 2   (b) 8   (c) 0   (d) −4
   (e) −0.4   (f) −7   (g) $2p$ (h) $4p$

2. (a) 2   (b) 8   (c) 0   (d) −4
   (e) −0.4   (f) −7   (g) $2p$ (h) $4p$

3. 4 and −4

4. (a) $y = 4x - 4$ (b) $y = -2x + 1$
   (c) $y = 2x - 3$ and $y = -2x - 3$
   (d) $y = -2$

5. (a) $2y = -x + 3$ (b) $4y = x + 22$
   (c) $x = 0$
   (d) $2y\sqrt{c} = -x + \sqrt{c}(4c + 1)$

6. $12y = -4x + 33$

7. $4y = 4x + 3$

8. $\left(-2\frac{1}{4}, 5\frac{1}{16}\right)$

Exercise 5C (page 58)

1. (a) $2x$ (b) $2x - 1$ (c) $8x$
   (d) $6x - 2$ (e) −3   (f) $1 - 4x$
   (g) $4 - 6x$ (h) $\sqrt{2} - 2\sqrt{3}x$

2. (a) 3   (b) $-6x$ (c) 0
   (d) $2 + 6x$ (e) $-2x$ (f) $6 - 6x$
   (g) $2 - 4x$ (h) $4x + 1$

3. (a) 6   (b) 3   (c) −3   (d) 8
   (e) −8   (f) −6   (g) 4   (h) −17

4. (a) $\frac{3}{4}$ (b) $\frac{1}{2}$ (c) $-\frac{3}{2}$
   (d) −1   (e) $\frac{3}{2}$ (f) $\frac{1}{2}$

5. (a) $y = -2x - 1$ (b) $y = -x$
   (c) $y = 2x - 1$ (d) $y = 6x + 10$
   (e) $y = 1$ (f) $y = 0$

6. (a) $2y = x - 3$ (b) $4y = -x + 1$
   (c) $8y = -x - 58$ (d) $x = 0$
   (e) $2y = x + 9$ (f) $x = \frac{1}{2}$

7. $4y = 4x - 1$

8. $y = 0$

9. $y = -2x$

10. $12y = 12x - 17$

11. $x = 1$

12. $7y = -x + 64$

14. (a) 0.499 875 ...   (b) 0.500 012 ...
    (c) 0.249 968 ...   (d) 0.250 015 ...
    (e) 0.999 999 ...   (f) 1.000 001 ...

Exercise 5D (page 61)

1. (a) $3x^2 + 4x$ (b) $-6x^2 + 6x$
   (c) $3x^2 - 12x + 11$ (d) $6x^2 - 6x + 1$
   (e) $1 + 3x^2$ (f) $-3x^2$

2. (a) −10   (b) 6   (c) 58
   (d) −1   (e) 8   (f) 12

3. (a) −2, 2   (b) $-\frac{4}{3}, 2$ (c) −5, 7
   (d) 1   (e) $-1, -\frac{1}{3}$ (f) No values

4. (a) $\frac{1}{\sqrt{x}}$ (b) $\frac{1}{\sqrt{x}} + 1$ (c) $1 - \frac{1}{4\sqrt{x}}$
   (d) $1 - \frac{1}{\sqrt{x}}$ (e) $1 + \frac{1}{x^2}$ (f) $2x + 1 - \frac{1}{x^2}$
   (g) $1 - \frac{2}{x^2}$ (h) $1 + \frac{1}{\sqrt{x}}$

5. $y = 4x + 2$

6. $y = x + 2$

7. $4y = x + 4$

8. $4y = -x + 4$

9. $x = 1$

11. $y = -2x - 6$

12. $y = -a^2 x,\ y = 2a^2 x + 2a^3,\ y = 2a^2 x - 2a^3$

13. $\left(\frac{1}{2}, -2\right)$

Exercise 5E (page 68)

1. $f'(p) = 3p^2$

2. $f'(p) = 8p^7$

3. $f'(p) = -\dfrac{2}{p^3}$

Miscellaneous exercise 5 (page 68)

1. $y = 13x - 16$

2. (a) −9   (b) $a = -\frac{19}{3}, 3$

3. $80y = 32x - 51$

4. $\left(-3, -\frac{1}{3}\right)$

5. $k = 2$

6. $\left(-\frac{1}{3}, -4\frac{17}{27}\right),\ (2, 13)$

7. $x + 19y - 153 = 0$

8. 13

9. (2,12)

10. $k = 2$

11. Both curves have gradient 12.

12. −183

6 Inequalities

Exercise 6A (page 73)

1. (a) $x > 14$ (b) $x < 4$ (c) $x \leqslant 2\frac{1}{2}$
   (d) $x \geqslant 7$ (e) $x > -4$ (f) $x \leqslant -3\frac{1}{5}$
   (g) $x < -3\frac{1}{2}$ (h) $x \leqslant -4$

2. (a) $x > 7$ (b) $x \leqslant 22$ (c) $x < -11\frac{1}{2}$
   (d) $x \leqslant 6$ (e) $x \geqslant -2\frac{3}{4}$ (f) $x > -2$
   (g) $x < 3\frac{1}{3}$ (h) $x \geqslant -4$

3 (a) $x \geq -4$ (b) $x \leq 4$ (c) $x > 9$

    (d) $x \geq -2$ (e) $x \geq \frac{1}{3}$ (f) $x < 1$

    (g) $x < 1\frac{2}{5}$ (h) $x > 2$

4 (a) $x > -7$ (b) $x \leq 2$ (c) $x < -6$

    (d) $x > 3$ (e) $x \geq 2\frac{3}{4}$ (f) $x < 19$

    (g) $x < 8\frac{1}{2}$ (h) $x \geq 9$

5 (a) $x \geq -9$ (b) $x \geq 4$ (c) $x > 6$

    (d) $x > 2\frac{1}{4}$ (e) $x \leq \frac{6}{7}$ (f) $x \geq -1$

    (g) $x < -\frac{3}{4}$ (h) $x > -3$ (i) $x \leq -\frac{1}{4}$

6 (a) $x > 5\frac{1}{2}$ (b) $x < -3$ (c) $x \geq -1\frac{5}{8}$

    (d) $x < -2$ (e) $x \leq 5$ (f) $x \leq 1\frac{7}{9}$

    (g) $x < -1\frac{2}{5}$ (h) $x \geq 4\frac{8}{13}$

Exercise 6B (page 76)

1 (a) $2 < x < 3$

    (b) $x < 4$ or $x > 7$

    (c) $1 < x < 3$

    (d) $x \leq -1$ or $x \geq 4$

    (e) $x < -3$ or $x > \frac{1}{2}$

    (f) $-2\frac{1}{2} \leq x \leq \frac{2}{3}$

    (g) $x \leq -2$ or $x \geq -1\frac{1}{4}$

    (h) $x < -3$ or $x > 1$

    (i) $x < 1\frac{1}{2}$ or $x > 5$

    (j) $-5 < x < 5$

    (k) $-1\frac{1}{3} < x < \frac{3}{4}$

    (l) $x \leq -\frac{2}{3}$ or $x \geq \frac{2}{3}$

2 (a) $3 < x < 6$

    (b) $x < 2$ or $x > 8$

    (c) $-5 \leq x \leq 2$

    (d) $x \leq -1$ or $x \geq 3$

    (e) $x < -1\frac{1}{2}$ or $x > 2$

    (f) $-5 \leq x \leq \frac{2}{3}$

    (g) $x \leq -3$ or $x \geq -\frac{4}{5}$

    (h) $x < -5$ or $x > 2$

    (i) $x < 2\frac{1}{2}$ or $x > 3$

    (j) $x \leq -\frac{1}{3}$ or $x \geq \frac{1}{3}$

    (k) $x < -1\frac{1}{3}$ or $x > \frac{2}{7}$

    (l) $x \leq -1\frac{2}{3}$ or $x \geq \frac{1}{3}$

3 (a) $x < \frac{1}{2}(-3 - \sqrt{29})$ or $x > \frac{1}{2}(-3 + \sqrt{29})$

    (b) True for no x

    (c) $\frac{1}{2}(5 - \sqrt{17}) < x < \frac{1}{2}(5 + \sqrt{17})$

    (d) True for all x

    (e) $-3 < x < 3$

    (f) $x = -1$ only

    (g) $\frac{1}{4}(3 - \sqrt{17}) < x < \frac{1}{4}(3 + \sqrt{17})$

    (h) $\frac{1}{2}(-3 - \sqrt{41}) < x < \frac{1}{2}(-3 + \sqrt{41})$

    (i) $x \leq \frac{1}{4}(-7 - \sqrt{41})$ or $x \geq \frac{1}{4}(-7 + \sqrt{41})$

4 (a) $x < -3$ or $x > -2$

    (b) $3 < x < 4$

    (c) $-3 \leq x \leq 5$

    (d) $x \leq -3$ or $x \geq 3$

    (e) $x \leq 1$ or $x \geq 1\frac{1}{2}$

    (f) $-\frac{2}{3} < x < 1\frac{1}{2}$

    (g) $x < \frac{1}{2}(-5 - \sqrt{17})$ or $x > \frac{1}{2}(-5 + \sqrt{17})$

    (h) $x < -\frac{1}{3}\sqrt{21}$ or $x > \frac{1}{3}\sqrt{21}$

    (i) True for no x

    (j) True for all x

    (k) $x < -\frac{3}{4}$ or $x > \frac{1}{3}$

    (l) $\frac{1}{6}(7 - \sqrt{37}) \leq x \leq \frac{1}{6}(7 + \sqrt{37})$

Miscellaneous exercise 6 (page 77)

1 $-6 \leq x \leq 7$

2 $-4 < x < 2$

3 $-4 < x < 3$

4 $-1 < x < 0$ or $x > 1$

5 $-3 \leq x \leq 0$ or $x \geq 2$

6 (a) $k < 0$ or $k > 8$

    (b) $-1\frac{1}{2} < k < 1\frac{1}{2}$ provided $k \neq 0$ (if $k = 0$ the equation is linear, and has just one root)

    (c) $k < -2$ or $k > 2$

7 (a) $0 \leq k < 5$ (b) $k = 0$

    (c) $-\frac{8}{25} < k < 0$

8 $k \leq 0$ or $k \geq \frac{4}{9}$

9 $x < -2$ or $x > \frac{2}{3}$

10 $-\frac{1}{2} < x < 0$ or $x > 2$

11 (a) $x < 2$ or $x > 2\frac{1}{2}$ (b) $1 - \sqrt{6} < x < 1 + \sqrt{6}$

Revision exercise 1
(page 78)

1 $(-4, -16)$

2 (a) $12\sqrt{3}$ (b) 48

4 $(x + 5)^2 + 13$;

    (a) 13; -5 (b) $x \leq -8$ or $x \geq -2$

5 $(-1, 6)$, $x + y = 5$

6 (a) $\frac{1}{2} < x < 2$ (b) $-\frac{1}{2} < x < \frac{7}{2}$ (c) $x \geq 6.3$

7 $9x - y = 16$

8 $\pm\sqrt{65}$

9 $(0, 0); (1, 1)$

10 $(-1, 7)$

11 $(1, 0)$

12 $£(12(x + y) + 15xy)$; $5z^2 + 8z - 4 = 0$; 0.4

13 $x + y = 5$; 7

14 (a) $x > \frac{4}{3}$ (b) $x > \frac{3}{2}$ (c) $x \leq 0$ or $x \geq 5$

15 $\left(-\frac{9}{4}, \frac{81}{16}\right)$

16 $\left(-\frac{1}{4},\frac{1}{16}\right), \left(2\frac{1}{4},5\frac{1}{16}\right)$

17 $0, 5$

18 25

19 $(2,1)$; the line is a tangent to the curve.

20 $2x+3y=7, 3x-2y=4$; $(4,4)$

21 (a) $2\sqrt{3}$ (b) $\frac{3}{2}$ (c) $2\sqrt{2}$

22 $48x+32y+65=0$

23 (a) $(3,-1)$ (b) 5 (c) $2\sqrt{6}-1$

24 (a) $x<-1$ or $x>2$ (b) $-1<x<2$ or $x>3$

25 $(1,1), (4,-1)$

26 $y+2x=3; \left(\frac{9}{4},-\frac{3}{2}\right)$

27 $2\sqrt{19}$ cm

7 Index notation

Exercise 7A (page 85)

1 (a) a^{12} (b) b^8 (c) c^4
(d) d^9 (e) e^{20} (f) x^6y^4
(g) $15g^8$ (h) $3h^8$ (i) $72a^8$
(j) p^7q^{15} (k) $128x^7y^{11}$ (l) $4c$
(m) $108m^{14}n^{10}$ (n) $7r^3s$ (o) $2xy^2z^3$

2 (a) 2^{26} (b) 2^{12} (c) 2^6 (d) 2^6
(e) 2^2 (f) 2^1 (g) 2^0 (h) 2^0

3 (a) $\frac{1}{8}$ (b) $\frac{1}{16}$ (c) $\frac{1}{5}$
(d) $\frac{1}{9}$ (e) $\frac{1}{10\,000}$ (f) 1
(g) 2 (h) 27 (i) $\frac{2}{5}$
(j) $\frac{1}{128}$ (k) $\frac{1}{216}$ (l) $\frac{27}{64}$

4 (a) $\frac{1}{2}$ (b) $\frac{1}{512}$ (c) $\frac{1}{32}$
(d) 8 (e) $\frac{1}{8}$ (f) 8

5 (a) $\frac{1}{10}$ (b) $\frac{2}{5}$ (c) $\frac{2}{5}$
(d) $\frac{1}{10}$ (e) 10 (f) 10

6 (a) a (b) b (c) c^{-6}
(d) 2 (e) e^{-9} (f) f^{-5}
(g) $3g^{-1}$ (h) $\frac{1}{9}h^{-4}$ (i) $\frac{1}{9}i^4$
(j) $8j^6$ (k) $8x^9y^{-3}$ (l) $p^{-8}q^{-16}r^{-12}$
(m) $2m$ (n) $9n^{-9}$ (o) $8x$
(p) $\frac{25}{2}a^7c^{-4}$ (q) $\frac{1}{64}q^6$ (r) $144x^{-2}y^4$

7 (a) $x=-2$ (b) $y=0$ (c) $z=4$
(d) $x=-2$ (e) $y=120$ (f) $t=0$

8 (a) 2.7×10^{-5} m^3 (b) 5.4×10^{-3} m^2

9 26.7 km h^{-1} (to 1 decimal place)

10 (a) 1.0×10^{-3} m^3 (to 2 significant figures)
(b) 101.9 m (to 1 decimal place)
(c) 5.6×10^{-3} m (to 2 significant figures)

11 (a) 4.375×10^{-4} (b) 4.5×10^{-7}

12 $x=-3$

13 (a) $(1,8)$
(b) $\left(3,\frac{1}{3}\right)$
(c) $\left(\sqrt{2},\sqrt{2}\right), \left(-\sqrt{2},-\sqrt{2}\right)$
(d) $\left(\frac{1}{2},32\right), \left(-\frac{1}{2},32\right)$
(e) $\left(\frac{1}{3},243\right), \left(-\frac{1}{3},-243\right)$
(f) $(2,4), (-2,4)$

14 (a) RQP (b) PQR (c) QPR (d) QRP

15 (a) $x>10$
(b) $x<-50$ or $x>50$
(c) $-\sqrt{10}/10 \leqslant x \leqslant \sqrt{10}/10$, $x\neq0$
(d) $x<-20$ or $x>20$

Exercise 7B (page 89)

1 (a) 5 (b) 2 (c) 6 (d) 2
(e) 3 (f) $\frac{1}{3}$ (g) $\frac{1}{2}$ (h) $\frac{1}{7}$
(i) $\frac{1}{10}$ (j) -3 (k) 16 (l) $\frac{1}{625}$

2 (a) 2 (b) $\frac{1}{16}$ (c) 16 (d) $\frac{1}{2}$
(e) 2 (f) $\frac{1}{2}$ (g) 16 (h) $\frac{1}{2}$

3 (a) 4 (b) 8 (c) $\frac{1}{27}$ (d) 81
(e) 4 (f) 8 (g) $\frac{1}{32}$ (h) 32
(i) $\frac{1}{1000}$ (j) 625 (k) $2\frac{1}{4}$ (l) $\frac{2}{3}$

4 (a) a^2 (b) $12b^{-1}$ (c) $12c^{3/4}$
(d) 1 (e) $4x^4y^5$ (f) 2
(g) $5pq^2$ (h) $4m^{5/4}n^{7/4}$ (i) $2^{5/4}x^{-1}y^{5/4}$

5 (a) 64 (b) 27 (c) 8 (d) 9
(e) $\frac{1}{4}$ (f) $\frac{1}{27}$ (g) 2 (h) 2

6 (a) 1.9 (to 1 decimal place)
(b) 2.2 m (to 1 decimal place)

7 6.5 cm (to 1 decimal place)

8 (a) $x=\frac{5}{2}$ (b) $y=-\frac{3}{2}$ (c) $z=\frac{1}{4}$ (d) $x=\frac{3}{2}$
(e) $y=\frac{4}{3}$ (f) $z=-\frac{7}{3}$ (g) $t=\frac{6}{5}$ (h) $y=-\frac{7}{4}$

9 (a) (i) $2.0082988...$ (ii) $0.082988...$
(iii) $\frac{1}{12}$ (iv) $12y-x=16$
(b) (i) $4.0332642...$ (ii) $0.332642...$
(iii) $\frac{1}{3}$ (iv) $3y-x=4$
(c) (i) $0.2479381...$ (ii) $-0.020618...$
(iii) $-\frac{1}{48}$ (iv) $48y+x=20$
(d) (i) $0.0614733...$ (ii) $-0.010266...$
(iii) $-\frac{1}{96}$ (iv) $96y+x=14$

10 (a) (i) $0.250000195...$
(ii) $\frac{1}{4}$ (iii) $4y-x=4$
(b) (i) $-0.062500244...$
(ii) $-\frac{1}{16}$ (iii) $16y+x=12$
(c) (i) $-0.03125039...$
(ii) $-\frac{1}{32}$ (iii) $32y+x=6$
(d) (i) $-0.011718994...$
(ii) $-\frac{3}{256}$ (iii) $256y+3x=16$

12 (a) $-\dfrac{1}{4x^2}$ (b) $-\dfrac{6}{x^3}$ (c) 0

    (d) $\dfrac{3}{4\sqrt[4]{x}}$ (e) $\dfrac{2}{\sqrt[3]{x^2}}$ (f) $-\dfrac{2}{\sqrt{x^3}}$

    (g) $-\dfrac{3}{x^2}-\dfrac{1}{x^4}$ (h) $10\sqrt{x^3}$ (i) $\tfrac{3}{2}\sqrt{x}$

    (j) $-\dfrac{1}{6\sqrt[3]{x^4}}$ (k) $\dfrac{4-x}{x^3}$ (l) $\dfrac{3x-1}{4\sqrt[4]{x^5}}$

13 (a) (i) 16 (iii) $-\tfrac{1}{4}$ (iv) 16
       (ii), (v), (vi) No value
    (c) q must be odd

Miscellaneous exercise 7 (page 91)

1 (a) 6 (b) $\tfrac{1}{16}$ (c) $\tfrac{1}{2}$ (d) $2\tfrac{10}{27}$

2 (a) $2p^{1/8}q^{-3/2}$ (b) $\tfrac{1}{10}b^{-3}$
    (c) $2xy^2$ (d) $m^{-2/3}n^{1/3}$

3 $\dfrac{1}{3a^2}$

4 $a^{-2/3}$

5 -1 and 8

6 $x=\tfrac{8}{7}$

7 (a) 2.5×10^{179} (b) 1×10^{292}
    (c) 2×10^{56} (d) 3×10^{-449}

8 (b) 1.5×10^{11} m (to 2 significant figures)

9 (a) $\tfrac{15}{4}\sqrt{2}$ (b) $\tfrac{13}{3}+\tfrac{40}{9}\sqrt{3}$

10 (a) 2^{71} (b) 2^{-399} (c) $2^{7/3}$
     (d) 2^{99} (e) $2^{3.3}$

11 $x=-\tfrac{5}{6}$

12 $mn=-1$

13 (a) $S=2^{2/3}3^{2/3}\pi^{1/3}V^{2/3}$
     (b) $V=2^{-1}3^{-1}\pi^{-1/2}S^{3/2}$

14 $\left(\tfrac{11}{20},\tfrac{4}{5}\right)$

15 $\left(\tfrac{67}{32},\tfrac{5}{8}\right)$

16 8×10^3 J, or 8000 J

8 Functions and graphs

Exercise 8A (page 96)

1 (a) $x\geqslant0$ (b) $x\leqslant0$
    (c) $x\geqslant4$ (d) $x\leqslant4$
    (e) $x\leqslant0$ and $x\geqslant4$ (f) $x\leqslant0$ and $x\geqslant4$
    (g) $x\leqslant3$ and $x\geqslant4$ (h) $x\geqslant2$
    (i) All real numbers except 2
    (j) $x>2$ (k) $x\geqslant0$
    (l) All real numbers except 1 and 2

2 (a) $f(x)\geqslant4$ (b) $f(x)\geqslant10$
    (c) $f(x)\geqslant6$ (d) $f(x)\leqslant7$
    (e) $f(x)\geqslant2$ (f) $f(x)\geqslant-1$

3 (a) $f(x)\geqslant1$ (b) $f(x)\geqslant-\tfrac{45}{4}$
    (c) $f(x)\geqslant\tfrac{7}{4}$ (d) $f(x)\geqslant-7$
    (e) $f(x)\geqslant-\tfrac{169}{12}$ (f) $f(x)\leqslant21$

4 (a) $0\leqslant f(x)\leqslant16$ (b) $-1\leqslant f(x)\leqslant7$
    (c) $0\leqslant f(x)\leqslant16$ (d) $4\leqslant f(x)\leqslant25$

5 (a) $f(x)>7$ (b) $f(x)<0$
    (c) $f(x)>-1$ (d) $f(x)>-1$
    (e) $f(x)>2$ (f) $f(x)\geqslant-\tfrac{1}{4}$

6 (a) $f(x)\geqslant0$ (b) all real numbers
    (c) all real numbers except 0
    (d) $f(x)>0$ (e) $f(x)\geqslant5$
    (f) all real numbers   (g) $0\leqslant f(x)\leqslant2$
    (h) $f(x)\geqslant0$

7 $0<w<12, 0<A\leqslant36$

8 $0<x<4$

9 (a) 7 (b) $\tfrac{1}{200}$ (c) 5
    (d) 5 (e) $\pi-3$ (f) $4-\pi$

10 (a) 2 (b) $\tfrac{1}{4}$ (c) 0
     (d) 2 (e) 1

11 (a) $0<y<0.0001$ (b) $y>10\,000$

12 (a) $|y|>10^{-9}$ (b) $|x|<0.1$

13 $|N-37\,000|<500$

14 $|m-n|\leqslant5$

15   The length is 5.23 cm correct to 2 decimal places.

Exercise 8B (page 99)

3 (a)   (b)

    (c)   (d)

4 (a)   (b)

Exercise 8C (page 104)

1 (a) $y=x^2-3x$
    (b) $y=x^2+3x+4$
    (c) $y=x^2-3x+4$

2 (a) $y=x^2-x+1$
    (b) $y=x^2-5x+2$
    (c) $y=x^2-x-4$

3 (a) 3 units in the positive x-direction
    (b) 3 units in the positive x-direction and
       -3 units in the positive y-direction, in
       either order

4 If $y = x^2$ is translated by -4 units in the positive x-direction and -2 units in the positive y-direction, in either order, the equation becomes $y = x^2 + 8x + 14$.

5 $y = \frac{4}{9}x^2$
   (a) Use a factor of $3\sqrt{2}/2$
   (b) Use a factor of $\frac{2}{9}$

6 (a) y-axis   (b) x-axis

7 y-axis

8 (a) $y = -\left(\frac{1}{3}x - 2\right)^2$ (b) $y = 4(x+3)^2$
   (c) $y = 2x^2 + 8$

9 A translation of -1 in the positive x-direction, then a stretch of factor 3 in the y-direction, finally a reflection in the x-axis

10 (a) Stretch, factor a in the y-direction
   (b) Translation a units in the positive y-direction
   (c) Translation $-a$ units in the positive x-direction
   (d) Stretch, factor $1/a$ in the x-direction

11 (a) Odd function, even derivative
   (b) Even function, odd derivative
   (c) Function, derivative neither even nor odd
   (d) Function neither even nor odd, even derivative

Miscellaneous exercise 8 (page 106)

1 (a) $f(x) \leq 9$ (b) all real values
   (c) $f(x) \geq -69$ (d) $f(x) \geq -36$

2 $y = -2x + 8$

3 $\frac{1}{4}, -2$

4 (a)   (b)

5 The curve remains the same.

6 (a) $f(x) \geq -7$
   (b) Translation by 2, in negative x-direction
      Stretch, y-direction, scale factor 5
      Translation by 7, in negative y-direction
   (c) Translation by 7, in positive y-direction
      Stretch, y-direction, scale factor $\frac{1}{5}$
      Translation by 2, in positive x-direction
   (e) Translation by 2, in negative x-direction
      Stretch, y-direction, scale factor 5

7 25; $f(x) \leq 25$

8 Translation by 1, in negative x-direction
   Stretch, y-direction, scale factor 2

9 $\frac{1}{2}\sqrt{7}$

10 (a)   (b)

11 $a = 6, b = -10$

12 $c = 3, d = -7$

13 $y = -f(-x)$; $f(x)$ is an odd function.

14 (a) $f(x) = 1$ (b) $f(x) = -1$

15 (a) The gradient at P' is the negative of the gradient at P. So $f'(-p) = -f'(p)$. The derivative of an even function is odd.

16 (a) $f(x) = \{-2, -1, 0, 1, 2, 3\}$
   (b) $0 \leq f(x) < 1$

17 $p = 5, q = 2, r = 8$

9 Applications of differentiation

Exercise 9A (page 113)

1 (a) $2x - 5, x \geq \frac{5}{2}$ (b) $2x + 6, x \geq -3$
   (c) $-3 - 2x, x \leq -\frac{3}{2}$ (d) $6x - 5, x \geq \frac{5}{6}$
   (e) $10x + 3, x \geq -\frac{3}{10}$ (f) $-4 - 6x, x \leq -\frac{2}{3}$

2 (a) $2x + 4, x \leq -2$ (b) $2x - 3, x \leq \frac{3}{2}$
   (c) $-3 + 2x, x \leq \frac{3}{2}$ (d) $4x - 8, x \leq 2$
   (e) $7 - 4x, x \geq \frac{7}{4}$ (f) $-5 - 14x, x \geq -\frac{5}{14}$

3 (a) $3x^2 - 12, x \leq -2$ and $x \geq 2$
   (b) $6x^2 - 18, x \leq -\sqrt{3}$ and $x \geq \sqrt{3}$
   (c) $6x^2 - 18x - 24, x \leq -1$ and $x \geq 4$
   (d) $3x^2 - 6x + 3$, all x
   (e) $4x^3 - 4x, -1 \leq x \leq 0$ and $x \geq 1$
   (f) $4x^3 + 12x^2, x \geq -3$
   (g) $3 - 3x^2, -1 \leq x \leq 1$
   (h) $10x^4 - 20x^3, x \leq 0$ and $x \geq 2$
   (i) $3(1 + x^2)$, all x

4 (a) $3x^2 - 27, -3 \leq x \leq 3$
   (b) $4x^3 + 8x, x \leq 0$
   (c) $3x^2 - 6x + 3$, none
   (d) $12 - 6x^2, x \leq -\sqrt{2}$ and $x \geq \sqrt{2}$
   (e) $6x^2 + 6x - 36, -3 \leq x \leq 2$
   (f) $12x^3 - 60x^2, x \leq 5$
   (g) $72x - 8x^3, -3 \leq x \leq 0$ and $x \geq 3$
   (h) $5x^4 - 5, -1 \leq x \leq 1$
   (i) $nx^{n-1} - n$; $x \leq 1$ if n is even, $-1 \leq x \leq 1$ if n is odd

5 The second answer in each part gives intervals for which the function is increasing. In the other intervals it is decreasing.

(a) $\frac{1}{2}x^{1/2}(5x-3)$, $x \geqslant \frac{3}{5}$

(b) $\frac{1}{4}x^{-1/4}(3-14x)$, $0 < x \leqslant \frac{3}{14}$

(c) $\frac{1}{3}x^{-1/3}(5x+4)$, $x \leqslant -\frac{4}{5}$ and $x \geqslant 0$

(d) $\frac{13}{5}x^{-2/5}(x^2-3)$, $x \leqslant -\sqrt{3}$ and $x \geqslant \sqrt{3}$

(e) $1 - \frac{3}{x^2}$, $x \leqslant -\sqrt{3}$ and $x \geqslant \sqrt{3}$

(f) $\frac{(x-1)}{2x\sqrt{x}}$, $x \geqslant 1$

6 (a) (i) $(4,-12)$ (ii) minimum (iv) $f(x) \geqslant -12$

(b) (i) $(-2,-7)$ (ii) minimum (iv) $f(x) \geqslant -7$

(c) (i) $\left(-\frac{3}{5},\frac{1}{5}\right)$ (ii) minimum (iv) $f(x) \geqslant \frac{1}{5}$

(d) (i) $(-3,13)$ (ii) maximum (iv) $f(x) \leqslant 13$

(e) (i) $(-3,0)$ (ii) minimum (iv) $f(x) \geqslant 0$

(f) (i) $\left(-\frac{1}{2},2\right)$ (ii) maximum (iv) $f(x) \leqslant 2$

7 (a) $(-4,213)$, maximum; $(3,-130)$, minimum

(b) $(-3,88)$, maximum; $(5,-168)$, minimum

(c) $(0,0)$, minimum; $(1,1)$, neither

(d) $(-2,65)$, maximum; $(0,1)$, neither; $(2,-63)$, minimum

(e) $\left(-\frac{1}{3},-\frac{11}{27}\right)$, minimum; $\left(\frac{1}{2},\frac{3}{4}\right)$, maximum

(f) $(-1,0)$, neither

(g) $(-1,-2)$, maximum; $(1,2)$, minimum

(h) $(3,27)$, minimum

(i) none

(j) $\left(\frac{1}{4},-\frac{1}{4}\right)$, minimum

(k) $\left(6,\frac{1}{12}\right)$, maximum

(l) $(-2,17)$, minimum

(m) $(1,3)$, maximum

(n) $(-1,-5)$, minimum

(o) $(0,0)$, minimum; $\left(\frac{4}{5},\frac{256}{3125}\right)$, maximum

8 (a) $f(x) \geqslant \frac{3}{4}$

(b) $f(x) \geqslant -16$

(c) $f(x) \leqslant -2$, $f(x) \geqslant 2$

Exercise 9B (page 119)

1 (a) Gradient of road

(b) Rate of increase of crowd

(c) Rate of increase of magnetic force with respect to distance

(d) Acceleration of particle

(e) Rate of increase of petrol consumption with respect to speed

2 (a) $\dfrac{dp}{dh}$, p in millibars, h in metres

(b) $\dfrac{d\theta}{dt}$, θ in degrees C, t in hours

(c) $\dfrac{dh}{dt}$, h in metres, t in hours

(d) $\dfrac{dW}{dt}$, W in kilograms, t in weeks

3 (a) $6t+7$ (b) $1-\dfrac{1}{2\sqrt{x}}$

(c) $1-\dfrac{6}{y^3}$ (d) $2t-\dfrac{1}{2t\sqrt{t}}$

(e) $2t+6$ (f) $12s^5-6s$

(g) 5 (h) $-\dfrac{2}{r^3}-1$

4 (a) Velocity

(b) (i) increasing   (ii) decreasing

(c) 9, occurs when velocity is zero and direction of motion changes

5 (a) $\dfrac{dx}{dt} = c$

(b) $\dfrac{dA}{dt} = kA$; A stands for the amount deposited

(c) $\dfrac{dW_M}{dt}$ and $\dfrac{dW_J}{dt}$ are both <0, $\dfrac{dW_M}{dt} < \dfrac{dW_J}{dt}$

(d) $\dfrac{dx}{dt} = f(\theta)$; x stands for diameter, θ for air temperature

6 80 km h^{-1}

7 20 m

8 36

9 $4\sqrt{5}$

10 Greatest $V = 32\pi$ when $r = 4$, least $V = 0$ when $r = 0$ or $h = 0$

11 $x = 25$

12 (b) 1800 m^2

13 $0 < x < 20$, 7.36 cm

14 20 cm

15 38400 cm^3 (to 3 significant figures)

16 2420 cm^3 (to 3 significant figures)

Miscellaneous exercise 9 (page 121)

1 Maximum at $(-2,-4)$; minimum at $(2,4)$; y increases with x for $x \leqslant -2$ and $x \geqslant 2$

2 (a) $\dfrac{dn}{dt} = kn$ (b) $\dfrac{d\theta}{dt} = -k\theta$

(c) $\dfrac{d\theta}{dt} = -k(\theta - \beta)$

4 $(20-4t) \text{ m s}^{-1}$, -4 m s^{-2}; for $0 \leqslant t \leqslant 5$

5 (a) 20 m (b) 6 s (c) 40 m s^{-1}

6 50

7 (a) $9\sqrt{2} \text{ cm}$ (b) $40\frac{1}{2} \text{ cm}^2$

8 (a) $(-1,-7)$; $(2,20)$
  (b) Graph crosses the x-axis three times.
  (c) $y=-5$ has three intersections with graph.
  (d) (i) $-20<k<7$ (ii) $k<-20$ and $k>7$

9 $(-2,4)$; $(2,-28)$; $-28 \leqslant k \leqslant 4$

10 $\left(-\frac{2}{3},\frac{4}{27}\right)$; $(0,0)$; $0<k<\frac{4}{27}$

11 $(-1,5)$, $(2,-22)$; $(0,10)$;
  (a) $5<k<10$ (b) $-22<k<5$ and $k>10$

12 $\left(\frac{1}{3},\frac{4}{27}\right)$, $(1,0)$; $k<-\dfrac{2}{3\sqrt{3}}$ and $k>\dfrac{2}{3\sqrt{3}}$

13 (a) $P=2x+2r+\frac{1}{2}\pi r$, $A=\frac{1}{4}\pi r^2+rx$
  (b) $x=\frac{1}{4}r(4-\pi)$

14 Maximum at $\left(2,\frac{1}{4}\right)$
  (a) $\left(2,5\frac{1}{4}\right)$
  (b) $\left(3,\frac{1}{2}\right)$; that is, when $x-1=2$

15 (a) $1100-20x$ (b) £$x(1100-20x)$
  (c) £$(24\,000-400x)$; £37.50

0 Integration

Exercise 10A (page 126)

1 (a) x^4+k (b) x^6+k
  (c) x^2+k (d) x^3+x^5+k
  (e) $x^{10}-x^8-x+k$ (f) $-x^7+x^3+x+k$

2 (a) $3x^3-2x^2-5x+k$
  (b) $4x^3+3x^2+4x+k$
  (c) $7x+k$
  (d) $4x^4-2x^3+5x^2-3x+k$
  (e) $\frac{1}{2}x^4+\frac{5}{2}x^2+k$
  (f) $\frac{1}{2}x^2+\frac{2}{3}x^3+k$
  (g) $\frac{2}{3}x^3-\frac{3}{2}x^2-4x+k$
  (h) $x-x^2-x^3+k$

3 (a) $\frac{1}{5}x^5+\frac{1}{3}x^3+x+k$
  (b) $\frac{7}{2}x^2-3x+k$
  (c) $\frac{2}{3}x^3+\frac{1}{2}x^2-8x+k$
  (d) $\frac{3}{2}x^4-\frac{5}{3}x^3+\frac{3}{2}x^2+2x+k$
  (e) $\frac{1}{6}x^4+\frac{1}{6}x^3+\frac{1}{6}x^2+\frac{1}{6}x+k$
  (f) $\frac{1}{8}x^4-\frac{1}{9}x^3+\frac{1}{2}x^2-\frac{1}{3}x+k$
  (g) $\frac{1}{2}x^2-x^3+x+k$
  (h) $\frac{1}{4}x^4+\frac{1}{3}x^3+\frac{1}{2}x^2+x+k$

4 $f(x)=4x^2-5x$

5 $y=2x^3-x-19$

6 $y=\frac{1}{8}x^4+\frac{1}{8}x^2+x-21$

7 $f(x)=5x^3-3x^2+4x-6$

9 (a) $-x^{-1}+k$ (b) $-x^{-3}+k$
  (c) $-3x^{-2}+k$ (d) $2x^2+3x^{-1}+k$
  (e) $-\frac{1}{2}x^{-2}+\frac{1}{3}x^{-3}+k$ (f) $-2x^{-1}-\frac{2}{3}x^3+k$

10 (a) $y=\frac{2}{3}x^{3/2}+k$ (b) $y=12x^{1/3}+k$
  (c) $y=\frac{3}{4}x^{4/3}+k$ (d) $y=\frac{4}{3}x^{3/2}-4x^{1/2}+k$
  (e) $y=\frac{15}{2}x^{2/3}+k$ (f) $y=-6x^{1/3}+k$

11 $y=4x^{3/2}-7$

12 $y=-4x^{-1}+13$

13 $y=x^{1/2}-2$

14 $y=\frac{3}{4}x^{4/3}+3x^{-2}+\frac{5}{4}$

15 (a) $y=x^3+3x^2+k$
  (b) $y=4x^3+2x^2-5x+k$
  (c) $y=2x^2-x^{-1}+k$
  (d) $y=\frac{2}{3}x^{3/2}+8x^{1/2}+k$
  (e) $y=\frac{1}{2}x^2+\frac{20}{3}x^{3/2}+25x+k$
  (f) $y=x+10x^{1/2}+k$

16 (a) 118 cm (to 3 significant figures)   (b) 27

17 17 months (to the nearest month)

18 192

Exercise 10B (page 132)

1 (a) $2x^2+k$ (b) $5x^3+k$ (c) $\frac{1}{3}x^6+k$
  (d) $9x+k$ (e) $\frac{1}{18}x^9+k$ (f) $\frac{2}{15}x^5+k$

2 (a) 7   (b) 84   (c) 4
  (d) 4   (e) $\frac{1}{16}$ (f) 2

3 (a) $3x^2+7x+k$
  (b) $2x^3-x^2-5x+k$
  (c) $\frac{1}{2}x^4+\frac{7}{2}x^2+k$
  (d) $\frac{3}{5}x^5-2x^4+3x^3-\frac{1}{2}x^2+4x+k$
  (e) $\frac{2}{3}x^3-\frac{3}{2}x^2-20x+k$
  (f) $\frac{1}{4}x^4-2x^2+k$

4 (a) 22   (b) 22   (c) 36
  (d) $7\frac{1}{6}$ (e) 210   (f) 0

5 72

6 15

7 195

8 80

9 80

10 $10\frac{2}{5}$

11 18

12 16

13 (a) 39   (b) $5\frac{1}{3}$ (c) $10\frac{2}{3}$
  (d) 10   (e) 500   (f) $5\frac{1}{3}$

14 (a) $-\frac{1}{2}x^{-2}+k$ (b) $\frac{1}{3}x^3+x^{-1}+k$
  (c) $\frac{2}{3}x^{3/2}+k$ (d) $\frac{18}{5}x^{5/3}+k$
  (e) $2x^3-5x^{-1}+k$ (f) $2x^{1/2}+k$

15 (a) 144   (b) $1\frac{1}{2}$ (c) 20
  (d) $6\frac{3}{4}$ (e) 16   (f) 3

16 $1\frac{3}{4}$

17 60

18 $3\frac{1}{3}$

19 7

20 5

21 (a) $22\frac{2}{3}$ (b) $2\frac{3}{8}$

22 96

24 $42\frac{7}{8}$

Exercise 10C (page 138)

1 -4

2 (a) $10\frac{2}{3}$ (b) 8   (c) $2\frac{1}{4}$ (d) $1\frac{5}{6}$

3 (a) $10\frac{2}{3}$ (b) 8   (c) 100

4 (a) $\frac{1}{4}$ (b) 6   (c) 100

5 $\dfrac{s^{1-m}-1}{1-m}$; $\dfrac{1}{m-1}$

6 $\dfrac{1-r^{1-m}}{1-m}$; $m<1$, $\dfrac{1}{1-m}$

7 12

8 $10\frac{2}{3}$

9 32

10 108

11 $42\frac{2}{3}$

12 $4\frac{1}{2}$

13 36

Miscellaneous exercise 10 (page 139)

1 $y=\frac{1}{6}x^3-\frac{1}{6}x^2+x+\frac{1}{3}$

2 ±2; 32

3 $4x\sqrt{x}+k$; 28

4 (a) $-\frac{1}{2}x^{-2}+\frac{1}{4}x^4+k$ (b) 6

5 $31\frac{1}{4}$

6 $50\frac{2}{15}$

7 7

8 $6\frac{3}{4}$

9 $1\frac{1}{3}$

10 0

11 (a) $\frac{1}{4}x^4-x^2+k$ (b) 2

12 (a) $y=-\frac{1}{2}x+\frac{3}{2}$ (b) $2\frac{29}{48}$

13 ±2

15 (a) 6   (b) 67   (c) —   (d) 45
    (e) 17   (f) -11 (g) 17   (h) 11

17 (a) $y=2x-2$ (b) $6\frac{3}{4}$

19 $(0,0),(\pm2,-16)$; 32.4

20 $\frac{1}{2}$

21 (a) $\frac{1}{27},0$ (b) (i) $(3,0)$ (ii) $\left(4,-\frac{1}{128}\right)$

11 Trigonometry

Exercise 11A (page 146)

1 (a) 0.9063,   0.4226,   0.4663
   (b) -0.5736,   0.8192, -1.4281
   (c) -0.7071, -0.7071,   1
   (d) 0.8192, -0.5736, -0.7002
   (e) -0.3420,   0.9397, -2.7475
   (f) 0.3843,   0.9232,   2.4023
   (g) -0.5721,   0.8202, -1.4335
   (h) -0.9703, -0.2419,   0.2493

2 (a) max 3 at $x=90$, min 1 at $x=270$
   (b) max 11 at $x=180$, min 3 at $x=360$
   (c) max 13 at $x=180$, min -3 at $x=90$
   (d) max 4 at $x=90$, min 2 at $x=270$
   (e) max 10 at $x=27\frac{1}{2}$, min 8 at $x=72\frac{1}{2}$
   (f) max 5 at $x=90$, min 1.875 at $x=450$

3 (a) 160   (b) 320   (c) 240
   (d) 50   (e) 220   (f) 340
   (g) 40, 140   (h) 30, 330   (i) 70, 250
   (j) 80, 100   (k) 160, 200   (l) 100, 280

4 (a) 160   (b) -40 (c) -120
   (d) 50   (e) -140 (f) -20
   (g) 40, 140   (h) 30   (i) $-110, 70$
   (j) 80, 100   (k) ±160 (l) $-80, 100$

5 (a) $\frac{1}{2}\sqrt{2}$ (b) $-\frac{1}{2}$ (c) $-\frac{1}{2}$ (d) $\sqrt{3}$
   (e) $-\frac{1}{2}\sqrt{2}$ (f) $\frac{1}{2}\sqrt{3}$ (g) -1 (h) $-\frac{1}{2}\sqrt{3}$
   (i) $-\frac{1}{2}\sqrt{2}$ (j) 0   (k) 1   (l) $\frac{1}{2}\sqrt{2}$
   (m) $-\frac{1}{2}$ (n) -1 (o) $-\frac{1}{2}$ (p) 0

6 (a) 60   (b) 240   (c) 120   (d) 30
   (e) 30   (f) 135   (g) 210   (h) 90

7 (a) 120   (b) 60   (c) -90 (d) 180
   (e) 60   (f) -30 (g) -45 (h) 0

8 (a) $A=5, B=2.8$
   (b) 7.42 m

Exercise 11B (page 149)

3 (a) 90   (b) 45   (c) 180   (d) 30
   (e) 360   (f) $11\frac{1}{4}$

Exercise 11C (page 153)

1 (a) 5.7, 174.3   (b) 237.1, 302.9
   (c) 72.0, 108.0   (d) 36.9, 323.1
   (e) 147.1, 212.9   (f) 35.3, 324.7
   (g) 76.0, 256.0   (h) 162.3, 342.3
   (i) 6.3, 186.3   (j) 203.6, 336.4
   (k) 214.8, 325.2   (l) 161.6, 341.6
   (m) 49.5, 160.5   (n) 240, 360
   (o) 10, 70

2 (a) 53.1, 126.9   (b) ±75.5
   (c) −116.6, 63.4   (d) −137.9, −42.1
   (e) ±96.9   (f) −36.9, 143.1
   (g) −128.7, 51.3   (h) ±45, ±135
   (i) 0, ±60, ±180

3 (a) 35.3, 144.7, 215.3, 324.7
   (b) 21.1, 81.1, 141.1, 201.1, 261.1, 321.1
   (c) 108.4, 161.6, 288.4, 341.6
   (d) 26.1, 63.9, 116.1, 153.9, 206.1, 243.9, 296.1, 333.9
   (e) 10.9, 100.9, 190.9, 280.9
   (f) 68.3, 111.7, 188.3, 231.7, 308.3, 351.7

4 (a) ±16.1, ±103.9, ±136.1
   (b) −125.8, −35.8, 54.2, 144.2
   (c) −176.2, −123.8, −56.2, −3.8, 63.8, 116.2,
   (d) ±37.9, ±142.1
   (e) −172.3, −136.3, −100.3, −64.3, −28.3, 7.7 43.7, 79.7, 115.7, 151.7
   (f) −78.5, −11.5, 101.5, 168.5

5 (a) ±96.4
   (b) −107.3, 162.7
   (c) −56.0
   (d) No roots in the interval
   (e) 35.4
   (f) −43.6

6 (a) 30, 90, 210, 270
   (b) 22.5, 112.5, 202.5, 292.5
   (c) 65, 85, 185, 205, 305, 325
   (d) 110, 230, 350
   (e) 85, 145, 265, 325
   (f) 80
   (g) No roots in the interval
   (h) 45, 105, 165, 225, 285, 345
   (i) 80

7 (a) −170.8, −9.2
   (b) −90, 90
   (c) −180, −135, 0, 45, 180
   (d) −173.4, −96.6, 6.6, 83.4
   (e) 11.3, 78.7
   (f) −150.5, −90.5, −30.5, 29.5, 89.5, 149.5

8 (a) 27, 63, 207, 243
   (b) 4, 68, 76, 140, 148, 212, 220, 284, 292, 356
   (c) 20, 80, 140, 200, 260, 320

9 0, 60, 120, 180

10 For example,
   (a) $\sin 4\theta°$, $\cos 4\theta°$, $\tan 2\theta°$
   (b) $\sin 18\theta°$, $\cos 18\theta°$, $\tan 9\theta°$
   (c) $\sin\frac{15}{2}\theta°$, $\cos\frac{15}{2}\theta°$, $\tan\frac{15}{4}\theta°$
   (d) $\sin 3\theta°$, $\cos 3\theta°$, $\tan\frac{3}{2}\theta°$
   (e) $\sin\frac{1}{2}\theta°$, $\cos\frac{1}{2}\theta°$, $\tan\frac{1}{4}\theta°$
   (f) $\sin\frac{3}{5}\theta°$, $\cos\frac{3}{5}\theta°$, $\tan\frac{3}{10}\theta°$

11 (a) 120   (b) 180   (c) 90
   (d) 540   (e) 720   (f) 720
   (g) 120   (h) 90

12 (a) 0.9863
   (b) $A = 12$, $B = 6$, 6 hours 7 minutes
   (c) Days 202, 345

13 (a) 30   (b) 3.25 m   (c) 27

Exercise 11D (page 157)

1 (a) $11; \frac{4}{5}, \frac{3}{5}, \frac{4}{3}$
   (b) $37.5; \frac{15}{17}, \frac{8}{17}, \frac{15}{8}$
   (c) $\sqrt{13}; \frac{3}{13}\sqrt{13}, \frac{2}{13}\sqrt{13}, \frac{3}{2}$
   (d) $11; \frac{5}{14}\sqrt{3}, \frac{11}{14}, \frac{5}{11}\sqrt{3}$
   (e) $17\sqrt{5}; \frac{22}{85}\sqrt{5}, \frac{31}{85}\sqrt{5}, \frac{22}{31}$
   (f) $12\sqrt{2}; \frac{1}{3}, \frac{2}{3}\sqrt{2}, \frac{1}{4}\sqrt{2}$

2 (a) $-\frac{11}{14}$ (b) $\frac{20}{29}$ (c) $\pm\frac{1}{2}\sqrt{3}$
   (d) $0, \pm 78.5$ (to 1 decimal place)

4 (a) 30, 150, 210, 330   (b) 0, 180, 360
   (c) 36.9, 143.1, 199.5, 340.5
   (d) 0, 51.0, 180, 309.0, 360

5 −116.6, −26.6, 63.4, 153.4

Miscellaneous exercise 11 (page 158)

1 (a) 360   (b) 90

2 (a) $\cos x°$ (b) $-\cos x°$

3 $(0,1), (\pm 180, 0)$

4 (a) 21.8, 201.8   (b) 11.8, 78.2, 191.8, 258.2

5 24.1, 155.9

6 (a) Examples are $\tan x°$, $\sin 2x°$, $\cos 2x°$
   (b) 10, 50, 130, 170

7 30, 270

8 (a) $2\sin 2x°$ (b) 105, 165, 285, 345

9 (a) 168.5   (b) 333.4   (c) 225   (d) 553.1

11 (a) 2, 0; 180, 90   (b) 9, 1; 240, 60
   (c) 49, 9; 105, 45   (d) 8, 5; 90, 180
   (e) 6, 3; 180, 360   (f) 60, 30; $7\frac{1}{2}, 52\frac{1}{2}$

12 (a) 0, 180, 360   (b) 0, 30, 150, 180, 360
   (c) $67\frac{1}{2}, 157\frac{1}{2}, 247\frac{1}{2}, 337\frac{1}{2}$
   (d) 30, 120, 210, 300

13 (a) 60   (b) 8.9, 68.9, 128.9
   (c) (i) 51.1 (ii) 21.1

14 (a) (i) Stretch in the y-direction, scale factor 4
     (ii) Translation of 3 units in the negative y-direction
   (b) (ii) 2

15 (a) $4.8 \pm 1.2 \sin 15t°$ or $4.8 \pm 1.2 \cos 15t°$
    (b) $21500 \pm 6500 \sin 36t°$ or
         $21500 \pm 6500 \cos 36t°$
    (c) $12 \pm 10 \sin t°$ or $12 \pm 10 \cos t°$

16 (a) 7.2
    (b) (i) $N - C$ (ii) $N + C$ after 37.5 weeks

17 $A = 0.5, B = 4.5, a = 1, \beta = 12$

12 Second derivatives

Exercise 12A (page 163)

1 (a) At $x = -1, 0, 1$ (b) $3x^2 - 1$
   (c) $6x$

2 (b) $3x^2 + 1, 6x$ (c) $x \geqslant 0$

4 (a) (i) $(0,0), \left(\pm\sqrt{2}, 4\right)$ (ii) $\left(\pm\frac{1}{3}\sqrt{6}, -\frac{8}{9}\right)$
   (b) (i) $(0,0), \left(-\frac{2}{3}, \frac{4}{27}\right)$ (ii) $\left(-\frac{1}{3}, \frac{2}{27}\right)$
   (c) (i) $(\pm 1, \pm 2)$ (ii) none
   (d) (i) none   (ii) none
   (e) (i) $(2,3)$ (ii) none
   (f) (i) $(-2,-3)$ (ii) none

5 (a) Rate of increase of inflation, positive

6 (a) $f'(x)+, f''(x)+$ (b) $f'(x)+, f''(x)-$
   (c) $f'(x)+, f''(x) 0$ (d) $f'(x)-, f''(x)+$
   (e) For $0 < x < 3$, $f'(x)+, f''(x)+$;
        for $x > 3$, $f'(x)-, f''(x)+$
   (f) For $x < -1, f'(x)+, f''(x)+$;
        for $-1 < x < 0, f'(x)+, f''(x)-$;
        for $0 < x < 1, f'(x)-, f''(x)-$;
        for $x > 1, f'(x)-, f''(x)+$

7 (a) Both positive, sudden change (drop in S),
        then $\dfrac{dS}{dt}$ is negative changing to positive with
        $\dfrac{d^2 S}{dt^2}$ positive.
   (b) Price rising sharply, sudden 'crash', price
        continues to drop but less quickly and then
        recovers to give steadier growth.

8 (b) $+, -, -, +$

9 (a) $\dfrac{dN}{dt} = -kN, k > 0$ (c) $+$

Exercise 12B (page 166)

1 (a) $(-1,-2)$ minimum; $(1,2)$ maximum
   (b) $(0,0)$ maximum; $(2,-4)$ minimum
   (c) $(0,1)$ minimum
   (d) $(-1,11)$ maximum; $(2,-16)$ minimum
   (e) $\left(2, -\frac{3}{8}\right)$ minimum
   (f) $(-1,2)$ minimum; $(1,2)$ minimum
   (g) $\left(2, \frac{1}{4}\right)$ maximum
   (h) $(2,22)$ inflexion

2 (a) $(-1,-8)$ minimum; $(0,-3)$ maximum;
        $(2,-35)$ minimum
   (b) $(1,6)$ inflexion
   (c) $\left(-\frac{4}{3}, -14\frac{2}{9}\right)$ minimum; $\left(\frac{4}{3}, 14\frac{2}{9}\right)$ maximum
   (d) $(-2,3)$ minimum
   (e) $(-2,-4)$ maximum; $(2,4)$ minimum
   (f) $\left(6, \frac{1}{12}\right)$ maximum
   (g) $(0,-7)$ inflexion
   (h) $(0,1)$ minimum; $(1,2)$ inflexion

Exercise 12C (page 169)

1 (a) $2x + 3, 2, 0, 0$
   (b) $6x^2 + 1 - \dfrac{1}{x^2}, 12x + \dfrac{2}{x^3}, 12 - \dfrac{6}{x^4}, \dfrac{24}{x^5}$
   (c) $4x^3, 12x^2, 24x, 24$
   (d) $\frac{1}{2}x^{-1/2}, -\frac{1}{4}x^{-3/2}, \frac{3}{8}x^{-5/2}, -\frac{15}{16}x^{-7/2}$
   (e) $-\frac{1}{2}x^{-3/2}, \frac{3}{4}x^{-5/2}, -\frac{15}{8}x^{-7/2}, \frac{105}{16}x^{-9/2}$
   (f) $\frac{1}{4}x^{-3/4}, -\frac{3}{16}x^{-7/4}, \frac{21}{64}x^{-11/4}, -\frac{231}{256}x^{-15/4}$

2 (a) $2x - 5, 2, 0, 0$
   (b) $10x^4 - 6x, 40x^3 - 6, 120x^2, 240x$
   (c) $-4x^{-5}, 20x^{-6}, -120x^{-7}, 840x^{-8}$
   (d) $6x - 6x^5, 6, -30x^4, -120x^3, -360x^2$
   (e) $\frac{3}{4}x^{-1/4}, -\frac{3}{16}x^{-5/4}, \frac{15}{64}x^{-9/4}, -\frac{135}{256}x^{-13/4}$
   (f) $\frac{3}{8}x^{-5/8}, -\frac{15}{64}x^{-13/8}, \frac{195}{512}x^{-21/8}, -\frac{4095}{4096}x^{-29/8}$

3 $n(n-1)(n-2) \ldots 3 \times 2 \times 1$

4 $(n+2)(n+1)n(n-1) \ldots \times 3x^2$

5 0

Miscellaneous exercise 12 (page 169)

3 (a) Subsonic: $\dfrac{dk}{dV}$ +, initially small then
        increasing; $\dfrac{d^2 k}{dV^2}$ +, decreasing to zero.
        Transonic: $\dfrac{dk}{dV}$ + at first, zero at velocity of
        sound, then −; $\dfrac{d^2 k}{dV^2}$ zero, −, zero again.
        Supersonic: $\dfrac{dk}{dV}$ −; $\dfrac{d^2 k}{dV^2}$ zero, then +.
   (b) At the boundaries between the regions.
   (c) Possibly levelling out, becoming constant
        again.

4 $(-1)^n (n+2)(n+1)n(n-1) \ldots \times 3x^{-(n+3)}$

5 $(-1)^{n-1} \times \dfrac{3 \times 5 \times 7 \times \ldots \times (2n-3)}{2^n} x^{-\frac{1}{2}(2n-1)}$ if $n \geqslant 3$

6 (a) $(1,15), (3,31)$ (b) $(1,2)$

7 (i) $\dfrac{dx}{dt}$ is $+,0,-$ with $\dfrac{d^2x}{dt^2}$ $-,0,+$

(ii) $\dfrac{dx}{dt}$ is $-$; $\dfrac{d^2x}{dt^2}$ is $+$

(a) Graph dips below $x=0$ with a minimum, then tends to $x=0$. Hence

$\dfrac{dx}{dt}$ is $-,0,+$ with $\dfrac{d^2x}{dt^2}$ $+,0,-$

(b) $\dfrac{dx}{dt}$ is $0,-$ with $\dfrac{d^2x}{dt^2}$ $-,0,+$

Revision exercise 2
(page 171)

1 (a) $22.5\,\text{cm}$ (b) $45\,\text{cm}$, $15\,\text{cm}$
(c) $0.33,\ 3.67$ (d) 15

2 $8x^2$

3 (a) $4x^{-\frac{2}{3}}$; $y=x+16$ (b) $23y-22x=360$
(c) $(-8,8)$

5 6

6 $(-4,8),(1,3); 20\frac{5}{6}$

7 $1-\dfrac{1}{x^2};\ \dfrac{1}{\sqrt{x}};\ \dfrac{-3}{2x^{\frac{3}{2}}};\ 1-\dfrac{1}{x^{\frac{3}{2}}}-\dfrac{2}{x^3}$

8 (a) $(-1,5),(1,1)$ (b) $(0,3)$
(c) $9y+x=7$ (d) 4

9 -4, maximum; -8, minimum

11 $\dfrac{n-1}{n+1}$

12 (a) $\pm 50.8, \pm 129.2$ (b) $-150.0, -30.0$
(c) $-166.7, -76.7, 13.3, 103.3$
(d) $\pm 165.0, \pm 15.0$

13 (a)   (b)

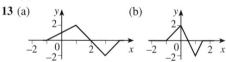

14 Maximum

15 (a) $15, 75, 105, 165, 195, 255, 285, 345$
(c) 180; for example, $(45,1.5)$

16 $y=\dfrac{5}{2}x^2+3x+4$

17 $\dfrac{1}{2}x^{-\frac{1}{2}}-\dfrac{1}{2}x^{-\frac{3}{2}};\ 1-x^{-2}$

18 0, Between $x=1$ and $x=3$, there is the same area above and below the x-axis.

19 Two roots

Mock examinations

Mock examination 1 for P1 (page 173)

1 $30-12\sqrt{6}$

2 $(x-2)^2+5, x=2\pm\sqrt{6}$

3 (i) $\left(0,\sqrt{1.5}\right),(-1.5,0)$ (ii) $\left(0,\sqrt{3}\right),(-1.5,0)$

4 $6x^2+\dfrac{1}{x^2}+\dfrac{1}{\sqrt{x}}$

5 $67.2, 112.8, 247.2, 292.8$

6 $£\left(24x-20x^2\right)$

7 $x=2,\ y=1$ or $x=-5,\ y=8$

8 $(-1,0)$; (i) $(3.2,6.4)$ (ii) 2

9 $(-1,1)$; (i) $10\frac{2}{3}$ (ii) $\frac{7}{12}$

Mock examination 2 for P1 (page 175)

1 $y=2x+1$

2 (ii) $a=\frac{1}{2}, b=2, c=\frac{1}{2}$

3 $(x+3)^2+7,\ (-3,7)$

4 $a=4, b=-3$

5 2

6 $y=\dfrac{4}{3}x^2+\dfrac{2}{x^2}-\dfrac{10}{3}$

7 (i) $5\,\text{m}$ (ii) $6\,\text{m}, 2\,\text{m}$
(iii) 7 p.m. to 11 p.m.

8 (i) $-1,0$ (ii) $-4\sqrt{3}<k<4\sqrt{3}$

9 $y+6x=8,\ 5\frac{1}{3}$

10 $1-\dfrac{2}{x^2},\ 2\sqrt{2}$, minimum. The value of $f'(x)$ is always increasing, so the curve bends upwards.

Answers to P2

1 Polynomials

Exercise 1A (page 181)

1. (a) 3   (b) 1   (c) 4
   (d) 0   (e) 1   (f) 0

2. (a) $4x^2 + 7x + 6$
   (b) $5x^3 + 3x^2 - 6x - 3$
   (c) $8x^4 - 3x^3 + 7x^2 - 3x + 1$
   (d) $2x^5 + 2x^4 - 5x^2 + 3$
   (e) $4 - 5x - 2x^2 - x^3$

3. (a) $2x^2 + x - 8$
   (b) $3x^3 + 7x^2 - 8x + 9$
   (c) $-2x^4 - x^3 + 7x^2 + 3x - 3$
   (d) $2x^5 - 2x^4 - 6x^3 + 5x^2 + 1$
   (e) $2 + 9x - 6x^2 - x^3$

4. (a) $2x^3 - 3x^2 + 9x - 2$
   (b) $3x^3 - 7x^2 + 16x - 13$
   (c) $x^3 - 4x^2 + 7x - 11$
   (d) $3x^3 - 8x^2 + 17x - 17$

5. (a) $6x^2 - 7x - 3$
   (b) $x^3 + x^2 - 7x + 2$
   (c) $2x^3 + 5x^2 - 3x - 9$
   (d) $12x^3 - 13x^2 + 9x - 2$
   (e) $x^4 + 2x^3 - 2x^2 + 2x - 3$
   (f) $8x^4 - 6x^3 - 15x^2 + 18x - 5$
   (g) $x^4 + 5x^3 + 5x^2 + 3x + 18$
   (h) $x^5 - 5x^4 + 3x^3 + 10x^2 - 8x + 5$
   (i) $3 + 8x - 4x^2 + 13x^3 - 4x^4 + 4x^5$
   (j) $8 - 22x + 19x^2 - 3x^3 - 3x^4 + x^5$
   (k) $6x^3 + 29x^2 - 7x - 10$
   (l) $2x^5 - 7x^4 + 6x^3 - 10x^2 + 4x - 3$

6. (a) $0, -1$ (b) $-11, -1$
   (c) $-3, -9$ (d) $25, -8$
   (e) $20, -21$ (f) $-16, 13$
   (g) $-17, -1$ (h) $-5, 11$
   (i) $5, -6$ (j) $-11, 8$

7. (a) $4, 1$ (b) $2, -3$
   (c) $2, 1$ (d) $3, -2$
   (e) $1, 2$ (f) $2, -3$
   (g) $2, 3$ (h) $2, -1$

Exercise 1B (page 184)

1. (a) $x - 3$ (b) $x + 17$
   (c) $3x + 11$ (d) $7x - 3$
   (e) $x - 3$ (f) $7x - 2$

2. (a) $1, -5, 22$ (b) $1, 8, -11$

   (c) $3, -4, 0$ (d) $3, -1, -4$
   (e) $4, 1, 4$ (f) $7, 1, 8$

3. (a) $1, -3, 5, 2$ (b) $1, -2, 4, 22$
   (c) $1, 1, -1, 3$ (d) $4, 1, -3, 11$
   (e) $2, 7, -1, 0$ (f) $3, 0, -5, 10$

4. (a) $2, -3, 4, -1, -2$ (b) $4, 1, 0, -2, 3$
   (c) $3, 1, -1, 2, 0$ (d) $1, -2, 5, -3, 2$

Exercise 1C (page 188)

1. (a) $x - 2, -4$ (b) $x + 1, -7$
   (c) $2x + 7, 13$ (d) $x + 2, 3$
   (e) $2x - 1, -1$ (f) $x, 0$

2. (a) $x^2 - 3, 7$
   (b) $x^2 + 2x + 15, 71$
   (c) $2x^2 - 6x + 22, -71$
   (d) $5x^2 + 20x + 77, 315$
   (e) $x^2 - x - 1, -6$
   (f) $2x^2 + 7x - 1, 3$

3. (a) $x^2 - 4x + 2, -x + 7$
   (b) $x^2 - 2x + 3, 2x + 5$
   (c) $2x - 6, 9x^2 + 4x + 11$
   (d) $3x^2 + 2x - 5, 30$

4. (a) -5 (b) 13 (c) 50 (d) -355
   (e) $\frac{7}{8}$ (f) $7\frac{13}{27}$ (g) 0 (h) 279

5. -1

6. -2

7. -5

8. 3

9. $5, -3$

10. $4, -3$

11. $2, 1$

12. $5, 3$

Exercise 1D (page 191)

1. (a) $(x+1)(x-2)(x+3)$ $-3, -1, 2$
   (b) $(x-1)(x-3)(x+1)$ $-1, 1, 3$
   (c) $(x-1)(x-5)(x+3)$ $-3, 1, 5$
   (d) $(x+1)^2(x-5)$ $-1, 5$
   (e) $(x-2)(x+2)(x+3)$ $-3, -2, 2$
   (f) $(2x+1)(x-1)(x+4)$ $-4, -\frac{1}{2}, 1$
   (g) $(3x-1)(x-2)(x+2)$ $-2, \frac{1}{3}, 2$
   (h) $(x+1)(2x-1)(3x+2)$ $-1, -\frac{2}{3}, \frac{1}{2}$
   (i) $(x-1)(x^2+3x-1)$ $1, \frac{1}{2}\left(\pm\sqrt{13}-3\right)$

2 (a) $(x-3)(x-1)(x+1)(x+2)$ $-2,-1,1,3$
(b) $(x-2)(x+1)(x+2)(x+3)$ $-3,-2,-1,2$
(c) $(x-3)(x-1)(x+2)(2x+1)$ $-2,-\frac{1}{2},1,3$
(d) $(x+1)(x-2)(2x+1)(3x+2)$ $-1,-\frac{2}{3},-\frac{1}{2},2$
(e) $(x-1)^3(x+1)$ $-1,1$
(f) $(x-2)^2(2x+1)^2$ $-\frac{1}{2},2$

3 (a) $(x-2)(x^2+2x+4)$
(b) $(x+2)(x^2-2x+4)$
(c) $(x-a)(x^2+ax+a^2)$
(d) $(x+a)(x^2-ax+a^2)$
(e) $(x-a)(x+a)(x^2+a^2)$
(f) $(x+a)(x^4-ax^3+a^2x^2-a^3x+a^4)$

4 (b) n must be odd;
$x^{n-1}-ax^{n-2}+a^2x^{n-3}-\ldots+a^{n-1}$

Miscellaneous exercise 1 (page 192)

1 $a=-3, b=1$

2 1

3 $3x+4$ and $2x+3$

4 $a=-1, b=-10$

5 $a=-6$

6 $x=-1,\frac{1}{2},-\frac{3}{2}$

7 (a) $a=2$
(b) $x=2,\sqrt{2},-\sqrt{2}$

8 $(x-3)(x^2+x+2)$; one root only as the discriminant of the quadratic is negative; one point only, as the equation for the intersections is the given cubic.

9 $x^2+4x+6=(x+2)^2+2$

10 $x^2-3; x^2+x+2$

11 (b) $p=-\sqrt{5}, q=\sqrt{5}$

12 $4x+7$

13 $x^2+2x+2, 0$

14 (a) $84,0$; $x-2$ is not a factor of $p(x)$, but $x+2$ is.
(b) $-2,-1\frac{1}{2},\frac{1}{2}$

15 (a) $a=-15$
(b) $(x+2)(x-5)(x+\sqrt{5})(x-\sqrt{5})$
(c) $x<-\sqrt{5}, -2<x<\sqrt{5}, x>5$

16 $A(-\sqrt{3},0), B(\sqrt{3},0)$; $(x-2)(x+1)^2$
(a) $x=2$
(b) They touch at $(-1,2)$.

17 (b) $6x-4$
(d) $x=1,1-\sqrt{2},1+\sqrt{2}$

2 Combining and inverting functions

Exercise 2A (page 199)

1 (a) 121   (b) 4   (c) 676

2 (a) 17   (b) 8   (c) 152

3 (a) 1   (b) 4   (c) $\frac{1}{2}$

4 (a) 1   (b) 4   (c) $6\frac{1}{3}$

5 (a) 0   (b) 21
(c) $-3\frac{3}{4}$ (d) x^2-4

6 (a) 27   (b) 8
(c) $3\frac{3}{8}$ (d) $(\cos x°+2)^3$

7 (a) 16   (b) 4
(c) 81   (d) $(2\sqrt{x}-10)^2$

8 (a) $\times, 4, +, 9$ (b) $+, 9, =, \times, 4$
(c) sq, $\times, 2, -, 5$ (d) $-5, =$, sq, $\times, 2$
(e) $\sqrt{\ }, -, 3, =$, cube
(f) $-, 2, =$, square, $+, 10, =, \sqrt{\ }$

9 (a) $\mathbb{R}, f(x) \geq 0$ (b) $\mathbb{R}, -1 \leq f(x) \leq 1$
(c) $x \geq 3, f(x) \geq 0$ (d) $\mathbb{R}, f(x) \geq 5$
(e) $x > 0, f(x) > 0$ (f) $\mathbb{R}, f(x) \leq 4$
(g) $0 \leq x \leq 4, 0 \leq f(x) \leq 2$
(h) $\mathbb{R}, f(x) \geq 6$ (i) $x \geq 3, f(x) \geq 0$

10 (a) 4   (b) -14 (c) -9 (d) 33
(e) 23   (f) -17 (g) 16   (h) 0

11 (a) 49   (b) 59   (c) 35
(d) $\frac{1}{16}$ (e) 9   (f) 899

12 (a) 7   (b) -19 (c) 1   (d) $\frac{1}{2}$
(e) $\frac{1}{2}$ (f) -1 (g) $3\frac{2}{3}$ (h) 2

13 (a) $x \mapsto 2x^2+5$ (b) $x \mapsto (2x+5)^2$
(c) $x \mapsto \dfrac{2}{x}+5$ (d) $x \mapsto \dfrac{1}{2x+5}$
(e) $x \mapsto 4x+15$ (f) $x \mapsto x$
(g) $x \mapsto \left(\dfrac{2}{x}+5\right)^2$ (h) $x \mapsto \dfrac{1}{(2x+5)^2}$

14 (a) $x \mapsto \sin x°-3$ (b) $x \mapsto \sin(x-3)°$
(c) $x \mapsto \sin(x^3-3)°$ (d) $x \mapsto \sin(x^3)°$
(e) $x \mapsto x-9$ (f) $x \mapsto (\sin x°)^3$

15 (a) fh   (b) fg
(c) hh   (d) hg or ggh
(e) gf or fffg   (f) gffh
(g) fgfg or ffffgg   (h) hf
(i) hffg

16 (a) $x \geqslant 0, \mathrm{gf}(x) \geqslant -5$

   (b) $x \geqslant -3, \mathrm{gf}(x) \geqslant 0$

   (c) $x \neq 2, \mathrm{gf}(x) \neq 0$

   (d) $\mathbb{R}, 0 \leqslant \mathrm{gf}(x) \leqslant 1$

   (e) $\mathbb{R}, \mathrm{gf}(x) \geqslant 0$

   (f) $-4 \leqslant x \leqslant 4, 0 \leqslant \mathrm{gf}(x) \leqslant 2$

   (g) $x \leqslant -2$ or $x \geqslant 3, \mathrm{gf}(x) \geqslant 0$

   (h) $x < -2, \mathrm{gf}(x) > 0$

17 (a) $-2\frac{2}{3}$ or 4   (b) 7   (c) 1

18 $a = 3, b = -7$ or $a = -3, b = 14$

19 $a = 4, b = 11$ or $a = 4\frac{1}{2}, b = 10$

Exercise 2B (page 206)

1 (a) $x \mapsto x - 4$ (b) $x \mapsto x + 5$

   (c) $x \mapsto \frac{1}{2}x$ (d) $x \mapsto 4x$

   (e) $x \mapsto \sqrt[3]{x}$ (f) $x \mapsto x^5$

2 (a) 10   (b) 7   (c) 3

   (d) 5   (e) -4

3 (a) 4   (b) 20   (c) $\frac{7}{5}$

   (d) 15   (e) -6

4 (a) 8   (b) $\frac{1}{8}$ (c) 512

   (d) -27 (e) 5

5 a, d, f, g, k

6 a, c, e, f, g, h, j

7 (a) 0   (b) -1 (c) $\frac{2}{3}$

   (d) 4   (e) -5 (f) -1

   (g) $1\frac{1}{2}$ (h) 1   (i) 4

8 (a) $x \mapsto \frac{1}{3}(x+1)$ (b) $x \mapsto 2(x-4)$

   (c) $x \mapsto \sqrt[3]{x-5}$ (d) $x \mapsto (x+3)^2, x > -3$

   (e) $x \mapsto \frac{1}{5}(2x+3)$ (f) $x \mapsto 1 + \sqrt{x-6}, x \geqslant 6$

9 (a) $y \mapsto \frac{1}{6}(y-5)$ (b) $y \mapsto 5y - 4$

   (c) $y \mapsto \frac{1}{2}(4-y)$ (d) $y \mapsto \frac{1}{2}(3y-7)$

   (e) $y \mapsto \sqrt[3]{\frac{1}{2}(y-5)}$ (f) $y \mapsto \dfrac{1}{y-4}, y \neq 4$

   (g) $y \mapsto \dfrac{5}{y} + 1, y \neq 0$

   (h) $y \mapsto \sqrt{y-7} - 2, y \geqslant 7$

   (i) $y \mapsto \frac{1}{2}(3 + \sqrt{y+5}), y \geqslant -5$

   (j) $y \mapsto 3 + \sqrt{y+9}, y \geqslant -9$

10 (a) $x \mapsto \frac{1}{4}x$ (b) $x \mapsto x - 3$

   (c) $x \mapsto x^2, x \geqslant 0$ (d) $x \mapsto \frac{1}{2}(x-1)$

   (e) $x \mapsto \sqrt{x} + 2, x \geqslant 0$ (f) $x \mapsto \frac{1}{3}(1-x)$

   (g) $x \mapsto \dfrac{3}{x}, x \neq 0$ (h) $x \mapsto 7 - x$

12 (a) $y \mapsto \dfrac{2y}{y-1}, y \neq 1$ (b) $y \mapsto \dfrac{4y+1}{y-2}, y \neq 2$

   (c) $y \mapsto \dfrac{5y+2}{y-1}, y \neq 1$ (d) $y \mapsto \dfrac{3y-11}{4y-3}, y \neq \frac{3}{4}$

13 (a) $\mathrm{f}(x) > -1$

   (b) $x \mapsto 2 + \sqrt{x+1}, x > -1, \mathrm{f}^{-1}(x) > 2$

14 (a) $\mathrm{f}(x) > 3$

   (b) $x \mapsto 2 + (x-3)^2, x > 3, \mathrm{f}^{-1}(x) > 2$

15 $k = -1$

   (a) $\mathrm{f}(x) \geqslant 5$

   (b) $x \mapsto -1 - \sqrt{x-5}, x \geqslant 5, \mathrm{f}^{-1}(x) \leqslant -1$

16 $a = \frac{1}{8}, b = \frac{3}{8}$

17 6

18 $x \mapsto \sqrt{x - 5\frac{3}{4}} - \frac{1}{2}, x > 6, \mathrm{f}^{-1}(x) > 0$

19 $x \mapsto 1 - \sqrt{-\frac{1}{2}(x+5)}, x < -5, \mathrm{f}^{-1}(x) < 1$

Miscellaneous exercise 2 (page 209)

1 (a) 29   (b) 61   (c) 2

   (d) -3 (e) 290   (f) 497

2 (a) $\mathbb{R}, \mathrm{f}(x) \leqslant 4$ (b) $\mathbb{R}, \mathrm{f}(x) \geqslant -7$

   (c) $x \geqslant -2, \mathrm{f}(x) \geqslant 0$ (d) $\mathbb{R}, \mathbb{R}$

   (e) $\mathbb{R}, \mathrm{f}(x) \geqslant 0$ (f) $x \geqslant 0, \mathrm{f}(x) \leqslant 2$

3 (a) $x \mapsto (1-2x)^3$ (b) $x \mapsto 1 - 2x^3$

   (c) $x \mapsto 1 - 2x^9$ (d) $x \mapsto 4x - 1$

   (e) $x \mapsto \frac{1}{2}(1-x)$

4 (a) 48   (b) 3   (c) -1

   (d) 4   (e) 4

5 (a) 12   (b) 27

6 $x \mapsto -3 + \sqrt{x-1}, x > 10$

7 $x \mapsto \sqrt[3]{\frac{1}{4}(x-3)}, x \in \mathbb{R}$

8 (a) $\sqrt{\frac{1}{3}(x+4)}$ (b) $3x^2 + 24x + 44$

9 (a) gf   (b) ff

   (c) g^{-1} (d) fgh or fhg

   (e) hfg   (f) f^{-1}

   (g) $\mathrm{g}^{-1}\mathrm{fgh}$ or $\mathrm{g}^{-1}\mathrm{fhg}$ (h) hf^{-1}

10 $\mathrm{f}^{-1}(x) = \sqrt{x-1}, x \geqslant 1$;

   $\mathrm{gf}(x) = x^2 - 2, \mathrm{gf}(x) \geqslant -2$

11 $1 \pm \sqrt{3}$

12 $k = 1; x \mapsto 1 - \sqrt{x-6}, x \geqslant 6$

13 $a = -2, b = 11$ or $a = 2, b = -13$

14 (b) $-\sqrt{1-x}, x \leqslant 1$ (c) $-\frac{1}{2}$

15 (a) $x \mapsto \frac{1}{4}(x-5)$ (b) $x \mapsto \frac{1}{2}(3-x)$

   (c) $x \mapsto -\frac{1}{8}(7+x)$ (d) $x \mapsto -8x - 7$

   (e) $x \mapsto -\frac{1}{8}(7+x)$

16 (a) $x \mapsto \frac{1}{2}(x-7)$ (b) $x \mapsto \sqrt[3]{x+1}$

   (c) $x \mapsto \sqrt[3]{\frac{1}{2}(x-5)}$ (d) $x \mapsto \frac{1}{2}(\sqrt[3]{x+1} - 7)$

   (e) $x \mapsto 2x^3 + 5$ (f) $x \mapsto (2x+7)^3 - 1$

   (g) $x \mapsto \sqrt[3]{\frac{1}{2}(x-5)}$ (h) $x \mapsto \frac{1}{2}(\sqrt[3]{x+1} - 7)$

17 (a) 3   (b) 7   (c) 3   (d) 7

18 (a) x (b) $\dfrac{x+5}{2x-1}$ (c) x

   (d) x (e) $\dfrac{x+5}{2x-1}$

19 (a) $\dfrac{4}{2-x}$ (b) $\dfrac{4}{2-x}$ (c) x

     (d) $\dfrac{2x-4}{x}$ (e) x (f) $\dfrac{2x-4}{x}$

3 Sequences

Exercise 3A (page 213)

1 (a) $7, 14, 21, 28, 35$ (b) $13, 8, 3, -2, -7$
     (c) $4, 12, 36, 108, 324$ (d) $6, 3, 1.5, 0.75, 0.375$
     (e) $2, 7, 22, 67, 202$ (f) $1, 4, 19, 364, 132\,499$

2 (a) $u_1 = 2, u_{r+1} = u_r + 2$

     (b) $u_1 = 11, u_{r+1} = u_r - 2$

     (c) $u_1 = 2, u_{r+1} = u + 4$

     (d) $u_1 = 2, u_{r+1} = 3u_r$

     (e) $u_1 = \frac{1}{3}, u_{r+1} = \frac{1}{3}u_r$

     (f) $u_1 = \frac{1}{2}a, u_{r+1} = \frac{1}{2}u_r$

     (g) $u_1 = b - 2c, u_{r+1} = u_r + c$

     (h) $u_1 = 1, u_{r+1} = -u_r$

     (i) $u_1 = \dfrac{p}{q^3}, u_{r+1} = qu_r$

     (j) $u_1 = \dfrac{a^3}{b^2}, u_{r+1} = \dfrac{bu_r}{a}$

     (k) $u_1 = x^3, u_{r+1} = \dfrac{5u_r}{x}$

     (l) $u_1 = 1, u_{r+1} = (1+x)u_r$

3 (a) $5, 7, 9, 11, 13; u_1 = 5, u_{r+1} = u_r + 2$
     (b) $1, 4, 9, 16, 25; u_1 = 1, u_{r+1} = u_r + 2r + 1$
     (c) $1, 3, 6, 10, 15; u_1 = 1, u_{n+1} = u_r + r + 1$
     (d) $1, 5, 14, 30, 55; u_1 = 1, u_{n+1} = u_r + (r+1)^2$
     (e) $6, 18, 54, 162, 486; u_1 = 6, u_{r+1} = 3u_r$
     (f) $3, 15, 75, 375, 1875; u_1 = 3, u_{r+1} = 5u_r$

4 (a) $u_r = 10 - r$ (b) $u_r = 2 \times 3^r$
     (c) $u_r = r^2 + 3$ (d) $u_r = 2r(r+1)$

     (e) $u_r = \dfrac{2r-1}{r+3}$ (f) $u_n = \dfrac{r^2+1}{2^r}$

Exercise 3B (page 216)

2 (a) r (c) $1^3 = t_1^2 - t_0^2, 2^3 = t_2^2 - t_1^2, \dots$

3 (a) 5040 (b) 6720 (c) 35

4 (a) $\dfrac{8!}{4!}$ (b) $\dfrac{12!}{8!}$ (c) $\dfrac{n!}{(n-3)!}$

     (d) $\dfrac{(n+1)!}{(n-2)!}$ (e) $\dfrac{(n+3)!}{(n-1)!}$ (f) $\dfrac{(n+6)!}{(n+3)!}$

     (g) $8!$ (h) $n!$

5 (a) 12 (b) $22 \times 22!$
     (c) $n+1$ (d) $n \times n!$

7 (a) $1, 5, 10, 10, 5, 1, 0, 0, \dots$
     (b) $1, 6, 15, 20, 15, 6, 1, 0, 0, \dots$
     (c) $1, 8, 28, 56, 70, 56, 28, 8, 1, 0, 0, \dots$

8 (a) $\dfrac{11!}{4! \times 7!}$ (b) $\dfrac{11!}{7! \times 4!}$ (c) $\dfrac{10!}{5! \times 5!}$

     (d) $\dfrac{12!}{3! \times 9!}$ (e) $\dfrac{12!}{9! \times 3!}$

10 $\dbinom{n}{r} + \dbinom{n}{r+1} = \dbinom{n+1}{r+1}$

11 The sum of the terms in the sequence is 2^n.

Exercise 3C (page 221)

1 (a) 3 (d) -2 (f) q (h) x

2 (a) $12, 2r$ (b) $32, 14 + 3r$
     (c) $-10, 8 - 3r$ (d) $3.3, 0.9 + 0.4r$
     (e) $3\frac{1}{2}, \frac{1}{2} + \frac{1}{2}r$ (f) $43, 79 - 6r$
     (g) $x + 10, x - 2 + 2r$ (h) $1 + 4x, 1 - 2x + xr$

3 (a) 14 (b) 88 (c) 36
     (d) 11 (e) 11 (f) 11
     (g) 16 (h) 28

4 (a) 610 (b) 795
     (c) -102 (d) $855\frac{1}{2}$
     (e) -1025 (f) $998\,001$
     (g) $3160a$ (h) $-15\,150p$

5 (a) $54, 3132$ (b) $20, 920$
     (c) $46, 6532$ (d) $28, -910$
     (e) $28, 1120$ (f) $125, 42\,875$
     (g) $1000, 5\,005\,000$ (h) $61, -988.2$

6 (a) $a = 3, d = 4$ (b) $a = 2, d = 5$
     (c) $a = 1.4, d = 0.3$ (d) $a = 12, d = -2.5$
     (e) $a = 25, d = -3$ (f) $a = -7, d = 2$
     (g) $a = 3x, d = -x$ (h) $a = p + 1, d = \frac{1}{2}p + 3$

7 (a) 20 (b) 12 (c) 16
     (d) 40 (e) 96 (f) 28

8 (a) 62 (b) 25

9 (a) £76   (b) £1272

10 (a) 5050 (b) $15\,050$ (c) $\frac{1}{2}n(3n+1)$

11 £813,000

Miscellaneous exercise 3 (page 222)

1 (a) (i) $1, 2, 5, 14, 41$ (ii) $2, 5, 14, 41, 122$
       (iii) $0, -1, -4, -13, -40$
       (iv) $\frac{1}{2}, \frac{1}{2}, \frac{1}{2}, \frac{1}{2}, \frac{1}{2}$

     (b) (i) $b = \frac{1}{2}$ (ii) $b = \frac{3}{2}$ (iii) $b = -\frac{1}{2}$
       (iv) $b = 0$

2 1444

3 (a) $3, 1, 3$; alternately 1 and 3
     (b) all terms after the first are 2 (c) 2

4 (a) alternately 0 and -1; 1, then alternately 0 and -1; gets increasingly large.

   (b) $\frac{1}{2}\left(1\pm\sqrt{5}\right)$

5 $n(2n+3)$

6 168

7 -750

8 $2n-\frac{1}{2}$

9 167 167; 111 445

10 40

11 (a) 991   (b) 50 045.5

12 (a) 18   (b) $2(2n+1)$
   (c) $a=6, d=4$, sum $=2\,004\,000$

13 71 240

14 (a) 47, 12 years left over   (b) £345,450

15 $a=\dfrac{10\,000}{n}-5(n-1)$; 73

16 (a) $0, 1, 4, 9, 16; r^2$ (b) $0, 1, 2, 3, 4; r$
   (c) $1, 2, 4, 8, 16; 2^r$

4 The binomial theorem

Exercise 4A (page 227)

1 (a) $4x^2+4xy+y^2$
   (b) $25x^2+30xy+9y^2$
   (c) $16+56p+49p^2$
   (d) $1-16t+64t^2$
   (e) $1-10x^2+25x^4$
   (f) $4+4x^3+x^6$
   (g) $x^6+3x^4y^3+3x^2y^6+y^9$
   (h) $27x^6+54x^4y^3+36x^2y^6+8y^9$

2 (a) $x^3+6x^2+12x+8$
   (b) $8p^3+36p^2q+54pq^2+27q^3$
   (c) $1-12x+48x^2-64x^3$
   (d) $1-3x^3+3x^6-x^9$

3 (a) 42   (b) 150

4 (a) 240   (b) 54

5 (a) $1+10x+40x^2+80x^3+80x^4+32x^5$
   (b) $p^6+12p^5q+60p^4q^2+160p^3q^3$
       $+240p^2q^4+192pq^5+64q^6$
   (c) $16m^4-96m^3n+216m^2n^2-216mn^3+81n^4$
   (d) $1+2x+\frac{3}{2}x^2+\frac{1}{2}x^3+\frac{1}{16}x^4$

6 (a) 270   (b) -1000

7 $1+2x+5x^2+4x^3+4x^4$

8 $x^3+12x^2+48x+64$
   $x^4+13x^3+60x^2+112x+64$

9 $72x^5+420x^4+950x^3+1035x^2+540x+108$

10 7

11 $x^{11}+11x^{10}y+55x^9y^2+165x^8y^3+330x^7y^4$
     $+462x^6y^5+462x^5y^6+330x^4y^7$
     $+165x^3y^8+55x^2y^9+11xy^{10}+y^{11}$

12 59 136

Exercise 4B (page 231)

1 (a) 35   (b) 28   (c) 126   (d) 715
   (e) 15   (f) 45   (g) 11   (h) 1225

2 (a) 10   (b) -56 (c) 165   (d) -560

3 (a) 84   (b) -1512 (c) 4032   (d) $-\frac{99}{4}$

4 (a) 3003   (b) 192 192
   (c) 560 431 872   (d) 48 048

5 (a) $1+13x+78x^2+286x^3$
   (b) $1-15x+105x^2-455x^3$
   (c) $1+30x+405x^2+3240x^3$
   (d) $128-2240x+16\,800x^2-70\,000x^3$

6 (a) $1+22x+231x^2$
   (b) $1-30x+435x^2$
   (c) $1-72x+2448x^2$
   (d) $1+114x+6156x^2$

7 $1+16x+112x^2$; 1.1712

8 $4096+122\,880x+1\,689\,600x^2$; 4220.57

9 $1+32x+480x^2+4480x^3$; 5920

10 $1-30x+405x^2$; 234

11 7

12 $2+56x^2+140x^4+56x^6+2x^8$;
   2.005 601 400 056 000 2

13 $a=4, n=9$

Miscellaneous exercise 4 (page 232)

1 $27+108x+144x^2+64x^3$

2 (a) $1+40x+720x^2$ (b) $1-32x+480x^2$

3 (a) $-48\,384$ (b) $\frac{875}{4}$

4 $2187+25515x+127575x^2$; 2455

5 $256+256x+112x^2+28x^3$; 258.571

6 $256-3072x+16128x^2$; 253

7 $x^6+3x^3+3+\dfrac{1}{x^3}$

8 $16x^4-96x+\dfrac{216}{x^2}-\dfrac{216}{x^5}+\dfrac{81}{x^8}$

9 $2x^6+\dfrac{15x^2}{2}+\dfrac{15}{8x^2}+\dfrac{1}{32x^6}$

10 48

11 20 000

12 495;   (a) 40 095   (b) 7920   (c) $\frac{495}{16}$

13 30

14 $1 + 40x + 760x^2$;
    (a) 1.040 76   (b) 0.923 04

15 $1024 - \dfrac{2560}{x^2} + \dfrac{2880}{x^4}$; 999

16 B; D

17 $\dfrac{7}{16}$

18 5376

19 $\dfrac{6435}{128}$

20 -2024

21 $1 + 12x + 70x^2$; 1.127

22 $270x^2 + 250$; $\pm\dfrac{4}{3}$

23 $\pm\dfrac{5}{6}$

24 (a) $1 + 5\alpha t + 10\alpha^2 t^2$ (b) $1 - 8\beta t + 28\beta^2 t^2$;
    $10\alpha^2 - 40\alpha\beta + 28\beta^2$

25 (b) (i) 4 or 7   (ii) 3 or 13
     (iii) 7 or 13   (iv) 17 or 28

27 (b) (i) $a = 3, b = 6, c = 8$
     (ii) $a = 6, b = 4, c = 9$

29 1.005 413 792 056 807

30 (a) $217 + 88\sqrt{6}$ (b) $698\sqrt{2} + 569\sqrt{3}$

31 (a) 568; 567 and 568   (b) 969 and 970

32 $2n(n+1)$

33 $a = -\dfrac{1}{6}, b = \dfrac{1}{2}, c = -\dfrac{1}{2}, d = \dfrac{1}{6}$

5 The trapezium rule

Exercise 5 (page 238)

1 (a) 2.12   (b) 0.75

2 5.73

3 3.09

4 (a) 1.26   (b) 0.94   (c) 0.8

5 8.04

6 1.034

8 2.86

9 3.14

10 (a) 19.40 (b) underestimates (c) 3.10

Miscellaneous exercise 5 (page 239)

1 10.6

2 3.28; overestimate

3 1.701

4 0.52

5 0.70

6 (a) 1.41

7 51

8 1140 m

9 8.15 km

10 (a) 0, 1.708, 2.309, 2.598, 2.582, 2.141, 0
    (b) 34.0 m^2 (c) 3400 m^3

11 0.55

12 (a) 0.622 m^2 (b) 12.4 m^3 (c) 3.9 m^3
    (d) (b) overestimate, (c) underestimate

13 (a) $\dfrac{592}{3}$ (b) $98 + 70\sqrt{2}$

14 $a = 10$, $(x+1)(x-2)(2x-5)$; 16; 18

15 0.535, 0.5; $T = \dfrac{3}{8}h - \dfrac{1}{4} + \dfrac{1}{2}h^{-2}$,
    $h = 2 \times 3^{-\frac{1}{3}}$, or 1.39

16 (a) $\dfrac{1}{3}$ (b) $\dfrac{1}{2}, \dfrac{3}{8}, \dfrac{11}{32}, \dfrac{43}{128}$ (c) $\dfrac{1}{6}, \dfrac{1}{24}, \dfrac{1}{96}, \dfrac{1}{384}$
    (d) $E_n = -\dfrac{1}{2n^2}$ (e) 708, or more

6 Extending differentiation and integration

Exercise 6A (page 243)

1 (a) $2(x+3)$ (b) $4(2x-3)$
   (c) $-9(1-3x)^2$ (d) $3a(ax+b)^2$
   (e) $-3a(b-ax)^2$ (f) $-5(1-x)^4$
   (g) $8(2x-3)^3$ (h) $-8(3-2x)^3$

2 $na(ax+b)^{n-1}$

3 (a) $10(x+3)^9$ (b) $10(2x-1)^4$
   (c) $-28(1-4x)^6$ (d) $15(3x-2)^4$
   (e) $-12(4-2x)^5$ (f) $72(2+3x)^5$
   (g) $10(2x+5)^4$ (h) $18(2x-3)^8$

Exercise 6B (page 247)

1 (a) $20(4x+5)^4$ (b) $16(2x-7)^7$
   (c) $-6(2-x)^5$ (d) $2\left(\dfrac{1}{2}x+4\right)^3$

2 (a) $-3(3x+5)^{-2}$ (b) $2(4-x)^{-3}$
   (c) $-6(2x+1)^{-4}$ (d) $-64(4x-1)^{-5}$

3 (a) $(2x+3)^{-\frac{1}{2}}$ (b) $2(6x-1)^{-\frac{2}{3}}$
   (c) $-2(4x+7)^{-\frac{3}{2}}$ (d) $-10(3x-2)^{-\frac{5}{3}}$

4 60

5 $(-6, 125)$

6 $y = -\dfrac{3}{4}x - \dfrac{5}{4}$

7 $y = -3x + 48$

8 (a) $\dfrac{1}{14}(2x+1)^7 + k$ (b) $\dfrac{1}{15}(3x-5)^5 + k$
   (c) $-\dfrac{1}{28}(1-7x)^4 + k$ (d) $\dfrac{2}{11}\left(\dfrac{1}{2}x+1\right)^{11} + k$

9 (a) $-\dfrac{1}{10}(5x+2)^{-2} + k$ (b) $\dfrac{2}{3}(1-3x)^{-1} + k$
   (c) $-\dfrac{1}{4}(x+1)^{-4} + k$ (d) $-\dfrac{1}{8}(4x+1)^{-3} + k$

10 (a) $\frac{1}{15}(10x+1)^{\frac{3}{2}}+k$ (b) $(2x-1)^{\frac{1}{2}}+k$

    (c) $\frac{6}{5}\left(\frac{1}{2}x+2\right)^{\frac{5}{3}}+k$ (d) $\frac{16}{9}(2+6x)^{\frac{3}{4}}+k$

11 (a) 820   (b) $\frac{26}{3}$ (c) $\frac{2}{15}$ (d) $\frac{16}{225}$

12 (a) 4   (b) 18

13 (a) $\frac{1}{4}$ (b) $\frac{5}{36}$

14 (a) $\frac{243}{10}$ (b) $4\frac{1}{2}$ (c) $\frac{2}{3}$ (d) 28

15 2.25

16 $a=-5, b=-2$ or $a=5, b=2$

17 $\left(4,8\frac{2}{3}\right)$, maximum

18 9.1125

19 $\frac{1}{20}$

Miscellaneous exercise 6 (page 251)

1 $80(4x-1)^{19}$

2 $8(3-4x)^{-3}$

3 $-\frac{4}{3}$

4 $8\frac{2}{3}$

5 $y=20x+11$

6 $\frac{1}{6}$

7 (a) 1, 2   (b) $10\frac{1}{8}$

8 (b) $25\frac{5}{6}$

9 $8x+5y-34=0$

10 $(2,-4)$; $(0,0),(4,0)$; $(0,16),(4,-16)$; $(2,0),\left(2\pm2\sqrt{3},0\right),(0,16)$

11 (a) $(-4,0),(0,2)$ (b) $5\frac{5}{6}$

12 $3\frac{1}{2}$

13 $438\frac{6}{7}$

14 $70\frac{7}{8}$

15 (a) minimum   (b) 20

16 $2\frac{1}{2}$

17 $\left(\frac{1}{2},\frac{1}{4}\right)$, maximum

18 $\left(2\frac{1}{2},6\right)$, minimum

19 (a) $(1,256),\left(2\frac{1}{3},0\right)$ (b) $-\frac{256}{45}$

20 4

7 Volume of revolution

Exercise 7 (page 258)

1 (a) $\frac{98}{3}\pi$ (b) $\frac{3093}{5}\pi$

   (c) $\frac{279\,808}{7}\pi$ (d) $\frac{3}{4}\pi$

2 (a) 504π (b) $\frac{3498}{5}\pi$

   (c) $\frac{15}{2}\pi$ (d) $\frac{16}{15}\pi$

3 (a) 4π (b) 9π

   (c) 3355π (d) $\frac{3}{10}\pi$

   (e) $\frac{648}{5}\pi$ (f) $\frac{9}{2}\pi$

   (g) 156π (h) $\frac{2}{3}\pi$

4 (a) $\frac{512}{15}\pi$ (b) $\frac{16}{15}\pi$

   (c) $\frac{1}{30}\pi$ (d) $\frac{81}{10}\pi$

5 (a) $\frac{2}{15}\pi$ (b) $\frac{1}{6}\pi$

6 (a) $\frac{2048}{15}\pi$ (b) $\frac{128}{3}\pi$

7 (a) $\frac{3}{10}\pi$ (b) $\frac{3}{10}\pi$

8 $\frac{1}{10}\pi$

9 9π

Miscellaneous exercise 7 (page 259)

1 $\frac{206}{15}\pi$

3 $\frac{4}{3}\pi ab^2$; $\frac{4}{3}\pi a^2 b$

4 (b) 3   (c) 3π (d) $\frac{1}{2}\pi$

5 (i) (a) infinite   (b) $1\frac{1}{2}$

      (c) 5π (d) $\frac{3}{7}\pi$

   (ii) (a) infinite   (b) $\frac{1}{3}$

      (c) infinite   (d) $\frac{1}{7}\pi$

6 (a) 36; 18 (b) $\frac{1296}{5}\pi$ (c) $\frac{81}{2}\pi$

7 4π

8 (a) $\frac{4}{3}a^2$ (b) $2\pi a^3$; $\frac{53}{240}\pi a^3$

Revision exercise 3
(page 261)

1 $(x+4)(x-2)(x-3)$

2 24π

3 $x\mapsto\dfrac{1-x}{1+2x}, x\in\mathbb{R}, x\neq-\frac{1}{2}$

4 $\frac{1}{2}(2n+1)$ (b) 20

5 (a) $x^8-8x^6+28x^4$ (b) 216

6 16.41

7 $-(2x+3)^{-\frac{3}{2}}$

8 (c) $(2x+1)(x-1)(x-3)$

9 (a) $(x-1)^2-2$; $-2\leqslant f(x)\leqslant14$
   (b) $x\geqslant1$

10 (b) 22

11 (a) 5   (b) $\frac{1}{2}$

12 25.5

13 18

14 (a) $f(x) \leqslant 4$ (b) Reflect in $y = 2$
   (c) $\sqrt{4-x}, x \leqslant 4$ (d) 1.56

15 (b) 2 (c) 4.37

16 1215

17 (a) $a = b = 2$
   (b) $(x-1)(x+1)(x-2)(x+2),\ \pm 1, \pm 2$

18 21

19 $k = 2.7$, correct to 2 significant figures

8 The logic of mathematics

Exercise 8A (page 267)

1 (a) All places except the first
   (b) All places except the first
   (c) All places except the second

2 (a) 1, 9
   (b) 5
   (c) 0
   (d) No solution

3 All of them

4 (a) $0 < x < 1$
   (b) Either $x \geqslant 0$ and $x \leqslant y$, or $x \leqslant 0$ and $x \geqslant y$
   (c) $x \geqslant 1$
   (d) Either $y \geqslant x$ and $y \geqslant -x$, or $y \leqslant x$ and $y \leqslant -x$

Exercise 8B (page 270)

5 (c) The sum of n consecutive integers is divisible by n if n is odd, and by $\frac{1}{2}n$ but not by n if n is even.

Exercise 8C (page 274)

1 Converses need not be unique. In each part two converses are given.
   (a) If the square of a number is odd, the number itself is odd. True
   (a) Every odd number is the square of an odd number. False, counterexample: 3
   (b) If the product of two numbers is odd, the two numbers are both odd. True
   (b) Every odd number is the product of two odd numbers. True
   (c) If the product of two numbers is even, the two numbers are both even. False: $6 = 2 \times 3$
   (c) Every even number is the product of two even numbers. False, counterexample: 2
   (d) If the product of two numbers is not prime, the two numbers are both prime. False, counterexample: $8 = 2 \times 4$

   (d) Every number which is not prime can be written as the product of two prime numbers. False, counterexample: 1
   (e) If the sum of two numbers is even, the two numbers are both odd. False: $6 = 2 + 4$
   (e) Every even number can be written as the sum of two odd numbers. True
   (f) If the sum of two numbers is odd, one of the numbers is even and the other is odd. True
   (f) Every odd number can be written as the sum of an even number and an odd number. True

2 (a) The set of points (x, y) which lie on a straight line satisfy the equation $y = mx + c$ for some values of m and c.
   Counterexample: points of the line $x = 0$
   (b) For any numbers a, b and c, the set of points (x, y) which satisfy the equation $ax + by + c = 0$ lie on a straight line.
   Counterexample: $a = 0, b = 0, c = 0$

3 $\sqrt{2}$ cannot be written as a rational number.

4 If you attempt to follow through with $\sqrt{4} = p/q$, you get $p^2 = 4q^2$, you can deduce that p^2 is a multiple of 4, but you cannot go on to deduce that p is a multiple of 4. It breaks down because 4 is not prime. A counterexample is that 4 divides 10^2, but 4 does not divide 10.

5 (a) In a circle, if an angle subtended by a chord is a right angle, the chord is a diameter. True
   (b) A line which is a perpendicular bisector of a chord of a circle passes through the centre. True
   (b) Alternatively, the line joining the centre to the mid-point of a chord is perpendicular to the chord. True
   (c) A line through a point on a circle perpendicular to the radius at that point is a tangent to the circle. True

Exercise 8D (page 276)

2 $x + 2y = 5$ and $y - x = 1$
   $\Leftrightarrow\ (x + 2y) + (y - x) = 5 + 1$
       and $y - x = 1$
   $\Leftrightarrow\ 3y = 6$ and $y - x = 1$
   $\Leftrightarrow\ y = 2$ and $y - x = 1$
   $\Leftrightarrow\ y = 2$ and $x = 1$.
   The point of intersection is therefore $(1, 2)$.

3 (a) S   (b) S   (c) N   (d) S
   (e) N&S   (f) S   (g) N

Miscellaneous exercise 8 (page 276)

3 11 divides $(a_0 + a_2 + \ldots) - (a_1 + a_3 + \ldots)$.

6 Pythagoras' theorem.
  If a line is perpendicular to two lines in a plane, it is perpendicular to all the lines in the plane.

7 (a) True
  (b) False, counterexample: $n = 6$
  (c) False, counterexample: $n = 4$

8 Cards 1 and 3

9 The modulus function

Exercise 9A (page 282)

3 (a) $2 < x < 4$ (b) $-2.1 \leqslant x \leqslant -1.9$
  (c) $1.4995 \leqslant x \leqslant 1.5005$ (d) $-1.25 \leqslant x \leqslant 2.75$

4 (a) $|x - 1.5| \leqslant 0.5$ (b) $|x - 1| < 2$
  (c) $|x + 3.65| \leqslant 0.15$ (d) $|x - 2.85| < 0.55$

5 $|a + b| \leqslant |a| + |b|$; $|a + b| \geqslant ||a| - |b||$

Exercise 9B (page 287)

1 (a) $3, -7$ (b) $8, -6$ (c) $0, 3$
  (d) $3, -3\frac{2}{3}$ (e) $4, \frac{2}{3}$ (f) $-2, \frac{1}{2}$
  (g) $-2, -8$ (h) $-4, 1\frac{3}{7}$

2 (a) $-3 < x < -1$ (b) $x < -2$ or $x > 8$
  (c) $-5 \leqslant x \leqslant -2$ (d) $x \leqslant -3\frac{1}{3}$ or $x \geqslant 2$
  (e) $x < -\frac{3}{4}$ or $x > \frac{1}{2}$ (f) $x < -3$ or $x > 2\frac{1}{3}$
  (g) $1 < x < 3$ (h) $x \leqslant 0$

3 (a) $-1 \leqslant x \leqslant 1$ (b) $x \geqslant 1$ (c) $x \leqslant -1$

4 (a) $x \geqslant 1$ (b) $x \leqslant 0$ (c) $0 \leqslant x \leqslant 1$

5 (a) True   (b) False

Miscellaneous exercise 9 (page 288)

1 $x < \frac{1}{2}$

2 3 and -2 respectively

3 $-10 < x < \frac{2}{3}$

4 $-\frac{1}{3}, -1$

5 $x < 1$

6 $-\frac{1}{3}, \frac{1}{5}$; $x < -\frac{1}{3}$ or $x > \frac{1}{5}$

7 Any value of x such that $-3 \leqslant x \leqslant 3$

8 (a) (ii) $0 \leqslant f(x) \leqslant 2$, $-1 \leqslant g(x) \leqslant 1$
  (b) $f(x)$ is periodic, with period 180; $g(x)$ is not periodic.

9 $x < 2.4$ and $x > 4$

10 (a) $2x + 1$ (b) 7   (c) $-2x - 1$

11 (a) $-2, \frac{4}{3}$ (b) No solution

12 (a) 8   (b) -3

13 (a) $y = 3x - 1$ (b) $y = 1 - x$

15 (a) $x < 1$ or $x > 1\frac{2}{3}$
  (b) $x < -\frac{5}{3}$ or $-1 < x < 1$ or $x > \frac{5}{3}$
  (c) $x < \frac{3}{5}$ or $x > \frac{5}{3}$

10 Geometric sequences and exponential growth

Exercise 10A (page 293)

1 (a) $2; 24, 48$ (b) $4; 128, 512$
  (c) $\frac{1}{2}; 4, 2$ (d) $-3; 162, -486$
  (e) $1.1; 1.4641, 1.61051$ (f) $\frac{1}{x}; \frac{1}{x}, \frac{1}{x^2}$

2 (a) $2 \times 3^{n-1}$ (b) $10 \times \left(\frac{1}{2}\right)^{n-1}$
  (c) $1 \times (-2)^{n-1}$ (d) $81 \times \left(\frac{1}{3}\right)^{n-1}$
  (e) x^n (f) $p^{2-n} q^{n+1}$

3 (a) 11   (b) 13
  (c) 7   (d) 14
  (e) 6   (f) 13

4 (a) $3; 1\frac{1}{3}$ (b) $2; 1\frac{1}{2}$ or $-2; 1\frac{1}{2}$
  (c) $\frac{1}{3}; 531\,441$ (d) $\pm\sqrt{2}; 4$
  (e) $\pm 7; \dfrac{16807}{(\pm 7)^{n-1}}$

5 (a) $59\,048$ (b) $-29\,524$
  (c) 1.9922 (d) 0.6641
  (e) $12\,285$ (f) 8.9998
  (g) $\dfrac{x(1 - x^n)}{1 - x}$ (h) $\dfrac{x(1 - (-x)^n)}{1 + x}$
  (i) $\dfrac{x^{2n} - 1}{x^{2n-3}(x^2 - 1)}$ (j) $\dfrac{x^{2n} - (-1)^n}{x^{2n-2}(x^2 + 1)}$

6 (a) 2047 (b) 683
  (c) $262\,143$ (d) $\dfrac{1023}{512}$
  (e) $\dfrac{29\,525}{39\,366}$ (f) $19.843\,75$
  (g) $\dfrac{341}{1024}$ (h) $2 - \left(\frac{1}{2}\right)^n$
  (i) $\frac{1}{3}\left(64 - \left(\frac{1}{4}\right)^n\right)$ (j) $\frac{1}{4}\left(243 + \left(-\frac{1}{3}\right)^n\right)$

7 $2^{64} - 1 \approx 1.84 \times 10^{19}$

8 £2,684,354.55

10 (a) 2   (b) 8th

11 (a) 3   (b) 14th

12 (a) $\dfrac{p}{q}; n$ (c) (i) np^{n-1} (ii) $-np^{-(n+1)}$

Exercise 10B (page 297)

1 (a) 2   (b) $\frac{3}{2}$ (c) $\frac{1}{4}$ (d) $\frac{1}{9}$

   (e) $\frac{3}{4}$ (f) $\frac{1}{6}$ (g) 3   (h) $\frac{1}{3}$

   (i) $\frac{20}{3}$ (j) 62.5   (k) $\frac{x}{1-x}$ (l) $\frac{1}{1+x^2}$

   (m) $\frac{x}{x-1}$ (n) $\frac{x^3}{x+1}$

2 (a) $\frac{4}{11}$ (b) $\frac{41}{333}$ (c) $\frac{5}{9}$ (d) $\frac{157}{333}$

   (e) $\frac{1}{7}$ (f) $\frac{2}{7}$ (g) $\frac{5}{7}$ (h) $\frac{6}{7}$

3 $\frac{1}{6}$

4 $-\frac{5}{6}$

5 3

6 19.2

7 2 m

8 0.375 m east of O, 1.5 m

9 10 seconds

10 19 m

11 (a) edge of table   (b) 8

Exercise 10C (page 303)

1 £7103.39

2 £1239.72

3 £317.23

4 £1167.70

5 £3747.15

6 (a) 63 000   (b) 36 200   (c) 19 700

7 (a) 5.83×10^7 (b) 5.65×10^7

8 (a) 17 800   (b) 29 100

9 (a) 85.1 kg   (b) 68.1 kg

10 (a) £2254.32   (b) 139

11 (a) 5.42   (b) 5.42

12 £2718.28

13 (a) $(8,24)$, $(9,48)$ (b) $(8,768)$, $(9,1536)$

Miscellaneous exercise 10 (page 304)

1 $6\frac{1}{4}$

3 $a = 3, r = -\frac{1}{4}; 2.4\left(1 - \left(-\frac{1}{4}\right)^n\right)$

4 62

5 $\frac{1}{999}, \frac{4}{37}$

6 $\frac{4}{5}; 18$

7 $8\left(1 - \left(-\frac{1}{2}\right)^n\right); 8, 13$

8 $r = 0.917; a = 40$

9 $20 \times 1.1^{n-1}; 17$

10 £56,007

11 (a) 20

12 $n = 45, 19.8$ seconds

13 100×1.054^5, yes

14 $r = -\frac{1}{3}$

16 $r = \frac{k-1}{k+1}$

11 Exponential and logarithmic functions

Exercise 11A (page 311)

1 (a) $8 = 2^3$ (b) $81 = 3^4$
   (c) $0.04 = 5^{-2}$ (d) $x = 7^4$
   (e) $5 = x^t$ (f) $q = p^r$

2 (a) $3 = \log_2 8$ (b) $6 = \log_3 729$
   (c) $-3 = \log_4 \frac{1}{64}$ (d) $8 = \log_a 20$
   (e) $9 = \log_h g$ (f) $n = \log_m p$

3 (a) 4   (b) 2   (c) -2
   (d) 0   (e) 1   (f) $-\frac{1}{3}$
   (g) $\frac{3}{4}$ (h) $\frac{3}{2}$ (i) 7

4 (a) 7   (b) $\frac{1}{64}$ (c) 4
   (d) $\frac{1}{10}$ (e) $4\sqrt{2}$ (f) 6
   (g) $\frac{1}{256}$ (h) -10 (i) $\frac{1}{3}\sqrt{3}$

5 (a) $\log p + \log q + \log r$
   (b) $\log p + 2\log q + 3\log r$
   (c) $2 + \log p + 5\log r$
   (d) $\frac{1}{2}(\log p - 2\log q - \log r)$
   (e) $\log p + \log q - 2\log r$
   (f) $-(\log p + \log q + \log r)$
   (g) $\log p - \frac{1}{2}\log r$
   (h) $\log p + \log q + 7\log r - 1$
   (i) $\frac{1}{2}(1 + 10\log p - \log q + \log r)$

6 (a) 2   (b) -1 (c) $\log 30\,575$ (d) 0
   (e) 3   (f) -3 (g) $\log 8$ (h) 0

7 (a) $r - q$ (b) $2p + q$ (c) $p + \frac{1}{2}r$
   (d) $-q$ (e) $p + 2q + r$ (f) $p - q + 2r$
   (g) $q - p - r$ (h) $4p + q - 2r$ (i) $p + q - 2r$

Exercise 11B (page 316)

1 (a) 1.46   (b) 1.56   (c) 1.14
   (d) 1.22   (e) 3.58   (f) 1.71
   (g) -2.21 (h) 3   (i) -0.20

2 (a) $x > 1.89$ (b) $x < 1.43$ (c) $x < -1.68$
   (d) $x > 9.97$ (e) $x > 8.54$ (f) $x < -2$
   (g) $x \geqslant -2$ (h) $x \leqslant -5.61$ (i) $x \geqslant 3.77$

3 37

4 14

5 27

6 7

7   9.56

8   (a)   0.89   (b)   12 days   (c)   19.9 days

9   9.49 a.m. Tuesday

10   390 years

11   71 months

12   (a)   1.79   (b)   2.37   (c)   0.486
     (d)   −7.97   (e)   1.04   (f)   2.32

13   (a)   1.76   (b)   0.685   (c)   −2.32

14   (a) $y = 2.51 \times 3.98^x$ (b) $y = 10^{12} \times 0.001^x$
     (c) $y = 5.01 \times 50.1^x$ (d) $y = 5.01x^2$
     (e) $y = \dfrac{0.316}{x^5}$

15   (a) $\log y = \log a + x \log b$;
        gradient $= \log b$, intercept $= \log a$
     (b) $\log y = \log a + b \log x$
        gradient $= b$, intercept $= \log a$

16 $a \approx 1, n \approx 1.5$

17   Investment $=$ £850, interest at 7.5%

Miscellaneous exercise 11 (page 318)

1   (a) $\dfrac{1}{\log a - 2}$ (b) $\sqrt{\dfrac{5a}{2}}$

2   0.774

3 $f^{-1} : x \mapsto e^x - 1, \quad x \in \mathbb{R}$

4 $2 - \log 2$

6 $\log 3 - \frac{1}{6}$

11 $\log_2 \dfrac{x+2}{x}, \ \frac{2}{7}$

12 $10\,000, 451$

12 Differentiating exponentials and logarithms

Exercise 12A (page 324)

1   (a) $3e^{3x}$ (b) $-e^{-x}$ (c) $6e^{2x}$
     (d) $16e^{-4x}$ (e) $3e^{3x+4}$ (f) $-2e^{3-2x}$
     (g) $-e^{1-x}$ (h) $12e^{3+4x}$

2   (a) $3e^2$ (b) $-2e$ (c) -1
     (d) -2

3   (a) $ey = x + 2$
     (b) $y = 3x - 1$
     (c) $y = \left(4 + 4e^4\right)x - \left(4 + 6e^4\right)$
     (d) $4y = -2x + 1 + 2\ln 2$

4   No stationary points

5   (a) $\frac{1}{3}e^{3x} + k$ (b) $-e^{-x} + k$
     (c) $\frac{3}{2}e^{2x} + k$ (d) $e^{-4x} + k$

     (e) $\frac{1}{3}e^{3x+4} + k$ (f) $-\frac{1}{2}e^{3-2x} + k$
     (g) $-e^{1-x} + k$ (h) $\frac{3}{4}e^{3+4x} + k$

6   (a) $\frac{1}{2}\left(e^4 - e^2\right)$ (b) $e - \dfrac{1}{e}$ (c) $e^5 - e$
     (d) $e^{10} - e^8$ (e)   6   (f) $\frac{3}{4}e$
     (g) $\dfrac{1}{\ln 2}$ (h) $\dfrac{1}{\ln 3}\left(3^9 - \frac{1}{27}\right)$

7 $\frac{1}{2}\left(e^4 - 1\right)$

8 $1 - e^{-N}$; 1

9   An overestimate

Exercise 12B (page 326)

1   (a) $\dfrac{1}{x}$ (b) $\dfrac{2}{2x-1}$ (c) $\dfrac{-2}{1-2x}$
     (d) $\dfrac{2}{x}$ (e) $\dfrac{b}{a+bx}$ (f) $\dfrac{-1}{x}$
     (g) $\dfrac{-3}{3x+1}$ (h) $\dfrac{2}{2x+1} - \dfrac{3}{3x-1}$
     (i) $-\dfrac{6}{x}$ (j) $\dfrac{1}{x} + \dfrac{1}{x+1}$ (k) $\dfrac{2}{x} + \dfrac{1}{x-1}$
     (l) $\dfrac{1}{x-1} + \dfrac{1}{x+2}$

2   (a) $y = 2x - \ln 2 - 1$
     (b) $y = 2x - 1$
     (c) $y = -3x - \ln 3 - 1$
     (d) $ey = x + e\ln 3$

3   (a) $e - 1$, minimum
     (b) $\frac{1}{2} - \ln 2$, minimum
     (c)   1, minimum
     (d)   1, minimum

5 $2y = 2 - x$

6 $x > 6$, $\dfrac{1}{x-2} + \dfrac{1}{x-6}$ (a) $x > 6$ (b)   None

7   (i) $2 < x < 6$, $\dfrac{1}{x-2} - \dfrac{1}{6-x}$
        (a) $2 < x < 4$ (b) $4 < x < 6$
     (ii)   There are no points in the domain.

Exercise 12C (page 328)

1   (a) $y = \frac{1}{2}\ln x + k, \quad x > 0$
     (b) $y = \ln(x-1) + k, \quad x > 1$
     (c) $y = -\ln(1-x) + k, \quad x < 1$
     (d) $y = \frac{1}{4}\ln(4x+3) + k, \quad x > -\frac{3}{4}$
     (e) $y = -2\ln(1-2x) + k, \quad x < \frac{1}{2}$
     (f) $y = 2\ln(1+2x) + k, \quad x > -\frac{1}{2}$
     (g) $y = -2\ln(-1-2x) + k, \quad x < -\frac{1}{2}$
     (h) $y = 2\ln(2x-1) + k, \quad x > \frac{1}{2}$

2   (a) $\ln 2$ (b) $\ln 2$ (c) $\ln 2$ (d) $\ln 2$

3 (a) $\ln 2$ (b) $\frac{1}{2}\ln 3$ (c) $\frac{2}{3}\ln\frac{13}{7}$

   (d) $\ln\dfrac{5e-7}{4e-7}$ (e) $\ln 2$ (f) $8+\ln 5$

4 $2\ln\frac{3}{2}$

5 $\frac{1509}{1976}=0.763\ldots$, overestimate, $2\ln\frac{19}{13}=0.758\ldots$

6 $\pi\ln\frac{5}{2}$

7 $\frac{1}{2}\pi\ln 3$

8 $y=\frac{3}{2}\ln\left(\frac{1}{3}(2x+1)\right)$

9 $y=2\ln(4x-3)+2$

10 $2\pi\ln 2$

Exercise 12D (page 333)

1 (a) $-\ln 4$ (b) $-\frac{1}{2}\ln 3$ (c) $\frac{2}{3}\ln 5-\ln 4$

   (d) $\ln\dfrac{7-2e}{7-e}$ (e) $-\ln\frac{5}{3}$ (f) $2-\ln 2$

2 $\ln 7,\ -\frac{2}{7}$

3 $2^x\ln 2,\,3^x\ln 3,\,10^x\ln 10,\,-\left(\frac{1}{2}\right)^x\ln 2$

4 For example, 13

5 (a) They all approach 0.

Miscellaneous exercise 12 (page 333)

1 (a) $\dfrac{3}{3x-4}$ (b) $\dfrac{-3}{4-3x}$ (c) $3e^{3x}$

   (d) $-e^{-x}$ (e) $\dfrac{1}{3-x}-\dfrac{1}{2-x}$ (f) $\dfrac{-6}{3-2x}$

2 Overestimates; the graph lies below the straight line at the top of the trapezia.

3 $\left(\frac{1}{2},8\right),(4,1)$; $15\frac{3}{4}-12\ln 2$

4 (a) $\frac{2}{3}e-\frac{1}{6}e^{-2}-\frac{1}{2}$ (b) minimum

5 $2x-e^{-x}+k$

6 $x=\frac{1}{2}$, minimum

8 $y=x+4$

9 $y=-\frac{1}{2}x+\frac{1}{4}$

10 (a) $\dfrac{2}{x-1}$ (b) $3\ln 2$

12 (a) -1 (b) 1

13 (a) $2-e^{-a}=a$ (b) $\displaystyle\int_0^a\left(2-e^{-x}-x\right)dx$

14 (a) $e^{-2a}-3a=0$

    (d) $\frac{1}{2}-\frac{3}{2}a^2-\frac{1}{2}e^{-2a}$

15 $\frac{1}{2}e$

16 Stretch in the y-direction with scale factor e; translation of 1 unit in the negative x-direction. Reflection in the line $y=x$.

17 (a) 3.00 (b) 1.22×10^6

13 The chain rule

Exercise 13A (page 338)

1 (a) $30(5x+3)^5$ (b) $\frac{5}{2}(5x+3)^{-\frac{1}{2}}$

   (c) $\dfrac{5}{5x+3}$

2 (a) $-20(1-4x)^4$ (b) $12(1-4x)^{-4}$

   (c) $-4e^{1-4x}$

3 (a) $15x^2\left(1+x^3\right)^4$ (b) $-12x^2\left(1+x^3\right)^{-5}$

   (c) $\dfrac{3x^2}{1+x^3}$

4 (a) $24x\left(2x^2+3\right)^5$ (b) $-4x\left(2x^2+3\right)^{-2}$

   (c) $-2x\left(2x^2+3\right)^{-\frac{3}{2}}$

5 $24x^3\left(3x^4+2\right)$

6 (a) $72x^8+72x^5+18x^2$ (b) $18x^2\left(2x^3+1\right)^2$

7 (a) $20x^4\left(x^5+1\right)^3$ (b) $48x^2\left(2x^3-1\right)^7$

   (c) $12e^{2x}\left(e^{2x}+3\right)^5$ (d) $\frac{5}{2}x^{-\frac{1}{2}}\left(\sqrt{x}-1\right)^4$

8 (a) $8x\left(x^2+6\right)^3$ (b) $45x^2\left(5x^3+4\right)^2$

   (c) $28x^3\left(x^4-8\right)^6$ (d) $-45x^8\left(2-x^9\right)^4$

9 (a) $2(4x+3)^{-\frac{1}{2}}$ (b) $12x\left(x^2+4\right)^5$

   (c) $-36x^2\left(6x^3-5\right)^{-3}$ (d) $3x^2\left(5-x^3\right)^{-2}$

10 (a) $\dfrac{6}{x}(\ln x+1)^5$ (b) $-\dfrac{4}{x^2}\left(\dfrac{1}{x}+2\right)^3$

    (c) $\dfrac{2x^3}{2+x^4}$ (d) $-15e^{-x}\left(e^{-x}+1\right)^4$

11 (a) $-\frac{4}{25}$ (b) 0

12 $\frac{3}{8}$

13 $-3\frac{3}{4}$

14 (a) $6\left(x^2+3x+1\right)^5(2x+3)$

    (b) $\dfrac{3x^2+4}{x^3+4x}$

    (c) $-3\left(x^2+5x\right)^{-4}(2x+5)$

    (d) $2e^{x^2+x+1}(2x+1)$

15 $y=12x-25$

16 $x+4y=8$

17 $x+6y=23$

18 $6x\left(x^2-1\right)^{-\frac{1}{2}}\left(\sqrt{x^2-1}+1\right)^5$

19 $-x\left(1-x^2\right)^{-\frac{1}{2}}e^{\sqrt{1-x^2}}$

20 $(0,3)$; minimum

Exercise 13B (page 342)

1   1.215×10^4 h^{-1}

2   $0.76°$ min^{-1}

3   (a)   4.8 cm s^{-1} (b)   24 cm^2 s^{-1}

4   (a)   240 mm^2 s^{-1} (b)   2400 mm^3 s^{-1}

5   942 mm^2 s^{-1}

6   0.25 m min^{-1}

7   0.0076 m s^{-1}

8   0.011 m s^{-1}

9   0.0025 cm s^{-1}

Miscellaneous exercise 13 (page 343)

1   $40x^3(x^4+3)^4$

2   $24x + y = 49$

4   $-\dfrac{10}{27}$

5   $\left(0, \tfrac{1}{4}\right)$

6   $3x + 4y = 18$

7   0.377 cm^2 s^{-1}

8   (a) $\dfrac{10}{\sqrt{\pi}}$ cm   (b) $\dfrac{1}{4\sqrt{\pi}}$ cm s^{-1}

9   4 m^2 s^{-1}

10   (a) $\tfrac{1}{2}\left(x+\dfrac{1}{x}\right)^{-\frac{1}{2}}\left(1-\dfrac{1}{x^2}\right)$ (b) $\dfrac{1}{2x+\sqrt{x}}$

11   $y = 2x - 3$

12   (a) $-12t(3t^2+5)^{-3}$ (b) $-\dfrac{2}{t}$

13   $(3,0)$

14   (a) $\dfrac{2-x}{\sqrt{4x-x^2}}$, $(2,2)$

15   $\dfrac{3}{20\pi}$ cm s^{-1}

16   0.052 m s^{-1}

17   $\left(-3, e^{-81}\right)$; $(0,1)$; $\left(3, e^{-81}\right)$

18   $\left(-\sqrt{3}, -4\right)$ minimum; $(-1,0)$ maximum; $(0,-4)$ minimum; $(1,0)$ maximum; $\left(\sqrt{3}, -4\right)$ minimum

14 Solving equations numerically

Exercise 14A (page 349)

2   2

3   $1.91, -29.6$; as the graph is continuous there is at least one root in the interval $3 < x < 4$.

4   (a)   (i) -2 (ii) -1.71
     (b)   (i)   2   (ii)   2.63

     (c)   (i)   1   (ii)   1.33
     (d)   (i)   6   (ii)   6.30
     (e)   (i) -8 (ii) -7.86
     (f)   (i)   4   (ii)   4.53

5   The graph of the function f may have a break in it. $f(x) = \dfrac{1}{x}$ has $f(-1)f(1) < 0$, but $f(x) = 0$ has no root between -1 and 1.

Exercise 14B (page 351)

1   Here are three possible examples for each part.

     (a) $x = \sqrt[5]{5x-6}$; $x = \tfrac{1}{5}(x^5+6)$; $x = \sqrt{\dfrac{5x-6}{x^3}}$

     (b) $x = 5e^{-x}$; $x = \ln 5 - \ln x$; $x = \sqrt{5xe^{-x}}$

     (c) $x = \sqrt[5]{1999 - x^3}$; $x = \sqrt[3]{1999 - x^5}$; $x = \sqrt[3]{\dfrac{1999}{x^2+1}}$

2   (a)   (i) $f(x) = x^{11} - x^7 + 6 = 0$ (ii) -1.1769, -1.2227, -1.2338, -1.2367, -1.2375
         (iii) converging to a root
         (iv) x_5 is an approximate root of $f(x) = 0$
     (b)   (i) $f(x) = x^4 - x^3 - 34x^2 + 289 = 0$
         (ii)   7.1111, 22.283, 463.11, 214 440, 4.598×10^{10} (iii) diverging
     (c)   (i) $f(x) = x^4 - 500x - 10 = 0$ (ii)   7.9446, 7.9437, 7.9437, 7.9437, 7.9437
         (iii) converging to a root
         (iv) x_5 is an approximate root of $f(x) = 0$

3   1.6198, 1.8781, 1.6932, 1.8208, 1.7304, 1.7933; converging

4   (b)   0.7895 correct to 4 significant figures; it is convergent to another root.

5   $x_{n+1} = \sqrt[3]{e^{x_n} + 2}$ with $x_0 = 2$ converges to 2.27 in 11 steps;

     $x_{n+1} = \dfrac{e^{x_n} + 2}{x_n^2}$ with $x_0 = 2$ converges to 2.27 in 3 steps.

6   (a)   9   (b)   6

Exercise 14C (page 355)

1   (a)   no convergence; $F^{-1}(x) = \dfrac{3}{x+1}$, 1.303

     (b)   no convergence; $F^{-1}(x) = \tfrac{1}{3}\ln(5-x)$, 0.501

     (c)   converges to 2.277

     (d)   no convergence; $F^{-1}(x) = -\sqrt[6]{300 - 10x}$, -2.6237

     (e)   converges to 13.1998

     (f)   no convergence; $F^{-1}(x) = \sqrt{20 - \dfrac{3}{x}}$, 4.3952

2 (a) 5, 1.179   (b) −13, 6.730
  (c) 10, −1.896   (d) −3.485, 12.87

Miscellaneous exercise 14 (page 356)

1 5, 13;   (a) There exists a root between $x = 1$
  and $x = 2$.   (b) $1\frac{5}{8}$

2 2

3 2.15

4 $0.381 < x < 0.382$

5 5.0

6 (b) 0.77

7 (a) Two solutions

8 233.1

9 (a) $x + 15y + 30 = 0$
  (b) One graph is increasing from $-\infty$ to ∞, and
    the other decreasing, in $-90 < x < 90$. Hence
    there is a point of intersection, and only one.
  (c) −35

10 1.76

11 1.210

12 6.72

13 (a) 1, 1.389. There could be an even number of
    roots in the interval.
  (b) 0.310 or 0.756   (c) 0.62, 1.51

14 (b) 3.111 11, 3.103 32, 3.103 84, 3.103 80;
    3.104

15 (b) The second, as its derivative is numerically
    less than 1 between $x = 2$ and $x = 3$; 2.93

16 (a) 3   (b) $F(t) = 1 + \dfrac{\ln(9t)}{\ln 4}$, $F^{-1}(t) = \frac{1}{9}4^{t-1}$ or
    vice versa; $t = F(t)$; 3.486

17 (b) −5   (c) $k = -63$, $\alpha = -4.4188$

18 (a) $\left(\pm\sqrt{5}, \pm\sqrt{5}\right)$
  (c) The function g is self-inverse.
  (d) 2.236 068

19 (b) 30, 40 (c) 30, 35 (d) 32.5, 35
  (e) $a_r = 30$, 30, 32.5, 33.75, 34.375, 34.375,
    34.531 25, 34.609 375, 34.648 437 5,
    34.667 968 75
    $b_r = 40$, 35, 35, 35, 35, 34.6875, 34.6875,
    34.6875, 34.6875, 34.6875
    $\alpha = 34.7$ correct to 1 decimal place.

20 (a) 1.324 72   (b) 0.111 83, 3.577 15

15 Radians

Exercise 15 (page 362)

1 (a) $\frac{1}{2}\pi$ (b) $\frac{3}{4}\pi$ (c) $\frac{1}{4}\pi$ (d) $\frac{1}{6}\pi$
  (e) $\frac{2}{5}\pi$ (f) $\frac{1}{10}\pi$ (g) $\frac{2}{3}\pi$ (h) $\frac{1}{8}\pi$
  (i) 4π (j) $\frac{10}{3}\pi$ (k) $\frac{3}{2}\pi$ (l) $\frac{1}{180}\pi$

2 (a) 60°   (b) 9°   (c) 36°   (d) $22\frac{1}{2}°$
  (e) 20°   (f) 120°   (g) $112\frac{1}{2}°$ (h) 108°
  (i) 4°   (j) 1080°   (k) −90°   (l) 50°

3 (a) $\frac{1}{2}\sqrt{3}$ (b) $\frac{1}{2}\sqrt{2}$ (c) $\frac{1}{3}\sqrt{3}$ (d) 0
  (e) $-\frac{1}{2}\sqrt{2}$ (f) $-\frac{1}{2}\sqrt{3}$ (g) $-\sqrt{3}$ (h) $\frac{3}{4}$

4 (a) $s = 8.4$, $A = 29.4$ (b) $s = 7.35$, $A = 12.8625$
  (c) $\theta = 1.5$, $A = 48$ (d) $r = 20$, $A = 140$
  (e) $\theta = 2.4$, $s = 12$ (f) $s = 8$
  (g) $r = 8$, $\theta = 2$ (h) $\theta = \frac{5}{3}$

5 (a) 2.26 cm^2 (b) 1.47 cm^2 (c) 830 cm^2
  (d) 9.05 cm^2 (e) 0.556 cm^2

6 6.72 cm^2

7 28.2 cm

8 (b) 2.31

9 2.74

10 26.3 cm^2

11 (a) $1.61r$ (b) $0.32r$

12 15.5 cm, 14.3 cm^2

Miscellaneous exercise 15 (page 363)

1 3.6 cm, 10.8 cm^2

2 $\frac{1}{4}$

3 r^2

4 $\frac{2}{3}\pi$, $\frac{1}{3}\pi - \frac{1}{4}\sqrt{3}$

5 17 cm^2

6 $\frac{1}{2}r^2(\theta - \sin\theta)$, $1.2 < \theta < 1.3$

7 $DE = 2r - 2r\cos\theta$

8 $2\pi - \dfrac{s}{r}$

9 1.4

Revision exercise 4
(page 366)

1 (a) −2   (b) 1   (c) 3   (d) ±3

2 (a) £16,600   (b) Year 9
  (c) £$\left(475n^2 + 12325n\right)$ for $0 \leqslant n \leqslant 9$:
    £$(20400n - 34200)$ for $n > 9$
  (d) £$13,500 \times 1.05^{n-1}$
  (f) Year 10

3 (a) $3(3x^2+2)(x^3+2x-1)^2$ (b) $3e^{3x-1}$

   (c) $\dfrac{2x}{x^2-1}$ (d) $-x(x^2+1)^{-\frac{3}{2}}$

4 (a) $2\pi\times10^{15}$ km^3 s^{-1} (b) $4\pi\times10^9$ km^2 s^{-1}

5 (a) $\frac{1}{2}e^6-\frac{1}{2}$ (b) $\frac{1}{4}\pi e^{12}-\frac{1}{4}\pi$

6 (a) 13.97, 15   (b) 21

7 $-1.17, 0.69, 2.48$

8 (a) $3\frac{1}{2}$ (b) 3.21

9 (a) At 3.49 hours   (b) After 15 hours
   (c) 2.51×10^5

10 (a) $(6x-6)e^{3x^2-6x}$ (b) $(1,e^{-3})$, minimum
   (c) $x+6y=8$

11 2π cm, $2(\pi-\sqrt{3})$ cm^2

12 (a) $e-1$ (b) $\frac{1}{2}(e-(e-1)\ln(e-1))$

Mock examinations

Mock examination 1 for P2 (page 368)

1 $x>\dfrac{\ln 3}{\ln 2}$

2 $1, 1\frac{2}{3}$

3 $8, x^2+2x+4$

4 $\frac{1}{12}\pi(3k-1)^4, 1.81$

5 $d=3a; 590a, \frac{1}{3}a(4^{20}-1)$

6 (i) $f(x)\geqslant\frac{1}{3}$ (ii) 0
   (iii) $g^{-1}(x)=\frac{1}{2}(x+1)$ (iv) $\frac{2}{3}$

7 2

8 (i) $10e^{-\frac{1}{20}}\approx9.51$ units,
   (ii) $\frac{1}{10}e^{-\frac{1}{20}}\approx0.0951$ units s^{-1}
   69.3 seconds

9 $\frac{1}{4}+\frac{1}{2}\sqrt{e}+\frac{1}{4}e$, overestimate; $e-1$

Mock examination 2 for P2 (page 370)

1 $\ln(36e)$

2 $81x^4+216x^3+216x^2+96x+16$

3 (i)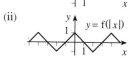

   (ii)

4 $A=2, B=5$

5 $3, 4, 5; (n-1)b-(n-2)a$

6 2.613

7 (i) $f(x)\in\mathbb{R}$ and $f(x)\neq1$; $g(x)\geqslant-1$
   (ii) g has no inverse because it is not one–one;
      for example, $g(-1)=g(1)=2$
   (iii) $x\mapsto\frac{1}{3}\dfrac{x+1}{1-x}, x\in\mathbb{R}, x\neq1$

8 (i) $-2xe^{-x^2}$,
   (ii) $\ln\frac{5}{3}$

9 10.7 cm, 6.64 cm^2

10 36π cm^3

Index

The page numbers refer to the first mention of each term, or the shaded box if there is one.